"Much of the history of African Americans in Minnesota has fortunately been preserved for the ages thanks to the pioneering work of Walter Scott, whose publications from the 1950s, '60s, and '70s have recently been reissued by the Minnesota Historical Society as *The Scott Collection*. Now, Mr. Scott's children, who are board members of Minnesota's Black Community Project, have undertaken a continuation of their father's work by bringing his treasures of historical preservation up to date.

"Their new collection, *Minnesota's Black Community in the 21st Century*, continues the documentation of Black excellence by highlighting contemporary successful African Americans engaged in a broad range of crafts and professions. The book's short biographies and photos capture as nothing else can all there is to celebrate in the present generation of Minnesota's African American community. Together with Walter Scott's legacy, we are blessed with a panoramic vision of a people's indomitable pride, dignity, and steady advance. To experience this vision is to be inspired and filled with pride and hope for our future. Enjoy the books, see the vision, and give thanks."

—Jerry Freeman, senior editor, *Minnesota Spokesman-Recorder*

"Our history as a people is one that must be told, learned, and recorded. *Minnesota's Black Community Project in the 21st Century* is a wonderful and needed continuation of Mr. Walter Scott's publications. It is a valuable public resource as well as a great reference for educators at all levels."

—Benjamin Mchie, founder and president, African American Registry

"*Minnesota's Black Community in the 21st Century* continues the important work of Walter Scott and his profiles of prominent African Americans in Minnesota from the 1960s and '70s. The biographies in this work, compiled by Minnesota's Black Community Project, will give today's readers an excellent overview of key figures in the state's African American community, while also providing vital information for future researchers."

—Edward Hathaway, manager, Special Collections, Archives,
    Preservation and Digitization, Hennepin County Library

"All too often, Minnesota history has been whitewashed as the story of voyageurs and senators, and the vibrant cultural and artistic life of Minnesota's Black community is presented only as an 'add-on' to a white narrative. In this crucial and necessary book, we see the current and future faces of our state excelling across all dimensions of human endeavor. It is a valuable documentation of where we are now and the promise of our future."

—Stephen Brookfield, John Ireland Endowed Chair, University of St. Thomas

"Without documentation, history cannot be preserved. Minneapolis publisher Walter R. Scott Sr. knew this when he set out to record the lives and work of Black Minnesotans in the 1950s, '60s, and '70s. Collectively the photos and biographical sketches in his three books provide more than snapshots of vibrant lives—they give us the feel of an era. *Minnesota's Black Community in the 21st Century* extends Scott's extraordinary vision and puts in our hands the joys and accomplishments of today's Black professionals in Minnesota, ensuring that Minnesota's Black history will endure. This highly anticipated publication will serve as an essential resource on Black history in Minnesota and is a welcome addition to the shelves of the Gary Sudduth African American History and Culture Collection at Sumner Library."

—Natalie Hart, adult services librarian, Hennepin County Library Sumner Branch

"When it comes to researching and preserving the history of postwar African American life in Minnesota, Walter Scott's pioneering trilogy of books—now reissued as *The Scott Collection*—has proven invaluable. *Minnesota's Black Community in the 21st Century* builds on Walter Scott's legacy as a forward-thinking journalist and chronicler of everyday Black excellence, bringing the project into the modern age by highlighting the contributions being made right here, right now."

—Andrea Swensson, radio host for 89.3 The Current and author of
Got to Be Something Here: The Rise of the Minneapolis Sound

"I have lived in the Twin Cities since the early '70s, and I had been exposed to Walter Scott's books shortly after arriving. When I met Anthony Scott sometime later, I was surprised to hear his father was the author of those books. I'm elated to see those books updated into the 21st century. I know his father is proud that the legacy continues."

—William C. Crutcher III, retired assistant general counsel,
chief environmental counsel, General Mills

"The publication of *Minnesota's Black Community in the 21st Century* is both necessary and timely. The continued documentation of the progress made is also a reminder that the work is ongoing and continuing to progress. I applaud the efforts of the nonprofit Minnesota's Black Community Project in compiling such an important work."

—Michael T. Fagin, PhD, special presidential advisor,
Minnesota State University, Mankato

MINNESOTA'S BLACK COMMUNITY IN THE 21st CENTURY

MINNESOTA'S BLACK COMMUNITY in the 21st CENTURY

Anthony R. Scott, Charles E. Crutchfield III, MD,
and Dr. Chaunda L. Scott, editors

Foreword by Dr. Mahmoud El-Kati

MINNESOTA
HISTORICAL
SOCIETY PRESS

CLEAN
WATER
LAND &
LEGACY
AMENDMENT

mnhspress.org

The Minnesota Historical Society Press is a member of the Association of University Presses.

Front cover, *top row, left to right:* Wayne Glanton, George J. Scott, Willie Ruth Hall; *bottom row, left to right:* Bryson Glanton Scott, Arianna J. Crutchfield, Dr. Josie R. Johnson.
Photos by Olivia Samira Crutchfield

Manufactured in the United States of America

10 9 8 7 6 5 4 3 2 1

∞ The paper used in this publication meets the minimum requirements of the American National Standard for Information Sciences—Permanence for Printed Library Materials, ANSI Z39.48-1984.

International Standard Book Number
ISBN: 978-1-68134-131-6 (hardcover)

Library of Congress Cataloging-in-Publication Data
Names: Scott, Anthony R., editor. | Crutchfield, Charles E. III, editor. | Scott, Chaunda L., editor.
Title: Minnesota's Black Community in the 21st Century / Anthony R. Scott, Dr. Charles E. Crutchfield III, and Dr. Chaunda L. Scott, editors.
Description: Saint Paul : Minnesota Historical Society Press, 2020. | Includes index. | Summary: "*Minnesota's Black Community in the 21st Century* shines a spotlight on African American individuals and organizations who are helping to build a better Minnesota. This book highlights the contributions of contemporary black Minnesotans in the fields of the arts, beauty and fashion, community service, education, entertainment, finance, government, labor, law and law enforcement, media and communications, medicine and health care, religion, social services, sports, science and technology, and more"—Provided by publisher.
Identifiers: LCCN 2019047340 | ISBN 9781681341316 (hardcover)
Subjects: LCSH: African Americans—Minnesota.
Classification: LCC E185.93.M55 M565 2020 | DDC 977.6/0496073—dc23
LC record available at https://lccn.loc.gov/2019047340

To Minnesota's thriving African American community—
past, present, and future

CITY OF SAINT PAUL
Mayor Melvin Carter

390 City Hall
15 West Kellogg Boulevard
Saint Paul, MN 55102

Telephone: 651-266-8510
Facsimile: 651-266-8521

January 17, 2020

Mr. Anthony R. Scott
President, Minnesota's Black Community Project
400 E. 42nd Street
Minneapolis, Minnesota 55409

Dear Mr. Scott,

Thank you for the opportunity to offer this endorsement of the Minnesota's Black Community Project's new book *Minnesota's Black Community in the 21st Century.*

Passing down the stories of those who came before us has been a vital part of history since the dawn of time and the wisdom that we inherit from our ancestors is given new life each time we pass it on to the next generation. This book continues this rich tradition and ensures we carry forward the legacy that has been bestowed upon us.

Congratulations to you, your board members, and the staff of Minnesota's Black Community Project for compiling this living history of the African-American community in Minnesota. This work serves as an inspiration for all of us.

Sincerely,

Melvin Carter
Mayor of Saint Paul

Minneapolis
City of Lakes

September 25th, 2018

Mr. Anthony R. Scott
President, Minnesota's Black Community Project
400 E. 42nd St
Minneapolis, MN 55409

Dear Mr. Scott,

I am excited for the new publication sponsored by Minnesota's Black Community Project entitled *Minnesota's Black Community in the 21st Century*, which will recognize the accomplishments of Minnesota's 21st century African American community. This publication is important for the recognition and recording of Minnesota's history. As the Mayor of Minneapolis, I know how important the entrepreneurship and innovation of our African American community has been in making Minneapolis a vibrant and successful city. I look forward to supporting the programs sponsored by Minnesota's Black Community Project.

It is with sincere delight that I congratulate you, Mr. Scott, and the board members of Minnesota's Black Community Project, on crafting this 21st century publication. Your work will help Minnesotans celebrate the many ways that African Americans across the state continue to help shape our history, culture, and future.

With best regards,

Jacob Frey

Mayor

CONTENTS

FOREWORD

First, let us begin by offering a hearty hail and salute to Minnesota's Black Community Project for its creative and visionary spirit and offering of this work. This volume honors Black people in Minnesota and is a treasure to behold. It is a much-needed, life-giving counterpoint to the "social death" that Black communities across America have endured for centuries. The images, messages, and symbols herein presented are sources of education, inspiration, and celebration. This panoramic view of Black life in the state of Minnesota is close to a work of art. Indeed, it is akin to Duke Ellington's music. That is to say, it is beyond category.

To boot, *Minnesota's Black Community in the 21st Century* gives us an arresting gaggle of pictorial literature of Black Minnesota life. In 1860, the population of Black people in Minnesota was 259, living mainly in St. Paul. In 1960, the population of Black people was 22,263, primarily located in the two major cities of St. Paul and Minneapolis. Today, with more than 300,000 Black people in the state, African American citizens can be found living and working in nearly two-thirds of the cities in Minnesota! Black people are living in at least 534 cities in Minnesota. This intrastate migration has led many of the metro suburbs to become significantly populated with Black people, to the degree that some are "majority-minority" cities. This movement of middle- and professional-class Black people that has taken place over the last several decades is due to their quest for better housing,

better schools, and better jobs. These significant changes and other dynamics make one wonder, "What are Black folks doing in all these places? Who are they and how did they get there?"

When I was asked to write the foreword for this volume, I was pleased to learn that Minnesota's Black Community Project was sponsoring it. I was also pleased to hear that this volume would be a contemporary extension of Walter R. Scott's research on Minnesota's Black community done in the 1950s, '60s, and '70s. Scott's renowned historical research eloquently captured nearly every aspect of Black community life during those yesteryears. In the postwar era, due to new opportunities brought on by civil rights struggles, a new middle and professional class emerged and was diversely composed of medical doctors, lawyers, engineers, architects, educators, a sturdy clergy, and pockets of business owners, as well as social service, civic and fraternal, and civil rights organizations. The words and images that Scott used dutifully reminded us of the local individuals who played significant roles in fighting for human and civil rights for all. The activist segment of the Black community was deeply aware of what hovered over us all and continues to threaten the ideals of democracy: racism and the American doctrine of white supremacy. One cannot thank Walter Scott enough for the historical research he provided about Minnesota's Black community.

The population of Black Minnesotans in the 21st century has evolved into a thriving community of men, women, teenagers, and children who are rising in achievement and success like never before. Black Minneapolitans, for example, much like the rest of Black America, have persevered, in spite of this nation's roadblocks. Great gains have been made in the opportunities for jobs, education, and even housing with the breaking of restrictive covenants, a clever racist trick that prevented Black citizens from securing housing in many areas. Now that such racial barriers have somewhat subsided compared to past decades, Black Minneapolitans are no longer bound to live in the only three areas of the city previously open to them, in south Minneapolis, Near North Minneapolis, and first-ring suburbs. Black families and individuals now work and live in almost every section of the metropolitan area.

This compilation by Minnesota's Black Community Project salutes a cross-section of highly successful Black citizens, including civic and political leaders, an enlightened clergy, actors, artists, educators, lawyers, business professionals, entertainers, and sports stars.

Thank you, Minnesota's Black Community Project, for this volume entitled *Minnesota's Black Community in the 21st Century*. It serves as a gift to all Black Minnesotans, especially our children. As they grow into life, they will appreciate and honor this legacy, which will help them to understand and value and build upon who they are, as a deeply rooted part of the making of Minnesota and America.

Lastly, the emotional undertone of this volume represents something that is complexly and compellingly human. There is something strangely and hauntingly beautiful, too. It is suggestive of the sentiment of Black America's finest poet laureate, Langston Hughes:

I, Too

I, too, sing America.
I am the darker brother.
They send me to eat in the kitchen
When company comes,
But I laugh,
And eat well,
And grow strong.

Tomorrow,
I'll be at the table
When company comes.
Nobody'll dare
Say to me,
"Eat in the kitchen,"
Then.

Besides,
They'll see how beautiful I am
And be ashamed—

I, too, am America.

Mahmoud El-Kati
Professor Emeritus of History
Macalester College, St. Paul

INTRODUCTION

For more than 165 years, a small population of African Americans in Minnesota has lived and thrived in communities in and around Minneapolis and St. Paul. Toward the end of World War II, in the spring of 1945, the Governor's Interracial Commission submitted to Minnesota governor Edward Thye a report on the condition of Black people in Minnesota. It was later published as a booklet entitled *The Negro Worker in Minnesota*. During the period from 1950 to 2015, distinguished researchers and scholars Walter R. Scott Sr., Dr. David Vassar Taylor, and Dr. William Green, among others, began documenting and publishing the historical contributions of Black Minnesotans of the 19th and 20th centuries.

Significantly, Walter R. Scott and the Scott Publishing Company produced a series of books in the 1950s, '60s, and '70s that highlighted what Black success looked like in Minnesota. Through pictorial résumés or, more specifically, photographs and brief biographical sketches, the books profiled the Black trailblazers working in professional occupations in Minnesota during this crucial pre– and post–civil rights period. The three self-published works were *Centennial Edition of the* Minneapolis Beacon (1956), *Minneapolis Negro Profile* (1968), and *Minnesota's Black Community* (1976). Even though Water Scott had limited financial resources and no technological support, the three volumes he produced are indispensable documents of African American history in post–World War II Minnesota. His

series provided one of the most important collections on African American residents in any state of the union, during any time period.

Today, however, research and literature highlighting contemporary African American success in Minnesota during the 21st century are scarce. Moreover, the majority of reporting on African Americans by the media in Minnesota and throughout the United States is negative. As a way to begin reversing this trend in the state, Minnesota's Black Community Project (MBCP) was established in 2016 as a nonprofit organization by two African American families from the Twin Cities: the Scotts and the Crutchfields.

MBCP is thrilled and honored to build upon Walter Scott's earlier research by introducing its first major project: *Minnesota's Black Community in the 21st Century.* (Throughout this volume, please note that the terms *Black* and *African American* will be used interchangeably.) Utilizing the "pictorial résumé" approach of Walter Scott's books from previous decades, this volume provides a glimpse into the African American men and women in Minnesota who are making valuable contributions in a variety of professions and fields, including arts and entertainment, business and entrepreneurship, community service, education, government and public affairs, law and law enforcement, media and communications, medicine and health care, religion, and sports. It also recognizes and applauds our Rising Stars, the young African American individuals who are emerging talents, whether they be school-age or up-and-coming professionals.

MBCP's goal is to make the information in this book widely accessible to the public, in Minnesota and around the globe, in order to shed light on a community that is too often left out of historical and contemporary profiles of the state. One cannot talk about Minnesota history and life without including its African American citizens. We hope this book serves to illustrate this point and educate all readers on the positive influence that African Americans have in our state. With this understanding, we can all move closer to unity and a better appreciation of and for all Minnesotans.

This book adds to the historical record by providing an overview look at African Americans in Minnesota in the 21st century, focusing on the professional, cultural, economic, and educational contributions of a range of individuals and organizations. It is intended to serve as a primary reference for scholars, researchers, and students conducting research on African Americans in contemporary Minnesota. The book deserves a place in elementary schools, middle schools, high schools, and colleges and universities in Minnesota and globally, and it will be of lasting value to the official record of the State of Minnesota and the Minnesota Historical Society. This publication will also be of value to public libraries and, in particular, libraries, centers, and institutes that have a strong focus on African Americans.

Perhaps most importantly, by sharing the stories of today's Black community in Minnesota, we hope to inspire African American children, youth, and adults to strive toward academic and professional success so that their accomplishments and contributions can further advance the health, wealth, and well-being of our state and someday be chronicled as a part of Minnesota's rich African American history.

The board members and staff of MBCP are ecstatic to offer this groundbreaking book to you. In compiling the photos and biographies for this celebratory volume, we had the pleasure of connecting and reconnecting with members of Minnesota's vibrant and diverse African American community. We were pleasantly overwhelmed by the support from the Twin Cities community regarding the importance of this book project.

What our board members most appreciated from working on this project is that Minnesota, our home state, has an exceptionally talented and thriving African American community that is worthy of being recognized and celebrated on an ongoing basis. We want to thank the many people who participated in this history-making endeavor. Without you, this book would not have been possible.

Of course, this book offers just a snapshot look at the hundreds of thousands of talented African Americans who live and work in Minnesota, specifically in Minneapolis and St. Paul, and is intended to offer a representative sampling of the myriad ways in which African Americans are an integral part of the Minnesota experience. We fully acknowledge that African Americans live in every corner of the state, and we hope to share their stories and accomplishments in future projects. We further acknowledge that there may be unintentional oversights and omissions in this volume despite our best efforts to produce a worthy publication. Moreover, we want our readership to know that this publication, along with our companion website, is part of an ongoing MBCP endeavor. Therefore, if you were not featured in this book, don't fret as additional opportunities are forthcoming for you to be acknowledged and celebrated. For more information, visit MinnesotasBlackCommunityProject.org.

On behalf of Minnesota's Black Community Project, we want to thank the countless numbers of people and organizations who helped to make this critical book possible. We are also grateful for the financial support we received for the research behind this book from a Minnesota Historical and Cultural Heritage Grant from the Minnesota Historical Society, a Pollination Project Foundation Grant, and the Crutchfield Dermatology Foundation. The Minnesota's Black Community Project board members and members at large would like to sincerely thank Ted Hathaway, the special collections, preservation, and digitization manager at the Hennepin County Library in downtown Minneapolis; Natalie Hart, head librarian at the Sumner Library in north Minneapolis; the Sabathani Community Center in Minneapolis; the Golden Thyme Café in St. Paul; Jerry Freeman, senior editor, and Tracey Williams-Dillard, CEO/publisher of the *Minnesota Spokesman-Recorder*; and Traci Bransford, partner, general counsel, and business and entertainment attorney at Stinson Leonard Street law firm in Minneapolis for helping to get the word out to the community about this book project. We also wish to thank Professor Mahmoud El-Kati for his outstanding foreword; our excellent support staff, Allison Cortez and Kelly McGuire;

our biography writers, George J. Scott and Nel Yomtov; our contributing literary writer, Dr. Jeanetta D. Sims; and our phenomenal photographers, Bruce Palaggi, Olivia Crutchfield, and Bryson Scott. Last, but not least, we want the thank Josh Leventhal, director of the Minnesota Historical Society Press, for helping MBCP make the release of *Minnesota's Black Community in the 21st Century* possible.

The MBCP board members also want to salute Walter R. Scott for his earlier books that extolled the contributions and achievements of African Americans in Minnesota in previous decades. We hope that this book, like those before it, serves as a lasting memento of the hopes and strengths of Minnesota's African American community in the present and for the future. We accept the responsibility of furthering Walter Scott's work on applauding and celebrating African American success in Minnesota with honor and pride as we move through the 21st century. Quoting Walter Scott's statement about his own publications, this book is "an earnest attempt to present pictorially, not merely facts, but facts in their proper proportion and perspective."

Dr. Chaunda L. Scott
Secretary
Minnesota's Black Community Project

Anthony R. Scott
President
Minnesota's Black Community Project

Charles E. Crutchfield III, MD
Vice President
Minnesota's Black Community Project

ABOUT THE "WE ARE HERE" SERIES
BY DR. JEANETTA D. SIMS

This groundbreaking book provides a visual representation of what inter-generational African American success looks like in 21st-century Minnesota. Through the book's photographs and biographical sketches, African Americans in Minnesota have an opportunity to introduce themselves to the world, be discovered, and be rediscovered. Indeed, as this profound volume illustrates, we are here.

The "We Are Here" series is a collection of poems and prose by Dr. Jeanetta D. Sims that celebrates the multifaceted presence of African Americans in local communities. Selections from this series open each section of the book, simultaneously honoring the past, present, and future contributions of African Americans in the particular fields. No finer time exists to claim, reclaim, and remind the world of the African American presence and its contributions to society.

ARTS AND ENTERTAINMENT

Can You Appreciate Us

Can you hear us?
Soulful, sweet sultry sounds of music.

Can you see us?
Passionate portrayals of poetic performances.

Can you laugh with us?
Commanding comics carrying casual conversations.

Can you appreciate us?
Suspending and mirroring reality to enhance
Black lives.

We are here.

We sing.
We act.
We joke.
We entertain.

The laughter, enjoyment, and fun of African American entertainment is hearty. The swelling music and soulful sounds are reminiscent of a lively family reunion. The abilities appear effortless, even as the portrayals are skillful. We are motivated by how they move us. And, as audiences, we are the primary benefactors of their expertise. The artistry of African Americans in the fine arts and writing professions is equally charismatic. Their passion holds audiences captive for years, the memorable impact outliving the length of the performance or the work. We smile in moments of reflection on their work. And we are grateful they endured the effort to share their talents for our enjoyment.

African American singers, musicians, actors, writers, storytellers, and artists have been enriching the Minnesota arts and culture scene for generations. Today, the community boasts creative people working in both traditional and avant-garde styles, across a range of media. The list is far greater than what we are able to highlight here.

Ta-coumba Aiken

Ta-coumba Aiken is an artist, arts administrator, educator, and community activist. He has created or helped create more than 300 murals and public art sculptures, many of which shape the visual experience of the Twin Cities. Aiken has served on the boards of the Minneapolis Arts Commission and the St. Paul Art Collective, among others, and has acted as an advisor on the arts for both the City of St. Paul and the City of Minneapolis. He has received fellowships from the Pollock-Krasner Foundation and the Bush Foundation. His works can be experienced in many public spaces across the Twin Cities as well as in the collections of the Walker Art Center, the McKnight Foundation, and General Mills.

Ta-coumba Aiken

Leslie Barlow

Leslie Barlow is a visual artist and educator who works primarily in the medium of oil painting. Born and raised in Minneapolis, Barlow received her bachelor of fine arts degree in 2011 from the University of Wisconsin–Stout and her master of fine arts degree in 2016 from the Minneapolis College of Art and Design, the same year *City Pages* chose her as an Artist of the Year. In 2019, she was awarded both the McKnight Visual Artist Fellowship and the Springboard 20/20 Fellowship. In 2016 and 2018, Barlow received the Minnesota State Arts Board Artist Initiative Grant, and in 2018, she received the Minnesota Museum of American Art Purchase Award in the Minnesota State Fair juried exhibition. Barlow directs Studio 400, a space for artists in Northeast Minneapolis, and teaches university and community classes. She also leads artist and arts programming for the MidWest Mixed conference.

Lou Bellamy

Lou Bellamy is the founder and artistic director emeritus of Penumbra Theatre in St. Paul. He is also an Obie Award–winning director and an accomplished actor, and he taught theater and dance at the University of Minnesota for 38 years. Founded in 1976, Penumbra is the largest Black theater in the country and one of the premier venues focusing on the dramatic exploration of the African American experience. During Bellamy's four decades at Penumbra, the theater has produced nearly 40 world premieres, including August Wilson's first professional production. Penumbra has produced more plays by

Lou Bellamy

Sarah Bellamy

the Pulitzer Prize–winning Wilson than any other theater in the world.

Sarah Bellamy

Sarah Bellamy is the artistic director of Penumbra Theatre. The daughter of Lou Bellamy, she has taken the torch from her father in leading the highly regarded and influential African American theater. Sarah Bellamy is also a playwright and director. She leads Penumbra's community engagement initiatives, including the Summer Institute, a leadership development program for teens to practice art for social change. A graduate of Sarah Lawrence College, Bellamy holds a master's degree from the University of Chicago and has taught at Macalester College, the University of Minnesota, and United Theological Seminary of the Twin Cities.

Blackout Improv

Blackout Improv was founded and is owned by Alsa Bruno, Joy Dolo Anfinson, Andy Hilbrands, John Gebretatose, and Kory LaQuess Pullam. Blackout is dedicated to comedy, social justice, and arts access with a cast of performers that includes comedians, musicians, actors, dancers, poets, writers, storytellers, and educators who all want to see more Black performers on more stages, to create comedic dialogue around serious truths, and to facilitate access to improvisational comedy for Black students. In addition to performing, Blackout has spent many thousands of hours putting on trainings, workshops, and performances for nonprofits, colleges, and corporations all over the globe.

Trevor Bowen

■ Trevor Bowen

Trevor Bowen is a costume designer who has outfitted a variety of productions in the Twin Cities. His clients have included Theater Latté Da, Park Square Theatre, the History Theatre, the Guthrie Theater, and many others. A native of Oklahoma, Bowen was named emerging artist of the year at the 2016 Ivey Awards.

■ R. Terrance Briscoe

Rising Star

R. Terrance Briscoe has been performing on Twin Cities stages since the age of four. His acting career began at the Children's Theatre Company, where he starred in *The Wind in the Willows*, *How the Grinch Stole Christmas*, and

R. Terrance Briscoe

Not Without Laughter. Briscoe has also worked alongside Lou Bellamy at Penumbra Theatre, where he starred in *Black Nativity* and *Canned Goods.* In 2019, Briscoe starred in the Youth Performance Company's 30th anniversary production of *Periphery: The Student Sit-ins of 1960,* inspired by the sit-in movement of Greensboro, North Carolina, during the civil rights movement. It was his second performance with the Youth Performance Company, his first being *The Day King Died: The Final Chapter.* In addition to acting, Briscoe has been a part of several award-winning choirs and has walked the runway as a model for Nordstrom department stores. A Minneapolis native, Terrance is married to Phyllis Briscoe, and they have two sons.

Brandi Brown

■ Brandi Brown

Brandi Brown is a stand-up comic and a writer. She performs and emcees regularly at Minneapolis's Acme Comedy Club and has opened for such notable comics as Maria Bamford, Hannibal Buress, and Michael Che. A native of Minneapolis, Brown was a finalist in the Nickelodeon Studios Auditions tour when she was just eight years old. Years later, she was a finalist in Acme's "Funniest Person in the Twin Cities" contest. She is a cohost of the "Bill Corbett's Funhouse" podcast.

Carlyle Brown

◾ Carlyle Brown

Carlyle Brown is a playwright, a performer, and the artistic director of Carlyle Brown & Company. He has written 11 original plays, and many of his productions have been performed at St. Paul's Penumbra Theatre as well as at Children's Theatre Company, Mixed Blood Theatre, and Park Square Theatre in the Twin Cities. He has also received commissions from theaters throughout the country. Brown is a core writer and board member of the Playwrights' Center in Minneapolis, and he is an alumnus of New Dramatists in New York. He has also served on the board of the Jerome Foundation.

◾ Shá Cage

Shá Cage is an actress, director, playwright, spoken-word artist, educator, and activist. She is the senior curator at Catalyst Arts, a producing arts team committed to providing space for traditionally marginalized artists and communities of color. She has written five solo works and six plays collaboratively, and she has performed onstage at a range of Twin Cities theaters, including Penumbra, the Guthrie, Pangea, Mixed Blood, Ten Thousand Things, and more. In 2019, Cage directed the play *African School Girls* at the Jungle Theater and coproduced the film documentary *39 Seconds*, about Black baseball player John Donaldson. She was named a 2017 "Artist of the Year" by *City Pages*, a leading artist of her generation by *Insight News*, a "Change Maker" by the Minnesota Women's Press, and a "Mover and Maker" by *Mpls.St.Paul Magazine*. Cage cofounded Mama Mosaic Theater and the MN Spoken Word Association. Her work and activism have taken her across the country as well as overseas to Africa, Asia, and Europe.

◾ Calonna Carlisle
Rising Star

Calonna Carlisle is a gifted dancer, athlete, musician, singer, student, and spokesmodel. She is already a star, with even greater stardom ahead.

Calonna Carlisle with her mom, Sara Carlson

◾ Donte Collins

Donte Collins is a Black, Queer American poet. Named the inaugural Youth Poet Laureate of St. Paul in 2017, they

Donte Collins

also received the 2016 "Most Promising Young Poet" award from the Academy of American Poets, the 2016 John R. Mitchell Prize in poetry from Augsburg University, and the McKnight Artist Fellowship for Spoken Word in 2018. Collins's poetry collection *Autopsy* was published in 2017.

Bill Cottman

Bill Cottman, who worked for several decades as an electrical engineer, found his true calling as an artist and photographer. His photographic work has been exhibited in galleries across the Twin Cities since the early 1970s. He has developed several books of his photography and poems and has received many grants, including from the Minnesota State Arts Board and a McKnight Artist Fellowship for Photography in 2002. Born and raised in Salisbury, Maryland, Cottman moved to the Twin Cities after graduating from Howard University School of Engineering in 1967 and went on to a 20-year career at Honeywell in various management roles.

Ladonna Craelius
Rising Star

Ladonna Craelius participates in all manner of creative pursuits, both in front of and behind the camera. Born and raised in Chicago, Craelius has had a lifelong love for the arts. Her childhood home was filled was books, art, music, and dance. She began her career as a model, which blossomed into acting. Her deepest wish is to leave behind a legacy of art and creativity that will inspire people long after she is gone.

Ladonna Craelius

Olivia S. Crutchfield
Rising Star

Olivia S. Crutchfield is a photographer from Mendota Heights and a student at the Stern School of Business at New York University. She started taking pictures as a teenager in 2014 and enjoys shooting nature and portrait photography. Crutchfield shares her photos through Instagram (35,000 followers) and has worked as a photojournalist for the *Minnesota Spokesman-Recorder* newspaper and as a member of the photo team of Minnesota's Black Community Project. She was editor in chief

Olivia S. Crutchfield

of the Eagan High School newspaper and director of the school yearbook. Crutchfield was a two-time national champion in the Young Business Professionals of America, a member of the National Honor Society, and a photographic intern for National Geographic during a four-week trip to Australia. She is also an accomplished pianist and has a black belt in karate.

Danielle Daniel

Danielle Daniel is an actress, storyteller, author, and educator. Her storytelling programs and tour shows have been presented in Europe and around the United States. She has worked in many schools, colleges, and community organizations using the art of storytelling to entertain, educate, motivate, and empower people of all ages and encourage students to develop their own creative voice and style. During her career, Daniel has received a Jim Dusso Artist Award, a Minnesota State Arts Board Fellowship, a Many Voices Award from the Playwright

Center, and a Jerome Fellowship. She is the author of a children's book, *The Ghost of Old Man Willie*, and five plays. She received a bachelor of arts degree from the University of Minnesota and completed the Kennedy Performance Arts Center "Artist as Educators" program.

Mary Moore Easter

Mary Moore Easter is an award-winning poet and the founder, former director, and emeritus professor of the dance program at Carleton College in Northfield. She published the chapbook *Walking from Origins* in 1993 and the poetry collection *The Body of the World* in 2018. Among her many honors are a Bush Artist Fellowship, multiple McKnight Artist Fellowships, a Cave Canem Fellowship, a Loft Creative Nonfiction Award, and a Pushcart Prize nomination for poetry.

Keno Evol

Keno Evol (Antoine Duke) is a poet and educator born in Chicago, Illinois, and raised in south Minneapolis. He is the founder and executive director of Black Table Arts, a company focused on arts education, professional development, and creative opportunities for Black artists, and also hosts the annual Because Black Life Conference. He is editor of his company's anthology, *A Garden of Black Joy: Global Poetry from the Edges of Liberation and Living*. Evol won first place in the 2017 Sonia Sanchez–Langston Hughes Poetry Contest. He was an honorable mention for both the 2017 Spoken Word Immersion Fellowship and the 2018 McKnight Artist Fellowship for spoken word at the Loft Literary Center in Minneapolis. He has been published in *Split This Rock*, *Radius Lit*, and *Vinyl*.

Shannon Gibney

Shannon Gibney is an educator, activist, and award-winning author who has published books for both adults and children. Her acclaimed *Dream Country* won the 2019 Minnesota Book Award for Young Adult Literature, and *See No Color* won the 2016 Minnesota Book Award for Young People's Literature. Gibney is a professor of English at Minneapolis Community and Technical College, and she teaches courses on writing at the Loft Literary Center in Minneapolis and elsewhere. She also writes and speaks extensively on issues relating to race, gender, class, power, and identity.

Shannon Gibney

Beverly Tipton Hammond

Beverly Tipton Hammond is a visual artist, dancer, writer, singer, and songwriter. Her paintings have been displayed in Hennepin County exhibitions and at the Minnesota African American Heritage Museum and Gallery. Her "Hattitude" series pays homage to the cultural and spiritual significance of women's hats, or church hats, in the African American community. Hammond also serves as a worship leader at Gethsemane Lutheran Church in north Minneapolis.

Beverly Tipton Hammond

H. Adam Harris

H. Adam Harris is an actor, director, teaching artist, and cultural equity consultant. He is a member of the Penumbra Theatre Company and the theater's associate director of programming. He has appeared in numerous productions with the Children's Theatre Company as well as at such venues as the Guthrie Theater, Park Square Theatre, Pillsbury House Theatre, Seattle Children's Theatre, and New Conservatory Theatre Center in San Francisco. Harris also is a board member of Ten Thousand Things Theater Company; education coordinator at the Playwrights' Center; a resident teaching artist with the Guthrie; and an equity, diversity, and inclusion consultant for various organizations. He is a graduate of the University of Minnesota/Guthrie Theater BFA Actor Training Program.

Carolyn Holbrook

Carolyn Holbrook is a writer, educator, and advocate for the arts. Her passion for providing grassroots accessibility to the literary arts inspired her to found in 1993 SASE: The Write Place, where she served as artistic/executive director until 2006. In 2015, she established "More Than a Single Story," a series of public conversations with writers of color centered on themes of race and narrative voice. That year she was named a "Change Maker" by the Minnesota Women's Press. Her essays and writings have been published in numerous collections, including *A Good Time for the Truth: Race in Minnesota,* and in 2010 she won the prestigious Kay Sexton Award at the Minnesota Book Awards. Holbrook is an adjunct professor of creative writing at Hamline University's College of Liberal Arts/ Creative Writing Programs, as well as a creative writing instructor at the Loft Literary Center. Her newest collection, *Tell Me Your Names and I Will Testify,* was published in 2020.

Carolyn Holbrook

Ernie Hudson

Ernie Hudson

Ernie Hudson is a longtime film, television, and stage actor. Perhaps best known for his role in the original *Ghostbusters* movie of 1984 and its 1989 sequel, he has more than 230 screen credits, including recurring roles on HBO's *Oz* and Netflix's *Grace and Frankie* and guest appearances on such popular shows as *Modern Family, Grey's Anatomy,* and *Key and Peele.* Hudson is the father of four boys and divides his time between homes in Minneapolis and Los Angeles.

Kelechi Jaavaid

Kelechi Jaavaid, aka K Jay the Comedian, is a multitalented artist best known for his comedy work at comedy clubs and festivals. He has film and TV credits, and he performs as a spoken word artist as the character Late Nite Poet. Jaavaid is also a former teacher who has developed

Kelechi Jaavaid

Marlon James

a program using arts as a conflict-resolution tool to help students examine decision-making skills and life options.

◼ Marlon James

Marlon James is an award-winning novelist and associate professor of English at Macalester College in St. Paul. He won the Man Booker Prize in 2015 for his novel *A Brief History of Seven Killings*, which also won a Minnesota Book Award and many other accolades. His fourth novel, *Black Leopard, Red Wolf*, was published in 2019 as the first of a planned trilogy of fantasy fiction. A native of Jamaica, James joined the Macalester English department in 2007 and, in 2016, was named the college's first writer-in-residence.

◼ Seitu Ken Jones

Seitu Ken Jones is a visual artist from Minneapolis. Working on his own or in collaboration, Jones has created more than 30 large-scale public art works during his career. He has been awarded a Minnesota State Arts Board Fellowship, a McKnight Visual Artist Fellowship, a Bush Artist Fellowship, a Bush Leadership Fellowship, and a National Endowment for the Arts/Theater Communication Group Designer Fellowship. Jones also received a Loeb Fellowship at the Harvard Graduate School of Design in 2001–02 and was the artist-in-residence at the Harvard Ceramics Program. He was Millennium artist-in-residence for 651 Arts in Brooklyn, New York, and was the first artist-in-residence for the city of Minneapolis. In 2014, he integrated artwork into three stations for the new Greenline Light Rail Transit system in the

Twin Cities. A 2013 Joyce Award from Chicago's Joyce Foundation allowed Jones to develop CREATE: The Community Meal, a dinner for 2,000 people at a table a half a mile long. The project focused on issues relating to access to healthy food. Jones worked with members of his neighborhood to create Frogtown Farm, a five-acre farm in a St. Paul city park. He was awarded a Forecast Public Art Grant to build a floating sculpture to act as a research vessel for the Mississippi River. He received the 2017 Distinguished Artist Award from the McKnight Foundation.

Jones is a retired faculty member of Goddard College in Port Townsend, Washington. He holds a bachelor's degree in landscape design and a master's of library science degree in environmental history. He is also a member of the board of managers for the Capitol Region Watershed District.

Seitu Ken Jones

Tish Jones

Tish Jones is a poet, performer, educator, and organizer from St. Paul. She is the founder and executive director of TruArtSpeaks, a nonprofit organization whose mission is to cultivate literacy, leadership, and social justice through the study and application of spoken-word and hip-hop culture. She has directed the Brave New Voices Festival and has performed on national and local stages, including the Walker Art Center, the Cedar Cultural Center, and TEDxMinneapolis. Her work has also appeared in print and audio formats for the Minnesota Historical Society Press and the Loft Literary Center, respectively. Jones was the curating artist for the Twin Cities Public Television segment *ART IS . . . My Origin.* She has held fellowships with Art Matters, Springboard 20/20, and the International Leadership Institute.

Ray "Fancy Ray" McCloney

Ray "Fancy Ray" McCloney is a comedian, television personality, and flamboyant showman and the self-proclaimed "Best Looking Man in Comedy." McCloney had his own talk

Ray "Fancy Ray" McCloney

show, *The Fancy Ray Show*, on public access television in the 1980s and '90s. He has performed in concert with Richard Pryor, Chris Rock, and Little Richard and appeared on *The Tonight Show*, *Last Comic Standing*, and *America's Got Talent*, as well as in dozens of commercials, including a 2016 Super Bowl ad. In 1998, he declared his candidacy for governor of Minnesota and appeared on the ballot, only to lose to Jesse Ventura. Fancy Ray is also ordained by the Universal Life Church and officiates weddings, life celebration ceremonies, and spiritual services.

■ Shaina McCoy

Shaina McCoy is a painter and artist from Minneapolis. She attended the Perpich Center for Arts Education in Golden Valley and then Normandale Community College before graduating with an associate of arts degree from Minneapolis Community and Technical College. Her work has been included in group exhibitions at Art4Shelter, PLOT, Venture North, and City Wide Artists Gallery in Minneapolis and at Gildar Gallery in Denver. McCoy had her first solo exhibition, "A Family Affair," in 2019 at Ever Gold [Projects], a gallery located, appropriately, on Minnesota Street in San Francisco.

■ Neese Parker

Neese Parker is the youth engagement manager at Youthprise, a resource for youth-serving organizations in Minnesota. She is committed to providing technical assistance to youth of color who wish to earn sustainable income from their art. Using innovative strategies, she hopes to make

Neese Parker

an impact for young artists around the world and create examples for future generations.

■ Junauda Petrus-Nasah

Junauda Petrus-Nasah is a creative activist, writer, playwright, and performance artist focused on the *corde lisse*. Alongside Erin Sharkey (see page 19), in 2011 Petrus-Nasah cofounded Free Black Dirt, an experimental artist collective based in Minneapolis. In 2016, *City Pages* dubbed her an Artist of the Year. In addition to writing, choreographing, and directing performance pieces, Petrus-Nasah was lead artist with Heart of the Beast Theatre's May Day parade for two years. She has received two travel and study grants from the Jerome Foundation, a Givens Foundation fellowship, the Playwrights' Center Many Voices Mentorship, and the Naked Stages residency at Pillsbury House. She is the writer and director of the poetic film series *Sweetness of Wild*, and in 2019, she published her first book, *The Stars and the Blackness Between Them*, a queer love story about two Black girls, one from Trinidad, the other from Minneapolis. The book received a Coretta Scott King Honor Award and is a finalist for a 2020 Minnesota Book Award. Petrus-Nasah was born in Minneapolis.

T. Mychael Rambo

◼ T. Mychael Rambo

T. Mychael Rambo is an award-winning actor, vocalist, arts educator, and community organizer. One of the area's finest and most experienced stage actors, he is a longtime member of the Penumbra Theatre Company and has performed at such Twin Cities theaters as the Guthrie, the Ordway, Illusion, Mixed Blood, Park Square, Ten Thousand Things, and the Minnesota Opera, among others. In addition, he has appeared on stages around the world as well as in television commercials, feature films, and television series. Rambo has also released two music albums. Among his many accolades are the 2010

Sally Award for Arts Educator from the Ordway, a 2010 Minnesota Black Music Award, a McKnight Theater Artist Fellowship, a Minnesota State Arts Board Artist Fellowship, and the University of Minnesota Century Council Community Award and Outstanding Community Service Award.

◼ Robyne Robinson

Robyne Robinson is principal consultant at Five X Five Art Consultants, working with artists, developers, and public and private clients to plan and execute public art installations. She is also a jewelry designer at Rox Minneapolis Jewelry and was previously the arts and culture director for the Minneapolis–St. Paul International Airport. Prior to becoming an arts consultant and advocate, Robinson spent 20 years as a reporter, anchor, and producer for KMSP/Fox 9; she is a two-time Emmy Award winner and in September 2018 became the first

Robyne Robinson

person of color to be inducted into the Minnesota Broadcasting Hall of Fame. A graduate of Loyola University in Chicago, Robinson ran for Minnesota lieutenant governor in 2010, with arts advocacy as a central initiative in her campaign. She is an accomplished public speaker and has served on numerous art boards, including at Walker Art Center and the Minneapolis College of Art and Design.

Bobby Rogers

Bobby Rogers is a photographer, visual artist, and the resident photographer at Walker Art Center. His work often centers on his multiple identities as a Black, millennial Muslim while exploring narratives of resilience and pride in Black culture. The Minneapolis native earned a bachelor of fine arts degree from the Minneapolis College of Art and Design. In 2016, he was named a "Top Visual

Artist to Watch" by *Minnesota Monthly*; in 2017, *City Pages* named him one of the "Artists of the Year." Rogers's work has been shown at the International Center of Photography, the Minneapolis Institute of Art, Public Functionary, and the Minnesota Museum of American Art, among other spaces, and he has been featured in publications ranging from Vice and *Juxtapoz* to the *New York Times* and the Huffington Post.

Dua Saleh, on the cover of their EP release, *Nūr*

Bobby Rogers

Dua Saleh

Dua Saleh is a singer, poet, actor, and activist. Born in Sudan, Saleh moved to the Twin Cities as a child and was raised in St. Paul's Rondo neighborhood. They began writing poetry as a teenager and then in college at Augsburg University. Their performance of the poem "Pins and Needles" at a Button Poetry Live event went viral on YouTube. Saleh eventually turned their attention to music. Their debut EP from 2019, *Nūr*, incorporates themes of race, gender, and personal experiences.

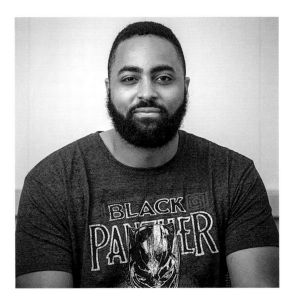
Bryson Glanton Scott

Bryson Glanton Scott
Rising Star

Bryson Glanton Scott earned a bachelor of fine arts in screenwriting from Metropolitan State University in 2014. Since then, he has been involved in film and photography projects for several community organizations, including the Sabathani Community Center and Hennepin County Library. He is also a freelance photographer in Minneapolis and a guitarist. Scott is employed by Hennepin County as a correctional officer. He is the son of Anthony and Jackie Scott and the grandson of Walter R. Scott Sr. and Margaret A. Scott and Wayne and Clodeal Glanton.

Erin Sharkey

Erin Sharkey is a writer, producer, educator, and graphic designer. She teaches classes at the Loft Literary Center and Metropolitan State University and has taught for the Minnesota Prison Writing Workshop. Sharkey cofounded Free Black Dirt, an experimental-arts collective, and

in 2015 helped start the Black Market Reads podcast on Black literature. She was a 2016/17 Loft Mentor Series winner in creative nonfiction, a 2016 VONA/Voices Travel Writing fellow, a 2015 African American Literature Emerging Writers fellow with the Givens Foundation, and a Coffee House Press "In the Stacks" artist-in-residence at the Givens Collection at the University of Minnesota, where she helped promote Umbra Search, a digital search tool for African American memory. Sharkey received her master of fine arts degree in creative writing from Hamline University.

Austene Van

Austene Van is an actor, director, writer, and choreographer. She is the founder and artistic director of New Dawn Theatre Company, which is dedicated to illuminating and supporting cutting-edge works by underrepresented communities. She also works as a director at Yellow Tree Theatre in Osseo and

Austene Van

is theater director at Skylight Music Theatre in Milwaukee, Wisconsin. Van has worked at virtually every major theater in the Twin Cities area.

Chaun Webster

Chaun Webster is a poet and graphic designer. His creative work draws from his interest in the sign of graffiti, the layering of collage, simultaneity, and the visuality of text. He utilizes these methods to investigate race, specifically the instability of blackness and black subjectivities, geography, memory, and the body. Webster's first book, *GeNtry!fication: or the scene of the crime*, was published in 2018 and won the Minnesota Book Award for Poetry.

Regina Williams

Regina Williams is an acclaimed actor and singer who has performed at nearly every major theater in the Twin Cities. She is a member of the Penumbra

Regina Williams

Theatre Company and a core member at Ten Thousand Things Theater. She earned an Ivey Award for her role as Mama Nadi in the Mixed Blood Theatre production of *Ruined*. Williams has also recorded three solo music albums.

Nothando Zulu

Nothando Zulu

Nothando Zulu is a master storyteller who has been performing in the Twin Cities since the late 1970s. She shares stories that entertain, educate, motivate, and inspire, drawing from an extensive reserve of colorful characters whose antics leave audiences amused and pondering life's lessons. She and her husband, Vusumuzi (Vusi), founded the Minnesota chapter of the Black Storytellers Alliance, a national nonprofit group dedicated to maintaining the art of storytelling and spreading stories of the African diaspora. Since 1991, Nothando and Vusi have produced the three-day storytelling festival Signifyin' & Testifyin'. Nothando is also a wife, mother, grandmother, and great-grandmother and a community and political activist.

MUSICIANS

■ Tre Aaron

Tre Aaron is a country music artist. Tre Aaron and the Sidewalk Blues Boys have performed at events and venues around the Twin Cities, including the May Day Festival in Powderhorn Park, Fern's Bar & Grill in St. Paul, Palmer's Bar in Minneapolis, and the Lake Harriet Band Shell.

Tre Aaron

■ Stefon "P.O.S." Alexander

Stefon Alexander, better known as P.O.S., is a rapper, hip-hop artist, producer, musician, and "punk philosopher." The Minneapolis native is a founding member of the Doomtree hip-hop collective, formed in 2001. He has also

Stefon "P.O.S." Alexander

been in the punk bands Degenerates and Building Better Bombs, the local supergroup Gayngs, and the experimental noise band Marijuana Deathsquads. P.O.S. has released three studio albums with Doomtree and five solo albums. He has also made guest appearances on numerous recordings by fellow hip-hop and rock artists.

■ Bernard Allison

Bernard Allison is a guitar player and a true son of the blues, having followed in the footsteps of his blues legend father, Luther Allison. Allison's 17th album, *In the Mix*, was recorded at Winterland Studios in Minneapolis with core band members George Moye on bass, Mario Dawson on drums, and José James on sax and guest Mark Leach on keyboards. His latest album, *Let It Go*, was released in 2018 and peaked at number nine on the *Billboard* charts.

Bernard Allison (see page 21)

Astralblak

Astralblak is a funk, soul, R&B, and hip-hop collective. Originating in 2014 under the name Zuluzuluu, the band consists of MMYYKK (Mychal Fisher), Greg Grease (Greg Johnson), DJ Just

Astralblak

Nine (Kenichi Thomas), elliott (Elliott Surber), and Proper-T (Taylor Johnson), each of whom is a producer, songwriter, and multi-instrumentalist. In 2016, they released the EP *What's the Price?* and followed with the 2018 album *Seeds.*

Aisha Baker

Aisha Baker is singer-songwriter of pop, rock, and jazz music. She started singing in nightclubs with her dad as a chaperone. Baker wrote two songs that appeared in the Robert Townsend films *The Meteor Man* and *The Five Heartbeats.* Baker is also a clinic nurse at Park Nicollet Health Services in Minneapolis.

Aisha Baker

Chastity Brown

Chastity Brown is a singer, songwriter, and musician. Born in Tennessee, she grew up surrounded by country and soul music, styles that can be heard in her own compositions along with folk, blues, and pop influences: she has been referred to as a "banjo-playing soul singer." Since moving to Minneapolis in 2006, Brown has released five studio albums (as of 2019). She is also involved in many charitable causes around the Twin Cities.

Chastity Brown

Walter Chancellor Jr.

◼ Walter Chancellor Jr.

Walter Chancellor Jr. is a multi-instrumentalist and renowned saxophonist in the Twin Cities. Specializing in contemporary jazz and rhythm and blues music, he has performed and recorded with various national and local acts, including providing the sax work for Prince's 1996 platinum-selling album, *Emancipation*. In addition, Chancellor has worked with such artists as Chaka Khan, Bobby Lyle, Thomasina Petrus, and Debbie Duncan, to name a few. Through his own production company, Chancellor Music, Chancellor provides music production, songwriting, and session work for local and national artists working in the film and advertising industries as well as corporate groups and other private entities.

◼ Bobby Commodore

Bobby Commodore is a renowned drummer who has played with many local ensembles in a range of genres. In 1974, he began a 20-year affiliation with the Grammy Award–winning group Sounds of Blackness, with whom he toured the United States and recorded several albums. It is also where he met his wife, Ginger Commodore, who is a singer with the Sounds. Working with Sounds of Blackness led to many other musical opportunities for Bobby in the Twin Cities gospel community. It also led him into the world of jazz and a 12-year affiliation as drummer and business manager for Moore by Four. With Moore by Four, Commodore has played to sold-out houses across the Midwest, toured the world playing at prestigious jazz festivals, and appeared on several PBS

Bobby Commodore

Commodore has traveled the world, performing across the United States, Europe, and Japan. She has expanded her career by producing and performing in tribute shows in the Twin Cities. Artists she has paid tribute to include Stevie Wonder, Aretha Franklin, and Natalie Cole. She serves as an instructor with Penumbra Theatre's Summer Institute as well.

specials featuring the ensemble. Commodore has also performed at the Guthrie Theater, Orchestra Hall, the Ordway Center for the Performing Arts, and the Fitzgerald Theater. He continues to refine his skills while serving as musical director and drummer for his wife and her band, GCQ. Commodore defines his playing style as "being in the pocket, in the groove."

■ Ginger Commodore

Ginger Commodore is a singer, songwriter, and actress in the Twin Cities. She and her husband, drummer Bobby Commodore, are original members of the Grammy Award–winning ensemble Sounds of Blackness and several local gospel groups. Ginger is also an original member of the vocal jazz ensemble Moore by Four. She's shared the stage with such artists as Doc Severinsen, Patrice Rushen, Kenny Loggins, and Rachelle Ferrell. Commodore has also been in several theatrical productions with the Minnesota Opera Company, the Mixed Blood Theatre, the Children's Theatre Company, Hey City Theatres, the Penumbra Theatre Company, and the Chanhassen Dinner Theaters.

Ginger Commodore

■ Mike De'cole

Mike De'cole is a vocalist and soulful crooner based in Minneapolis. He released his debut album, *So It Was Written*, in 2016. In 2017, he collaborated with songwriter Mosi Dorbayani on the six-track EP *May, and Everything After* on the World Academy of Arts, Literature, and Media (WAALM) label. A second EP, *Simply Wonderful*, was released in the UK in 2019.

Mike De'cole

Dem Atlas

Dem Atlas, born Joshua Evans Turner, is a hip-hop artist from the Twin Cities. He released his debut EP, *Charle Brwn*, in 2013 and followed with the full-length *Embrace the Sun*, recorded with fellow rapper Guante and producer Rube as the group Sifu Hotman. Dem Atlas has two solo albums—*mF deM* from 2016 and *Bad Actress* from 2018—both on the Rhymesayers Entertainment recording label.

DJ Keezy

DJ Keezy is a hip-hop DJ who curates dance and hip-hop events at clubs around the Twin Cities, notably a recurring dance night called the Klituation, emphasizing female empowerment behind an all-female lineup of DJs, artists, and performers. Born Akeena Bronson in north Minneapolis, DJ Keezy was named "Best Club DJ" by *City Pages* in 2017. Her DJing style focuses on hip-hop and rap but has heavy doses of jazz and R&B, including both throwback music and current hits.

Ashley DuBose

Ashley DuBose is a singer, songwriter, voice-over actress, and model. She also works as a substitute teacher and has a bachelor's degree in mathematics. DuBose began singing and writing music at the age of 10, and she rose to fame when she appeared on season five of the hit TV show *The Voice*, in 2013. In 2014, she was named "Best Vocalist (Female)" by *City Pages*. Her albums *Somethin' More* and *Be You* have amassed millions of streams by fans in more than 130 countries.

Ashley DuBose

Debbie Duncan

Debbie Duncan, also known as the "First Lady of Song," is a renowned jazz vocalist who has shared her phenomenal vocal talent in the Twin Cities and

Debbie Duncan

at jazz festivals throughout the United States. In addition to being a distinguished jazz vocalist and flutist, she teaches voice lessons at Walker West Music Academy in St. Paul and works with youth at We Care Performing Arts. In 2018, Duncan released a new jazz album entitled *Full Circle.*

PaviElle French

PaviElle French is a singer, songwriter, pianist, and artist. Hailing from St. Paul's Rondo neighborhood, French came from a musical family and honed her artistry at Mississippi Creative Arts School, Walker-West Music Academy, Penumbra Theatre, and SteppingStone Theater. In 2015, she was voted "Best R&B Vocalist" by *City Pages,* named one of First Avenue's "Best New Bands," and

PaviElle French

featured on TPT's "Lowertown Line" series, for which she received an Upper Midwest Emmy Award. She won a 2016 Sage Award for Outstanding Performance for her solo dance work, "Ovarian Fortitude." Best known for her soulful, R&B style of vocals, in 2019, she composed a symphony—commissioned by and performed with the St. Paul Chamber Orchestra—called "A Requiem for Zula," to honor her mother, Zula Young, and her Rondo roots. French performs regularly at music venues throughout the Twin Cities, including the Cedar Cultural Center, First Avenue, Icehouse, the Dakota, and more.

George Scott Trio

The George Scott Trio offers smooth jazz mixed with funk. The group features George Scott on lead guitar and bass, Aaron Bellamy on drums, and MC Alan C on keyboards. George Scott is also a

George Scott

George Scott Trio

producer and composer and has long been a part of the Minneapolis music scene. He has shared the stage with such notables as Prince, Musiq Soulchild, Sheila E., Ray Charles, Larry Graham, and more. He is an inspired instrumentalist who speaks through music. Steeped in a long line of jazz, R&B, funk, and fusion acts, Aaron Bellamy is a longtime warrior of the college and state fair circuits, performing with Shangoya, Backbeat, and Soul Explosion. Multitalented songwriter and master of ceremonies Alan C completes the musical foundation of this exciting trio. His fat keyboard sounds and vocals are surpassed only by his class act as emcee.

◼ Soli Hughes

Soli Hughes is a gifted guitarist who has performed around the world as a solo artist and with the groups Moore by Four and Sounds of Blackness. He has appeared at the renowned jazz festivals in Perugia, Italy, and Espoo, Finland. He also performed with Flyte Tyme, Shirley King, the Jackson 5, the 5th Dimension, Bobby Lyle, and Roy Ayers. His playing style is described as intensely emotional.

Soli Hughes

◼ Maurice Jacox

Maurice Jacox has been a top singer on the Twin Cities' R&B scene since the early 1970s. He was lead vocalist for the legendary act Willie and the Bees as well as the Butane Soul Review and the Soul Tight Committee. His combination of smooth falsetto voice, powerful stage presence, and broad musical experience rivals that of some of the greatest names in soul music.

Maurice Jacox

◼ Cynthia Johnson

Cynthia Johnson is a multitalented singer, saxophonist, and songwriter and the voice behind the worldwide smash hit "Funkytown," by the disco/funk band Lipps Inc. A native of St. Paul, Johnson was named Miss Black

Cynthia Johnson

Minnesota USA in 1976. She was the vocalist for the influential Twin Cities band Flyte Time for seven years and has performed with Sounds of Blackness, Maceo Parker, Aretha Franklin, and Prince. Johnson recorded three albums with Lipps Inc., whose other hits include "Rock It," "How Long," and "Designer Music." In 2013, Johnson released her debut solo album, *All That I Am*, for which she wrote and produced all the songs.

◼ Kathleen Johnson

Kathleen Johnson is the original vocalist of Best Kept Secret (BKS) and founder of Musicians4Musicians. In 1981, Johnson formed the band Myst with her sisters Mocha Johnson and Karen Johnson, which later morphed into BKS. She has worked live and in the studio with a wide range of artists, including Prince, Alexander O'Neal, Tevin Campbell, Billy McLaughlin, Sam Moore, Jordin Sparks, Carmen Electra, Billy Holloman, Paul Peterson, and more. She has performed at countless Twin Cities music venues, country clubs, and special events. She mentors up-and-coming artists and contributes her talents to numerous fundraisers and philanthropic events.

■ Dahlia Jones

Rising Star

Dahlia Jones is an R&B and gospel artist, guitar player, and songwriter. She was born and raised in Minneapolis and has backgrounds in many artistic outlets, such as classical choir music and musical theater. She was a contestant on the final season of *American Idol* in 2016.

Dahlia Jones

■ Lady Midnight

Lady Midnight, born Adriana Rimpel, is a vocalist, songwriter, and multi-disciplinary artist. She was named "Best Twin Cities Vocalist" of 2017 by *City Pages.* After working with the Afro-Cuban band Malamanya and the electronic trio Vandaam, Lady Midnight pursued a solo career and, in 2019, released her first album, *Death Before Mourning.* She has also appeared on recordings by such artists as P.O.S., Brother Ali, and Bon Iver and regularly performs onstage with musicians around the Twin Cities and beyond. Born in St. Paul, Rimpel earned a BFA degree in photography from the Minneapolis College of Art and Design. She also works as an arts educator for youth.

Lady Midnight, on the cover for her *Death Before Mourning* album

■ Lakame

Rising Star

Lakame is a gifted musician, singer, and guitar player. A student at the High School for Recording Arts in St. Paul, he has already been invited to perform at significant national concerts, including Austin City Limits. Several seasoned musicians have commented that he reminds them of a young Prince.

Lakame

■ Annie Mack

Annie Mack is a jazz and blues vocalist. The north Minneapolis native has shared her talents at such Twin Cities venues as the Dakota, Aster Cafe, Bunker's Music Bar and Grill, First Avenue, and the Fitzgerald Theater. She has also appeared at national and international festivals, such as the John Coltrane International Jazz and Blues Festival in North Carolina, the Lancaster Roots and Blues Festival in Pennsylvania, and the Thunder Bay Blues Festival in Ontario, Canada.

Annie Mack

■ Kiana Marie

Kiana Marie is a singer/songwriter who coproduces her projects through her company Songstress Productions. An alumna of MacPhail Center for Music, she is a frontline vocalist for Universoul, Musicians4Musicians, and Raising the Bar—An Artist's Loft. Some of her proudest accomplishments include writing a song featuring Grammy nominee

Kiana Marie

Stokley Williams of Mint Condition and appearing on Beyoncé's *I Am World Tour* DVD doing the "Single Ladies" dance. Marie's mentor, vocalist Kathleen Johnson (page 28), describes her as having a sound of her own, with strong undertones of a young Beyoncé and a young yet seasoned Etta James.

■ Maxx Band's Soul Experience

Maxx Band's Soul Experience (MBSE), formerly known as the Maxx Band, was formed in 1999 by Jeffrey Craig and Curtis Jackson, two lifelong friends from Gary, Indiana. MBSE is a live performance act based out of Minneapolis specializing in old- and new-school R&B, funk, and dance music and featuring some of the most sought-after vocalists in the Twin Cities area, including Ray Covington, Kendra Glenn, and Jamecia Bennett. Maxx has been the opening act and/or supporting band for such

Maxx Band's Soul Experience

national artists as S.O.S. Band, Cameo, Con Funk Shun, the Dazz Band, Rose Royce, Troop, Alexander O'Neal, Lenny Williams, and others. MBSE has performed at many of the top Twin Cities venues, past and present, as well as at countless public and private events.

◾ Muja Messiah

Muja Messiah is a Twin Cities–based rapper whose style is rooted in street-rap traditions while touching on topics ranging from his rap superiority to movie characters to politics. He has released six studio albums, including *9th House*, a collaboration with fellow Minneapolis rapper I Self Devine. He also collaborated with singer Maria Isa on two full-length albums as the duo Villa Rosa.

Muja Messiah

■ Mankwe Ndosi

Mankwe Ndosi is multidisciplinary musician, performance artist, singer, and songwriter. Describing herself as a "song maker, culture worker, and wild plant woman," she uses music, dance, theater, and spoken-word art forms to connect her audiences to performance, to each other, and to nature. She performs nationally and internationally and is a member of the Association for the Advancement of Creative Musicians, a historic African collective of musicians and composers dedicated to nurturing, performing, and composing original music. Ndosi's 20 years of creative community work has included program development, design, facilitation, teaching, hosting festivals, community organizing, and nonprofit leadership.

Sherri Orr

■ Sherri Orr

Sherri Orr is a vocalist, songwriter, workshop facilitator, and choir director. She began her music career at an early age, forming youth groups and youth choirs, and her music leadership has spanned nearly four decades. Orr has shared the stage with many local and national artists, including Ray Charles and Mick Sterling, among others. Orr's latest project is "For His Glory," a concert of original music.

■ Destiny Roberts

Destiny Roberts is a musician, rapper, singer, and producer in the Twin Cities. She was born and raised in St. Paul in a musical family, and she began performing and releasing music at the age of 13. Primarily a hip-hop artist, her influences range from soul and R&B to jazz.

Mankwe Ndosi

Destiny Roberts

Sabathanites Drum and Bugle Corps

The Sabathanites Drum and Bugle Corps, out of the Sabathani Community Center in south Minneapolis, performs regularly at parades, festivals, openings, and other celebrations around the Twin Cities. The corps was created in 1964 as a youth organization of the Sabathani Baptist Church. It was originally composed of more than 50 individuals from both north and south Minneapolis, employing a variety of drummers, buglers, and majorettes. More than half a century after the corps was formed, several original members still perform with the Sabathanites.

Sabathanites Drum and Bugle Corps

Davu Seru

◼ Davu Seru

Davu Seru is a drummer, composer, author, and educator. Although he plays in a range of genres, he is best known for his free jazz improvisations and compositions. He is composer and bandleader for the ensembles Motherless Dollar and No Territory Band, and he has performed and recorded with musicians and composers throughout the United States and France. Seru has received awards from the Jerome

Foundation, American Composers Forum, the Metropolitan Regional Arts Council, and the Minnesota State Arts Board, and he has earned commissions from the Zeitgeist Ensemble and Walker Art Center. In addition to his musical pursuits, he is the author of *Sights, Sounds, Soul: The Twin Cities through the Lens of Charles Chamblis* and a visiting professor at Hamline University. Originally from north Minneapolis, Seru now lives in St. Paul. He earned his bachelor's degree in English and African American literature from Hamline and a master's degree in English from the University of Minnesota.

◼ Soul Tight Committee

The Soul Tight Committee is a 10-piece band that specializes in old-school soul, R&B, and dance music, mostly from the '70s. The band's mission is to provide listeners with the very best soul and dance music in a lively and engaging stage show. Soul Tight has been

Soul Tight Committee

performing at nightclubs, festivals, weddings, and corporate functions in the Minneapolis–St. Paul greater metro area for many years, with its roots extending back to 1991. Regulars at such clubs as the Minnesota Music Cafe and Bunkers, the Soul Tight Committee continues to be a consistent draw.

◼ Sounds of Blackness

Sounds of Blackness is an award-winning vocal and instrumental ensemble that has been performing jazz, blues, spirituals, rock 'n' roll, R&B, gospel, hip-hop, and soul music since 1971. Led by music director Gary Hines, Sounds of Blackness has performed for everyone from presidents and queens to orphans and prison inmates. They have played at the Olympics, the World Cup, the Ryder Cup, the Super Bowl, and many other sporting events, as well as at concert halls, schools, community centers, corporate events, festivals, and benefit concerts all over the world. Sounds of Blackness has appeared with Quincy Jones, Oprah Winfrey, Michael Jackson, Aretha Franklin, Stevie Wonder, Kirk Franklin, Shirley Caesar, Yolanda Adams, Sting, Prince, Elton John, Maya Angelou, Usher, Harry Belafonte, Aloe Blacc, Common, John Legend, and many more. They've won an NAACP Image Award, a Soul Train

Sounds of Blackness

Music Award, seven Stellar Awards, an International Time for Peace award, and three Grammy Awards. Two of their singles have reached number one on the US dance chart: "The Pressure Part 1" (1991) and "I Believe" (1993). Sounds of Blackness glorifies God by uplifting people through Black music.

■ The Steeles

The Steeles are an accomplished musical family consisting of five siblings: J. D., Fred, Jearlyn, Jevetta, and Billy. Originally from Gary, Indiana, they have been an integral part of the Minneapolis sound for decades. The Steeles have recorded and performed with Prince as well as with super-producers Jimmy Jam and Terry Lewis. They have shared the stage with Mavis Staples, George Clinton, Maurice White of Earth, Wind & Fire, the Blind Boys of Alabama, Donald Fagen, Morgan Freeman, the Saint Paul Chamber Orchestra, the Minnesota Orchestra, and many others throughout their long and storied career.

The Steele siblings have recorded gold and platinum albums, and they received the Sally Award for Education from the Ordway Center for the Performing Arts. They have taken their bold, heartfelt, melodic sounds far and wide, including to corporate and nonprofit projects throughout the United States and around the world. The Steeles have also contributed to several soundtracks, including the award-winning documentary *Hoop Dreams* and the films *Graffiti Bridge*, *Blankman*, and *Corrina, Corrina*.

The Steeles

Jason Tanksley

Jason Tanksley is an adjunct instructor in music at St. Olaf College in Northfield and a Rosemary and David Good Fellow with the Minnesota Orchestra as a tuba player. Tanksley has performed with the Cleveland Orchestra, the Detroit Symphony Orchestra, the Jacksonville Symphony, the Michigan Opera Theatre, and other ensembles.

Jason Tanksley

BUSINESS AND ENTREPRENEURSHIP

Owning Ourselves

Wrestling with numbers,
Exchanging services for dollars,
Probing location through research,
Hustling people for insight.

Transitioning plans like trapeze artists
Tackling issues like linebackers
Hurdling obstacles like Olympians
Balancing priorities like gymnasts.

We preserve our own path.
We chart our own direction.
We re-claim our own finances.
We re-position our own resources.

We are here.

We grow profits from meager starts.
We carry wealth across generations.
We invest willingly in communities.
We risk to enjoy owning ourselves.

Business acumen and the preservation of business districts are stimulated when African American professionals work in, own, and successfully launch local companies. Active entrepreneurship propels growth—both for the community and for the individual. The community gains a corporate advocate and employer. The professional gains personal fulfillment and a greater vested interest in the future of the local and state economies. We salute those who build wealth and who reinvest in the African American community. Included here are a selection of men and women who have made or are making their mark in a range of fields in Minnesota, from finance and high-tech industries to restaurants and fashion.

■ DJ Baker

DJ Baker is the owner of Firm Facility Service, a company that provides facility maintenance services for businesses. Baker is passionate about partnering with other entrepreneurs around business design and planning. He aspires to support up-and-coming entrepreneurs of color as they embark on careers in business. He is currently designing a volunteer program for high school students who are interested in learning business planning.

■ Ronald Bellfield

Ronald Bellfield, now retired, worked at the Metropolitan Council of the Twin Cities and was chief boiler operator at Walker Art Center. He attended Mankato State College in 1972, Saint Paul Technical College in 1996, and the University of California in 1998, earning a Class B Wastewater Treatment License. His brother Donald (page 65) was active in community service for many years.

Ronald Bellfield (right) with his brother Donald

Mama Sheila Brathwaite

Frederick Brathwaite

■ Mama Sheila Brathwaite and Frederick Brathwaite

Mama Sheila Brathwaite and her husband, Frederick Brathwaite, are co-owners and managers of Mama Sheila's Soul Food Kitchen on Bloomington Avenue South in Minneapolis. The restaurant offers a variety of delicious soul food meals.

Frank Brown

Frank Brown is a printing industry professional with more than thirty years of experience. A resident of north Minneapolis, Brown graduated with a bachelor's degree in business and accounting from Central Washington University and a master's in business administration from Seattle University. Disappointed by the way larger print companies treated their employees, he opened a Minuteman Press franchise in Uptown Minneapolis in 2015, choosing racial, social, and economic justice as the guiding principles for his business. Brown's is the only minority-owned union shop in Minnesota. Within one year of business, the Neighborhood Development Center in Minneapolis named Brown a finalist for its entrepreneur of the year award. Outside work, Brown is a leader in many organizations, including TakeAction Minnesota, Jewish Community Action, ISAIAH, and the Main Street Alliance of Minnesota.

Laurie Ann Saddler Crutchfield

Laurie Ann Saddler Crutchfield is the CFO for Crutchfield Dermatology, a company with 50 employees. A graduate of Michigan State University, she worked for many years as a computer engineer at IBM, American Express Financial Advisors, Lockheed Martin, and Northwest Airlines. She has three children and is married to Dr. Charles E. Crutchfield III (page 132).

Lachelle Cunningham

Lachelle Cunningham is the chef and owner of Chelle's Kitchen catering service and was the founding chef at Breaking Bread Café in north Minneapolis. Her mother's family has roots in the Rondo neighborhood of St. Paul, and her father's family hails from Minneapolis's north side. Cunningham brings a global perspective to her local roots to create innovative, high-quality, and healthy soul food, while stressing the

Laurie Ann Saddler Crutchfield

Lachelle Cunningham

healing power of food. Her "Healthy Roots" philosophy seeks to reclaim the narrative around soul food and healthy eating and use it to help improve the economic well-being of the community. Cunningham also teaches culinary classes at Saint Paul College and offers food-business training, consulting, and apprenticeships at Chelle's Kitchen.

Martin Daniels

■ Martin Daniels

Martin Daniels had a long career working in computers and network systems for state services before his retirement in 2014. A native of Tarrytown, New York, Daniels moved to Minnesota to attend Macalester College. After graduating, he was employed by TIES, a computing consortium for Minnesota school districts. He first worked on mainframe computers and later joined a team introducing IBM personal computers for administrative work in public schools. He also taught computing classes at Saint Mary's University, Hennepin

Technical College, and Saint Paul Community College. In the mid-1980s, he left TIES to work for the State of Minnesota's Department of Human Services, where he eventually became the systems supervisor for network and server computing. Daniels was a key member of the team that oversaw the Y2K conversion for DHS. In the 2000s, he joined the Minnesota Medical Information Systems unit, where he managed the server infrastructure team. He became a Certified Information Systems Security Professional. Daniels and his wife raised two daughters in Minneapolis.

■ Brett Davis

Brett Davis started working in the liquor business at Ken and Norm's Liquor store on Chicago Avenue in south Minneapolis. The store was owned by his father, Norm Davis, and Ken Jones. Davis has worked in the liquor business for more than 30 years and plans to retire in the same business.

Brett Davis

Tommie Daye

Tommie Daye is the owner of Tommie's Pizza in St. Paul's Merriam Park neighborhood. Daye has worked in food and beverage management for more than 30 years. Opened in October 2018, Tommie's Pizza is a family-run business; Tommie's wife, Dana, and several of their children work at the shop. It is the only Black-owned pizzeria in the Twin Cities.

Richard Doten

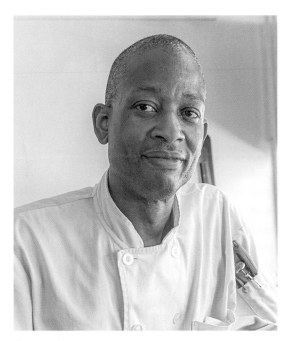

Tommie Daye

Richard Doten

Richard Doten and his wife, Janice, are owners of LaDoten Custom Guitars in Minneapolis. A guitarist himself, Richard had a lifelong passion and dream to open a guitar establishment. He assists professional and novice guitarists in perfecting the style and sound of their music.

Reese M. Dyer

Reese M. Dyer worked as a credit manager at Ecolab in St. Paul for 43 years until retiring in 2016. A native of Chicago, he moved to Minneapolis in March 1968. He is a graduate of North High School and Macalester College, where he earned a bachelor of science degree in psychology. In August 1973, he married Elaine Glanton of Minneapolis; they had two sons, Maurice and Marcel. Dyer has also served as an executive board member of the Prince Hall Grand Lodge of Minnesota.

Reese M. Dyer

April Estes with Tracy Wesley, CEO and funeral director of Estes Funeral Chapel

Richard Estes and April Estes

Richard Estes and April Estes opened Estes Funeral Chapel in 1962 on Plymouth Avenue in north Minneapolis. The husband-and-wife team wanted to offer quality funeral services to African Americans in Minnesota at a time when such services were provided only by white-owned funeral chapels. In 2013, Richard passed away, leaving Estes Funeral Chapel in the capable and experienced hands of family members.

Debra Williams Jones

Debra Williams Jones had a successful career of 39 years at Honeywell International, where she served as senior contract manager. Jones worked with the US government and with domestic and international clients. A graduate of Augsburg University with a bachelor of arts degree in business administration and accounting, Jones is now retired.

Debra Williams Jones

Estes Funeral Chapel

■ Ashley Lauren

Rising Star

Ashley Lauren is the owner and designer of Diva Rags & Suavé Clothing and founder of the Diva/Suavé Project charity. Diva Rags & Suavé was established in 1999 and offers intricately hand-painted scarves, custom-designed clothing and accessories, and apparel featuring legendary artists Prince, Bob Marley, Jimi Hendrix, and John Lennon, as well as aromatherapy oils and jewelry.

In addition to the Diva Rags & Suavé business, Lauren established the Diva/Suavé Project charity in 2006 to honor her grandfather, Danny Davis, aka "Mr. Wonderful," a community advocate, a Golden Gloves boxing champion during the 1950s, and a member of the Minnesota Boxing Hall of Fame. Youth participants in the Diva/Suavé Project are taught self-sufficiency, financial literacy, nutrition, urban agriculture, customer service, teamwork, entrepreneurship, leadership, and social responsibility. Lauren has received many awards for her work, such as the Outstanding Student Award at Metropolitan State University, Grand Prize Winner—Zion Rootswear, the Woman of Peace Award from the Peacepower Foundation, the Stephanie Ball-Bailey Youth Leadership Award from the City of Minneapolis, and the EDIT: Art for Change Award. In addition, the Diva/Suavé Project has been acknowledged by CNN, KSTP News, and the *Star Tribune*.

■ Channon L. Lemon

Channon L. Lemon is vice president of economic development for the Saint Paul Area Chamber of Commerce, focused on strategic visioning for economic vibrancy

Channon L. Lemon

in the east metro and in the city's central business district. Lemon guides the chamber and its members on increasing diversity in the boardroom, the workforce, and the vendor pool. Lemon holds a master of business administration from the University of Minnesota's Carlson School of Management and a bachelor of business administration in insurance from Howard University. Lemon's father, James McCoy Willis, and his father were activists and civil rights leaders, while her mother, Montez MaryLee Willis, was a community advocate and her grandfather a church planter.

■ Cerise D. Washington Lewis

Cerise D. Washington Lewis is a chemical engineer at Ecolab Inc. in St. Paul, where she has worked since 2008. Prior to that she worked in product development at 3M. Lewis is a graduate of Hampton University and the daughter of Gregory and Barbara Washington.

Wendell Maddox

Wendell Maddox is the CEO and president of the ION Corporation, based in Eden Prairie. Founded by Maddox in 1984, the ION Corporation aids the aerospace industry with high-tech electronic equipment and related services. Maddox was born in Chicago but grew up in Minneapolis and graduated from Central High School. He attended the University of Toledo, the University of Minnesota, and Dartmouth College. He received a degree in electrical engineering.

Peter McCullar

Wendell Maddox

Peter McCullar

Peter McCullar has served as the director of service at Leeds Precision Instruments Inc. in the Twin Cities since the 1990s. Established in Minneapolis in 1986, Leeds designs, manufactures, and sells comparison microscopes and imaging systems to forensic laboratories in the United States and around the world.

Benjamin Mchie

Benjamin Mchie is a historian, author, educational consultant, and video and film producer. In 1999, he founded the African American Registry (aaregistry .org), one of the most comprehensive databases of African American history, culture, and heritage in the world. Born in south Minneapolis, Mchie received a bachelor of arts in speech communications at Long Beach State University. He is a seven-time Emmy Award–winning videographer and two-time MTV Video Award nominee.

Kenya McKnight-Ahad
Rising Star

Kenya McKnight-Ahad is a resident of north Minneapolis and a master of business administration student at Saint Mary's University in Halifax, Canada, studying the management of cooperatives and credit unions centering on global economies and cooperative economics. From 2013 to 2017, McKnight-Ahad served as the first African American to be appointed as a Metropolitan Council representative

Kenya McKnight-Ahad

on the Transportation Advisory Board. McKnight-Ahad is also the president and founder of the Black Women's Wealth Alliance in Minnesota.

Andre McNeal

Andre McNeal is the CEO of Bachelor Boy Entertainment Group, an events promotion company in the Twin Cities. In addition to being a successful African American entrepreneur, McNeal is

a human services worker, a community service advocate, and the father of six children and also a grandfather.

Linda K. Mizen

Linda K. Mizen worked for many years at 3M and has received patents for her work in film-coating technology and graphics. A native of Detroit, Michigan, she was the first African American woman to earn a bachelor of science degree in biochemistry from the University of Michigan–Dearborn. She also earned a master of science degree in macromolecular science and engineering at the University of Michigan in Ann Arbor. For nine years, Mizen chaired the Science Training Encouragement Program (STEP) at 3M, which offers training, mentoring, and hands-on experience for minority high school students who have an interest in science and technology. She also started a 3M STEP laboratory in post-apartheid South Africa. After leaving 3M, Mizen taught mathematics, chemistry, and physical science part-time at the high school and university levels.

Andre McNeal

Linda K. Mizen

◾ Kim Nelson

Kim Nelson is the former senior vice president of external affairs for General Mills, where she worked for 29 years before retiring in 2017. Nelson has a master of business administration from the Columbia Business School in New York City and completed her undergraduate studies at Georgetown University in Washington, DC.

Rosemary Nevils-Williams and Raeisha Williams

Kim Nelson

◾ Rosemary Nevils-Williams and Raeisha Williams

Rosemary Nevils-Williams and Raeisha Williams, a mother-daughter team, were co-owners of Heritage Tea House & Café on University Avenue in St. Paul. One of the few Black-owned businesses in the city's old Rondo neighborhood, the café opened in December 2017 with the intention of being a community gathering space. Nevils-Williams and Williams offered a variety of tea and coffee drinks as well as a selection of soul food dishes. Heritage Tea House won the 2018 People's

Choice Award in the Saint Paul Business Program. The café closed in 2020.

◾ Brian Palaggi
Rising Star

Brian Palaggi is an emerging digital marketing leader from the Twin Cities. Palaggi believes that every creation is an opportunity for innovation. He infuses bold artistry into his work, harnessing the potency of his background in social media, modern design, and technology. Palaggi has digital marketing experience with large international brands, local e-commerce businesses, and world-renowned entertainers. He

Brian Palaggi

has also contributed social media marketing research that is currently being used by St. Paul's Concordia University. "Our world is ever changing, and technology is becoming crucial to our everyday lives," Palaggi says. "To continue to grow and make meaningful connections with each other we must recognize and embrace change with a sense of curiosity. I believe that we as humans must view technology holistically instead of autonomously to understand our daring, new world."

Gail Peterson

Gail Peterson is the vice president of marketing for global health care at Ecolab in St. Paul. Prior to joining Ecolab, she spent more than a decade in various roles at General Mills. She earned a bachelor of arts degree at Princeton University and a master of business administration from Harvard Business School. In March 2019, Peterson was inducted into the Executive Leadership Council, a member organization dedicated to the development of Black global leaders and to increasing the number of Black executives worldwide; she is one of only 19 ELC members from the Twin Cities. Peterson is also on the board of the Minnesota Children's Museum.

Nicole Pillow

Nicole Pillow is a speaker, writer, educator, and personal empowerment coach. She serves as the education director at Tandem, a nonprofit organization that cultivates a community of hope and provides resources and support for thousands of women and children in crisis every year. Pillow is also a media ambassador and leader for Weight Watchers

Nicole Pillow

International, equipping hundreds of people each week with the skills and mind-set needed for a healthy and fulfilling lifestyle.

Anika Robbins

Anika Robbins is the founder of ANIKA International Cosmetics and owns ANIKA & Friends, an event management and marketing agency. She is the founder and executive director of the ANIKA Foundation and founder of Black Votes Matter MN. Robbins owns and operates Robbins Urban Wellness Retreat in the Camden neighborhood of north Minneapolis along with her husband, Dr. Juneau Robbins. She serves as a civil rights commissioner for the City of Minneapolis and as the chair of the Cultural Engagement Complete Count Committee for the State of Minnesota and is a member of the Our Census MN co-creation table. She is also the secretary of the Black Civic Network.

Don Samuels

Don Samuels is the CEO of Micro-Grants, a nonprofit company that provides small and medium-sized grants to support low-income individuals seeking to develop a small business or secure stable employment. A former Minneapolis city councilmember, Samuels ran unsuccessfully for mayor of Minneapolis in 2013. He also served for one term on the Minneapolis school board. In 2003, Samuels cofounded the PEACE Foundation, which became the Northside Achievement Zone (NAZ). His wife, Sondra Samuels (page 73), is currently the president and CEO of NAZ.

Don Samuels

Anthony R. Scott

Anthony R. Scott spent 20 years as a supervisor with the Hennepin County Child Protection Unit. He also worked as a vocational expert on a contract basis with the Social Security Office of Hearings and Appeals for five years. Scott established and owned Scott Rehabilitation, a registered qualified rehabilitation firm that provided return-to-work services to injured workers under the Minnesota workers' compensation laws.

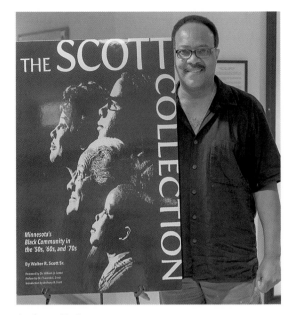

Anthony R. Scott

He earned a bachelor of arts degree in urban studies and a master's degree as a Hubert H. Humphrey Scholar in rehabilitation counseling from Mankato State College.

Scott is the president of Minnesota's Black Community Project, a nonprofit organization that highlights and celebrates the accomplishments of African Americans in Minnesota through presentations, seminars, workshops, articles, books, documentaries, and exhibits. He is also a talented and well-known bass guitarist in the Twin Cities. He resides in Minneapolis and has two adult sons, Anthony R. Scott II (see page 85) and Bryson Glanton Scott (see page 19).

Carolyn Smallwood

Carolyn Smallwood is the CEO of Way to Grow, an early childhood and elementary education nonprofit organization. Deeply committed to issues concerning children, she sat on Governor Mark Dayton's Early Learning Council for four years and was cochair of Minneapolis mayor Betsy Hodges's Cradle to K Cabinet. Smallwood has served on numerous local boards, including the African American Leadership Forum, Minnesota Comeback, and MinneMinds. Prior to joining Way to Grow in 2004, she was vice president for sales and marketing at Twin Cities RISE! and executive director of the Minnesota Minority Supplier Development Council. In 2014, Smallwood was named one of the Twin Cities' "Top African Americans of Influence" by the *Star Tribune.*

Carolyn Smallwood

◼ Leon Tazel III

Leon Tazel III is the founder and CEO of the Tazel Institute, a Minnesota company focused on exposing young African American men to different businesses and industries. The Tazel Institute works with African American male students in grades 9 through 12 in various districts

in the Twin Cities metro area. The institute has been recognized as a unique way of introducing young men to new opportunities.

Tazel is also a certified human resources professional through the Society of Human Resources Management and the Human Resources Certification Institute. He has more than 29 years of experience in the human resources field, including work in alternative dispute resolution, problem-solving, team building, and more.

Tazel is a first-generation college graduate from Slippery Rock University of Pennsylvania, where he earned a bachelor of arts in communications. He holds a master of arts degree in management from the College of St. Scholastica.

Leon Tazel III

Camille A. Thomas

Camille A. Thomas

Camille A. Thomas is the founder and owner of Vision Investment, a coaching and consulting firm established in 2015. She became a certified personal and professional life coach at the Adler Graduate School in Minnetonka in 2009. She has coached and consulted with more than 5,000 employees in various positions at Fortune 100 companies, and she also coaches national and international entrepreneurs.

Thomas has served on boards of directors for several organizations and currently serves on the board of the Minnesota Black Chamber of Commerce. She is the cofounder of Fearless Commerce, a company that works to highlight Black women business owners through books and live events. Thomas is also the founder of the Activate Network, a community that supports women of color business owners and entrepreneurs. Thomas was recognized as a "Young Entrepreneur Under 35" by *Minnesota Business* magazine and was

named among the top "Women in Business" by *Minneapolis/St. Paul Business Journal* in 2018. Thomas holds a bachelor's degree in community health education and a master's degree in holistic health studies.

Robert Thomas

Robert Thomas moved to Minnesota in 1970 from Kansas City, Missouri. In 1972, he was among the first small group of African American men to be admitted to an apprenticeship program in Minnesota, where he learned a professional trade in painting and plastering.

Robert Thomas

John Trotman

John Trotman is a quality manager at General Dynamics, a global aerospace and defense company. Originally from Guyana, Trotman came to the Twin Cities via Howard University in 1973 after landing a job as an engineer with Honeywell. He was joined by his soul mate, Yvette, in 1974, and they have a son, Devol.

John Trotman

Maurice Tyner

Maurice Tyner is a longtime mortgage analyst specializing in mortgage financing, lending, and escrow analysis. He holds a bachelor of business administration degree from National University and is a Certified Master Mortgage

Maurice Tyner

Underwriter with a NMLS license. He is a Vietnam-era veteran and spent six years in the US Air Force as a security defense officer and a meteorologist. Tyner also is the award-winning author of the book *Manchild*, written under the pseudonym Bekila Tyner. He is an original member of the Sabathanites Drum Corps.

Mychael and Stephanie Wright

Mychael Wright and Stephanie Wright

Mychael Wright and Stephanie Wright are co-owners of Golden Thyme Coffee and Café on Selby Avenue in St. Paul. When Golden Thyme opened in March 2000, it served only coffee and pastries. Today, Golden Thyme is a popular African American community spot that serves mouthwatering dishes including homemade breakfast selections, soups and sandwiches, red beans and rice, and their famous Golden Thyme chicken and spaghetti, in addition to pastries and coffee drinks. Golden Thyme also offers entertainment and hosts weekly community workshops and seminars. Moreover,

Golden Thyme Coffee and Café on Selby Avenue in St. Paul

Golden Thyme is the unofficial head-quarters for the annual Selby Avenue Jazz Fest.

Rodney Young

Rodney Young is CEO and president of Delta Dental of Minnesota, one of the largest dental benefit providers in the nation. He has served on the board of Delta Dental since 1998 and has continued in that role since becoming CEO in January 2012. Delta Dental of Minnesota serves 8,800 Minnesota- and North Dakota–based employer groups and 4.1 million members nationwide. Young is considered a strategic and visionary executive leader with a solid background of business experience.

Rodney Young

BEAUTY AND FASHION

Jacqueline Amissha Addison

Jacqueline Amissha Addison is a free-lance designer who works under the label AkuaGabby, a combination of her parents' first names. Her interest in fashion design was inspired by her father, who was a tailor in their native Ghana. After graduating high school, Addison came to Minnesota and studied graphic design at North Hennepin Community College. She later enrolled at the Art Institutes International Minnesota, where she earned a bachelor's degree in fashion design.

Jacqueline Amissha Addison

Tiffany Blackwell

Tiffany Blackwell is the founder and owner of V.I.P. Hair and Nail Salon in Minneapolis. A successful entrepreneur, she began working in salons while in high school before going to school to become a licensed cosmetologist. Blackwell opened V.I.P. in 1993. She is married to Jerry Blackwell.

Shirlee Callender

Shirlee Callender

Shirlee Callender has been modeling professionally in the Twin Cities for several decades. In 2017, when she was in her eighties, Callender was crowned Queen of the Northlands at the Saint Paul Winter Carnival and participated

Fresh Cuts Barber Shop, on Fourth Avenue South and 38th Street East in Minneapolis

in the 34th Annual Rondo Days Parade in St. Paul. Callender moved to Minnesota from her native Des Moines, Iowa, in 1951 after she finished high school.

■ Cameron Cook

Rising Star

Cameron Cook is the owner and operator of Fresh Cuts Barber Shop, located on the corner of 38th Street and Fourth Avenue in south Minneapolis. Cook established Fresh Cuts in 2012 because he was inspired by the Young Brothers Barber Shop that operated across the street from his shop for many years.

Cameron Cook with client

David Harper

David Harper owned an independent barbershop in St. Paul and previously was the manager at Gifted Hanz Salon and Spa. A graduate of Mechanic Arts High School, Harper was also involved in acting.

David Harper

Thandisizwe Jackson-Nisan

Rising Star

Thandisizwe Jackson-Nisan was named Miss Black Minnesota in 2017 and Miss Plus America in 2016, and she was a finalist for Miss Minnesota USA in 2017. She represented Minnesota at the 2018 Miss Black USA competition. Jackson-Nisan was born in north Minneapolis. Her South African first name means "hope for the people and lover of the nation." Jackson-Nisan says, "It is my pleasure and honor to compete in pageants that recognize young women of African descent with emphasis on community service."

Thandisizwe Jackson-Nisan

Andrea Pryor

Andrea Pryor is the owner of Exterior Image Barber and Beauty Salon on Chicago Avenue South in Minneapolis. Patrons of this establishment find it to be economical, relaxing, and friendly. In 2018, Exterior Image celebrated its 20th year in business.

Andrea Pryor

Samantha Rei

Samantha Rei is a fashion designer and illustrator. She began her fashion career with her label Blasphemina's Closet in 2000 and subsequently founded the eponymous Samantha Rei label in 2013. Influenced by such designers as Alexander McQueen, Vivienne Westwood, Hirooka Naoto, John Galliano, and Anna Sui, the Minnesota native attained celebrity status after appearing on the reality television show *Project Runway* in 2017.

Rei enrolled at the Perpich Center for Arts Education in Golden Valley in 1998 to hone her skills as an illustrator and painter in order to pursue comic book art. After graduating in 1999, she attended the College of Visual Arts in St. Paul to major in illustration before continuing her education in the apparel technologies program at Minneapolis Community and Technical College. Rei has been featured in such publications as Huffington Post, *Shojo Beat*, the *Gothic & Lolita Bible*, *Gothic Beauty*, *Glamour UK*, and *Vogue UK*. She was named one of 2014's "Artists of the Year" by *City Pages* and earned Readers' Choice honors for "Best Local Fashion Designer" in 2016 and 2017. In 2015, she authored and illustrated a how-to book on subculture fashion design called *Steampunk and Cosplay Fashion Design and Illustration*.

Sara Rogers

Sara Rogers

Sara Rogers is a Twin Cities model, television personality, and fashion expert. She is the senior consultant at Sara Rogers Style, providing fashion, image, and style consultation for men and women.

Samantha Rei

Dimensions in Hair, in Near North Minneapolis, is owned by Michael and Doris Spicer.

■ Michael Spicer and Doris Spicer

Michael Spicer and Doris Spicer are the owners of Dimensions in Hair beauty salon and barbershop, which opened in 1991 on West Broadway in Near North Minneapolis. Michael is a master barber with more than 30 years of experience. Their daughter, Lisa Spicer Wade, is the salon manager.

■ Nathaniel Talton

Nathaniel Talton is the owner of Upper Cutz Barbershop in Eagan. Talton attended Park Center Senior High School in Brooklyn Park. A master barber, he received professional training at the Minnesota School of Barbering in Minneapolis.

Nathaniel Talton

Houston White

Houston White is the founder and owner of H. White Men's Room, a clothing store, barbershop, and coffee bar located in the Camden neighborhood of north Minneapolis. He also runs the HWMR clothing line based around the branding "Black Excellence." White is a graduate of North High School, after which he attended barber school. He is a strong advocate of neighborhood development, and his shop has become a community gathering space.

Eddie Withers Jr.

Eddie Withers Jr. is a barber and the owner of Eddie's Barber Shop on Fourth Avenue South in Minneapolis. Withers opened his barbershop in 1970. He became a barber because he wanted to emulate his father, Eddie Withers Sr., who owned a barbershop in the Rondo neighborhood of St. Paul. Withers and his father worked there together for many years. Eddie's Barber Shop is a staple of the African American community in south Minneapolis.

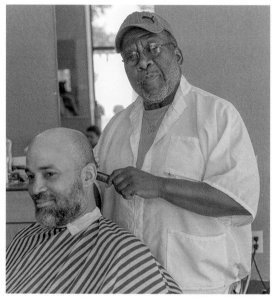

Eddie Withers Jr. with client

Eddie's Barber Shop in south Minneapolis

Teqen Zéa-Aida and Nathan Yungerberg

Teqen Zéa-Aida and Nathan Yungerberg founded the modeling agency Vision Management Group Inc. in 1996 to promote diversity in the media and modeling industries. Supporting the careers of countless models, industry insiders, and actresses, Vision helped to foster a fresh image of modern American beauty and redefine the idea of what is beautiful. Vision models worked for clients such as Target, Dayton's, Best Buy, and Aveda as well as Vogue, Prada, Tommy Hilfiger, and Versace. Vision closed in 2016. Zéa-Aida went on to run the art gallery City Wide Artists in downtown Minneapolis and has since entered city politics. Yungerberg moved to New York City, where he works as a photographer and is an award-winning playwright.

Teqen Zéa-Aida and Nathan Yungerberg

COMMUNITY SERVICE

Serving Beyond Self

How kind to consider others,
Valuing people beyond the self.

How astute to market missions,
Enlisting volunteers to act beyond egos.

How thoughtful to sacrifice time,
Choosing to invest beyond personal agenda.

How appropriate to share wealth,
Giving resources beyond personal family needs.

Considering, enlisting, sacrificing, and sharing,
As supporters of community,
We are here.
Moving beyond self to serve.

Nestled in the strongest communities are active, ordinary, everyday citizens willing to dedicate their time and resources to advance the needs of others. African American communities are no exception. Though often lost amid the celebrity of athletes and entertainers, thoughtful, committed African American people serve. Through their efforts, they have altered the course of countless families, individuals, and organizations as they place importance on serving others beyond self.

Community service can take many forms, whether it is work addressing individual economic or employment needs, health and safety concerns, or larger issues of racial equity and community pride, among other activities. The work is central to building and maintaining a strong and vibrant African American community in Minnesota.

Cavis Adams

Cavis Adams is a full-time fire captain for the City of Minneapolis Fire and Rescue. He also freelances as an English/Spanish medical interpreter for Hennepin County. He holds a bachelor of arts degree with a Spanish major from the University of Minnesota. Adams is the author of the novel *Granddaddy*.

Cavis Adams

Louis Alemayehu

Louis Alemayehu is a writer, educator, administrator, poet, performer, and activist of African and Native American heritage. Alemayehu was raised on the South Side of Chicago and moved to Minnesota to attend Concordia College in 1964. His work toward environmental and social justice in the state spans decades. He has organized for the Mississippi River Revival, North American Water Office, Women's Environmental

Institute, and Environmental Justice Advocates of Minnesota, among many other organizations. Alemayehu is a cofounder of the Native Arts Circle, the oldest Native American artists' organization in the Upper Midwest. Both the Loft Literary Center and Intermedia Arts have honored him as a spoken word artist and creative writer. He received a leadership grant from the St. Paul Companies Awards and a commendation for lifelong commitment to social justice from the Headwaters Foundation. In 2009, the Minnesota Spoken Word Association recognized Alemayehu with an Urban Griot award for 30 years performing spoken word.

Marvin Roger Anderson

Marvin Roger Anderson is a community leader, former librarian, and cofounder of Rondo Avenue Inc. (RAI). RAI is dedicated to preserving, conserving, and honoring the history of St. Paul's Rondo neighborhood and the contributions of its residents, past and present. RAI hosts the annual Rondo Days parade and festival and is developing the Rondo Commemorative Plaza in the heart of the old neighborhood to commemorate this essential African American community that was torn apart by the construction of I-94 beginning in the 1950s.

Born and raised in St. Paul, Anderson graduated from Morehouse College in 1962 and received his juris doctorate from Hastings College of Law in San Francisco in 1966. He volunteered for the Peace Corps in Senegal and later worked as an ordinance drafter in Minneapolis's Department of Civil Rights. Anderson returned to school in 1974 to earn a master's degree in library science from the University of Minnesota. He worked as a reference librarian at the university's law library for four years before being appointed State Law Librarian in 1980, a position he held for 22 years. In recognition of his service, the room housing the library's rare books was renamed "The Marvin R. Anderson Special Collections Room." He has received many awards in celebration of his work in the community.

Patricia Anderson

Patricia Anderson

Patricia Anderson has been a community leader for more than two decades, working with at-risk youth and their families. She worked for many years at City, Inc., in north Minneapolis as the program director. After City, Inc., closed its doors due to lack of funding, Anderson went to work at Sabathani Community Center in south Minneapolis, serving the same population at a different location.

Donald Bellfield

Donald Bellfield worked for the Metropolitan Council in the Twin Cities as a human resources consultant and has served on various committees, including the Council on Black Minnesotans (governor appointee), the Minneapolis Civilian Police Review Authority (mayoral appointee), and the Minneapolis Office of Police Conduct Review (mayoral appointee). He attended Mankato State College and the University of Minnesota's Hubert H. Humphrey Institute of Public Affairs. (See page 40 for his photograph.)

Steven Belton

Steven Belton is the president and CEO of the Minneapolis Urban League. Prior to that, he held various executive roles in both the nonprofit and private sectors, including several positions with Minneapolis Public Schools. He was a partner at Stinson Leonard Street law firm, executive director of the State Council on Black Minnesotans, and

Steven Belton

The Minneapolis Urban League, on Plymouth Avenue in north Minneapolis

president/CEO of the Urban Coalition of Minneapolis. He also serves as a youth minister at Park Avenue United Methodist Church in south Minneapolis. A graduate of Minneapolis Central High School, Belton earned a bachelor's degree in political science from Washington University in St. Louis and a juris doctorate from the University of Michigan Law School. He is married to Sharon Sayles Belton (page 92), the former mayor of Minneapolis, with whom he has three adult children. Steven Belton was named Minneapolis Urban League president in 2015.

The **Minneapolis Urban League** has been a source of strength and encouragement in the Twin Cities since 1926, playing an essential advocacy role on issues affecting African Americans.

Through employment opportunities, educational programs, and community engagement activities, it aims to assist the African American community in achieving economic empowerment and self-sufficiency to build wealth that can be passed down to future generations. The MUL is located on Plymouth Avenue in north Minneapolis.

■ Cindy Booker

Cindy Booker is the executive director of Sabathani Community Center in south Minneapolis. A native of Minneapolis, she was a student at Hale Elementary School when it merged with Field School as part of the city's desegregation efforts. She went on to graduate from Washburn High School and then earned a bachelor's degree in economics from St. Cloud State. Booker worked at Minnesota State University, St. Olaf College, and North High School before entering the corporate world as a finance executive with Target, where she spent 14 years. Booker became the executive director of Sabathani in 2013.

Cindy Booker

Sabathani Community Center on East 38th Street in south Minneapolis

Sabathani Community Center was founded in 1966 by concerned residents and members of Sabathani Baptist Church who wanted to provide a recreational space for neighborhood kids. Sabathani quickly outgrew its initial, single purpose and began offering a range of direct services to support basic community needs. Since moving into the former Bryant Junior High School building on East 38th Street in 1979, Sabathani has remained a focal point for community identity, empowerment, and social change, offering a place where young children and seniors from the surrounding neighborhoods can gather in a welcoming environment to build community, conduct business, and participate in programs and services that move people forward.

■ Melvin Whitfield Carter Jr.

Melvin Whitfield Carter Jr. is the founder and executive director of Save Our Sons, a nonprofit organization dedicated to helping African American

Melvin Whitfield Carter Jr.

youth follow a positive life path. Prior to that he spent nearly 30 years with the St. Paul Police Department. Carter grew up in the Rondo neighborhood of St. Paul and attended St. Paul Central High School. His wife, Toni Carter (page 93), is a Ramsey County commissioner, and they are the proud parents of three children, including Melvin Carter III, the mayor of St. Paul (page 92).

Tiffany Casey

Tiffany Casey

Rising Star

Tiffany Casey is a youth librarian at the Sumner Library branch of Hennepin County Library in north Minneapolis. Casey works with the community on a wide range of programs and services for youth, families, and schools, and she manages the youth portion of the Sudduth African American History and Culture Collection, which are books written about and by African Americans. She also works on system-wide teams at Hennepin County Library that focus on advancing racial equity, Black history, and teen parenting outreach. Her work on these teams involves training staff on racial equity and assisting with the development of diverse support programs that meet the needs of the communities that Sumner Library serves.

Duchesne Drew

Duchesne Drew is the community network vice president at the Bush Foundation. A key part of his role is community engagement, building partnerships with related organizations and leaders, and helping to expand formal and informal networks across the region. A veteran newspaper reporter, editor, and manager, Drew previously worked at the Minneapolis *Star Tribune* and the *Dallas Morning News*. In addition to serving on the board of the Saint Paul Area Chamber of Commerce, Drew is a member of the Itasca Project's working team, and he is on the steering committee for Greater MSP's "BE MSP" initiative, which is focused on retaining professionals of color within the Twin Cities region. Drew's other board commitments include the African American Leadership Forum, the Monitors Club, the Leadership Learning Community, the *Columbia Daily Spectator*, and the advisory board of Ujamaa Place.

Suluki Fardan

Suluki Fardan worked several years as an education assistant for the Minneapolis Public Schools and later worked for the Minneapolis Urban League before retiring. Currently, he is an active member of the Sabathanites Drum Corps. Fardan is the grandson of Anthony B. Cassius, owner of the Dreamland Café in south Minneapolis and, later, Cassius Bar and Café in downtown Minneapolis. Opened in 1949, Cassius Bar and Café was the first African American–owned establishment in Minneapolis to be granted a liquor license.

Suluki Fardan

■ Robin Hickman

Robin Hickman is a social activist, TV and film producer, and arts advocate. She is the founder and creative director/artist at A Celebration of Soulful Dolls; director and organizational strategist of Taking Our Place Centerstage at Ordway Center for the Performing Arts; and founder/CEO/executive producer

of SoulTouch Productions. Her production company has been involved with numerous award-winning television shows. Hickman is a graduate of St. Paul Central High School and has a degree in communications from Howard University. She is the daughter of Bobby Hickman, a St. Paul activist who was the director of St. Paul's Inner-City Youth League. Her mother, Patricia Frazier-Hickman, was a leader in the fight for equal rights and educational equity in St. Paul. Hickman has established a scholarship in her mother's name for child development at Saint Paul College.

Rowena D. Holmes

■ Rowena D. Holmes

Rowena D. Holmes is a crime prevention specialist with the City of Minneapolis and has worked in law enforcement for nearly three decades. She brings neighborhood and community stakeholders together to identify nuisances and other problems and conflicts, while building sustaining relationships and long-term

Robin Hickman

solutions. Holmes considers herself a lifelong learner and a servant leader, striving to be compassionate, nonjudgmental, and someone who always looks for the greater good. She earned a bachelor's degree in theology and a master's degree in organizational leadership.

◼ Neda Kellogg

Neda Kellogg is the CEO of Successful Connections, a coaching and consulting firm, and the founding executive strategist of the nonprofit Project DIVA, a supportive coaching program that prepares young Black women from third to twelfth grade for life after high school. For more than 20 years, Kellogg has focused her work on equipping women and girls for financial well-being as well as academic, social, emotional, and career success. In 2018, Kellogg received a fellowship from the Bush Foundation to deepen her work against the systemic and personal barriers facing young Black women in Minneapolis.

◼ Nick (Davis) Khaliq

Nick (Davis) Khaliq is a well-known and well-respected St. Paul community activist and former president of the St. Paul NAACP. He was good friends with and an activist partner of St. Paul civil rights pioneer Katie McWatt.

◼ Amoke Kubat

Amoke Kubat is a Yoruba priestess, teacher, artist, and writer who partners with community artists, activists, and organizations. She is a north side resident, and the Mississippi River is a key focal point for Kubat, who believes local African Americans have lost their connection to the river. She has brought many people to experience the Mississippi, whether from its banks or on a boat. Kubat is also the organizer of Yo Mama's House, an art-based support group and cooperative designed to empower mothers. Kubat has authored short stories, a memoir, and a play. She grew up in California but has lived in Minneapolis for more than three decades, teaching for 20 years in Minneapolis Public Schools. She holds a bachelor's degree in creative writing and feminist studies from Immaculate Heart College and a master of religious leadership and black church leadership degree from United Theological Seminary in New Brighton.

◼ Brittany Lewis

Dr. Brittany Lewis is the founder and CEO of Research in Action, an urban research, strategy, and engagement firm. She is also a senior research associate for the Center for Urban and Regional Affairs (CURA) at the University of Minnesota and previously worked as a research fellow at the Federal Reserve Bank of Minneapolis and as a visiting assistant professor in American studies and political science at Macalester College. Her specializations include US Black empowerment politics and policymaking in urban housing, employing a critical race and gender studies lens to examine the political economy of race, gender, and place. Dr. Lewis was the principal investigator for CURA's "The Illusion of Choice: Evictions and Profit in North Minneapolis" report and co–principal investigator on "The Diversity of Gentrification: Multiple Forms of Gentrification in Minneapolis and St. Paul." Her research was used in a Minnesota Supreme Court case to expand rights for tenants facing evictions, as direct testimony at the Minnesota state legislature, and to inform the human services and public safety impact agenda within Hennepin County and the City of Minneapolis. Dr. Lewis serves on the Metropolitan Council Livable Communities Advisory Committee, the City of Minneapolis Advisory Committee on Housing, and the State of Minnesota Working Group on Police-Involved Deadly Force Encounters. Dr. Lewis is the author of a number of state and city reports, has been featured in academic journals, and has been honored with several research fellowships.

Rose McGee

Rose McGee is a pie philanthropist and creator of the Sweet Potato Comfort Pie approach—a catalyst for caring and strengthening community. McGee has a TEDx Talk on the "Power of Pie" and is featured in the national PBS documentary *A Few Good Pie Places*. During the racial disturbance in Ferguson, Missouri, following the murder of Michael Brown by a police officer in 2014, McGee baked 30 sweet potato pies, loaded them into her car, and drove to Ferguson to offer comfort. Upon returning to Minnesota, she followed a deeper calling to get something done at home. Sweet Potato Comfort Pie has become a cornerstone service activity during the Martin Luther King Jr. holiday weekend, when dozens of volunteers of all ages and ethnicities bake pies and distribute them to individuals and organizations throughout the community.

McGee is the author of the book *Story Circle Stories* and *Kumbayah: The Juneteenth Story*, as well as the

Rose McGee

forthcoming children's book *Can't Nobody Make a Sweet Potato Pie Like Our Mama*. She is a two-time Charlie Awards nominee, a Minnesota's 50 over 50 honoree, a Celebrating the Sistas honoree, and a member of Delta Sigma Theta Sorority. Her home community of Golden Valley bestowed on her the Bill Hobbs Human Rights Award in 2018 and named her "Citizen of the Year."

Jonathan Palmer

Jonathan Palmer is the executive director of the Hallie Q. Brown Community Center in St. Paul. Palmer's early years were spent in the Washington, DC, metro area before he moved to the Twin Cities in 1989. He earned a bachelor's degree in psychology with a minor in theater from Morehouse College in

Jonathan Palmer

Hallie Q. Brown Community Center

1994. Raised by a family committed to public service and political work, Palmer began his career at the grass-roots level in Minneapolis with three Neighborhood Revitalization Programs to develop strategies to reduce crime and to expand affordable housing options. Palmer has served as executive director of the Jordan Area Community Council and director of the Minneapolis Empowerment Zone, a federally funded community renewal initiative. In 2008, Palmer assumed his present position at Hallie Q. Brown. Palmer is currently earning a master's degree in public affairs from the Humphrey Institute at the University of Minnesota. He lives in north Minneapolis with his wife and daughters.

In operation for more than ninety years, the **Hallie Q. Brown Community Center** is an African American, nonprofit social service agency open to all, primarily serving the Summit-University area of St. Paul and the Twin Cities metro area with a wide variety of programs addressing the community's critical needs. Hallie Quinn Brown

(1845–1949) was an African American educator, elocutionist, women's suffrage leader, and author. The community center has evolved from an independent human services provider at its founding in 1929 to a multiservice center as the administrative body of the Martin Luther King Center, which houses eight other agencies and programs, including the nationally recognized Penumbra Theatre Company.

Phyllis Wheatley Community Center

Phyllis Wheatley Community Center was established in 1924 by the Women's Cooperative Alliance as a settlement house in a mostly black neighborhood in north Minneapolis. Known at the time as the Phyllis Wheatley House, it provided services, a community center, and programs focused on recreation, education, and the arts for African Americans in a city divided by segregation. In 1929, a newly constructed Wheatley House opened with a new library, day care,

Mural at Phyllis Wheatley Community Center

medical clinic, and lodging. The organization became a boardinghouse for black college students, who were not allowed in the University of Minnesota dorms. In 1962, the house became the Phyllis Wheatley Community Center. The 1929 building was demolished in 1970 because of I-94 construction, and another facility was built in north Minneapolis. Today the Phyllis Wheatley Community Center continues to provide programs in lifelong learning for children, youth, and adults as well as family services for the diverse greater Minneapolis community.

Thomas Redd

Rising Star

Thomas Redd is a patron experience supervisor at Sumner Library in north Minneapolis. Redd graduated from Hamline University in 2014 with a bachelor's degree in sociology and a minor in religion. His creative outlets include singing, photography, and writing. He is also a youth worker at the Safe House, an emergency youth shelter in St. Paul.

Thomas Redd

Redd is a native Minnesotan and a first-generation Liberian American.

Sondra Samuels

Sondra Samuels is president and CEO of the Northside Achievement Zone (NAZ). Formed in 2003 as the PEACE Foundation, NAZ is a collaborative of partner organizations, schools, and community members working to end multigenerational poverty in north Minneapolis and build a culture of achievement through educational success and measurable academic outcomes. In 2011, NAZ was named a federal Promise Neighborhood and received a grant from the US Department of Education to help build the program. Under Samuels's leadership, NAZ has become a nationally recognized model for community and systems change.

■ Darrell Thompson

Darrell Thompson is the president of Bolder Options, a nonprofit organization uniting one-on-one mentoring with goal setting, physical activity, tutoring, and leadership opportunities to build confidence, maximize potential, and encourage healthy life skills in 10- to 14-year-olds. Thompson has worked with Bolder Options for more than two decades. Each year the organization engages with nearly 3,000 children in Minneapolis, St. Paul, and Rochester. Born in St. Louis, Missouri, Thompson relocated to Rochester with his family when he was just a year old. Thompson played football for the Minnesota Golden Gophers and for five years in the NFL for the Green Bay Packers. In 1997, Thompson was selected into the Gophers Hall of Fame. He is the radio color commentator for Gopher football broadcasts.

■ Mary Whitney

Reverend Dr. Mary Whitney is a speaker and educator in the areas of domestic violence, employment training, and restorative justice. Her mission is to provide victims of abuse with personal peer counseling that encourages open discussion, helps clients cope with traumatic experiences, and gives advice on using spiritual inspiration to build confidence. Whitney won the 2010 Presidential

Mary Whitney

Lifetime Volunteer Service Award, the 2010 Spirit of Peace Award, and the 2010 Governor's Faith Based and Community Service Initiative Award, and she was the honoree for the Women's Appreciation Award at the fourth annual Women Unite to Win in 2012.

■ Winfred "Fred" Woods

Winfred "Fred" Woods worked in the social services profession in Minnesota for nearly two decades as the programs director at the Dorothy Day Center, an organization run by Catholic Charities of St. Paul and Minneapolis that provides meals, shelter, and other assistance to the homeless.

Winfred "Fred" Woods

EDUCATION

Teaching the Future Today

What is the cost of an ignorant people?
We do not know, because we choose learning.

What is the challenge of the illiterate?
We do not know, because we prioritize reading.

What is the problem with feeble-minded thinking?
We do not know, because we pursue critical analysis.

What is the loss of unexamined phenomena?
We do not know, because we chase intellectual curiosity.

What is the reason for an ill-equipped community?
We do not know, because we teach the future today.

We are learners.
We are readers.
We are thinkers.
We are researchers.
We are teachers.
We are here.

The power of education in the lives of African Americans cannot be overstated. By placing education in a preeminent role in the community, educators offer lifelong learning opportunities for the youngest and oldest members of society.

African Americans have long contributed to the educational system in Minnesota as teachers, administrators, counselors, and more. Included here are just some of the men and women currently working in or recently retired from elementary schools, high schools, and colleges and universities.

Joy Ellis Bartlett

Joy Ellis Bartlett is a retired public-school teacher and former professor at Augsburg College who also worked as a model, author, and educational television personality. Her mother, Mary Jackson Ellis, was the first African American schoolteacher in the Minneapolis Public Schools.

Rose M. Brewer

Rose M. Brewer

Rose M. Brewer is a professor and past chairperson of the department of African American and African studies at the University of Minnesota. Her specialties include African American women's studies, Black family life, race, class, gender, and social change. She is a coauthor of the book *The Color of Wealth: The Story Behind the U.S. Racial Wealth Divide* and author of many essays, articles, and refereed publications. Dr. Brewer received her master's degree and PhD from Indiana University and did postdoctoral studies at the University of Chicago. She is a University of Minnesota College of Liberal Arts Dean's Medalist, a member of

the Academy of Distinguished Teachers, a 2013 winner of the American Sociological Association's Distinguished Contributions to Teaching Award, and a recipient of the Josie Johnson Social Justice Award.

A social activist and scholar, Brewer is the resource co-coordinator for the Black Midwest Initiative, a collective of scholars, students, artists, and community organizers committed to advocating for the lives of African Americans in the Midwest and Rust Belt regions. Prior to that, she has served as a member of the board of Project South: Institute for the Elimination of Poverty and Genocide, as a board member of United for a Fair Economy, and as a founding member of the Black Radical Congress.

Tonyus Chavers

Tonyus Chavers is a 30-year veteran of the Minneapolis Public Schools and a former physical education teacher at the Richard R. Green Central Park Elementary School in Minneapolis. In 2015 she

Tonyus Chavers

received the Fox9 Top Teacher Award. Chavers was also the first Black female high school basketball coach in Minneapolis. She played in the Women's Professional Basketball League (1978–81), a forerunner of the WNBA, and in 2018 she was inducted into the Women's Basketball Hall of Fame as a member of the trailblazing league.

Mahmoud El-Kati

Mahmoud El-Kati

Mahmoud El-Kati is a lecturer, author, and commentator on the African American experience. He is professor emeritus of history at Macalester College in St. Paul and the author of *Politically Considered: 50th Commemoration of the Supreme Court Decision of 1954*, *The Hiptionary: A Survey of African American Speech Patterns with a Digest of Key Words and Phrases*, *Haiti: The Hidden Truth*, and *The Myth of Race/The Reality of Racism: Critical Essays*. He is also the editor of *Towards an African Education*, a collection of essays by Minnesotans about the education of African American people and children. El-Kati

hosts a weekly public affairs radio show called "Reflections and Connections" on KMOJ/89.9 FM radio.

As a guiding elder to the social activist and educational organization Solidarity–Twin Cities, El-Kati stays active in the upliftment and liberation of the African American community. He is an instructor for the Nu Skool of Afrikan American Thought, a monthly community forum hosted at the High School for Recording Arts in St. Paul.

Clayton Ellis

Clayton Ellis is the associate principal of Oak Point Elementary in Eden Prairie. Born in Bloomington, Ellis attended Minnesota State University Mankato for his undergraduate studies and later his educational leadership specialist degree. He also holds a master's degree in education from Saint Mary's University of Minnesota.

Clayton Ellis

David Ellis

David Ellis is the founder and director of the High School for Recording Arts in St. Paul, one of the nation's most successful charter schools for at-risk youth. He is developing novel educational curricula that will positively affect students across the United States. A longtime resident of St. Paul, Ellis is a graduate of St. Paul Open School. He attended the University of Minnesota and earned a pilot's degree and license from Embry-Riddle Aeronautical University.

David Ellis

Artiera Evans

Artiera Evans is a veteran educator with Minneapolis Public Schools. She currently teaches third grade at Emerson Spanish Immersion Learning Center. In 2019, she received a national teaching award from the nonprofit organization Honored. Evans earned bachelor's and master's degrees from the University of Minnesota.

Artiera Evans with student

Donna Gingery

Donna Gingery is an educator in Prior Lake and the author of *Red's Adventures: The Egg Pie*, a children's book based on her life growing up in Selma, Alabama. Gingery holds a bachelor's degree from the University of Minnesota, a master's degree in educational leadership from Saint Mary's University, and an administration license in K-12 education from the University of Minnesota.

Donna Gingery

William D. Green

William D. Green

Dr. William D. Green is professor of history at Augsburg College. A leading scholar of African American history in Minnesota, he is the author of three books chronicling the early history of Blacks in the state: *A Peculiar Imbalance: The Fall and Rise of Racial Equality in Minnesota, 1837–1869*; *Degrees of Freedom: The Origins of Civil Rights in Minnesota, 1865–1912*; and *The Children of Lincoln: White Paternalism and the Limits of Black Opportunity in Minnesota, 1860–1876*. He has also published numerous articles, op-ed pieces, and book chapters on history, law, and education. He earned a bachelor of arts degree in history from Gustavus Adolphus College in St. Peter and received his master's, PhD, and juris doctorate from the University of Minnesota. Dr. Green served on the board of directors of Minneapolis Public Schools from 1993 to 2001 and as the school district's superintendent from 2006 to 2009.

Donna Kay Harris

Donna Kay Harris is an advisor in the academic world and has completed her coursework toward a doctorate degree in leadership at Saint Mary's University

in St. Paul. She is also the author of three books: *Spiritual Secrets for Successful Single Parenting, Spiritual Poems*, and *How to Heal from Sophisticated Slavery*. Her books seek to inspire readers and help anyone who needs encouragement.

Donna Kay Harris

Duchess Harris

Dr. Duchess Harris is a professor of American studies at Macalester College in St. Paul and was named the first chair of the American Studies Department in 2003. She was a Mellon Mays Fellow at the University of Pennsylvania, where

Duchess Harris

she earned a degree in American history. She earned a PhD in American studies from the University of Minnesota. She did postdoctoral fellowships at the Institute on Race and Poverty at the University of Minnesota Law School and at the Womanist Studies Consortium at the University of Georgia. She earned a juris doctorate in January 2011 and has an expertise in civil rights law. In 2015, the Minnesota Association of Black Lawyers bestowed on her the Profiles in Courage Award.

In 2018, Dr. Harris launched the Duchess Harris Collection, a line of books that offers scholarly expertise and authoritative content for students in grades 3 through 12. The books cover a range of topics from African American history to current events and other subjects. She is also the author of academic works for adults, such as *Black Feminist Politics from Kennedy to Trump*, as well as many journal articles. At Macalester, Harris helped to launch the "Human Computers at NASA" digital archive, honoring the African American women who worked as mathematicians at NASA in the 1940s through the 1960s, including Harris's grandmother, Miriam Daniel Mann.

Professor Harris resides in Vadnais Heights with her husband, their three children, and their cats and poodle.

■ Delores Henderson

Delores Henderson spent more than 40 years as an educator with the St. Paul Public Schools, including as the principal at J. J. Hill Elementary School and at Hazel Park Preparatory Academy. She dedicated herself to improving educational opportunities for all students, believing that, with the proper tools and resources, every child can learn

Delores Henderson

and flourish. Dr. Henderson earned master's and specialist degrees in curriculum and instruction from the University of Minnesota, as well as a PhD in education administration.

■ Nerita Griffin Hughes

Nerita Griffin Hughes is the dean of business, technology, career, and workforce development at North Hennepin Community College. After serving as interim dean for six months, she was officially named to the position in May 2018, becoming the first African American

Nerita Griffin Hughes

dean at the college. A native of south Minneapolis, Hughes attended Grambling State University in Louisiana and later received an MBA and a doctorate of education from Saint Mary's University.

Josiah Jackson

Dr. Josiah Jackson is an educator, author, chef, speaker, actor, intercessor, and evangelist. She received a bachelor's degree in education from HBCU Lincoln University in Jefferson City, Missouri; a culinary certificate from Le Cordon Bleu; a master's degree in education from Saint Mary's University in Winona; a master of divinity from Interdenominational Theological Center, Atlanta, Georgia; and a doctorate in education at Bethel University, St. Paul. Dr. Jackson also taught elementary and high school in the Minneapolis Public Schools. She has published two books, *God Called Her Josiah Jackson: An Autobiography of Josiah Jackson* and *Leap of Faith*.

Bonita Jones

Bonita Jones is an elementary teacher and labor advocate who has dedicated her professional life working to create the schools that students and educators deserve. After serving hundreds of students in the classroom in Minneapolis Public Schools, she went on to support her colleagues as peer assistance and review mentor for tenured teachers. Currently, she's on staff at the Minneapolis Federation of Teachers. Jones's mother and father were among the first African Americans to move to south Minneapolis in the 1950s, and she still lives in her family home in the Bryant neighborhood. She is a graduate of Carleton College and earned a master's degree in early childhood education from Concordia College in St. Paul.

Robert J. Jones

Dr. Robert J. Jones is the chancellor of the University of Illinois Urbana-Champaign, the first African American to hold that position. Earlier in his career, he spent 34 years at the University of Minnesota, including as a professor in agronomy and plant genetics, an administrator, executive vice provost, and senior vice president for academic administration. The University of Minnesota's Urban Research and Outreach-Engagement Center in north Minneapolis is named after Dr. Jones. During his time in Minnesota, he was also a member of Sounds of Blackness musical ensemble for several years.

Dr. Jones is married to Dr. Lynn Hassan Jones, and they have five children.

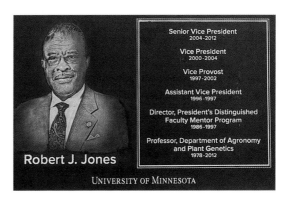

Robert J. Jones

Eric Mahmoud

Eric Mahmoud is the CEO and founder of Harvest Network of Schools, based in north Minneapolis. The charter management organization consists of the Best Academy, a K-8 school founded in 2008, and the Mastery School, a K-6 school

Eric Mahmoud

founded in 2012. Harvest Preparatory School, a K-4 school founded in 1992, merged with Best Academy in 2018. Together the schools serve nearly a thousand predominantly low-income African American students.

Keith Mayes

Dr. Keith Mayes is an associate professor in the African American and African studies department at the University of Minnesota. He teaches various courses on African American history and has special expertise on social and political movements and current issues of race and perception. He is the author of *Kwanzaa: Black Power and the Making of the African-American Holiday Tradition*, published in 2009. Dr. Mayes earned a PhD in history from Princeton University.

Fayneese Miller

Dr. Fayneese Miller is the 20th president of Hamline University in St. Paul. In her first four years since assuming the role in 2015, the university has dramatically increased enrollment among first-generation students and students of color, produced two Truman Scholars

and two Minnesota Teachers of the Year, and become one of 10 campuses in the United States to receive a Truth, Racial Healing and Transformation designation.

A native of Danville, Virginia, Dr. Miller received her master's and doctorate in experimental psychology from Texas Christian University, has a bachelor's degree in psychology from Hampton University, and performed postdoctoral work at Yale University. She previously served as dean of the College of Education and Social Services at the University of Vermont. Miller is a member of the NCAA Division III President's Council and serves ex officio on the boards of the Minnesota Private College Council, the Mitchell Hamline School of Law, and the New American Colleges and Universities national consortium.

Fayneese Miller

Lilene Elizabeth "Liz" Moore

Lilene Elizabeth "Liz" Moore

Lilene Elizabeth "Liz" Moore was a longtime Minneapolis Public School social worker and worked with special education students for more than 20 years. Moore also taught social work to graduate and undergraduate students at the University of Minnesota and Augsburg College in Minneapolis. Perhaps most notably, she was selected as a delegate from Minnesota to the first National Women's Conference, held in Houston, Texas, in 1977.

Originally from Des Moines, Iowa, Moore received her high school diploma from North Community High School in Minneapolis. She earned her bachelor of arts and master of arts degrees in social work from the University of Minnesota. Moore was granted a principal licensure certificate from Saint Mary's University in 1996.

Moore is a very spiritual woman, and her advice to all is, "In all thy ways, acknowledge [God] and he shall direct thy path." She is also involved in many community organizations and activities.

Samuel Myers Jr.

Dr. Samuel Myers Jr. is the Roy Wilkins Professor of Human Relations and Social Justice at the University of Minnesota's Humphrey School of Public Affairs and director of the Roy Wilkins Center for Human Relations and Social Justice. He specializes in the impacts of social policies on the poor and has consulted with such organizations as the National Commission for Employment Policy, the US Commission on Civil Rights, and the US Congressional Committee on the Judiciary, Subcommittee on Crime. Myers is a past president of the Association of Public Policy and Management and of the National Economic Association, and he has served on the boards of several national scientific and economic foundations. Locally, he has served on the boards of Catholic Charities of St. Paul and Minneapolis, the Breck School, and the Catholic Community Foundation of Minnesota. Dr. Myers received a PhD in economics from MIT.

Samuel Myers Jr.

◼ Beverly Propes

Beverly Propes is a licensed school nurse and consultant at Minneapolis Public Schools. She has been a community activist and champion for wellness and health around the Twin Cities for many years and an active member of the Minnesota Association of Black Physicians for more than 25 years.

Beverly Propes

◼ Alana Ramadan

Alana Ramadan is the Direct Instruction reading coordinator at north Minneapolis's Harvest Preparatory and the Best Academy, a charter school that serves 800 students of African American and East African descent in grades K-8. Ramadan coordinates the foundational reading program for students in grades K-2 and is responsible for initial placement of students in the Direct Instruction program, tracking student progress, and training and assigning instructors. During her 24 years at Harvest Preparatory and the Best Academy, Ramadan has served as preschool teacher, preschool curriculum coordinator, kindergarten teacher, teaching assistant, substitute

Alana Ramadan

teacher, latchkey coordinator, supervisor of educational assistants, and kindergarten and first grade level team facilitator.

◼ Elmore Roundtree

Elmore Roundtree has worked as a football, baseball, and basketball coach at various high schools in the Twin Cities. In 2006, he became the first Black football coach at Eagan High School. Born

Elmore Roundtree

and raised in South Carolina, Roundtree moved to Minneapolis after earning a bachelor of science degree in criminal justice and mass communications at Bemidji State University. He was hired as a childcare worker at St. Joseph's Home for Children in 1982 and eventually became lead childcare worker and then shelter supervisor. In 1994, he accepted a position with Dakota County Community Corrections as a probation officer. He is the cofounder and chair of the Dakota County Black Employee Network (BEN), the first employee resource group of its kind within Dakota County. The group's mission is to foster the inclusion and advancement of Black employees at Dakota County while building a network of support for individual and collective concerns. Roundtree and his wife, Alane, have two adult sons, Alex and Aaron.

Anthony R. Scott II

Anthony R. Scott II

Anthony R. Scott II is a 14-year veteran with Minneapolis Public Schools as a special education assistant and associate educator and a family and community liaison. He currently serves as a job coach for young adults with special needs. A native Minnesotan, Scott attended Pilgrim Lutheran Elementary School, DeLaSalle High School, Minneapolis Community and Technical College, and Metropolitan State University, where he earned a bachelor of arts degree in urban entrepreneurship. He is the treasurer for Minnesota's Black Community Project, a member of the Reverend Dr. Martin Luther King Jr. Park Legacy Council, and a board member for the Sabathani Community Center in Minneapolis. In addition, Scott owns a micro-event planning company.

Chaunda L. Scott

Dr. Chaunda L. Scott is an associate professor of organizational leadership and the diversity and inclusion specialist for the office of the dean at Oakland University in Rochester, Michigan. She also serves as the secretary for Minnesota's Black Community Project in Minneapolis. Dr. Scott has coauthored six books on workforce diversity along with numerous scholarly articles and chapters on diversity education and workforce diversity. She has also received several teaching and research awards in these areas and has presented her research in locations across the globe.

In 2013, she was recognized as one of the Top 25 Education Professors in Michigan by Online Schools Michigan. In 2015, she received a prestigious Fulbright Specialist Scholarship at Cape Peninsula University of Technology in Cape Town, South Africa, where she engaged in diversity education research and provided diversity

Chaunda L. Scott

education professional development seminars to administrators, faculty, and staff.

Scott is a native Minnesotan and the daughter of Walter R. Scott and Margaret A. Scott. She received a bachelor of science degree in human resource development from the University of Detroit in Michigan; a master's degree in administration, planning, and social policy from the Harvard Graduate School of Education in Cambridge, Massachusetts; and a doctorate degree in organizational leadership and adult education with a focus in diversity education from Teachers College/Columbia University in New York City.

■ Walter Scott Jr.

Walter Scott Jr. taught physical education in Minneapolis schools for more than 30 years and coached baseball teams at both North High School and Central High School. A graduate of

Central High School, Scott went on to earn a bachelor of science degree in physical education from Alabama State University in Montgomery. As an outfielder on the Alabama State baseball team, he played for legendary coach and Negro League baseball player Herbert "Hot Dog" Wheeler.

From 1990 through 2016, Scott was a rope power coach with the Minneapolis Public School's Rope Power Program. He also taught rope power skills at Putnam, Shingle Creek, and Jenny Lind elementary schools in Minneapolis. Now retired from teaching, Scott is known on talk radio as the "Secretary of Insight." Several years ago, he was selected as the number-one call-in guest and hosted his own show on KFAN. He is also an active member of the Sabathanites Drum Corps.

Walter Scott Jr.

■ Carlos Sneed

Carlos Sneed is the associate dean of students at Hamline University in St. Paul and director of the Hedgeman Center for Student Diversity Initiatives and Programs. As director, Sneed supervises

Carlos Sneed

staff, mentors students, advises student organizations, and coordinates diversity education initiatives for students, staff, and the Hamline University community. Sneed is active in the Minnesota College Personnel Association and served a three-year term as its president. In 2007, he received the MCPA's Linda Schrempp Alberg Award for Outstanding Contribution to Minnesota Higher Education, and in 2009 he received the Hamline University John Wesley Outstanding Service Award for Staff. Originally from Tennessee, Sneed earned a bachelor's degree in African and Afro-American studies and psychology from Washington University in St. Louis and a master's degree in higher education and student affairs from Bowling Green State University in Ohio.

◼ Jason Sole

Jason Sole is an adjunct professor of criminal justice at Hamline University and former president of the Minneapolis NAACP. He is a staunch advocate for reforming the criminal justice system and for motivating Black youth to excel

beyond the stereotypes of violence, drugs, and crime. He cofounded the Humanize My Hoodie Movement, which challenges perceptions about African American men through clothing, art exhibitions, and workshops. A formerly incarcerated individual, Sole published his own story of redemption, *From Prison to Ph.D.: A Memoir of Hope, Resilience, and Second Chances,* in 2014.

Jason Sole

◼ David Vassar Taylor

David Vassar Taylor is a trustee at Northwestern Health Sciences University and was the dean of the General College of the University of Minnesota for 16 years. He has also held administrative positions at Morehouse College in Atlanta and Dillard University in New Orleans. Taylor grew up in the Rondo neighborhood of St. Paul and is among the leading experts on African American history in the state. He is the author of *African Americans in Minnesota* and *Cap Wigington: An Architectural Legacy in Ice and Stone.*

Michael Walker

■ Michael Walker

Michael Walker is the director of Black Male Student Achievement for Minneapolis Public Schools. From 2006 to 2009, he served as a career and college center coordinator for AchieveMpls at Roosevelt High School and then became Roosevelt's dean of students (2009–11) before serving as assistant principal from 2011 to 2014. A product of Minneapolis Public Schools, Walker earned his undergraduate degree in physical education from Southwest Minnesota State University, his master's degree in counseling from the University of Wisconsin–River Falls, and his administrative license from St. Cloud State.

Walker is the inaugural director for the Office of Black Male Student Achievement, which focuses on changing outcomes for Black males who attend Minneapolis Public Schools. The office engages with students, families, teachers, and community members to overcome disparities in the school system and foster a climate of equity and support.

■ Floyd Williams

Floyd Williams is an instructor of Kemetic yoga and has multiple certifications in yoga teacher training. Williams is an advocate of Ma'at (truth), justice, harmony, and balance. He is the author of three books: *The Holy Black Papyrus, The Origin of Racism,* and *Unspoken Truth.*

Floyd Williams

■ Terrion Williamson

Dr. Terrion Williamson is an associate professor of African American and African studies at the University of Minnesota, with appointments in gender, women and sexuality studies and American studies. Her research and teaching specializations include black feminist theory, 20th- and 21st-century African American literature, black cultural studies, media studies, and racialized gender violence. A native of Peoria, Illinois, she received her bachelor's degree in English and African American studies from the University of Illinois at Chicago and

Terrion Williamson

a juris doctorate from the University of Illinois Urbana-Champaign, where she served as executive editor of the *University of Illinois Law Review*. She earned a master's degree and PhD in American studies and ethnicity from the University of Southern California. Dr. Williamson is also a founder and director of the Black Midwest Initiative, a collective of scholars, students, artists, and community organizers committed to advocating for the lives of African Americans in the Midwest and Rust Belt regions. Her first book, *Scandalize My Name: Black Feminist Practice and the Making of Black Social Life*, was published in 2016.

▨ Josef Woldense

Dr. Josef Woldense is an assistant professor of African American and African studies and affiliated faculty in the department of political science at the University of Minnesota. He received a PhD in political science from Indiana University. His research interests are in the areas of African politics, comparative politics, public policy, political institutions, authoritarian regimes, and social network analysis, with a geographical focus on Africa. He joined the University of Minnesota faculty in 2018.

Josef Woldense

GOVERNMENT AND PUBLIC AFFAIRS

For the Love

For the love of country,
We engage in the array of public affairs.

For the love of community,
We pursue the path of politics.

For the love of duty,
We serve through obligations of self.

For the love of honor,
We seek excellence with a higher ethos.

For the love of Black lives,
For the value of Black representation,
For the importance of impacting Black history,
For the necessity of equal opportunity,
We are here.

African American professionals have answered the call for leadership through governmental engagement. From positions as mayors and city councilmembers to statewide and national roles in public office, African Americans have contributed to the development of political agendas and to the landscape of legislation in Minnesota and beyond.

Sharon Sayles Belton

Sharon Sayles Belton

Sharon Sayles Belton is an activist, politician, and community leader. She was elected mayor of Minneapolis in 1993, becoming the first African American and the first woman to hold that office. She was reelected in 1997 and served two full terms. She is currently the vice president of community relations and government affairs for Thomson Reuters, a media and legal business based in Eagan.

Born in St. Paul, Belton later moved to Minneapolis and graduated from Minneapolis Central High School. She attended Macalester College, where she received a bachelor of science degree in biology. She soon shifted her focus to community service. In 1978, Belton cofounded the Harriet Tubman Shelter for Battered Women in Minneapolis and later helped establish the National Coalition Against Sexual Assault. She won her first elected office in 1983 when she was voted to the Minneapolis City Council. She became city council president in 1990.

Belton has received the Rosa Parks Award from the American Association for Affirmative Action and the Gertrude E. Rush Distinguished Service Award presented by the National Bar Association. In 2017, Belton was honored with a bronze bust in Minneapolis City Hall to honor her eight years as the city's mayor. She is married to Steven Belton (page 65).

Melvin Carter III

Melvin Carter III is the mayor of St. Paul, the first African American to hold that office. He previously was a member of the St. Paul City Council from 2008 to 2013 and served as vice chair for much of his tenure. He then served as the director of the Office of Early Learning with the Minnesota Department of Education and as executive director of the Minnesota Children's Cabinet. Carter grew up in St. Paul's Rondo neighborhood and graduated from Central High School. He earned

Melvin Carter III

a master's degree in public policy from the Hubert H. Humphry Institute of Public Affairs at the University of Minnesota and an undergraduate degree from Florida A&M University. He and his wife live in St. Paul and are the parents of five children. Carter is the son of former St. Paul police officer Melvin Whitfield Carter Jr. (page 67) and county commissioner Toni Carter.

Toni Carter

Toni Carter has been a Ramsey County commissioner since 2005 and was the first African American to serve on a county board in Minnesota. She is co-chair of the Minnesota Human Services Performance Council and the Ramsey County Juvenile Detention Alternatives Initiative Stakeholder Committee. Carter has previously worked as a middle school teacher and a systems engineer at IBM, and she has been on the boards of many community organizations. Hailing from Bessemer, Alabama, she attended Concordia University and Carleton College. She is married to Melvin Whitfield Carter Jr. (page 67) and is the mother of St. Paul mayor Melvin Carter III.

Toni Carter

Bobby Joe Champion

Bobby Joe Champion

Bobby Joe Champion is an attorney and a member of the Minnesota Senate, representing District 59 for the DFL Party. He previously served two terms in the state house of representatives, from 2008 to 2012. Champion graduated from Minneapolis North High School, Macalester College, and William Mitchell College of Law. Prior to elective office, he served as assistant attorney general under Hubert "Skip" Humphrey III and Mike Hatch. Champion also has been involved in music with Flyte Tyme Productions and cofounded the Excelsior Choir.

Phillipe Cunningham

Phillipe Cunningham is the Minneapolis city councilperson serving Ward 4, located in the city's northwest corner. Born and raised in Illinois, Cunningham worked as a special education

Phillipe Cunningham

teacher in the Chicago Public Schools before moving to Minnesota, where he became active in youth policy issues. He was appointed to the City of Minneapolis Youth Violence Prevention Executive Committee and later served as Mayor Betsy Hodges's senior policy aide for education, youth success, racial equity, and LGBTQ rights. He was one of the first openly transgender men to be elected to public office, defeating 20-year incumbent Barb Johnson in the 2017 city council elections.

◼ Jeremiah Ellison

Jeremiah Ellison is the Minneapolis city councilperson for Ward 5 on the city's north side, where he was born and raised. He has been an artist, community organizer, youth counselor, and workers' rights advocate. Ellison was elected to the city council in 2017. He is the son of Minnesota attorney general Keith Ellison.

◼ Keith Ellison

Keith Ellison is the attorney general of Minnesota, winning election as a member of the DFL Party in 2018. Before that, he was the US representative for Minnesota's Fifth Congressional District for 12 years. Ellison was the first Muslim to be elected to the US Congress. A native of Detroit, Michigan, Ellison received his juris doctorate from the University of Minnesota Law School. He worked for many years as an attorney in civil rights and defense law, including spending five years as the executive director of the Legal Rights Center, a community-driven nonprofit law firm specializing in adult and juvenile criminal defense and restorative justice practices and advocacy.

Keith Ellison

John Mark Harrington

John Mark Harrington is commissioner of the Minnesota Department of Public Safety under Governor Tim Walz. He was chief of the St. Paul Police Department from 2004 to 2010 and chief of Metro Transit Police for Minneapolis–St. Paul from 2012 to 2019. In between, he served one term in the Minnesota Senate, representing District 67, which includes portions of St. Paul. Born and raised in Chicago, Harrington received a bachelor of arts degree from Dartmouth College and a master's in education from the University of St. Thomas in St. Paul. In all, Harrington worked for 33 years in the St. Paul Police Department.

Jeff Hayden

Jeff Hayden is the Minnesota state senator representing District 62 in south Minneapolis. He serves on several senate committees and is the ranking member on the Human Services Reform Finance and Policy Committee. He was first elected as a state representative in 2008 and then joined the senate following a special election in 2011. Hayden has been involved in many community service organizations, including as manager of Hearth Connection, a nonprofit dedicated to eliminating homelessness, and as housing coordinator for the Minnesota Supportive Housing Consortium, among others. Hayden is also on the board of the Amateur Sports Commission, the Council on Black Minnesotans, and the Midwestern Legislative Conference innovations selections committee. He lives in the Bryant neighborhood of Minneapolis with his wife, Terri, and their two children.

Jeff Hayden

Andrea Jenkins

Andrea Jenkins is the city councilperson for Minneapolis's Ward 8. Her historic election in 2017 made her the first African American openly transgender woman to be elected to office in the United States. A published author, performance artist, poet, and activist, Jenkins has worked for many years in community development and social services. She is from Chicago and first came to Minnesota in 1979 to attend the University of Minnesota. She worked for the Hennepin County government for a decade and was a staff member on the Minneapolis City Council for 12 years. Jenkins was curator of the Transgender Oral History Project at the University of Minnesota's Jean-Nickolaus Tretter Collection in Gay, Lesbian, Bisexual and Transgender Studies. She holds a master's degree in community development from Southern New Hampshire University, a master of fine arts in creative

Andrea Jenkins

Rena Moran

writing from Hamline University, and a bachelor's degree in human services from Metropolitan State University. Jenkins has received numerous awards and fellowships, including being named a 2011 Bush Fellow to advance the work of transgender inclusion.

■ Rena Moran

Rena Moran represents District 65A in the Minnesota House of Representatives and is the deputy minority leader for the DFL Party. First elected in 2010, she serves on the education, health and human services reform, and job growth and energy affordability committees. She is a Chicago native and received a bachelor of science degree in early childhood education from Southern Illinois University. Moran faced

homelessness when she came to Minnesota in the early 2000s but soon found a job and housing for herself and her children. She is an active community organizer and recipient of a Bush Fellowship in 2013.

■ Erin Maye Quade

Erin Maye Quade is a former member of the Minnesota House of Representatives and was the DFL-endorsed candidate for lieutenant governor in 2018 with running mate Erin Murphy. Quade was the first openly LGBTQ candidate to receive a major party endorsement for statewide office in Minnesota. Prior to winning election to the state legislature in 2016, she worked on the staff of US representative Keith Ellison. Quade is a graduate of the University of St. Thomas in St. Paul.

Erin Maye Quade

Angela Steward-Randle

Colonel Angela Steward-Randle was the director of human resources, manpower, and personnel for the Minnesota National Guard. Her 30-year military career made her one of the most senior African American women in the history of the organization. As a senior officer, Colonel Steward-Randle worked closely with her fellow service members, teaching them the skills they needed to thrive and succeed in the National Guard.

Chris Taylor

Chris Taylor is the Chief Inclusion Officer for the State of Minnesota. In this role, he provides strategic direction to advance inclusion and equity initiatives and culture in state government agencies and operations while helping to establish equitable policies, programs, and community engagement. In addition, he supports agencies and staff charged with carrying out recruitment and hiring, procurement, and economic development responsibilities. He also serves as chair of the One Minnesota Council for Inclusion and Equity to address diversity, inclusion, and equity in state government practices. Prior to his appointment as CIO by Governor Tim Walz in April 2019, Taylor directed the Department of Inclusion and Community Engagement at the Minnesota

Angela Steward-Randle

Chris Taylor

Historical Society. He first joined MNHS in 2005 as the diversity outreach manager. He developed and facilitated undergraduate museum fellowship programs and was a cocreator of the Heritage Studies and Public History program, a partnership between the Minnesota Historical Society and the University of Minnesota.

Taylor received his bachelor's degree from the University of St. Thomas and a master's degree from the Cooperstown Graduate Program for Museum Studies. He earned his doctorate of education in the Organization Development and Change program at the University of St. Thomas. Taylor has served on the boards of the Minnesota Council of Nonprofits, the East Side Freedom Library, the Minnesota Association of Museums, and the Ramsey County Historical Society. He has also served on the Diversity, Equity, Access, and Inclusion Task Force for the American Alliance of Museums and the Diversity and Inclusion Task Force for the American Association for State and Local History.

Neva Walker

■ Neva Walker

Neva Walker was the first African American woman elected to the state legislature in Minnesota. She served four terms in the house of representatives for District 61B, from 2001 to 2009. In 2008, *City Pages* named her "Best Politician." During her eight years in office, Walker was an advocate for prisoners' rights, AIDS prevention programs, and sex education in schools. She earned a bachelor's degree in social and public policy from Metropolitan State University.

LAW AND LAW ENFORCEMENT

To Protect and to Defend

We promise to protect and to serve,
To yield our lives for others.

    We swear to defend and uphold,
    To risk ourselves for others.

Out of duty, we protect honorably.
Out of love, we defend with integrity.
Out of sacrifice, we enforce admirably.

    Pursuing the life the law grants
      For all people
    While defending the rights the law asserts
      For all people

We are protectors and defenders.
We are risk-takers and enforcers.
We are here.

African American communities and local law enforcement benefit when gifted African American men and women work in law and law-related professions. From suiting up in uniform to providing legal counsel, this group of professionals offers immediate examples for others to emulate. Whether working as police officers, lawyers, or judges, African Americans have enjoyed increasing roles in law and law enforcement in Minnesota in recent decades.

Charlie Adams

Commander Charlie Adams oversees the Minneapolis Police Department's Procedural Justice Division, which consists of the Community Engagement Team, the Police Community Support Team, and the Cedar-Riverside/West Bank Safety Center. He has been with the MPD since 1986 and has served in four of the city's five police precincts, as well as in the internal affairs, homicide, and minority recruitment units. Commander Adams is a well-respected and credible leader both within the MPD and in the community, making him well suited to lead the Procedural Justice Unit. His brother, son, and daughter are also members of the Minneapolis Police Department.

Charlie Adams

Pamela Alexander

Pamela Alexander served the Fourth Judicial District in Minnesota for more than 30 years, until her retirement in 2018. A fourth-generation Minnesotan who grew up in south Minneapolis, she was the first female Black judge in the state. Alexander earned a bachelor of arts degree at Augsburg College and received her juris doctorate from the University of Minnesota Law School. After several

Pamela Alexander

years working as an attorney, she was appointed to the Hennepin County Municipal Court in 1983 and became a Hennepin County District Court judge in 1986. In the 1990s, she helped create the district court's Equal Justice Committee and helped produce the Racial Bias Task Force Report. She teaches at the University of St. Thomas School of Law.

Judge Alexander has been a member of many professional and community organizations, such as the Minnesota Association of Black Lawyers, Minnesota Women Lawyers, National Association of Women Judges, National Bar Association Judicial Council, Minnesota Association of Black Women Lawyers, National Association of Juvenile and Family Court Judges, Children's Defense Fund Black Community Crusade for Children—Judges Advisory Board, and the Governor's Council on Police Community Relations. She has received dozens of awards, from the NAACP Profile in Courage Award to the 2017 Sabathani Leadership Award.

Medaria Arradondo

Medaria Arradondo is the 53rd chief of the Minneapolis Police Department. He joined the MPD in 1989 as a patrol officer in the Fourth Precinct on the city's north side and worked his way up the ranks before being appointed inspector of the First Precinct in 2013. He also served as a school resource officer, commander of the internal affairs unit, deputy chief, and assistant chief before being nominated as chief by Mayor Betsy Hodges in 2017. Chief Arradondo sits on several community boards and is a member of national and international police associations. He served as MPD's liaison to the National Initiative for Building Community Trust and Justice, overseeing the execution of initiatives on procedural justice, implicit bias, and reconciliation training. His work has helped positively transform the MPD culture and position the department as a national leader in police service excellence.

Medaria Arradondo

James Bransford

James Bransford

James Bransford is a longtime legal and criminal justice advocate. He is a community outreach specialist for the St. Paul–based Nurturing House, which helps find counseling support services for African Americans and African immigrants who are experiencing substance abuse issues or personal and social violence. Although Bransford does not have a law degree, his knowledge, skills, and experience in the criminal justice field have helped numerous individuals get the help they need. Both of Bransford's daughters work in the criminal justice field.

Tanya M. Bransford

Tanya M. Bransford has served as a district court judge in Hennepin County since 1994. She currently manages felony drug and property cases for the Fourth Judicial District. As the presiding juvenile court judge from 2006 to 2008, Judge Bransford led the Juvenile Detention Alternatives Initiative, which dramatically reduced the number of young

Tanya M. Bransford

people in detention while preserving public safety. Prior to that, she became the first Black woman to serve as a district court referee for Hennepin County's Juvenile Division and the first Black female workers' compensation judge with the Office of Administrative Hearings. Her efforts to improve the criminal justice system extend to her work as chair of the equal justice committee in Hennepin County District Court, as a founding member of the Minnesota Judicial Council's equality and justice committee, and as board member of the National Consortium of Racial and Ethnic Fairness in the Courts.

A graduate of North St. Paul High School, Bransford did her undergraduate studies at Gustavus Adolphus College in St. Peter before earning her juris doctorate at Hamline University School of Law. Judge Bransford began her legal career in private practice working in the areas of personal injury, criminal defense, and workers' compensation.

■ Traci V. Bransford

Traci V. Bransford is a partner at the law firm of Stinson Leonard Street, where she serves as outside general counsel to prominent public figures in sports, entertainment, and media. With more than 25 years' experience in entertainment law, Bransford guides her clients through many aspects of business and nonprofit entity formation and management, including strategizing and structuring their businesses, negotiating contracts, and counseling them on intellectual property matters.

Bransford earned her law degree from the New York University School of Law and her bachelor's degree from Spelman College in Atlanta. She began her legal career in California and was ultimately recognized by the Los Angeles County Board of Supervisors for her diverse litigation skills by being appointed a hearing officer to the Los Angeles County Civil Service Commission,

Traci V. Bransford

where she presided over employment and labor disputes. Bransford also practiced law in New York City before coming home to Minnesota. Bransford is involved in many civic and nonprofit organizations and is a sought-after speaker on entertainment, sports, and diversity matters. She is the proud mother of two children, Russell Todd Bullock and Rose Elizabeth Bullock.

◼ Tina Burnside

Tina Burnside is a senior trial attorney at the Equal Employment Opportunity Commission, where she has worked since 1997. She earned her juris doctorate from the University of Wisconsin Law School. She has practiced law in federal courts in Minnesota, Wisconsin, Iowa, North Dakota, North Carolina, and Louisiana. She is a frequent speaker at employment law seminars on various litigation and enforcement issues

Tina Burnside

under the Americans with Disabilities Act, Title VII of the Civil Rights Act of 1964, and the Age Discrimination in Employment Act of 1967. She is also a writer and editor for employment law handbooks published by the Minnesota State Bar Association, Continuing Legal Education.

In addition to her legal work, Burnside has served on many boards, including the Minneapolis Arts Commission, the Minnesota Black Women Lawyers Network, the Minneapolis Urban League, and the Central Area Neighborhood Development Organization (CANDO). She has volunteered as a guardian ad litem, serving as an advocate for abused and neglected children in Hennepin County juvenile court.

In 2018, Burnside teamed up with Coventry Cowens to found the Minnesota African American Heritage Museum and Gallery on Penn Avenue in north Minneapolis. MAAHMG seeks to preserve, record, and highlight the achievements, contributions, and experiences of African Americans in Minnesota through exhibits, workshops, and events.

◼ James Cannon

James Cannon has been a workers' compensation judge for the state of Minnesota since 1987. As a judge with the Office of Administrative Hearings, he conducts settlement conferences to facilitate agreements, presides over hearings, and issues decisions regarding all workers' compensation claims. He spent more than a decade as an attorney before becoming a judge. Judge Cannon is married to Lois Cannon (page 130), who is a certified nurse midwife, and they have two children.

James Cannon (see page 103)

■ Sam Clark

Sam Clark is an attorney at Greene Espel and served as city attorney of St. Paul under Mayor Chris Coleman from 2015 to 2018. Clark attended Cretin–Derham Hall High School in St. Paul and received his undergraduate degree from Harvard University and a law degree from Yale Law School. He clerked for Chief Judge Michael J. Davis in the US District Court for the District of Minnesota and then joined Greene Espel in 2009 before leaving to work in politics. Clark worked as the counsel for US senator Amy Klobuchar on the Senate Judiciary Committee and then was state director of her Minnesota office.

■ Al Coleman

Al Coleman is a partner at the law firm of Saul Ewing Arnstein & Lehr in Minneapolis. Advising clients in a broad range of corporate and transactional matters, he focuses on representing private equity sponsors and domestic and international companies in mergers and acquisitions, divestitures, and joint ventures. Coleman is a financial management graduate of the University of St. Thomas and a graduate of the University of Minnesota Law School, where he remains involved in various business law programs.

Among his professional accolades, Coleman was named to the *Minneapolis/ St. Paul Business Journal*'s list of "40 under 40" in 2006 and *Minnesota Business Magazine*'s "Power 50" in 2016, and he received a client choice award in 2018 recognizing his excellent customer service. He is the author of the career development guide *Secrets to Success*. A frequent lecturer to students and young professionals, Coleman has shared his success principles with thousands of men and women across the country.

■ Carleton B. Crutchfield

Carleton B. Crutchfield has a private law practice in St. Paul and is a professor in the Business Law Department at St. Cloud State University. He grew up in the Highland Park neighborhood in

Carleton B. Crutchfield

St. Paul and graduated from St. Paul Central High School. After attending Morehouse College, he completed a master's degree in public policy at Princeton University and earned a law degree from Columbia Law School. Crutchfield is engaged in several educational endeavors with children and adults in need.

Christopher Ellis Crutchfield

Christopher Ellis Crutchfield is the deputy director of community relations and external affairs for Ramsey County Community Corrections, a position he has held since 2006. He is also an attorney and an adjunct professor at St. Cloud State University, where he teaches media law. Crutchfield is active in his community and in local politics. He serves on the Minnesota Department of Natural Resources Parks and Trails Legacy Advisory Committee. For more than 25 years, Crutchfield has conducted Underground Railroad reenactments and other cultural

Christopher Ellis Crutchfield

simulations. An outdoor enthusiast, he loves to fish in the lakes and rivers of Minnesota and Wisconsin. Crutchfield has five children.

Ayodele Jessica Famodu

Captain Ayodele Jessica Famodu is a member of the Minnesota Army National Guard 34th Infantry Division Judge Advocate General (JAG) Team. She is assigned as a team chief with A Company, Division Headquarters, and Headquarters Battalion. Captain Famodu was commissioned as an army reserve officer in 2011 and assigned to the 214th Legal Operations Detachment out of Fort Snelling. From 2014 to 2016, Captain Famodu served as a special victim's counsel (SVC) and was selected as one of the initial SVC regional program managers and advisors for the Reserve Program. As an SVC, she handled her own cases from outset to courts martial proceedings and maintained oversight of the numerous cases assigned to other SVCs in her 18-state area of operation.

In her civilian career, Famodu serves on the felony trial team at the Ramsey County Attorney's Office in St. Paul. Her prior litigation experience includes working as an assistant public defender for Hennepin County, handling both misdemeanor and felony cases, from 2011 to 2017; a medical malpractice defense associate with Barker & Castro in Chicago from 2008 to 2010; and an assistant corporation counsel for the City of Chicago from 2003 to 2008. Captain Famodu is a summa cum laude graduate of the University of Pittsburgh and a 2003 graduate of William Mitchell College of Law. She is also a proud mother of two young girls and married to a former marine.

David C. Higgs

David C. Higgs was appointed to the Second Judicial District by Governor Jesse Ventura in May 2002 after practicing civil litigation in the Twin Cities area for more than 20 years. He served on the court until retiring in March 2019. Higgs received his juris doctorate from the University of Minnesota Law School in 1981. Throughout his 17 years on the bench, the Honorable Judge Higgs presided over a wide range of civil, criminal, juvenile, child protection, and civil commitment and family law cases. He has served on the board of directors of Southern Minnesota Regional Legal Services, Neighborhood House, Minnesota Minority Lawyers Association (predecessor to the Minnesota Association of Black Lawyers), and Minnesota Board of Law Examiners. He was a member of the Minnesota Supreme Court Racial Bias Task Force and served on numerous other Minnesota judicial branch committees.

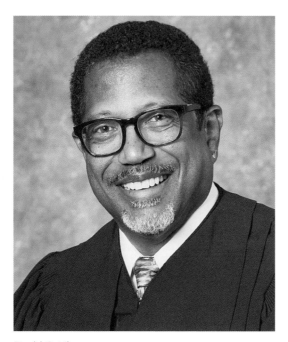

David C. Higgs

Ronald E. Hunter

Ronald E. Hunter

Ronald E. Hunter is a retired captain in the US Navy and a former assistant vice president at Cargill. He graduated from the University of Minnesota Law School with his juris doctorate in 1978. Hunter has earned several awards, such as the Minnesota Association of Black Lawyers President's Award, 2010; the Cargill Chairman's Award for High Performance, 2004; and "hero" recognition by Heroes in Our Midst, 2006. He holds membership at the St. Olaf College Board of Regents, the Minnesota Association of Black Lawyers board of directors, the National Bar Association, the Urban Coalition of Minneapolis board of directors, the Minnesota Minority Lawyers Association board of directors, and the Association of the US Navy. Hunter is also the founder of the Cultural Union for Black Expression at St. Olaf College, and he led the creation and development of the Cargill Law Department's intellectual property team.

Lee A. Hutton III

Lee A. Hutton III is a trial attorney and partner at Hutton Kluz Evans. He specializes in entertainment and sports law as well as general litigation. Hutton was named "Attorney of the Year" by *Minnesota Lawyer* in 2010. He received his juris doctorate from William Mitchell School of Law in St. Paul. Hutton is married to attorney and entrepreneur Diana Hutton.

Herbert A. Igbanugo

Herbert A. Igbanugo is the founding shareholder of Igbanugo Partners International Law Firm, where he heads the international trade law practice group and its consulting division Afrique Sub-Sahara Strategies LTD. He was also a founding partner of Blackwell Igbanugo PA, the largest Black-controlled US law firm between 2003 and 2006. Born in Nigeria, he received undergraduate degrees in international relations and economics from the University of Minnesota and his juris doctorate from Hamline University School of Law. He is a member of the Minnesota and New York State Bar Associations and is admitted to practice before numerous US courts, including the Supreme Court.

Herbert A. Igbanugo

Shawn Renee Kennon

Shawn Renee Kennon has been an attorney with the Hennepin County Public Defender's Office since 1993. Having focused in the juvenile courts for 19 years, defending termination of parental rights petitions, gang certification defense, and juvenile delinquencies, she currently practices criminal defense law in the suburban courts. A native of Omaha, Nebraska, Kennon received her bachelor of arts degree, magna cum laude, from Brown University. She graduated from the University of Michigan Law School in 1984.

In 1992, she was interim executive director of the Minneapolis Civilian Police Review Authority before joining the conflicts panel of the Hennepin County Public Defender's Office. Additionally, in 1993, she became the first Black woman selected to serve as a panel member on the Hennepin County Commitment Defense Project, defending mentally ill and chemically dependent clients. Kennon is or has been a member of the American Bar Association, the National, Federal, Minnesota, and Hennepin County Bar Associations, the Minnesota Association of Black Lawyers, the Chrysalis Center for Women board, the Breck School alumni board, the Alpha Kappa Alpha Sorority, and the Minneapolis–St. Paul Chapter of the Links, Inc.

LaJune Thomas Lange

LaJune Thomas Lange is a retired judge of the Fourth Judicial District in Minnesota and a recognized expert in human rights and international development. She is the founder and president of the International Leadership Institute, dedicated to building global leaders and citizens. Raised in Minneapolis,

Lange graduated from Augsburg University and received her juris doctorate from the University of Minnesota Law School. She has received awards from the American Bar Association and the Minnesota Association of Black Lawyers and the General Mills MLK Profiles in Courage Award, among others. The Honorable Judge Lange serves as Honorary Consul for the Republic of South Africa in Minnesota, and she was selected by the US State Department to travel around the world as an expert on the rights of women, African American history, and judicial decision-making.

■ Nekima Levy Armstrong

Nekima Levy Armstrong is a renowned civil rights attorney, ordained reverend, former law professor, freedom fighter, legal scholar, author, and national expert on issues at the intersections of race, public policy, economic justice, public education, juvenile justice, and the criminal justice system. She received her law degree from the University of Illinois at Urbana-Champaign. Levy Armstrong has

Nekima Levy Armstrong, with her husband, Marques Armstrong

earned many accolades, including being named 2014 "Attorney of the Year" by *Minnesota Lawyer* and one of "50 under 50 Most Influential Law Professors of Color in the Country" by *Lawyers of Color* magazine. She taught law at the University of St. Thomas Law School for 13 years, served as president of the Minneapolis NAACP, and was an adviser to Black Lives Matter Minneapolis. She ran for mayor of Minneapolis in 2017. Her husband, Marques Armstrong, is president and CEO of Hope & Healing Counseling Services.

Jada Lewis

■ Jada Lewis

Jada Lewis is a trial attorney in the business and commercial litigation division of Stinson Leonard Street. Before joining the firm, she was an assistant Ramsey County attorney representing the state and county in felony jury trials, civil litigation, and administrative hearings. Lewis received a bachelor of arts degree from the University of St. Thomas and her juris doctorate from

Hamline University in St. Paul. During law school, she completed an externship with the Honorable Donovan Frank of the US District Court, District of Minnesota. Lewis also worked as a law clerk to the Honorable Tanya M. Bransford (page 101) of the Minnesota Fourth Judicial District as well as in the juvenile division of the Hennepin County Attorney's Office.

Kevin Lindsey

Kevin Lindsey is an attorney with Lindsey Law and Consulting and serves as the CEO of the Minnesota Humanities Center, a statewide nonprofit located in St. Paul that collaborates with organizations and people to inspire community conversations and illuminate diverse voices across the state. From 2011 to 2018, Lindsey served as the commissioner of the Minnesota Department of Human Rights. He has 25 years of legal experience through his work as an attorney at private law firms, as an executive in business, and in the public sector. He

received his juris doctorate and bachelor of arts from the University of Iowa, where he served as editor in chief of the *Iowa Law Review*. Lindsey was honored by his alma mater with the 2017 Iowa Law Review Distinguished Alumni Award. He was also an AARP Minnesota and Pollen 2018 "50 over 50" honoree and received the 2017 Minnesota Lawyer Diversity and Inclusion Award. Lindsey has held numerous governmental and nonprofit board roles, including board chair and interim executive director of Walker West Music Academy and board member for Growth and Justice, an organization seeking to create inclusive employment and business practices for all in Minnesota.

Jeff Martin

Jeff Martin is deputy director for the Office of Human Rights and Equal Economic Opportunity for the City of St. Paul. A longtime Ramsey County resident and community advocate, Martin graduated from William

Kevin Lindsey

Jeff Martin

Mitchell College of Law. He has also worked in private practice and formerly served as associate city attorney in the office of the St. Paul City Attorney. He was an assistant public defender for the State of Minnesota Board of Public Defense in the Second Judicial District. Martin served as president of the St. Paul Branch of the NAACP from 2011 to 2017.

Marie F. Martin

Marie F. Martin is a bankruptcy attorney at Martin and Hedervare, located in Little Canada. Her guiding philosophy is to use the practice of law to make life better for her clients. Martin received degrees in accounting and banking and finance from North Carolina A&T State University and received her juris doctorate from Mitchell Hamline School of Law in St. Paul.

Michelle A. Miller

Michelle A. Miller

Michelle A. Miller is vice president and chief counsel for employment law at Medtronic, Inc. Her role is designed to proactively identify and address workplace legal, policy, immigration, and employee relations issues, as well as provide appropriate legal guidance and resources for senior management. Miller earned her law degree from the University of Minnesota Law School. She also received a master's degree from Southern Methodist University and a bachelor's degree from Indiana University.

Marie F. Martin

Maria Mitchell

Maria Mitchell has worked as an assistant attorney for Ramsey County and as an assistant in the Hennepin County

Public Defender's Office. A native Minnesotan, she graduated from the University of Minnesota Law School. Mitchell is a member of the Minnesota Association of Black Lawyers, Alpha Kappa Alpha Sorority, Minnesota Women Lawyers, and St. Paul Human Rights and Equal Opportunity Commission, which she serves as chair. She has also provided legal commentary on Minnesota Public Radio and BBC radio.

Maria Mitchell

◼ Adine S. Momoh

Rising Star

Adine S. Momoh is a partner and trial attorney at Stinson Leonard Street. She represents clients in various aspects of litigation before state and federal courts across the country, from case development and strategy, to discovery, to motion practice, to trial, to appeal in matters involving securities and banking litigation, estates and trusts litigation,

and creditors' rights and bankruptcy. In her eight years of practice, Momoh has been recognized both locally and nationally for her community involvement, public service, and professional achievements. Most notably, she was selected by the National Conference of Bankruptcy Judges as a Blackshear Presidential Fellow in 2016, was honored as a finalist for the American Bar Association's National Outstanding Young Attorney Award in 2015, and received the Minnesota State Bar Association's (first) Outstanding New Lawyer of the Year Award in 2014. In 2018, Momoh became the 100th president of the Hennepin County Bar Association, the first Black woman and youngest attorney to lead the organization, which is the largest county bar in Minnesota and one of the largest in the country, with more than 8,000 members. Momoh has a bachelor's degree in business administration–legal studies in business, psychology, and pre-law from the University of St. Thomas and a law degree from William Mitchell College of Law. She previously clerked for the Honorable Jeanne J. Graham of the US District Court for the District of Minnesota.

◼ Roger New

Roger New is the chief of the Eagan police department and a 24-year veteran of the department. The Eagan City Council named New as chief by unanimous vote in May 2018, making him the city's first African American police chief. He holds bachelor's and master's degrees and is a graduate of the prestigious FBI National Academy. Starting in 1994 as an Eagan police officer, New rose to the rank of patrol sergeant in

Roger New

Nnamdi A. Okoronkwo

2004 and just two years later was promoted to lieutenant. He was appointed deputy chief in 2016. He now leads Eagan's 89-person department.

Nnamdi A. Okoronkwo

Nnamdi A. Okoronkwo is an assistant city attorney for Minneapolis, serving as the Fourth Precinct community attorney. He was appointed by the city attorney's office to address crime in Fourth Precinct neighborhoods. Okoronkwo attended the Blake School in Minneapolis before receiving his bachelor's degree from Augsburg University and a juris doctorate from William Mitchell College of Law.

Alan Page

Alan Page is a former justice of the Minnesota Supreme Court and a Hall of Fame professional football player. After

starring for the University of Notre Dame Fighting Irish football team and earning a bachelor's degree in political science, Page was a first-round pick of the Minnesota Vikings in the 1967 NFL draft, and he went on to play 11.5 seasons with the team. As a defensive tackle on the vaunted "Purple People Eaters" defensive line, he helped lead the Vikings to four Super Bowl appearances (all losses) between 1970 and 1977. He spent his final three and a half seasons with the Chicago Bears before retiring in 1981. During his career, Page earned All-Pro honors six times and was voted to nine consecutive Pro Bowls; in 1971 he became the first defensive player ever to be named NFL Most Valuable Player. He was inducted into the Pro Football Hall of Fame in 1988 and the NCAA College Football Hall of Fame in 1993.

While playing for the Vikings, Page attended the University of Minnesota Law School, where he earned his juris

Alan Page

doctorate degree in 1978. After working as an attorney for a Minneapolis
law firm and then in the state attorney general's office, he was elected
to the Minnesota Supreme Court
in 1992, becoming the first African
American to serve on the state's highest court. He was reelected three more
times and served until 2015, when he
reached the mandatory retirement
age of 70.

In 1988, Justice Page and his wife,
Diane Sims Page, started the Page Education Foundation. Seeking to encourage
the educational goals of young people of
color throughout Minnesota, the foundation's programs offer financial support
and positive mentor relationships for
youth. Justice Page is also the author of
three children's picture books: *Alan and
His Perfectly Pointy Impossibly Perpen-
dicular Pinky*, *The Invisible You*, and
Grandpa Alan's Sugar Shack, all written with his daughter, Kamie Page.

■ Artika Tyner

Dr. Artika Tyner is a civil rights attorney, educator, award-winning author,
public speaker, and advocate for justice. In 2019, she was announced as the
director of the newly established Center
on Race, Leadership and Social Justice
at the University of St. Thomas School
of Law. Dr. Tyner previously worked as
the associate vice president for diversity
and inclusion at St. Thomas, and she
holds three degrees from the university:
a doctorate of education in leadership,
a master of public policy and leadership, and a juris doctorate. She earned
a bachelor's degree in English from
Hamline University. Tyner is also the
coauthor of the children's book *Justice
Makes a Difference: The Story of Miss
Freedom Fighter, Esquire*.

Artika Tyner

▪ Ira W. Whitlock

Ira W. Whitlock is the founder and lead attorney of Whitlock Law Office. He has practiced criminal law for more than 20 years, representing clients in both state and federal court, including felonies and misdemeanors. He also handles state and federal criminal appeals, including post-conviction relief, forfeiture, and expungement cases. Whitlock is respected in the legal community as an aggressive criminal lawyer who fights vigorously for his clients.

Whitlock received his bachelor of arts degree from the University of Minnesota in Morris and went on to study law at William Mitchell College of Law in St. Paul, where he obtained a doctor of jurisprudence degree in 1993. Whitlock worked various law clerk jobs, as a research assistant for Professor Eric Janus at William Mitchell, as a certified student attorney at Neighborhood Justice Center, and most notably as a clerk for the Honorable J. Thomas Mott of Ramsey County District Court, all of which gave him the experience necessary to open his own practice.

Ira W. Whitlock

MEDIA AND COMMUNICATIONS

Mediated Realities

On screen.
On print.
On camera.
On television.

Depicting characters.
Telling stories.
Communicating narratives.
We are here.

In film.
In papers.
In magazines.
In devices.

Challenging reality.
Augmenting reality.
Making reality.
Reflecting reality.
Creating mediated realities.
We are here.

A hallmark accomplishment of African American professionals in the media and communication industry is the dualistic nature of making and shaping realities. Mediated reality permeates African American life, and African American life shapes mediated reality. Across the spectrum of channels and platforms, we impact trends, music, and so much more.

African Americans have achieved prominent roles in a range of local media, from newspapers to radio and television to the internet. Two Black newspapers, the *Minnesota Spokesman-Recorder* and *Insight News*, have a long-standing presence in the community and have played key roles in reporting on the lives and histories of Minnesota's African Americans.

◼ Walter "Q Bear" Banks

Walter "Q Bear" Banks has been a radio personality for 89.9 KMOJ for more than 40 years. He started working at KMOJ when it was still a low-power AM station. Q Bear currently serves as the operations coordinator and co–program director at KMOJ, and he hosts the station's *Afternoon Drive* show from 2:00 PM to 6:00 PM, Monday through Friday.

Lissa Jones (see page 121) and Walter "Q Bear" Banks

◼ Roxane Battle

Roxane Battle is a veteran television journalist, award-winning author, and mom. Following a successful television news career, most notably as an anchor and reporter at the Minneapolis NBC affiliate KARE-11 TV for 15 years, Battle now works as a creative consultant and contributing host on Fox 9, KMSP-TV. She is a national speaker, frequently delivering keynotes on the topics of finding joy, navigating life transitions, and work-life balance.

Roxane Battle

Battle was featured on the cover of *Working Mother* magazine and has been profiled in *Ebony* magazine, the Minneapolis *Star Tribune*, and the *St. Paul Pioneer Press*. Her memoir, *Pockets of Joy: Deciding to Be Happy, Choosing to Be Free*, was published in 2017 and became an Amazon best seller in multiple categories. A native of St. Paul, Battle is a graduate of the University of Minnesota–Twin Cities, where she studied journalism and theater arts. She completed her master's degree in journalism at the University of Missouri-Columbia. As a Minnesota State Arts Board grantee, Battle was tapped as an assistant director for a Dowling Studio production at the world-renowned Guthrie Theater in 2018. In her free time, she enjoys cycling around the Minneapolis Chain of Lakes and runs 5K races. She has also completed four consecutive Iron Girl duathlons.

Freddie Bell

Freddie Bell is a broadcast journalist and the general manager at 89.9 KMOJ, the "People's Station." He hosts three radio programs, two of which air in the Twin Cities and the third across the country in syndication. Bell began his professional career as a television broadcast journalist for the ABC News affiliate KETV in Omaha, Nebraska, and has worked in markets such as Tampa, Florida, and Washington, DC. *The Morning Show* with Freddie Bell and Chantel Sings airs every weekday morning on KMOJ.

Daniel Bergin

Daniel Bergin is senior producer and partnership manager at Twin Cities PBS, where he has worked since 1991. His 2019 documentary, *Jim Crow of the North*, explored the history of housing discrimination in the Twin Cities and the legacy of redlining, for which he received an Upper Midwest Emmy Award. Among his other notable previous productions are *North Star: Minnesota's Black Pioneers, Lowertown: The Rise of an Urban Village*, and *Out North: MNLGBTQ History*. He has won several Upper Midwest Emmy awards for writing, editing, and producing. His *Literature & Life: The Givens Collection* was named Best History Documentary at the Prized Pieces International Black Film Festival, and *With Impunity: Men & Gender Violence* was named Best Documentary of 2012 by *Mpls/St. Paul Magazine*. He has produced many short narrative films that have screened nationwide, as well as PSAs and other shorter works.

A Minneapolis native and resident, Bergin received his bachelor of arts degree from the University of Minnesota.

He attended the esteemed PBS Producers Academy and has served as a director on the boards of several community media organizations, including Intermedia Arts, St. Paul Neighborhood Network, Hennepin Theatre Trust, and IFP MN. Bergin has been recognized as a Minnesota State Arts Board Fellow, a *Twin Cities Business Journal* "40 under 40" in 2003, a *City Pages* Artist of the Year in 2004, and a Bush Leadership Fellow for his work in community media.

Adrienne Broaddus

Adrienne Broaddus is the co-anchor of KARE-11 *News* weekdays at 11:00 AM. She joined KARE-11 in 2014 from WISH-TV, a CBS affiliate in Indianapolis, Indiana. A graduate of Michigan State University, Broaddus previously worked at stations in Lansing and Saginaw, Michigan. She is an active member of the National Association of Black Journalists. She received a 2018 Upper Midwest Emmy Award for news anchor and a 2019 Emmy for general assignment reporting.

Adrienne Broaddus

Reg Chapman

Reg Chapman

Reg Chapman has been a reporter for WCCO-TV since 2009. One of the station's most experienced reporters, he previously worked for television networks in New York City, Pittsburgh, Dayton, Omaha, and Sioux City, as well as at KSTP-TV in Minneapolis. A graduate of the University of Nebraska, he has received an Edward R. Murrow Award for investigative reporting and several Associated Press awards. Chapman donates his time to the Urban League, the NAACP, and the YMCA.

Angela Davis

Angela Davis is the host of *MPR News with Angela Davis*, a daily radio program that explores life in Minnesota and how the state is changing. Prior to her radio career, she was an anchor and reporter for WCCO-TV and KSTP-TV. She has won five regional Emmy Awards for anchoring and covering breaking news. Davis holds a journalism degree from the University of Maryland and is a longtime member of the National Association of Black

Journalists. Davis is also an active volunteer with organizations dedicated to helping Minnesota students achieve academic success. She is married to Duchesne Drew (page 68), vice president of the Bush Foundation in St. Paul. The couple has two children.

Angela Davis

Charles M. Dillon

Charles M. Dillon, aka "Chaz Millionaire," is a longtime radio personality, DJ, and host of *Jazz Reflections* on 89.9 KMOJ radio. Born and raised in Minneapolis, Dillon was mentored by such legendary DJs and broadcasters as Kyle Ray, Michael "Professor Funk" Hill, Pharaoh Black, and James "DJ Pres" Demmings. Professor Funk gave Dillon his first break in 1981 on the show *Soul on the South Side* on KFAI radio. He has traveled the world with music legends, including Alexander O'Neal, Cherelle, Patti LaBelle, and Stephanie Mills, among many others. As a White

Charles M. Dillon

Kiya Edwards

House press-credentialed photographer, he covered President Barack Obama and First Lady Michelle Obama. Dillon is a lifelong supporter of the arts, a committed activist, and a mentor to youth in Minneapolis.

◼ Kiya Edwards

Kiya Edwards is a news reporter at KARE-11. A Minneapolis native, she joined the station in June 2018 from KARE's sister station KSDK in St. Louis. She previously reported for KWQC-TV6 News in Davenport, Iowa. After graduating from the University of Minnesota, Edwards moved to Nairobi, Kenya, where she reported for the weekly show *Africa Journal,* covering stories across the African continent.

◼ Ron Edwards

Ron Edwards wrote a weekly column for the *Minnesota Spokesman-Recorder* and was the host of the cable TV show *Black Focus,* the longest-running program on the Minneapolis Telecommunications Network. He was a longtime civil rights advocate and activist, the

Ron Edwards

former head of the Minneapolis Civil Rights Commission and of the Minneapolis Urban League, and author of the book *The Minneapolis Story, Through My Eyes.* Edwards passed away in January 2020 at the age of 81.

■ Maury Glover

Maury Glover describes himself as a "reporter, raconteur, and Renaissance man." Glover is a news and features reporter for Fox 9 News, bringing poignant and personal stories of people from all walks of life. Born, raised, and educated in Minnesota, Glover is the son of Gleason Glover, the former executive director of the Minneapolis Urban League.

Maury Glover

■ Amy Hockert

Amy Hockert is a special projects reporter and anchor for Fox 9 News, KMSP-TV. A Minnesotan through and through, Hockert delivers in-depth, long-form feature stories to viewers and fills in on the anchor desk

Amy Hockert

as needed. She received a 2018 Upper Midwest Emmy for health reporting and a 2017 Emmy for general assignment reporting. Prior to joining Fox 9 in 2015, she worked as a weekend anchor for KARE-11 TV. Hockert and her husband have two children.

■ Ethan Horace

Ethan Horace, also known as "Mr. Music," is a musician, broadcaster, and journalist. In February 2017, he won the journalism award at the Beautiful

Ethan Horace

Humans Awards, a show that recognizes individuals who have helped shape the Twin Cities entertainment industry in fashion, music, journalism, photography, and production. Horace is the host of Power Hour 2.0 on KFAI radio and the producer of Somali Link Radio. He is also a production manager and occasional on-air personality for WFNU. He graduated from the High School for Recording Arts in St. Paul.

Wallace Jackman

Wallace Jackman is the president of Minnesota Black Pages, a premier community resource and business directory, which he founded in the 1990s. He is the former copublisher of the *Minnesota Spokesman-Recorder*. In 1962, Jackman's mother, Launa, married Cecil Newman, founder of the *Spokesman* and *Recorder* newspapers, and Jackman joined the paper a few years later. Born in Des Moines, Iowa, Jackman moved to Minneapolis at age 15.

Lissa Jones

Lissa Jones is executive producer and host of the *Urban Agenda* program on KMOJ radio and host of the *Black Market Reads* podcast, a project of the Givens Foundation for African American Literature highlighting African American writers (see photo page 116).

Samuel King

Samuel King covers political stories for FOX 9 News. A graduate of the Medill School of Journalism at Northwestern University, King worked as a reporter at WSFA-TV in Montgomery, Alabama, his home state. As a child, King dreamed of

Samuel King

being a reporter. His first job was tutoring elementary schoolchildren.

Al McFarlane

Al McFarlane is the president of McFarlane Media Interests and publisher of *Insight News*, a community newspaper serving Minnesota's African American residents and located on Bryant Avenue North in Minneapolis. McFarlane attended Morehouse College and the University of Minnesota School of Journalism, where he graduated with

Al McFarlane

a bachelor's degree in mass communications. After working as a reporter at the *St. Paul Pioneer Press* and then as community relations coordinator at General Mills, McFarlane was hired by Graphic Services as vice president of the Midwest Public Relations division. He became editor in chief at *Insight News* in 1974 and purchased the paper a year later. Since 1997, McFarlane has hosted *Conversations with Al McFarlane*, a series of forums and conversations with community leaders, produced in partnership with KFAI radio.

McFarlane has served as chairman of the Minnesota Multicultural Media Consortium, as president of the Black Publishers Coalition, and as president and CEO at Midwest Black Publishers Coalition Inc. In 1996, he formed the Minnesota Minority Media Coalition, comprising owners of ethnic newspapers in the state. From 2015 to 2017, McFarlane was chair of the National Newspaper Publishers Association Foundation board of directors.

■ La Velle E. Neal III

La Velle E. Neal III is the Major League Baseball beat writer for the Minneapolis *Star Tribune*. He has covered the Minnesota Twins on and off the field for more than 20 years, as well as providing basketball and football coverage during the baseball off-season. A native of Chicago and a graduate of the University of Illinois-Chicago, Neal covered the Kansas City Royals for the *Kansas City Star* from 1995 to 1997. He is a former president of the Baseball Writers Association of America.

La Velle E. Neal III

■ Lea B. Olson

Lea B. Olson is a longtime sports broadcast journalist and the founder of Rethink the Win, a resource for athletes, parents, and coaches aimed at creating a positive experience and environment for youth sports. She has worked as a game analyst for the Minnesota Lynx on Fox Sports Net; as an analyst, broadcaster, and host for prep sports on KSTC 45; and as a sideline reporter and pregame host for the Minnesota Timberwolves. Before her journalism career, Olson played basketball for the University

Lea B. Olson

of Minnesota Gophers. She has been a public advocate for women in the media, served on the Minnesota Twins Community Foundation board and on the Minnesota State High School League board, and been a mentor for African American athletes at the University of Minnesota.

Bisi Onile-Ere

Bisi Onile-Ere joined the Fox 9 News team as a reporter in December 2017 after working for Al Jazeera America as a correspondent and fill-in anchor. She previously reported for stations in Detroit and Flint, Michigan, and in Duluth. A Minneapolis native and graduate of the University of Minnesota–Twin Cities, Onile-Ere won two Emmy Awards and an Associated Press Award during her time in Michigan.

Bisi Onile-Ere

Brandi Powell

Brandi Powell is a weekend anchor/reporter with KSTP-TV in Minneapolis–St. Paul. She joined the news team in January 2014. Powell previously reported at KNSD-TV in San Diego, California, and has worked as a reporter in Austin,

Brandi Powell

Texas, and Bismarck, North Dakota. A graduate of George Washington University, Powell has won several Emmy Awards for team reporting and earned individual Emmy nominations. She lives in Minneapolis with her husband.

Maria Reeve

Maria Reeve is the assistant managing editor for news at the *Star Tribune*, where she has worked since 2011 in a variety of roles, including as features

Maria Reeve

writer, head of east metro coverage, and deputy metro editor. Prior to that, she spent 18 years as a politics editor and reporter for the *St. Paul Pioneer Press* and two years as a reporter for the *Bradenton Herald* in Florida. Reeve did her undergraduate studies at Davidson College and received her master's in journalism from the University of Maryland. She has been a member of the National Association of Black Journalists since 1994, and she served as president of Twin Cities Black Journalists from 2016 to 2019.

Pete Rhodes and Kimberly Bedell Rhodes

Pete Rhodes and Kimberly Bedell Rhodes are the principals of the Urban Mass Media Group. Producers of cultural media and arts programming for urban markets since 1980, this husband-and-wife team has offered diversity in content by spotlighting amazing people and their contributions in the community.

The Rhodeses founded the Minnesota Black Music Awards in 1982 to recognize local and national Black music genres and artists. In 1984 the couple founded CBLS Cable Radio, a 24-hour Black music station, which evolved into the video cable channel Black Music America Networks and the popular website BlackMusicAmerica.com. From 2014 to 2017, the Rhodeses produced the regional Emmy-nominated weekly community affairs show *Urban Perspectives.* In 2016, Pete Rhodes and Kimberly Bedell Rhodes became the first African Americans to be honored as members of the Upper Midwest Emmy Silver Circle, recognizing people with twenty-five years or more in the industry.

Jonathan Rozelle

Jonathan Rozelle

Jonathan Rozelle is a reporter for KSTP 5 Eyewitness News. Prior to joining KSTP in May 2018, he worked for KARK/FOX 16 in Little Rock, Arkansas. Rozelle began his professional journalism career at KSWO-TV in Lawton, Oklahoma, and then worked at KHBS/KHOG in Fayetteville, Arkansas. Rozelle graduated from Cal State University, Los Angeles with a degree in broadcast journalism.

Kimberley Bedell Rhodes and Pete Rhodes

Norman Seawright III

Norman Seawright III is the sports news anchor for WCCO-TV. Seawright did his undergraduate study at the University of Mississippi, majoring in broadcast journalism with a minor in Spanish. Working as a reporter and play-by-play broadcaster for the Ole Miss department of intercollegiate athletics inspired him to pursue a degree at Syracuse University's S. I. Newhouse School of Public Communications in broadcast and digital journalism with an emphasis in sports communication.

Dawn Stevens

Dawn Stevens is an anchor and reporter on the FOX 9 *Morning News* and on FOX 9 *Buzz*, and she reports on big, late-breaking stories of the day. The daughter of an air force major, Stevens grew up in Nebraska and has lived in the Midwest her entire life. She joined Fox 9 in 2006 and became the morning anchor in 2010.

Dawn Stevens

Camille Williams

Camille Williams

Camille Williams was a weekend news anchor for KARE-11 TV from 2015 to 2018, alongside her husband, Cory Hepola. Born in Canada to Jamaican parents, Williams previously worked as a public relations officer at the Harris County District Attorney's Office in Texas and as an anchor/reporter in Texas, New York, and Florida. The award-winning journalist lives in Plymouth with her husband and three children.

Tracey Williams-Dillard

Tracey Williams-Dillard is the CEO and publisher of the *Minnesota Spokesman-Recorder* newspaper and the granddaughter of the paper's founder, Cecil Newman. Williams-Dillard has worked at the paper for more than 40 years.

Established in 1934 to highlight African American issues that would otherwise go unnoted in the mainstream press, the **Minnesota Spokesman-Recorder** began as two separate

Mural on the side of the *Spokesman-Recorder* building

Tracey Williams-Dillard

papers—the *Minneapolis Spokesman* and the *St. Paul Recorder*—until they merged in 2007. The *Minnesota Spokesman-Recorder* is the oldest Black-owned newspaper in Minnesota and one of the oldest family-owned newspapers in the entire country. Its offices are located at 3744 Fourth Avenue South in Minneapolis, and the building was designated a local historic landmark in 2015.

■ Todd Wilson

Todd Wilson is a reporter for Channel 5 Eyewitness News on KTSP-TV. Born and raised in south Minneapolis, he joined KSTP in August 2012 after working at WESH 2 News in Orlando, Florida. Wilson has also worked at stations in South Carolina, Ohio, and Arkansas. He graduated from Roosevelt High School in Minneapolis and is a graduate of Morris Brown College in Atlanta. He and his wife, Melissa, have three children.

Todd Wilson

MEDICINE AND HEALTH CARE

Gifted Presence

A dose of care.
An ounce of prevention.
A diagnostic listening ear.
A gifted surgeon for correction.

A thoughtful office visit.
A troubling follow-up phone chat.
A comforting pill to swallow.
A proactive wellness plan.

In clinics and hospitals.
In pharmacies and assisted living centers.
In management and teaching.
In first- and multigenerational presence.

We are here.

We care for our own.
We alleviate the anxiety of patients.
We prevent further systemic pain.
We educate for behavior change.

Physicians and medical professionals who care for the vitality and health of those in African American communities are a blessing. Through expertise and specialized knowledge, this group of professionals offers insight and prescriptive support for ailments, accidents, and activities that are both routine and novel. Their gifted presence and willingness to serve as a trusted resource provide comfort to the community.

▨ Wanda Adefris, MD

Dr. Wanda Adefris is an obstetrician-gynecologist (OB/GYN) physician and surgeon at Adefris & Toppin Women's Specialists in Woodbury. She received her undergraduate degree from Brown University in 1984, then earned her medical degree from Temple University in 1988. Her internship and residency were completed in 1992 at Emory University. After working in private practice in Atlanta, Dr. Adefris and her family relocated to Minneapolis in 1994. She is board certified and is a fellow of the American College of Obstetricians and Gynecologists.

Kimberly Anderson, OTR/L

Wanda Adefris, MD

▨ Kimberly Anderson, OTR/L

Kimberly Anderson is an occupational therapist and certified hand therapist at Park Nicollet. After completing her graduate studies at the University of Minnesota in 2005, Anderson has practiced as a hand occupational therapist for metro primary care and hand orthopedic and plastic surgery providers in rehabilitation of post-surgery and non-surgery conditions of the hand to shoulder, including arthritis, fractures, and tendonitis. Anderson became interested in her profession through a high school sports medicine class. She enjoys treating the full spectrum of hand and arm conditions and places a personal emphasis on thorough physical examinations, extensive patient education, evidence-backed rehab, and quick return to function (daily life, work, and sports). She makes it a priority to keep current with the latest literature on the science of pain and holistic treatment approaches.

■ Melvin Ashford, MD

Melvin Ashford is a physician in obstetrics and gynecology at the Minnesota Women's Care clinic located in Maplewood. His specialty is in female pelvic medicine and reconstructive surgery (urogynecology). Originally from Detroit, Michigan, he is a graduate of the Boston University School of Medicine. Dr. Ashford has received several awards and has been recognized by *Mpls.St.Paul Magazine* as a "Top Doctor" every year from 2014 to 2019. He is a member of several medical societies. Ashford and his wife, Jackie, are the parents of four children.

Joel L. Boyd, MD

Melvin Ashford, MD

■ Joel L. Boyd, MD

Dr. Joel L. Boyd is an associate professor in the Department of Orthopaedic Surgery at the University of Minnesota. He is a graduate of Temple University School of Medicine and completed his orthopedic surgery residency at the Cleveland Clinic in Ohio and his fellowship at the University of Western Ontario. His clinical interests include sports medicine, specializing in knee surgery including arthroscopy, ACL injuries, multiple ligament injuries, and partial and total joint arthroplasty. Dr. Boyd is the team physician for the Minnesota Wild and for the University of Minnesota football team. He also has been involved with USA Hockey as national head team physician and was the team physician of the NFL's Vikings for nine years and of the WNBA's Lynx for 15 years. His primary practice is at Tria Orthopaedic Center in Bloomington and the University of Minnesota.

LaPrincess C. Brewer, MD, MPH, FACC, FASPC

■ LaPrincess C. Brewer, MD, MPH, FACC, FASPC

Dr. LaPrincess C. Brewer is a cardiologist and assistant professor of medicine within the Mayo Clinic division of preventive cardiology, Department of Cardiovascular Medicine in Rochester. She has clinical expertise in prevention, women's health, cardiac rehabilitation, and telecardiology. Her primary research focus is on developing strategies to reduce and ultimately eliminate cardiovascular disease health disparities in racial and ethnic minority populations and in underserved communities through health promotion and community-based participatory research.

Dr. Brewer completed clinical fellowships in cardiovascular diseases and preventive cardiology at the Mayo Clinic Department of Cardiovascular Medicine. She is an active member of the American Heart Association, American College of Cardiology, National Medical Association, and Association of Black Cardiologists, and she serves on several committees. She was part of the inaugural class of the "40 under 40" Leaders in Health distinction from the National Minority Quality Forum for her heart disease prevention intervention in African American churches in Rochester and Minneapolis–St. Paul. She was named the 2016 Person of the Year in Health Care by the Rochester *Post-Bulletin*. Her research and community engagement initiatives have earned her a number of prestigious awards, including the 2017 Minnesota American College of Physicians Volunteerism Award. Her community health advocacy efforts have been featured on both local and national media outlets such as the Mayo Clinic News Network, ABC, CBS, PBS, CNN, Reuters, and the Huffington Post.

■ Lois Cannon

Lois Cannon is a certified nurse midwife and has worked for HealthPartners since 2002. Cannon moved from California to Minneapolis in 1984. She is a

Lois Cannon

graduate of California State University at Hayward (now Cal State East Bay) and the University of Minnesota, where she earned a master of nursing in midwifery degree in 1996. As a professional midwife, Cannon provides primary maternity care services to help women of all ages and their newborns attain, regain, and maintain health. She also emphasizes health promotion and education, disease prevention, and informed decision-making. Cannon is married to the Honorable Judge James Cannon (page 103) and has two children.

Blanche Chavers, MD

Blanche Chavers, MD

Dr. Blanche Chavers is a professor of pediatrics at the University of Minnesota Masonic Children's Hospital. She attended medical school at the University of Washington, Seattle. She was the first African American female graduate from the University of Washington School of Medicine and the first African American professor of pediatrics at the University of Minnesota. She has earned the University of Minnesota Clinical Research Scholar Award and is a member of the American Society of Pediatric Nephrology and the American Society of Transplantation. Dr. Chavers is originally from Clarksdale, Missouri; she is married to Gubare Mpambara, and they have a son, Kaita Mpambara.

Iris H. Cornelius, PhD

Dr. Iris H. Cornelius is a nationally known psychologist, teacher, and consultant specializing in child and family psychology, integrative practices, coaching, and leadership development. She has devoted her professional practice as a psychologist to mental health in schools, hospitals, and community treatment programs with an emphasis on creating and improving systems that develop belonging and cultural identity within families and work groups. Dr. Cornelius received her undergraduate degree in psychology from Brown University, a master of science degree in psychology from Howard University, and her PhD in clinical psychology from the University of Washington.

In 2004, Dr. Cornelius founded a nonprofit organization, I AM Resources, focused on increasing learning outcomes for students of color. Now serving more than 400 students, I AM Resources brings psychological services and integrative mind-body programming to children, teachers, and parents in three school sites within St. Paul Public Schools.

Charles E. Crutchfield Sr., MD

Charles E. Crutchfield Sr., MD

Dr. Charles E. Crutchfield Sr. is a retired obstetrician-gynecologist. He practiced OB/GYN medicine for several decades and was affiliated with multiple hospitals in the St. Paul area, including Allina, HealthEast, Regions, and United. Born in a small town in rural Alabama, he moved to north Minneapolis as a teenager to live with his aunt and grandmother. After graduating from North High School, he went to the University of Minnesota and, at the age of 19, enrolled in the University of Minnesota Medical School, where he earned his medical degree at the age of 23. Dr. Crutchfield was a captain in the air force for two and a half years during the Vietnam War. Dr. Crutchfield became the first Black OB/GYN to open a private practice in Minnesota. In more

than 50 years of practice, he delivered 9,000 babies and performed 6,000 surgical procedures.

Charles E. Crutchfield III, MD

Dr. Charles E. Crutchfield III is a physician and the founder of Crutchfield Dermatology in Eagan. The son of two physicians, he grew up in St. Paul, and his family were the first African Americans to move into the city's Highland Park neighborhood. Dr. Crutchfield graduated from Minnehaha Academy in Minneapolis, Carleton College in Northfield, and the Mayo Clinic Graduate School and Medical School in Rochester. He completed his transitional internship at the Gundersen Clinic and his dermatology residency at the University of Minnesota. He was the first African American dermatologist to practice privately in Minnesota. Dr. Crutchfield is also a clinical professor of dermatology at the University of Minnesota Medical

Charles E. Crutchfield III, MD

School and Distinguished Benedict Professor of Biology at Carleton College. He writes a weekly health column for the *Minnesota Spokesman-Recorder* newspaper, has coauthored a textbook of dermatology, and has published more than 300 scholarly and informative medical articles. He has received numerous recognition honors from his peers. Dr. Crutchfield is a member of the Alpha Omega Alpha National Honor Medical Society and is the current president of the Minnesota Association of Black Physicians. He is a founding member of Minnesota's Black Community Project, the driving force behind this book.

■ Susan Ellis Crutchfield-Mitsch, MD

Dr. Susan Ellis Crutchfield-Mitsch is a retired family medicine physician. In 1963, she became the first African American woman to graduate from the University of Minnesota Medical School. At age 22, she was also the youngest person to graduate from the University of Minnesota Medical School. Dr. Crutchfield-Mitsch engaged in private practice for many years and was an assistant professor at the University of Minnesota. She was also the senior vice president of Prudential Life Insurance Company in charge of medical affairs. She later became the medical director of Metropolitan Health Plan and chair of the board of Children's Hospitals.

■ Michael "Mike" England, MD

Dr. Michael "Mike" England is a surgeon with Minnesota Surgical Associates in St. Paul. A native of Highland Park, Dr. England obtained his medical degree from Mayo Medical School in Rochester in May 1986. He completed his internship and residency at Mayo Clinic department of surgery in July 1991 and received board certification from the American Board of Surgery a year later. He entered private practice in August 1991 and has been with Minnesota Surgical Associates since 1994. He is the brother of Dr. Stephen England, and the son of Dr. Rodney England, a pioneering African American physician in Minnesota.

■ Stephen England, MD, MPH

Stephen England is a pediatric orthopedic surgeon with Tria Orthopedic Center. He grew up in St. Paul and received a bachelor of arts degree in biology at the University of Minnesota. He attended Cornell University Medical College in New York City for medical school and his surgical residency. Dr. England earned a master of public health degree at Johns Hopkins Bloomberg School of Public Health. He is the brother of Dr. Michael "Mike" England, and the son of Dr. Rodney England, a pioneering African American physician in Minnesota.

■ Sean Ennevor, MD

Dr. Sean Ennevor is an anesthesiology consultant and philanthropist. Originally from Freehold, New Jersey, he graduated from the University of California, Los Angeles School of Medicine. He received a scholar award from the department of surgery at UCLA School of Medicine. Dr. Ennevor has worked for 20 years in clinical medicine, been published in scientific journals and textbooks, and served as a medical editor. Ennevor and his wife, Bridgett, have two children.

Sean Ennevor, MD (see page 133)

Alyse Marie Hamilton, MD

Dr. Alyse Marie Hamilton is the founder and medical director of Advanced Health and Vitality Center in Edina, where she also practices. She specializes in bioidentical hormone replacement therapy, nutritional

Alyse Marie Hamilton, MD

assessment/therapy, advanced Lyme disease, natural infusion therapies for immune system, and nutritional support. Born in Chinle, Arizona (Navajo Reservation), Dr. Hamilton graduated from Macalester College in St. Paul and received her medical degree from the University of Minnesota Medical School. She holds memberships at the American Academy of Anti-Aging and Regenerative Medicine and Minnesota Holistic Medical Group. Hamilton and her husband, Michael, have one child and six grandchildren.

David Hamlar, MD, DDS

David Hamlar, MD, DDS

Dr. David Hamlar is an assistant professor in the Department of Otolaryngology, Head and Neck Surgery at the University of Minnesota. He specializes in craniofacial skull base surgery. He attended Howard University College of Dentistry and the Ohio State University

College of Medicine. Dr. Hamlar came to Minnesota for his fellowship in facial plastic and reconstructive surgery. He is a retired Minnesota National Guardsman, achieving the rank of major general.

Dionne Hart, MD

Dr. Dionne Hart is the medical director of Care from the Hart, which provides patient advocacy and psychiatric consultation services. She is board certified in both addiction medicine and psychiatry and works as an adjunct assistant professor at the Mayo Clinic School of Medicine. In 2013, Dr. Hart received the Minnesota Medical Association's Minority Affairs Meritorious Service Award. In 2014, she was named the Minnesota Psychiatric Society's Psychiatrist of the Year. In 2016, she became the first African American woman to be elected to the Minnesota Medical Association's board of trustees. In 2017, Dr. Hart was one of five psychiatrists in the nation to receive the National Alliance on Mental Illness Exemplary Psychiatrist Award. That same year, she was elected into the American College of Psychiatrists, an honorary medical organization. She also received the Minnesota Medical Association's President's Award. In 2018, she was named a distinguished fellow of the American Psychiatric Association.

Mark Holder, MD

Dionne Hart, MD

Mark Holder, MD

Dr. Mark Holder is a board-certified family medicine doctor in Minneapolis and St. Paul. A graduate of the University of Minnesota in physiology, Morehouse School of Medicine, and the University of Miami Family Medicine Residency Program, he founded Mperial Health after practicing in a variety of clinical environments, from Atlanta, Georgia, to Gbanga and Monrovia, Liberia, to Miami, Florida. Mperial Health is a patient-centered private practice that creates a paradigm shift to deliver high-quality, affordable health services in Minneapolis.

Jerone Kennedy, MD

■ Jerone Kennedy, MD

Dr. Jerone Kennedy is a neurosurgeon in St. Cloud and is affiliated with St. Cloud Hospital. He received his medical degree from Stanford University School of Medicine and received his internship and neurological surgery residency training at the University of Minnesota. Dr. Kennedy has been in practice for more than 20 years and is well respected by doctors across the state and the country.

■ Andrew Kiragu, MD

Dr. Andrew Kiragu has served as medical director of the Pediatric Intensive Care Unit (PICU) at Hennepin Healthcare since 2003. Dr. Kiragu has considerable experience and expertise in neurocritical care and the management of neurotrauma. He is co–medical director of the Pediatric Brain Injury Program, which has served more than 4,000 children with acquired brain injuries since 1989. Dr. Kiragu also provides pediatric critical care at Children's

Minnesota and Gillette Children's Specialty Healthcare as an associate of the children's respiratory and critical care specialists group.

Dr. Kiragu was awarded a grant through the Robert Wood Johnson Foundation to establish an Injury Free Coalition for Kids (IFCK) site in Minneapolis at Hennepin Healthcare, with a goal of studying and promoting injury prevention across the state. He serves on the national board of IFCK and is also a member of the American Academy of Pediatrics council on injury, violence, and poison prevention. Locally, he serves on the advisory board of Safe Kids Minnesota and is past president of the Minnesota chapter of the American Academy of Pediatrics.

Andrew Kiragu, MD

Valerie Lemaine, MD

■ Valerie Lemaine, MD

Dr. Valerie Lemaine is board certified and a diplomate of both the American Board of Plastic Surgery and the Royal College of Physicians and Surgeons of Canada. She studied at the University of Montreal Medical School, and her credentials also include reconstructive microsurgery and clinical research fellowships at Memorial Sloan Kettering Cancer Center in New York as well as a master of public health from Columbia University.

An accomplished plastic surgeon, Dr. Lemaine began her career in 2010 at the prestigious Mayo Clinic in Rochester, Minnesota, where she expanded the breast reconstruction program. Dr. Lemaine joined Plastic Surgery Consultants in 2018. Her special interests are cosmetic surgery of the face, breasts, and body; reconstructive surgery for breast cancer, skin cancer, and gynecologic cancer; and gender affirmation surgery.

Dr. Lemaine has been named "Top Doctor" and "Best Doctor for Women" by *Minnesota Monthly* every year since 2014. She is a nationally and internationally invited lecturer in plastic surgery and breast reconstruction topics and has authored numerous plastic surgery peer-reviewed publications and book chapters. Dr. Lemaine is the cocreator of the YouTube channel 2breastsurgeons, which covers a variety of topics such as breast health, plastic surgery, and women's health.

Barbara Leone, MD

■ Barbara Leone, MD

Dr. Barbara Leone practices at HealthEast Walk-in Care Clinic in Maplewood and Woodbury, with a specialty in urgent care. She grew up in Minneapolis and St. Paul and graduated from Harvard Medical School. Dr. Leone is a member of the American Academy of Family Physicians. She taught at the University of Minnesota family medicine residency program from 2000 to 2013. Leone and her husband, Pastor Steven Brown, have four children and eight grandchildren.

Chip Martin, MD

■ Chip Martin, MD

Dr. Chip Martin is a pediatric cardiologist at the University of Minnesota. He attended the University of Michigan Medical School and completed his residency and fellowship at the University of Minnesota.

■ Zeke J. McKinney, MD, MHI, MPH

Dr. Zeke J. McKinney is a board-certified occupational and environmental medicine physician who works as the primary OEM provider at the HealthPartners Riverway Clinic in Anoka. He is additionally board certified in public health and general preventive medicine, as well as in clinical informatics, which is the practice of optimizing information in the delivery of health care. He grew up in north Minneapolis, then finished high school at Phillips Academy Andover in Massachusetts. Dr. McKinney received a

bachelor of science degree in computer science from the University of Illinois at Urbana-Champaign College of Engineering. He attended medical school at the University of Minnesota, where he completed a dual-degree MD/master of health informatics program. McKinney began his graduate medical education in a general surgery internship at Hennepin County Medical Center in Minneapolis, followed by OEM training at the HealthPartners/University of Minnesota OEM residency in St. Paul.

Zeke J. McKinney, MD, MHI, MPH

■ Tamiko Morgan, MD, MPH, FAAP

Dr. Tamiko Morgan is corporate medical director at WellCare Health Plans. She grew up in the Chicago area and attended medical school at the University of Illinois before completing her pediatric residency at the University of Minnesota. Her specialty areas are pediatrics, health policy, public health, and managed care. She holds memberships at the Minnesota National Medical

Tamiko Morgan, MD, MPH, FAAP

Association and the American Academy of Pediatrics. Dr. Morgan is also the founder of the wellness company 2 E.D.I.F.Y., dedicated to social justice and equity in health care. Morgan and her spouse have one daughter.

David Olson, MD

Dr. David Olson is faculty in the Program in Sports Medicine at the University of Minnesota Medical School and is associate director of the university's Sports Medicine Fellowship. He also directs the sports medicine curriculum at the university's North Memorial Family Medicine Residency and co-directs the Twin Cities Sports Medicine Conference. Dr. Olson is a primary care sports medicine physician at Twin Cities Orthopedics specializing in a wide range of sports medicine concerns, including diagnosis and management of concussions and acute and chronic musculoskeletal issues. He enjoys providing team care for high school, college, and professional sports teams, including the Minnesota Vikings, the University of Minnesota Gophers, Minneapolis Community and Technical College, and Roseville Area High School.

Rahshana Price-Isuk, MD

Dr. Rahshana Price-Isuk practices family medicine and is medical director at Neighborhood HealthSource. She earned her medical degree at the University of Maryland, Baltimore, and did her residency at the University of Minnesota Broadway Family Medicine Clinic and North Memorial Health Hospital. She specializes in outpatient family medicine and enjoys providing comprehensive care from birth through end of life, particularly working with adolescents to address their social and mental health needs.

Inell Rosario, MD

Dr. Inell Rosario is board certified in otolaryngology, head and neck surgery, and sleep medicine, and she is the president of Andros ENT & Sleep Center. She was born and raised on Andros, an island in the Bahamas. She

Inell Rosario, MD

graduated from Macalester College in 1987 with a bachelor of arts degree and attended medical school at the University of Minnesota. She completed her internship and residency at the Medical College of Wisconsin. She is a former president of the Minnesota Association of Black Physicians. When she isn't working at the clinic, Dr. Rosario likes to exercise, play basketball, and do mission work. She is married and has two children. Her husband, Luis, is the director of the Ramsey County Assessor department.

Nneka Sederstrom, PhD, MPH

■ Nneka Sederstrom, PhD, MPH

Dr. Nneka Sederstrom is the director of the clinical ethics team at Children's Minnesota. Originally from Florence, Alabama, she received her bachelor's degree in philosophy from George Washington University in 2001. She volunteered in the Center for Ethics at Medstar Washington Hospital Center while continuing her academic career,

receiving her master's in philosophy in 2003 and PhD in medical sociology in 2008, both from Howard University. Dr. Sederstrom served as director of the Center for Ethics and director of the Spiritual Care Department at Medstar Washington until joining Children's Hospital of Minnesota in March 2016. Her academic credentials include a master of public health degree in global health management. Sederstrom is married to Charlie Sederstrom and they have one son.

■ Barbara Toppin, MD

Dr. Barbara Toppin is an obstetrician-gynecologist physician and surgeon at Adefris & Toppin Women's Specialists in Woodbury and a board-certified OB/GYN with many years of experience in women's health care. She graduated from Wellesley College and received her medical degree from the University of Cincinnati in 1982. She completed her residency at Harlem Hospital, serving

Barbara Toppin, MD

as executive chief resident in her fourth year. Dr. Toppin's professional experience includes serving as clinical instructor at Columbia University College of Medicine, as medical director of the Ossining Open Door clinic in upstate New York, and in private practice in White Plains, New York.

■ Traci E. Troup, MD

Dr. Traci E. Troup practices urgent care medicine at Allina Urgent Care. She grew up in Minneapolis and Shoreview and is a graduate of the University at Buffalo School of Medicine. Dr. Troup is a member of the American Academy of Family Physicians and the American Board of Family Medicine. She and her husband, Riley Washington, have two daughters.

Traci E. Troup, MD

RELIGION

Give and Bear Fruit

In pulpits and quiet places of prayer,
We are reminded to count our blessings.
Through the words of preachers and pastors,
We are comforted by God's sacrificial love for us.

In personal study and private meditation,
We are lifted and renewed in spirit.
Through worship and song,
We praise the One who grants us life.

In circle of family and friends,
We are joined to produce Godly seed.
Through acts of kindness and care,
We are privileged to support others in giving.

We remember and are blessed.
We comfort and are comforted.
We renew and are restored.
We praise and remain faithful.
We give and bear fruit.

We are here.

The power of religion and faith has sustained African American communities for generations. In these spirit-filled places, preachers, pastors, ministers, elders, and others all contribute to the development of a more moral people bound with love and support for one another. Spiritual leadership guides communities with eternal consequence rather than short-term outcomes. From this leadership perspective, individuals who give of themselves in this way have immeasurable, lasting value.

SALUTING LONG-STANDING AFRICAN AMERICAN CHURCHES IN MINNESOTA

This section salutes African American churches in Minnesota that have stood the test of time and played a major role in supporting the African American community in a variety of ways. We also recognize 21st-century African American ministers and ministries in the Twin Cities.

AFRICAN AMERICAN CHURCHES IN MINNEAPOLIS

■ Bethesda Baptist Church

Founded 1887
1118 South Eighth Street
Minneapolis, MN 55404
Reverend Dr. Arthur Agnew
Bethesda Baptist Church was founded in 1887 by an escaped former slave. The original church fell to fire in 1961, and members rebuilt it. Bethesda Baptist is one of the oldest African American churches in Minneapolis.

■ El Bethel Baptist Church

Founded 1976
3949 Fourth Avenue South
Minneapolis, MN 55409
Reverend Willis L. Gilliard

■ Emmanuel Tabernacle Church of God in Christ

Founded 1956
2501 East 22nd Street
Minneapolis, MN 55104
Reverend Mark Frazier

El Bethel Baptist
Church

Greater Friendship Missionary Baptist Church

Fellowship Missionary Baptist Church

Founded 1992
3355 North Fourth Street
Minneapolis, MN 55412
Reverend Albert Gallmon Jr.

Grace Temple Deliverance Center

Founded 1957
1908 Fourth Avenue South
Minneapolis, MN 55404
Reverend Willa Grant Battle

Greater Friendship Missionary Baptist Church

Founded 1960
3805 Third Avenue South
Minneapolis, MN 55409
Reverend Billy G. Russell

Macedonia Baptist Church

Founded 1980
3801 First Avenue South
Minneapolis, MN 55404
Reverend Dr. Herbert Thomas

New Creation Baptist Church

Founded 2001
1414 East 48th Street
Minneapolis, MN 55417
Pastor Dr. Daniel B. McKizzie Sr.

Park Avenue United Methodist Church

Founded 1893
3400 Park Avenue South
Minneapolis, MN 55407
Reverend Dr. Will Healy

Park Avenue United
Methodist Church

■ St. James African Methodist Episcopal Church

Founded 1863
3600 Snelling Avenue
Minneapolis, MN 55406
Reverend Marchell Hallman

■ St. Peter's African American Episcopal Church

Founded 1880
401 East 41st Street
Minneapolis, MN 55409
Reverend Carla Mitchell

■ Shiloh Temple International Ministries

Founded 1931
1201 West Broadway Avenue
Minneapolis, MN 55411
Bishop Richard D. Howell Jr.

■ Wayman African Methodist Episcopal Church

Founded 1919
1221 Seventh Avenue North
Minneapolis, MN 55411
Reverend Richard H. Coleman

■ Zion Baptist Church

Founded 1910
621 Elwood Avenue North
Minneapolis, MN 55411
Reverend Brian Herron

St. Peter's African American Episcopal Church

AFRICAN AMERICAN CHURCHES IN ST. PAUL

◼ Camphor United Memorial Methodist Church

Founded 1921
585 Fuller Avenue
St. Paul, MN 55103
Reverend Gloria Roach Thomas

◼ Mount Olivet Baptist Church

Founded 1922
451 Central Avenue West
St. Paul, MN 55103
Reverend James C. Thomas

Camphor
United
Memorial
Methodist
Church

Mount Olivet
Baptist
Church

■ New Hope Baptist Church

Founded 1952
711 Burr Street
St. Paul, MN 55130
Reverend Runney D. Patterson Sr.

■ Pilgrim Baptist Church

Founded 1863
732 Central Avenue West
St. Paul, MN 55104
Reverend Dr. Charles Gill
Pilgrim Baptist is the oldest
Black church in St. Paul.

New Hope
Baptist
Church

Pilgrim Baptist Church

Progressive Baptist Church

Founded 1992
1505 Burns Avenue
St. Paul, MN 55106
Reverend Dr. Melvin G. Miller

St. James African Methodist Episcopal Church

Founded 1876
624 Central Avenue West
St. Paul, MN 55104
Reverend Stacy Smith

Progressive Baptist Church

St. James
African
Methodist
Episcopal
Church

■ St. Peter Claver Church

Founded 1888
369 Oxford Street North
St. Paul, MN 55104
Father Erich Rutten
St. Peter Claver was the first
Black Catholic church in Minnesota.

■ Shiloh Missionary Baptist Church

Founded 1967
501 Lawson Avenue West
St. Paul, MN 55117
Reverend Steve Daniels Jr.

St. Peter
Claver
Church

Shiloh
Missionary
Baptist
Church

Arthur Agnew

The Reverend Dr. Arthur Agnew has led Bethesda Baptist Church in downtown Minneapolis since 1992. He and his wife, Bobbie Jean Agnew, came to Bethesda from Chicago, where he was head of the associate ministers training program at Fellowship Baptist Church. During his 25 years at Bethesda, Agnew established "Discussions That Encounter," a forum on bridging the racial gaps in the area.

Charles Gill

Arthur Agnew and Bobbie Jean Agnew

Charles Gill

The Reverend Dr. Charles Gill is the pastor at Pilgrim Baptist Church in St. Paul. In 2016, he was inducted into the Martin Luther King Board of Preachers at Morehouse College. His greatest joy is to serve his risen savior as an ambassador, speaking boldly, making known the mystery of the gospel (Ephesians 6:19, 20). Originally from Brooklyn, New York, Reverend Gill is married to Adrian Gill.

Brian Herron

Reverend Brian Herron is the pastor at Zion Baptist Church in Minneapolis. Formerly he was a politician and Minneapolis city councilmember. Reverend Herron attended Clark Atlanta University, an HBCU.

Brian Herron

Eleanor M. Hunsberger

The Reverend Eleanor M. Hunsberger is a retired ELCA minister who served several Lutheran congregations. She was the first African American, male or female, ordained and "called" into ministry in the state of Minnesota. She is a former resident of the Sumner Olsen Housing Projects and a graduate of North High School. Hunsberger worked at the telephone company for 17 years, and after that she worked for more than 10 years in the field of chemical dependency. Along with Jimmy Evans and Peter Bell, she cofounded the Minnesota Institute on Black Chemical

Eleanor M. Hunsberger

Abuse (MIBCA). Several years later, Hunsberger continued her education and received undergraduate degrees from Metro State University (1980) and a master of divinity from Luther Northwestern Seminary in St. Paul (1985). Reverend Hunsberger has spent many years speaking at national youth gatherings and working in the field with seminary students during their third year of preparing for the ministry.

Timothy P. Jackson and Jessica Lynn Jackson

Timothy P. Jackson, affectionately known as "Pastor Tim," and Jessica Lynn Jackson are the pastors at IMPACT LIVING Christian Center (ILCC), located in the Seward neighborhood of south Minneapolis. God united Tim with his soul mate, Jessica, in marriage on August 15, 2003, and launched them into ministry two years later, in July 2005. Jessica is an accomplished employment attorney, ordained minister, mediator, executive leadership coach,

Jessica Lynn Jackson and
Timothy P. Jackson

organizational development consultant,
dynamic speaker, and skilled facilitator.
Pastors Tim and Jess are known as a
"dynamic duo" by their IMPACT family
and throughout the Twin Cities community. As the founders and visionary
leaders of ILCC and their nonprofit We
IMPACT!, the Jacksons joyfully serve
together as co-laborers with Christ.

Daniel B. McKizzie Sr.

Daniel B. McKizzie Sr. is the founder
and senior pastor at New Creation
Baptist Church in south Minneapolis,
established in 2001. A native of Minneapolis, he graduated from Washburn
High School, attended the University of
Minnesota College of Liberal Arts, and
earned his master of divinity at Luther
Seminary. Pastor McKizzie received
an honorary doctor of divinity degree
from St. Thomas Christian College in
May 2009.

Daniel B. McKizzie Sr.

Billy G. Russell

Billy G. Russell is senior pastor of
Greater Friendship Missionary Baptist
Church in Minneapolis. He has served
as a pastor since 1982, and he is the
president of the Minnesota Baptist
State Convention. He also worked as
a school administrator for more than
20 years. Reverend Russell has served
on the Sabathani Community Center

Billy G. Russell

board, the Urban League board, and the Here's Life Inner City advisory board and for Isaiah Transportation and Financial Equity Networks. He received a bachelor of science degree in physical education with a minor in earth science from the University of Southern Mississippi in Hattiesburg; a master's degree in education administration from William Carey College, also in Hattiesburg; and a master's degree in Christian counseling at Faith Seminary in Tacoma, Washington. He is working on a doctorate degree in strategic leadership from Faith Seminary.

■ Thomas Van Leer

Reverend Thomas Van Leer is the chaplain for the Minnesota Timberwolves and a student advisor at Summit Academy, a vocational school in north Minneapolis. He is the author of three books, most recently *The Conversation: Who's Talkin?*

Thomas Van Leer

SPORTS

Making Change and Millions

We dunk on the court.
We kneel on the field.
We catch on the grass.
We sprint on the track.

We slide into home.
We serve over nets.
We balance on beams.
We protest and play.

We are here.

Winning games and championships,
Negotiating contracts and causes,
Entertaining youth and adults,
Modeling athleticism and mission,

Supporting teammates and towns,
Impacting lives and communities,
Competing for interests and titles,
Making change and millions.

The athleticism and accomplishments of Black athletes have inspired and amazed people for generations. Their strength and power in performance elicits smiles, cheers, nods, and "stank" faces. These men and women show their skills on the basketball court, the baseball diamond, the football field, and the running track and in a range of other athletic pursuits. Their advocacy for national and international causes prompts debate and signals the breadth of their reach beyond sport. They are graceful, determined competitors who entertain us. Simultaneously, they are purposeful, trained specialists who have broad impact on their communities, and they work in the front offices and on the sidelines as leaders and entrepreneurs behind the scenes. Sports is an integral facet of American life, and Black athletes impress spectators and command attention.

Seimone Augustus

Seimone Augustus

Seimone Augustus is a guard for the Minnesota Lynx of the WNBA. She was selected by the Lynx as the first overall pick in the 2006 WNBA draft and was named the league's rookie of the year at the end of that season. As of 2019, she has played in seven WNBA All-Star Games, helped the Lynx to four league championships, and won three Olympic gold medals with Team USA. As a collegiate star for Louisiana State University, Augustus won numerous NCAA awards, and in 2010 she became the first female athlete to have her jersey number retired by LSU.

Joey Browner

Joey Browner played 10 seasons in the NFL (1983–92), nine of those with the Minnesota Vikings. The six-time Pro Bowl defensive back is a member of the Vikings' "Ring of Honor." Since his retirement, Browner has remained active in the community through youth coaching and mentoring activities and through the Joey Browner Foundation, a charitable organization based in Eagan.

Byron Buxton

Byron Buxton is the center fielder for the Minnesota Twins. He began his minor league career in the Twins organization at the age of 18 in 2012 and made his major league debut in 2015. He combines speed, power, and great fielding on the diamond.

Byron Buxton

Rodney "Rod" Carew

Rodney "Rod" Carew played 19 seasons in Major League Baseball, his first 12 with the Minnesota Twins, as a second baseman and first baseman. He was selected to the all-star team in all but the final season of his career, was named the American League rookie of the year in 1967, and was the league's Most Valuable Player in 1977. A seven-time batting champ, Carew was inducted

Noah Croom and kids

Rodney "Rod" Carew

into the National Baseball Hall of Fame
in 1991, his first year of eligibility.
Following his playing career, he has
spent many years working as a coach
and advisor for the Twins organization,
as well as for other teams. Carew has
been an advocate for a variety of
health-related causes, especially heart-
health awareness with the American
Heart Association, following a heart
attack he suffered in 2015.

Gregory Coleman

Gregory Coleman is the KFAN sideline
reporter for the Minnesota Vikings. In
his 12-year NFL career, he played for the
Cleveland Browns, the Minnesota Vikings, and the Washington Redskins, one
of the first African American punters in
the league. His Greg Coleman Celebrity
Golf Tournament benefits underserved
students in the Twin Cities area in con-
junction with the YWCA. He and his
wife, Eleanor, have two adult children.

Noah Croom

Noah Croom is the assistant general
manager of the Minnesota Timberwolves of the NBA. A graduate of the
University of Virginia Law School, he
previously served as an associate counsel for the NBA and as assistant general manager and legal counsel for the
Vancouver Grizzlies basketball team.
Croom has also worked for a private law
firm, and from 2002 to 2016 he was vice
president, general counsel of Goodwin
Sports Management.

Stefon Diggs

Stefon Diggs is a wide receiver for the
Minnesota Vikings of the NFL. He was
born in Gaithersburg, Maryland, and
played college football for the University

Stefon Diggs

of Maryland. Diggs tied for the team lead with nine touchdowns during the 2018 season.

■ Larry Fitzgerald Jr.

Larry Fitzgerald Jr. is a wide receiver for the Arizona Cardinals of the NFL. He has been selected to the Pro Bowl in 11 of his first 15 seasons and ranks first among active players in career touchdowns. Fitzgerald was born in Minneapolis and attended Academy of Holy Angels in Richfield. Off the playing field, the Larry Fitzgerald First Down Fund supports youth programs across the country, and in Minneapolis it purchased computers for five schools and refurbished the basketball court at Martin Luther King Jr. Park, among other philanthropic efforts. The fund also supports research toward preventing, treating, and curing breast cancer.

Sylvia Fowles

■ Sylvia Fowles

Sylvia Fowles is the center for the WNBA's Minnesota Lynx. A star collegiate player at Louisiana State University, she was selected with the second overall pick by the Chicago Sky in the 2008 WNBA draft. Fowles joined the Lynx in 2015 and helped lead the team to a WNBA championship that season, during which she was named finals MVP. Fowles earned the regular-season league MVP award in 2017, which ended with another Lynx title and another finals MVP award for Fowles. She is a three-time WNBA Defensive Player of the Year, and in 2018 she set a single-season record for most rebounds. Fowles has also won three Olympic gold medals with Team USA.

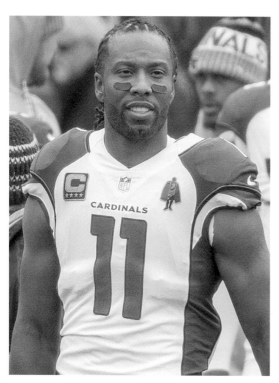

Larry Fitzgerald Jr.

Jordan Greenway

Jordan Greenway is a forward for the Minnesota Wild in the National Hockey League, joining the team in 2018. He played high school hockey for Shattuck–St. Mary's in Faribault. Greenway represented the United States at the 2017 International Ice Hockey Federation World Championship and the 2018 Winter Olympics, the first African American named to a US Olympic hockey roster.

Eric Hudson

Eric Hudson is the senior director of ticket sales and service for the Minnesota Twins. He has been with the team since 2000. Hudson has a degree in economics from the University of Minnesota.

Eric Hudson and kids

Tre Jones

Tre Jones is a point guard for the Duke University Blue Devils. He led Apple Valley High School to class 4A state

Tre Jones

titles in 2015 and 2017 and was named a McDonald's All-American and Minnesota Mr. Basketball after his senior season in 2018. He is the younger brother of NBA player Tyus Jones.

Tyus Jones

Tyus Jones is a point guard for the Minnesota Timberwolves of the NBA. The Burnsville native was a star player at Apple Valley High School and led the team to the class 4A state championship during his junior year. He first became a varsity starter when he was in eighth grade and went on to earn numerous accolades during his high school career, including being named a McDonald's All-American and Minnesota

Tyus Jones

Maya Moore

Mr. Basketball in 2014. Jones began receiving college scholarship offers when he was in ninth grade, and he ultimately chose Duke University, where he won an NCAA national championship in his lone collegiate season. After being selected by the Cleveland Cavaliers in the first round of the NBA draft, he was traded to his hometown Timberwolves on draft night.

■ Maya Moore

Maya Moore is a forward with the Minnesota Lynx of the WNBA. A two-time college player of the year, Moore led the University of Connecticut to back-to-back NCAA championships in 2009 and 2010 while not losing a single game in either season. She was chosen by the Lynx with the number one overall pick in the 2011 WNBA draft and went on to be named league rookie of the year. She won the league MVP award in 2014 and has been an all-star five times. With Moore as one of the team leaders, the Lynx claimed four WNBA titles from 2011 to 2017. She has also won two Olympic gold medals and two FIFA World Championships with Team USA.

■ Sianneh Mulbah

Sianneh Mulbah is chief people officer for the Minnesota Timberwolves and Minnesota Lynx, overseeing talent acquisition, diversity and inclusion, organizational development, benefits administration, employee engagement, and training and development. She received her bachelor's degree in psychology from Bemidji State University and her master of business administration and master of arts in organizational management/human resources from Concordia University in St. Paul. Mulbah serves on the boards of Girls on the Run Twin Cities and the Twin Cities chapter of Women in Sports and Events (WISE) and is a past member of the Minneapolis Downtown Council.

■ Tony Oliva

Tony Oliva played 15 seasons in Major League Baseball, all with the Minnesota Twins, as a right fielder and designated hitter; he later coached the Twins. After moving to the United States from Cuba in 1961, he became one of the game's best hitters and an all-star during his first eight seasons. Oliva was the 1964 American League Rookie of the Year, an AL batting champion during three seasons, an AL hit leader five seasons, and a Gold Glove winner. He is regarded as one of the best players not yet inducted into the Baseball Hall of Fame.

■ Dan Strong

Dan Strong is a senior executive in ticket sales for the Minnesota Twins. He graduated from the University of Wisconsin-Stout with a bachelor's degree in business administration and also was an all-American in track and field. Prior to joining the Twins' staff, he worked for the Minnesota Timberwolves.

Dan Strong

Karl-Anthony Towns Jr.

■ Karl-Anthony Towns Jr.

Karl-Anthony Towns Jr. is a forward for the NBA's Minnesota Timberwolves. He played college basketball for the Kentucky Wildcats and was drafted by the Timberwolves with the number one overall pick in the 2015 NBA draft. He won the rookie of the year award following the 2015–16 season and played in the 2018 and 2019 NBA All-Star Games.

Trent Tucker

Kevin Warren

Kevin Warren was named commissioner of the Big Ten Conference in 2019. Prior to that, he spent 15 years in the Minnesota Vikings organization, including the last four as its chief operating officer, the first African American COO in NFL history. Before joining the Vikings, he held front-office positions with other NFL teams and worked as a sports and entertainment lawyer. Warren earned his juris doctorate from the University of Notre Dame Law School, a master of business administration from Arizona State University, and a bachelor's degree from Grand Canyon University. He has been active in philanthropy and community issues around the Twin Cities, donating money and time toward improving education and health care in the region.

Trent Tucker

Trent Tucker is a former professional basketball player and a television and radio commentator. He played for the University of Minnesota Golden Gophers before launching his 11-year NBA career. Known as a three-point specialist, Tucker played mostly for the New York Knicks, and he won an NBA title with the Chicago Bulls in his final season of 1993. After his playing career, he became a broadcast analyst for the Minnesota Timberwolves and currently does commentary for KFAN radio. He is also involved in coaching and youth mentoring and active in many charitable and philanthropic organizations. Tucker spent five years as the director of athletics for Minneapolis Public Schools.

Frank White

Frank White is the founder and CEO of Respect Sports and a coordinator of the RBI (Reviving Baseball in the Inner Cities) program sponsored by the Minnesota Twins. He is a graduate of Mechanic Arts High School in St. Paul and

Frank White

attended the University of Minnesota. He has been involved in countless community athletic programs and charity organizations and is a participating associate/consultant of the Minnesota Historical Society. White is the author of *They Played for the Love of the Game: Black Baseball in Minnesota* and an expert on Minnesota sports history.

Bob "Jumping Jack" Williams

■ Bob "Jumping Jack" Williams

Bob "Jumping Jack" Williams spent two seasons with the Minneapolis Lakers of the National Basketball Association. When he joined the team in 1955, he was the franchise's first Black player and one of just seven Black players in the NBA. He spent his off-seasons traveling the world with the Harlem Globetrotters alongside such legends as Meadowlark Lemon. Williams is a member of the Black Legends of Professional Basketball, an organization dedicated to honoring and celebrating the achievements and contributions of the Black pioneers of professional basketball from 1900 to 1960. Williams resides with his wife, Marietta, in Rosemount. They have five children, 20 grandchildren, 24 great-grandchildren, and three great-great-grandchildren.

■ Dave Winfield

Dave Winfield is a former professional baseball player and member of the National Baseball Hall of Fame. A native of St. Paul, Dave and his brother, Steve, developed their skills playing ball at the Oxford playground for coach Bill Peterson. Dave Winfield played baseball for and graduated from St. Paul's Central High School before heading to the University of Minnesota on a baseball scholarship. He played both baseball and basketball for the Golden Gophers. Winfield was drafted by teams in four different professional sports leagues: Major League Baseball, the National Basketball Association, the American Basketball Association, and the National Football League—even though he never played collegiate football. Over his 23-year professional baseball career, Winfield spent time with six different teams, including two seasons with the Minnesota Twins. A 12-time all-star, he was elected to the hall of fame in his first year of eligibility; he is also a member of the NCAA College Baseball Hall of Fame.

Since retiring, he has worked as a television analyst, as an executive with

Dave Winfield

the San Diego Padres baseball team, and for the Major League Baseball Players Association. Always giving back to the community, he started the David M. Winfield Foundation for Underprivileged Youth in 1977. The foundation has wide-reaching educational, health care, and social welfare programs that benefit underprivileged youth and families. Although he lives in California most of the year, Winfield remains a pillar of the Twin Cities community.

■ Steve Winfield

Steve Winfield is a baseball coach, sports booster, and valued mentor to countless youth athletes in the Twin Cities. He has also worked as a local journalist covering baseball in Minnesota. He played minor league and semipro baseball. The older brother

Steve Winfield

of baseball hall of famer Dave Winfield, Steve has championed and been closely involved with the Winfield Foundation, which has benefited unprivileged youth in St. Paul since 1977.

ABOUT MINNESOTA'S BLACK COMMUNITY PROJECT

In 2015, eight professional African Americans from two prominent Minnesota families, the Scott family and the Crutchfield family, came together and filed an application to start a 501(c)(3) nonprofit organization called Minnesota's Black Community Project. MBCP was awarded active nonprofit status in June 2016.

The central aims of MBCP are 1) to highlight and celebrate the historical and contemporary contributions of African Americans in Minnesota through publications and community programs throughout the Twin Cities, and 2) to fill a void in the research by highlighting the modern-day achievements of African Americans in Minnesota across a range of occupations.

The founding board members of MBCP are Anthony R. Scott Sr., president; Dr. Charles E. Crutchfield III, vice president; Dr. Chaunda L. Scott, secretary; and Anthony R. Scott II, treasurer. Members at large are Dr. Charles Crutchfield Sr., George J. Scott, Christopher Crutchfield, Walter R. Scott Jr., and Olivia Crutchfield.

PROJECT STAFF

Chaunda L. Scott

COEDITOR, PROJECT MANAGER, RESEARCH ADVISOR, AND BIOGRAPHY WRITER

Dr. Chaunda L. Scott is an associate professor of organizational leadership and the diversity and inclusion specialist for the office of the dean at Oakland University in Rochester, Michigan. She also serves as the secretary for Minnesota's Black Community Project in Minneapolis. Dr. Scott has coauthored six books on workforce diversity along with numerous scholarly articles and chapters on diversity education and workforce diversity. She has also received several teaching and research awards in these areas and has presented her research in locations across the globe. (See page 85 for full bio.)

Anthony R. Scott

COEDITOR AND PROJECT ADMINISTRATOR

Anthony R. Scott Sr. spent 20 years as a supervisor with the Hennepin County Child Protection Unit. He also worked as a vocational expert on a contract basis with the Social Security Office of Hearings and Appeals for five years. Scott established and owned Scott Rehabilitation, a registered qualified rehabilitation firm that provided return-to-work services to injured workers under the Minnesota workers' compensation laws. Scott is the president of Minnesota's Black Community Project. He also is a talented and well-known bass guitarist in the Twin Cities. (See page 50 for full bio.)

Chaunda L. Scott

Anthony R. Scott

Charles E. Crutchfield III, MD

Kelly McGuire

Charles E. Crutchfield III

COEDITOR AND BIOGRAPHY WRITER

Dr. Charles E. Crutchfield III is a physician and the founder of Crutchfield Dermatology in Eagan. He was the first African American dermatologist to practice privately in Minnesota. Dr. Crutchfield is also a clinical professor of dermatology at the University of Minnesota Medical School and Distinguished Benedict Professor of Biology at Carleton College. He writes a weekly health column for the *Minnesota Spokesman-Recorder* newspaper, has coauthored a textbook of dermatology, and has published more than 300 scholarly and informative medical articles. He is a founding member of Minnesota's Black Community Project, the driving force behind this book. (See page 132 for full bio.)

Kelly McGuire

PROJECT SPECIALIST

Kelly McGuire is the executive assistant to Dr. Charles E. Crutchfield III at Crutchfield Dermatology and the Crutchfield Dermatology Foundation. She has worked with Dr. Crutchfield for over a decade. McGuire became the first certified dermatology tech in the country. She is passionate about helping and caring for people, making her employment at Crutchfield Dermatology a perfect fit. Outside of work she enjoys spending time with her family and friends and being outdoors. She is a big sports fan, and she especially loves baseball.

Allison Cortez

EXECUTIVE ADMINISTRATIVE ASSISTANT

Allison Cortez served as the executive administrative assistant for Minnesota's Black Community Project. She was born in Queens, New York, and moved to

Minnesota in 2001. She currently works full-time as the associate executive assistant to Dr. Charles E. Crutchfield III at Crutchfield Dermatology. Cortez has played various essential administrative roles in the health care industry for the past 10 years. She is also a proud mother of two.

Bruce Palaggi

Allison Cortez

Bruce Palaggi

LEAD PHOTOGRAPHER

Bruce Palaggi is the lead photographer for Minnesota's Black Community Project and a professional freelance photographer in St. Paul. Palaggi's photography has been shown at gallery exhibits, and several of his images are part of professional stock photo collections. For more than two decades, Palaggi has built an extensive catalog of travel photographs, photographed weddings, and participated in art festivals throughout the Twin Cities.

Olivia S. Crutchfield

PHOTOGRAPHER

Olivia S. Crutchfield is a photographer from Mendota Heights and a student at the Stern School of Business at New York University. She started photography as a teenager in 2014 and has worked as a photojournalist for the *Minnesota Spokesman-Recorder* newspaper. She is a member of the photo team of Minnesota's Black Community Project. (See page 10 for full bio.)

Olivia S. Crutchfield

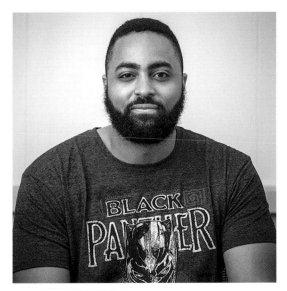

Bryson Glanton Scott

George J. Scott

Bryson Glanton Scott

PHOTOGRAPHER

Bryson Glanton Scott is employed by Hennepin County as a correctional officer. He has also been involved in film and photography projects for several community organizations, including the Sabathani Community Center and Hennepin County Library. He is a freelance photographer in Minneapolis and a guitarist. (See page 19 for full bio.)

George J. Scott

BIOGRAPHY WRITER

George J. Scott is a board member at large for Minnesota's Black Community Project and a biography writer for this book. He is also a renowned smooth jazz and R&B guitarist and bassist who has been a part of the Twin Cities music scene for more than 25 years. He is a songwriter and lyric editor who produces soundtracks for recording artists throughout the United States, as well as his own original works.

Nel Yomtov

BIOGRAPHY WRITER

Nel Yomtov is an award-winning writer of children's books and graphic novels from New York City. He specializes in writing about American history, country studies, science, and biography.

Nel Yomtov

Jeanetta D. Sims

CONTRIBUTING LITERARY WRITER

Dr. Jeanetta D. Sims is the dean of the Jackson College of Graduate Studies and a professor of marketing in the College of Business at the University of Central Oklahoma in Edmond. She is the first woman and first African American woman to hold this deanship in the institution's more than 125-year history. In 2007, she founded Diverse Student Scholars as a robust interdisciplinary program of student research engagement at UCO. Dr. Sims is also accredited in public relations. An avid writer, researcher, and reader, she has authored more than 50 books, chapters, reviews, refereed journal articles, and proceedings publications and received Top Paper Awards from marketing, management, and communication associations. She contributed the "We Are Here" series of original poems, and accompanying descriptive text, to this publication.

Jeanetta D. Sims

PHOTO CREDITS

Olivia S. Crutchfield: 41 (Laurie Ann Saddler Crutchfield), 55 (Shirlee Callender), 61 (Teqen Zéa-Aida and Nathan Yungerberg), 64 (Cavis Adams), 65 (Patricia Anderson), 69 (Suluki Fardan), 77 (Clayton Ellis), 78 (David Ellis), 85 (Anthony R. Scott II), 102 (Tanya M. Bransford), 104 (James Cannon, Carleton B. Crutchfield), 105 (Christopher Ellis Crutchfield), 128 (Wanda Adefris), 129 (Melvin Ashford, Joel L. Boyd), 130 (Lois Cannon), 131 (Blanche Chavers), 132 (Charles E. Crutchfield Sr.), 134 (Sean Ennevor, Alyse Marie Hamilton), 135 (Dionne Hart), 136 (Jerone Kennedy), 137 (Barbara Leone), 138 (Chip Martin, Zeke J. McKinney), 139 (Tamiko Morgan), 140 (Nneka Sederstrom, Barbara Toppin), 141 (Traci E. Troup)

Minnesota Spokesman-Recorder: 8 (Trevor Bowen), 12 (Beverly Tipton Hammond), 21 (Tre Aaron), 25 (Mike De'cole), 29 (Dahlia Jones), 30 (Annie Mack), 31 (Muja Messiah), 33 (Destiny Roberts), 37 (Jason Tanksley), 55 (Jacqueline Amissha Addison), 58 (Samantha Rei), 78 (Artiera Evans, Donna Gingery), 80 (Nerita Griffin Hughes), 82 (Eric Mahmoud), 87 (Carlos Sneed, Jason Sole), 113 (Artika Tyner), 120 (Ethan Horace), 126 (Tracey Williams-Dillard)

Bruce Palaggi: 6 (Ta-coumba Aiken), 15 (Ray "Fancy Ray" McCloney), 19 (Bryson Glanton Scott), 20 (Nothando Zulu), 23 (Walter Chancellor Jr.), 24 (Bobby Commodore, Ginger Commodore), 26 (Debbie Duncan), 27 (George Scott Trio, Soli Hughes), 28 (Cynthia Johnson), 31 (Maxx Band's Soul Experience), 32 (Sherri Orr), 33 (Sabathanites Drum and Bugle Corps), 40 (Ronald and Donald Bellfield, Mama Sheila Brathwaite, Frederick Brathwaite), 42 (Martin Daniels, Brett Davis), 43 (Tommie Daye, Richard Doten, Reese M. Dyer), 44 (April Estes with Tracy Wesley, Estes Funeral Chapel), 46 (Peter McCullar), 47 (Andre McNeal), 48 (Brian Palaggi), 50 (Anthony R. Scott), 53 (John Trotman, Maurice Tyner, Mychael and Stephanie Wright), 54 (Golden Thyme Coffee and Café), 56 (Fresh Cuts Barber Shop, Cameron Cook), 57 (Andrea Pryor), 60 (Eddie Withers Jr., Eddie's Barber Shop), 66 (Minneapolis Urban League), 67 (Sabathani Community Center, Melvin Whitfield Carter Jr.), 68 (Tiffany Casey), 69 (Rowena D. Holmes), 72 (Jonathan Palmer, Hallie Q. Brown Community Center), 73 (Phyllis Wheatley mural, Thomas Redd), 74 (Mary Whitney, Winfred "Fred" Woods), 79 (William D. Green, Donna Kay Harris), 81 (Robert J. Jones), 83 (Lilene Elizabeth "Liz" Moore), 84 (Beverly Propes, Alana Ramadan), 86 (Walter Scott Jr.), 88 (Floyd Williams), 92 (Melvin Carter III), 101 (James Bransford), 110 (Marie F. Martin), 116 (Lissa Jones and Walter "Q Bear" Banks), 119 (Charles M. Dillon, Ron Edwards), 126 (Spokesman-Recorder mural), 144 (El Bethel Baptist Church), 145 (Greater Friendship Missionary Baptist Church), 146 (Park Avenue United Methodist Church, St. Peter's African American Episcopal Church), 147 (Camphor United Memorial Methodist Church, Mount Olivet Baptist Church), 148 (New Hope Baptist Church, Pilgrim Baptist Church), 149 (Progressive Baptist Church, St. James African Methodist Episcopal Church), 150 (St. Peter Claver Church, Shiloh Missionary Baptist Church), 152 (Eleanor M. Hunsberger), 153 (Jessica Lynn Jackson and Timothy P. Jackson), 166 (Anthony R. Scott Sr.), 168 (Allison Cortez), 169 (Bryson Glanton Scott)

Paul Battaglia: 96 (Andrea Jenkins)
Andrea Canter: 32 (Mankwe Ndosi), 34 (Davu Seru)
Charles E. Crutchfield III, MD: 46 (Wendell Maddox), 59 (Nathaniel Talton)
FOX 9: 121 (Samuel King), 123 (Bisi Onile-Ere), 125 (Dawn Stevens)
High School for Recording Arts, St. Paul: 29 (Lakame)
Gary Hines: 35 (Sounds of Blackness)
Insight News: 121 (Al McFarlane)
KARE 11: 117 (Adrienne Broaddus), 119 (Kiya Edwards), 125 (Camille Williams)
KMSP: 120 (Amy Hockert)
KSTP-TV: 123 (Brandi Powell), 124 (Jonathan Rozelle), 126 (Todd Wilson)
Macalester College: 14 (Marlon James)
Mayo Clinic: 130 (LaPrincess C. Brewer)
Minneapolis Star Tribune: 122 (La Velle E. Neal III)
Minnesota House of Representatives: 98 (Neva Walker)
Minnesota Humanities Center: 109 (Kevin Lindsey)
Minnesota National Guard, photo by Master Sgt. Blair Heusdens: 97 (Angela Steward-Randle)
Minnesota Public Radio: 118 (Angela Davis)
Minnesota Twins: 157 (Rodney "Rod" Carew)
Margie O'Loughlin: *The Monitor*
Brian Palaggi: 168 (Bruce Palaggi)
Rhymesayers: 21 (Stefon "P.O.S." Alexander)
Bryson Glanton Scott: 52 (Robert Thomas), 86 and 166 (Chaunda L. Scott)
George Scott: 34 (Soul Tight Committee)
Kathleen Tauer: 17 (T. Mychael Rambo)
Walker Art Center, photo by Bobby Rogers: 22 (Astralblak)
WCCO-CBS Minnesota: 118 (Reg Chapman)
University of Minnesota: 76 (Rose M. Brewer), 83 (Samuel Myers Jr.), 89 (Terrion Williamson, Josef Woldense)
US House Office of Photography: 94 (Keith Ellison)

Creative Commons
Keith Allison (CC-BY-SA-2.0): 157 (Stefon Diggs), 158 (Larry Fitzgerald Jr.)
David on Flickr (CC-BY-2.0): 156 (Byron Buxton)
Frenchieinportland (CC-By-SA-4.0): 160 (Tyus Jones)
Keenan Hairston (CC-BY-SA-2.0): 159 (Tre Jones)
Dan Kelly (CC-BY-2.0): 93 (Bobby Joe Champion)
Susan Lesch (CC-BY-4.0): 158 (Sylvia Fowles), 160 (Maya Moore), 161 (Karl-Anthony Towns Jr.)
Arturo Pardavila III (CC-BY-2.0): 163 (Dave Winfield)
Lorie Shaull (CC-BY-SA-2.0): 97 (Erin Maye Quade)
Lorie Shaull (CC-BY-SA-4.0): 156 (Seimone Augustus)
Gage Skidmore (CC-BY-SA-3.0): 13 (Ernie Hudson)
Slipperypulse (CC-BY-SA-3.0): 23 (Chastity Brown)
Tony Webster (CC-BY-SA-2.0): 94 (Phillipe Cunningham), 95 (Jeff Hayden)
Tony Webster (CC-BY-SA-3.0): 50 (Don Samuels)

If not listed above, photos were provided by the featured individuals.

INDEX

The text of *Minnesota's Black Community in the 21st Century* has been set in Anko, a typeface designed by Eko Bimantara. The name heads have been set in Acumin Pro, a typeface designed by Robert Slimbach.

Book design by Wendy Holdman.

Civil Procedure

RICHARD L. MARCUS

Distinguished Professor of Law and
Horace O. Coil Chair in Litigation
University of California, Hastings College of the Law

THOMAS D. ROWE, JR.

Elvin R. Latty Professor Emeritus of Law
Duke University School of Law

Eighteenth Edition

Gilbert Law Summaries is a trademark registered in the U.S. Patent and Trademark Office

Printed in the United States of America

ISBN: 978-1-68328-101-6

Summary of Contents

Capsule Summary

I. PERSONAL JURISDICTION AND RELATED MATTERS

A. INTRODUCTION

1. Types of Personal Jurisdiction

Personal jurisdiction is a state's power to hear a case and enforce its judgment.

a. In Personam Jurisdiction

In personam jurisdiction permits a court to enter a judgment that is ***personally binding*** on defendant. Courts in other states must give ***full faith and credit*** to a valid judgment.

b. In Rem Jurisdiction

In rem jurisdiction permits a court to adjudicate the rights of ***all possible claimants in a specific piece of property***.

c. Quasi in Rem Jurisdiction

There are two types of quasi in rem jurisdiction. The first type permits a court to determine rights of ***particular parties*** in property under its control. The second type permits a court having jurisdiction over defendant's property, but not over defendant personally, to use the property to satisfy plaintiff's personal claim against defendant. Use of this latter type as a basis for jurisdiction over nonresident defendants has been severely limited.

2. *Pennoyer v. Neff* and the Traditional Power Theory

Under *Pennoyer v. Neff*, a state's jurisdiction was generally limited to persons served with process or property seized in the state.

3. Shift to Minimum Contacts

With *International Shoe*, the Court shifted from an emphasis on in-state service to a requirement of ***minimum contacts*** with the forum state "such that the maintenance of the suit does not offend traditional notions of fair play and substantial justice."

B. CONTEMPORARY CONSTITUTIONAL GROUNDS FOR STATE-COURT JURISDICTION

1. Contacts with Forum

International Shoe generated a two-stage approach to personal-jurisdiction problems, looking first to whether the defendant ***purposely availed*** himself of the privilege of conducting activities in the forum and then at the ***reasonableness*** of permitting jurisdiction.

a. Purposeful Availment—Minimum Contacts

Purposeful-availment inquiry focuses solely on ***activities of defendant***, looking for some voluntary action by defendant establishing a ***beneficial relationship*** with the forum state.

(1) Foreseeability

Mere foreseeability of contact with the forum is important but insufficient; defendant's conduct with respect to the forum state must be such that he should reasonably *anticipate being haled into court there* (*e.g.*, long-term relationship with forum or seeking to serve forum market).

(2) Relationship Between Contacts with Forum and Claim Asserted

The Court assumes "specific" jurisdiction is proper with regard to claims that are related to forum contacts that satisfy the purposeful-availment requirement, but jurisdiction may also be proper when the claim arises from contacts that do not satisfy the purposeful-availment requirement, but is of the same type as claims that do. This result might be rationalized by focusing on foreseeability of facing claims of this type in this state.

(3) Commercial vs. Noncommercial

Purposeful availment is more easily found with regard to defendant's commercial activity.

(4) Choice of Law Distinguished

That a particular state's law may apply under choice-of-law "center of gravity" principles does not alone satisfy the purposeful-availment requirement as to that state.

(5) Reasonableness Insufficient to Satisfy Purposeful-Availment Requirement

Factors such as a lack of inconvenience to defendant cannot outweigh the requirement of purposeful availment.

b. Fair Play and Substantial Justice—Reasonableness

In the reasonableness inquiry, consideration of *plaintiff's interests* is proper. But reasonableness by itself, while necessary, is not sufficient; the defendant must have constitutionally adequate minimum contacts with the forum.

(1) Factors

Factors considered when determining the reasonableness of jurisdiction are: (i) defendant's burden in defending the suit in the forum, (ii) the forum state's interest in adjudication, (iii) plaintiff's interest in obtaining convenient and effective relief, (iv) the judicial system's interest in resolving the suit effectively, and (v) states' shared interest in furtherance of fundamental substantive social policies.

c. Application to Internet Activities

Although still an evolving area, the same minimum-contacts analysis applies to Internet activities, but the *purposeful-availment requirement* is emphasized and *the reasonableness requirements are probably relaxed*.

2. Presence of Defendant's Property in Forum

Presence of defendant's property in the forum will often establish a constitutionally sufficient contact between defendant and the forum, ordinarily because it establishes relevant contact as to the property between defendant and forum.

a. **Location of Property**

Tangible property is located in a state if it is physically present there. Intangible property may be considered located in a jurisdiction if some transaction related to the property occurred there, but if embodied in an instrument, it is usually said to be located where the instrument is. This issue is usually governed by *state law*.

b. **Presence of Property Supports Jurisdiction**

The presence of property in a state may support jurisdiction as to issues pertaining to that property by providing contacts among the forum, defendant, and litigation.

(1) **True in Rem**

States continue to have power to exercise true in rem jurisdiction, as in condemnation proceedings.

(2) **Claim Related to Rights and Duties Arising from Ownership**

Property provides sufficient contact if the claim is related to rights or duties related to the property (*e.g.*, absentee owner might be sued for injuries sustained on property located in the forum).

(3) **Absence of Another Forum**

The Court has not ruled on the scope of jurisdiction by necessity, which may exist when defendant's property is located in the forum and no other forum is available to plaintiff.

c. **Presence of Unrelated Property Insufficient for Jurisdiction**

When property is completely *unrelated* to plaintiff's claim, its presence alone will not support jurisdiction.

3. **General Jurisdiction**

Courts distinguish between *general personal jurisdiction*, which subjects defendant to suit in the forum on any claim, and *specific personal jurisdiction*, which confers jurisdiction only for claims related to defendant's contact with the forum.

a. **Natural Persons**

General jurisdiction is available in the state of a natural person's *domicile*.

b. **Corporations**

A corporation is subject to general jurisdiction in (i) its *state of incorporation*, (ii) if different, its *principal place of business*, and (iii) in very limited extensions, *additional states in which it is essentially "at home."*

4. **Consent**

Defendant may consent to jurisdiction in a forum.

a. **Express Consent**

Defendant may expressly consent to jurisdiction, either before or after suit is filed.

b. **Implied Consent**

By filing suit in a forum, plaintiff consents to jurisdiction as to any related counterclaim by defendant.

c. Appearance

Depending on prevailing rules, jurisdiction may be supported by a party's voluntary appearance in court to contest issues other than jurisdiction.

5. Service Within Jurisdiction

Traditionally, service within the jurisdiction was ***presumptively sufficient*** to support jurisdiction.

a. Possible Minimum-Contacts Requirement

After *Shaffer v. Heitner*, many thought that transient jurisdiction (jurisdiction obtained solely on the basis of service on a defendant present in the forum) was invalid absent minimum contacts, but the Supreme Court has since upheld transient jurisdiction. *Note*: The Court has left open the question whether service would be sufficient if defendant were not present voluntarily.

b. Fraudulent Inducement

If defendant is served with process after being fraudulently induced to enter the state, the court will ***not*** exercise jurisdiction.

6. Territorial Jurisdiction of Federal Courts

In most cases, the territorial jurisdiction of a federal court is no broader than that of the state where it is located.

a. Constitutional Limitations on Nationwide Service

Subject to possible due-process limitations, Congress could constitutionally give federal courts nationwide personal jurisdiction.

b. National Contacts

The Court has not decided whether an alien defendant's contacts with this country may be aggregated to support jurisdiction.

C. STATUTORY AUTHORIZATION FOR JURISDICTION

1. Long-Arm Statutes

It is not enough that an exercise of jurisdiction is constitutionally authorized; there must also be a statute or rule authorizing jurisdiction. After *International Shoe*, state legislatures began to enact long-arm statutes extending the reach of their courts' jurisdiction. Some long-arm statutes authorize jurisdiction whenever it would not violate the Constitution, but most such statutes list specific acts that warrant the exercise of jurisdiction.

2. Federal-Court Jurisdiction

In general, federal courts exercise jurisdiction no broader than that authorized by the long-arm statute of the state where the federal court is located.

D. LITIGATING JURISDICTION

1. Default

If a party believes the court lacks personal jurisdiction, she may default and later argue that the judgment should not be given full faith and credit because the court did not have jurisdiction.

2. Appearance to Litigate Jurisdiction

In federal court and in most states, defendant may raise lack of personal jurisdiction along with other defenses in her answer or pre-answer motion. A few states require a special appearance.

3. Binding Effect

Once defendant has appeared and litigated jurisdiction, she cannot relitigate the issue in another court, but she can appeal it after a final decision is rendered or, in some states (*e.g.*, California), immediately after her challenge to personal jurisdiction is rejected in the trial court.

E. VENUE

1. Introduction

Venue is a statutory limitation on the *geographic location* of litigation to prevent a plaintiff from suing where it would be burdensome for the defendant to appear and defend.

2. Federal Venue Limitations

a. Defendant's Residence

In federal courts, venue lies where *any defendant resides* if all defendants reside in the same state. A *corporation's* residence is any district in which it is subject to personal jurisdiction. Venue for *unincorporated associations and partnerships* is proper where they are doing business.

b. Location of Substantial Part of Events or Omissions or of Property

Venue is also proper where a substantial part of the events or omissions giving rise to the claim occurred or where a substantial part of the property subject to the litigation is located.

c. Fallback Venue

If no other district is available, venue is proper where any defendant is subject to personal jurisdiction.

d. Special Venue Statutes

Congress has enacted venue options or requirements for certain types of cases, *e.g.*, statutory interpleader.

e. Removed Cases

Venue for a case removed from state court to federal court is in the district encompassing that state court.

3. Litigating Venue

Improper venue may be *waived* unless the issue is properly raised (*e.g.*, by timely motion).

4. Federal Transfer Provisions

A federal case may be transferred to another federal court in the following cases.

a. Venue or jurisdiction improper in original court

If venue or jurisdiction is improper, the court may transfer the case to a proper federal court or may dismiss.

b. Transfer for convenience

A court generally will respect plaintiff's choice of forum, but may, for the convenience of the parties and witnesses, in the interest of justice, transfer a case to another district where it might have been brought, or to any district to which all parties have consented.

F. FORUM NON CONVENIENS

Even if jurisdiction and venue are proper, a court may decline to exercise jurisdiction if the venue selected by the plaintiff is *grossly inconvenient*.

1. Adequate Alternative Forum Available

The court *cannot dismiss* if there is no adequate alternative forum available to the plaintiff.

G. NOTICE

1. Constitutional Requirements

Due process requires that *reasonable efforts to provide notice* be made with regard to persons whose interests are to be determined. Notice must inform the defendant of the *nature and place* of the proceeding.

a. Method

Service of notice is usually by personal delivery, first class mail, or publication (when the person cannot be located). If service by these methods is impossible, the court may authorize service via e-mail.

2. Service of Process

The usual method of giving notice is serving a summons and complaint on defendant, directing that he file an answer or suffer a default.

a. Methods of Service

Depending on the rules of the jurisdiction, service of process may be made by personal delivery, by mail (including waiver of service), or by leaving it at defendant's home or office.

b. Immunity from Service

In some jurisdictions, rules immunize from service those persons who are present in the state only to participate in a legal proceeding.

3. Timing of Notice—Prejudgment Seizures

At common law, defendant's property could be seized, even before defendant had notice of the action, to provide security for any judgment plaintiff might obtain.

a. State-Law Requirements

States have placed various limits on prejudgment seizures.

b. Procedural Due Process Requirements for Prejudgment Seizure

Supreme Court decisions on prejudgment seizures *without* notice or advance hearing when the claimant's interest in the property *does not antedate the suit* seem to require proof of *exigent circumstances* and a factual setting in which *claims can reliably be evaluated* on documentary proof.

II. SUBJECT-MATTER JURISDICTION OF THE FEDERAL COURTS

A. INTRODUCTION

1. Nature of Subject-Matter Jurisdiction

Subject-matter jurisdiction involves a court's *authority* to rule on a particular type of case.

2. Personal Jurisdiction Distinguished

Subject-matter jurisdiction limits a court's power based on *case type*, while personal jurisdiction limits a court's power over persons based on *geographic location.*

3. Defects Not Waivable

Lack of subject-matter jurisdiction is not waivable. *Grounds* for subject-matter jurisdiction must be alleged in a federal-court complaint.

a. Defendant May Raise Objection at Any Time

Lack of subject-matter jurisdiction may be raised at any time, even after final judgment.

b. Court to Raise Sua Sponte

If the parties do not raise lack of subject-matter jurisdiction, the court may raise it on its own motion.

c. Resolution Before Merits of Suit

Whether the court has subject-matter jurisdiction must be resolved *before* consideration of the merits of the case. However, personal-jurisdiction challenges may be resolved before challenges to subject-matter jurisdiction.

(1) Forum Non Conveniens Dismissal Permitted Before Resolving Jurisdiction

A district court can dismiss on grounds of forum non conveniens without first resolving any jurisdictional challenges if the defendant can justify dismissal.

4. State Courts

Except for matters within the exclusive jurisdiction of the federal courts, state courts are usually considered courts of general jurisdiction, *i.e.*, some state court is available for every type of claim.

a. Concurrent Jurisdiction of Federal Claims

State courts generally have jurisdiction concurrent with federal courts to hear federal claims, except for some types of cases falling within the exclusive jurisdiction of federal courts, *e.g.*, patent claims.

5. Federal Courts' Jurisdiction

Jurisdiction of federal courts is limited by the *constitutional grant* set forth in Article III and by the statute vesting the federal courts with jurisdiction.

B. DIVERSITY JURISDICTION

1. Constitutional Authorization

Article III., Section 2 authorizes diversity jurisdiction to provide a forum for persons who might be victims of *local prejudice.* The Constitution requires only *minimal diversity* (*i.e.*, that diversity exist between one plaintiff and one defendant).

2. **Diversity Statute**

The statute contains two prerequisites to diversity jurisdiction: diversity of citizenship and a minimum amount in controversy.

a. **Complete Diversity Requirement**

The diversity statute requires complete diversity (*i.e.*, that *no defendant have the same citizenship as any plaintiff*).

(1) **Statutory Exceptions to Complete Diversity**

Diversity jurisdiction is permissible even in the absence of complete diversity in (i) statutory interpleader actions, (ii) certain class actions governed by the Class Action Fairness Act, and (iii) cases governed by the Multiparty, Multiforum Trial Jurisdiction Act.

(2) **Alienage Diversity Jurisdiction**

Federal courts have subject-matter jurisdiction over cases involving a United States citizen and a citizen of a foreign country and cases involving completely diverse United States citizens and a citizen of a foreign country.

b. **How Citizenship Determined**

For *natural persons*, including *permanent resident aliens*, citizenship is generally the same as *domicile.* A *corporation* is a citizen of every state in which it is incorporated and of the state of its *principal place of business.* A corporation organized under the laws of another country is a citizen of that country for alienage diversity jurisdiction, but is also a citizen of an American state if its principal place of business is in the United States. Unincorporated associations are citizens of *each state in which any member is a citizen.*

(1) **Class Actions**

In class actions not within the Class Action Fairness Act, only the citizenship of the *named representatives* is considered.

(a) **Class Action Fairness Act Cases**

The Act gives district courts original jurisdiction over certain class actions when there is minimal diversity between any class member and any named defendant.

(2) **Executors, Guardians, and Trustees**

Legal representatives of decedents or incompetents are deemed citizens of the *same state as the person represented.*

(3) **Fictitious Defendants**

A 1988 federal statute permitted cases with fictitious defendants (John/Jane Doe cases) to be removed to federal court, but the diversity statute was not similarly amended. There is a split among federal courts as to whether such cases can be brought under diversity jurisdiction.

c. **Time for Determination**

Diversity need exist only at the *commencement of the action.*

(1) Partial Exception—Removal

For removed cases, diversity must exist **both** at the time of filing the suit **and** at the time the removal notice is filed.

d. Realigning Parties

In considering diversity, the court looks to the **real interests** of the parties and may realign them accordingly as plaintiffs or defendants; *e.g.*, in shareholder derivative cases, the corporation may likely be realigned as a defendant.

e. Efforts to Create Diversity

Diversity cannot be created by collusively or improperly joining a party or by **assigning a claim** without sufficient consideration.

f. Efforts to Defeat Diversity

Plaintiffs are allowed some latitude in taking steps to defeat diversity (*e.g.*, adding bona fide claims against nondiverse defendants).

g. Dismissing Party to Preserve Diversity

A plaintiff may sometimes preserve diversity by dismissing a nondiverse defendant, but may not proceed in federal court without a required party, *infra*.

h. Jurisdictional Amount

More than $75,000 must be in controversy in a diversity case, computed as of the date of **commencement** of the suit.

(1) Legal Certainty Test

The amount claimed by plaintiff is determinative unless defendant shows to a legal certainty that the minimum cannot be met. That judgment is ultimately entered for a lesser amount does not affect diversity jurisdiction. **Interest and costs are excluded** in computing the minimum amount.

(2) Aggregation of Claims to Satisfy Requirement

Separate claims can be aggregated to satisfy the requirement in the following situations:

(i) **All claims of a single plaintiff against a single defendant**, even if the claims are unrelated;

(ii) The **claims of a single plaintiff against several defendants only if all defendants are jointly liable**;

(iii) Claims of **several plaintiffs against one defendant only** if plaintiffs have a **common undivided ownership interest** in the claims; and

(iv) The claims of class members in **cases governed by the Class Action Fairness Act**, provided the amount in controversy for the entire class **exceeds $5 million**.

(a) Counterclaims

Counterclaims generally cannot be aggregated with plaintiff's claim. (Note that compulsory counterclaims, *infra*, need not meet the amount-in-controversy requirement providing plaintiff's claim does.)

i. Exceptions to Diversity Jurisdiction

Courts decline to exercise diversity jurisdiction over cases involving domestic relations and probate actions.

j. Class Action Fairness Act of 2005

The Act grants a federal court original jurisdiction over a class action based on state law if:

(i) There is *minimal diversity* between the class members and the named defendants;

(ii) The aggregate claims of all class members exceed *$5 million*; and

(iii) There are at least *100 members* in the class.

(1) Excluded Actions

The federal court will not have jurisdiction when a *state, state official, or other governmental entity is the primary defendant* or in claims solely based on *federal securities laws* or that relate to the *internal affairs of a corporation.*

(2) Decline of Jurisdiction

A district court *must* decline jurisdiction under the Act if: (i) more than two-thirds of the plaintiff class members are citizens of the state in which the action was filed, (ii) a defendant from whom significant relief is sought is a citizen of that state, and (iii) the principal injuries were incurred in that state. It *may* decline jurisdiction if the primary defendants and more than one-third but less than two-thirds of the plaintiff class are citizens of the state in which the action was filed.

C. FEDERAL-QUESTION JURISDICTION

1. Constitutional Grant

Article III, Section 2 extends the federal judicial power to cases *arising under* the Constitution, the laws of the U.S., and treaties; cases affecting ambassadors, consuls, etc.; admiralty cases; and cases to which the U.S. is a party. This power is viewed broadly.

2. Federal-Question Statute

a. Statute Interpreted More Narrowly than Constitution

The language of the federal-question statute is very similar to that in Article III, but has been interpreted more narrowly.

(1) State-Court Jurisdiction over Cases Raising Federal Questions

State courts have *concurrent* jurisdiction over most federal-question issues.

b. Standards for Determining Whether Federal Question Is Raised

A federal question may be raised when federal law has created the claim sued upon (inclusive of implied rights of action) or when an "embedded" federal-law element in a state-law claim is necessarily raised, actually disputed, substantial in the sense of being important to the federal system as a whole, and capable of resolution in federal court without disrupting the federal-state balance approved by Congress.

c. Well-Pleaded Complaint Rule

The federal question must appear in the properly pleaded allegations in the complaint. If federal law did not create the claim sued upon, the federal issue must be a *required element of the state-law claim.*

(1) Anticipation of Defense Insufficient

A federal question is not sufficiently raised by plaintiff's allegation that defendant will rely on a defense based on federal law.

(2) Federal Counterclaim Insufficient

A counterclaim based on federal law does not bring a case within federal-question jurisdiction.

(3) Removed Cases

The well-pleaded complaint rule applies to cases sought to be removed from state to federal court by a defendant. However, a plaintiff usually can elect not to assert an available federal claim in order to avoid federal-question jurisdiction and, thus, prevent removal.

(a) Federal Counterclaim Insufficient

A case cannot be made removable to federal court by bringing a federal-law counterclaim in state court.

(4) Declaratory-Judgment Cases

In declaratory-judgment cases, rather than examining the actual complaint, a court determines whether jurisdiction exists by considering if a hypothetical, well-pleaded complaint for a coercive remedy, *e.g.,* injunction or damages, would have presented a federal question.

(5) Supreme Court Jurisdiction Compared

The well-pleaded complaint rule does not apply to cases appealed from state courts to the United States Supreme Court.

d. Plausible Assertion of Federal Right Sufficient

If the plaintiff purports to assert a claim created by federal law, the court has jurisdiction unless the claim is frivolous or made solely to bring about jurisdiction. If the court dismisses a case for failure to state a federal claim, the decision is on the merits.

e. Jurisdictional Amount

In most federal-question cases, there is ***no required minimum*** amount in controversy.

D. SUPPLEMENTAL JURISDICTION

1. Introduction

When jurisdiction is proper, federal courts have jurisdiction over ***all issues in the case***, not just claims that provide the basis for original jurisdiction.

2. Background—Pendent and Ancillary Jurisdiction

The supplemental jurisdiction statute arises from the decisional concepts of ancillary jurisdiction and pendent jurisdiction.

a. Ancillary Jurisdiction

The doctrine of ancillary jurisdiction gave federal courts the power to hear claims brought by parties other than the plaintiff related to the plaintiff's claim, such as counterclaims, crossclaims, interpleader claims, and claims by intervenors.

b. Pendent Jurisdiction

The doctrine of pendent jurisdiction gave federal courts the power to hear nonfederal claims against a nondiverse defendant as long as the claims arose from the same event as the federal claim.

c. Lack of Statutory Basis

In 1989, the Supreme Court called the validity of ancillary and pendent jurisdiction into doubt, at least with regard to claims against added parties, because there was no statutory basis for such jurisdiction and all exercises of federal-court jurisdiction have been said to require a statutory basis.

3. Supplemental-Jurisdiction Statute

In 1990, Congress adopted the Supplemental Jurisdiction Statute, which grants federal courts that have original jurisdiction over a claim supplemental jurisdiction over all other claims that form *part of the same case or controversy* under Article III. Thus, any claim that is part of the same constitutional case may be added, including claims that involve the joinder or intervention of additional parties.

a. Standard

In determining whether supplemental jurisdiction is proper, a federal court will ask whether:

(i) The *federal claim is sufficiently substantial*;

(ii) The federal and nonfederal claims arise from a *common nucleus of operative fact*; and

(iii) The federal and nonfederal claims are such that they would ordinarily be tried in *one judicial proceeding.*

b. Exception for Diversity Cases

When federal subject-matter jurisdiction is founded *solely* on diversity, there is no supplemental jurisdiction over claims *by plaintiffs* against persons made parties under Rule 14 (impleader), Rule 19 (required party joinder), Rule 20 (permissive party joinder), or Rule 24 (intervention), or over claims *by persons proposed to be joined* under Rules 19 or 24.

(1) Distinguish—Rule 20 Joinder

Claims *by plaintiffs joined permissively pursuant to Rule 20* are not excluded by the supplemental jurisdiction statute. However, claims *against defendants joined under Rule 20* are excluded from supplemental jurisdiction.

(2) Distinguish—Class Actions

Supplemental jurisdiction extends to class members' claims even if they do not satisfy the minimum amount-in-controversy requirement; the claims of these class members are appended to the jurisdictionally sufficient claims of the plaintiff class representatives.

c. Discretionary Decline of Jurisdiction

A federal court can decline to exercise supplemental jurisdiction when: (i) a novel or complex issue of state law is involved; (ii) the nonfederal claim predominates; (iii) all original-jurisdiction claims are dismissed; or (iv) in other extraordinary circumstances.

d. Tolling of Limitations

The limitations period for claims asserted under supplemental jurisdiction, or for any other claim in the same action voluntarily dismissed, is tolled while the case is pending in federal court and for 30 days after dismissal by the federal court.

E. REMOVAL

1. Grounds for Removal

In general, a state-court action that plaintiff *could originally have filed in federal court* can be removed there by defendant.

a. Federal Question

The *well-pleaded complaint rule* governs the removal of a federal-question case by defendant, *e.g.*, a federal defense in an answer is insufficient for removal. *Supplemental jurisdiction* permits a defendant to remove a federal-claim case even if it also includes defendants against whom only state-law claims are asserted.

b. Diversity of Citizenship

Complete diversity is required for removal of diversity cases. However, removal is not permitted if any defendant is a citizen of the state in which the action is brought (*i.e.*, a *forum defendant*) unless it is a class-action claim based on state law that could have been filed in federal court under the Class Action Fairness Act. *Fictitious defendants* are disregarded in determining complete diversity for removal purposes. The *jurisdictional-amount* requirement applies to removed cases.

c. Separate and Independent Federal Claim

When a federal-question claim is joined in state court to an unrelated state-law claim or a nonremovable claim, and the action is removed to federal court, the court must sever claims that are not within original or supplemental jurisdiction, or that are made nonremovable by statute, and remand them to state court.

d. Special Removal Statutes

Special removal statutes apply to certain types of cases, *e.g.*, *federal civil rights* regarding racial equality when protection in state court is inadequate, or actions that could have been filed in federal court under the Multiparty, Multiforum Trial Jurisdiction Act.

e. Removal Forbidden in Employment-Injury Cases

Actions brought in state court pursuant to the Federal Employers' Liability Act or under state workers'-compensation laws cannot be removed to federal court. However, an action brought under the Fair Labor Standards Act can be removed to federal court.

f. Removal Under the Class Action Fairness Act

Class-action claims that could have been filed in federal court under the Class Action Fairness Act can be removed to federal court.

2. Procedure for Removal

Defendant removes by filing a notice of removal in the appropriate federal district court and notifying the other parties and the state court.

a. **Only Defendant Can Remove**

Plaintiff may not remove under any circumstances, including on the basis of defendant's assertion of a counterclaim.

b. **All Defendants Must Join**

Unless an individual defendant has a *separate and independent claim against him*, all defendants who have been served must join in filing for removal. However, actions filed pursuant to the Class Action Fairness Act can be removed *without* the consent of all the defendants.

c. **Timing**

Upon *service of process*, a defendant has 30 days to file a notice of removal unless the case becomes removable later, in which case the 30 days begins running from that point. The case is considered removed as soon as the notice is filed and served.

3. **Remand**

The federal court should remand an improperly removed case to state court, or it may remand only *claims within supplemental jurisdiction* if the other claims are dismissed, or if it declines to exercise supplemental jurisdiction. Orders of remand based on lack of subject-matter jurisdiction or for defects in removal procedure are *not reviewable*, although a remand motion *erroneously denied* may be appealed. If the action was filed under the Class Action Fairness Act, the appellate court has discretion to review on appeal an order granting or denying a remand.

4. **No "Reverse" Removal**

Presently, there is no method to remove a case originally filed in federal court to state court. However, federal courts may apply the *abstention* doctrines.

III. RELATION BETWEEN STATE AND FEDERAL LAW

A. STATE LAW IN THE FEDERAL COURTS

1. **Rules of Decision Act**

Under the Act, the *laws of the states* are the rules of decision in federal courts, except when the Constitution or federal laws or treaties provide otherwise.

2. **Former Rule—*Swift v. Tyson***

Under *Swift v. Tyson*, "laws" in the Rules of Decision Act was held not to include much state common law. Thus, federal courts followed their own view of what the "general" common law was or should be.

3. **Overruling of *Swift* by *Erie***

Erie held that state common-law principles should govern when Congress had not provided otherwise.

a. **Reasoning of *Erie***

The Court *found* that the Rules of Decision Act was not intended to exclude all state general common law and that *Swift* had led to a *lack of uniformity and resulting discrimination.* But more importantly, the Court *held* that the Constitution did *not* give federal courts the power to declare the substantive common law that would apply in a state.

b. ***Erie* as Part of Practice Revolution**

Erie coincided with adoption of the Federal Rules of Civil Procedure. Thus, at the same time federal courts increased *application of state substantive law*, they also began using *uniform federal procedural law.*

c. **Principal Cases Developing *Erie***

Cases after *Erie* have attempted to implement the general guideline that *state substantive law* and *federal procedural law* should govern state-law actions in the federal courts.

(1) ***Guaranty Trust Co. v. York***

York, in holding that a state statute of limitations took precedence over a more flexible federal laches approach, articulated an *"outcome determination"* test; *i.e.*, a federal law is substantive if application of the federal law instead of the state law will *significantly affect the outcome of the litigation.* It was hard to know where to stop in applying this doctrine, since almost any rule could qualify as substantive under the test, especially if disobeyed.

(2) ***Byrd* and the "Interest-Balancing" Approach**

Byrd adopted a balancing test that considered (i) the *relation between the state rule and the underlying state right*; (ii) the *interests of the federal judicial system*; and (iii) the *outcome-determination* effect of each choice. This approach suffers from difficulties of weighing nonequivalent interests.

(a) **Status of *Byrd* test**

After ignoring the *Byrd* test for nearly 40 years, the Court revived it to a limited extent, invoking it when the possibly applicable federal law was purely decisional *and* was an essential characteristic of the federal-court system.

4. **Approach Under *Hanna v. Plumer***

Hanna gave preference to the Federal Rules in a conflict between a state requirement of personal service and the federal allowance of substituted service.

a. ***Erie* Dictum in *Hanna***

In dicta, *Hanna* confirmed the scaling back of the *York* test, but suggested that the test be applied in light of the *twin aims* of the *Erie* rule: "discouragement of forum shopping and avoidance of inequitable administration of the laws." The Court held, however, that this approach should be applied only to unguided *Erie*-choice problems and not to cases such as the one here, where Congress had established guidelines by statute.

b. **Holding with Respect to Validity of Federal Rules**

The Court held that under the Rules Enabling Act the Federal Rules are to be applied if they deal, as the Act specifies, with practice or procedure. It mentioned but did not invoke the Act's limitation that Federal Rules are not to abridge, enlarge, or modify a substantive right, noting that that language is not addressed to merely "incidental" effects on the rights of litigants.

5. **Modern Approach Under *Erie* and *Hanna***

The modern approach to federal-state law choice issues employs a two-stage analysis.

a. **Conflict-Determination Stage**

It should first be determined whether there is any ***direct conflict*** between the federal and state rules.

b. **Conflict-Resolution Stage**

If a true conflict is found, the ***source*** of the federal rule should be considered.

(1) **Federal Constitution**

Rules that derive from the Constitution always govern state-law actions in federal courts; *e.g.*, right to jury trial.

(2) **Acts of Congress**

Statutes governing federal courts prevail over state law ***if*** the federal statute is "arguably procedural."

(3) **Federal Rules**

Federal Rules are judged according to the standards of the Rules Enabling Act (*i.e.*, they will be applied if they are procedural). ***Incidental effects on state substantive law*** are disregarded.

(4) **Judge-Made Federal Procedural Rules**

Decisional rules present ***unguided* Erie *choices*** and are judged according to whether they meet *Erie*'s twin aims of discouraging forum shopping and avoiding inequitable administration of the laws.

6. **Which State's Law Applies?**

Under *Klaxon Co. v. Stentor Manufacturing Co.*, in ***diversity cases*** requiring application of state law, the court will apply ***the law of the state in which it sits***, ***including that state's choice-of-law rules.***

7. **Determining Applicable State Law**

A problem may arise if a state's highest court has not recently ruled on the point of law in question.

a. **General Guideline—"Proper Regard" to State-Court Rulings**

The federal court must give "proper regard" to state-court precedents, but is not necessarily bound by rulings of intermediate state courts.

b. **Implementation in Light of *Erie* Aims**

Unclear state law should be approached with *Erie*'s twin aims in mind, and not with simplistic or rigid tests. Where certification is authorized by state law, a federal court may seek an authoritative answer to uncertain questions of state law from the state's highest court.

B. **FEDERAL COMMON LAW**

Although there is ***no federal general common law***, federal courts have authority to create common law in ***particular areas of federal authority or interest.***

IV. PLEADINGS AND MOTION PRACTICE

A. INTRODUCTION

The basic purpose of pleading is to give notice of the general character of the controversy between the parties. Under *code pleading* (used in California, New York, Illinois, and some other states), pleadings are also intended to narrow and frame the issues.

B. HISTORY OF PLEADING

1. Common-Law Pleadings

Pleadings at common law had to fit within one of the recognized *forms of action* (*e.g.*, case, trespass, assumpsit, etc.). A plaintiff was thus forced to shape the out-of-court transaction into the mold of a theory of substantive law expressed in one of the forms, resulting in numerous pleadings and counter-pleadings in an effort to fashion a single issue. Amendments to change from one form to another were not permitted.

a. Distinguish—Equity Pleading

Equity courts were governed by different procedures. Equitable relief was available only when there was no right to recover under any forms of action at law, *i.e.*, no adequate remedy at law. In equity, a plaintiff went outside the forms of action and recited *facts* showing his grievance. This *fact pleading* became the basis of code pleading.

2. Code Pleading

The New York Code of 1848 (Field Code) originated code pleading. It was later adopted or adapted by a majority of the states and is still used in several today. Code pleading departed from common-law pleading rules in several important ways.

a. Single Form of Action

The fundamental principle of code pleading is that plaintiff's claim is a *statement of facts showing a right to a remedy.* Code pleading abolished forms of action; a plaintiff could recover under any legal theory applicable to the facts he pleaded and proved.

b. Merger of Law and Equity

Code pleading generally eliminated separate courts of law and equity, a change persisting to modern practice. However, while procedural distinctions have been abolished, legal and equitable *remedies* remain distinct.

c. Limited Number of Pleadings

Far fewer pleadings are allowed under code pleading than under the common law, and no attempt is made to reduce a case to a single issue.

d. Fact Pleading

A pleading under the codes must set forth the *ultimate facts* constituting the *cause of action* in ordinary and concise language.

3. Pleading Under the Federal Rules

The Federal Rules, now adopted by most states, *further liberalize* pleading rules and eliminate the technicalities of the Field Code.

a. Pleadings Permitted

Fewer pleadings are permitted under the Federal Rules than in code states. A *motion to dismiss* is used instead of demurrer.

b. Notice Pleading

The Federal Rules eliminate the requirement of "facts constituting a cause of action." Now, all that is needed is a *"short and plain statement of the claim showing that the pleader is entitled to relief."*

C. COMPLAINT

In most jurisdictions, filing of the complaint commences a civil action.

1. Form

The essential parts of the complaint are as follows.

a. Caption

The complaint must set forth the name of the court, the number assigned to the action, a designation of the pleading (*e.g.*, Complaint for Damages), and the names of the parties.

b. Jurisdictional Allegations

In *federal court*, the complaint must allege the ground(s) upon which federal jurisdiction is invoked. Failure to do so results in a dismissal if the complaint is not amended to supply the ground(s). (Pleading jurisdiction is *not* normally required in *state courts* because they are usually courts of general jurisdiction.)

c. Body

There must also be a statement of ultimate facts constituting the cause of action (code pleading) or a short and plain statement of the claim showing that the pleader is entitled to relief (Federal Rules). Each claim or cause of action should be set forth in a separate group of paragraphs, and each paragraph should be limited to a single set of facts.

(1) Direct Allegations

The allegations should be *simple, concise, and direct.* A plaintiff who *lacks personal knowledge* as to some element of the claim may plead that "to the best of his knowledge, information, and belief," the claim is "well-grounded in fact," but in federal court, reasonable inquiry must first be made pursuant to Rule 11. Similarly, in code-pleading states, allegations may be *denied* on lack of information and belief.

(2) Alternative and Inconsistent Allegations

A plaintiff may plead in the alternative by alleging facts based on *inconsistent legal theories*; he may also allege *inconsistent facts* if he has reason for not knowing which version is true. However, an *election of remedies* must be made *before* judgment.

(3) Defenses Need Not Be Anticipated

Ordinarily, plaintiff's complaint need not anticipate defendant's defenses.

d. Prayer for Relief

The pleading must set forth a prayer for relief. If a defendant *defaults* by failing to defend, the relief granted cannot exceed what is requested. In *contested* cases, on the other hand, relief is *not* limited to that which is requested, with a few exceptions. In *federal court*, a prayer determines the *amount in controversy* for jurisdictional purposes. In *state court* (and state-law actions in federal court), the prayer may determine the nature of the action (legal vs. equitable) on which the **right to jury trial** depends.

e. Subscription

The complaint must be signed by the attorney, or by a party if she has no attorney. In federal practice, the signature certifies that: (i) to the best of the attorney's knowledge formed after reasonable inquiry, the evidentiary contentions have evidentiary support or are likely to have support after discovery, (ii) the claims or defenses are warranted by existing law or a good-faith argument for change in existing law, and (iii) the complaint is not presented for any improper purpose.

(1) Verification

A verified pleading contains an affidavit at its end averring that the pleading is true to the best of affiant's knowledge, information, or belief. Verification is not required in federal practice unless so specified by rule or statute, *e.g.*, shareholders' derivative suits.

2. Form Complaints

In many jurisdictions, complaint forms for specific types of claims are presumptively sufficient.

3. Splitting of Claims

A pleader cannot split a single claim or cause of action into several parts and file separate suits on each. If suit is brought on only one part of a claim, **claim preclusion** (*infra*) bars later suit on the omitted claim(s).

4. Joinder of Claims

Except for the effect of claim preclusion, there is **no compulsory** joinder of claims. Practically, however, plaintiffs usually join related claims because of the danger of claim preclusion, *infra*.

a. Permissive Joinder

At common law, joinder was permitted only if all claims were in the same form of action and there was complete identity of parties to each claim. Under the **Federal Rules**, adopted by most states, a single plaintiff may join **as many claims** as he has against a single defendant, **regardless of the subject matter.** However, in **multi-party** cases, **at least one** of the claims by or against each party must arise out of the same transaction **and** must involve a common question of law or fact.

5. Consolidation of Separate Actions

A trial judge has power to order joint trials of separate lawsuits or may consolidate them if they involve a common question of law or fact. If such cases are pending in **different courts**, many jurisdictions permit **transfer**, in whole or in part, so the cases can be consolidated or joined.

D. CHALLENGES TO COMPLAINT

A defendant can challenge the legal sufficiency of the complaint **before** responding to the factual allegations in it.

1. Common Law

At common law, defects in the pleadings could be raised by two kinds of demurrer.

a. General Demurrer

This challenged the *substantive sufficiency* of the causes in the complaint.

b. Special Demurrer

This demurrer challenged *specific matters of form.*

2. State Practice

In the Field Code, the demurrer was preserved. Elsewhere, a motion to dismiss or a motion to make more definite and certain is used.

a. General vs. Special Demurrer

A general demurrer is used for a failure to plead facts sufficient to constitute a cause of action. A demurrer on any other ground is a special demurrer.

b. Rulings on Demurrer

Rulings must be *based on grounds* raised by the demurring party. If a demurrer is overruled, defendant must answer within the time ordered by the court or take a default; if sustained, the court usually grants plaintiff leave to *amend* the complaint.

c. Effect of Failure to Raise Ground for Demurrer

Grounds for demurrer are *waived* unless raised in the defendant's initial pleading (demurrer or answer). *Exceptions*: *Failure to state facts* sufficient to constitute a cause of action and the court's *lack of subject-matter jurisdiction* are *never* waived.

(1) Waiver of Objections to Personal Jurisdiction and Process

A general demurrer results in a waiver of objections to personal jurisdiction and sufficiency of process; however, these objections may be preserved in some states (*e.g.*, California) if defendant simultaneously files a motion to quash service of process.

d. Motion to Strike

A motion to strike reaches defects not subject to demurrer (*e.g.*, irrelevant or redundant matter in the complaint) and *extends the time* to file an answer.

3. Federal Practice

a. Motion to Dismiss

In federal practice, a motion to dismiss is the basic challenge to the legal sufficiency of adversary pleadings and is *always optional* with the defendant. It can be made on grounds such as lack of subject-matter or personal jurisdiction, improper venue, or a failure to state a claim. [Fed. R. Civ. P. 12(b)] If the motion is *granted*, a court has discretion to allow the plaintiff to *amend* the complaint.

(1) Test for Sufficiency of Complaint

The standard for failure to state a claim is more liberal than under code pleading: The claim must set forth the legal basis for the plaintiff's claims and contain sufficient detail (*e.g.*, dates, circumstances, etc.) to apprise the defendant of the claims against her. Starting with a decision in 2007, the Supreme Court has required that federal-court complaints meet a standard of "plausibility," which must rise above mere speculation but does not require a standard of probability. The complaint must allow "the court to draw the reasonable inference that the defendant is liable for the misconduct alleged." Some states with federal-style rules have followed these decisions, while others have not.

(a) Fraud or Mistake

Fraud and mistake must be *pleaded with particularity.* Also, under the Private Securities Litigation Reform Act, most federal securities-fraud claims must specify any misleading statements, state why the statements are misleading, and provide specific facts giving rise to a strong inference that defendant acted with any required state of mind.

(b) Lower Courts' Requirements

Lower federal courts require more specificity in pleadings involving cases *analogous to fraud*, *e.g.*, inequitable conduct, and in suits against government officials who claim *qualified immunity.*

(2) Rulings on Motion to Dismiss

If a motion to dismiss is *granted*, the court has discretion to grant plaintiff leave to *amend*, which is liberally granted. If the motion is *denied*, defendant must answer and proceed, but can raise the denial on appeal *after* final judgment.

b. Motion for More Definite Statement

This motion permits a very limited attack on the *form* of pleadings. It is granted when a pleading is so *vague* that it would be *unreasonable* to require the moving party to reply to it. [Fed. R. Civ. P. 12(e)]

c. Motion to Strike

Either party may move to strike any insufficient defense or any redundant, immaterial, impertinent, or scandalous material from the other's pleadings. [Fed. R. Civ. P. 12(f)] A motion to strike may also be used to attack separate *portions* of the complaint that are insufficient as a matter of *law* or when defendant raised an affirmative defense inapplicable to plaintiff's claim.

d. Time for Motion

A Rule 12 motion must be filed within the time for answering, and its filing extends the time to answer.

e. Waiver of Defenses

If a defendant fails to file a Rule 12 motion or, if she files but fails to include all available *defenses*, she waives objections to the *form* of the complaint and defenses of lack of venue, personal jurisdiction, or sufficiency of process. However, the defenses of lack of *subject-matter jurisdiction*, failure to join a *party required under Rule 19(b)*, and *failure to state a claim* are *not* waived.

4. Additional Rules of Pleading

The following apply in both state and federal practice.

a. Pleading Considered on Its Face

A challenge by demurrer or motion to dismiss usually considers only the sufficiency of a complaint itself. Reference to other matters will not be made (with a few exceptions).

(1) Conversion to Summary Judgment

If a motion to dismiss is accompanied by supporting evidentiary materials, and the court does not exclude them, the court must treat it as a motion for summary judgment, *infra*.

b. Anticipatory Defenses

A complaint need *not* anticipate affirmative defenses that might be raised. However, if it does so, it must plead facts to avoid the defenses.

(1) "Built-in" Defenses

If a plaintiff's allegations provide support for a defense, the defendant may raise it on a motion to dismiss for failure to state a claim.

E. ATTORNEY'S DUTY TO INVESTIGATE CLAIMS AND DEFENSES

1. Certification Requirement

Federal Rule 11 requires that every paper filed in court be signed by an attorney, or by the party herself if unrepresented.

2. Matter Certified by Signature

By signing, a person certifies that:

(i)   She has made an *inquiry reasonable under the circumstances* to support the factual and legal positions taken;

(ii) The *factual assertions have evidentiary support*;

(iii) The claim, defense, or other legal position is *supported by existing law* or makes a *nonfrivolous argument* for changing existing law or establishing new law; and

(iv) The paper was *not filed for an improper purpose.*

3. Sanctions

Imposition of sanctions for violation of Rule 11 is *discretionary.* Sanctions can be monetary or nonmonetary, but in any event are to be limited to what is necessary to *deter repetition* of such conduct. Law firms should be held *jointly liable* for sanctions along with the firm members who violate Rule 11.

4. Procedure

A party may move for sanctions, but must give the nonmoving party notice and 21 days to withdraw or correct the sanctionable paper. The court also has power to impose sanctions on its own initiative.

F. ANSWER

1. Denials

A defendant's answer must contain *effective* denials to put plaintiff's allegations at issue. Material allegations *not denied* are *deemed admitted.*

a. General Denials

A defendant may deny all the allegations of a complaint in a single denial. However, this response is no longer good practice in most jurisdictions, because *federal* (and similar state) *practice* has a basic pleading requirement of *good faith*; thus, a general denial is *rarely proper* because there is usually something in a complaint (*e.g.*, allegations about plaintiff's identity) that defendant should admit.

b. Specific Denials

Anything less than a general denial is a specific denial, *e.g.*, denial by *parts* (paragraphs or sentences in complaint); merely *negating* an allegation ("defendant was not drunk"); or alleging a *lack of sufficient information* to respond.

(1) Damages

In federal practice, damages are at issue even if not effectively denied. Most state jurisdictions are contra.

2. Affirmative Defenses

Any defense or objections constituting new matter or an affirmative defense must be pleaded in the answer; a simple denial is not sufficient to raise these. New matter is anything that defendant must prove to *avoid* plaintiff's claim. The test usually is whether defendant would bear the *burden of proof* on the issue at trial; if so, it is new matter.

a. Application

The following new matter *must* be specially pleaded in most states and *in federal practice.*

(1) Tort Cases

New matter includes the defenses of self-defense, consent, justification or other privilege, contributory negligence and assumption of risk, privilege or license (defense to trespass), and consent (defense to conversion). *Lack of proximate cause* is *not* new matter.

(2) Contract Cases

Fraud, mistake, duress, incapacity, release, waiver, estoppel, condition subsequent, payment, Statute of Frauds (federal and most states), statute of limitations, and pleas in abatement (assert a reason why action should be put off or not heard) must usually be specially pleaded.

b. Effect of Failure to Plead New Matter

If new matter is not pleaded in the answer, defendant *may not offer evidence* of such defenses *unless* plaintiff fails to object to the introduction of the evidence or the court allows leave to *amend.* A motion to amend *cannot revive* waiver of personal jurisdiction, venue, or manner of service.

3. Procedure in Answering Complaint

Requirements for allegations in a complaint also apply to allegations in an answer. Rule 11 requires a signature, and defendant may deny based on "a lack of information and belief." A federal defendant must file her answer within 20 days after service, absent a Rule 12(b) motion; if she waives service, defendant has 60 days after the waiver request was sent to answer.

4. Allegations of Answer Deemed Controverted

In federal practice, *no reply* to an answer is permitted unless the answer contains a counterclaim. However, some federal courts now require a reply when a defendant asserts a qualified-immunity defense. Plaintiff may avoid any new matter in defendant's answer by the introduction of evidence without further pleading.

5. **Challenges to Answer**

Plaintiff may challenge the legal sufficiency of an affirmative defense by *demurrer* (state practice) or *motion to strike* (federal practice). A motion for summary judgment or judgment on the pleadings may also be used.

G. COUNTERCLAIMS AND CROSSCLAIMS

1. Federal Practice

a. Counterclaims

A defendant may set forth as counterclaims in the answer any claims she has against plaintiff, even *if not related* to plaintiff's claims in the complaint.

(1) Subject-Matter Jurisdiction

If a *compulsory* counterclaim is based on the same transaction or occurrence as plaintiff's claim, it falls within the court's supplemental jurisdiction. However, a *permissive* counterclaim must satisfy subject-matter jurisdictional requirements, *i.e.*, must be based on some federal question or on diversity.

(2) Pleading

The sufficiency of a counterclaim is tested by the same rules used to test the sufficiency of a complaint.

(3) Joinder of Other Parties

Although a counterclaim is against the plaintiff, it can give rise to joinder of other parties. Joinder can be permissive, with an independent basis for subject-matter jurisdiction, or the court may order joinder.

(a) Voluntary Dismissal by Plaintiff

The assertion of a counterclaim bars plaintiff's dismissal of the action without *defendant's consent.*

(4) Permissive vs. Compulsory

If defendant's counterclaim is *unrelated* to plaintiff's claims, it is *permissive.* A *compulsory* counterclaim arises out of the *same transactions* as set forth in the complaint and must be asserted in the action or is barred in a later action.

(5) Statute of Limitations

The majority view finds that if a counterclaim arises out of the *same transaction*, it will not be barred if the complaint was timely filed.

b. Crossclaims

A defendant may set forth in the answer any claims that she has against a *co-defendant* that relate to the *transaction or occurrence* (or to any property) that is the subject of plaintiff's complaint, *e.g.*, crossclaim for contribution or indemnification.

(1) Impleader

Impleaders are claims against a *third person* not a party to the original action and are limited to indemnification and contribution claims.

2. **State Practice—Cross-Complaint**

Most state rules follow the Federal Rules. A few states provide that a defendant's claims against *any* party (plaintiff, co-defendant, or a third person) may be asserted in a cross-complaint, which is a pleading *separate* from an answer.

H. AMENDED AND SUPPLEMENTAL PLEADINGS

1. Amendments Before Trial

a. As a Matter of Course

In federal court either party may amend its pleading *once* as a matter of course within 21 days of serving it or, if a responsive pleading is required, 21 days after service of the responsive pleading or 21 days after service of a motion under Rule 12(b)–(e), –(f), whichever is sooner.

b. By Permission of Court

In any other situation, amendment may be made only by leave of court unless the opposing party consents. However, such permission is usually granted freely before trial.

c. Permissible Scope of Amendment

(1) State Practice

Today, an amendment is permitted if it is based on the *same general set of facts* as were set forth in the original pleading.

(2) Federal Practice

Under the Federal Rules, the determinative question is whether the amendment results in *prejudice* to the opposing party.

d. "Relation-Back Doctrine"—Statute of Limitations Problems

When a plaintiff seeks to amend the complaint after the applicable statute of limitations would otherwise have run, the question arises whether the amendment relates back to the date of filing the original complaint. In most jurisdictions, it relates back if the claim asserted in the amended pleading arose out of the *same conduct, transaction, or occurrence* as in the original complaint. In *diversity cases*, the question is procedural and is governed by the Federal Rules, *supra*.

e. Amendment Supersedes Original Pleading

An amended pleading supersedes the original, so the original has no further effect as a pleading. It may, however, still be used in *evidence* against the pleader (*e.g.*, as an admission).

2. Amendments at Trial

a. Background—Doctrine of Variance

At common law, the slightest variance between the facts pleaded and those proved was often fatal to recovery.

b. Code-Pleading Practice

Pleading rules today are usually more relaxed. When the evidence offered at trial is only a *partial* variance from the pleadings, leave to amend is usually granted if no prejudice will result.

c. Federal Practice

Because pleadings are now less important, amendments are liberally allowed; the doctrine of variance is effectively *abolished.*

3. Amendments After Trial

In federal practice, pleadings can be amended to conform to the proof at any time, even after entry of judgment or on appeal.

4. Supplemental Pleadings

The function of supplemental pleadings is to call attention of the court to material facts that have occurred *after* the filing of the complaint. The right to file a supplemental pleading is at the court's *discretion*, but is liberally given. A supplemental pleading *adds to*, but does not modify, the original pleading.

I. DEFAULT PROCEDURE

1. In General

If a defendant fails to answer or otherwise timely plead, a default can be entered.

2. Effect of Default Entry

Defendant's failure to plead is considered an *admission* of the claim against her.

3. Obtaining Judgment

After entry of a default, plaintiff must proceed to obtain a default judgment. *Relief is limited* to the amount or type that was sought in the prayer. The defendant is *not* entitled to appear in the proceeding.

4. Setting Aside Default

Once a default is entered, defendant's remedy is to move the court to set it (and any judgment entered pursuant to it) aside. In *federal practice*, the motion can be made at any time before judgment is entered. Thereafter, the motion must be made within *one year* after entry of the judgment or order. The defendant must show that she has a *valid excuse* for the default *and* a *meritorious defense* to the action and that *plaintiff will not be prejudiced.*

J. JUDGMENT ON THE PLEADINGS

1. Purpose

A motion for judgment on the pleadings is analogous to a demurrer or motion to dismiss, and challenges the adversary's pleadings on the ground that they are insufficient to establish any valid claim or defense.

2. Making the Motion

Either party may move for judgment on the pleadings at any time after the pleadings have closed, but not so late as to delay trial.

3. Issues Raised

Originally, the motion raised only sufficiency of the pleadings. Under modern practice, if the moving party presents matters beyond the pleadings, the motion is treated as a motion for summary judgment.

K. VOLUNTARY DISMISSAL BY PLAINTIFF

1. Common Law

At common law, plaintiff could dismiss his own case without prejudice at any time before verdict.

2. Code Practice

Code-pleading states provided that plaintiff could dismiss his own case without prejudice only before trial began; otherwise it was with prejudice.

3. Federal Practice—Notice of Dismissal (Voluntary)

Under federal practice, plaintiff may voluntarily dismiss his case *once* without prejudice by giving notice, if he does so *before* defendant has filed an answer or motion for summary judgment. Thereafter, plaintiff may dismiss only with defendant's consent or court permission.

4. Federal Practice—Dismissal by Leave of Court

The court can grant the plaintiff's motion for leave to dismiss without prejudice at any time before judgment, *unless* a defendant who has filed a counterclaim that cannot be independently adjudicated objects to the dismissal.

V. PARTIES

A. REAL PARTY IN INTEREST RULE

1. Background

At common law, the party having the legal right was the proper party to bring suit at law. Modern procedure requires that a civil action be prosecuted only by the "real party in interest."

2. Definition

The person bringing suit (i) must use his own name as plaintiff (except when he has court permission to use a fictitious name), *and* (ii) must have a legal right to enforce the claim under the applicable substantive law.

a. Under Federal Rules and State Rules

The following parties have a right to sue as representatives even though they may have no beneficial interest in the claim: an executor, administrator, guardian, or trustee of an estate; a party to a contract made for the benefit of another; and a private claimant suing in the name of the United States Government if such a claim is expressly authorized by statute.

b. In All Other Cases

In *all* other cases, the real party in interest is determined by reference to the applicable substantive law. In diversity actions, it is determined by reference to the applicable state law.

3. Determination of Real Party in Interest

a. Assignments

Whether the assignee is the real party in interest depends on the nature of the assignment. If the assignment is of the *entire* interest, the assignee is the real party in interest; this is so even for gratuitous assignments. If the assignment is of a *partial* interest, at common law the assignee could not enforce a claim; the modern rule is that partial assignees and the assignor are *required parties*.

b. Subrogation

Subrogation is equitable and results in an assignment by operation of law so that one who pays another for loss or injury caused by an act of a third person becomes entitled to enforce (as subrogee) the claim that the injured person (subrogor) had against the third party.

c. Trusts

The trustee, as holder of legal title, is the real party for redress of any wrong to the *trust estate.* But a beneficiary may sue the trustee to protect her beneficial rights.

d. Executors and Administrators

These are the proper parties to sue on behalf of decedents' estates.

e. Principal and Agent

If the obligation is owed to the *principal alone*, he is the only proper plaintiff. If the obligation is owed to *both the agent and the principal*, either may sue.

f. Third-Party Beneficiary

A third-party beneficiary who has enforceable rights under a contract is a real party in interest. If a promise was given for the benefit of a third party, *both* the promisee and third party would have enforceable rights.

B. CAPACITY OF PARTY TO SUE OR BE SUED

1. Definition

"Capacity" is the legal competence of a party to sue or be sued.

2. Individuals

A person's capacity is determined by the law of her domicile. If she lacks capacity (*e.g.*, is a minor), suit must be filed by a guardian or conservator.

3. Corporations

The capacity of a corporation to sue (or be sued) is determined by the law of the state in which it is organized.

4. Partnerships

a. Federal Practice—Entity vs. Aggregate

In federal court, a partnership can always sue or be sued as an *entity if the litigation involves a federal question.* However, in other actions, including diversity cases, the partnership's capacity is determined by the law of the state in which the court is located.

b. State Law Varies

Some states permit a partnership to sue *or* be sued as an entity. Many states permit a partnership to be sued, but *not* to sue, as an entity (in the partnership name). In those states, an action on behalf of the partnership must be brought in the names of the individual partners.

5. Unincorporated Associations

At common law, unincorporated associations lacked capacity to sue or be sued as entities.

a. State Practice

Many states now treat unincorporated associations like corporations.

b. Federal Practice

An unincorporated association has capacity to sue or be sued when a *federal right* is being enforced by or against the association. But when a *state* law is being enforced (*e.g.*, in a diversity action), the capacity of the unincorporated association is determined by the law of the state in which the federal action is brought.

6. Attacking Lack of Capacity

When lack of capacity appears on the face of the complaint, the complaint is subject to a *motion to dismiss.* If it is not raised by the time of the answer, the defect is *waived.*

C. JOINDER OF PARTIES

1. Permissive Joinder

a. Early Approach

Under the original codes, a plaintiff could join plaintiffs or defendants only if they *all* had an interest in the subject of the action *and* the relief sought.

b. Modern approach

Today, a person may join or be joined if:

(i) A right to relief is asserted by (or against) her *jointly, severally, or in the alternative*;

(ii) The right to relief *arises out of the same transaction or series of transactions*; *and*

(iii) There is *at least one question of law or fact common to all parties* sought to be joined.

(1) Additional Unrelated Claims

As long as the above requirements are met, a party may assert as many claims as she has against an opposing party, but the court has discretion to sever.

c. Subject-Matter Jurisdiction

In addition to the requirement of personal jurisdiction, federal subject-matter jurisdiction requirements must be satisfied as to *all* parties.

2. Required Joinder

Joinder is required for any person who has a *material interest* in the case and whose absence would result in *substantial prejudice* to him or to other parties.

a. Traditional Approach

Traditionally, a distinction was made between *necessary* parties (those who ought to be joined *if possible*; interests are *severable*) and *indispensable* parties (interests are *nonseverable*; action would have to be dismissed without them).

b. Modern Approach

The focus now is on the *practical consequences* of an interested person's absence. Any interested person should be joined if his absence would prevent *complete relief* from being given to other parties *or* if his absence would *substantially prejudice* his or other parties' interests. If a person who should be joined cannot be made a party, the court has discretion to determine whether to proceed or dismiss.

c. Procedure for Compelling Joinder

Defendant can raise the existence of unjoined required parties in a motion to dismiss or in the answer. The court will order joinder *unless* this would destroy subject-matter jurisdiction or the court lacks personal jurisdiction over the necessary parties. If an added party successfully objects to *venue*, she *must* be dismissed.

d. Waiver of Right to Compel Joinder

An objection to nonjoinder must be raised at the first opportunity or it is waived. However, objection to nonjoinder of an *indispensable* party may be raised at any time.

3. Impleader

Impleader is a procedure that permits the defendant to bring into the lawsuit a third person who is or may be *liable to the defendant for all or part of plaintiff's claim* against the defendant. Impleader is *limited* to situations in which the defendant has a *right to indemnity* against the impleaded third party. Whether such a right exists is determined by applicable *substantive law.*

a. Pleadings and Procedure

Leave of court is not required for impleader if the defendant (third-party plaintiff) files a third-party complaint within *14 days* after he serves his original answer. Thereafter, leave of court is required. The impleaded party may also file a *counterclaim or crossclaim* against existing parties, or may implead any person who may be liable to him.

b. Effect on Jurisdiction and Venue

An impleader claim usually is considered ancillary and thus has no effect on jurisdictional and venue requirements.

c. Distinguish—Crossclaim

Impleader can be asserted only against a person *not yet a party*; a *crossclaim* is by one party against *another party.* Unlike impleader, a crossclaim need not be based on a claim for indemnification.

4. Intervention

By intervening, a nonparty becomes a party to protect his interest from being adversely affected by a judgment in the action. Whether intervention is allowed depends on a balancing of two conflicting policies: (i) plaintiff alone should generally be allowed to join parties, with or against him, as he wishes; and (ii) other interested parties and the court have an interest in avoiding multiplicity of litigation or inconsistency of results.

a. Types of Intervention in Federal Cases

(1) Intervention of Right

Intervention is granted as a matter of right if the unconditional right to intervene is conferred by a federal statute, *or* when the *disposition* of the action without the applicant would likely *impair or impede* his ability to protect an interest relating to the subject of the action, unless existing parties would adequately protect the applicant's interest.

(2) Permissive Intervention

Permissive intervention is granted at a court's broad discretion when a *federal statute* gives a conditional right to intervene or when the applicant's claim or defense has a *question of law or fact in common* with the action.

b. Effect of Intervention in Federal Cases

(1) Subject-Matter Jurisdiction

In actions based solely on diversity, there is no supplemental jurisdiction over claims by intervenors or by plaintiffs against persons who intervene. When jurisdiction is not based solely on diversity, there usually is supplemental jurisdiction over claims by or against intervenors of right.

(2) Venue

The intervening party cannot object to venue in the original action.

(3) Judgment

Judgment rendered after intervention is binding on the intervenor as though he had been an original party, and he has a right to appeal if injured by the judgment.

5. Consolidation of Separate Actions

Even if joinder rules do not permit addition of new parties, almost the same result may be achieved by consolidating suits pending in the same court. The court has broad discretion to consolidate actions with common issues.

6. Interpleader

Interpleader enables a party against whom conflicting claims to the same debt or property are asserted (the "stakeholder") to join all adverse claimants in one action and to require them to litigate among themselves to determine who, if anyone, has a valid claim to the involved property. Once the stakeholder deposits the funds or property in the court, he can be discharged from the litigation, unless he also claims the asset.

a. Procedure

The party against whom conflicting claims are asserted may institute an interpleader action naming all claimants as defendants. If sued by one claimant, or fewer than all claimants, the stakeholder may invoke interpleader by filing a *counterclaim*, *infra*, naming remaining claimants as additional defendants.

(1) Deposit "Stake" with Court

In a statutory-interpleader action, the stakeholder must *deposit with the court*, or give security for, the entire disputed amount in his possession. Rule 22 interpleader does not require deposit.

b. Types of Federal Interpleader Actions

(1) Statutory Interpleader

Interpleader is permitted by 28 U.S.C. section 1335 if two or more *claimants of diverse citizenship* (minimal diversity) are making adverse claims to the same property, debt, or instrument and it has a *value of at least $500.*

(2) Rule 22 Interpleader

Rule 22 permits interpleader in an action that meets the normal jurisdictional requirements in federal court. Unlike statutory interpleader, there must be *complete diversity* between the stakeholder and *all* of the adverse claimants, and the jurisdictional amount must be in excess of $75,000, or a federal question must be involved.

(3) Limits of Process

In *statutory* interpleader, the reach of process is nationwide. Under *Rule 22*, service of process is the same as in other civil actions.

(4) Crossclaims and Counterclaims

Interpleaded claimants often crossclaim against each other, counterclaim against plaintiff, and implead third parties. Any additional claims that relate to the original interpleaded claim should fall within supplemental jurisdiction. Any other claims can be asserted only if there is an independent basis for subject-matter jurisdiction.

(5) Venue

In statutory interpleader, proper venue is the district where *any* claimant resides. Under Rule 22, venue is the same as in any other civil action.

D. CLASS ACTIONS

1. In General

One or more members of a class of persons similarly situated may *sue or be sued* on behalf of all members of that class if such action is justified by considerations of *necessity or convenience.*

2. Background

Class actions were originally permitted *only in equity*, and then only if it was shown that joinder of all parties was *impractical* and a few members could fairly represent all of the class. Later, under *code pleading*, class actions were allowed if there were "questions of common or general interest of many persons," or if the parties were so numerous as to make it impractical to join all of them.

a. Class Action Fairness Act

The Act gives federal courts subject-matter jurisdiction over certain class actions involving claims based on state law.

3. Prerequisites to Class Action

Under Fed. R. Civ. P. 23(a), the class must be adequately defined, and *all four* of the following conditions must be met:

a. Numerous-Parties Requirement

The trial court has considerable discretion in this issue because there is *no fixed minimum* needed to make a class. However, the class must be definitely *ascertainable* and it must be *manageable.* In some cases, all members must be given *individual notice* of the action. Class actions falling within the scope of the Class Action Fairness Act must have *more than 100 members.*

b. Common-Question Requirement

There must be "questions of law or fact common to the class."

c. Typical-Claim Requirement

The representative's claim must be typical of those of the class so that she will be motivated to protect the class interests.

d. Adequate-Representation Requirement

Similar to the typical-claim requirement, this condition also focuses on whether there is any *actual or potential conflict of interest* between the representative and the class. To ensure adequate representation, a court may divide a class into *subclasses* based on divergent interests.

4. Three Grounds for Class Actions

If the above *four conditions are met*, a class action may be based on *any one* of the following grounds:

a. Prejudice from Separate Actions

A class suit is permitted if the prosecution of separate actions would create the risk of *establishing incompatible standards of conduct* for defendant through inconsistent adjudications, or of *substantially impairing the interests* of other class members.

b. Equitable Relief

A class action is also proper if the basis on which the opponent has acted is generally applicable to the class and *declaratory or injunctive* relief would benefit the class as a whole.

c. Predominant Common Questions

The most common basis for a class action occurs when common questions of law or fact *predominate* over questions affecting only individual members, and, *on balance, a class action is superior* to other available methods for adjudication. Such class actions usually involve large numbers of damage claims.

5. Jurisdictional Requirements in Class Suits

a. Diversity of Citizenship

Only the citizenship of the *representative* is considered in actions not covered by the Class Action Fairness Act (CAFA). In CAFA actions minimal diversity between any class member and any defendant suffices.

b. Jurisdictional Amount

Generally, for original diversity jurisdiction the separate claims of individual class members must be at least *$75,000 and cannot be aggregated.* However, supplemental jurisdiction will apply to claims of unnamed members of a plaintiff class in a diversity action even if their claims do not exceed $75,000. Class-action claims that fall within the scope of the Class Action Fairness Act must *exceed $5 million, and the claims can be aggregated.*

c. Personal Jurisdiction

Although it has been held that in a nationwide class action, a state court could assert personal jurisdiction over absent members of the class who chose not to opt out, it is ***unclear*** whether a ***right to opt out*** is a requirement for the assertion of personal jurisdiction.

6. **Procedure in Conducting Class Suits**

    a. **Certification Hearing**

    The court must determine whether to certify an action as a class action soon after the filing of suit. If the court declines certification, the suit may proceed as an individual action.

    b. **Appointment of Class Counsel**

    The court must appoint class counsel to fairly and adequately represent the interests of the class after it certifies a class. Factors that the court must consider when appointing counsel are: (i) investigation of possible claims in the action, (ii) experience with complex litigation, (iii) knowledge of applicable law, and (iv) resources that will be committed to representing the class.

    c. **Statute of Limitations**

    The filing of a suit as a class action suspends the running of the statute of limitations for all putative members of the class until class certification is decided. The period begins to run again if certification is denied or members opt out.

    d. **Notice Requirements**

    Individual notice is ***mandatory*** in a ***damages class*** action based on a predominant question common to the class, and also before any type of class action may be ***settled or dismissed.*** In most other class actions, the form of notice to individual members is ***discretionary*** with the court, and no specific form for notice is required, but it must advise the member of the suit's existence, the nature of the claim and the relief requested, provisions for costs of suit, and the identity of the class representative.

    (1) Costs of Notice

    Plaintiff must pay the costs of giving notice, but can recover them from defendant if plaintiff wins.

    e. **Opting out by Class Members**

    Under Rule 23(b)(3), unnamed members of the class may opt out, and thus avoid the binding effects of the class action. There is no opt-out right in other Rule 23 class actions. Class members who have opted out may not use the issue-preclusive effects of a successful class action in their individual actions.

    f. **Intervention by Class Members**

    Intervention by class members in a class action is allowed on the same terms that govern intervention otherwise.

    g. **Discovery**

    Class members are "quasi-parties" for discovery purposes. An opponent cannot depose each member, but may use interrogatories and depositions to assess such issues as the typicality of claims, individual damages, etc.

    h. **Communications with Class Members**

    To prevent overreaching, the court may regulate communications between litigants or their counsel and unnamed class members.

i. Dismissal and Compromise

No dismissal or compromise may be made without *notice* to class members and *court approval.*

(1) Settlement Before Certification

If the purpose of the settlement is to *resolve class claims*, then Rule 23 applies and the court must scrutinize class certification and perform a full examination of the fairness of the proposed settlement. If the settlement purports to *settle only individual claims of the class representatives*, the court is not required to perform a fairness review.

(2) Objections by Class Members

A class member can object to the adequacy of the settlement but cannot subsequently *withdraw* the objection without court approval.

(3) Protections Under the Class Action Fairness Act

(a) Coupon Settlements

The court can approve a settlement that provides class members with coupons for goods or services from the defendant *after a hearing and determination that the settlement is fair.*

(b) Protection Against Loss by Class Members

A court can approve a settlement that is less than the amount that some class members paid in attorneys' fees if supported by a written finding that the *nonmonetary benefits substantially outweigh the monetary loss.*

(c) Protection Against Discrimination Based on Geographic Location

A court cannot approve a settlement that provides larger payouts for some class members based solely on geographic location.

(d) Notification of Federal and State Officials

Defendants must provide notice of proposed settlements to identified federal and state officials, and approval will not be issued until 90 days after the notice is served. A class member who shows that notice was not provided can elect not to be bound by the settlement.

j. Distribution of Proceeds of Action

Usually, a judgment settlement fund is created, with class members being notified to file claims to establish their shares.

k. Award of Attorneys' Fees

The legal fees incurred in obtaining a common fund for the benefit of class members are awarded out of the proceeds recovered by the class; the plaintiff who hired the attorney should not bear the entire legal expense.

7. Effect of Judgment in Class Action

The central issue is whether the judgment binds members of the class who were not before the court.

a. State Rules

In states retaining the distinctions among the three types of class ("true," "hybrid", and "spurious," as per the original Federal Rule), the "nature" of the action determines whether all members are bound.

b. Federal Rule

In federal courts, a valid judgment in any class action *binds all* class members *who do not request exclusion* ("opt out").

8. Defendant Class Actions

Suits may be brought against a defendant class under the same rules as for plaintiff class actions. There is a split among the courts whether such an action may be maintained under Rule 23(b)(2) (for injunctions or declaratory relief against the party opposing the class).

VI. DISCOVERY

A. INTRODUCTION

1. Purpose and Effect of Discovery Procedures

a. Obtaining Factual Information

A party who has effectively used discovery can go to trial with the best evidence for his contentions and knowledge of his adversary's case, thus avoiding delay or surprise, and the chance of a judgment resting on an accurate finding of fact is enhanced.

b. Narrowing and Simplifying

Discovery eliminates fictitious issues, claims, and defenses. Additionally, since pleadings are no longer the sole source of information, pleadings are simplified.

2. Problems in Discovery

Some concerns regarding discovery include *nonlitigation use* of discovery information, *harassing* an opponent into settlement, and *failure to respond* to requests in a timely or thorough manner.

B. BASIC DISCOVERY DEVICES

1. Prediscovery Disclosure

Federal Rule 26(a) requires certain disclosures to be made *before* formal discovery begins.

a. Early Conference of Counsel

Counsel are required to meet as soon as practicable to develop a proposed discovery plan that is then presented to the court. Generally, formal discovery cannot commence until *after* this meeting.

b. Disclosure of Materials Disclosing Party May Use

Prediscovery disclosure is required with respect to witnesses and documents that the disclosing party may use to support its claims or defenses. Materials that are to be used *solely for impeachment purposes* are not subject to disclosure.

c. Material to Be Disclosed

Each party is required to disclose:

(i) The ***names and, if known, addresses and phone numbers*** of persons with discoverable information that the disclosing party may use to support its claim or defense;

(ii) Copies or descriptions of ***all documents*** that the party possesses which it may use to support its claim or defense;

(iii) A ***computation of damages*** and the ***documents*** on which the computation is based; and

(iv) Any insurance agreement that might cover the claim.

d. Timing of Disclosures

These disclosures are to be made at or within 14 days after the early meeting of counsel and must be signed by an attorney.

e. Sanctions for Failure to Disclose

A party failing to disclose is subject to sanctions, such as a prohibition against using the undisclosed material as evidence.

2. Depositions

A deposition is an examination of a witness under oath in the presence of a court reporter. Parties have the right to be represented by counsel, who may examine and cross-examine the witness. Subject to deferral until a discovery plan is discussed, a party may take a deposition ***at any stage*** of a pending action after the parties' early discovery conference, but ***before*** an action is filed (or while an appeal is pending) a deposition may be taken only by leave of court ***to perpetuate testimony.***

a. Numerical Cap

Under the Federal Rules, each side may take only 10 depositions and a witness may be deposed only once. Each deposition is limited to one seven-hour day. These limitations may be changed by the parties' stipulation or by court order.

b. Compulsory Appearance of Witness

Witnesses must appear at a deposition when served with a ***subpoena.*** However, no subpoena is needed for an ***adverse party.***

c. Notice to Parties

Before taking a deposition, the party must give written notice to ***every other party***, including the deponent. The notice must include the time and place of the deposition and must do so ***reasonably*** in advance of the deposition. A ***nonparty witness*** is notified by a subpoena.

d. Production of Documents

The notice or subpoena may direct the witness to bring specified documents to the deposition, in which case 30-day notice is required.

e. Questioning of Deponent

Examination of deponents is usually ***oral***, but the questions may be ***written.*** If a witness ***objects*** to a question and refuses to answer it, the examining party may seek a court order compelling an answer.

f. Review of Transcript

If requested before completion of the deposition, a deponent is entitled to review and correct the transcript of his testimony. In federal court, other means of transcription (*e.g.*, videotape) may be used if the party noticing the deposition so chooses.

g. **Use of Deposition Testimony at Trial**

Statements in depositions are hearsay and thus are usually inadmissible *except* when used: (i) by one party against an adverse party as an *admission*; (ii) for *impeachment purposes*; or (iii) when the *deponent is unavailable.*

3. **Interrogatories**

Interrogatories are written questions *from one party to another* requiring written responses.

a. **Who Must Answer**

Parties are obliged to answer; a nonparty witness is not subject to interrogatories.

b. **Numerical Limit**

Interrogatories are limited to 25 per party, including subparts, but that limit may be changed by stipulation or court order.

c. **Duty to Respond**

A party must respond (or object) to interrogatories within 30 days of their service with all the information under her control (*i.e.*, in her files or by questioning employees). A *motion to compel* is available for incomplete or evasive answers.

4. **Requests for Admissions**

This is a device that imposes a duty on the party served to acknowledge facts not in doubt which thus need not be proved at trial. A request for admission may be served by any party *on any other party.*

a. **Subject of Request**

A request may ask for the admission of the *genuineness* of a document, the truth of factual allegations, or the applicability of legal concepts to facts. The admissions requested may include *conclusions of law*, *ultimate facts* (under Federal Rules), matters of opinion, or facts that are outside the responding party's knowledge.

b. **Appropriate Responses**

A requested admission, if made, binds the responding party in the present action. A party may always *deny*, but may be liable for full costs of proof if the denial is unjustified. Refusal to respond at all is rarely justified. If no timely response is made, the matter is deemed *admitted.*

c. **Withdrawal or Amendment**

The court may allow withdrawal or amendment of an admission when it would promote presentation of the merits.

5. **Requests for Inspection of Documents and Other Things**

A party can seek production from another party of *documents* (*e.g.*, writings, charts, etc.), *electronically stored information* (*e.g.*, recordings or images), and *tangible items.* Examination of the items may include testing and sampling of materials, entering onto the property of a party, or accessing a party's electronic information system (*e.g.*, computer).

a. **Making Request for Inspection**

A party may serve a request without prior court order or a showing of good cause unless the other party objects. In federal practice, a request may be served at any time after the Rule 26(f) conference; some states are more restrictive. Some showing of *necessity* is generally required for *inspection of premises.*

b. **Designation of Items**

The description of the items to be produced must be clear enough to allow a person of ordinary intelligence to know what is sought. The request must also specify the *time, place, and manner* of making the inspection.

c. **Form for Producing Electronically Stored Information**

A party can specify in her request the form in which the electronically stored information is to be produced, although the responding party may object to using the designated form. If the party does not make such a request, the producing party may choose the form so long as it is reasonably usable.

d. **Objection to Requests**

Written objections to requests must be filed within 30 days after service of a request.

e. **"Inaccessible" Electronically Stored Information**

A responding party does not have to produce electronically stored information if it can show the court that the information is from an inaccessible source because of undue burden or cost; however, the court may still order production for good cause.

f. **Organization of Produced Materials**

In federal court and some state courts, the responding party must produce requested materials either as they are normally kept or organized to correspond to the request.

g. **Failure to Respond**

A failure to respond exposes a party to sanctions, including the striking of pleadings and a determination of the facts on the assumption that inspection would have provided the requesting party with persuasive evidence.

h. **Materials in Possession of Nonparties**

Under the Federal Rules and in some states, a subpoena can order a nonparty to permit inspection and copying of documents in its control or inspection of premises. Some states require a showing of good cause as a condition precedent to issuance of the subpoena.

6. **Medical Examinations**

In federal court, a court order is required to examine a party whose physical or mental condition is in issue. The *condition in issue* must be raised directly by the pleadings or in discovery. A showing of *good cause* is required, and *only parties* (or persons in the custody or control of parties) are subject to examination.

a. **Qualifications of Examiner**

In federal court, examinations may be conducted by any *suitably licensed or certified examiner*, not always a medical doctor. The examiner is usually selected by the party requesting the examination. Upon objection, the court may choose an impartial examiner.

b. Type of Procedure

If the sought information is important, a novel or even uncomfortable procedure may be allowed, as long as it is reasonably safe.

c. Presence of Counsel or Other Observer

Absent compelling circumstances, a *majority of federal courts* do *not allow* the presence of counsel, a third party, or an unattended videotape machine. Other courts permit observers, while still others decide on a case-by-case basis.

d. Copies of Reports

Upon request, an examinee has the right to receive a copy of the examiner's report. However, if such a request is made, the examinee *waives* the doctor-patient privilege as to any previous examination of the same condition by the patient's own physician. Remember that even without a request, a plaintiff in a personal-injury case waives the privilege as to the injury at issue.

7. Duty to Supplement Discovery Responses

a. Federal Practice

Prior discovery disclosures or responses must be supplemented if in some *material respect they are incomplete* or incorrect or if *additional or corrective information* has been obtained since the disclosure or response was made.

b. State Practice Compared

In states not following the Federal Rules, *supplemental interrogatories* or other procedures may be used to obtain the same information.

C. SCOPE OF DISCOVERY

1. Relation of Discovery to Proof

Usually, discovery may inquire into all nonprivileged information *relevant* to the *claim or defense of any party* (whether or not admissible as proof), although a few jurisdictions limit discovery to admissible evidence. Federal courts, becoming increasingly uneasy with broad discovery, have moved to limit it.

a. Scope of Discovery in Federal Court

Note that the 2000 amendments changed the scope of relevancy to "any party's claim or defense," thus prohibiting parties from using discovery to develop new claims or defenses.

b. Proportionality Requirement

The general definition of the scope of discovery in federal court now requires that it be "proportional to the needs of the case," taking into account several factors including importance of the issues, the amount at stake, the parties' resources, and the relative weight of burden and expense in relation to likely benefit.

2. **Scope of Relevant Material**

   a. **Meaning of Relevance**

   Information is relevant if it tends to make the existence of any fact that is of consequence to the determination of the action more probable or less probable than it would be without the evidence.

   b. **Relation to Claims and Defenses**

   Although the scope of federal discovery has been narrowed, it need only relate to the claims and defenses and is not limited to information needed to satisfy a party's burden of proof.

   c. **Information About Witnesses**

   The identity and location of witnesses is discoverable, as is information relating to a witness's *credibility*.

   d. **Insurance Coverage**

   Although not admissible, such coverage is discoverable in most jurisdictions.

   e. **Financial Status**

   A defendant's ability to satisfy a judgment is usually not discoverable. However, in some cases, both a defendant's and plaintiff's financial conditions are pertinent and thus discoverable.

3. **Privilege**

   Privileged material is excluded from obligatory disclosure through discovery. The attorney-client privilege is the most frequently invoked.

   a. **Requirements for Attorney-Client Privilege**

   The privilege applies only to communications made *in confidence while seeking legal advice from a lawyer*, and it is *waivable* by the client.

   b. **Federal vs. State Law**

   In federal court, when a federal claim or defense is involved, absent contrary provision the common law as interpreted by the federal courts governs claims of privilege; if a state-law claim or defense is involved, privilege issues are determined in accordance with state law.

   c. **Corporate Clients**

   Questions as to which corporate employees are covered by the attorney-client privilege may be determined, depending on the jurisdiction, by the older *control-group* test or by the newer **Upjohn** *test*, which potentially extends coverage to *any* employee if certain requirements are met.

   d. **Other Communicational Privileges**

   Other privileges protect certain communications between spouses, doctors and patients, priests and penitents, and psychotherapists (even if not doctors) and patients.

4. **Trial Preparation Materials**

   a. **"Work Product"**—*Hickman v. Taylor* **rule**

   Materials prepared by or under the direction of a party or her attorney in anticipation of litigation are subject to discovery *only if* the seeker can show substantial need and an inability to obtain equivalent material by other means; *i.e.*, it is a *qualified privilege.*

(1) Matters Protected

The Federal Rule covers any materials prepared *in anticipation of litigation or for trial.* Materials such as accident reports might not be protected if they are regularly made and usable for purposes other than litigation.

(2) Special Protection for Mental Impressions of an Attorney

Federal Rule 26(b)(3) and similar state provisions protect absolutely against disclosure of the mental impressions and legal theories of an attorney.

(3) Trial Preparation by Nonlawyers

The work-product privilege also applies to the work product of claims agents, insurers, sureties, indemnitors, and some statements of witnesses to lawyers.

b. Expert Reports

Experts may help the lawyer prepare for trial, or may testify at trial to support the party's case.

(1) Nontestifying Experts

Facts known to and opinions held by nontestifying experts are discoverable only in exceptional circumstances. When discovery is ordered, the discovering party must pay a portion of the expert's fee. District courts are split on whether the identity of nontestifying experts is discoverable.

(2) Testifying Experts

At least *90 days before trial*, each party must identify each person that the party will call as an expert witness and must provide a detailed report of the witness's testimony and the basis therefor, qualifications, and compensation.

(3) Unaffiliated Experts

On occasion, experts who have not consented to assist either side may be compelled by subpoena to testify, although they probably must be paid a fee.

D. PROTECTIVE ORDERS

1. Introduction

The purpose of a protective order is to *prevent undue burdens* due to discovery.

2. Requirement of Good Cause

A protective order should be granted only on a showing of good cause by the party seeking protection.

a. Confidential Information

A protective order may be entered to protect trade secrets or other confidential research, development, or commercial information.

(1) Showing Required

The party seeking protection must show that the information has in fact been held in confidence and that a specific harm is likely to flow from discovery of the information.

(2) Format—"Umbrella" Orders

A common type of order allows the producing party to designate material as confidential, and requires the other party to hold it in confidence and use it only for trial preparation.

b. Inconvenient Place of Examination

Protective orders may be issued if a deposition has been scheduled at an inconvenient place; to prevent a litigant from conducting a deposition that is annoying, embarrassing, or oppressive; and to limit discovery that is burdensome in relation to the importance of the case.

E. FAILURE TO DISCLOSE OR TO COMPLY WITH DISCOVERY

1. Order Compelling Response—Necessary Prerequisite

Before discovery sanctions can be imposed, a party seeking discovery must usually obtain an order compelling it.

a. Exception—Failure to Respond or Disclose

If a party *completely* fails to respond to a valid discovery request or to attend his deposition, sanctions can *immediately* be sought. Failure to make Rule 26(a) disclosures or to supplement disclosures and discovery responses allows the court to *exclude undisclosed materials* in addition to imposing other sanctions.

b. Conference Before Motion

Before filing a motion to compel, a party must confer with the opposing party in an effort to secure compliance with discovery.

2. Sanctions for Failure to Comply with Order

The court has discretion in choosing from among a variety of options available as sanctions, including orders that establish facts in favor of the party seeking discovery, disallowance of claims or defenses, grant of dismissal or default, or a finding that a party is in contempt.

3. Culpability Necessary for Sanctions

Due process limits the power of the court to impose sanctions that affect the merits of a case. The court will ordinarily consider whether the party was guilty of willfulness, bad faith, or other fault. If a lawyer's misconduct is involved, most courts will consider the extent of the *client's involvement* in the litigation before imposing harsh sanctions on the client. In the case of loss, because of failure to take reasonable steps to preserve it, of electronically stored information that should have been preserved in anticipation or conduct of litigation, if the court finds intent to deprive another party of the information it may presume, or may instruct the jury to presume, that the information was unfavorable, or may dismiss or enter default.

4. Imposition of Costs of Discovery Proceedings

The losing party generally bears the opposing party's expense of making or defending against a motion to compel. A party who fails to obey a discovery order may be required to pay the other party's costs of seeking sanctions. A party who fails to attend a deposition that he scheduled bears any expenses related to that deposition.

5. Contempt Power

Contempt is an appropriate sanction *only* if the party or witness refuses to make disclosure in *defiance of a prior court order.* The contempt sanction may be *civil* (party may purge himself of the contempt by providing the information) or *criminal.* *No* contempt sanction of either kind may be used to compel a *medical examination.*

6. Distinguish—Sanctions for Improper Certification

Federal Rule 26(f) makes the attorney's signature on a discovery paper a certification that the material in it *is supported by law*, *has a proper purpose*, and *is reasonable*. If a paper is signed in violation of the Rule, the court is to sanction the offending person.

F. APPELLATE REVIEW OF DISCOVERY ORDERS

1. Orders Usually Not Appealable

Most discovery orders are not final, and thus in most jurisdictions are not appealable. Neither are discovery orders considered collateral to the main action, nor are they injunctions.

2. Modes of Review

a. Certified Appeal

In federal practice, a trial court may certify an important discovery question to the appellate court.

b. Mandamus or Prohibition

These writs may be issued by an appellate court (in both state and federal practice) in *extraordinary situations* to correct or prevent a trial judge's *abuse of discretion* in discovery.

c. Review After Judgment

Failure of the trial court to compel effective disclosure *may* be the basis for reversal if the ruling was *prejudicial.*

d. Sanction as Final

If the sanction is in the form of a final disposition (*e.g.*, judgment of dismissal), the judgment is final and appealable.

e. Review of Contempt Order

A civil-contempt order against a party is not final and appealable; a conviction of criminal contempt *is* final and appealable.

G. USE OF DISCOVERY AT TRIAL

1. Statements of Adversary

Admissions by a party in a deposition or in response to interrogatories are admissible and, in some cases, are conclusive proof of facts admitted. The *right to object* is retained at all times by the party whose statement is used at trial.

2. Statements of Other Witnesses

Prior inconsistent statements of a witness may be shown by a deposition admitted at trial. A *deponent's unavailability* also permits a deposition to be admitted. A *party's own deposition* may be used by the party if he is *genuinely* unavailable for trial.

H. PRIVATE INVESTIGATION

Civil litigants may conduct their own private investigation of the facts; *i.e.*, they are *not* required to use formal discovery procedures. Such litigants may use proof obtained, even by tortious means, since they are not subject to Fourth Amendment limits on searches.

VII. SUMMARY JUDGMENT

A. INTRODUCTION

1. Purpose

Summary judgment enables a court to look behind the pleadings to determine whether some *contentions are so lacking in substance* that judgment can be rendered against the party making them without the expense and delay of a full trial.

2. Impact on Right to Trial

Although the traditional belief is that a litigant has a right to test her claims at trial, there is no such right when there is no genuine factual dispute.

3. Trend Favoring Use of Summary Judgment

The advent of notice pleading has helped the motion for summary judgment supplant the motion to dismiss.

B. STANDARD FOR GRANT OF SUMMARY JUDGMENT

The court is to grant summary judgment if there is *no genuine dispute as to any material fact*.

1. Relation to Standard for Judgment as a Matter of Law

The Supreme Court has stated that in federal court the standard is the same at the summary-judgment stage as at the judgment as a matter of law stage.

a. Moving Party with Burden of Proof

If the moving party has the burden on the issue, summary judgment should be granted only if the jury could not reasonably disbelieve the moving party's evidence.

b. Opposing Party with Burden

If the moving party does not have the burden, summary judgment should be granted only if the opposing party does not present sufficient evidence to permit a jury reasonably to find for her.

2. Case-by-Case Determination

The evaluation of motions for summary judgment is done case by case, based not on specific rules but rather on general principles.

a. All Reasonable Inferences in Favor of Opposing Party

The court makes all reasonable inferences in favor of the opposing party, and views evidence in the light most favorable to that party.

b. Court May Not "Weigh" Evidence

The court may not judge the relative persuasiveness of conflicting versions of events.

c. **Role of Higher Burden of Proof**

The Supreme Court has held that when a party will bear a higher burden of proof at trial, that standard should be used in deciding the motion for summary judgment.

d. **Witness Credibility**

Witness credibility is not ordinarily assessed in deciding a motion for summary judgment.

(1) **Uncontradicted Interested Witness**

Even if uncontradicted, an *interested* witness's testimony will usually not be sufficient to support summary judgment because it might not be believed by the jury.

(2) **Disinterested Witness**

Some courts have held that an uncontradicted affidavit of a *disinterested* witness will support summary judgment for the party with the burden of proof.

e. **Motive, Intent, and State of Mind**

When mental state is at issue, summary judgment is usually *inappropriate.*

f. **"Slightest Doubt" Standard Contrasted**

The notion that summary judgment should be avoided whenever there was the "slightest doubt" about the outcome at trial has been *repudiated.*

C. PROCEDURE

1. Initial Showing

The court must first evaluate the moving party's showing to determine whether it justifies pretrial scrutiny of the evidence.

a. **Moving Party's Burden**

The moving party must show that there is no factual dispute and that he is entitled to judgment.

(1) **Moving Party with Burden of Proof**

If the moving party has the burden of proof, he must produce evidence such that *no reasonable jury* could find for the opponent.

(2) **Moving Party Without Burden of Proof**

The Supreme Court has rejected the early view that a moving party without the burden of proof must make a showing of the same strength as a party with the burden. The exact requirements are not clear, but a bald assertion that the opposing party lacks sufficient evidence is not enough; and the moving party should at least point to portions of the record showing the absence of factual disputes. In any event, a moving party without the burden need not (although it may) produce evidence affirmatively supporting a finding in its favor. In some cases, the content (or lack thereof) of the opposing party's required initial disclosures may be used to support the motion.

b. Opposing Party's Burden

If the moving party has not made the required initial showing, the opposing party technically need not make any showing in response. If the moving party has made an initial showing, the opponent has the burden of *coming forward with sufficient evidence* to support a jury verdict in his favor.

2. Notice

The opposing party is entitled to notice of the motion for summary judgment and must be given an opportunity to submit opposing materials.

3. Time for Motion

Unless otherwise provided by local rule or ordered by the court, parties may file summary-judgment motions at any time until 30 days after the close of all discovery.

4. Materials Considered on Motion

A court deciding a motion for summary judgment may consider *admissions* contained in the pleadings, *affidavits* made on personal knowledge, and *discovery materials.* Oral testimony is rarely used.

a. Admissibility

Materials considered in deciding a motion for summary judgment must generally be capable of admission as evidence, and the court will entertain objections to admissibility before considering the materials.

(1) Possible Relaxation for Opposing Party

The opposing party might not be held to the requirement of admissibility if it can show that it will have admissible evidence at trial.

5. Partial Summary Judgment

The court can grant summary judgment as to some but not all of the claims or defenses before it.

6. Inability to Provide Responsive Materials

The court may *continue* the hearing on the motion for summary judgment to allow time for the opposing party to obtain evidence. The evidence with respect to which the continuance is sought must be *material* to the motion and reasonably *obtainable.*

7. Appellate Review

The appellate court uses a *plenary standard* of review, giving no deference to the trial court decision.

a. Timing

If full summary judgment is not granted, review may be delayed until the final decision of the case.

b. Order Denying Motion

If summary judgment is mistakenly denied, the order is not reviewable until after trial, at which time it may be *harmless error* if the trial was properly conducted.

VIII. MANAGERIAL JUDGING, SETTLEMENT PROMOTION, AND ARBITRATION

A. PRETRIAL CONFERENCES AND MANAGERIAL JUDGING

1. Historical Background

The original Federal Rule 16 authorized a pretrial conference to be held shortly before trial for the purpose of organizing it. Amendments in the 1980s and 1990s provided for mandatory meet-and-confer sessions among the parties, more numerous pretrial conferences, discovery conferences, and a final pretrial conference.

2. Scheduling

Federal district courts are required, after consulting the parties, to enter a *scheduling order* within 90 days after a defendant's appearance and within 120 days after service of the complaint. This order sets time limits for joinder, amendments, discovery, and motions. A district may, by local rule, *exempt* certain types of cases inappropriate for the scheduling rule.

3. Discovery Control

Judges are required to limit discovery that is unduly cumulative, delayed, or burdensome.

a. Conference by Parties

At least 21 days before the Rule 16 scheduling conference or order, the parties are to hold a conference regarding the nature and basis of their claims and defenses and to develop a discovery plan. Within 14 days after the meeting, they are to submit a written report to the court. Cases exempted from the initial disclosure requirements are also exempt from the conference rule.

b. Court's Pretrial Order

Based on the parties' submission, the court is to enter an order limiting the time to complete discovery.

4. Issue Simplification

By the time a pretrial conference is held, the parties know more about their case and are in a better position to simplify the issues for trial. The court may not compel admissions, but may pressure parties to abandon unsupportable positions.

5. Settlement Promotion

Judges were once reluctant to become involved in settlement discussions, but Rule 16 now explicitly authorizes it.

a. No Power to Dictate Terms of Settlement

The court may suggest but not dictate the terms of settlement.

b. Ambiguity of Judicial Role

It is unclear how the judge's role in settlement comports with her usual role of deciding disputed matters according to legal standards. It is also unclear what role her pretrial opinion of the relative strengths of the cases should play.

c. Promotion of Alternative Dispute Resolution

The judge may discuss special procedures to assist in resolving the dispute at a pretrial conference when authorized by local rule or by statute.

6. **Final Pretrial Conference—Purpose**

The final pretrial conference seeks to resolve as much as possible before trial and to give notice of the subjects to be covered at trial.

a. **Required Pretrial Disclosures**

At least 30 days before trial, each party is to: (i) *disclose the names of witnesses* the party expects to present, (ii) *designate witnesses whose testimony will be presented by deposition*, and (iii) *identify documents and other exhibits* the party expects to offer.

b. **Topics Covered**

The *final pretrial order* encompasses the matters covered at the pretrial conference. It controls at trial and can be *modified only to prevent manifest injustice.*

7. **Sanctions**

Federal courts have *explicit authority* to use sanctions with regard to their pretrial supervision of cases.

B. **COURT-ANNEXED SETTLEMENT DEVICES**

To promote settlement, courts began experimenting with other ways of facilitating settlement.

1. **Mandated Alternative Dispute Resolution**

Under 1998 legislation, *federal district courts* must devise and implement an ADR program that all *civil* litigants must consider using in promoting a settlement. Each district must maintain a *panel of neutrals* to serve in ADR proceedings.

2. **Mediation**

Mediation involves a neutral third party who attempts to find a common ground on which the *parties can reach an agreement.* Since *formal legal rules are not binding* in mediation, the mediator can devise a solution that would not be available in litigation. Mediation procedures are also available in state courts.

3. **Early Neutral Evaluation**

This is an ADR device, used early in a case, that relies on an experienced neutral lawyer to advise the parties on their prospects after both sides have presented their positions.

4. **Summary Jury Trial**

Generally held after normal pretrial activities have concluded, an SJT is an abbreviated trial held before a jury summoned in the usual manner. Lawyers present summaries of the evidence at the SJT, which is usually *held in secret.* Occasionally, parties can stipulate that an SJT will be binding. Courts are split on the issue of compulsory participation.

5. **Court-Annexed Arbitration**

With consent of the parties, a federal court can refer any *civil* action for *nonbinding arbitration*, *except* cases involving *civil rights claims*, alleged *violations of constitutional rights*, or *damages exceeding $150,000.* Some states have also set up arbitration programs.

a. **Hearing**

The arbitration decision is based on a hearing at which the rules of evidence and procedure may be relaxed.

b. **Award**

The arbitrator's award ***becomes the judgment unless a trial de novo*** is demanded. The party who demands a trial may be required to ***reimburse*** the opposing party for certain costs if the party demanding trial does not receive a result more favorable than the award.

C. FORMAL OFFER-OF-JUDGMENT RULES

1. Federal Rule of Civil Procedure 68

a. Basic Provisions and Purpose

Federal Rule of Civil Procedure 68 provides that a defending party may offer to allow judgment to be entered against it on specified terms, with costs then accrued. The opposing party has 14 days in which to accept; if it does, the court clerk must enter judgment. If it does not accept and does not obtain a ***more favorable*** judgment, it must pay the costs incurred after the offer was made. The rule is generally regarded as intended to encourage settlements, but it applies only to formal, served offers and not to settlement offers made in negotiation.

b. Applicability

Rule 68's cost-shifting feature comes into play only if the offeree wins some recovery, but not more than the unaccepted offer. It does not apply if the offeror wins outright; in that case, usual cost provisions apply.

c. Effect on Liability for Attorneys' Fees

Rule 68 can affect parties' liability for attorneys' fees, as opposed to non-fee "costs," only if an applicable statute authorizes an award of attorneys' fees as part of "costs." An offeree otherwise entitled to a fee award who wins a judgment not better than an unaccepted offer loses its entitlement to post-offer attorneys' fees. But most courts hold that such an offeree, having obtained some recovery, is not liable for the offeror's post-offer fees.

d. No Mooting of Offeree's Claim by Non-Acceptance of Full-Satisfaction Rule 68 Offer

An unaccepted Rule 68 offer that would give an individual plaintiff all that it might legally gain in a judgment does not, given the Rule's language that an "unaccepted offer is considered withdrawn," moot either individual or putative class claims.

e. Other Key Features of Federal Rule 68

Four other significant features of Federal Rule 68 are (i) that successive offers are permissible; (ii) that it can apply in cases seeking other forms of relief than money damages; (iii) that it authorizes formal offers of damages after a judgment of liability; and (iv) that it is available only to parties defending against claims, not to claimants.

2. **State Offer Rules and Their Applicability to State-Law Claims in Federal Court**

State offer rules that differ from Federal Rule 68 have mostly been held inapplicable to defending parties' offers, which are governed by the federal rule. But when a state rule lets a claimant make a formal demand, and provides for cost or fee consequences if the defendant does not do better than the demand, such rules have generally been held applicable to state-law claims in federal court.

D. THE FEDERAL ARBITRATION ACT AND ITS IMPACT ON REGULATION OF ARBITRATION

1. Applicability of General Contract-Validity Provisions

The Federal Arbitration Act (FAA) of 1925 makes written arbitration provisions in contracts involving commerce "valid, irrevocable, and enforceable, save upon such grounds as exist at law or in equity for the revocation of any contract."

2. General Trend in Supreme-Court Decisions

Over the last few decades the Supreme Court has decided several cases on the FAA's impact on state- or federal-law provisions bearing on the enforceability of arbitration agreements. Generally these decisions have been favorable to upholding such agreements, including not just cases involving peer-to-peer agreements to arbitrate rather than adjudicate but also contracts of adhesion between the likes of consumers or employees and their service providers or employers.

3. Decisions Affecting Class Arbitration

Businesses often include in contracts provisions that both require arbitration rather than adjudication and specify that arbitration cannot take the form of a class proceeding, making arbitration on an individual basis the only avenue of redress for what may be a small claim. The Supreme Court has held that the FAA preempts state law holding waivers of class arbitration unconscionable. It has also held that an arbitration agreement waiving class-wide arbitration in a credit-card arbitration clause did not impermissibly limit plaintiffs' ability to pursue their federal antitrust claims.

IX. TRIAL

A. RIGHT TO TRIAL BY JURY

1. Source of Right

In federal courts, the right to a jury trial in civil actions at law is derived from the **Seventh Amendment** and, if that does not apply, the right may be provided by **Congress.** In **state courts**, the right to a jury trial in civil cases is **not** a due process right protected by the Fourteenth Amendment. However, there may be a federal statutory right to jury trial in state-court actions that are governed by federal law. Note that most **state constitutions** have provisions similar to the Seventh Amendment of the U.S. Constitution.

2. Cases in Which Right Exists

a. Basic Historical Test

The historical test used to determine whether a right to jury trial exists in civil cases in federal court is whether the claim involved is **legal or equitable** as those terms were understood in 1791 (when the Seventh Amendment became effective).

b. **Present Federal Standards for Right to Jury Trial**

The right was observed in English law courts but not in Chancery (equity). Modern actions that are *counterparts to actions at law* (*e.g.*, personal-injury claims) are triable to a jury. Actions that are *counterparts to equity suits* (*e.g.*, injunctions) do *not* give rise to a jury trial. Proceedings to enforce statutory rights in federal court are triable to a jury when the relief sought is a *legal remedy.*

c. **Declaratory Relief**

As a *statutorily created right*, declaratory relief is historically neither legal nor equitable. Generally, federal courts examine the underlying non-declaratory claim and permit a jury trial if that claim is triable by jury.

d. **Punitive Damages**

A federal civil jury's determination of punitive damages does not involve fact-finding within the Seventh Amendment, so that appellate review of a punitive damages award does not involve constitutionally impermissible reexamination of a jury finding.

3. **Proceedings in Which Right to Jury Applies in Part**

a. **Actions Joining Legal and Equitable Claims**

In federal court, actions involving both legal and equitable claims are to be structured to preserve a jury trial on issues common to the legal and equitable aspects of the case, even if the equitable aspects predominate. Some states are contra and allow nonjury disposition of minor legal matters under the equitable "clean-up" doctrine.

(1) **Priority of Issues at Trial**

The order in which issues are tried can be important because it may determine the outcome. In *federal* court, issues respecting a claim for legal relief ordinarily must be tried *first.* In *state* courts, the order is often within the *discretion* of the trial judge.

b. **Equitable Proceedings Seeking Legal Relief**

Federal courts focus on the *nature of the underlying claim* in determining the right to jury trial.

c. **Issues of Law and Fact for Same Claim**

Even when a right to jury trial exists, some issues may be questions of law for the judge while others are issues of fact for the jury. If the legal issue is dispositive, there is no jury trial.

4. **Right to Jury Trial Depends on Timely Demand**

a. **State Practice**

The right to jury trial usually must be exercised by a written demand at the time the case is set for trial; if demand is not timely made, the right is waived.

b. **Federal Practice**

In federal court, a jury must be demanded in writing not later than 14 days after service of the last pleading directed to the issue for which the jury is demanded.

5. When Jury Trials Are Discretionary with Court

A court may order a jury trial on any or all issues when the right *has been waived*, when a claim is not jury triable (with both parties' *consent*), or to obtain an *advisory verdict.*

B. SELECTION OF THE JURY

1. Summons of the Venire

Prospective jurors ("veniremen") are summoned by the court. The venire must be selected by a method that does not systematically exclude any religious, racial, ethnic, or political group.

2. Number of Jurors Required

The venire is usually at least two to three times larger than the number of jurors needed. Common law required a jury of 12. However, today *12 is not required* by either due process or the Seventh Amendment. In federal civil cases, there must be at least six. The Sixth Amendment *does* require at least six jurors in a *criminal* case, and some states also allow six jurors in *state civil trials*, but this depends entirely on state law.

3. Voir Dire Examination of Jurors

The examination of prospective jurors as to possible biases is known as voir dire.

a. Challenge for Cause

A prospective juror may be challenged if it appears that he or a member of his family has a financial interest in the litigation, or for other reasons indicating he will not be an impartial juror. There is *no limit* to the number of challenges for cause.

b. Peremptory Challenge

Each party is entitled to a limited number of challenges *without* a showing of cause, but peremptory challenges cannot be based on the juror's race or sex.

C. DISQUALIFICATION OF JUDGE

1. Grounds for Disqualification

Grounds include any basis that may affect a judge's impartiality; *e.g.*, personal bias, personal knowledge of facts, previous involvement as a lawyer, financial interest, or family relationship. The disqualifying reason must be based on *matters outside the courtroom.* A judge must disqualify herself if adequate grounds exist.

2. Procedure for Disqualification

a. Federal Practice

A party seeking disqualification files an affidavit of bias setting forth the necessary facts. If the facts are legally sufficient to disqualify the judge, she must excuse herself and reassign the case.

b. State Practice

Most states require an actual showing by affidavit on grounds for disqualification. In some states, each party has an absolute right to disqualify *one* judge by simply stating in an affidavit that a fair trial cannot be obtained before that judge.

D. ORDER OF TRIAL

1. Right to Speak First and Last

The general rule is that the party that has the ***burden of proof*** as to the principal issues (usually the plaintiff) speaks first and last. However, the trial judge usually has the discretion whether to accord that right.

2. Stages of Jury Trial

The normal sequence in a civil trial is plaintiff's opening statement; defendant's opening statement; presentation of direct evidence by plaintiff, with cross-examination of each witness by defendant, followed by re-direct and re-cross, whereupon ***plaintiff rests***; presentation of direct evidence by defendant, with cross-examination, re-direct, and re-cross and then ***defendant rests***; rebuttal evidence by plaintiff, and then by defendant; plaintiff's argument to jury; defendant's argument to jury; plaintiff's closing argument; instructions to jury by judge; and the jury verdict.

3. Nonjury Trial

In a nonjury trial, the order is usually the same as above until the evidence has been presented, whereupon the parties may propose specific findings of facts and conclusions of law to the court.

E. PRESENTATION OF EVIDENCE

1. Control over Presentation

The presentation of evidence is usually the responsibility of the parties and their counsel, although most courts give a judge discretion to call his own witnesses.

2. Rules of Evidence

Federal-court proceedings are governed by the Federal Rules of Evidence. Many states' rules follow the Federal Rules. Some states have their own evidence codes, while others rely on common-law rules.

3. Objections and Exceptions

Failure to object to admission of evidence waives the objection. If no objection is made to evidence that raises new issues, the pleadings (or pretrial order) are treated as if amended to include those issues (***amendment by proof***).

4. Burden of Producing Evidence

The plaintiff and defendant must offer sufficient evidence proving each element of the prima facie case or defense. Plaintiff's failure to provide such evidence entitles the defendant to a dismissal or judgment as a matter of law.

F. PRE-VERDICT MOTIONS

1. In General

At the close of proof, motions may be used to determine whether a party has carried the burden of producing evidence.

2. Jury Trial—Motion for Judgment as a Matter of Law (Directed Verdict)

Either party may make such a motion after the adversary has been fully heard with respect to the issue in question.

a. **Standard for Grant**

The standard looks to whether *the jury could reasonably find for the nonmoving party*. If the moving party has the burden of proof, the evidence favoring him must be of *such compelling strength* that the jury could not reasonably find for the opponent. If the party opposing the motion has the burden, that party must have *no substantial evidence* (no "scintilla" of evidence in some states) that would permit a jury to find in her favor.

b. **Case-by-Case Determination**

Evaluation is case-by-case, using general principles rather than fixed rules.

(1) **All Reasonable Inferences Indulged in Favor of Opposing Party**

The court is to view evidence in the *light most favorable to the opposing party*, and is to make all *reasonable inferences* in that party's favor.

(2) **Court May Not "Weigh" Evidence**

The court may not "weigh" conflicting versions of events as to persuasiveness.

(3) **Demeanor Evidence**

If the moving party has the burden of proof and relies on witnesses whom the jury could disbelieve, it is generally not entitled to judgment as a matter of law, even if there is no conflicting evidence. There is a possible exception for occasions when the witness is *disinterested* and *unimpeached.*

c. **Distinguish—Renewed Motion for Judgment as a Matter of Law**

In federal court, a party cannot make a renewed motion after an unfavorable verdict unless she moves for judgment as a matter of law after the opposing party was *fully heard on an issue* and before submission of the case to the jury. The same standard is used for both motions. Practical considerations relating to possible appellate dispositions may influence the trial judge to wait for the jury's verdict rather than granting a pre-verdict motion, and then to consider a renewed post-verdict motion.

3. **Jury Trial—Motion for Nonsuit**

In some states, the defendant may move for a nonsuit at the close of plaintiff's opening statement (or at close of plaintiff's proof) if the statement of proof reveals that plaintiff's case is *legally insufficient.*

4. **Nonjury Trial—Motion for Judgment as a Matter of Law**

In a nonjury trial, after a party has been fully heard with respect to an issue, the court may enter a judgment against that party if it finds the party's proof is *unpersuasive.* The motion is analogous to the common-law *demurrer* to the evidence. Today, some states call it a *motion to dismiss*, while in others it is a *motion for judgment.*

G. **ARGUMENT TO JURY**

1. **Time for Argument**

In federal practice and most state courts, counsels' arguments take place at the close of the evidence and *before* the jury receives the judge's instructions.

2. Right to Argue

Counsel have an absolute right to argument in a jury trial. However, the trial judge has discretion to control the duration and manner of argument.

3. Limitations on Argument

Counsels' comments must be *based on the evidence*, the argument must be within the limits of the *governing substantive law*, and counsel may *not appeal to the passions or prejudices* of the jurors.

H. INSTRUCTIONS TO JURY

1. In General

Before a jury deliberates, the judge instructs it on certain relevant matters.

2. Issues of Fact

A *judge* determines issues of *law* (*e.g.*, interpretation of statute), while a *jury* decides disputed issues of *fact.* Questions of fact are specific and pertain to past events.

3. Burden of Persuasion

a. Assigning the Burden

The judge must explain to the jury which party has the burden of persuasion concerning each issue of fact the jury must decide.

b. Degree of Persuasion

In a civil case, the usual burden of persuasion is by *preponderance of the evidence.* However, some issues such as fraud, duress, or undue influence must be shown by *clear and convincing proof.*

4. Comment on the Evidence

Generally, a judge may comment to the jury on the quality of the evidence presented.

5. Instructions Requested by Counsel

Although the responsibility for instructions rests with the judge, counsel has a duty to propose instructions that present the theory of the case. Proposed instructions must be *written* and served on opposing counsel. They must be filed by the close of evidence. Each party must be given the *opportunity to object* to an adversary's proposed instructions.

6. Appellate Review of Jury Instructions

Generally, errors in instructions are waived unless objections are timely made. Traditionally, courts have held that egregious ("*plain*") error may be reversible even without a timely objection, but some courts hold that there is no plain-error exception.

I. JURY DELIBERATION AND VERDICT

1. Types of Verdicts

a. General Verdict

The most common form of verdict, a general verdict, is a decision in favor of one party or the other, with amount of damages if claimant prevails.

b. Special Verdict

This verdict consists of the jury's *answers to specific factual questions* that it is instructed to decide; it is not a direct decision as to which party should prevail.

c. General Verdict with Written Questions

This verdict *combines the two forms* above. The jury makes a general decision as to which party should prevail on the law while simultaneously answering specific questions of fact. If there is an *inconsistency* between the *special findings and the general verdict*, a judge may ignore the verdict and enter judgment based on *the special findings.* However, inconsistency among the special findings usually requires a new trial.

2. Requirement of Unanimity

The general rule in federal and most state courts is that the jury must render a unanimous verdict unless the parties otherwise agree.

3. Jury Deliberation and Impeachment of Verdict

a. Standards of Jury Conduct

Only information presented at trial may be considered by the jury; any communication from the judge must be received in the *presence of counsel.* Each juror must make up his own mind; there can be no verdict of the average or by lots. *No coercion* by the judge is allowed.

b. Impeachment of Verdict for Juror Misconduct

At *common law*, juror misconduct had to be established by the testimony of a person *other than* a juror. The federal rule today is that a juror may testify to any "extraneous prejudicial information" or "outside influence." Some states allow jurors to testify to *any* improper influence, either inside or outside the jury room.

c. Usually No Impeachment for Matters "Internal" to Jury's Deliberations

The Supreme Court has refused to allow verdict impeachment for use of intoxicants during jury deliberations, or for information revealed in deliberations making it appear that a juror had not responded honestly to questions during voir dire. It has, however, allowed impeachment for reliance during deliberations on racial stereotypes or animus.

d. Announcement of Verdict

The verdict must be announced in open court. At the request of either party, the jury may be *polled.* If the verdict is incomplete, the court may direct the jury to continue its deliberations.

J. MOTIONS AFTER VERDICT OR JUDGMENT

1. Renewed Motion for Judgment as a Matter of Law (Judgment N.O.V.)

A renewed motion for judgment as a matter of law is granted after a verdict when the trial judge concludes that there is *no substantial evidence* supporting the decision.

a. Procedural Requirements

In federal practice, a renewed motion can be entered *only* on motion of a *party*; in some states it can be entered *by the court* sua sponte. The federal rule requires the motion to be made within 28 days after judgment was entered on the verdict; state requirements vary.

(1) Prior Motion

In federal court, a renewed motion cannot be considered unless the moving party made a motion for judgment as a matter of law after the opposing party had been fully heard on the issue raised by the motion.

2. Motion for New Trial

A trial judge has the power to order a new trial on all or some of the contested factual issues.

a. Grounds for Motions—Jury Trial

A federal court may order a new trial in a jury case "for any reason for which a new trial has heretofore been granted in an action at law in federal court." Some state statutes are more explicit in specifying when a new trial is appropriate. Appropriate grounds include *prejudicial misconduct*, such as improper jury argument. Prejudicial error is *waived* if known and not raised prior to verdict. Some other grounds are surprise, newly discovered or improper evidence, verdict contrary to law, and a verdict contrary to the evidence.

b. Grounds for Motion—Nonjury Trial

In a nonjury trial, such a motion may be granted on grounds of newly discovered evidence, erroneous findings of fact, and/or error in the conduct of the trial.

c. Procedural Requirements

A federal court may order a new trial on its own motion; some states require a party to make the motion. In federal practice, the motion must be served not later than 28 days after the entry of judgment; state time limits vary.

d. Order

In nonjury cases, a court may order a full or partial new trial; in jury cases, the court must grant or deny the motion but may do so in parts or on conditions. In federal court, a judge need not specify grounds on which the new trial is granted; in some states, grounds must be stated. Grounds include *excessive or inadequate damages and insufficiency of proof.*

(1) Conditional New Trial

A *remittitur* is an order for a new trial unless plaintiff consents to a *reduction* of the damage award. An *additur* (not allowed in federal court) orders a new trial unless defendant consents to an *increase* in the verdict amount.

3. Motion to Alter or Amend Judgment

This motion is used to reopen judgments in both jury and nonjury cases and is used to correct *errors of law only.* Such a motion is subject to the same time limits as a motion for a new trial.

4. Motion for Relief from Judgment

Such a motion may be made in federal court to correct a clerical error (no time limit); or within one year on the grounds of mistake, inadvertence, or surprise; excusable neglect; newly discovered evidence; fraud or misconduct; or within a reasonable time on grounds of void judgment, change of circumstances, and for any other reason justifying relief. State rules vary.

a. Distinguish Independent Suit to Set Aside Judgment

Such a suit is an equitable proceeding usually based on *jurisdictional defects* or *fraud.* The independent suit may be filed in a different court while a motion for relief from a judgment is made to the court that entered the judgment. Grounds for an independent suit are narrower and more strictly applied. Relief in federal court is authorized only *"to prevent a grave miscarriage of justice."*

5. Coram Nobis

Abolished in federal courts, the common-law writ of coram nobis is still available in some states. It is *cautiously applied* and is granted only when it is absolutely clear that a fact previously determined to be true is false and that the fact was crucial to the outcome of the case.

X. APPEAL

A. RIGHT TO APPEAL

1. Status as Right

At *common law*, there was no right to appeal; a writ of error was discretionary with the court. Also, the Due Process Clause does not guarantee a right of appeal, at least in civil cases. However, the right to appeal is *statutorily created* in every state, and federal courts have a general right of appeal.

2. Waiver of Right

The right of appeal may be lost through an express waiver, an untimely assertion, voluntary compliance with a judgment, or acceptance of benefits under the judgment.

B. COURTS OF REVIEW

1. The Federal System

Most appeals from district courts and proceedings to review decisions by federal administrative agencies are taken to one of the 13 United States Courts of Appeals. The United States Supreme Court has limited original jurisdiction, and primarily hears appeals from district courts (in very limited circumstances), the United States Courts of Appeals (by writ of certiorari or certification), and state courts (must involve federal law and the litigant must have exhausted state-court appeal procedures).

C. APPELLATE PROCEDURE

1. Filing of Appeal

In the federal system, an appeal is commenced by filing a *notice of appeal* in the appellate or trial court within 30 days after entry of judgment (60 days if the United States is a party). State rules vary. In any case, time limits are jurisdictional and usually *cannot be waived.*

2. Appeal Bonds

An appeal bond must generally be filed to secure the adversary's costs if the judgment is affirmed. Assurance that a judgment will be satisfied if affirmed may also have to be given by posting a *supersedeas bond*, which keeps the judgment from taking effect pending appeal.

3. **Record on Appeal**

Review on appeal is usually limited to the trial record.

4. **Stay of Proceedings Below**

While an appeal from a final judgment is pending, the trial court generally has *no power* to alter or vacate its judgment, and very limited power to make any other order affecting the rights of the parties with respect to the case on appeal.

D. RULINGS SUBJECT TO APPEAL

1. **Final-Decision Requirement**

   a. **General Rule**

   At *common law*, a writ of error could be taken only from a final judgment—*i.e.*, judgment that stated the outcome of the proceedings and manifested that the proceedings were complete. Now, the final-decision rule is the basic rule, but it is subject to exceptions.

   b. **Jurisdictional Character of Rule**

   The final-decision rule is jurisdictional in that it *cannot be waived.*

2. **Exceptions to Final-Decision Requirement**

   a. **Partial Final Decisions**

   If multiple claims or parties are involved in an action, an order disposing of fewer than all claims is usually not a final judgment unless the trial court enters a partial final judgment (when that is authorized).

   b. **Review of Equitable Remedies**

   In early equity practice, the rule was not applied because personal orders (*e.g.*, injunctions), if erroneous, might result in irreversible consequences. Thus, immediate appellate review was permitted. Modern practice preserves the right to interlocutory review from orders that might result in irreparable consequences, *e.g.*, grant or denial of a preliminary injunction.

   c. **Ruling on Remand of Case Under Class Action Fairness Act**

   An order to remand a case to state court after removal to federal court under the Class Action Fairness Act is reviewable by the court of appeals if application is made "not more than 10 days" after entry of the order.

   d. **Liability Determination in Removed Multiparty, Multiforum Cases**

   An appeal of a district court order determining liability and certifying intent to remand to state court a case under the Multiparty, Multiforum Trial Jurisdiction Act must be taken within 60 days after entry of the order.

   e. **Discretionary Review**

   Interlocutory appeals are also permitted in the federal system when the *trial court certifies* that determination of a controlling question of law would speed the ultimate resolution of the case, *and* the court of appeals *grants leave* to appeal. Appellate jurisdiction extends to any question included in the certified order and is not limited to the specific question formulated by the district judge.

f. Orders Regarding Class Certification

Such orders are immediately reviewable if application for review is made within 14 days. Whether to accept the application is completely within the appellate court's discretion and does not require district-court certification.

g. Collateral Orders

In federal court, an immediate appeal is permitted from orders as to collateral matters if (i) the issue the order concerns is an important one that is completely separate from the merits of the underlying case; (ii) deferred review would effectively destroy appellant's rights; and (iii) the trial court has made its final decision on the challenged issue. The collateral-order exception is limited to a *small class of cases.*

h. Practical Construction of "Finality"

The United States Supreme Court has held that the final decision rule should be construed practically, not technically.

E. SCOPE OF APPELLATE REVIEW

1. In General

Appellate review does not extend to retrying facts or supplanting the trial judge's decision in discretionary matters.

2. Findings of Fact Subject to Limited Review

a. Jury Verdicts

The role of the appellate court is to oversee the jury's adherence to the law. Verdicts must be supported by *substantial evidence.*

b. Judicial Findings in Nonjury Trials

A judge's findings in a nonjury trial may be set aside if in *clear error.* Note that this is a less restrictive test, permitting reversal more often than the test for jury verdicts.

c. "Fact" and "Law" Distinguished

Only findings of fact are entitled to deference. *Errors of law* (*e.g.*, improper jury instructions, erroneous conclusions of law by judge) are reviewed de novo and, if not harmless, result in reversal. The distinction between law and fact can be difficult, and there is no satisfactory test.

3. Review of Discretionary Rulings

A trial judge is entrusted by law with discretion as to certain matters, especially procedural questions. An appellate court will not reverse such decisions absent a clear *abuse of discretion.*

4. "Harmless Error" Standard

The general rule is that an appellate court will not reverse any judgment unless the trial court's error was *prejudicial* (*i.e.*, affected substantial rights of the parties) or the error was *egregious.*

5. **Waiver of Objections in Lower Court**

   a. **General Rule**

   An appellate court will not reverse a judgment to correct any error that might have been avoided or corrected if the appellant had made a timely objection in the trial court.

   b. **Exceptions**

   An appellate court may review despite the lack of a timely objection if: (i) the trial court lacked *subject-matter jurisdiction*, or (ii) error is so clear and fundamental that it would be *unjust* to let the judgment stand.

6. **Trial de Novo**

   Sometimes legislatively authorized for appeals from state courts of limited jurisdiction and informal procedures such as small-claims courts, this is, in effect, a new trial in a court of general jurisdiction.

F. **APPELLATE REVIEW BY EXTRAORDINARY WRIT**

1. **Prerogative Writs**

   The available writs, depending on the court system, are:

   (i) *Mandamus*—an order directing a judge to perform her legal duty; and

   (ii) *Prohibition*—an order enjoining a judge from conduct exceeding her lawful authority.

2. **Source of Power to Issue Writs**

   State-court writs are usually based on common-law practice. Federal courts are statutorily empowered to issue prerogative writs.

3. **Discretionary Character of Writ**

   The issuance of a prerogative writ is always discretionary with the appellate court. There is *no right* to a hearing.

4. **Grounds for Issuance**

   A writ may issue for abuse of discretion, excess of jurisdiction, or refusal to exercise jurisdiction. There must be a *need for immediate review*, *i.e.*, when petitioner has no right to a present appeal and would suffer undue hardship or substantial prejudice if review was delayed until after a final judgment.

5. **Common Uses of Writs**

   The courts of appeals use discretionary writs to correct erroneous denials of jury trial, to prevent the improper delegation of judicial power, and to prevent unlawful remand to state court.

6. **Supervisory Mandamus**

   In rare circumstances, mandamus may be used to resolve *issues of first impression* that may be important in a significant number of cases.

7. **Availability**

   The increased availability of these writs in some states makes them equivalent to a device for seeking review of an interlocutory order.

XI. PRECLUSIVE EFFECTS OF JUDGMENTS

A. INTRODUCTION

1. In General

Preclusion has two main components: claim preclusion and issue preclusion.

2. Claim Preclusion (Also Called Res Judicata)

A final judgment on a claim or cause of action *precludes reassertion of that claim* or cause of action in a subsequent suit. If the judgment was for plaintiff, there is a *merger* of the claim in the judgment; if judgment was for defendant, it is a *bar* against plaintiff's suing again on the same claim.

3. Issue Preclusion (Also Called Collateral Estoppel)

A decision regarding an *issue of fact* may be binding in later litigation between the same parties, or sometimes against a prior party (but usually not against a prior nonparty).

4. Purposes

The purpose of the res judicata doctrine is to avoid the time and expense of multiple litigation on the same matter, and it stabilizes the result of adjudication by preventing inconsistent outcomes.

B. CLAIM PRECLUSION

1. In General

Before any judgment can have claim-preclusive effect it must be final, "on the merits" (a prerequisite often taken much too literally), and valid.

2. Policy Basis

Litigants should be compelled to litigate their entire claim their first time in court, for policy reasons related to judicial efficiency, prevention of vexation of defendants, and consistency.

a. Effect

The effect of claim preclusion may be to foreclose related claims that were never litigated because they were never raised in the first litigation.

3. Meaning of Claim—Breadth of Preclusion

Unless the claim in the second suit is the *"same,"* claim preclusion does not apply (although issue preclusion might).

a. Traditional Tests

Traditionally, the courts applied preclusion when the second claim involved the *same primary right and duty*, turned on essentially the *same evidence*, or *merely changed the legal theory.*

b. Modern Approach—Transactional Test

Under the Restatement, claim preclusion applies to all or part of the transaction or series of connected transactions out of which the action arose. Preclusion of a related claim that was omitted in a previous proceeding is referred to as the rule against "claim splitting."

    c.   **Claims by or Against Different Parties**

        Such claims are *usually not foreclosed* by claim preclusion, although it may apply if the parties are in privity.

4.   **"Final"**

    a.   **Effect of Appeal**

        Whether a judgment on appeal is final for claim-preclusion purposes is determined by the *law of the jurisdiction* in which the judgment was rendered.

    b.   **Modifiable Judgments**

        Such judgments (*e.g.*, alimony awards, child custody) are preclusive *until modified.*

    c.   **Conflicting Judgments**

        If two judgments conflict, usually the *later in time* controls.

5.   **"On the Merits"**

    A judgment is "on the merits" if the claim has been tried and determined, and includes dispositions such as summary judgment, directed verdict, nonsuit, etc. Note that a *dismissal* that does *not* relate to the merits (*e.g.*, for lack of jurisdiction) does not bar subsequent action, although *some non-"merits" dispositions* such as for misconduct in litigation (*e.g.*, as a sanction for discovery abuse), defaults, and settlements *can have claim-preclusive effect*. The "on the merits" phrase can be dangerously misleading, and the Restatement (Second) of judgments does not use it. In any event, it should not be taken too literally.

6.   **"Valid"**

    A judgment is valid *unless* the court lacked subject-matter or territorial *jurisdiction*, or notice to defendant did not conform to *due process* requirements. However, if the question of validity was *litigated* in the original action, that determination is usually preclusive.

7.   **Attachment Jurisdiction**

    Attachment jurisdiction (restricted, but not eliminated, by *Shaffer v. Heitner*) is gained by seizing local property as a basis for collecting an obligation unrelated to the property. A judgment based on attachment jurisdiction does *not* extinguish the claim except to the extent of the property seized. However, *issues* actually litigated are *conclusive* on the parties if the amount of the attached property gave them a fair incentive to litigate.

8.   **Exceptions to Claim Preclusion**

    Exceptions to the doctrine are recognized only under *extraordinary* circumstances (*e.g.*, fraud on the court). There is a *very strong policy* against relitigation.

9.   **Defenses and Counterclaims**

    a.   **Effect of Compulsory-Counterclaim Rules**

        A defendant must assert any counterclaim she has against plaintiff that arises from the same transaction as plaintiff's claim. If defendant fails to do so, with very limited exceptions she is barred from later asserting it, either as a defense or as a basis for relief in an independent action.

b. When No Compulsory-Counterclaim Rule Involved

In such cases, claim preclusion does not prevent a defendant from asserting the same matter first as a defense, and later in a separate suit as a basis for independent relief against the former plaintiff (although issue preclusion may apply).

C. ISSUE PRECLUSION

1. Direct Estoppel

Issues actually litigated *between the parties* are binding on them in subsequent actions concerning the *same claim.*

2. Collateral Estoppel

If a second suit involves a different claim (thus no merger, bar, or direct estoppel), the first judgment may be invoked as to all matters *actually litigated and determined in the first action and essential to its determination.*

a. Identical Issue

The issue in the first adjudication must be identical to the one presented in the subsequent action.

b. Exceptions

Issue preclusion might not be applied if any of the following apply: the initial action was not appealable, the court proceedings were informal or expedited in the first suit, the stakes are much higher in the second suit, the issue in the second suit is one of law and the claim is substantially unrelated to the claim in the first suit, the burden of proof in the second suit is materially different, *or* there is a clear need for a new determination in the second suit.

D. PERSONS PRECLUDED BY JUDGMENTS

1. Parties and Privies

A party to a judgment is bound by claim preclusion *and* issue preclusion; a privy is usually bound to the *same extent.* Privity with a party is a legal conclusion, encompasses a number of relationships, and may be substantive or procedural.

2. Nonparties Not Bound

Generally, a nonparty is not bound by a judgment because to do so would violate due process.

a. Nonparty May Benefit

A nonparty to an action may benefit from the judgment.

(1) Claim Preclusion

If a relationship of *vicarious liability* (but *not* joint liability) exists, a judgment exonerating either potential defendant precludes an action on the same claim against the other.

(2) Issue Preclusion

Generally, a person who litigates an issue against one party and loses may not relitigate that issue with another party, but this preclusion may be limited when the issue would not be conclusive between the parties to the original action or when unjust under the circumstances.

E. INTERJURISDICTIONAL PRECLUSIVE EFFECTS OF JUDGMENTS

1. Basic Rule

If judgments are rendered in different court systems, generally the preclusion principles of the court system that rendered the first judgment should be used to determine its preclusive effect in the second jurisdiction.

a. State-Court Judgments

State-court judgments are given effect in other states by the Full Faith and Credit Clause and also are given effect in other state courts, and in federal court, by federal statute.

b. Federal-Court Judgments

Federal-court judgments are entitled to preclusive effect according to *federal common law*, but in diversity cases, the federal common law requires following the preclusive effect that the judgment would be given by the courts of the state in which the federal court rendering the judgment sat.

2. Prohibition Against Broader or Narrower Preclusion

The Supreme Court has interpreted the Full Faith and Credit Clause as forbidding a federal court from giving more or less effect to a state court judgment than would the preclusion rules of that state.

Approach to Exams

Examination questions on civil procedure can concern a wide range of issues. The issues that you are most likely to encounter are discussed below and can be analyzed in the following sequence. (Note that these issues are discussed in greater detail in the Key Exam Issues section at the beginning of each chapter.)

1. **Jurisdiction**

   Does the court have *authority* to render judgment in the present action, consistent with constitutional requirements of due process?

   a. Does the court have jurisdiction *over the parties* (territorial jurisdiction of the state)?

   b. Does the court have jurisdiction *over the subject matter* (over the particular type of action)?

   c. Has *adequate notice* been given to all parties?

2. **Venue**

   Assuming the court does have jurisdiction, is it the *proper place* for trial of the action under the rules governing venue?

   a. If the action was originally filed in a court having proper venue, are there grounds for *transfer* or change of venue to another court?

3. **State and Federal Law**

   a. If the action is in federal court, does it concern a state-law matter (usually this means it is a diversity case)? If so, the court will generally follow *state substantive law* and *federal procedural law.*

   b. Is there an *Erie* problem—*i.e.*, is there a *true conflict* between federal and state rules of law? (Only if there is a true conflict do you need to consider which rule, state or federal, applies.)

4. **Pleadings**

   a. Does the complaint contain a *valid substantive legal claim*?

   b. Does the complaint state the elements of a *prima facie case*?

   c. Is the complaint *sufficiently specific* so as to give fair notice of the basis of the claim(s) made?

   d. Does the answer properly admit or deny the complaint's allegations? Does it properly raise any applicable defenses?

   e. Is there a ground for allowing an *amendment*?

5. **Parties**

   a. Are the named parties proper (*real party in interest and capacity to sue or be sued*)?

   b. Are the named parties *properly joined?*

   c. Are there *other parties* who should be joined under the required-party rule or who may become parties by intervention or impleader?

d.   Can the parties assert ***claims against each other*** in addition to those in the complaint—*i.e.*, counterclaims or crossclaims? Can the parties implead other parties?

e.   Is a ***class action*** appropriate?

6.   Discovery

Is there a controversy as to either party's right to obtain pretrial discovery from the other party or from some third person? If so, consider:

a.   Have the parties satisfied the requirement of ***disclosure***?

b.   Is the information sought within the ***permissible scope*** of discovery (*i.e.*, is it relevant to the claim or defense of a party, not privileged, and proportionate to the needs of the case)?

c.   Is the information protected by a ***privilege*** or as ***work product***?

d.   Is the ***proper mechanism*** used (*e.g.*, deposition, interrogatory, etc.)?

e.   What limitations by ***protective order*** are needed to prevent abuse?

f.   If a discovery order was violated, or if a disclosure obligation was not met, is a ***sanction*** appropriate?

7.   Trial

a.   Is there a ***right to a jury trial?***

b.   Are the issues before the court within the ***scope*** of the pleadings or pretrial order, or properly in issue because evidence on them was received without valid objection?

c.   Who has the ***burden of proof*** as to a particular issue, and has the burden been met?

d.   Were ***instructions*** properly given to the jury, and were they substantially correct?

e.   Was there ***improper conduct*** by the judge, a counsel, party, witness, or juror?

f.   Did plaintiff put on sufficient evidence to survive a ***motion for judgment as a matter of law?***

8.   Post-Trial

a.   Is there relief that the ***trial court*** can give?

(1)   Motion for a ***new trial*** (to overcome procedural error or if the verdict is against the weight of the evidence).

(2)   ***Renewed motion for judgment as a matter of law*** (if the verdict is unsupported by sufficient evidence).

(3)   ***Extraordinary relief*** (*e.g.*, if newly discovered evidence, fraud).

b.   Can the ***appellate court*** provide relief?

(1)   Is there a ***final judgment*** or other appealable order?

(2)   Is ***discretionary appeal*** available?

(3)   May review be obtained by ***extraordinary writ***?

c.   Does ***claim preclusion*** (res judicata) or ***issue preclusion*** (direct or collateral estoppel) bar relitigation of this matter in later trials?

Civil Procedure

Eighteenth Edition

Chapter One

Personal Jurisdiction and Related Matters

CONTENTS

Key Exam Issues

Most civil-procedure courses include consideration of where a suit may be brought. In a country the size of the United States, that can prove very important. Those issues raise questions of personal jurisdiction (*i.e.*, a court's authority over the **parties** in the lawsuit) and venue (*i.e.*, the **geographic location** where the case is heard). (Note that a different jurisdictional question—whether a suit may be brought in federal court—is covered in Chapter Two.)

Examination questions about whether a suit may proceed in the location selected by the plaintiff are very frequent. When you face such a question, ask yourself the following questions:

1. **Is There a Statute or Rule That Gives the Court a Basis for the Exercise of Jurisdiction?**

   There must be some "enabling legislation" that authorizes the court to exercise jurisdiction. The traditional method for gaining jurisdiction is service within the state, but all states have adopted statutory or rule authorizations for exercise of jurisdiction even if there is no such in-state service, called **long-arm statutes**. Under these statutes, jurisdiction often depends on whether the defendant has done something in relation to the state or one of its residents. As a result, you frequently must analyze the specific wording of the statute or rule involved to determine whether the allegations of the suit satisfy its provisions. Moreover, some long-arm statutes have been interpreted to extend as far as is permitted under the Constitution even though their express terms do not say so. In federal court, the same statutory jurisdictional provisions apply as in state court except in a few special circumstances.

2. **Is This Exercise of Jurisdiction Constitutional?**

   The Due Process Clause of the Fourteenth Amendment limits a state court's power to compel a defendant to respond to a suit. Your analysis may require you to look to one or more of a number of grounds for satisfying this constitutional requirement:

   a. Does the defendant have **minimum contacts** with the state where the court is located (the "forum") that are sufficient to support the exercise of jurisdiction with regard to the claim in this case? This analysis is often called **specific jurisdiction** because it depends on the specific claim being asserted. You should consider whether the defendant has **purposefully availed** himself of the benefits and protections of the forum state by voluntarily establishing an affiliation with the state. Also determine whether the exercise of jurisdiction is **reasonable** in light of the state's interest, the burden on the defendant, and the plaintiff's interest in a remedy in the state, among other factors.

   b. Can the forum state exercise **general jurisdiction**? Every defendant should have a "home base" where it is fair that he be subject to suit no matter where the events giving rise to the claim occurred. For natural persons, this is ordinarily the **domicile** of the person. For businesses, general jurisdiction exists in a corporation's state of incorporation and principal place of business. Beyond that, the Supreme Court has said that general jurisdiction is proper only when the defendant's affiliations with the state are so "continuous and systematic" as to render it "essentially at home" in the forum state.

   c. Has **property** belonging to the defendant been seized within the state? Seizure of the defendant's property in the state may be a sufficient ground for the exercise of jurisdiction there. However, in order for the property to support the exercise of jurisdiction, it must be **related to the claim**, either because the property itself is the object of the claim or because the property was involved in the events giving rise to the claim. Seizure of totally unrelated property does not support jurisdiction, except possibly to secure a judgment rendered by a court elsewhere that does have personal jurisdiction over the defendant.

d.   Has the defendant ***consented*** to jurisdiction in the forum state? Consent may result from making a ***general appearance*** to defend the case (in some states a defendant who contests jurisdiction must make a ***special appearance***, raising only the issue of jurisdiction). A defendant may also consent in advance ***by contract***.

e.   Was the defendant ***personally served*** within the forum state? If so, jurisdiction is usually established. The defendant may be able to overcome jurisdiction in very unusual circumstances if his presence in the state was not ***intentional*** or ***knowing***. And ***fraudulent inducement*** into the state may be a ground for disregarding service.

3.   Is Venue Proper?

Besides constitutional limitations on the location of litigation, there are statutory limitations on the venue for suits, often focused on the ***residence*** of the defendants. In addition, venue statutes frequently permit suit where the ***events underlying the suit*** have occurred.

4.   Is Another Location Far Superior?

Even though the location selected for the suit is not so unreasonable that it is unconstitutional to proceed there, it may be that another location is very clearly superior. If so, a state court may dismiss the case for ***forum non conveniens*** if the preferred forum is in another state or outside this country. Within the federal-court system, the court may ***transfer*** to a federal court in another district to solve the problem or dismiss if the preferred court is in another country.

5.   Was Proper Notice Given?

For a court to enter a judgment binding on a defendant, the plaintiff must have made reasonable efforts to give the defendant notice of the lawsuit. Ordinarily satisfactory notice is given by ***service of process***—the summons to appear before the court and the complaint against the defendant—in accord with the pertinent rules or statutes on service. In unusual circumstances, the defendant may be able to argue that the authorized manner of service is not ***reasonably calculated to provide actual notice*** and that entry of judgment would therefore violate due process.

A. Introduction

1. Jurisdiction—Historical Perspective

In the 19th century, the law on personal jurisdiction focused largely on the power of a state to compel a response to a suit before its courts. Under the prevailing view, "in personam" jurisdiction could be exercised only if the defendant was personally served with process inside the state. Alternatively, a state could exercise "in rem" jurisdiction whenever it could seize property of the defendant and use that property to satisfy any resulting judgment.

a. Effects of Early Jurisdiction Rules

In operation, these 19th-century attitudes toward jurisdiction could produce anomalous results. Unless a defendant had property in a state, he often could not be sued there even if the suit arose from something the defendant had done in the state to a plaintiff citizen of the state. This limitation seemed to constrict jurisdiction too much, and tempted plaintiffs to lure prospective defendants into a state so they could be served there, but courts would often refuse to exercise jurisdiction on the ground that the defendant had been tricked into the state. On the other hand, if the defendant's property could be seized in the state, the court could exercise jurisdiction up to the value of the property even if the lawsuit had nothing to do with the property and was based on a claim that had nothing to do with the state. Because intangible property—such as a bank account—could be subject to seizure in a number of places, this method seemed to overextend a state's jurisdiction.

b. Reformulation by Supreme Court

Eventually, the Supreme Court rejected the requirement for personal service in the state to justify in personam jurisdiction, and ruled that a nonresident defendant could be subject to jurisdiction on a claim related to his contacts with the state if he had minimum contacts with the state. It also curtailed the exercise of "in rem" jurisdiction based on seizure of property, limiting it to cases in which there is a relationship between the claim and the property.

2. Types of Personal Jurisdiction

Personal jurisdiction (sometimes called territorial jurisdiction) refers to a state's power to hear a case and enforce its judgment over the particular parties or property involved. This power is based on the state's connection to the parties or property. Personal jurisdiction is divided into three categories:

a. In Personam Jurisdiction

In personam jurisdiction permits a court to enter a judgment that is *personally binding* on the defendant, either ordering her to do or refrain from doing a certain act (equitable or injunctive relief) or decreeing that the plaintiff may collect a certain amount of damages from the defendant (legal relief). Courts in other states must enforce such a judgment because the Constitution requires them to give *full faith and credit* to the judgment.

b. In Rem Jurisdiction

In rem jurisdiction permits a court *to adjudicate the rights of all possible claimants to a specific piece of property*, as in a condemnation proceeding. This authority originated from a state's power to determine controversies regarding real property within its borders: "The well-being of every community requires that the title to real estate therein shall be secure, and that there be convenient and certain methods of determining any unsettled questions respecting it." [**Arndt v. Griggs,** 134 U.S. 316 (1890)]

c. Quasi in Rem Jurisdiction

Quasi in rem jurisdiction formerly included cases of two types. The first category included cases involving *individual disputes related to property under the court's control* (such as actions for specific performance of a contract to purchase land). This type of quasi in rem jurisdiction continues to provide a constitutional basis for the exercise of jurisdiction. The second category of cases involved essentially *personal disputes when the court could not assert personal jurisdiction over the defendant*, but had jurisdiction over property belonging to the defendant. That property would be seized at the request of the plaintiff and used to satisfy the claim if the plaintiff prevailed. The use of this second category of quasi in rem jurisdiction to provide a basis for exercise of jurisdiction over nonresident defendants has been severely limited on constitutional grounds. (*See infra*, pp. 20–23.)

3. *Pennoyer v. Neff* and the Traditional Power Theory

In **Pennoyer v. Neff,** 95 U.S. 714 (1878), the Court held that for the state to exercise power over individuals or property there must be *valid service of process* on the individual (in in personam cases) *or attachment of property* in the state (in in rem actions). The methods by which jurisdiction may be obtained have broadened since *Pennoyer*.

a. The *Pennoyer* Decision

In 1865, attorney Mitchell sued Neff in an Oregon state court, alleging that Neff owed him about $250 for legal work performed. Neff, a resident of California, was not personally served; instead, service was by publication based on Mitchell's assertion that Neff owned property in Oregon. When Neff did not appear in the action, Mitchell obtained a default judgment. A month later, Neff acquired title to a tract of land in Oregon, and Mitchell had the sheriff seize and sell the land to satisfy the judgment. Mitchell bought the land at the sheriff's sale and transferred title to Pennoyer shortly thereafter. Many years later, Neff sued Pennoyer in federal court, arguing that the sale was invalid because the Oregon court lacked jurisdiction to enter the judgment against him. The Supreme Court agreed, stating that there had been no in personam jurisdiction over Neff because he was never served with process, and there was no in rem jurisdiction because the court did not attach any Oregon property owned by Neff before the entry of judgment in the suit. Thus, the court had no jurisdiction over Neff or his property, and the judgment was invalid.

(1) Relation to Due Process

Because the Fourteenth Amendment did not become effective until 1868, after Mitchell had Neff's property sold, the Fourteenth Amendment Due Process Clause was not involved in the case. However, the Court made it clear in dictum that in the future, *due process would apply the same limitations on exercise of jurisdiction*.

b. Territorial Limits on Process

In keeping with its concept of a state's power being limited by its borders, the Court in *Pennoyer* determined that a state cannot serve an individual domiciled in another state with process and summon that person to respond to a lawsuit against him. This basic limitation on the power of state courts to exercise in personam jurisdiction over out-of-state defendants has been relaxed by the modern shift to a minimum-contacts analysis. (*See infra*, pp. 7–8.)

c. Methods to Obtain Jurisdiction

(1) Service Within State Sufficient

Under *Pennoyer*, service of process on a defendant within the state is sufficient for jurisdiction. This conclusion is implicit in *Pennoyer's* reasoning, and is the basis for what has come to be known as *transient jurisdiction*; *i.e.*, a court may obtain jurisdiction over a defendant if the defendant is served when he is physically present in the state even if his presence is temporary. It has been carried to great lengths.

e.g. **Example—Service in Airplane**: Passenger was on a nonstop scheduled commercial airline flight from Memphis, Tennessee, to Dallas, Texas. While the plane was over Pine Bluff, Arkansas, he was served with process. The service was held to be sufficient to establish jurisdiction in Arkansas. [**Grace v. MacArthur,** 170 F. Supp. 442 (E.D. Ark. 1959)]

(a) Limitation—Fraudulent Inducement into Foru

However, courts decline transient jurisdiction when the defendant was fraudulently lured into the jurisdiction. [*See, e.g.,* **Wyman v. Newhouse,** 93 F.2d 313 (2d Cir. 1937)—service in Florida was invalid when defendant was enticed to Florida by plaintiff who falsely told him that she was leaving the country permanently and would like to see him one last time; *and see infra,* p. 29]

(b) Constitutional Validity

A number of legal authorities questioned the constitutional validity of transient jurisdiction in the wake of **Shaffer v. Heitner,** 433 U.S. 186 (1997) (*see infra,* p. 29), but the Supreme Court upheld the practice in **Burnham v. Superior Court,** 495 U.S. 604 (1990).

(2) Seizure of Defendant's Property

Pennoyer indicated in dictum that ***prejudgment seizure*** of a defendant's property was sufficient to permit a state to dispose of that property to satisfy ***claims not related to the property***. When such seizure was accomplished, the court had power to control disposition of the property, even absent service of process within the jurisdiction. This is an application of the second category of ***quasi in rem jurisdiction*** discussed above. (*See supra,* p. 4.)

(a) Need for Prejudgment Seizure

Quasi in rem jurisdiction was not available in *Pennoyer* itself because in the first action, the plaintiff, Mitchell, did not attach defendant Neff's property ***before*** entry of the judgment. The Court held that seizure after judgment was insufficient to support jurisdiction.

(b) Scope of "Property"

1) Debt as Property

In **Harris v. Balk,** 198 U.S. 215 (1905), the Court upheld assertion of quasi in rem jurisdiction over a debt owed to the defendant by a temporary visitor to the state. The Court reasoned that "[t]he obligation of the debtor to pay his debt clings to and accompanies him wherever he goes." Therefore, the debt was sufficiently "present" to permit its seizure to provide a basis for exercise of jurisdiction to the extent of the debt.

2) Insurance Policies

Some states extended this idea to justify the seizure of an insurer's obligation to defend and indemnify its insured. The obligation was said to be property of the insured, present wherever the insurer could be served, thereby justifying jurisdiction. [*See* **Seider v. Roth,** 17 N.Y.2d 111 (1966)] However, the Supreme Court ***invalidated this practice*** in **Rush v. Savchuk,** 444 U.S. 320 (1980) (*see infra,* p. 23).

d. Exceptions to In-State Service or Prejudgment-Seizure Requirement

In *Pennoyer,* the Court recognized some exceptions to its rigorous rules:

(1) Status

Even absent service within the state, the *Pennoyer* Court acknowledged that a state court could determine the status of one of its citizens toward a nonresident. This exception bore principally on divorce cases and gave rise to the "Nevada divorce," in which one spouse would move to Nevada for the period required to establish residency and obtain a divorce there. Jurisprudentially, it led to the concept of the **divisible divorce**, under which the marital status was treated as a res that could be the subject of adjudication by the state in which either spouse resided, but alimony, child support, and other financial matters were viewed as in personam and beyond the authority of a state that had not obtained jurisdiction by personal service.

(2) Consent

Pennoyer suggested that states could require noncitizens to consent to suit as a condition for conducting activities in the state. As explained in *Pennoyer*, this authority depended on the state's right to forbid or exclude the activity. However, there were limitations on the power of a state to exclude noncitizens, and there gradually arose a doctrine of **implied consent**, which holds that a defendant's **in-state activities** are sufficient to justify service for suits **related to the activities**, despite doubts about the power to forbid them.

> **e.g.** **Example—Nonresident Motorist Statutes**: In **Hess v. Pawloski**, 274 U.S. 352 (1927), the Court upheld jurisdiction based on a statute that treated driving within the state as implied appointment of a local official as defendant's agent for service of process in the state in any suit in that state on claims arising from that driving.

e. Notice

Pennoyer had an ambivalent attitude toward the need for notice to the defendant of the pendency of the action.

(1) Notice Not Sufficient to Establish Jurisdiction

The Court proceeded from the notion that a state's power over individuals ends at its borders, so that process from a state's courts cannot run into another state and force persons domiciled there to appear in a legal proceeding. Therefore, notice to Neff in California of the suit filed by Mitchell in Oregon would not have any effect on the power of the Oregon court to enter a binding judgment.

(2) Notice Not Required to Establish Jurisdiction

Pennoyer similarly did not indicate that notice was required for entry of a valid judgment. Instead, it indicated that prejudgment seizure of the defendant's property would be sufficient. *Rationale*: the law presumes that property is always in the possession of its owner, and therefore its seizure will inform the owner "that he must look to any proceedings authorized by law upon such seizure for its condemnation and sale." For examination of the current requirement that notice be given, *see infra*, p. 48 *et seq.*

4. Shift to Minimum Contacts

In **International Shoe Co. v. Washington**, 326 U.S. 310 (1945), the Court shifted away from *Pennoyer's* insistence on service within the state to support in personam jurisdiction. Instead, it held that to subject a defendant to a judgment in personam, due process requires only that "he have certain minimum contacts with [the forum] such that the maintenance of the suit does not offend 'traditional notions of fair play and substantial justice.' "

a. Systematic and Continuous Activity

The Court has upheld in personam specific jurisdiction over a nonresident defendant based on *systematic and continuous contacts with the state*. In *International Shoe*, the defendant was a Delaware corporation headquartered in St. Louis, Missouri. It employed 11 to 13 salespeople in Washington, who were authorized only to solicit orders. The orders could be accepted or rejected only by the home office. Although it had no permanent office in Washington, the sales efforts there generated commissions of at least $31,000 per year. The state claimed that International Shoe was obligated to contribute to the state's unemployment compensation fund in amounts proportional to the activities of its salespeople there. The Court upheld Washington's jurisdiction, an easy decision given the volume and systematic and continuous nature of the contacts with the state, as well as the fact that the claim was directly related to the defendant's activities in the state. Contrast general jurisdiction with regard to claims unrelated to defendant's in-state activity, permitted only where a corporation is incorporated or has its principal place of business or when a defendant's affiliations with the state are so continuous and systematic as to render it "essentially at home" in the forum state. (*See infra*, p. 23 *et seq*.)

b. Single Contact

The Court has also upheld jurisdiction over a nonresident (Texas) defendant based on a *single contact with the forum* (California)—sending a contract for reinsurance to an insured in California. [**McGee v. International Life Insurance Co.,** 355 U.S. 220 (1957)] The Court emphasized that there was a trend toward expanding the permissible scope of state jurisdiction, based on a fundamental change in the national economy to a more nationalized form of commerce. This development reduced the burden on a defendant of defending in any state in which it engages in economic activity. The Court indicated that it was sufficient that the contract sued on in *McGee* had "a substantial connection with the State." This conclusion was based in part on the presence in California of witnesses to the company's defense of suicide, and also on the existence of pervasive regulation of insurance companies in California. *McGee* is regarded by many as a high-water mark for expansive state-court jurisdiction.

c. Purposeful-Availment Limitation

The Court cautioned, however, that "it is a mistake to assume that this trend heralds the eventual demise of all restrictions on the personal jurisdiction of state courts." [**Hanson v. Denckla,** 357 U.S. 235 (1958)] In *Hanson*, the Court said that there must be "some act by which the defendant *purposefully avails* itself of the privilege of conducting activities within the forum state, thus invoking the benefits and protections of its laws."

d. Post-*International Shoe* Trend

For 30 years after *International Shoe* was decided, state courts and legislatures expanded state-court jurisdiction. The usual impetus behind such expansions was to provide a forum for local plaintiffs claiming injury due to products or services provided by distant defendants. Given elastic limitations on jurisdiction, there were strong pressures to open the doors of the local courts to such plaintiffs.

B. Contemporary Constitutional Grounds for State-Court Jurisdiction

1. Contacts with Forum

International Shoe's approach has generated a two-stage analysis for determining whether the exercise of specific jurisdiction over a nonresident defendant is proper. The first stage looks to the ***purposeful-availment*** requirement introduced in *Hanson, supra*, which is usually the harder requirement to satisfy. If that is satisfied, the analysis turns to questions of ***reasonableness***.

a. Purposeful Availment—Minimum Contacts

This criterion is the requirement on which the Supreme Court has usually relied in overturning overbroad extensions of specific jurisdiction by the lower courts. Usually the lower courts justified extensions of jurisdiction on grounds of reasonableness, lack of burden to the defendant, state interest in local adjudication, and convenience to the plaintiff. It is important to keep in mind that, unlike the reasonableness inquiry (*see infra*, pp. 16–18), the purposeful-availment inquiry focuses solely on ***the activities of the defendant*** and not on the interests of the plaintiff.

(1) Definition

Although far from absolutely clear, the purposeful-availment inquiry looks to some ***voluntary action by the defendant*** establishing a ***relationship with the forum***, usually one in which the defendant seeks to benefit from the relationship with the forum state.

(2) Rationale

This requirement gives defendants "fair warning that a particular activity may subject [them] to the jurisdiction of a foreign sovereign." [**Burger King Corp. v. Rudzewicz,** 471 U.S. 462 (1985)] It thereby "gives a degree of predictability to the legal system that allows potential defendants to structure their primary conduct with some minimum assurance as to where that conduct will and will not render them liable to suit." [**World-Wide Volkswagen Corp. v. Woodson,** 444 U.S. 286 (1980)]

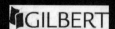

Look **only at defendant's activities** to see if the defendant has **purposefully availed** himself of jurisdiction in the forum state, such as by:

- Having entered into a long-term relationship with the forum state;

- Serving or seeking to serve the forum market;

- Delivering products into stream of commerce with the expectation that they will be purchased in the forum state (but additional conduct directed toward the forum might be required); or

- Targeting activities or intending effects in the forum (limited to wrongful or commercial activity).

NO

YES

No Jurisdiction

Look at defendant's activities **and** plaintiff's interests to see if it is **reasonable to assert jurisdiction** over defendant; consider factors such as:

- **Burden on defendant** to defend in the forum;

- **Forum state's interest** in adjudicating the dispute because plaintiff is a citizen of the state or because the state has an interest in regulating defendant's activity giving rise to the claim;

- **Plaintiff's interest** in obtaining convenient and complete relief;

- The interstate **judicial system's interest** in obtaining the most efficient resolution of controversies; and

- The **shared interest of the several states** in furthering fundamental substantive social policies.

NO

YES

Minimum Contacts Exist

(3) Foreseeability

Standing alone, the reasonable foreseeability that a suit might be filed in a forum is not sufficient. "[T]he foreseeability that is critical to due process analysis . . . is that the defendant's conduct and connection with the forum State are such that he should reasonably anticipate being haled into court there." [**World-Wide Volkswagen Corp. v. Woodson,** *supra*]

(a) Unilateral Act of Plaintiff—Insufficient

It is said that the unilateral act of the plaintiff in bringing a product to the forum or relocating in the forum is insufficient to establish the requisite connection.

e.g. **Example—Relocation to Forum**: The settlor of a trust lived in Pennsylvania when she set up the trust. The trustee was a Delaware bank. Several years after creating the trust, the settlor moved to Florida. That unilateral act did not justify Florida's assertion of jurisdiction over the Delaware trustee even though the move was foreseeable and the bank corresponded with the settlor after she moved. [**Hanson v. Denckla,** *supra*, p. 8]

e.g. **Example—Taking Product to Forum**: Plaintiffs bought a car in New York and drove it to Oklahoma, where they were in an accident and suffered severe injuries allegedly caused by a defective design and placement of the car's gas tank. This action by plaintiffs (driving the car to Oklahoma) did not establish a contact between the New York retail seller and Oklahoma. [**World-Wide Volkswagen Corp. v. Woodson,** *supra*]

e.g. **Example—Plaintiffs' Connections to Forum**: Although plaintiffs had long-term connections with Nevada, those connections did not support jurisdiction for a suit in Nevada against a law-enforcement officer who seized $97,000 in cash from them in the Atlanta, GA, airport, and allegedly later provided a false affidavit about that seizure to a court in Georgia, causing delays in return of the money to plaintiffs. [**Walden v. Fiore,** 134 S. Ct. 1115 (2014)]

(b) Entering into a Long-Term Relationship with a Forum Resident

When the defendant has established a *long-term relationship* with a forum resident, that may suffice to establish minimum contacts.

e.g. **Example—Franchise Agreement**: A Michigan defendant entered into a 20-year franchise agreement with a Florida fast-food corporation that required him to adhere to a detailed set of specifications in the operation of his franchised restaurant, to send payments to Florida, and to agree to the application of Florida law in construing the contract. The Court stated that Florida jurisdiction was proper because the defendant reached "out beyond Michigan and negotiated with a Florida corporation for the purchase of a long-term franchise and the manifold benefits that would derive from affiliation with a nationwide organization." [**Burger King Corp. v. Rudzewicz,** *supra*]

e.g. **Example—Acceptance of Corporate Directorship**: When defendants have accepted directorships in a corporation incorporated in the forum state, they may be subject to jurisdiction in that state. [*See* **Armstrong v. Pomerance,** 423 A.2d 174 (Del. 1980)] The rationale is that the defendants' status as directors and their power to act in that capacity arise exclusively under the forum state's laws. The Delaware court held that the directors accepted their directorships with explicit statutory notice that they could be haled into the forum state's courts "to answer for alleged breaches of the duties imposed on them by the very laws which empowered them to act in their corporate capacities."

(c) Seeking to Serve

In *World-Wide Volkswagen, supra*, the Court indicated that Oklahoma contacts would have been sufficient to support jurisdiction if it were shown that the defendants "regularly sell cars at wholesale or retail to Oklahoma customers or residents or that they indirectly, through others, *serve or seek to serve* the Oklahoma market."

1) Single Act

A single act seeking to serve the forum market has been held sufficient to support jurisdiction in an action asserting a claim growing out of that act. [*See* **McGee v. International Life Insurance Co.,** *supra*, p. 8]

(d) Stream of Commerce

The Court has also said that a forum state may assert personal jurisdiction over a corporation that "delivers its products into the stream of commerce with the expectation that they will be purchased by consumers in the forum State." [**World-Wide Volkswagen Corp. v. Woodson,** *supra*]

1) Retail Seller

In *World-Wide Volkswagen*, the Court held that the stream of commerce ends with the retail sale of the product, even if it is foreseeable that the purchaser will take the product to another state. (Note that a retail seller who regularly serves customers from a given state would be said to "seek to serve" that state's market even if located in another state.)

2) Manufacturer or Component Supplier

In *World-Wide Volkswagen*, the Court cited with seeming approval **Gray v. American Radiator & Standard Sanitary Corp.,** 176 N.E.2d 761 (Ill. 1961), which upheld jurisdiction over a component supplier whose product was sent into the forum state as part of a product manufactured by its customer. However, the Court later failed to resolve a similar issue involving a Japanese component manufacturer and a Taiwanese tire manufacturer whose product failed in California. [**Asahi Metal Industry Co. v. Superior Court,** 480 U.S. 102 (1987)] Justice O'Connor's opinion in *Asahi* (not for a majority of the Court) indicated that placing a product in the stream of commerce is not sufficient, and that some "additional conduct" by which the defendant indicates "an intent or purpose to serve the forum state" is essential. The circumstances under which a manufacturer will be found subject to jurisdiction in a state because its product is sold there remain unclear.

In 2011, the Court again failed to resolve the question of when a manufacturer is subject to jurisdiction for injuries caused in the forum by its product. In **J. McIntyre Machinery, Ltd. v. Nicastro,** 564 U.S. 873 (2011), the Court held that a New Jersey state court's reliance on the stream-of-commerce theory did not support jurisdiction because the evidence showed no direct sales by defendant to purchasers in the forum state. Justice Kennedy's plurality opinion asserts that the stream-of-commerce "metaphor" does not support jurisdiction even though plaintiff was injured by defendant's product in the forum. Justice Breyer's concurring opinion "adhere[s] strictly to our precedents" and stresses that the facts did not show a "regular flow" of defendant's products into the forum, or "regular course" of sales into the forum. The sale to New Jersey was from defendant's exclusive American distributor, an Ohio company that was in bankruptcy. Justice Ginsburg, joined by two others, urged adoption of a stream-of-commerce theory.

(e) Targeting or Intending Effects in Forum

The Court has indicated that, at least for *intentional torts*, jurisdiction can be obtained over a nonresident defendant in a forum if the defendant intended that his actions could have an effect in that forum. [**Calder v. Jones,** 465 U.S. 783 (1984)—Court indicated that the editor and author of an allegedly libelous story about a California plaintiff were subject to jurisdiction in California because "California is the focal point, both of the story and of the harm suffered"]

1) Generally Focused on Wrongful or Commercial Activity

The Court has stated that the effects test (above) "was intended to reach *wrongful activity* outside of the State causing injury within the State or *commercial activity* affecting State residents." [**Kulko v. Superior Court,** 436 U.S. 84 (1978)]

e.g. **Example**: In *Kulko*, an ex-wife moved from New York to California and then sued her New Yorker ex-husband in California to modify child-custody and child-support arrangements (*see supra*, p. 7, regarding divisible divorce). The Court held that the ex-husband's act of buying the couple's daughter a ticket to move to California, at her request, was not sufficient to support California jurisdiction, even though the ex-husband could have foreseen effects there. The Court reasoned that the ex-husband did not purposefully derive any benefits from activities related to California, and he had no other relevant contact with California. Thus, he could not reasonably anticipate being haled into court there.

cf. **Compare**: A lower court upheld California jurisdiction over French defendants who obtained a French court order directing a California Internet service provider to take actions in California or face significant financial penalties. The French litigants were found to have sufficient contact with the forum state of California based upon the French order to satisfy the purposeful-availment test. [**Yahoo! Inc. v. La Ligue Contre Le Racisme et L'Antisemitisme,** 433 F.3d 1199 (9th Cir. 2005)—"We do not read *Calder* necessarily to require in purposeful direction cases that all (or even any) jurisdictionally relevant effects have been caused by wrongful acts."]

2) Not Applicable to All Intentional Torts

The effects test may not apply to all intentional torts. [*See* **IMO Industries, Inc. v. Kiekert AG,** 155 F.3d 254 (3d Cir. 1998)—for jurisdiction to be upheld, plaintiff must have felt brunt of harm of intentional tort in forum, and defendant must have expressly aimed its conduct at the forum]

Example: Plaintiffs' allegations that defendant law-enforcement officer improperly seized $97,000 from them at the Atlanta, GA, airport and intentionally submitted a false affidavit in Georgia to justify this seizure, causing delay in the return of plaintiffs' money, did not suffice to support jurisdiction for their suit against defendant in Nevada even though plaintiffs had long-term connections to Nevada and were en route there. The same due-process jurisdictional principles apply when intentional and negligent torts are involved, and defendant's actions were not in any way targeted toward Nevada even though he may have been aware that plaintiffs had a significant contact with that state. [**Walden v. Fiore**, *supra*]

(4) Relationship Between Contacts with Forum and Claim Asserted

The Supreme Court has assumed that jurisdiction is proper for claims *related to the forum contacts* that satisfy the purposeful-availment requirement. This involves what has been called *specific jurisdiction*. [*See* **Burger King Corp. v. Rudzewicz**, *supra*, p. 9] For a discussion of the concept of general jurisdiction, *see infra*, pp. 23–26. However, some cases present difficult problems that are often raised on examinations. Consider the following cases in which the claim was not directly related to the forum contacts:

Example: Recall that in **World-Wide Volkswagen Corp. v. Woodson**, *supra*, the plaintiffs purchased an Audi in New York, drove it to Oklahoma, were involved in an accident in Oklahoma, and alleged that they were injured because of design defects in the car. It seemed to be assumed that Oklahoma had specific jurisdiction for the plaintiffs' claim over Audi, the German manufacturer, and Volkswagen of America, the importer of Audi cars for the entire country, because both "seek to serve" the Oklahoma market. However, it is difficult to see how the plaintiffs' claim was related to Audi's and VW's contacts with Oklahoma (*i.e.*, their efforts to serve Oklahoma), since the car in question was sold in New York.

Example: In **Buckeye Boiler Co. v. Superior Court**, 71 Cal. 2d 893 (1969), the plaintiff was injured in California when a boiler manufactured by the defendant exploded. The defendant regularly supplied boilers to a California purchaser, but these were of a different type from the one that injured the plaintiff, and nobody could explain how that boiler got to California. The California court upheld jurisdiction, finding that the plaintiff's claim appeared to arise from the defendant's economic activity in California: the totality of its sales of tanks to California customers or to other customers for foreseeable resale or use in California.

(a) Possible Resolution

One resolution of this problem of similar claims not evidently connected with the forum contacts is to focus on the foreseeability elements mentioned above. (*See supra*, p. 11.) If the claim actually asserted is of the type the defendant should have foreseen in the forum, it is not unfair to subject the defendant to jurisdiction even if this particular claim does not arise from the defendant's contacts. [*See* Twitchell, *The Myth of General Jurisdiction*, 101 Harv. L. Rev. 610, 661–62 (1988)] However, consider the "tricky problem of what constitutes adequate similarity. Must it be the identical product that is distributed? A similar make or model? . . . Would assertion of specific jurisdiction require that a similar product sent into the forum state have an identical defect?" [Brilmayer, *Related Contacts and Personal Jurisdiction*, 101 Harv. L. Rev. 1444 (1988)]

(5) Commercial vs. Noncommercial

Purposeful availment may be found more easily with regard to a defendant's commercial activity than with regard to noncommercial activity. In assessing a defendant's contacts with the state, it is significant whether a defendant seeks "commercial benefit from solicitation of business" from a resident of the forum state.

e.g. **Example—Franchising Agreement**: In *Burger King*, *supra*, the defendant, a Michigan citizen, dealt face-to-face with the Michigan office of Burger King regarding opening a Burger King franchise in Michigan. However, he also negotiated with the Florida headquarters and agreed to send payments and notices there. Noting that the defendant was a "***commercial actor***," the Court held that the Florida contacts constituted purposeful availment and thus upheld jurisdiction at Burger King's home in Florida.

cf. **Compare—Suits Against Consumers**: In *Burger King*, the Court indicated that suits against consumers to collect payments due on personal purchases would not be permitted at the distant sellers' locations.

cf. **Compare—Family Law**: A court is less likely to find minimum contacts when the defendant has not sought any commercial benefits from contacts with the forum. Thus, the Court held that a divorced father who sent his daughter to live with his ex-wife did not thereby become subject to California jurisdiction in an action to modify support and child-custody arrangements. The Court reasoned that "[a] father who agrees, in the interests of family harmony and his children's preferences, to allow them to spend more time in California than was required under a separation agreement can hardly be said to have 'purposefully availed himself' of the 'benefits and protections' of California's laws." [**Kulko v. Superior Court,** *supra*, p. 13]

(6) Choice of Law Distinguished

The Court has repeatedly emphasized that the fact that a given state's law may apply to a case under its conflict-of-laws rules is not relevant to whether the purposeful-availment requirement is satisfied. [**Kulko v. Superior Court,** *supra*—that California may be the "center of gravity" for choice-of-law purposes does not mean that California has personal jurisdiction over the defendant]

(a) Distinguish—Choice of Law Clause

However, the parties' election that a certain state's law will govern their relations may support jurisdiction in that state. Thus, in *Burger King*, *supra*, the Court stated that the inclusion of a provision selecting Florida law in the parties' contract, although not sufficient of itself to support jurisdiction, "reinforced [defendant's] deliberate affiliation" with Florida.

(7) No Relation to Federalism

The Supreme Court has sometimes suggested that the limitations on personal jurisdiction are related to principles of interstate federalism, specifically to issues of a state's sovereignty vis-a-vis other states. [*See* **World-Wide Volkswagen Corp. v. Woodson,** *supra*, p. 14] However, the Court has since stated that the requirement of personal jurisdiction ultimately arises from the Due Process Clause and is unaffected by notions of federalism. If it were otherwise, it would not be possible for a defendant to waive the personal-jurisdiction requirement, because this would interfere with state sovereignty. [*See* **Insurance Corp. of Ireland, Ltd. v. Compagnie des Bauxites de Guinee,** 456 U.S. 694 (1982)]

cf. **Compare—Contacts with Entire Nation Compared to Contacts with a Given State**: A plurality of the Supreme Court has suggested that a non-American defendant may be subject to jurisdiction in a federal court due to national contacts even though it does not have sufficient contacts to support jurisdiction in a state court. [**J. McIntyre Machinery, Ltd. v. Nicastro,** *supra*—"Because the United States is a distinct sovereign, a defendant may in principle be subject to the jurisdiction of the courts of the United States but not of any particular State."]

(8) Reasonableness Insufficient to Satisfy Purposeful-Availment Requirement

The Court has rejected the idea that other factors can outweigh the importance of the purposeful-availment requirement: "Even if the defendant would suffer minimal or no inconvenience from being forced to litigate before the tribunals of another State; even if the forum State has a strong interest in applying its law to the controversy; even if the forum State is the most convenient location for litigation, the Due Process Clause . . . may sometimes act to divest the State of its power to render a valid judgment." [**World-Wide Volkswagen Corp. v. Woodson,** *supra*]

b. Fair Play and Substantial Justice—Reasonableness

Besides focusing on the defendant's contacts with the forum, the jurisdictional inquiry takes account of a number of other factors that bear together on whether the *exercise of jurisdiction in the state is reasonable*. On this question, *consideration of the plaintiff's interests is proper*.

EXAM TIP   **GILBERT**

Remember to distinguish between the *purposeful availment* and *reasonableness* portions of your due-process discussion. Don't include discussion of plaintiff's convenience, etc., under purposeful availment, but focus on these concerns in relation to reasonableness. There are some circumstances supporting reasonableness in most exam questions.

---

(1) Factors

The Supreme Court has identified a variety of factors that may bear on the reasonableness of jurisdiction:

(a) The *burden on the defendant* to defend the litigation in the forum;

(b) The *forum state's interest* in adjudicating the dispute;

(c) The *plaintiff's interest* in obtaining convenient and effective relief;

(d) The *interstate judicial system's interest* in obtaining the most efficient resolution of the dispute; and

(e) The *shared interest of the several states* in furthering fundamental substantive social policies.

(2) Overlap

The same facts may be relevant to more than one of the above factors. For example, if the action arises out of an injury to the plaintiff in the forum, that may bear on the state's interest in adjudicating the dispute, and on the plaintiff's interest in obtaining convenient and effective relief, given the likely presence in the forum of important witnesses to the event. Similarly, the judicial system's interest in efficient resolution of the dispute could favor local resolution where potential witnesses are located and also could favor local resolution if there are local defendants who could not be sued elsewhere—a factor that would also bear on the plaintiff's interest in effective relief. That the injury occurred outside the forum state may indicate not only that witnesses are not conveniently located, but also that the primary substantive interests involved are those of the state where the event occurred.

(3) None Critical

That certain factors do not support forum jurisdiction is not fatal to jurisdiction. Thus, for example, the plaintiff need not be local for jurisdiction to be valid. [**Keeton v. Hustler Magazine, Inc.,** 465 U.S. 770 (1984)] Similarly, that the defendant has conducted only one piece of business in the state does not by itself defeat jurisdiction over a claim arising out of that business. [**McGee v. International Life Insurance Co.,** *supra*, p. 12]

(4) Easy to Satisfy

"[W]here a defendant who purposefully has directed his activities at forum residents seeks to defeat jurisdiction, he must present a compelling case that the presence of some other considerations would render jurisdiction unreasonable." [**Burger King v. Rudzewicz,** *supra*, p. 15]

e.g. **Example**: In **Keeton v. Hustler Magazine, Inc.,** *supra*, plaintiff sued in New Hampshire after her first suit in Ohio was dismissed. She had no prior contact with New Hampshire, but sued there only because the limitations period had expired in all other states. The Court found that the defendant's regular sale of 10,000 to 15,000 magazines in the state constituted purposeful availment and upheld jurisdiction as reasonable even though the plaintiff sought to recover damages for defamation worldwide under the "single publication rule." (*See* Torts Summary.)

(5) Greater Concern with Burden on Foreign Defendants

The Court has indicated that it may be relevant that the defendant is a foreigner, recognizing the "unique burdens placed upon one who must defend oneself in a foreign legal system." [**Asahi Metal Industry v. Superior Court,** *supra*, p. 12]

e.g. **Example**: In *Asahi*, the Court held that it was unreasonable for California to exercise jurisdiction over a cross-complaint for indemnity by a Taiwanese manufacturer against a Japanese component maker. In addition to the extra burdens placed on foreign defendants, the Court placed weight on the fact that the California plaintiff had settled his claim, leaving only the indemnification claim to be decided, and that it could be decided equally conveniently in Japan or Taiwan, where the dealings between the parties occurred.

(a) Caution

It is not clear whether *Asahi* indicates that as a general matter there is greater concern with the reasonableness of jurisdiction over foreign defendants. It may be that the Court would have viewed things differently had the California plaintiff been pursuing a claim against the Japanese component manufacturer who objected to jurisdiction.

(6) First Amendment Concerns

Some lower courts felt that in certain defamation cases the risk of chilling the exercise of First Amendment rights warranted more demanding scrutiny of the reasonableness of jurisdiction. However, in **Calder v. Jones,** *supra*, p. 13, the Court rejected this reasoning: "[T]he potential chill on protected First Amendment activity stemming from libel and defamation actions is already taken into account in the constitutional limitations on the substantive law governing such suits. To reintroduce those concerns at the jurisdictional stage would be a form of double counting."

c. Application—Internet Activities

The greatly increased use of the Internet in recent decades has produced rulings on the scope of personal jurisdiction in resulting litigation. Because this development is recent, this is an *evolving area* and the *emerging rules remain unclear*. For purposes of illustration, however, some specifics can be provided.

(1) Same General Analysis Applied

The same minimum-contacts analysis that is used for other litigation applies to suits arising from Internet activities as well (*see supra*, p. 7).

EXAM TIP   **GILBERT**

Note that, like the regular minimum-contacts analysis, the more important consideration in Internet cases (and usually the more difficult one to satisfy) is whether the *purposeful-availment requirement* has been satisfied.

(a) Contracts via Internet

As in *Burger King* (*supra*, p. 9), entering into an *ongoing contract* via Internet communications usually will suffice to support jurisdiction at the forum of either party for an action alleging breach of contract against the other. [*See* **CompuServe, Inc. v. Patterson,** 89 F.3d 1257 (6th Cir. 1996)—Ohio jurisdiction proper in suit based on software distribution agreement entered into on line between Ohio plaintiff and Texas defendant]

e.g. **Example—Regular On-Line Marketing**: A Michigan plaintiff who successfully bid on two paintings offered by a New York business in an on-line auction could sue in Michigan for breach of contract when the paintings were not delivered even though plaintiff had paid for them. Defendant's use of eBay was "regular and systematic," and supported jurisdiction in the purchaser's state. [**Dedvikaj v. Maloney,** 447 F. Supp.2d 813 (E.D. Mich. 2006)]

e.g. **Example—"One-Shot" On-Line Sale**: Defendants from Wisconsin made an on-line sale of a 1964 Ford Galaxie to a purchaser in San Francisco for over $34,000, claiming that it was in excellent condition. After delivery in San Francisco, the buyer found that it was in poor condition, and sued in California for fraud. Because this online sale was a "one-shot affair," due process precluded suit in California. [**Boschetto v. Hansing,** 539 F.3d 1011 (9th Cir. 2008)]

(b) Causing Effects in Forum via Internet Activities May Suffice

Activities via the Internet have been reviewed under the "effects test" of *Calder* (*supra*, p. 13) to determine whether the defendant should have realized that the effect in the forum would lead to suit there.

Example: A federal court held that D.C. had jurisdiction over a defamation suit against a California-based electronic gossip columnist because numerous D.C. readers had the defendant's column e-mailed to them, reader contributions from D.C. were solicited, stories in the column focused on D.C., and the defendant visited D.C. to promote the column. [**Blumenthal v. Drudge,** 992 F. Supp. 44 (D.D.C. 1998)]

Compare: The California Supreme Court held that a college student who posted a program that could be used to duplicate DVDs, despite encryption designed to prevent duplication, did not sufficiently target California entertainment companies or the California computer industry to permit a California court to exercise jurisdiction in a suit for an injunction against alleged misappropriation of the program. [**Pavlovich v. Superior Court,** 29 Cal. 4th 262 (2002)]

(c) Relation to State Long-Arm Statute Requirements

Courts apply their usual long-arm analysis when determining personal jurisdiction in Internet cases. A state has long-arm jurisdiction when the defendant commits an act enumerated in the long-arm statute and thereby submits to the state's personal jurisdiction for any claim arising out of that act. (*See infra*, p. 31.) [*See, e.g.*, **Bensusan Restaurant Corp. v. King,** 126 F.3d 25 (2d Cir. 1997)—alleged trademark infringement on passive Web page set up in Missouri did not constitute tortious act committed in New York under its long-arm statute; *compare* **Blumenthal v. Drudge,** *supra*—defendant's interactive Web page satisfied long-arm statute in defamation case due to the impact of the story in D.C., and to defendant's "persistent course of conduct" consisting of contacts with forum residents in connection with subjects addressed on the Web page, as well as solicitation of information from D.C. residents for use in the online column]

(2) Specific Issues Relating to Internet

(a) Ability of Forum Residents to Access Internet Site Usually Not Sufficient

Most courts hold that the ability of forum residents to access a Web page does not, standing alone, support forum jurisdiction. [*See* **GTE New Media Services, Inc. v. BellSouth Corp.,** 199 F.3d 1343 (D.C. Cir. 2000)—that forum residents could access defendant's Web page was not sufficient to uphold jurisdiction; *compare* **Inset Systems, Inc. v. Instruction Set, Inc.,** 937 F. Supp. 161 (D. Conn. 1996)—foreign corporation's advertising via Internet was solicitation of sufficient repetitive nature to satisfy solicitation of business provision of long-arm statute]

(b) Level of Interaction and Nature of Web Page Relevant

Courts often look to the level of interaction of a Web page to determine whether or not the purposeful-availment requirement has been met. If the Web page is *passive* (*e.g.*, merely provides information), jurisdiction will usually not be found. [*See* **Bensusan Restaurant Corp. v. King,** *supra*—local Missouri club with Web page could not be subject to trademark suit under New York long-arm statute by New York club with same name] Even a Web page that permits interaction may not support jurisdiction if it is essentially "local" in nature. [*See* **Millennium Enterprises, Inc. v. Millennium Music, L.P.,** 33 F. Supp. 2d 907 (D. Or. 1999)—defendant's interactive Web page about its retail outlets in North Carolina insufficient to support jurisdiction in Oregon because content was essentially local, and when it became aware of plaintiff's trademark concerns, defendant posted notice saying it would not fill orders from Oregon]

1) Criticism

Certain "passive" Web sites may still be said to target the forum. Consider, *e.g.*, an imaginary Web site www.BombTheBridge.org, containing the plans for the construction of the Golden Gate Bridge, detailed instructions on how and where to place bombs to destroy the bridge, and specific instructions on how to build such bombs. Even if such a Web site were entirely passive, a court might well hold that it targeted San Francisco.

(3) Possible Relaxation of Reasonableness Requirements

Because communication via the Internet is easier than by other means, the advent of this new mode of communication may cause courts to relax the reasonableness requirements. [*See* **McGee v. International Life Insurance Co.,** *supra*, p. 8—in upholding jurisdiction, Court emphasized the "fundamental transformation of our national economy" and the fact that "modern transportation and communication have made it much less burdensome for a party sued to defend himself in a State where he engages in economic activity"]

2. Presence of Defendant's Property in Forum

Quasi in rem and in rem jurisdiction have been curtailed since **Harris v. Balk,** *supra*, p. 6. Nevertheless, the presence of the defendant's property in the jurisdiction often may suffice to make jurisdiction constitutional, but ordinarily only because it establishes a relevant contact between the defendant and the forum.

a. Location of Property

(1) Tangible Property

Tangible property (*e.g.*, real estate, chattels) is located in a state if it is *physically present* therein.

(2) Intangible Property

Generally, states may declare that intangible property is located within their jurisdiction if some transaction related to the property occurred within the state. When intangible property is embodied in an instrument (*e.g.*, negotiable paper), however, it is usually said to be located in the state where the instrument is located.

e.g. **Example**: A *debt* (such as a bank account) may be deemed located where the debtor (the bank) is located, but generally shares of stock are said to be located where the certificate is located.

(a) Absence of Constitutional Limitations

The Court has placed no constitutional limitations on the power of a state to declare intangible property present within its borders. It has upheld multiple death taxation of property by different states that all claim the property is within their jurisdiction [**Blackstone v. Miller,** 188 U.S. 189 (1903)], but has held that when a debt may be located in more than one state, due process forbids a state from declaring the property escheated unless it can guarantee that no other state would make a conflicting and duplicative claim. [**Western Union Telegraph Co. v. Pennsylvania,** 368 U.S. 71 (1961)]

e.g. **Example—Corporate Stock**: In **Shaffer v. Heitner,** *supra*, p. 6, Delaware, unique among the 50 states, declared that shares of stock in corporations it chartered were located in that state rather than where the certificate was located. The Court did not question this view.

e.g. **Example—Insurer's Duty to Defend and Indemnify**: In **Rush v. Savchuk,** *supra*, p. 6, the Court did not question the state's conclusion that the insurer's obligation to defend and indemnify the insured constituted property in the state, while holding that contact insufficient to support jurisdiction.

b. Contacts Test

Shaffer held that the minimum-contacts analysis of *International Shoe* should be applied to jurisdiction over property, reasoning that jurisdiction over a thing is an "elliptical way of referring to jurisdiction over the interests of *persons* in a thing" and should therefore be viewed as analogous to personal jurisdiction in terms of protection of those interests.

c. Presence of Property Supports Jurisdiction

In *Shaffer*, the Court recognized that "the presence of property in a State may bear on the existence of jurisdiction by providing contacts among the forum State, the defendant, and the litigation."

(1) True in Rem Cases

The Court appeared to leave untouched the state's power to exercise true in rem jurisdiction, which "affects the interests of all persons in designated property." Therefore, the state would have jurisdiction based on the presence of the property in true in rem cases (*e.g.*, condemnation).

(2) Preexisting Claim to Property

Actions for specific performance or otherwise to perfect a claim to the property (*e.g.*, actions to remove a cloud on title) should also still be permissible in the state where the property is located. Note that the legal right asserted must be to recover the specific property located in the forum state, as in a replevin action. Property attached as security for an eventual money judgment would not suffice.

(3) Claim Related to Rights and Duties Arising from Ownership

The Court also noted that jurisdiction could be sustained on the basis of presence of the property where the **claim relates to the duties of the owner**.

e.g. **Example**: In **Dubin v. Philadelphia,** 34 Pa. D. & C. 61 (1938), jurisdiction was upheld in a suit against an absentee owner of property for injuries sustained on the property. The court reasoned that "[i]t is just as important that nonresident owners of Philadelphia real estate should keep their property in such shape as not to injure our citizens as it is that nonresident owners of cars should drive about our streets with equal care. It is only a short step beyond this to assert that defendants in both classes of cases should be answerable in this forum."

(a) Movable Property

Note that injuries may be inflicted by movable property, such as construction equipment or an airplane. If that produces a claim against the owner, seizure of the property may support jurisdiction even if the owner did not cause the property to be in the forum (*e.g.*, because the property was leased).

(b) Distinguish—Property Unrelated to Claim

In **Rush v. Savchuk,** *supra*, the Court held that the presence of "property" (the insurer's obligation to defend and indemnify the insured) was jurisdictionally insignificant since "[t]he insurance policy is not the subject matter of the case . . . nor is it related to the operative facts of the negligence action."

(4) Absence of Another Forum

In a footnote in *Shaffer*, the Court noted that "[t]his case does not raise, and we therefore do not consider, the question whether the presence of a defendant's property in a State is a sufficient basis for jurisdiction when no other forum is available to the plaintiff." This statement may sanction **jurisdiction by necessity**.

e.g. **Example**: In **Mullane v. Central Hanover Bank & Trust Co.,** 339 U.S. 306 (1950), the Court upheld New York jurisdiction to determine the interests of all beneficiaries (including possible claims of mismanagement by the trustee) in trusts established in New York without examining the beneficiaries' personal affiliation with New York. Eschewing an attempt to categorize this jurisdiction as in rem or in personam, the Court reasoned that "the interest of each state in providing means to close trusts that exist by the grace of its laws and are administered under the supervision of its courts is so insistent and rooted in custom as to establish beyond doubt the right of its courts to determine the interests of all claimants, resident or nonresident, provided its procedure affords full opportunity to appear and be heard." The *scope* of this "jurisdiction by necessity" is **unclear**.

(5) Securing Judgment in Another Forum

In *Shaffer*, the Court rejected the argument that quasi in rem jurisdiction is necessary to prevent a defendant from moving his assets to a state in which he is not subject to suit. The Court suggested that in such a situation it might be proper for the plaintiff to attach the property as security for a judgment being pursued in a state that has in personam jurisdiction over the defendant. (For an example upholding jurisdiction to attach defendant's assets pending judgment in a jurisdiction that has personal jurisdiction over defendant, *see* **National Union Fire Insurance Co. v. Kozeng,** 115 F. Supp. 2d 1231 (D. Colo. 2000).)

(6) Enforcing Valid Judgment

Similarly, the Court noted that once a judgment is entered by a court with in personam jurisdiction, it is proper for another state to enforce the judgment, even if it did not have jurisdiction to decide the case as an original matter. [*See* **Shaffer v. Heitner,** *supra*]

d. Presence of Unrelated Property Insufficient for Jurisdiction

Shaffer holds that when property is "*completely unrelated to the plaintiff's cause of action*" its presence alone will not suffice to support jurisdiction. This holding *overrules* **Harris v. Balk,** *supra*, p. 6.

e. Insurance Obligations

States cannot obtain jurisdiction over nonresident defendants in automobile tort actions by treating the defendant's insurer's obligation to defend and indemnify as property in the state and garnishing the insurer. [**Rush v. Savchuk,** *supra*, p. 22]

f. In Personam Alternative

Whenever the defendant may be subject to in rem jurisdiction, it is important to consider in personam jurisdiction as well.

Example: In *Shaffer*, Justice Brennan, while agreeing that *International Shoe* should be applied to quasi in rem jurisdiction, argued that the defendants' acceptance of positions as officers or directors in Delaware corporations should support jurisdiction over them in Delaware. After the decision in *Shaffer*, the Delaware legislature promptly enacted a statute so providing, and such exercise of in personam jurisdiction was upheld. [**Armstrong v. Pomerance,** *supra*, p. 11]

3. General Jurisdiction

a. Introduction

The Supreme Court distinguishes between *specific* and *general* personal jurisdiction. If general jurisdiction is justified, the defendant is subject to suit on *any claim* in the forum. Specific jurisdiction, on the other hand, gives rise to jurisdiction only for *claims related to the jurisdictional contact* with the state. [*See* **Burger King Corp. v. Rudzewicz,** *supra*, p. 9]

(1) Relation to Claim

The general-jurisdiction analysis usually becomes important when the relation between the defendant's contacts with the jurisdiction and the claim sued upon is not sufficient for specific jurisdiction. (*See supra*, p. 14, for purposeful-availment focus on relation between contacts and claim.) When there is not a sufficient relation between the contacts and the claim, one may look for a basis to exercise general jurisdiction.

Example: In **Helicopteros Nacionales de Colombia v. Hall,** 466 U.S. 408 (1984), the plaintiffs sued in Texas to recover for the deaths of workers killed in a helicopter crash in Peru. The helicopter was operated by the defendant, a Colombian company. The parties conceded that the claims did not arise out of the defendant's contacts with Texas, so there was no basis for specific jurisdiction. Neither did the Court find a basis for general jurisdiction.

(2) Rationale

Since *International Shoe* forbids jurisdiction only where it would violate fair play and substantial justice for the state to exercise jurisdiction, one might well question the need for general jurisdiction in other cases. The general idea is to provide a "*safe harbor*" where the plaintiff may bring suit without the worry that a court might later question the existence of sufficient contacts under *International Shoe*.

b. Natural Persons

General jurisdiction is available in the state of a person's *domicile*. [**Milliken v. Meyer,** 311 U.S. 457 (1940)] One acquires a domicile by *being present* in a state *with the intent* to make it one's home for a permanent or indefinite period.

(1) Distinguish—Diversity of Citizenship Subject-Matter Jurisdiction

Domicile is also important for determining diversity of citizenship in connection with the subject-matter jurisdiction of federal courts. (*See infra*, p. 67.) Be sure to keep the concepts of personal jurisdiction and subject-matter jurisdiction separate.

c. Corporations

A corporation is subject to general jurisdiction in its *state of incorporation* and in the state in which its *principal place of business* is located, if different from its state of incorporation. This latter concept may produce problems if the executive offices are in one state and the manufacturing headquarters are in another. (*See infra*, p. 68 *et seq.*, regarding citizenship of corporation for diversity purposes.)

(1) Continuous and Systematic Contacts Rendering Corporation "Essentially at Home" in the Forum State

Beyond the paradigm bases for general jurisdiction over a corporation, state of incorporation and principal place of business, the Supreme Court has announced that "[a] court may assert general jurisdiction over foreign (sister state or foreign country) corporations to hear any and all claims against them when their affiliations with the State are so 'continuous and systematic' as to render them essentially at home in the forum state." [**Goodyear Dunlop Tires Operations, S.A. v. Brown,** 564 U.S. 915 (2011)] It has added that general jurisdiction over a foreign corporation is appropriate "only when the corporation's affiliations with the State in which suit is brought are so constant and pervasive 'as to render [it] essentially at home in the forum State.' " [**Daimler AG v. Bauman,** 134 S. Ct. 746 (2014)] These cases reflect a *narrowing* of the prior concept of general jurisdiction. [*See also* **Nichols v. G.D. Searle & Co.,** 991 F.2d 1195 (4th Cir. 1993)—because specific jurisdiction has "expanded tremendously," general jurisdiction, "which functioned primarily to ensure that a forum was available for plaintiffs to bring their claims [has] been rendered largely unnecessary. Thus, broad constructions of general jurisdiction should generally be disfavored."]

(a) Temporary Headquarters in Forum

In **Perkins v. Benguet Consolidated Mining Co.,** 342 U.S. 437 (1952), a Philippine corporation was unable to operate due to the Japanese occupation of the Philippines during World War II. Its president and general manager maintained an office in Ohio that seems to have functioned as a substitute head office. The Court stated that defendant had functioned as "carrying on in Ohio a *continuous and systematic*, but limited, part of its general business."

Jurisdiction in Ohio over a claim not related to the state was upheld. Note that *Perkins* is the only case in which the Supreme Court has ever upheld beyond-paradigm general personal jurisdiction.

Caution: Before the Supreme Court's recent *Goodyear* and *Daimler* decisions, the simple formulation "continuous and systematic" had become deeply embedded in the minds of many as describing the contacts that sufficed for beyond-paradigm general personal jurisdiction. But the Court pointed out in *Daimler* that *International Shoe* had used the term in the context of specific, rather than general, jurisdiction as describing one type of situation in which specific jurisdiction can exist when the in-state activities gave rise to the liabilities sued on. And its formulations in the recent general-jurisdiction cases have been much more demanding, referring to "continuous and systematic general business contacts" and requiring that the corporation's in-state activities be such as to render it "essentially at home" in the forum.

(b) Ongoing Operations in Forum

In older cases in some lower courts, even a relatively small office of a defendant corporation would suffice to uphold general jurisdiction, but the Supreme Court has tightened those requirements.

e.g. **Example**: In **Bryant v. Finnish National Airline,** 15 N.Y.2d 426 (1965), the New York Court of Appeals upheld jurisdiction over a claim for injuries sustained in Europe based on defendant's operation of a one-and-a-half room office in New York, staffed by three full-time and four part-time employees, and maintenance of a bank account in New York, even though defendant had no flights to or from American airports. Under contemporary standards, this level of activity would not suffice to support general jurisdiction.

Problem—nationwide business activities: In *Rush, supra,* p. 23, the Supreme Court stated that State Farm Insurance Co. was subject to garnishment in Minnesota because "State Farm is 'found,' in the sense of doing business, in all 50 states." The propriety of basing general jurisdiction over companies with nationwide business activities is unclear.

(c) Distinguish—Occasional Local Sale of Defendant's Other Products by Affiliates

In **Goodyear Dunlop Tires Operations, S.A. v. Brown,** *supra,* the Supreme Court held that indirect European subsidiaries of an American corporation were not subject to American jurisdiction in a suit by American citizens seeking to recover for deaths caused by an accident near Paris, France, allegedly due to faulty tires manufactured overseas by the subsidiaries for the European and Asian market. The particular type of tire involved was not marketed in the United States. The distribution of a small percentage of other types of the European subsidiaries' tires by still other affiliates of the American corporation did not support general jurisdiction.

(d) Distinguish—Local Subsidiary Subject to General Jurisdiction

In **Daimler AG v. Bauman,** *supra,* a suit against the German corporation that manufactures Mercedes Benz automobiles, the Supreme Court held that even if defendant's U.S. subsidiary, MBUSA, a Delaware limited-liability corporation, were subject to general jurisdiction in California, that did not provide a basis for subjecting the parent company to suit in California. Plaintiffs sued the German parent company for alleged actions of its Argentinian subsidiary causing harm to Argentinian residents during the "dirty war" in Argentina between 1976 and 1983. The German company's "slim contacts with the State [of California] hardly render it at home there."

(e) Distinguish—Purchase of Equipment and Execution of Contract in Forum

In **Helicopteros Nacionales de Colombia v. Hall,** *supra*, p. 23, the defendant, a Colombian corporation, had contracted to provide transportation services in Peru, in connection with a project being built there by a Texas-based joint venture, and had been paid over $5 million for its services under the contract. The defendant had also purchased most of its helicopter fleet from a Texas manufacturer and sent its pilots to Texas for training. The Court held the defendant's contacts with Texas to be *insufficient* as a basis for general jurisdiction over the defendant.

(f) Regular Purchases in Forum

Similarly, in **Rosenburg Bros. & Co. v. Curtis Brown Co.,** 260 U.S. 516 (1923), an Oklahoma retailer's purchase of a large portion of its merchandise in New York was held *not to be sufficient* for jurisdiction, even when coupled with regular visits to New York in connection with the purchases. The Supreme Court cited this case with approval in *Helicopteros*.

(g) Rejection of Reasonableness Limit for General Jurisdiction

The multi-factor reasonableness test that can defeat specific personal jurisdiction in cases like *Asahi*, *supra*, even when a defendant has sufficient minimum contacts with the forum, has no role in general-jurisdiction analysis. "When a corporation is genuinely at home in the forum State . . . any second-step [reasonableness] inquiry would be superfluous." [*Daimler*, *supra*]

4. Consent

A defendant may consent to jurisdiction in the forum. This consent may be *express*, *implied*, or due to the making of a *general appearance* in the minority of states that do not follow federal practice.

a. Express Consent

Express consent can be made either before or after suit is filed, and suffices to support jurisdiction without reference to other contacts with the forum.

e.g. **Example**: In **National Equipment Rental, Ltd. v. Szukhent,** 375 U.S. 311 (1964), Michigan farmer defendants signed the plaintiff's form lease for farm equipment providing that one Florence Weinberg of Long Island would be their agent for service of process in New York. The defendants did not know Weinberg, who was the wife of an officer of the plaintiff, but the Court upheld the effectiveness of service on her to establish jurisdiction in New York.

Knowing when to discuss "minimum contacts" in detail on your exam can sometimes be tricky. It's easy to forget that the traditional bases of jurisdiction—**consent, domicile, and service within the state**—can justify the exercise of personal jurisdiction without regard to a minimum-contacts analysis. Therefore, if the facts of an exam question **strongly** support the assertion of personal jurisdiction on one of these traditional grounds, you should **stress that traditional ground** in your answer. **Be alert, however, for facts indicating that the traditional ground may not be satisfied**—e.g., facts are given that show that the defendant may have been fraudulently induced into the forum for service of process, which would nullify reliance on service within the state as a basis for personal jurisdiction. In such a case, after discussing the traditional basis and why it might not be available under the facts of your question, you should discuss minimum contacts in detail as sort of a backup plan.

(1) Registration by Corporation

In many states, foreign corporations that engage in business in the state are required to register and appoint an agent for service of process in the state, thereby consenting to suit there.

(a) Commerce-Clause Limitations

The power of a state to insist on consent to general jurisdiction may be questionable to the extent that it unreasonably burdens interstate commerce. [*Compare* **Pennsylvania Fire Insurance Co. v. Gold Issue Mining & Milling Co.**, 243 U.S. 93 (1917)—state could require corporations wishing to do business to consent to jurisdiction on unrelated claims—*with* **Bendix Autolite Corp. v. Midwesco Enterprises, Inc.**, 486 U.S. 888 (1988)—state may not deny protection of statute of limitations to foreign corporation that refuses to consent to jurisdiction on unrelated suits]

(b) Possible Due Process Limitations

The Supreme Court has limited general jurisdiction over corporate defendants to states in which the corporation is "essentially at home." *See* p. 24 *supra*. The lower courts are divided about whether corporate registration alone suffices to support general jurisdiction. [*Compare* **Cossaboon v. Maine Medical Center**, 600 F.3d 25 (1st Cir. 2010)—"Corporate registration in New Hampshire adds some weight to the jurisdictional analysis, but it is not alone sufficient to confer general jurisdiction"—*with* **Bane v. Netlink, Inc.**, 925 F.2d 637 (3d Cir. 1991)—by registering to do business in Pennsylvania, defendant purposefully availed, and its subsequent withdrawal of its authorization to do business in the state did not change that conclusion]

(c) Implied Consent Contrasted

As an adjunct to the registration requirements, states often treat conduct of business in the state to be impliedly appointing a state official, often the secretary of state, as agent for service of process. This view is not based on a true consent theory, but on the constitutionality of exercise of state jurisdiction over claims arising from the corporation's activities in the state.

(2) Limitation—Local Actions

In cases involving title to land, courts may proceed only if the land is located in the jurisdiction. (*See infra*, p. 40.) In such cases *consent of the parties is insufficient*.

b. Implied Consent

By filing suit, the plaintiff is deemed to have consented to the jurisdiction of the forum for the purpose of a counterclaim by the defendant. [**Adam v. Saenger,** 303 U.S. 59 (1938)] However, this implied consent does not extend to a counterclaim unrelated to the subject matter of the plaintiff's claim against the defendant.

(1) Consent in Class Actions

In class actions, the failure of unnamed *plaintiff class* members to opt out of the class action constitutes consent to adjudication of their claims in the forum. [**Phillips Petroleum Co. v. Shutts,** 472 U.S. 797 (1985)] The Supreme Court has not resolved the question whether the same reasoning would apply to a defendant class.

c. Appearance

A party's voluntary appearance, except when it is making a "special appearance" only to contest jurisdiction in a state that follows such a procedure, in an action is *sufficient by itself* to support jurisdiction.

(1) What Constitutes an Appearance?

In general, an appearance occurs when the defendant *defends litigation on the merits*. Depending on the prevailing rules in the jurisdiction, the issue turns on the extent to which the defendant raises issues other than jurisdiction.

(a) State Courts

In some states, a defendant who wishes to preserve objections to personal jurisdiction must make a *special appearance* raising *only jurisdictional issues*. Raising any other matter subjects the defendant to the risk of having made a general appearance and thereby consenting to jurisdiction. In some states requiring a special appearance, however, the defendant may simultaneously raise other defenses so long as it immediately challenges personal jurisdiction. [*See, e.g.*, Cal. Civ. Proc. Code § 418.10(e)(1)—defendant who files a motion to quash service of process challenging personal jurisdiction may simultaneously answer, demur, or move to strike the complaint without waiving its objection to jurisdiction]

(b) Federal Courts

In federal courts and in most state courts, a defendant need not make a special appearance; all grounds of defense, including lack of personal jurisdiction, can be asserted in a motion or answer. [*See* Fed. R. Civ. P. 12(b)]

1) Waiver

However, if the defendant fails to raise personal jurisdiction in her *initial motion* or answer, that objection is waived. [Fed. R. Civ. P. 12(h)(1)]

2) Consent to Jurisdiction to Decide Jurisdiction

By moving to dismiss for lack of personal jurisdiction, the defendant consents to the power of the court to decide that question, ***including the power to order discovery pertinent to the jurisdictional question.*** [Insurance Corp. of Ireland, Ltd. v. Compagnie des Bauxites de Guinee, *supra*, p. 15]

a) Binding Effect

A defendant who appears and litigates jurisdiction may not later raise jurisdiction as a bar to full faith and credit. (*See infra*, p. 35.) To preserve the jurisdictional objection as a ground for resisting full faith and credit, defendant must default. (*See infra*, p. 29.)

(c) Extent of Jurisdiction Conferred

A general appearance may be limited to the claims made or issues raised in the action at the time of the appearance.

(d) Alternative of Default

A defendant who believes that jurisdiction in the forum is improper may disregard the suit and permit a default judgment to be taken against him. When the plaintiff later attempts to enforce the default judgment in another jurisdiction under the Full Faith and Credit Clause, the defendant can then challenge on the ground that the rendering court lacked jurisdiction. If the enforcing court finds jurisdiction was proper, however, there will be no further opportunity to defend on the merits. (*See infra*, p. 34.)

5. Service Within the Jurisdiction

Under *Pennoyer, supra*, p. 4, service of process within the jurisdiction was presumptively sufficient to support jurisdiction.

a. Possible Minimum-Contacts Requirement

In *Shaffer, supra*, p. 21, the Court stated that "all assertions of state court jurisdiction must be evaluated according to the standards set forth in *International Shoe.*" However, in **Burnham v. Superior Court**, 495 U.S. 604 (1990), the Supreme Court, without a majority opinion but with no dissents, **upheld** the constitutionality of "***transient jurisdiction***," obtained by service on a nonresident ***temporarily*** within the state, even though the suit was unrelated to the defendant's activities in the state. **Caution:** This ground for jurisdiction may not suffice, according to some Justices' opinions, if the defendant's presence in the state was not ***intentional*** or ***voluntary***. Also, actual use of transient jurisdiction is not common.

b. Fraudulent Inducement

When the defendant is personally served in the, forum state, the court will ***not*** exercise jurisdiction on that ground if the defendant was lured into the jurisdiction by the plaintiff's ***false statements***. [*See* **Wyman v. Newhouse**, *supra*, p. 6]

(1) Distinguish—Trickery to Effect Service

Although fraudulently inducing a defendant into the jurisdiction is generally a defense to the assertion of jurisdiction on the basis of that service, using trickery ***to*** *effect service* on a defendant already in the jurisdiction generally *does not interfere with the effectiveness of service*.

(2) In Rem Cases

When the plaintiff relies on seizure of the defendant's movable property to establish jurisdiction, the seizure should be disregarded if the *property is moved* to the forum as the result of some *trickery by the plaintiff*. [*See* **Commercial Air Charters v. Sundorph,** 57 F.R.D. 84 (D. Conn. 1972)—jurisdiction refused because plaintiff's friend "rented" defendant's airplane, misrepresenting his intentions, and took it into forum so that plaintiff could levy attachment]

■GILBERT

A COURT WILL HAVE JURISDICTION OVER A DEFENDANT IF:

☑ Defendant has sufficient *minimum contacts* with the forum so that the forum's exercise of jurisdiction over defendant is reasonable;

☑ Defendant's *property has been seized within the forum* and there is an appropriate relationship between the property and the claim;

☑ Defendant's contacts with the forum are *so continuous and systematic* that jurisdiction on *unrelated claims* can be exercised (general jurisdiction) because defendant is *essentially at home* in the forum state;

☑ Defendant expressly, impliedly, or by appearance *consented* to forum's exercise of jurisdiction; or

☑ Defendant was *personally served within the forum*.

---

6. Territorial Jurisdiction of Federal Courts

In most cases, federal courts *do not exercise nationwide jurisdiction*. Except in a few situations when such powers are conferred by rule or statute, the territorial jurisdiction of a federal court is usually no broader than that of the courts of the state in which the federal court is located. (*See infra*, p. 33 *et seq.*)

a. Constitutional Limitations on Nationwide Service

It appears that Congress *could* constitutionally create nationwide personal jurisdiction for the federal courts. [*See* **United States v. Union Pacific Railroad,** 98 U.S. 569 (1878)—asserting that Congress could have created a single federal district court with nationwide jurisdiction] There may, however, be *limitations under the Due Process Clause* of the Fifth Amendment on extremely inconvenient exercises of jurisdiction. [*Compare* **Republic of Panama v. BCCI Holdings,** 119 F.3d 935 (11th Cir. 1997)—finding nationwide exercise of jurisdiction subject to Fifth Amendment due process limitations—*with* **FTC v. Jim Walter Corp.,** 651 F.2d 251 (5th Cir. 1981)—rejecting argument that Fifth Amendment Due Process Clause does not permit federal-court personal jurisdiction based on contacts with United States as a whole]

b. National Contacts

Some have argued that in actions against aliens, contacts with the United States should be *aggregated* in order to determine whether together they would support jurisdiction in this country, even though no one state has sufficient contacts to justify jurisdiction. The

Supreme Court has not passed on this argument. [*See* **Omni Capital International v. Rudolf Wolff & Co., Ltd.,** 484 U.S. 97 (1988); **Mwani v. bin Laden,** 417 F.3d 1 (D.C. Cir. 2005)—terrorist group's bombing of United States embassy in Nairobi, Kenya, provided a basis for United States jurisdiction because it was targeted at the United States] A Supreme Court plurality opinion has suggested that a non-American defendant may be subject to jurisdiction in a federal court due to national contacts even though it does not have sufficient contacts to support jurisdiction in a state court. [**J. McIntyre Machinery, Ltd. v. Nicastro,** *supra*—"Because the United States is a distinct sovereign, a defendant may in principle be subject to the jurisdiction of the courts of the United States but not of any particular State."]

C. Statutory or Rule Authorization for Jurisdiction

1. Introduction

For a court to assert jurisdiction over an out-of-state defendant, there must be a statute or rule that gives the court the authority to exercise jurisdiction. In state court, such authority is usually in the form of a ***long-arm statute***, which operates as ***enabling legislation***. Thus, the ***first step*** in a jurisdictional analysis (*i.e.*, before any analysis of minimum contacts or other jurisdictional basis) is to examine this legislation and determine whether it covers the case presented. This often involves a problem of ***statutory interpretation***—deciding what the legislators or rule-makers meant by the words selected for the statute or rule.

2. Long-Arm Statutes

In the wake of *International Shoe*, legislatures began to enact statutes extending the reach of their courts' jurisdiction ("the long arm of the law").

a. Full-Power Statutes

Long-arm statutes in a few states explicitly authorize exercise of jurisdiction ***whenever it would not violate the Constitution***. [*See, e.g.*, Cal. Civ. Proc. Code § 410.10] In such states, the only question that need be considered is the constitutionality of jurisdiction. Note that some courts have interpreted statutes that do not expressly provide this broad jurisdiction nevertheless to have this effect. (*See infra*, p. 32.)

b. Specific Acts

Many long-arm statutes ***designate specific acts*** as warranting the exercise of jurisdiction. Common examples include claims arising from:

(i)   The transaction of any business within the state;

(ii) The commission of a tortious act within the state;

(iii) Ownership, use, or possession of real property within the state;

(iv) Contracting to insure any person, property, or risk located in the state at the time of contracting; and

(v)   The maintenance of a marital domicile in the state in an action for divorce.

With such a statute, one must consider (i) whether the defendant's activities fall within the terms of the statute and (ii), if so, whether the exercise of jurisdiction in this case is constitutional.

(1) Common-Sense Reading

In general, courts say that they will give the words of the rule or statute their ordinary meaning. In some instances, however, they seem to overextend that reading. Thus, in **Gray v. American Radiator & Standard Sanitary Corp.,** *supra*, p. 12, the court read the Illinois statute's provision of jurisdiction for "the commission of a tortious act within this State" to cover the manufacture in Ohio of an allegedly defective valve that was shipped to a manufacturer in Pennsylvania and incorporated into a boiler made there. [*Compare* **Feathers v. McLucas,** 15 N.Y.2d 443 (1965)— language "tortious act within the state" too clear to include tortious act outside the state that causes an injury within the state]

(2) Different Legal Theory

If the defendant's specific act is within the statute, claims based on the same act but a different legal theory usually can also be asserted in the action. [**Mack Trucks, Inc. v. Arrow Aluminum Castings Co.,** 510 F.2d 1029 (5th Cir. 1975)—products liability suit based on "tortious act" long-arm provision can assert both negligence and breach of contract theories]

(3) "Arising out of" Requirement

Usually, long-arm statutes that designate specific acts require that claims arise out of that act. This presents a problem similar to that in determining whether there is a relationship between the claim and the contacts on a minimum-contacts analysis (*supra*, p. 14) and whether specific or general jurisdiction is being invoked (*supra*, p. 23). However, in this instance, the analysis made is of the relationship between the contacts and the claim as a matter of state law, rather than as a matter of federal constitutional law.

(4) "Tortious Act"

The tortious-act requirement is generally held to be satisfied whenever the plaintiff *alleges* that the defendant's act was tortious. [**Nelson v. Miller,** 11 Ill. 2d 378 (1975)] If an actual tortious act were required and the defendant won the case on the ground that the act was not tortious, that could mean that there was no jurisdiction.

(5) Full Power Through Interpretation

Some long-arm statutes specifically extend jurisdiction to the constitutional limit. (*See supra*, p. 31.) In those states that have specific-act statutes, some courts have interpreted the statutes to extend jurisdiction to the constitutional limit. [*See* **World-Wide Volkswagen Corp. v. Woodson,** *supra*, p. 16—Oklahoma statute interpreted as conferring jurisdiction to the limits permitted by constitution; **Nelson v. Miller,** *supra*—same with regard to Illinois statute]

(a) Rationale

Often the reasoning behind such extensions is that the legislature had no reason to deny residents access to the courts in cases in which jurisdiction would be constitutional.

(b) Caution

States that have taken this approach sometimes balk at pursuing it as far as possible. Thus, after *Nelson*, *supra*, the Illinois Supreme Court cautioned that "[a] statute worded in the way ours is should have a fixed meaning without regard to changing concepts of due process." [**Green v. Advance Ross Electronics Corp.**, 427 N.E.2d 1203 (Ill. 1981)] *But note*: Illinois later amended its long-arm statute to extend to the constitutional limit. [*See* Ill. Code Civ. P. § 2–209(c)]

3. Federal-Court Jurisdiction

In general, federal courts exercise jurisdiction no broader than that authorized by state long-arm statutes.

a. In Personam Jurisdiction

(1) Subject to Jurisdiction of State Court

Process from a federal court will confer jurisdiction over a defendant if the defendant would be subject to jurisdiction of a court of general jurisdiction in the state in which the federal court is located. [Fed. R. Civ. P. 4(k)(1)(A)] In other words, if the defendant could be served in a suit in the state where the federal court is located, the defendant can also be served in a federal-court suit.

(a) Constitutionality

When this authority is the ground for exercise of personal jurisdiction, the constitutionality of that exercise is the same as if the case were in state court.

(2) Rule 14 or Rule 19 Joinder

Even if local law does not permit service, a party who is served within a judicial district and within 100 miles of the place from which the summons was issued is subject to jurisdiction if joined under Rule 14 (impleader, *see infra*, p. 226 *et seq.*) or Rule 19 (required parties, *see infra*, p. 221 *et seq.*). [Fed. R. Civ. P. 4(k)(1)(B)] This authority is commonly known as *"bulge jurisdiction."* **Caution**: "Bulge jurisdiction" cannot be used to initiate an action, but only to add parties to an existing action.

(3) Interpleader or Other Federal Statutory Basis

Sometimes a federal statute authorizes *nationwide jurisdiction*. If so, federal courts can exercise jurisdiction even though state courts could not. Examples include interpleader [28 U.S.C. § 2361] and securities-fraud actions [15 U.S.C. § 78aa]. [Fed. R. Civ. P. 4(k)(1)(C)] Service in actions within the federal courts' multiparty, multiforum jurisdiction (*see, e.g.*, 28 U.S.C. § 1369—civil cases involving at least 75 individuals' deaths from a single accident at a discrete location) may be made at any place within the United States or anywhere outside the country if otherwise authorized by law. [28 U.S.C. § 1697]

(4) Minimum Contacts with United States

For *claims arising under federal law*, federal courts can exercise jurisdiction even though the defendant is *not subject* to the jurisdiction of the courts of general jurisdiction *in any state*, if this exercise would be consistent with the Constitution. [Fed. R. Civ. P. 4(k)(2)] This situation usually involves a foreign defendant.

(a) National vs. State Contacts

This provision could apply if the defendant's national contacts permit exercise of jurisdiction although no state has sufficient contacts to support it. [*See, e.g.*,

Go-Video, Inc. v. Akai Electric Co., 885 F.2d 1406 (9th Cir. 1989)] A Supreme Court plurality opinion has suggested that a non-American defendant might be subject to jurisdiction in a federal court on a nonfederal claims due to national contacts even though it does not have sufficient contacts to support jurisdiction in a state court. [**J. McIntyre Machinery, Ltd. v. Nicastro,** *supra.*]

(b) Narrow Long-Arm Statute

Alternatively, this provision could apply if the state in which the court is located has a narrow long-arm statute that does not apply to the circumstances presented in the case although there are constitutionally sufficient grounds for exercise of jurisdiction.

(c) Showing Defendant Not Subject to Jurisdiction in Any District

A plaintiff who invokes this ground of jurisdiction must certify that, based on available information, the defendant cannot be sued in any district. To avoid jurisdiction on this basis, the burden is then on the defendant to show that it is subject to suit in some district. [*See* **United States v. Swiss American Bank,** 191 F.3d 30 (1st Cir. 1999)]

b. In Rem Jurisdiction

The federal court may assert jurisdiction by seizing a defendant's assets found within the district only if *defendant cannot be served by an otherwise authorized means*, and then only in the *manner provided by the law of the state* in which the district court is located. [Fed. R. Civ. P. 4(n)(2)] *But note*: It may still be possible to challenge the seizure under **Shaffer v. Heitner.** (*See supra*, p. 21 *et seq.*)

c. No Court-Created Authority

In **Omni Capital International v. Rudolf Wolff & Co., Ltd.,** *supra*, p. 30, the Court rejected arguments that it should authorize nationwide service of process in connection with a federal claim for which Congress had not provided for such service. The Court found it "likely that Congress has been acting on the assumption that federal courts cannot add to the scope of service of summons Congress has authorized." The addition of Rule 4(k)(2) (*supra*, p. 33) provided the authority the Court had found lacking.

D. Litigating Jurisdiction

1. Introduction

Implicit in the idea of consent (*supra*, pp. 26–29) is the need for the defendant to raise personal-jurisdiction objections in a timely fashion. In reality, the defendant faces a variety of options.

2. Default

A party served with summons who believes that the court lacks personal jurisdiction or authority to serve process on her may disregard the process and allow her default to be taken. If an effort is later made to enforce the resulting default judgment, she can argue that full faith and credit should not be given to the judgment because it was entered by a court without jurisdiction. However, if this argument is rejected, the defendant may not then defend on the merits.

3. Appearance to Litigate Jurisdiction

The defendant can appear in the action and litigate jurisdiction in the court in which the suit was filed. In federal court and in most state courts, the jurisdictional objection can be raised along with other defenses (*see supra*, p. 28), but in a few states, the defendant would have to enter a special appearance (*see supra*, p. 28), which raises only the jurisdictional issue.

4. Discovery

When factual issues (*e.g.*, defendant's level of contacts with the forum) are pertinent to resolution of a personal-jurisdiction objection, the court may order discovery regarding those issues. By making a *personal-jurisdiction objection*, the defendant *consents to the court's jurisdiction with respect to such discovery*. [**Insurance Corp. of Ireland, Ltd. v. Compagnie des Bauxites de Guinee,** *supra*, p. 29]

5. Binding Effect

Once the defendant has appeared and litigated jurisdiction, she may not re-raise the issue collaterally to resist full faith and credit; she is estopped from re-litigating the issue. [**Baldwin v. Iowa State Traveling Men's Association,** 283 U.S. 522 (1931)]

a. Appellate Review

A defendant whose jurisdictional objections are rejected can appeal that decision in the court system in which the decision was made. However, in the federal courts and many state systems, appellate review is available only after a final decision is rendered, usually after a trial. (*See infra*, p. 425 *et seq.*) In some state systems, earlier review is possible. [*See* Cal. Civ. Proc. Code § 418.10(c)—defendant whose motion to quash service is denied must petition for writ of mandate within 10 days or enter a general appearance and waive jurisdictional objection]

E. Venue

1. Introduction

Venue is a statutory limitation on where a suit may be brought. It may prevent a plaintiff from bringing suit in a particular court even though the court has jurisdiction. The venue rules are designed to prevent the plaintiff from suing where it would be burdensome for the defendant to appear and defend. Venue usually is considered after it is determined that there is statutory authorization for the exercise of jurisdiction and that the exercise of jurisdiction is constitutional.

a. Federal System

Venue statutes in the federal system limit the *federal districts* in which suit may be brought. In the federal judicial system, venue "refers to the geographic specification of the proper court or courts for the litigation of a civil action that is within the subject-matter jurisdiction of the district courts in general, and does not refer to any grant or restriction of subject-matter jurisdiction." [28 U.S.C. § 1390(a)]

b. State Courts

Venue statutes in state court systems usually limit the *counties* in which suit may be brought.

Don't confuse venue with jurisdiction. Jurisdiction involves the **power** of the court to decide a case (subject-matter jurisdiction) and to exercise its power over a particular defendant or piece of property (personal jurisdiction). Venue involves the **proper place** to bring the action. Remember that you need not even consider whether venue is proper until you have already determined that the court has jurisdiction. If so, then you look at the particular venue statute to see if venue is proper.

2. Federal Venue Limitations

The same venue provisions apply to all civil actions in federal district court. [28 U.S.C. § 1391(a)(1)] Before amendment in 2011, the venue statute had different provisions for *transitory actions* and *local actions* (cases involving land). These differences were *abolished* by amendment in 2011. [28 U.S.C. § 1391(a)(2)]

cf.   **Compare—State Local-Action Restrictions**: In many states, venue for actions involving real property is still limited to the court where the property is located. *E.g.,* Cal. Code Civ. Proc. § 392(a)—actions for recovery of real property, determination of an interest in real property, or foreclosure of a lien or mortgage on real property must be brought in the county where the real property is situated.

a. Defendant's Residence

Venue is proper in a judicial district where any defendant resides, if all defendants reside in the state where the district is located, whether federal subject-matter jurisdiction is based on diversity of citizenship or a federal question. [28 U.S.C. § 1391(b)(1)]

(1) Residence of Natural Person

The residency of a natural person refers to domicile—the place she resides with intent to remain permanently or indefinitely. In this sense, it is analogous to citizenship for purposes of diversity jurisdiction. (*See supra*, p. 24.) [28 U.S.C. § 1391(c)(1)]

(2) Residence of Entities

A defendant entity, whether or not incorporated, that has the capacity to sue or be sued is deemed to reside in any judicial district in which it is subject to the court's personal jurisdiction with respect to the action in question. A plaintiff entity is deemed to reside only in the district in which it maintains its principal place of business. [28 U.S.C. § 1391(c)(2)] (Where a plaintiff resides, though, is usually irrelevant for federal venue purposes.)

(3) Residence of Corporations in States with Multiple Districts

A corporation is deemed to reside in any district within a multiple-district state with which its contacts would be sufficient to subject it to personal jurisdiction if that district were a separate state. If there is no such district, the corporation is deemed to reside within the district with which it has the most significant contacts. [28 U.S.C. § 1391(d)]

(4) Defendant Not Resident in United States

A defendant that is not resident in the United States may be sued in any judicial district; and the joinder of such a defendant in a suit is disregarded in determining whether venue is proper if it is sued along with other defendants. [28 U.S.C. § 1391(c)(3)]

b. Location of Substantial Part of Events or Omissions or of Property

Venue is proper in "a judicial district in which a substantial part of the events or omissions giving rise to the claim occurred, or a substantial part of property that is the subject of the action is situated," whether federal subject-matter jurisdiction is based on diversity of citizenship or a federal question. [28 U.S.C. § 1391(b)(2)] These provisions are intended to cope with the problem of *venue gaps*, which could arise when there are multiple defendants and there is no state that is the residence of all of them.

(1) Distinguish—Where Claim Arose

Until 1990, venue was proper "where the claim arose." This term had generated substantial litigation to determine which of several districts was the *single one* "where the claim arose" in cases involving multiforum transactions, and the term received a narrow interpretation by the Supreme Court. [**Leroy v. Great Western United Corp.,** 443 U.S. 173 (1979)] Unlike this narrow interpretation, the amended venue statute contemplates that in a number of cases venue may be proper on this ground in *more than one district.*

(2) Application

Problem areas in the application of the 1990 statutory provision include the following:

(a) "Giving Rise"

It is not clear whether Congress intended that the pertinent events be only those on which liability is predicated under the relevant substantive law. For example, in a products-liability action against a manufacturer, it is likely that the retail sale of the product would not be an element of the claim, but the place of retail sale may nevertheless be a proper venue even if the injury occurred in another district.

(b) "Substantial Part"

Although the amended statute contemplates that more than one district may qualify, it is not clear how many events (or omissions) suffice as a "substantial part."

Example: When a creditor's demand letter was forwarded to a district by the Postal Service from plaintiff's old address, receipt of the letter in the district was held to satisfy the venue requirements for an action under the Fair Debt Collection Practices Act [15 U.S.C. §§ 1692 *et seq.*]. The harm Congress sought to protect against occurred when the letter was received. [**Bates v. C & S Adjusters, Inc.,** 980 F.2d 865 (2d Cir. 1992)]

Example: A government enforcement action against a defendant that had mailed 15 million postcards nationwide could be brought in Iowa, where 200,000 postcards were directed. [**United States v. Hartbrodt,** 773 F. Supp. 1240 (S.D. Iowa 1991)]

(3) "Property Present"

The problem of location of property is similar to the question of location of property for purposes of personal jurisdiction (*see supra*, pp. 20–21), but turns in this instance on the intent of Congress, which may be to have the federal courts develop federal rules regarding the location of property for venue purposes.

(a) Property Subject of the Action

The property must be the subject of the action for this venue provision to apply.

c. Fallback Venue—Used When Other Venue Requirements Cannot Be Satisfied in Any District

If there is no other district in which an action may otherwise be brought as provided in 28 U.S.C. § 1391(b)(1) or (2), it may be brought in "any judicial district in which *any defendant is subject to the court's personal jurisdiction* with respect to such action." [28 U.S.C. § 1391(b)(3)]

(1) Application—As a Fallback Only

A plaintiff who wishes to rely on the fallback provision must demonstrate that venue cannot be established in any other district.

(a) Defendant's Residence

The fallback provision may not be used if all defendants are residents of a single state, since section 1391(b)(1) would apply. In single-defendant cases, resort to the fallback is not justified if defendant is a resident of another state and personal jurisdiction can be obtained there.

(b) Substantial Portion of Acts Giving Rise to the Claim

The fallback venue provision cannot apply if there is any district in which a substantial portion of the acts or omissions giving rise to the liability occurred, because that would suffice for venue under section 1391(b)(2). Often, the fallback provision would apply only if the acts or omissions giving rise to the liability occurred outside this country, although there could be cases in which they occurred in this country but there is no district in which a "significant portion" of them occurred.

(2) Fallback Ensures Venue Is Proper in Some District

By adopting the fallback venue provision, Congress meant to provide that there would always be some federal district court in which venue would be proper when personal jurisdiction was proper. [**Atlantic Marine Constr. Co. v. U.S. District Court,** 134 S. Ct. 568 (2013)—"The statute [§ 1391(b)(3)] ensures that so long as a federal court has personal jurisdiction over the defendant, venue will always lie somewhere."]

(3) Multidefendant Cases

In multidefendant cases, the fallback venue provision may apply if venue is proper as to only one defendant in that district, even if it is not otherwise proper as to one or more additional defendants. [28 U.S.C. § 1391(b)(3)—referring to any judicial district in which *any* defendant is subject to personal jurisdiction]

(4) Admiralty Cases Excluded

Cases in federal court under 28 U.S.C. § 1333, dealing with admiralty and prize cases, are mostly excluded from the operation of the general venue statutes. [28 U.S.C. § 1390(b)]

Remember that in venue questions you must analyze venue under the first bases for venue—defendant's residence and location of a substantial part of the events or omissions or of the property—*before* considering the fallback provision. *Only if neither of the first bases applies* do you consider using the fallback provision.

d. Special Venue Statutes

Congress has altered the general rules of venue in connection with certain types of cases:

(1) Additional Venue Options

In some types of cases, venue may be proper in certain locations in addition to the districts allowed under the general rules.

(a) Patent-Infringement Actions

In *addition* to the districts specified by the general venue statutes, venue in a patent-infringement action is also proper in the district where the defendant committed acts of infringement if the defendant has a "regular and established place of business" in that district. [28 U.S.C. § 1400(b)] The general venue statute's provision that a corporation resides in any district in which it is subject to personal jurisdiction (*see supra*, p. 36) does not apply to patent-infringement actions. [**TC Heartland LLC v. Kraft Food Groups Brands LLC,** 137 S.Ct. __ (2017)]

(b) Copyright Suits

Similarly, in *addition* to the districts specified by the general venue statutes, venue in copyright suits is proper in any district in which the defendant or her agent may be found. [28 U.S.C. § 1400(a)]

(2) Substitute Venue

In a few types of cases, venue is proper *only* in the districts specified by the special statute.

(a) Federal Tort Claims Actions

Venue for federal tort claims actions is proper only in the district where the plaintiff resides or where the act complained of occurred. [28 U.S.C. § 1402(b)]

(b) Statutory Interpleader

In statutory interpleader actions, venue is proper only in a district where a claimant to the fund resides. [28 U.S.C. § 1397]

e. Persons Not Resident in the United States

In a suit against a person not resident in the United States, suit may be filed in any judicial district, and the joinder of such a defendant is disregarded in determining where the action may be brought with respect to other defendants. [28 U.S.C. § 1391(c)(3)]

f. Removed Cases

When a case is removed from state court to federal court, it goes to the district encompassing the state court in which the action was pending, regardless of the residence of the parties. [28 U.S.C. § 1309(c); 28 U.S.C. § 1441(a)] In a sense, removal creates its own venue.

g. Local Actions

Until 2011, the federal venue statutes distinguished between "local actions" about real property, which had to be filed where the real property was located, and "transitory actions," which were subject to the rules described above. In 2011, this *distinction was abolished*. [28 U.S.C. § 1391(a)(2)—"the proper venue for a civil action shall be determined without regard to whether the action is local or transitory in nature"] Accordingly, venue cannot be defeated on the ground that the suit should be classified as a "local action."

(1) Compare—District in Which a "Substantial Part" of Property Subject to the Action Is Located

Venue may be proper because a "substantial part" of the property subject to the action is located in the district in which the action was filed. [28 U.S.C. § 1391(b)(2)] This is similar to, but different from, the local-action rule, which limits venue to the property's location.

(2) Transitory and Local Actions in State Venue Law

Venue law in many states has distinguished between transitory and local actions, requiring "local" actions to be brought where the property is located while permitting "transitory" actions to be brought in other places, such as the county where the defendant resides, even if the events took place elsewhere. But states may have different standards for determining which actions are "local" actions, some limiting the category to actions regarding title to real property and others including claims for damage to land. If state venue provisions apply, be alert to these possibilities.

(3) But Note: 2011 Federal Venue Amendment May Not Abolish Local-Transitory Distinction

Regarding the local-action doctrine as going to subject-matter jurisdiction rather than venue (a point on which division and uncertainty exist), the Ninth Circuit has held that the 2011 venue amendment did not abolish the distinction between local and transitory actions. [**Eldee-K Rental Props., LLC v. DirecTV, Inc.,** *supra*]

h. Forum-Selection Clause Irrelevant to Statutory Venue

The existence of a valid forum-selection clause that specifies a different location for the litigation is not a ground for dismissal for improper venue; whether venue is "wrong" or "improper" under the venue statutes depends exclusively on the statutory requirements. [**Atlantic Marine Constr. Co. v. U.S. District Court,** *supra*]

3. State Venue Limitations

State venue provisions involve similar considerations to federal venue rules.

a. Defendant's Residence

Traditionally, in personam actions can be brought in the county where the defendant resides; and when multiple defendants are sued, the action may be proper in any county where one of them resides. [*See* Cal. Civ. Proc. Code § 395]

b. Where Claim Arose

In some jurisdictions, most or some types of claims (*e.g.*, tort claims) can be brought where the claim arose. [*See* Cal. Civ. Proc. Code § 395(a)—in action for personal injury, venue is proper in county where injury occurs]

c. Actions Affecting Real Property

When the action affects title to real property, venue is usually in the county where the property is located. [*See* Cal. Civ. Proc. Code § 392(a)(1)]

d. Nonresident Defendant

In general, nonresidents are regarded as having no venue rights, and the plaintiff may often sue them in any county. [*See* Cal. Civ. Proc. Code § 395(a)]

(1) Equal Protection Challenge Rejected

A state may allow an out-of-state corporation to be sued in *any* county without violating the Equal Protection Clause, even when it limits suits against an in-state corporation to the county of its principal place of business. It is rational to weigh differently (i) the inconvenience of a domestic corporation in defending a suit in a forum distant from its principal place of business and (ii) the burden on an out-of-state corporation that must defend away from home in any event. [**Burlington Northern Railroad v. Ford,** 504 U.S. 648 (1992)]

4. Litigating Venue

As with personal jurisdiction, improper venue may be *waived* unless raised in the proper way. In federal court, for example, it is waived unless it is raised in the first Rule 12 motion or in the answer if there is no Rule 12 motion. [*See* Fed. R. Civ. P. 12(h)(1)]

a. Effect of Timely Venue Objection

When the defendant timely objects to venue and the court finds it improper, the court *cannot proceed* with the case. It may dismiss, but in most jurisdictions it can also transfer the case to a court that is a proper venue. (*See infra.*)

b. Possible Effect of Failure to Object to Personal Jurisdiction

Under the "fallback" venue provision, it is possible that failure to timely object to personal jurisdiction would preclude a challenge to venue if the plaintiff can show venue would not be proper in any other district—because venue would then be proper in any district in which defendant is "subject to the court's personal jurisdiction with respect to such action." [28 U.S.C. § 1391(b)(3)] Failure to object to personal jurisdiction waives that objection [Fed. R. Civ. P. 12(h)(1)], and could be held to make venue proper under the fallback provision as well.

5. Federal Transfer Provisions

A federal case may be transferred to another federal court in the following circumstances:

a. Venue or Jurisdiction Improper in Original Court

When venue or personal jurisdiction is improper in the court selected by the plaintiff and the defendant properly objects, the court *may transfer the case to a proper court* rather than dismiss it. [28 U.S.C. § 1406(a)]

(1) Transfer When Jurisdiction Also Improper

Although the statute talks of transfer only when venue is improper, the Supreme Court has held that it authorizes transfer when both jurisdiction and venue are improper. [**Goldlawr, Inc. v. Heiman,** 369 U.S. 463 (1962)]

(2) Transfer When Venue Proper but Jurisdiction Lacking

Lower courts have upheld transfer from a district where venue is proper but there is no personal jurisdiction. [**Bentz v. Recile,** 778 F.2d 1026 (5th Cir. 1985)]

(3) Court May Dismiss, Not Transfer

Although the district court may choose to relieve the plaintiff of some adverse consequences of filing suit in a district in which venue or jurisdiction is improper by transferring to a proper venue, it may dismiss instead of transferring. [*See* **Nichols v. G.D. Searle & Co.,** *supra,* p. 24—district court acted within its discretion when it dismissed rather than transferred when plaintiff's attorney committed "obvious error" in filing suit in the wrong court, and thereby imposed substantial unnecessary costs on defendant and the legal system]

b. Transfer for Convenience

When venue and jurisdiction are proper in the court selected by the plaintiff, the court can transfer the action "for the convenience of the parties and witnesses, in the interest of justice." [28 U.S.C. § 1404(a)]

(1) Distinguish—Forum Non Conveniens

This transfer provision considers many factors that bear on the question whether to dismiss on forum non conveniens grounds (*see infra,* p. 45), but it permits transfer on a *lesser showing of inconvenience.* [**Norwood v. Kirkpatrick,** 349 U.S. 29 (1955)] As the Supreme Court has explained, "[f]or the federal court system, Congress has codified the doctrine and has provided for transfer, rather than dismissal, when a sister federal court is the more convenient place for trial of the action." [**Sinochem International Co. v. Malaysia International Shipping Corp.,** 549 U.S. 422 (2007)]

(2) Proper Transferee Court

The statute authorizes transfer to any district in which the action *might have been brought* or to a district to which *all parties have consented.* [28 U.S.C. § 1404(a)]

cf. **Compare—Former Law**: Under the statutory language before amendment in 2011 that permitted party consent to transfer to a specific district, the Supreme Court held that transfer was permitted only to a district that would be *proper venue* and would have *valid personal jurisdiction.* [**Hoffman v. Blaski,** 363 U.S. 335 (1960)] Those requirements still apply *in the absence of consent.*

(3) Procedure

(a) Proper Moving Parties

Either the plaintiff or the defendant can move to transfer under this section. [**Ferens v. John Deere Co.,** 494 U.S. 516 (1990)—plaintiffs moved to transfer, arguing that they had sued in an inconvenient district] A defendant who has removed a case from a state court can also move to transfer after removal. [**Lynch v. Vanderhoef Builders,** 237 F. Supp. 2d 615 (D. Md. 2002)]

(b) Showing Required

In general, the *plaintiff's initial choice of forum should be respected*, and transfer is proper only when the balance of conveniences *strongly favors transfer*. This showing should look to the identity and location of witnesses, access to items of real evidence, and any other factor that would make trial in the transferee forum more convenient.

(4) Forum-Selection Clause

On a § 1404(a) motion to transfer, a valid and applicable forum-selection clause should be "given controlling weight in all but the most exceptional cases." The private-interest factors should not be weighed at all, since the parties have already assented to the agreed location for litigation, and public-interest factors should rarely defeat a transfer motion. [**Atlantic Marine Constr. Co. v. U.S. District Court,** *supra*]

c. Multidistrict Litigation

When cases pending in different districts raise a common question of law or fact, they can be transferred to one district. [28 U.S.C. § 1407]

(1) Showing Required

All that need be shown is that the actions share *a common question of fact or law*; unlike transfers for convenience under section 1404(a) (*supra*, p. 43), there is no preference for plaintiff's choice of forum.

(2) For Pretrial Purposes Only

This transfer is for pretrial purposes only; the cases should be remanded to the original court for trial. [28 U.S.C. § 1407(a)] The transferee court has full power to pass on any pretrial matters, however.

(3) Follow-up Transfer for Trial Not Authorized

Despite widespread support for the practice among lower courts, the Supreme Court has held that section 1407(a) does not authorize the judge who receives a multidistrict transfer to use section 1404(a) to transfer cases to her court for trial. [**Lexecon, Inc. v. Milberg Weiss Bershad Hynes & Lerach,** 523 U.S. 26 (1998)]

(4) Procedure

Motions for transfer are directed to the *Judicial Panel on Multidistrict Litigation*, which holds hearings and has the authority to transfer to any district *without reference to venue or jurisdiction*.

d. Effect on Choice of Law

In cases in federal court on grounds of diversity of citizenship, the transfer could affect choice of law because in such cases the federal court is required to look to the choice-of-law rules of the state in which it sits to determine choice of law issues. [**Klaxon Co. v. Stentor Electric Manufacturing Co.,** 313 U.S. 487 (1941)]

(1) Venue and Jurisdiction Proper in Original Court

When the plaintiff sues in a court that has proper venue and jurisdiction, a transfer for the convenience of the parties *does not affect choice of law* because the transferee court is to apply the same choice-of-law rules that the transferor court would have applied. [**Van Dusen v. Barrack,** 376 U.S. 612 (1964)] The *Van Dusen* rule applies even when the transfer is on motion of the plaintiff who chose the inconvenient forum in the first place and thus could shop for more favorable law. [**Ferens v. John Deere Co.,** *supra*, p. 43]

(2) Venue or Jurisdiction Improper in Original Court

If the plaintiff could not have overcome the defendant's venue or jurisdiction objections in the original court, the *choice-of-law rules of the transferee state should usually be applied*. [**Wisland v. Admiral Beverage Corp.,** 119 F.3d 733 (8th Cir. 1997)]

(3) Federal Claims

Because the federal circuits sometimes disagree on issues of federal law, it is possible for similar choice-of-law problems to arise when a claim is transferred from one circuit to another. Ordinarily, the interpretation of the transferee circuit is applied in this circumstance. [*In re* **TMJ Implants Products Liability Litigation,** 97 F.3d 1050 (8th Cir. 1996); *In re* **Korean Air Lines Disaster of Sept. 1, 1983,** 829 F.2d 1171 (D.C. Cir. 1987), *aff'd on other grounds sub nom.* **Chan v. Korean Air Lines,** 490 U.S. 122 (1989)]

(4) Effect of Forum-Selection Clause

When the parties have agreed to a valid forum-selection clause and transfer results, the rule in **Van Dusen v. Barrack,** *supra*, p. 44, should not apply. When a party bound by a forum-selection clause flouts its contractual obligation and files suit in a different forum, a transfer under § 1404(a) does not carry forward the original venue's choice-of-law rules. [**Atlantic Marine Constr. Co. v. U.S. District Court,** *supra*]

6. Transfer in State Court

State courts often have transfer provisions analogous to the federal ones. [*See, e.g.,* Cal. Civ. Proc. Code §§ 396—transfer when jurisdiction lacking, 397(c)—transfer for convenience of witnesses; Cal. Rules of Court §§ 3.501 *et seq.*—coordination of actions involving common questions of fact or law]

F. Forum Non Conveniens

1. Background

Even when jurisdiction and venue are proper, courts may decline to exercise jurisdiction on the ground that the location the plaintiff selected for the case is *grossly inconvenient*. This ancient common-law doctrine was endorsed by the Supreme Court as a matter of federal common law in **Gulf Oil Corp. v. Gilbert,** 330 U.S. 501 (1947), and is recognized in almost all state courts.

2. Present Use

a. Federal Courts

When the inconvenience problem can be solved by transfer to *another federal district*, the court may not dismiss; but if the proper forum is in another country, the federal court is to dismiss. [**Piper Aircraft Co. v. Reyno,** 454 U.S. 235 (1981); *In re* **Union Carbide Corp. Gas Plant Disaster at Bhopal, India,** 809 F.2d 195 (2d Cir. 1987)]

b. State Courts

When the more convenient court is not within the state and transfer is therefore not possible (*see supra*, p. 44, regarding in-state transfer) forum non conveniens remains an important device.

3. Rationale

Courts are not required to make their jurisdiction available to parties who engage in unfair forum shopping and thereby impose substantial inconvenience on other parties and expense and burden on the courts of the forum selected by the plaintiff.

4. Procedure

The defendant must make a *motion to dismiss* on grounds of inconvenience.

a. Showing Required

The defendant must show that the plaintiff has selected a *grossly inconvenient* location for the suit.

(1) Distinguish—Transfer

In federal court, the showing necessary to justify transfer is not as compelling as the showing needed to justify dismissal on forum non conveniens grounds.

b. Factors

The court is to consider a number of private and public factors in making a decision whether to dismiss on forum non conveniens grounds. (*See* chart, *infra*.)

c. Weight Given Plaintiff's Choice

Usually *substantial weight* is given to the plaintiff's choice to sue in a forum where venue and jurisdiction requirements are satisfied. When the plaintiff is foreign, however, that deference is not warranted. [**Piper Aircraft Co. v. Reyno,** *supra*, p. 45]

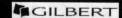

PRIVATE FACTORS

- ☑ *Relative ease of access to sources of proof*—*i.e.*, will access to needed proof be significantly easier in another forum?

- ☑ *Availability of compulsory process*—*i.e.*, as to **unwilling witnesses** whose testimony is important, will there be compulsory process to compel them to attend trial in another forum that is not available in the forum chosen by the plaintiff?

- ☑ *Cost of obtaining attendance of willing witnesses*.

- ☑ *Need to view premises*—*i.e.*, will having the jury view the premises involved in the litigation be important at trial? If so, this factor weighs in favor of having the trial near the premises.

PUBLIC FACTORS

- ☑ *Local interest* in having localized controversies decided at home;

- ☑ *Interest in having trial in forum familiar with the law* to be applied;

- ☑ *Avoiding unnecessary problems with conflict of laws*; and

- ☑ *Unfairness of burdening citizens* of an unrelated forum with jury duty.

d. Change in Substantive Law

That the law in the more convenient forum is less favorable to plaintiffs usually has no significant weight. [**Piper Aircraft Co. v. Reyno,** *supra*]

e. Adequate Alternative Forum Available

The court *cannot dismiss* unless an adequate alternative forum is available to the plaintiff.

(1) Adequate Remedy

The alternative forum must offer an adequate remedy; if there is no possibility of foreign judicial relief, the American court may conclude that the forum is inadequate. But the remedy need not be the same as in an American court, and the procedure of the foreign court may differ from that of the American court. [**Piper Aircraft Co. v. Reyno,** *supra*—dismissal upheld even though alternative forum was Scotland, where plaintiffs would not be able to rely on products-liability theories; *compare* **Phoenix Canada Oil Co. v. Texaco, Inc.,** 78 F.R.D. 445 (D. Del. 1978)— alternative forum in Ecuador might not be willing to hear the case, and there was no generally codified Ecuadorian legal remedy for the unjust-enrichment and tort claims asserted]

(2) Jurisdiction

The alternative forum must have jurisdiction over the defendant, but this problem can be solved by a stipulation by the defendant to submit to jurisdiction there.

f.   Conditions on Dismissal

The court can condition the dismissal to protect against unfairness to the plaintiff. A common example is insistence on a stipulation by the defendant that the statute of limitations will be deemed tolled as of the time suit was filed in the inconvenient forum, so that plaintiff does not risk a limitations defense based on the delay between the filing of the original case and the filing of suit in the preferred forum.

5.   Effect on Choice of Law

Because forum non conveniens results in a dismissal, the plaintiff must file a new suit, and the choice-of-law rules that apply are determined by the forum of the new suit.

6.   Contractual Limitations on Forum

Dismissal in favor of litigation in another forum can also occur when the dispute arises out of a contract in which the parties have agreed to litigate in a specific forum, but transfer to that forum is not possible.

a.   Federal Law—Generally Enforceable

The Supreme Court has held that "a proper application of § 1404(a) requires that a forum-selection clause be 'given controlling weight in all but the most exceptional case.' " [**Atlantic Marine Constr. Co. v. U.S. District Court**, *supra*] The Court has also declared that, as a matter of federal common law, such clauses are generally enforceable even when they result in dismissal because the forum chosen is in another country. [*See* The **Bremen v. Zapata Off-Shore Co.**, 407 U.S. 1 (1972)—clause should be enforced absent showing that doing so "would be unreasonable and unjust, or that the clause was invalid for such reasons as fraud or overreaching"] Moreover, the Supreme Court has held that a forum selection clause on a ***printed passenger ticket*** is enforceable even though not the subject of bargaining, unless enforcing it would violate fundamental fairness. [**Carnival Cruise Lines, Inc. v. Shute**, 499 U.S. 585 (1991)] *Note*: Congress invalidated such clauses in ship passenger tickets [46 U.S.C. App. § 183c], but later re-amended the statute to restore the original language, although apparently intending still to change the result in *Carnival Cruise Lines*. Such clauses may be valid in other consumer situations, however.

b.   State Law—Enforcement Limited

In many states, the enforcement of such clauses is limited, on the theory that the parties cannot by agreement "oust" a court with jurisdiction to decide the dispute. [*See, e.g.*, **Stewart Organization, Inc. v. Ricoh Corp.**, *supra*, p. 43—"Alabama looks unfavorably upon contractual forum-selection clauses"]

c.   Choice Between State and Federal Rules in Federal Court

When state-law claims are presented in federal court, there may be a serious problem determining whether to apply state or federal common law. The Supreme Court has not decided this question. [*See* **Stewart Organization, Inc. v. Ricoh Corp.**, *supra*] It has, however, decided that when transfer to the selected forum is possible under 28 U.S.C. section 1404(a), the existence of such a clause is a significant factor in deciding whether to transfer.

G. Notice

1. Introduction

In addition to personal jurisdiction and venue, problems of notice should be considered. Notice is not a substitute for these other factors, but is essential to a valid judgment.

2. Constitutional Requirements

Due process requires that *reasonable efforts to provide notice* be made with regard to persons whose interests are to be determined. [**Mullane v. Central Hanover Bank & Trust Co.,** *supra*, p. 22]

a. In Rem Cases

The notice requirement applies even to pure in rem actions. [**Walker v. City of Hutchinson,** 352 U.S. 112 (1956)]

b. Method

The method of giving notice must have a *reasonable prospect of giving actual notice*: "The means employed must be such as one desirous of actually informing the absentee might reasonably adopt to accomplish it." [**Mullane v. Central Hanover Bank & Trust Co.,** *supra*]

(1) Personal Delivery

Personal delivery of the notice (ordinarily the summons and complaint) is the traditional method of giving notice.

(2) First-Class Mail

In *Mullane, supra,* the Court required mailed notice to those whose addresses were known, reasoning that "the mails today are recognized as an efficient and inexpensive means of communication."

(a) Class Actions

In class actions brought under Federal Rule 23(b)(3) (common-question suits), there must be individual notice to all class members who can be identified with reasonable effort. [**Eisen v. Carlisle & Jacquelin,** 417 U.S. 156 (1974)]

(b) Notice to Prisoner

Notice of a forfeiture proceeding mailed to a prisoner was constitutionally sufficient because the prison used reasonable means to deliver mail to prisoners. [**Dusenbery v. United States,** 534 U.S. 161 (2002)]

(3) Posted Notice

Notice by posting on the defendant's residence may *not* be sufficient. [**Greene v. Lindsey,** 456 U.S. 444 (1982)—state procedure for giving notice of eviction proceedings by posting on the front door of apartment invalid in light of testimony that notices were often torn off doors; notice by mail required]

(4) Service via E-Mail

Under Federal Rule 4(f)(3), a court may authorize service via e-mail when service by more conventional means has been shown to be impossible. [**Rio Properties, Inc. v. Rio International Interlink, Inc.,** 284 F.3d 1007 (9th Cir. 2002)—defendant had announced to the world that it preferred to receive communication through its e-mail address, and plaintiff's numerous attempts to serve defendant by other means had been thwarted by defendant's manner of doing business]

(5) Service via Social Media

Service via social media has been attempted in rare cases, and may become more common. [**St. Francis Assisi v. Kuwait Fin. House,** 2016 WL 5725002 (N.D. Cal., Sept. 30, 2016)—service via Twitter; **Baidoo v. Blood-Dzraku,** 48 Misc. 3d 309 (Supreme Court, New York County 2015)—service via Facebook]

c. Effort to Identify

Reasonable efforts to identify and locate affected persons are required. As to named defendants, the identification issue should not be a problem, but in other instances, such as in rem actions, it can prove more difficult.

Example—Mortgagee: When property was sold for nonpayment of taxes, the mortgagee with a mortgage on file with the county recorder **was held entitled to notice of the sale. [Mennonite Board of Missions v. Adams,** 462 U.S. 791 (1983)]

Example—Creditor of Decedent: Application of a state requirement that claims against a decedent be presented to his executor within two months of publication of notice of the commencement of probate proceedings was held to violate due process when it cut off rights of creditors whose identity was reasonably ascertainable to a decedent's executor and who were not given notice. [**Tulsa Professional Collection Services, Inc. v. Pope,** 485 U.S. 478 (1988)]

(1) Class Actions

In class actions, the Court has accepted failure to identify significant numbers of class members. [*See* **Eisen v. Carlisle & Jacquelin,** *supra*—inability to locate more than half of six million class members] *Rationale*: In **Mullane v. Central Hanover Bank & Trust Co.,** *supra*, the Court explained that "notice reasonably certain to reach most of those interested in objecting is likely to safeguard the interests of all, since any objection sustained would inure to the benefit of all."

(a) Distinguish—Future-Claims Class Action

In a class action involving "future" claims by class members who had not yet manifested illness due to exposure to asbestos, the Supreme Court cautioned that providing adequate notice to such individuals might be impossible due to problems of identification and to the uncertainty caused for those who may not even know of the asbestos exposure at the time of any notice that is given. [**Amchem Products, Inc. v. Windsor,** 521 U.S. 591 (1997)]

d. Contents

The notice must intelligibly advise the defendant of the ***nature and place*** of the proceeding.

e. Constructive Notice

Sometimes when a person cannot be located *after reasonable efforts*, published or other constructive notice will suffice. [*See, e.g.,* Cal. Civ. Proc. Code § 415.50—service by publication when party cannot by reasonable diligence be served another way]

f. Effect of Failure to Receive

If a constitutionally valid procedure is used, the *judgment is binding* even if some interested parties do not actually receive notice. Due process requires reasonable efforts to provide notice, but Supreme Court cases "have never required actual notice." [**Dusenbery v. United States,** *supra,* p. 48]

g. Duty to Make Further Efforts If Notice Not Received

When the plaintiff learns that its initial efforts at giving notice failed even though they were reasonable, it must take reasonable additional steps to provide notice. [**Jones v. Flowers,** 547 U.S. 220 (2006)—when certified letter notifying homeowner that house would be sold to pay overdue taxes was returned, due process required the state to take reasonable additional actions to notify the owner before selling the house]

3. Service of Process

The usual method for giving notice is service of a *summons* and complaint on the defendant directing that the defendant file an answer to the complaint or suffer a default.

a. Jurisdiction Distinguished

Although service of process implies an exercise of jurisdiction, the questions of jurisdiction and method of service should be kept separate. Even when the method of service is proper, the defendant can still challenge the exercise of personal jurisdiction; although some forms of service may by themselves suffice to establish personal jurisdiction. [**Burnham v. Superior Court,** *supra,* p. 6—personal service in state sufficient to establish jurisdiction]

b. Methods of Service

Service of process can be accomplished by the following methods:

(1) Personal Delivery

Process may be served on the person. In the case of a corporation, partnership, or unincorporated association, service may be made on an officer or managing agent, or on an agent authorized by law.

(2) Substituted Service

Other means of service may be authorized by statute or court rule.

(a) Federal Rules

1) At Defendant's Home

A copy of the summons and complaint can be left at the "usual place of abode" of the person to be served with a "person of suitable age and discretion" residing therein. [Fed. R. Civ. P. 4(e)(2)(B)]

2) In Accordance with State Law

Service also may be made pursuant to the law of the *state in which the district court is located*, or pursuant to the law of the *state in which service is effected*. [Fed. R. Civ. P. 4(e)(1)]

EXAM TIP

To be proper, service of process must be by the book; therefore, you have to check the facts carefully to see that the rules were followed. Keep in mind that **personal service is best**—the defendant cannot claim that she did not receive notice—but it is not always possible. In that case, **substituted service** may be allowed, but be sure that the facts show that it was proper. Things to consider include:

- **Where** the service is made—is if the defendant's "usual abode" and not a vacation home, her mother's house, etc.?

- Check on **how** service was made—tacking a copy of the summons and complaint to the door of the home is not sufficient under most statutes; the papers must be left with a person at the home.

- And consider the person **who accepts** the papers; he must be of "suitable age and discretion," which means that leaving the papers with defendant's spouse would most likely be fine, but leaving them with her four-year-old son would not.

The technical rules must be followed, or the service is improper and the notice requirement not met.

---

3) Waiver of Service

A federal-court plaintiff may ask a defendant to waive formal service. This is done by sending a request for waiver of service to the defendant by first-class mail. Because a defendant has a duty to avoid unnecessary costs of service, a defendant located within the United States who fails to waive service without good cause can be liable for the costs of formal service. A defendant who waives service receives additional time to answer the complaint compared to one who is served in the usual manner. [Fed. R. Civ. P. 4(d)]

4) On Defendant in Foreign Country

A defendant served in another country may be served by an internationally agreed means or, if there is not an agreed means, as directed by the law of the place of service, including, unless forbidden by the law of that country, personal delivery or any form of mail requiring a signed receipt, or as directed by the court. [Fed. R. Civ. P. 4(f)] It has been held that service by e-mail is not an authorized means under the Hague Convention. [**Elobied v. Baylock,** 299 F.R.D. 105 (E.D. Pa. 2014)] But the Convention does not forbid service by postal mail, if the receiving state does not object. [**Water Splash, Inc. v. Menon,** 137 S.Ct. 1240 (2017)]

(b) State Law

State law on substituted service varies. For example, in California such service may be accomplished in the following ways:

1) At Defendant's Office or Home

A copy of the summons and complaint can be left at the person's office or abode *plus* mailing a copy to that place. [Cal. Civ. Proc. Code § 415.20]

2) By Mail Within State

A copy of the summons and complaint can also be mailed to a person within the state, if the person executes and returns an acknowledgment of service. [Cal. Civ. Proc. Code § 415.30]

3) By Mail Outside State

A copy of the summons and complaint can be served on a person outside the state by using return-receipt mail, without the need for execution of an acknowledgment by the defendant. [Cal. Civ. Proc. Code § 415.40]

(3) Service in Diversity Cases

In diversity cases, the service authorized by *Federal Rule 4* will suffice even if state-law requirements for service are different (*supra*, pp. 50–51). [**Hanna v. Plumer,** 380 U.S. 460 (1965)]

c. Immunity from Service

Some jurisdictions have rules that forbid service of process on a person who is in the state only to participate in a legal proceeding. *Rationale*: This immunity is designed to protect against the risk of people being unwilling to attend trials for fear of being served with process. These rules have been severely limited in recent times.

4. Timing of Notice—Prejudgment Seizures

a. Introduction

At common law, a plaintiff could have a defendant's property seized as a method of coercing the defendant to appear for trial. Over time, this seizure—variously called replevin, attachment, garnishment, or sequestration—came to be used to provide *security for any judgment* the plaintiff might obtain in the action. Very often, such prejudgment remedies were available before defendant was given notice of the action.

b. State-Law Requirements

Partly in response to constitutional decisions (*see infra*, p. 53 *et seq*.), states placed *limits on such prejudgment remedies*. Thus, before considering possible constitutional objections to state procedures, first consider whether the prejudgment seizure sought by the plaintiff is authorized by state law.

Example—California: In California, attachment is available only in contract actions for more than $500 for a fixed or readily ascertainable amount. In an action against a natural person, attachment is available only if the claim arises out of the defendant's conduct of a trade, business, or profession. [Cal. Civ. Proc. Code § 483.010]

Example—New York: Prejudgment attachment is allowed in New York only upon a showing that the defendant has assigned, disposed of, or encumbered or secreted property with intent to defraud creditors, or that the defendant is a non-domiciliary, or a resident who cannot be served in the state. [New York Civ. Prac. Law § 6201]

(1) Federal Courts

Federal courts **must apply state law** concerning the availability of prejudgment remedies, unless a federal statute provides a prejudgment remedy. [Fed. R. Civ. P. 64]

c. Procedural Due Process Requirements for Prejudgment Seizure

In a series of cases, the Supreme Court has considered the constitutional requirements for procedures attending issuance of prejudgment remedies. Because these cases are difficult to reconcile, it is worthwhile to consider them one by one.

(1) Sniadach—Garnishment of Wages

In **Sniadach v. Family Finance Corp.,** 395 U.S. 337 (1969), the Court held that the state violated a defendant's due process rights by allowing prejudgment garnishment of wages. The opinion contained suggestions that wages might be viewed as a **special type of property** because they are essential to everyday life.

(2) Fuentes—Seizure of Chattels

In **Fuentes v. Shevin,** 407 U.S. 67 (1972), the Court invalidated Florida and Pennsylvania procedures for writs of replevin that authorized the seizure of property, because there was no provision for **notice and a preseizure hearing**.

(a) Purpose of Hearing

The Court emphasized that the notice and hearing requirement ensured a "fair process of decisionmaking," but it was not clear on whether this position was limited to reducing the risk of erroneous issuance of writs of replevin.

(b) Alternative Safeguards Against Error

The 4–3 majority viewed alternative safeguards against error as significant factors in determining the type of hearing afforded, but the safeguards were "far from enough by themselves to obviate the right to a prior hearing of some kind." The dissent argued that the bond requirement, coupled with the creditor's desire to have the transaction completed, should provide sufficient protection.

(c) Unimportance of Cost of Hearing

The Court placed little importance on the possible cost of more elaborate hearing procedures, noting that "[t]he Constitution recognizes higher values than speed and efficiency."

(d) Exception for "Extraordinary Situations"

The Court recognized in dictum that the right to preseizure notice and hearing could be overcome in "extraordinary situations." It specified three factors that appeared to be necessary:

1) Such seizures should be **directly necessary** to secure an **important governmental or general public interest**, e.g., **public health** or **the war effort**.

2) Such seizures without notice may occur only when **delay would be inimical to the public interest**; and

3) Such seizures should be limited to circumstances in which the **state controlled the initiation of proceedings**.

(3) Mitchell

In **Mitchell v. W.T. Grant Co.,** 416 U.S. 600 (1974), the Court **upheld** Louisiana's procedure allowing the seller of several household appliances to obtain a writ for their seizure when the defendant missed payments.

(a) Fuentes Overruled?

One could argue that *Mitchell* overruled *Fuentes* since the situation was difficult to fit within the "extraordinary situations" analysis of *Fuentes*. (In dissent, the author of the *Fuentes* opinion asserted that the case had been overruled.)

(b) *Mitchell*'s Requirements—*Fuentes* Distinguished

However, the majority in *Mitchell* said that it was applying *Fuentes*, and that the Louisiana procedures were different in ways that made them constitutional because:

1) They **required more than the conclusory claims of ownership** called by the state procedures at issue in *Fuentes*;

2) Where this case arose, the practice was that a **judge** (rather than a clerk) **would pass on the application** for the writ;

3) "**Narrowly confined" issues** were presented by the application for the writ in Louisiana in contrast to the broad "fault" standard applicable in the statutes at issue in *Fuentes*; and

4) The defendant in Louisiana had a **right to an immediate hearing** on whether the plaintiff was entitled to the writ, and the burden remained on the plaintiff to justify the issuance of the writ.

(c) Explanation for Shift

The easiest explanation for the shift from *Fuentes* to *Mitchell* is that two new Justices—Powell and Rehnquist—were added to the Court in the interim.

(4) *Di-Chem*

In **North Georgia Finishing, Inc. v. Di-Chem, Inc.,** 419 U.S. 601 (1975), the Court struck down Georgia garnishment procedures. Its description of the distinguishing factors that made the case different from *Mitchell* provide a guide to important constitutional criteria.

(a) Property Not Subject of Suit

Unlike *Fuentes* and *Mitchell*, the property in *Di-Chem* (a bank account) had no intrinsic relation to the claim.

(b) Purpose of Due Process Requirements

The majority opinion found that the procedure in *Fuentes* was unconstitutional because the seizures there were "carried out without *notice* and without opportunity for a *hearing or other safeguard against mistaken repossession*." This phrasing seemed to revise the thrust of the *Fuentes* opinion, which treated the presence of safeguards as bearing on the type of hearing required, not the need for preseizure notice at all.

(5) *Doehr*

In **Connecticut v. Doehr,** 501 U.S. 1 (1991), the Court struck down Connecticut's provision for attachment of real property without prior notice and an opportunity for a hearing "as applied in this case." The Court followed a three-step analysis based on **Mathews v. Eldridge,** 424 U.S. 319 (1976).

(a) Private Interest

The Court held that the interests of a homeowner were *significantly affected* by attachment even though it did not interfere with possession of the property because attachment can cloud title, impede sale, and interfere with borrowing on the property.

(b) Risk of Erroneous Deprivation

The Court found that there was a *substantial risk of an erroneous deprivation* because the state practice allowed decisions based on a conclusory affidavit without prior notice and adversary hearing, and the underlying issue in the case (an alleged assault) did not lend itself to documentary proof.

(c) Governmental Interest

Connecticut had *no significant interest* in allowing a private plaintiff to attach defendant's property without notice or a showing of exigent circumstances, in view of the fact that other states have more exacting requirements for seizure without notice.

(6) Post-*Doehr* Decisions

(a) Application to Drug-Forfeiture Seizure

In **United States v. James Daniel Good Real Property,** 510 U.S. 43 (1993), the Court held that seizure of defendant's home after his conviction for drug trafficking there violated due process because he did not receive preseizure notice and an opportunity to be heard. The seizure deprived him of use of the property, created an unacceptable risk of error because owners are entitled to an affirmative defense of innocent ownership, and was unnecessary to protect the government's interest because real property cannot abscond.

(b) Application to Asset Freeze Based on Grand-Jury Determination of Probable Cause

In **Kaley v. United States,** 134 S. Ct. 1090 (2014), the Court held that a federal statute authorizing a court-ordered freeze of all defendant's assets on the basis of an ex parte application to the court does not violate due process if the grand jury has determined that there is probable cause to charge defendant with a crime. Because the only issue was whether the seizure was supported by probable cause, the Court regarded the utility of an additional hearing as speculative.

(c) Cognovit Notes

Related issues arise in connection with cognovit notes, in which the debtor agrees that in the event of a default in payments, the creditor may immediately and without notice obtain a judgment against the debtor. The Supreme Court has held that if such arrangements are the result of arm's-length negotiation between sophisticated commercial entities, they are enforceable over procedural due process objections. [**D.H. Overmyer Co. v. Frick Co.,** 405 U.S. 174 (1972)]

(d) Delay in Hearing

Although unreasonable delay in holding a post-deprivation hearing might violate due process, administrative needs may justify a delay of up to 30 days. [*See* **City of Los Angeles v. David,** 538 U.S. 715 (2003)—30-day delay on hearing regarding the return of money plaintiff had to pay to recover his car after it was towed was reasonable]

(7) Effect of *Doehr*

Doehr, *supra*, appears to have the following effects besides prescribing the three-part analysis of *Mathews*, *supra*:

(a) Exigent Circumstances

The Court's opinion suggests that proof of exigent circumstances may be ***constitutionally necessary*** to permit seizure without notice. (*Compare supra*, p. 53, regarding "extraordinary situations" under *Fuentes*.)

(b) Effect of Preexisting Interest in Property

The Court distinguished its summary affirmance in another case involving a mechanic's lien, suggesting that ***less rigorous standard***s might apply when the plaintiff is asserting an interest in the property that ***antedates the suit***.

(c) Type of Claim

The Court's emphasis on the difficulty of evaluating the assault claim before it on the basis of filings by plaintiff suggests that only claims that can be ***reliably evaluated*** on ***documentary proof*** may be the basis for seizure without notice.

(d) Due Process Limitations if Hearing Held Before Seizure

Even if a hearing is held before seizure, procedural due process may limit seizure unless the above criteria are satisfied.

Chapter Two

Subject-Matter Jurisdiction of the Federal Courts

CONTENTS	PAGE

Key Exam Issues

Like personal jurisdiction, subject-matter jurisdiction is covered in most civil-procedure courses. Although the topic has the same title—"jurisdiction"—and like personal jurisdiction deals with a court's power to hear a case—it relates to a very different concern and should be kept separate. Rather than focusing on the geographic location for litigation, subject-matter jurisdiction usually concerns whether a *type of case* may be brought in federal court. In every state, there is a state court of "general jurisdiction." This term means that cases of any type may be brought in that court. (Thus, the term "general jurisdiction" means something very different in regard to subject-matter jurisdiction from what it does concerning personal jurisdiction.)

Federal courts are courts of limited subject-matter jurisdiction. Article III of the Constitution does not create any lower federal courts, although it permits Congress to do so. Also, Article III limits the sorts of cases that Congress could authorize the federal courts to decide, requiring that they be courts of limited jurisdiction.

There are two main constitutional headings of federal-court civil jurisdiction: diversity jurisdiction and federal-question jurisdiction. *Diversity jurisdiction* is authorized by the Constitution whenever there is a party on one side of the litigation (plaintiffs) who is of "diverse" citizenship from a party on the other side of the litigation (defendants). *Federal-question* jurisdiction is authorized when a claim arises under federal law. (A third significant basis for federal-court civil jurisdiction, cases involving the federal government or its agencies or officers, is not covered in most first-year civil-procedure courses.)

The first Congress created lower federal courts and assigned them jurisdiction over certain cases. Since then, the statutory grants of jurisdiction have been modified, generally to expand the federal courts' authority to hear cases. But the statutory grants of jurisdiction are usually interpreted to be narrower than the maximum authority the Constitution permits Congress to assign to the lower federal courts. Accordingly, when you have an examination question about the subject-matter jurisdiction of a federal district court, it is important to focus on the following statutory grants of jurisdiction:

1. **Is Jurisdiction Available Under the General Diversity-Jurisdiction Statute?**

   a. **Complete Diversity**: Under the statute, there must be complete diversity. This requirement means that *no plaintiff* may have the same citizenship as *any defendant*. For this reason, you will need to determine the appropriate citizenship for each plaintiff and each defendant to the case, even if there are numerous parties. Keep in mind that some of those parties may be regarded as citizens of more than one state for purposes of diversity of citizenship. For example, corporations have the citizenship of every state in which they are incorporated and also of the state in which they have their principal place of business. Other groupings of people—such as partnerships or labor unions—may be considered to have the citizenship of each of their partners or members.

   b. **Jurisdictional Amount**: The diversity statute also requires that there be *more than $75,000* in controversy for jurisdiction to be available. If the plaintiff has claimed more than this amount in the complaint, this question ordinarily involves determining whether the claim was made in good faith. If the court can say to a "legal certainty" that this amount could not be recovered, this requirement is not satisfied.

   c. **Do Special Jurisdictional Provisions Apply to This Case?** For some types of cases, special jurisdictional provisions may apply. Certain *class actions* may be brought in federal court on grounds of minimal diversity. Similarly, *interpleader* actions may be brought in federal court on minimal diversity (*i.e.*, any claimant who is diverse from another claimant) grounds.

2. **Is Jurisdiction Available on the Ground That the Suit Raises a Federal Question?**

    a. **Federal Claim**: If the plaintiff is asserting a claim created by federal law, this ground for jurisdiction should be satisfied. The claim may be *expressly created* by federal statute, or *implied by federal courts* for violation of a prohibition in a federal statute. Even if the federal claim is subject to dismissal for failure to state a claim, it suffices to support federal-question subject-matter jurisdiction unless the court finds that it is wholly frivolous and made solely to obtain federal jurisdiction.

    b. **State-Law Claim Raising Federal Issue**: Even if the plaintiff is not asserting a claim created by federal law, there may be grounds for federal-court jurisdiction if the assertion of a state-law claim turns on the *resolution of a federal issue*. Assuming the complaint alleges a federal issue, the question is whether it meets the *well-pleaded complaint* test— *i.e.*, whether the inclusion of the federal issue is necessary as a matter of pleading to state a claim. Thus, plaintiff's *anticipation of a defense* based on federal law that defendant is certain to raise is *not sufficient* to establish federal-court jurisdiction. Also, if the federal ingredient is necessary to a plaintiff's claim, the federal issue must be *substantial*, because the determination of the state-law claim turns on resolution of the federal issue, and it may be important to ask whether there is a *federal interest* in having the claim heard in federal court.

3. **If the Case Was Originally Filed in State Court, Have Defendants Properly Removed It to Federal Court?**

    In general, defendants may remove a case to federal court whenever the plaintiff could *originally have filed* the case in federal court on grounds either of diversity or federal question. In a sense, this means that there is a preference for adjudication in federal court since the case will be heard in a federal forum whenever one side wants it in federal court. Thus, often a question about removal jurisdiction asks you first to address the issues raised above, and then you must consider some specialized aspects of removal:

    a. **Timely Notice of Removal by All Defendants**: There is a short time frame for removing a case to federal court, and *all defendants* must usually join in or consent to removing the case.

    b. **Whether Case was Within Federal Court's Original Jurisdiction**: Defendants ordinarily may remove the case only if it would have been within the federal court's original jurisdiction had plaintiff filed it in federal court. But note that sometimes this is not sufficient. For example, even if there is complete diversity of citizenship, removal is generally not available on grounds of diversity if one of the defendants is a citizen of the state in which the suit was filed.

    c. **Alternatively, Whether Case Involves a Separate and Independent Claim Arising Under Federal Law**: In one situation, removal jurisdiction is broader than original jurisdiction. If a defendant is sued on a claim arising under federal law that is entirely separate from claims not within federal jurisdiction that are also asserted in the case, it may remove the case on that ground even though plaintiff could not initially have filed the case in federal court.

    d. **Once Removed, Whether Case Is Subject to Remand to State Court**: If the case was improperly removed to federal court, the federal court may remand it. Even if removal was initially proper, if *all federal claims have been dismissed*, or if plaintiff was allowed to *amend to add nondiverse defendants* in a diversity case, the federal court may remand.

4. **Can Supplemental Jurisdiction Be Used to Add Claims or Parties to the Case?**

When a claim is properly before a federal court, the court may have "supplemental" jurisdiction over additional related claims against existing parties or additional parties. If you are presented with such additional claims or parties, consider the following issues:

a. **Constitutional Limits of Federal Judicial Power**: The federal court may exercise jurisdiction over the additional claims only if they are part of the *same constitutional case*, which usually depends on whether the additional claims arise out of the same *common nucleus of operative fact* as those within the federal court's original jurisdiction.

b. **Special Limits on Supplemental Jurisdiction in Diversity Cases**: To safeguard the complete-diversity requirement, supplemental jurisdiction is limited when plaintiffs want to use it in cases that fall within diversity jurisdiction. Thus, supplemental jurisdiction cannot be used to add *claims by plaintiffs* against any nondiverse person made a party through *third-party practice, joinder of required parties, permissive joinder, or intervention,* or over a claim by a nondiverse person sought to be joined as a required party or intervenor.

c. **Discretionary Decline of Jurisdiction**: Even if supplemental jurisdiction is authorized by statute, the district court has *discretion* to decline to exercise it due to the *complexity of state law*, because the *state-law claim substantially predominates*, or because the court has *dismissed* the claim over which it had original jurisdiction.

A. Introduction

1. Nature of Subject-Matter Jurisdiction

Historically—sometimes by mere accident—the courts obtained authority to decide only certain types of actions; *i.e.*, they had jurisdiction over only particular subject matters (*e.g.*, only cases involving claims in excess of a certain amount of money, or only claims involving land). Thus, whether a court has authority to hear a particular case may depend on the subject matter involved. The most significant limitations on subject-matter jurisdiction today, for purposes of this Summary, involve the subject-matter limitations on the federal courts. These limitations often reflect notions of the "proper" relation between federal and state power.

2. Personal Jurisdiction Distinguished

Subject-matter jurisdiction differs from personal jurisdiction. Personal jurisdiction limits the power of courts over persons based on geographic location. Subject-matter jurisdiction limits the power of courts based on *case type*. Subject-matter jurisdiction allocates authority between court systems (*e.g.*, only courts in the federal system have subject-matter jurisdiction over admiralty cases), or among courts of a given system (*e.g.*, some states provide that only state "family-law courts" have subject-matter jurisdiction over divorces). The two concepts of jurisdiction should not be confused. It is incorrect, for example, to say that the court "has diversity jurisdiction over the defendant" because diversity jurisdiction refers to jurisdiction over the type of case, not over the defendant. To proceed with a case, the court must possess *both personal jurisdiction* over the defendant and *subject-matter jurisdiction* over the claim.

3. Defects Not Waivable

Lack of subject-matter jurisdiction is not waivable, so it may be raised as a basis for dismissing a case at any time. It can lie in the background as a sort of "time bomb" in the plaintiff's lawsuit.

a. Plaintiff Must Allege Grounds for Subject-Matter Jurisdiction

Ordinarily, the plaintiff must include in the complaint allegations stating the subject-matter jurisdiction of the federal court. [*See* Fed. R. Civ. P. 8(a)(1)]

b. Parties May Raise Objection at Any Time

The defendant may raise lack of subject-matter jurisdiction *at any time* during the pendency of the case, even after final judgment has been entered and the case has been appealed on other grounds. [Fed. R. Civ. P. 12(h)(3)] Indeed, the defendant may even remove the case to federal court, lose there, and then raise lack of subject-matter jurisdiction as a ground for invalidating the judgment for the plaintiff. [*See* **American Fire & Casualty Co. v. Finn,** 341 U.S. 6 (1951)—After removing, defendant lost in federal court and then successfully moved to vacate the resulting judgment in favor of plaintiff and remand to state court] Further, a plaintiff who invoked federal jurisdiction may call attention to its absence, which sometimes happens when plaintiffs see a case going badly for them. Subject-matter jurisdiction defects sometimes can even be raised on "collateral" attack, after all appeals have been exhausted or waived and the judgment has become completely final.

(1) Distinguish—Personal Jurisdiction

The defendant's failure to raise *personal jurisdiction* at a required early time waives objections to personal jurisdiction. (*See supra*, p. 25.)

EXAM TIP

Be sure to remember the important distinction regarding waiver. Defects in *personal jurisdiction* can easily be waived—a defendant's mere failure to raise the issue in an initial motion or answer constitutes a waiver. However, defects in *subject-matter jurisdiction* are *not waivable*; a party can even raise the issue for the first time on appeal.

---

c. Court to Raise Sua Sponte

Even if the parties do not raise the issue, the court is to raise subject-matter jurisdiction on its own. [*See, e.g.,* **Louisville & Nashville Railroad v. Mottley,** 211 U.S. 149 (1908)—Court dismissed appeal for lack of subject-matter jurisdiction even though neither party raised issue]

d. Jurisdiction Must Be Resolved Before Court Addresses Merits of Suit

The question whether a court has jurisdiction must be resolved *before* the court may decide the merits of the case. [**Steel Co. v. Citizens for a Better Environment,** 523 U.S. 83 (1998)—rejecting "doctrine of hypothetical jurisdiction," followed by some circuits, under which a court would assume it had jurisdiction to decide the case on its merits when the merits question is more readily resolved than the jurisdiction question and the party that would prevail on the merits is the same party that would prevail if jurisdiction were denied]

(1) Personal-Jurisdiction Challenge May Be Resolved Before Subject-Matter Jurisdiction Challenge

Although a federal court must resolve challenges to its jurisdiction before deciding the merits of a case, there is no jurisdictional hierarchy requiring a federal court to resolve challenges to its subject-matter jurisdiction before resolving challenges to its personal jurisdiction. [**Ruhrgas AG v. Marathon Oil Co.,** 526 U.S. 574 (1999)—district court properly dismissed action removed from state court to federal court for lack of personal jurisdiction even though there were challenges to the court's removal jurisdiction]

(2) Forum Non Conveniens Dismissal Permitted Before Resolving Jurisdiction

Even though there are challenges to its jurisdiction, a district court may dismiss on grounds of forum non conveniens without first resolving those jurisdictional challenges if the defendant meets the "heavy burden" to justify dismissal on that ground. [**Sinochem International Co. v. Malaysia International Shipping Corp.,** 549 U.S. 422 (2007)]

4. State Courts

This chapter focuses on the *subject-matter jurisdiction of federal courts*. Except for claims within the exclusive jurisdiction of the federal courts (*infra*, p. 63), state-court systems usually exercise "general jurisdiction"; *i.e.*, a state court is available for every type of claim. Within the state-court system, however, there may be subject-matter jurisdiction limits that should be kept in mind:

a. Specialized Courts

Many states have specialized courts that deal exclusively with certain types of cases. For example, probate proceedings or matrimonial disputes may have to be raised before a specialized court, or a specialized division of the court.

b. Monetary Limits

Some states have courts with jurisdiction over claims below a certain dollar amount. These so-called *small-claims courts* have the authority to decide cases involving small sums [*see, e.g.*, Cal. Civ. Proc. Code § 116.220(a)—less than $5,000], using very informal procedures that may even forbid the participation of lawyers. In addition, there may be more formal courts with jurisdiction limited to claims under a certain amount.

c. General Jurisdiction

Each state has some court of "general jurisdiction." This means that *any type of claim* can be brought in this court, except those claims within the exclusive jurisdiction of the federal courts. (*See infra*, p. 63, regarding exclusive jurisdiction.)

d. Concurrent Jurisdiction of Federal Claims

Generally, state courts have jurisdiction concurrent with the federal courts to hear federal claims (as well as state-law cases that could come within federal diversity jurisdiction). If there is concurrent jurisdiction, a plaintiff may *choose* to file her case in either federal or state court. Indeed, under the Supremacy Clause of the Constitution [U.S. Const. art. VI, § 2], state courts may not refuse to enforce federal claims unless federal law provides otherwise: Thus, even if for some reason the plaintiff may not file her entire case in federal court, she can still file it in state court.

(1) Exception—Exclusive Federal-Court Jurisdiction

Federal law grants the federal courts *exclusive* jurisdiction over some types of cases, and state courts therefore cannot adjudicate such claims. Examples of such exclusive jurisdiction include the following:

(a) Patents and Copyrights

Federal courts have exclusive jurisdiction when the plaintiff's patent or copyright claim arises under a federal statute. [28 U.S.C. § 1338] State courts have concurrent jurisdiction, however, to decide claims arising under the common law (*e.g.*, for unfair competition) and to decide claims for breach of contract concerning the license, sale, or other disposition of patents, even if the validity of the patent is challenged. [**Lear, Inc. v. Adkins,** 395 U.S. 653 (1969)]

(b) Federal Antitrust Regulations

Claims for violation of the federal antitrust laws have been held to be within the exclusive jurisdiction of the federal courts. [*See* **Freeman v. Bee Machine Co.,** 319 U.S. 448 (1943)] States may, however, have parallel state-law antitrust provisions within the jurisdiction of the state courts.

(c) Federal Securities Acts

Federal jurisdiction is exclusive in actions brought under the Securities Exchange Act of 1934, including actions under *Rule 10b–5* for "manipulative or deceptive conduct" in connection with the purchase or sale of securities. [15 U.S.C. § 78a] States may, however, entertain claims for common-law fraud arising out of the same events.

(d) Distinguish—Federal Defense

When an issue of federal law arises *as a defense* to a state-law claim, the fact that a claim for affirmative relief on the federal ground would be subject to exclusive federal jurisdiction does *not* prevent the state court from considering the defense. Indeed, under the Supremacy Clause, the state; court cannot refuse to entertain the defense.

cf. **Compare—Exclusive State-Court Jurisdiction of Claim Created by Federal Law Rare:** Although Congress could divest the federal courts of jurisdiction over claims created by federal law, that will be found only if Congress expressly, or by fair implication, excludes federal-court jurisdiction, a rare occurrence. [**Mims v. Arrow Finan. Servs., LLC,** 565 U.S. 368 (2012)—federal Telephone Consumer Protection Act did not divest federal courts of authority to hear suits by private parties seeking redress for violation of provisions of the Act or its implementing regulations when it provided that such claimants may sue "in an appropriate court of [a] State."]

e.g. **Example—Suit Under Mining Patent Governed by Local Law:** In one case, the Supreme Court held that the federal courts did not have federal-question jurisdiction over claims based on a federal mining patent because the right asserted could be determined by "local rules or customs, or state statutes." [**Shoshone Mining Co. v. Rutter,** 177 U.S. 505 (1900)]

5. Federal Courts' Jurisdiction

a. Limited Jurisdiction

Unlike state courts, federal courts are courts of limited subject-matter jurisdiction.

(1) Constitutional Grant

Article III, section 1 of the United States Constitution establishes the Supreme Court and gives Congress the power to create inferior federal courts. Section 2 of Article III sets out the scope of the federal judicial power. It provides that, among others, the federal courts may hear cases: arising under the Constitution or federal law, affecting ambassadors, or between citizens of different states. To be constitutional, an exercise of jurisdiction by a federal court must be within the scope of power granted by Article III, section 2.

(2) Statutory Grant

It is not enough that an exercise of federal jurisdiction is merely permissible under the Constitution. There must also be some statutory grant by Congress vesting the federal courts with jurisdiction. Unless Congress has vested a federal court with jurisdiction, the fact that it might do so without violating the. Constitution is irrelevant.

	◪ GILBERT
DIVERSITY JURISDICTION	Under 28 U.S.C. § 1332, federal courts may hear cases when (i) no defendant is a citizen of the same state as any plaintiff in the case, **and** (ii) more than $75,000 is in controversy.
FEDERAL-QUESTION JURISDICTION	Under 28 U.S.C. § 1331, federal courts may hear cases involving a federal question. There is no amount in controversy requirement, but the federal question must appear in the plaintiff's well-pleaded complaint; allegations in the complaint anticipating a defense are not sufficient.
SUPPLEMENTAL JURISDICTION	Under 28 U.S.C. § 1367, once a federal court has jurisdiction over a claim under § 1331 or § 1332, it may hear claims that are related to the claims over which it has "original" jurisdiction.
REMOVAL JURISDICTION	Under 28 U.S.C. § 1441, a defendant may usually "remove" a case filed by plaintiff in state court if plaintiff could originally have filed the suit in federal court, provided defendant does so at the outset of the case or when it develops that the case has become removable.

b. Tactical Considerations

Litigants with a choice between state and federal court often prefer federal court for a variety of tactical reasons.

(1) Location

Federal courts are usually located in metropolitan areas, while many state courts are in less populated areas.

(2) Broad Discovery

Federal courts may afford broader opportunities for discovery (*i.e.*, pretrial devices to obtain information about a case—generally from the other party), although the breadth of federal discovery has been curtailed, *see infra*, pp. 296–297, and many state systems allow broad discovery.

(3) Speedy Trial

In some locations, state court dockets are backlogged and federal courts are able to offer parties shorter delays to trial. By the same token, where the delay is greater in federal court, a party desiring delay might want to litigate in federal court for that reason.

(4) Single Assignment System

In most federal courts, cases are assigned to a single judge from the outset. Some litigants believe that this arrangement is more efficient and effective than having the case assigned on a "master calendar" basis that assigns different aspects to different judges. Most states use the master calendar approach, although some are shifting to a single assignment system.

(5) Source of Jurors

Federal juries are drawn from the entire federal district, while state court juries are usually drawn from a more limited area, such as a county or part of a county.

(6) Manner of Selecting Judges

Federal district judges are nominated by the President and confirmed by the Senate. They may be removed only by impeachment and are relatively insulated from political pressures. Methods of selecting judges vary among states. In a few states, judges are appointed in a similar manner to the federal system. But most state judges are elected, and in many states the elections are either explicitly, or for practical purposes, partisan. In some states, judges may be regarded as more subject to political or other pressures than federal judges.

(7) Countervailing Considerations

Plaintiffs sometimes prefer state court for various reasons. Pleading requirements may not be as strict as in federal court; it may be harder for state-court defendants to get summary judgment; and plaintiffs may prefer state courts that do not require jury verdicts to be unanimous. Some state courts also have reputations for higher damage awards. Such considerations can lead plaintiffs to file their state-court cases in ways that make them hard or impossible to remove, as by including a "spoiler" diversity-destroying or in-state defendant in a state-law case.

B. Diversity Jurisdiction

1. Introduction

Most civil cases brought in federal courts are brought under one of two subject-matter jurisdiction statutes: the diversity statute [28 U.S.C. § 1332] or the federal-question statute [28 U.S.C. § 1331]. This section of the Summary will discuss diversity jurisdiction; federal-question jurisdiction will be discussed *infra*.

2. Constitutional Authorization

Article III, Section 2 of the Constitution provides that the judicial power of the United States may extend to controversies between two or more states, between a state and a citizen of another state, **between citizens of different states**, or between a state (or the citizens thereof) and foreign states, citizens, or subjects. The usual justification for creating diversity jurisdiction is to afford an alternative forum to out-of-state litigants who might be victims of local prejudice against outsiders.

a. What Constitutes Diversity

The plaintiff and defendant have diverse citizenship if one is a citizen of one state and the other is a citizen of another state or an alien or foreign national. There is **no diversity** jurisdiction, however, in a suit **between two aliens**, even if from different countries (*e.g.*, a citizen of India and a Canadian).

b. "Minimal" Diversity Constitutionally Required

The Constitution requires only that one plaintiff be of different citizenship from one defendant, even if there are co-parties who are not of diverse citizenship. [**State Farm Fire & Casualty Co. v. Tashire,** 386 U.S. 523 (1967)] Absent minimal diversity, the federal courts are forbidden to entertain a case unless it involves a federal question (discussed *infra*, p. 80 *et seq.*).

3. Diversity Statute

The First Congress not only created lower federal courts, but also vested them with diversity jurisdiction by passing the predecessor to 28 U.S.C. section 1332. That statute closely tracked the constitutional language. There are two main prerequisites to diversity jurisdiction under the statute: diversity of citizenship and a minimum amount in controversy.

a. Diversity of Citizenship

(1) Complete-Diversity Requirement

In 1806, the Supreme Court interpreted the diversity statute to **require complete diversity**, *i.e.*, that there be **no defendant** having the same citizenship as any plaintiff. [**Strawbridge v. Curtiss,** 7 U.S. 267 (1806)] Although it has made some changes to the statute since then, Congress has not tried to change this interpretation. The supplemental jurisdiction statute (granting federal courts jurisdiction to hear "supplemental" claims related to the claim over which they have "original" jurisdiction; *see infra*, p. 93 *et seq.*) appears to embrace the complete-diversity requirement, but could have been interpreted to weaken it; *see infra*, p. 93 *et seq.*

(2) Statutory Exceptions to Complete-Diversity Requirement

Congress has authorized exercise of federal-court diversity jurisdiction in some instances even though there is not complete diversity:

(a) Interpleader

The federal interpleader act permits a federal court to exercise jurisdiction in interpleader actions whenever any two or more adverse parties are of diverse citizenship. (28 U.S.C. § 1335(a)(1)] The Supreme Court has held that this "minimal diversity" jurisdiction is constitutional. [**State Farm Fire & Casualty Co. v. Tashire,** *supra*]

(b) Class Action Fairness Act

The Class Action Fairness Act of 2005 provides federal district courts with original jurisdiction over certain class actions in which there is minimal diversity between the class members and the named defendants. [28 U.S.C. § 1332(d)(2)]

(c) Multiparty, Multiforum Jurisdiction

The Multiparty, Multiforum Jurisdiction Trial Act confers jurisdiction on the federal district courts for actions arising from accidents that involve the deaths of at least 75 people so long as there is minimal diversity between adverse parties. [28 U.S.C. § 1369]

(3) Alienage Diversity Jurisdiction

Section 1332(a)(2) confers federal subject-matter jurisdiction over cases involving a citizen of the United States and a citizen of a foreign country, and section 1332(a)(3) confers federal subject-matter jurisdiction over cases involving completely diverse citizens of American states in which aliens are additional parties.

e.g. **Example**: Jacques, a citizen and resident of France, sues Bob, a citizen of Illinois. Assuming the amount-in-controversy requirement is met, the case could be in federal court under alienage jurisdiction because it is between a citizen of the United States and a citizen of a foreign country.

e.g. **Example**: Mary, a citizen and resident of New York, and Jacques, a citizen and resident of France, sue Bob, a citizen of Illinois. Assuming the amount-in-controversy requirement is met, the plaintiffs could invoke alienage jurisdiction because the case is between citizens of different states, with an alien as an additional party.

cf. **Compare**: Mary, a citizen and resident of New York, and Jacques, a citizen and resident of France, sue Roberto, a citizen and resident of Mexico. The case cannot be in federal court on grounds of diversity because both Jacques and Roberto are aliens.

(4) How Citizenship Is Determined

(a) Natural Persons

For United States nationals, "citizenship," in substance, has the same meaning as *domicile*. New citizenship may be established by physical presence in the new state and an intention to remain there permanently or indefinitely—*i.e.*, no present intent to reside elsewhere.

EXAM TIP   **GILBERT**

Although a person's domicile is important in determining both personal jurisdiction and diversity jurisdiction, be sure to keep these concepts separate. Personal jurisdiction gives a court *power over the defendant*, while diversity jurisdiction, a type of subject-matter jurisdiction, gives the court the authority to hear the *type of case*.

---

1) United States National Living Abroad

An American citizen permanently living abroad has no domicile within the United States and is *not a citizen of any state*. Such a person cannot be an original party to a diversity action in federal court.

2) Citizens of District of Columbia, Puerto Rico, and U.S. Territories

Although citizens of the District of Columbia, Puerto Rico, and U.S. territories might have suffered a similar fate to that of the expatriates, Congress instead provided that they should be *treated as citizens of states* for purposes of diversity jurisdiction, and the Supreme Court upheld this as constitutional. [28 U.S.C. § 1332(e); **National Mutual Insurance Co. v. Tidewater Transfer Co.,** 337 U.S. 582 (1949)] Thus, a citizen of Puerto Rico can sue a citizen of Mexico in federal court under alienage diversity jurisdiction.

(b) Corporations

For diversity purposes, a corporation is deemed to be a citizen of *every American state* and *every foreign state* in which it is *incorporated*, and of the American state or foreign state in which it has its *principal place of business*. [28 U.S.C. § 1332(c)(1)] Incorporation of a single corporation in more than one American state, however, is virtually or entirely nonexistent now.

1) "Principal Place of Business"

The principal place of business of a corporation is the state in which its *"nerve center"* is located. This standard looks to the state in which the corporation's officers *direct, control, and coordinate* the corporation's activities, which ordinarily will be the place where the corporation maintains its headquarters. That most of the corporation's employees or its main production facilities are located in other states would not change this conclusion. But note that the nerve center is not an office where the corporation merely holds board of directors' meetings involving officers and directors who have traveled there for that purpose. [*See* **Hertz Corp. v. Friend,** 559 U.S. 393 (2010)—Hertz was not a California corporation even though the amount of its activities in California was significantly greater than in any other state; its leadership was at its corporate headquarters in New Jersey] In some situations, there may be uncertainty, such as when the corporation's officers work at several different locations, perhaps communicating over the Internet; in such cases, courts should look to the center of overall direction.

e.g. **Example**: A New Hampshire corporation whose only business consisted of operating group homes in Maine, where it also had a State Director who controlled all day-to-day operations, nonetheless had its principal place of business in New Hampshire because the only two officers and directors of the corporation resided there, and they "set overall corporate policy and goals." [**Harrison v. Granite Bay Care, Inc.,** 811 F.3d 36 (1st Cir. 2016)]

2) Corporation as Alien

A corporation incorporated in a foreign state is a citizen of that foreign state for purposes of diversity of citizenship, as is any corporation that has its principal place of business in a foreign state. [28 U.S.C. § 1332(c)(1); *see also* **JPMorgan Chase Bank v. Traffic Stream (BVI) Infrastructure, Ltd.,** 536 U.S. 88 (2002)—even though British Virgin Islands is not recognized as an independent foreign state, a corporation organized under its law is an alien for purposes of diversity jurisdiction] *Note*: A corporation may be regarded as a citizen of multiple places, including both American states and foreign states, under these standards.

3) Distinguish—Venue

For venue purposes, a corporate defendant is usually treated as a resident of every state in which it is *subject to personal jurisdiction*, not merely its principal place of business. (*See supra*, p. 36.)

EXAM TIP

Remember that subject-matter jurisdiction and venue are two district concepts, and thus the rules regarding corporate citizenship are different. For purposes of *diversity jurisdiction*, the corporation is a citizen of its state(s) of *incorporation and* of the state of its *principal place of business*. For *venue* purposes, the corporation is deemed to reside in any federal district in which it is *subject to personal jurisdiction*, which allows venue in the state of incorporation, where its principal place of business is, and also in every other district where it *has sufficient contacts*.

(c) Other Artificial Entities

For purposes of diversity, unincorporated associations and other noncorporate artificial entities created by state law are viewed as citizens of *each state in which any member is a citizen*. As a result, complete diversity is often destroyed and diversity jurisdiction is unavailable.

1) Partnerships

A business partnership is viewed as an association for diversity purposes. Therefore, the citizenship of *each partner* must be considered. [**Cresswell v. Sullivan & Cromwell,** 922 F.2d 60 (2d Cir. 1990)—American law-firm partnership could not be sued in federal court on diversity grounds because it included partners who were United States nationals but were domiciled abroad, *see supra*, p. 68]

a) Limited Partnerships

In a general partnership, the partners have full individual liability for the partnership's debts. In a limited partnership, the liability of the "limited" partners is restricted to the amount of their investment and they have negligible power to control the partnership. Nonetheless, the Supreme Court has held that the citizenships of *all limited partners* must be taken into account for purposes of determining complete diversity. [**Carden v. Arkoma Associates,** 494 U.S. 185 (1990)]

b) Distinguish—Professional Corporation

Some enterprises (such as law firms) that formerly operated as partnerships now operate as "professional corporations" (mainly for tax reasons). Because the "shareholder" attorneys in such corporations remain individually liable for legal malpractice, arguably their citizenship should be considered for purposes of determining complete diversity. Lower federal courts have held, though, that only the citizenship *of the professional corporation* should be considered. [*See, e.g.,* **Cote v. Wadel,** 796 F.2d 981 (7th Cir. 1986)]

2) Labor Unions

The Supreme Court has held that unions are unincorporated associations for purposes of diversity jurisdiction, and thus the citizenship of *all union members* is considered. [**United Steel Workers v. R.H. Bouligny, Inc.,** 382 U.S. 145 (1965)]

3) Underwriting Syndicate

Lloyd's of London, the underwriting syndicate, has been held to have the citizenship, for purposes of diversity, of every "name" (*i.e.,* investor). [**Indiana Gas Co. v. Home Insurance Co.,** 141 F.3d 314 (7th Cir. 1998); *but see* **Certain Interested Underwriters at Lloyd's of London v. Layne,** 26 F.3d 39 (6th Cir. 1994)—as real party in interest, only Lloyd's itself need be considered in determining whether there is diversity]

4) Business Trusts

Business trusts involve investments by "shareholders" who entrust their investments to trustees who control the activities of the trust. Although this arrangement might make the shareholders of a trust seem like the shareholders of a corporation, Congress has not defined state citizenship for unincorporated entities as opposed to corporations. Accordingly, *all shareholders* of a business trust, as "members" of the trust, *must be considered* in determining its citizenship for purposes of diversity. [**Americold Realty Trust v. ConAgra Foods, Inc.,** 136 S. Ct. 1012 (2016)]

cf. **Compare—Suit by Trustees in Their Own Names**: When state law confers authority on trustees of a trust to sue in their own names in connection with trust affairs, and they file such a suit, *only the citizenship of the trustees* and not that of the nonparty shareholders is considered in determining whether diversity of citizenship exists. [**Navarro Savings Association v. Lee,** 446 U.S. 458 (1980)]

5) National Banks

Under 28 U.S.C. section 1348, a national bank chartered by the Comptroller of the Currency of the United States Treasury, rather than by a state, is deemed a citizen of the state in which its main office is located. [**Wachovia Bank v. Schmidt,** 546 U.S. 303 (2006)]

6) Class Action Fairness Act Cases

In cases governed by the Class Action Fairness Act, an unincorporated association is deemed to be a citizen of the state in which it has its principal place of business *and* of the state under whose laws it is organized. [28 U.S.C. § 1332(d)(10)]

(d) Permanent Resident Aliens

The district courts do not have diversity jurisdiction of actions between citizens of an American state and citizens of a foreign state who are *lawfully admitted for permanent residence* in the United States and are domiciled in the same state as an opposing party. [28 U.S.C. § 1332(a)(2)]

1) "Green Card" Required

The permanent-resident-alien provision applies only to those aliens who have been given "green cards" authorizing permanent residence. [**Foy v. Schatzman & Aaronson, P.A.,** 108 F.3d 1347 (11th Cir. 1997)]

2) Former Law—Permanent Resident Aliens as "Citizens" of State of Domicile

Until 2011, the statute provided that permanent resident aliens would be "citizens" of the state in which they were domiciled. This provision raised possible *constitutional objections* because it could allow a resident alien to be regarded as diverse from an alien opposing party, even though the Constitution does not treat a suit between aliens as within diversity jurisdiction.

(e) Class Actions

In a class action (*i.e.*, an action brought by representatives on behalf of a class consisting of a large number of persons), only the citizenship of the *named representatives* is considered in determining diversity. [**Supreme Tribe of Ben Hur v. Cauble,** 255 U.S. 356 (1921)]

EXAM TIP   **GILBERT**

Note that because only the citizenship of the *named representatives* is considered in determining diversity in a class action, it is irrelevant that some members of the class are citizens of the defendant's state; diversity still exists. Don't be fooled by a fact pattern in which the defendant is a large company, like Firestone, and members of the plaintiff class live in every state. Diversity may be preserved by carefully selecting the class representatives. Moreover, if the Class Action Fairness Act applies, only minimal diversity is required.

---

1) Class Action Fairness Act Cases

The Class Action Fairness Act of 2005 provides district courts with original jurisdiction over certain class actions in which there is *minimal diversity* between any class member and any named defendant, so long as other prerequisites are also met. [28 U.S.C. $1332(d)(2)]

(f) Executors, Guardians, and Trustees

The legal representative of an estate or of an infant or incompetent is deemed to have the citizenship of the decedent, infant, or incompetent. [28 U.S.C. § 1332(c)(2)]

(g) Fictitious Defendants

When the plaintiff in a civil case is unable to ascertain the name of a potential defendant, some states allow the plaintiff to sue the unknown defendant under a fictitious name (*e.g.*, "John Doe"). A number of federal courts have held that such cases could not be heard under diversity jurisdiction because of the uncertainty of the citizenship of the unnamed defendant. [*See, e.g.*, **Othman v. Globe Indemnity Co.,** 759 F.2d 1458 (9th Cir. 1985)] In 1988, a federal statute [28 U.S.C. § 1441; *see infra*, p. 100] providing for removal of cases from state court to federal court was amended. The amendment provides that for purposes of removal, the citizenship of defendants sued under fictitious names is to be disregarded. The diversity jurisdiction statute [28 U.S.C. § 1332] was *not* similarly amended. Nevertheless, it has been held that inclusion of a fictitious defendant neither destroys diversity jurisdiction nor requires that the fictitious defendant be named or dropped from the case. [*See, e.g.*, **Fat T, Inc. v. Aloha Tower Assoc. Piers 7, 8, and 9,** 172 F.R.D. 411 (D. Haw. 1996); *but see* **Howell v. Tribune Entertainment Co.,** 106 F.3d 215 (7th Cir. 1997)— fictitious defendants are not permitted in federal diversity suits] The Supreme Court has not yet resolved the issue.

(5) Time for Determination

Diversity need exist only as of the *commencement* of the action.

(a) Change Before Filing

It is immaterial that the parties had the same citizenship when the claim arose, and a party may even move to another state to create diversity, as long as there is a *genuine* change of citizenship.

(b) Change After Filing

Similarly, a change in either party's citizenship after the filing of the suit does not deprive the court of jurisdiction, nor will it cure a lack of diversity that existed when the suit was filed. [**Grupo Dataflux v. Atlas Global Group, L.P.,** 541 U.S. 567 (2004)—post-filing withdrawal of Mexican partners from Texas partnership did not cure lack of diversity that existed when suit against Mexican corporation was filed]

(c) Substituted Party

Sometimes after a case is filed, a plaintiff will transfer his interest in the case and the transferee will be substituted for the plaintiff. The general rule is still followed: Because diversity "is assessed at the time the action is filed," diversity is not destroyed even if the substituted plaintiff is a citizen of the same state as one of the defendants. [**Freeport-McMoRan, Inc. v. K N Energy, Inc.,** 498 U.S. 426 (1991)]

(d) Partial Exception—Removal

When an action is removed to federal court from state court on grounds of diversity, diversity must exist at the time of *filing of the suit and* on the date of *filing of the notice of removal*.

(6) Realigning Parties

In determining diversity, the court will look to the *real interests* of the parties and may realign them (as plaintiffs or defendants) according to their real interests. In general, the court will look to the *ultimate interests* of the parties in realigning them.

(a) Shareholders' Derivative Actions

In a shareholder derivative action (in which a shareholder brings a suit to enforce a right of the corporation because the officers of the corporation refuse to bring the suit directly), the corporation, even though nominally joined as a plaintiff, is likely to be realigned as a defendant for diversity purposes if (as is usually the case) it is controlled by persons antagonistic to the shareholder-plaintiff. [**Smith v. Sperling**, 354 U.S. 91 (1957)]

(7) Efforts to Create Diversity

28 U.S.C. section 1359 provides that there shall be no jurisdiction when a person has collusively or improperly been made a party or joined in order to invoke federal jurisdiction.

(a) Assignment of Claim

When a claim is assigned to establish diversity, or assigned without significant consideration, the assignment will not create diversity if diversity would not exist had the action been brought in the name of the assignor. [**Kramer v. Caribbean Mills, Inc.**, 394 U.S. 823 (1969)] However, if substantial consideration is given for the assignment, jurisdiction exists even though there would be no diversity between the assignor and the defendant.

(b) Appointment of Executor

Appointment of an out-of-state executor will not create diversity, because the executor is deemed to be a citizen of *the decedent's state*. (*See supra*, p. 72.)

(c) Distinguish—Change of Citizenship

A *genuine* change of citizenship can create diversity. (*See supra*, p. 72.)

(8) Efforts to Defeat Diversity

There is no similar statute forbidding efforts to defeat diversity, and plaintiffs have some latitude in doing so.

(a) Joinder of Nondiverse Defendants

Under federal practice, a plaintiff can bring a single action against a number of defendants, as long as the claims against the defendants arise out of the *same series of occurrences* or transactions and there is a *question of law or fact common* to all the parties. (*See infra*, pp. 218, 220.) Often the plaintiff may add claims against nondiverse defendants and thereby defeat diversity.

1) Limitation—Viable Claims

The plaintiff must have a viable claim against the nondiverse defendant or the presence of this defendant will be disregarded in making the diversity determination.

2) Limitation—Alternative Grounds for Federal Jurisdiction

Removal may be possible if nondiverse defendants are sued if federal jurisdiction can be justified on some other basis, such as federal-question jurisdiction (*i.e.*, a case arising under federal law; *see infra*, p. 81).

3) Limitation—Class Action Fairness Act Cases

In cases governed by the Class Action Fairness Act, joining a nondiverse defendant does not preclude federal subject-matter jurisdiction because the statute requires only *minimal diversity*. [28 U.S.C. § 1332(d)(2)]

(b) Appointment of Nondiverse Representative

The appointment of a nondiverse executor or administrator cannot defeat diversity because the citizenship of such persons is deemed to be the same as that of the decedent. (*See supra*, p. 72.)

(9) Effect of Lack of Diversity

(a) Dismissal of Nondiverse Party

The plaintiff often can solve the lack-of-diversity problem by dismissing the nondiverse party. [**Newman-Green, Inc. v. Alfonzo-Larrain,** 490 U.S. 826 (1989)]

(b) Required Party

When the nondiverse party is a required party (*i.e.*, a party needed for just adjudication, *see infra*, p. 221), the plaintiff may be unable to proceed in federal court. (*See infra*, p. 222—discussing decision whether to proceed with action in absence of required party.)

EXAM TIP

Remember to consider *other grounds* for federal jurisdiction if diversity is absent. For example, if a federal question is presented, the case may proceed in federal court even though there is no diversity.

---

b. Jurisdictional Amount

From the outset, the diversity statute limited federal jurisdiction to cases in which more than a certain *minimum amount* was *"in controversy."* Currently, diversity jurisdiction is limited to cases involving *more than $75,000*. *Rationale*: The monetary limitation seeks to ensure that only "substantial" cases will be brought in federal court.

(1) Time for Computing

The amount is computed as of the *date of commencement* of the action. Subsequent events (*e.g.*, part payment) do not defeat jurisdiction.

(2) Legal Certainty Test

The jurisdictional amount requirement is satisfied unless the plaintiff's complaint shows to a "legal certainty" that she could not recover *more* than the minimum amount. [**St. Paul Mercury Indemnity Co. v. Red Cab Co.,** 303 U.S. 283 (1938)]

(a) No Need to Itemize Damages in Complaint

The plaintiff ordinarily need not indicate in the complaint how she arrived at the amount of damages claimed.

1) But Note—Disclosure

Early in most cases the Federal Rules require that certain disclosures be made, including a computation of any damages claimed. (*See infra,* p. 275.)

(b) Good-Faith Limitation

The claim for damages set forth in the complaint is determinative of the amount in controversy if the claim was made in good faith; there need only be some *legal possibility* of recovering the minimum amount.

1) Removed Cases

Determination of the amount in controversy may be less strict in actions removed from state court to federal court under the removal statute, since the plaintiff would presumably have no incentive to inflate her claim to satisfy federal jurisdictional requirements when filing in state court.

(c) Effect of Judgment for Lesser Amount

That the actual recovery does not exceed the jurisdictional amount does not affect the jurisdiction of the court, as long as the claim was made in good faith. The court may, however, deny the plaintiff costs of suit or impose them on the plaintiff. [28 U.S.C. § 1332(b)] In practice, this power is rarely used.

(d) Valuing Claims for Nonmonetary Relief

When the remedy sought is not money (*e.g.,* when the plaintiff seeks an injunction ordering the defendant to refrain from doing some act) the courts are split on whether the relief should be valued from the *plaintiff's perspective* (value to the plaintiff) or the *defendant's perspective* (cost to the defendant) in cases in which the values would differ.

e.g. **Example—Plaintiff's Perspective:** Plaintiff sued to restrain defendant from erecting poles and wires in a way that would injure plaintiff's poles and wires. Although the cost to defendant of changing its operation would be less than the jurisdictional amount, the Supreme Court upheld jurisdiction because the value to plaintiff would exceed that amount. [**Glenwood Light & Water Co. v. Mutual Light, Heat & Power Co.,** 239 U.S. 121 (1915)]

e.g. **Example—Defendant's Perspective:** Plaintiffs sued a railroad to quiet title to water rights that were worth far less than the jurisdictional amount to plaintiffs, but a good deal more to defendant, and the court upheld jurisdiction. [**Ronzio v. Denver & Rio Grande Railroad,** 116 F.2d 604 (10th Cir. 1940)]

(e) Valuing Claims for Declaratory Relief

In declaratory-relief actions when the plaintiff seeks a determination that he is not liable to the defendant, the amount in controversy is the amount of the claim that would be asserted by the declaratory-relief defendant against the declaratory-relief plaintiff. With other sorts of declaratory claims (*e.g.*, that plaintiff may continue a course of conduct defendant claims is illegal), the analysis should resemble that for nonmonetary relief.

(f) Interest and Costs

Interest and costs are *excluded*. However, *attorneys' fees* that are recoverable by contract or by statute are considered part of the matter in controversy, rather than as costs, and are included.

(3) Aggregation of Claims to Satisfy Requirement

Whether separate claims for less than the jurisdictional amount can be aggregated to satisfy the jurisdictional-amount requirement depends on a number of factors.

(a) Claims of Single Plaintiff Against Single Defendant

All claims of the plaintiff against the defendant, whether or not related, *can be aggregated* to meet the minimum.

e.g. **Example**: Plaintiff sues defendant for $50,000 in damages arising from a car accident and for $30,000 arising from an unrelated breach of contract. These amounts may be aggregated to reach the jurisdictional amount.

(b) Claims of Single Plaintiff Against Several Defendants

Only claims for which all defendants are *jointly liable* to the plaintiff may be combined. "Joint liability" is defined narrowly for this purpose; claims arising from closely related conduct do not satisfy the test. "Joint" liability would arise in a few situations such as when the defendants are co-owners of property; it would not arise when the defendants are *joint tortfeasors*.

1) Note

When the plaintiff alleges that the defendants inflicted separate harms on her as part of a conspiracy, *allegations of conspiracy* may make defendants jointly liable and therefore *permit aggregation* of amounts.

(c) Claims of Several Plaintiffs Against Single Defendant

The claims of multiple plaintiffs can be aggregated only if they have a *common undivided ownership interest* in the claims.

e.g. **Example**: Peter and Penelope are tenants in common in a parcel of land (*i.e.*, each owns an "undivided" 50% interest). They sue Damon for trespass, alleging $120,000 in total damages to the property. Each plaintiff has suffered only $60,000 damage to his or her own interest, but the plaintiffs' undivided interest in the property has been injured. Under these circumstances, Peter and Penelope may aggregate their claims to meet the $75,000 requirement.

(d) Counterclaims

In general, the amount sought on a counterclaim cannot be aggregated with a plaintiff's small claim to satisfy the jurisdictional minimum. *But note*: A 1961 Supreme Court case [**Horton v. Liberty Mutual Insurance Co.,** 367 U.S. 348 (1961)] appears to look to the counterclaim as the basis for jurisdiction in a case involving Texas workers' compensation. However, it is regarded by many as limited to its quite unusual facts.

1) Distinguish—Jurisdiction over Counterclaim When Plaintiff Has Satisfied Minimum

When the defendant's counterclaim arises out of the same transaction and is therefore *compulsory* (*see infra*, p. 187), it need *not* satisfy the jurisdictional-minimum requirement because it is within the supplemental jurisdiction of the court (*see infra*, p. 94). With a *permissive* counterclaim (*see infra*, p. 187), however, there must be an *independent jurisdictional basis* and the jurisdictional-minimum requirement must therefore be satisfied.

2) Distinguish—Compulsory Counterclaim Sometimes Considered When Defendant Does Not Move to Dismiss

A few lower federal courts will allow the amount of defendant's compulsory counterclaim to be used to establish jurisdiction if: (i) the case was *originally filed* in federal court; (ii) the amount of the counterclaim satisfies the jurisdictional minimum of more than $75,000; and (iii) the defendant does not move to dismiss for lack of subject-matter jurisdiction. [*See, e.g.,* **Spectacor Management Group v. Brown,** 131 F.3d 120 (3d Cir. 1997)] But this approach does not justify using a counterclaim to satisfy the jurisdictional amount for *removal* because that would permit the defendant to override the plaintiff's choice to sue in state court. [*See, e.g.,* **Kaplan v. Computer Sciences Corp.,** 148 F. Supp. 2d 318 (S.D.N.Y. 2001)—emphasizing narrow construction required for removal jurisdiction]

(e) Class Action Fairness Act Cases

In cases governed by the Class Action Fairness Act, the claims of class members are *aggregated,* and federal-court jurisdiction exists if the amount sought for the class as a whole exceeds *$5 million*, even if the claims of no individual class member exceed $75,000. [28 U.S.C. § 1332(d)(6)]

c. Exceptions to Exercise of Diversity Jurisdiction

Although the diversity statute does not limit the subject matter of cases brought in federal court, the courts decline to exercise jurisdiction in some types of cases.

(1) Domestic Relations

As a matter of long-standing statutory construction, an exception to diversity jurisdiction *prohibits* issuance by a federal court of *divorce, alimony, or child-custody* decrees. However, the exception does not permit a federal district court to refuse to exercise diversity jurisdiction over a tort action for damages, even when the claims are brought by one divorced parent on behalf of children allegedly abused by the other parent. [**Ankenbrandt v. Richards,** 504 U.S. 689 (1992)]

(2) Probate Proceedings

Federal courts will not take jurisdiction over the *probate or annulment of a will or the administration of a decedent's estate*. They will also refrain from endeavoring to dispose of property that is in the custody of a state probate court. However, a federal court must exercise otherwise proper jurisdiction even though the issues may also be involved in litigation before a state probate court. [**Marshall v. Marshall,** 547 U.S. 293 (2006)—federal bankruptcy court had jurisdiction over a claim for damages for tortious interference with the testator's alleged intent to create a trust providing benefits to plaintiff Anna Nicole Smith, even though a state probate court had asserted that it had "exclusive jurisdiction" over the claim]

d. Proposals to Repeal Diversity Statute

For several decades, there have been calls for the repeal of the state-citizen diversity statute. Proponents of this move argue that any residue of prejudice against outsiders is insufficient to justify imposing the burden of deciding diversity cases on the federal courts. Those who favor retaining diversity jurisdiction urge that prejudice does persist, and that it is important to preserve options for litigants. It is impossible to forecast the future of this debate, although the litigating bar has been highly effective in opposing abolition proposals.

(1) Complex Litigation

Whatever the future of diversity jurisdiction generally, there is also sentiment favoring expanding it to cope with the demands of repeated litigation of related matters. This attitude is partly reflected in the adoption of the Class Action Fairness Act, which eased access to federal court. *See* p. 78 *infra*.

(2) Increase in Jurisdictional Minimum

As a partial compromise in the ongoing debate over the continued existence of diversity jurisdiction, Congress raised the jurisdictional amount from over $10,000 to over $50,000 in 1988 and then to over $75,000 in 1996, thus cutting down the number of cases that come within diversity jurisdiction.

e. Class Action Fairness Act of 2005

Congress found that class actions brought in state court and based solely on state law nonetheless often involved issues of national importance, and also that the class-action form itself was often abused in state court (*e.g.*, by "shopping" for a plaintiff-friendly state-court forum). To have issues of national importance heard in federal court, and to curb the alleged abuse of the class-action form in state courts, Congress adopted the Class Action Fairness Act of 2005. The Act expanded the federal courts' original jurisdiction over certain class actions based on state law and included some safeguards for settlements (discussed *infra*, p. 209 *et seq.*). For a federal court to have original jurisdiction over a class action under the Act, the following requirements must be met:

(1) Minimal Diversity

Under the Act, district courts have original jurisdiction over certain class actions in which there is *minimal diversity* between the class members and the named defendants. [28 U.S.C. § 1332(d)(2)] Specifically, there is minimal diversity under the Act if: (i) any member of a plaintiff class is a citizen of a state different from any defendant; (ii) any member of a plaintiff class is a citizen of a foreign country and any defendant is a citizen of a U.S. state; or (iii) any member of a plaintiff class is a citizen of a U.S. state and any defendant is a citizen of a foreign country.

(2) Aggregate Claims Exceeding $5 Million

Under the Act, the claims of all class members are *aggregated,* and the amount in controversy requirement is satisfied if the aggregate claims exceed *$5 million*. [28 U.S.C. § 1332(d)(6)]

(3) Minimum Class Size

There must be *at least 100 members* in the proposed class or classes. [28 U.S.C. $1332(d)(5)(B)]

(4) Excluded Actions

Certain class actions are specifically excluded under the Act:

(a) Primary Defendants Are States or Governmental Entities

There is no federal-court jurisdiction under the Act if the primary defendants are states, state officials, or other governmental entities against whom the court may be foreclosed from ordering relief (*see* Federal Courts Summary). [28 U.S.C. § 1332(d)(5)(A)]

(b) Claims Based on Securities Laws or Corporate Governance

There is no federal-court jurisdiction under the Act over a class action that *solely* involves a claim under *federal securities laws,* or that relates to the *internal affairs of a corporation* and is based on the laws of the state of incorporation. [28 U.S.C. § 1332(d)(9)]

(5) Decline of Jurisdiction

In some instances, the district court must or may decline jurisdiction over a class action even though the case falls within the jurisdiction provided for by the Class Action Fairness Act:

(a) Mandatory Decline

A district court *must* decline jurisdiction provided by the Act if: (i) *more than two-thirds* of the members of the proposed plaintiff class *are citizens of the state in which the action was filed*; (ii) *a defendant* from whom *"significant relief"* is sought is *a citizen of that state*; and (iii) the *"principal injuries"* were incurred *in the state in which the action was filed*. [28 U.S.C. § 1332(d)(4)]

(b) Discretionary Decline

A district court *may* decline jurisdiction provided by the Act if *more than one-third hut less than two-thirds* of the proposed plaintiff class are *citizens of the state in which the action was filed* and the *"primary defendants" are also citizens of that state*. In that case, the court considers a variety of factors, including whether the claims involve matters of national interest, whether the claims will be governed by the law of the state in which the action was filed, and whether the state has a "distinct nexus" with the class members, the alleged harm, or the defendants. [28 U.S.C. § 1332(d)(3)]

(6) Provisions for Protection of Class Members

The Class Action Fairness Act also included provisions designed to protect the interests of class members in connection with proposed settlements. (*See infra*, p. 261.)

(7) "Mass Actions"

The Class Action Fairness Act provides that a "mass action" must be treated as a class action if it is an action "in which monetary relief claims of 100 or more persons are proposed to be tried jointly on the ground that the plaintiffs' claims involve common questions of law or fact." [28 U.S.C. § 1332(d)(11)]

cf. **Compare—Action by State**: The Supreme Court has held that an action by a state to recover damages for injuries suffered by the citizens of the state is not a "mass action" because there is only one plaintiff, the state. [**Mississippi ex rel. Hood v. Au Optronics Corp.**, 134 S. Ct. 736 (2014)—action brought by State of Mississippi to recover for overcharges for liquid-crystal displays paid by the State's citizens due to defendants' cartel activities could not be removed under CAFA]

C. Federal-Question Jurisdiction

1. Constitutional Grant

a. Constitutional Provisions

Article III, Section 2 of the Constitution provides that federal judicial power shall extend to:

(1) Cases in law and equity *arising under the Constitution, the laws of the United States, and treaties* (this is the major area of federal-question jurisdiction);

(2) Cases affecting *ambassadors*, *consuls*, etc.;

(3) Cases involving *admiralty* and maritime jurisdiction; and

(4) Cases to which the *United States is a party*.

b. Broad View of Federal-Question Power

In 1824 the Supreme Court upheld a statute that it read to grant federal courts jurisdiction over any case to which the Bank of the United States (a private bank created by Congress) was a party. It found this acceptable because, even if the suit were about a state-law debt, the bank was a federal creation, and in every case there would be a question about whether it could legally sue—a federal question. That this question would not be important after it was resolved did not bother the Court: "The question forms an original ingredient in every cause. Whether it be in fact relied on or not, in the defense, it is still a part of the cause, and may be relied upon [to uphold federal-question jurisdiction]." [**Osborn v. Bank of the United States,** 22 U.S. 738 (1824)]

(1) Criticism

Some have criticized this broad view of federal question power as including too many cases in which the background federal question would not really be a viable issue in the case at all. Nevertheless, the *Osborn* holding stands and permits Congress to define federal-question jurisdiction extremely broadly. However, the courts have concluded that Congress has *not* defined federal-question jurisdiction this broadly under the *general* federal-question statute. [28 U.S.C. § 1331]

(2) Special Federal-Question Statutes

The Supreme Court has, however, found such broad definitions in some *special* "federal-question" jurisdiction statutes, such as the Foreign Sovereign Immunities Act, 28 U.S.C. section 1330 [**Verlinden B.V. v. Central Bank of Nigeria,** 461 U.S. 480 (1983)—congressional regulation of foreign sovereigns' immunity permits federal jurisdiction over alien's suit against foreign government entity even without any federal claim], and the federal statute chartering the American National Red Cross, 36 U.S.C. section 2 [**American National Red Cross v. S.G.,** 505 U.S. 247 (1992)—chartering statute's language confers original jurisdiction over suits involving the Red Cross, a private but federally chartered corporation, even in cases involving state law claims].

c. Claim Based on Federal Substantive Law

It may be that (except when a federal creation such as the Bank of the United States is involved, *see supra*) Congress can assign to the federal courts jurisdiction over claims it creates only by promulgating or providing for a body of federal substantive law to govern the claims or delegating authority to create such substantive law to the courts.

e.g. **Example—Labor Management Relations Act**: In the Labor Management Relations Act, Congress granted the federal courts jurisdiction over suits to enforce collective-bargaining agreements between employers and unions. The Court found this grant of jurisdiction valid despite lack of diversity, stressing the need for national uniformity in enforcement of such agreements and concluding that "the legislation does more than confer jurisdiction in the federal courts" because "the substantive law to apply in suits under [the Act] is federal law, which the courts must fashion from the policy of our national labor laws." [**Textile Workers Union v. Lincoln Mills,** 353 U.S. 448 (1957)]

2. Federal-Question Statute

a. Introduction

Initially, the lower federal courts mostly lacked jurisdiction to hear cases based on federal law (*i.e.*, "general federal-question jurisdiction") until Congress passed the predecessor to 28 U.S.C. section 1331 after the Civil War. The statute used language very similar to that in the Constitution, granting the federal courts jurisdiction to hear "all civil actions arising under the Constitution, laws, or treaties of the United States."

(1) Statute Interpreted More Narrowly than Constitution

Despite the similarity between the language of the statute and the Constitution, the Supreme Court has interpreted the statute more narrowly; the remainder of this section, therefore, examines the ways in which the Court has limited the reach of the statute.

(2) State-Court Jurisdiction over Cases Raising Federal Questions

As to most federal-question issues, jurisdiction in such cases is now *concurrent* between the state and federal courts. (*See supra*, pp. 62–63.)

(3) Supreme Court Review

Often, when the lower federal courts do not have jurisdiction under the federal-question statute, the Supreme Court has jurisdiction to review decisions of state courts involving federal-law issues. [*See* 28 U.S.C. § 1257]

b. Standards for Determining Whether a Federal Question Is Raised

The Supreme Court's decisions under the federal-question statute are sometimes difficult to reconcile, but look to two basic possibilities:

(1) Federal Law Creates Claim

If federal law creates the claim sued upon, there generally is no problem in finding that the federal courts have subject-matter jurisdiction. As Justice Holmes put it, "a suit arises under the law that creates the cause of action." [**American Well Works Co. v. Layne & Bowler Co.,** 241 U.S. 257 (1916)]

(a) Test Underinclusive

The Court has since recognized that this description is "more useful for describing the vast majority of cases that come within the district courts' original jurisdiction" than for distinguishing among cases in which jurisdiction is doubtful. [**Franchise Tax Board v. Construction Laborers' Vacation Trust,** 463 U.S. 1 (1983)]

(b) Implied Claims

Note that federal claims include claims implied by the courts in addition to private rights of action explicitly created by Congress. [*See, e.g.,* **J.I. Case Co. v. Borak,** 377 U.S. 426 (1964)—implied private right of action for securities fraud in violation of Federal Securities Exchange Act of 1934] However, the Supreme Court has taken a cautious attitude toward implying causes of action. (For details on implied claims, *see* Federal Courts Summary.)

(2) Nonfederal Claim That Turns on Construction of Federal Law

If the claim being sued upon is not one created by federal law but resolution of the suit turns on construction of federal law, application of the federal-question statute is more difficult. The Supreme Court has confirmed that federal-question jurisdiction can be proper "where the vindication of a right under state law necessarily turned on some construction of federal law." [**Merrell Dow Pharmaceuticals, Inc. v. Thompson,** 478 U.S. 804 (1986)]

e.g. **Example**: In a quiet-title action in state court, Plaintiff sought to regain title to real property that had been seized and sold to Defendant by the Internal Revenue Service to satisfy Plaintiff's tax delinquency. Plaintiff claimed that Defendant's title was invalid because the notice it received of the sale did not satisfy the requirements of the Internal Revenue Code. The Court ruled that the quiet-title action fell within federal-question jurisdiction because the question whether proper notice was given under the Internal Revenue Code involved a matter of substantial federal interest and was an essential element of the state law claim. [**Grable & Sons Metal Products, Inc. v. Darue Engineering & Manufacturing Co.,** 545 U.S. 308 (2005)]

e.g. **Example**: A landowner challenged building restrictions resulting from landmark designation based on state administrative-review law. The landowner's challenge to the administrative action was based on federal constitutional objections, and the right to relief under state law therefore required resolution of a substantial question of federal law. [**City of Chicago v. International College of Surgeons,** 522 U.S. 156 (1997)]

e.g. **Example**: A shareholder sued to enjoin a corporation in which he held stock from purchasing bonds issued by federal land banks. The shareholder asserted that under state law the corporation was forbidden to invest in bonds that were not legally issued. The only issue in the case was whether the bonds were validly issued under federal law, and the Supreme Court held that there was federal-question jurisdiction. [**Smith v. Kansas City Title & Trust Co.,** 255 U.S. 180 (1921)]

cf. **Compare**: A railroad employee sued his employer for injuries sustained on the job, which he alleged were caused by a defective uncoupling lever that did not comply with federal standards for safety equipment. The Supreme Court held that the fact that the alleged violation of the federal standard was an element of the state-law tort claim did not fundamentally change the state-law nature of the action and that jurisdiction was absent. [**Moore v. Chesapeake & Ohio Railway,** 291 U.S. 205 (1934)]

(a) Absence of Implied Federal Claim

In *Merrell Dow, supra,* the Court held that there was no federal-question jurisdiction over a state tort claim for negligent manufacture of a drug, although the claim relied on the defendant's alleged violation of the Federal Food, Drug, and Cosmetic Act ("FDCA"). The parties agreed that there was no implied federal cause of action, and the Court reasoned that in that circumstance it would "flout" the will of Congress to allow federal jurisdiction over a state-law claim turning on a violation of the FDCA. In a later case, however, the Court cautioned that "*Merrell Dow* should be read in its entirety as treating the absence of a federal private right of action as evidence relevant to, but not dispositive of, the determination whether there is federal question jurisdiction." [**Grable & Sons Metal Products, Inc. v. Darue Engineering & Manufacturing Co.,** *supra*]

(b) Substantial Bearing on Outcome

When federal law is an element of a state-law claim, it suffices to support federal question jurisdiction only when it is important to the outcome of the case: "The right or immunity must be such that it will be supported if the Constitution or laws of the United States are given one construction or effect, and defeated if they receive another." [**Gully v. First National Bank,** 299 U.S. 109 (1936)]

1) But Note—Constitutional Power

Under **Osborn v. Bank of the United States,** *supra,* p. 80, the unimportance of the question to the dispute before the court may not matter.

(c) Nature of Federal Interest

In *Merrell Dow, supra,* the Court suggested that it would be helpful to focus on the nature of the federal issues at stake and that this approach could reconcile the results in the *Moore* and *Smith* cases, *supra.* In *Smith,* jurisdiction was proper because the validity of an act of Congress was directly drawn into question, and there was a substantial federal interest in this question. On the other hand, in *Moore* the federal issue related to the employer's compliance at one place and time with one federal safety standard, and there was little federal interest in this isolated incident.

1) Federal Claim Not Necessary

The Supreme Court settled a circuit split over the interpretation of *Merrell Dow*, deciding that a federal right of action is not necessary for federal-question jurisdiction over a state law claim under *Merrell Dow*. The federal interest may have the nature and importance required by that decision in other ways. [**Grable & Sons Metal Products, Inc. v. Darue Engineering & Manufacturing Co.**, *supra*]

e.g. **Example**: Plaintiff's patent was held invalid in federal litigation, with the court ruling that his attorneys had waived a possible saving exception to an adverse patent-law rule. Plaintiff then sued his former attorneys for legal malpractice under state law in Texas state court, with the case turning on whether the attorneys' waiver of the federal-law exception cost him the federal lawsuit. The Texas Supreme Court held that under *Grable* (*supra*, p. 82), the embedded federal patent-law element in his state-law malpractice claim made federal-court jurisdiction over the claim exclusive under 28 U.S.C. § 1338(a). The U.S. Supreme Court reversed, distilling a four-point test from *Grable*: Federal-question jurisdiction over a state-law claim will lie if an embedded federal issue is 1) necessarily raised, 2) actually disputed, 3) substantial, and 4) capable of resolution in federal court without disrupting the federal-state balance approved by Congress. The federal-law element in plaintiff's claim satisfied the first two requirements; but it was not "substantial" in the relevant sense of the issue's importance to the federal system as a whole, rather than just its significance to the parties in the immediate case. There also appeared to be no significant threat to the development of uniform federal patent law from letting state courts decide such "fact-bound and situation-specific" issues in state-law malpractice claims; coupled with states' interest in maintaining standards in their licensed professions, upholding state-court jurisdiction posed no threat to the appropriate balance of federal and state judicial responsibilities. Accordingly, not only was federal jurisdiction not exclusive; federal-question jurisdiction did not exist at all. [**Gunn v. Minton**, 133 S. Ct. 1059 (2013)]

c. Well-Pleaded Complaint Rule

Generally, a federal court will not have federal-question subject-matter jurisdiction unless the federal question appears in the plaintiff's "well-pleaded complaint." Federal questions raised by an *answer* to a complaint are *not* sufficient. The well-pleaded complaint rule serves as a quick and reliable sorting device for allocating subject-matter jurisdiction between the state and federal courts.

(1) Federal Element of Nonfederal Claim Properly Included Under Pleading Rules

Sometimes a plaintiff who has a state-law claim will want to sue in federal court but cannot bring a diversity action. Such a plaintiff might try to get the case into federal court by injecting a federal-law issue into the complaint even though it is not required to be included by the rules governing pleading (*infra*, pp. 142–148). This tactic does not suffice to support federal-question jurisdiction. The federal issue must be an ***element of the state-law claim*** that is ***required to be included in the complaint to state a claim*** under the applicable rules of pleading, for that is what makes these allegations "well pleaded." [*E.g.*, Cal. Civ. Proc. Code § 431.10(a)— "A material allegation in a pleading is one essential to the claim or defense and which could not be stricken from the pleading without leaving it insufficient as to that claim or defense."]

(2) Anticipation of Defense Insufficient

Similarly, a plaintiff who wants to sue in federal court may try to raise a federal question to invoke jurisdiction by including in his complaint allegations relating to a federal-law defense that the defendant might raise. Such an allegation—in anticipation of a defense—is ***not*** a sufficient basis for federal-question jurisdiction. Under the well-pleaded complaint rule, allegations going to an anticipated defense are not required to be in a complaint.

Example: Plaintiffs sued Defendant railroad in federal court, alleging that the railroad had breached a contract to provide Plaintiffs with free lifetime passes to ride the railroad. Breach of contract is a state-law claim. The railroad had granted Plaintiffs the passes to settle Plaintiffs' personal-injury claims against it. Diversity jurisdiction was not available. In an attempt to invoke federal-question jurisdiction, Plaintiffs, in their complaint, alleged that Defendant would defend the breach-of-contract action by claiming that a newly enacted federal statute prohibited such lifetime passes. They further alleged that the statute should not apply to them or that the statute unconstitutionally deprived them of their property without due process of law. The Supreme Court held that the federal courts did not have federal-question jurisdiction over the case because the allegations relating to the federal statute were not essential to Plaintiffs' action for breach of contract; they merely anticipated a defense that the railroad would have to plead and prove. [**Louisville & Nashville Railroad v. Mottley,** *supra*, p. 61]

(3) Federal Counterclaim Insufficient

Like a federal defense to a state-law claim, a counterclaim based on federal law, ***even if compulsory***, does ***not*** create a federal question that justifies jurisdiction under section 1331. The defendant should not be able to defeat a plaintiff's right to have a state-law claim heard in state court by asserting a counterclaim based on federal law. [**Holmes Group v. Vornado Air Circulation Systems, Inc.,** 535 U.S. 826 (2002)]

(4) Removed Cases

As discussed earlier, usually state courts have concurrent jurisdiction to hear federal-question cases, and sometimes a plaintiff will choose to file a federal-law-based action in state court. As will be discussed later (*infra*, p. 99), in some circumstances a ***defendant*** has a right to remove such cases from the state court to federal court. In removal cases, the general rule discussed above applies: A case cannot be removed on the basis of federal-question jurisdiction unless the federal question appears on the face of the ***plaintiff's*** well-pleaded complaint. That the defendant has raised a ***federal defense is irrelevant***.

(a) Criticism

One of the reasons for the well-pleaded complaint rule that courts are not to consider an anticipated federal defense is that there is no way to be certain what defenses will be raised in a defendant's answer. Thus, there is no way to predict whether a federal question will actually be involved. But this argument loses its bite in removed cases, since removal must be on the defendant's motion, and the defendant can definitively establish whether he will raise a federal defense in his answer.

(b) Plaintiff's Election Not to Assert Federal Claim

To prevent the defendant from removing the case to federal court, a plaintiff might "artfully plead" her case to avoid a federal question. Generally, this is permissible on the rationale that the plaintiff is the master of her complaint and cannot be compelled to assert a claim that she chooses not to assert.

1) Partial Exception—Federal Displacement of State Law

The Supremacy Clause of the United States Constitution (making federal law the supreme law of the land) makes it possible for a state claim to be preempted by federal law. Ordinarily, preemption is a defense, and the possibility that federal law preempts a state-law claim does not provide a basis for federal-question jurisdiction. However, Congress may so completely preempt a particular area that any claim in that area is necessarily federal in character. This is *rare*; Congress has displaced state law in only a few statutory schemes. [*See, e.g.*, **Metropolitan Life Insurance Co. v. Taylor,** 481 U.S. 58 (1987)—state law "displaced" by Employee Retirement Income Security Act; *and see* **Avco Corp. v. Machinists,** 390 U.S. 557 (1968)—state-law disputes between employers and employees displaced by § 301 of Labor Management Relations Act] When Congress has so displaced state law in the area, a plaintiff may not—through artful pleading—elude federal jurisdiction by electing not to plead the federal claim because there is no other claim in the area. *The case may be removed on federal-question grounds because the only possible claim in the area is federal*.

e.g. **Example:** A state-court usury suit against a national bank could be removed because the National Bank Act, [12 U.S.C. § 85] provides the exclusive claim for usury against national banks, superseding claims based on state usury laws. [**Beneficial National Bank v. Anderson,** 539 U.S. 1 (2003)]

2) Distinguish—Federal Claim Preclusion

If a federal court enters a final judgment on a federal claim, under the doctrine of claim preclusion (or res judicata—*see infra*, pp. 445–453) any related claim is barred. But this effect does not "displace" state law in the same manner as Congress has done in the statutory schemes mentioned above, and claim preclusion is an affirmative defense. Hence, if a plaintiff later files a state-court suit asserting only a state-law claim based on the same events, that would usually be subject to claim preclusion, but that fact would not be a ground for removal. [**Rivet v. Regions Bank,** 522 U.S. 470 (1998)]

(c) Federal Counterclaim Insufficient

As with a counterclaim in federal court, a federal-law counterclaim in state court does not create federal subject-matter jurisdiction and does not provide a basis for removal. [**Holmes Group v. Vornado Air Circulation Systems, Inc.,** *supra*]

(5) Declaratory-Judgment Cases

Congress has adopted the Declaratory Judgment Act [28 U.S.C. § 2201], which allows parties to seek a declaration of rights rather than a coercive remedy. The Supreme Court has held that when actions are filed under the act, jurisdiction does not depend on whether a federal question appears in the complaint seeking the declaratory judgment. Instead, the federal court should essentially pretend that the action is for a coercive remedy (*e.g.*, an injunction, specific performance, damages) and determine whether a hypothetical, well-pleaded complaint for the coercive remedy would have presented a federal question. [**Skelly Oil Co. v. Phillips Petroleum Co.,** 339 U.S. 667 (1950)] The rationale is that the Declaratory Judgment Act was not intended to expand federal-court jurisdiction, and a well-pleaded complaint in a declaratory-judgment action might contain a federal question, but that federal question would be only a defense in a coercive action.

e.g. **Example:** If in *Louisville & Nashville Railroad, supra*, p. 85, the railroad had sued the Mottleys for declaratory relief, its complaint might have alleged that the Mottleys claimed a contract right to continue receiving free passes, but that an Act of Congress had invalidated such passes. Had this hypothetical suit been filed in federal court, the court should determine whether it had subject-matter jurisdiction by asking whether it would have jurisdiction over a breach-of-contract action brought by the Mottleys. As we have already seen, the impact of the federal legislation would be only a defense in such a suit, and it therefore would not provide a basis for jurisdiction over the railroad's hypothetical declaratory-relief action.

EXAM TIP

When answering an exam question, be sure to remember that in almost every case the ***plaintiff's complaint is the only pleading that is considered*** when determining whether federal-question jurisdiction is present. If the federal question arises in the plaintiff's well-pleaded complaint, there is federal-question jurisdiction. On the other hand, if the plaintiff artfully pleads a claim under state law so that no federal question appears in the complaint, there generally is no federal-question jurisdiction; a defendant may not remove the action to federal court alleging a federal defense. The only ***exception*** to the general rule arises when the plaintiff has artfully pleaded a state-law claim to avoid a federal question, and the defendant can show that federal law has completely replaced the state-law claim.

---

(6) Supreme Court Jurisdiction

The well-pleaded complaint rule is about original jurisdiction of federal district courts; the rule does not apply to cases appealed from state courts to the United States Supreme Court. Thus, even though a lower federal court does not have subject-matter jurisdiction to hear a case because the federal claim arises only as a defense, the Supreme Court may hear an appeal from a state-court judgment entered in essentially the same case. [28 U.S.C. § 1257; *and see* **Louisville & Nashville Railroad v. Mottley,** 219 U.S. 467 (1911)—Court reaches the Mottleys' federal arguments—that federal statute did not apply to them and that if it applied, it unconstitutionally deprived them of property—on merits on appeal from state-court judgment; *compare supra*, p. 422]

d. Nonfrivolous Assertion of Federal Right Sufficient

A federal claim or question is sufficient to vest the court with jurisdiction unless it "clearly appears to be immaterial or made solely for the purpose of obtaining jurisdiction, or where the claim is wholly insubstantial and frivolous." The litigant need not show that he will prevail on the merits of the claim; the federal claim need only be arguable. [**Bell v. Hood,** 327 U.S. 678 (1946)] *Rationale*: A court is not to delve too deeply into the merits of the federal claim at this point because the court is required to determine whether it has subject-matter jurisdiction *before* it considers the merits. [**Steel Co. v. Citizens for a Better Environment,** *supra*, p. 61]

Example: Under a statute requiring that a three-judge court be convened unless the claim was "insubstantial," a district court dismissed on the ground that plaintiff's complaint did not satisfy "plausibility" pleading standards, *see* p. 158 *infra*. The Supreme Court reversed: "We have long distinguished between failing to raise a substantial federal question for jurisdictional purposes . . . and failing to state a claim for relief on the merits; only 'wholly insubstantial and frivolous' claims implicate the former. Absent such frivolity, 'the failure to state a proper cause of action calls for a judgment on the merits and not for a dismissal for want of jurisdiction.' " [**Shapiro v. McManus,** 136 S. Ct. 450 (2015)]

Example: The plaintiff brought a Title VII claim and related state-law claims alleging employment discrimination. Title VII defines an employer as one that has more than 15 employees. After trial, the defendant moved to vacate a judgment in favor of the plaintiff and to dismiss both the Title VII claim and the related state-law claims for lack of subject-matter jurisdiction based on the contention, raised for the first time *after* the verdict, that it had fewer than 15 employees, which the defendant argued deprived the court of subject-matter jurisdiction. The Supreme Court held that the 15-employee requirement was a substantive element of the claim and not a jurisdictional requirement. Had the defendant raised this issue successfully by an early motion to dismiss for failure to state a claim or for summary judgment, the district court nonetheless might have exercised supplemental jurisdiction over the state law claims (*see infra*, p. 96). [**Arbaugh v. Y & H Corp.,** 546 U.S. 500 (2006)]

Example: In *Merrell Dow, supra*, p. 82, the Supreme Court accepted the parties' concession that the FDCA did not give rise to an implied federal claim and, therefore, provided no basis for exercise of federal-question jurisdiction. Yet when other plaintiffs sued, contending that the FDCA gave rise to implied claims, those were held sufficient to support federal-question jurisdiction: "Until this court or the Supreme Court holds that there is no implied private right of action under the FDCA, the opposite position cannot be deemed either frivolous or insubstantial." [*In re* **Bendectin Litigation,** 857 F.2d 290 (6th Cir. 1988)]

(1) Effect of Dismissal on Pleadings

Once the court has decided that a federal question is present, it has subject-matter jurisdiction over the case. If the court later dismisses the case for failure to state a federal claim, *the decision is on the merits*. There are differences between the effect of a dismissal for lack of subject-matter jurisdiction and dismissal for failure to state a claim.

(a) Claim Preclusion

If the court dismisses for failure to state a federal claim, that decision on the merits acts has claim-preclusive effect. (*See infra*, pp. 445–453, for discussion of claim preclusion.) A dismissal for lack of subject-matter jurisdiction has no claim-preclusive effect.

(b) Supplemental Jurisdiction

If a court dismisses for lack of jurisdiction, it cannot hear any part of the case. However, if the court decides it has jurisdiction and then dismisses for failure to state a federal claim, it may exercise supplemental jurisdiction (*see infra*) over related state-law claims and retain the case. But, because state-law claims should usually be dismissed as a matter of discretion if the federal claims are dismissed early in the action (*see infra*, p. 96), this possibility is rarely important.

e. No Jurisdictional Amount

When the court's federal-question jurisdiction is properly invoked, there is ***no minimum amount in controversy requirement*** (except in a few minor categories of cases).

D. Supplemental Jurisdiction

1. Introduction

a. Historical Basis

From an early date, the Supreme Court recognized that federal-question jurisdiction could not be limited to a decision of federal issues presented in a case. In 1824, the Court confirmed that a lower court exercising federal-question jurisdiction could decide all issues in a case, not just the federal questions. [**Osborn v. Bank of the United States,** *supra*, p. 80] *Rationale*: The basis for this reasoning was that the federal courts had jurisdiction over "*a whole case,* as expressed by the constitution." As joinder of claims and parties relaxed, the concept of the scope of the "constitutional case" expanded to encompass claims based on state law and claims against additional parties.

b. Goal

The goal of supplemental jurisdiction is to ***promote judicial economy and consistency of decision*** by removing obstacles to having all related controversies decided in one proceeding. As the Supreme Court put it, "Under the [Federal] Rules [of Civil Procedure], the impulse is toward entertaining the broadest possible scope of action consistent with fairness to the parties." [**United Mine Workers v. Gibbs,** 383 U.S. 715 (1966)]

c. Effect—Decision May Be Based on State Law Alone

Federal courts exercising federal-question jurisdiction can rest a decision entirely on issues of state law, without reaching issues of federal law. When federal constitutional issues are raised, this is often ***the preferable approach***, because it is said that courts should try to avoid unnecessary decision of matters of constitutional law. [**Siler v. Louisville & Nashville Railroad,** 213 U.S. 175 (1909)]

2. Background of Supplemental Jurisdiction—Pendent and Ancillary Jurisdiction

Supplemental jurisdiction, provided by statute in 1990, must be understood against the background of the preexisting doctrines of pendent and ancillary jurisdiction, which had developed in court decisions over several decades. (*Note*: Instructors have different preferences concerning the attention to be devoted to these topics. Your instructor might not emphasize these preexisting doctrines. In that case, you may find it best to skip from this point to p. 93, where discussion of the supplemental jurisdiction statute begins.)

a. Ancillary Jurisdiction

The doctrine of ancillary jurisdiction originated in cases where the federal court controlled property that was claimed by a litigant who was properly before the court. In such cases, ancillary jurisdiction allowed the court to entertain claims of others to the property even though the court had no independent basis for jurisdiction over those claims. [**Freeman v. Howe,** 65 U.S. 450 (1860)] Thereafter, the doctrine was expanded. Generally, ancillary jurisdiction involved assertion of a claim by a *party other than the plaintiff* that was related to the claim made by the plaintiff. The operation of ancillary jurisdiction is best understood from an examination of the various contexts in which it arose:

(1) Counterclaims

When a plaintiff brings a suit against a defendant, the defendant may file a counterclaim against the plaintiff. A counterclaim arising from the same transaction as the plaintiff's claim fell within the ancillary jurisdiction of the court. Note that under Federal Rule 13(a), such a counterclaim is compulsory, meaning that it would be barred by claim preclusion unless asserted. *Compare*: If a counterclaim did not arise from the same transaction as the plaintiff's claim (a "permissive counterclaim" under Fed. R. Civ. P. 13(b)), it was not within the court's ancillary jurisdiction and there had to be an independent basis for federal jurisdiction.

(2) Third-Party Practice—Impleader

Federal Rule 14 permits the *defendant* to assert a claim against another person not originally a party (called a third-party defendant) to the action, seeking indemnity in whole or in part for the claim the plaintiff has asserted against the defendant. There was ancillary jurisdiction over the third-party claim.

(a) Distinguish—Claim by Plaintiff Against Third-Party Defendant

If the *plaintiff* asserted a claim against the third-party defendant in a diversity case, however, there had to be an *independent basis for federal jurisdiction over that claim*.

Example: Plaintiff sued a power district for causing the death of her husband when a crane hit a high-tension wire. The power district impleaded the operator of the crane and later obtained summary judgment against Plaintiff's claim. Plaintiff amended her complaint to assert a claim against the operator of the crane, but there was no diversity between Plaintiff and the third-party defendant. The Supreme Court held that there was no jurisdiction over Plaintiff's claim against the third-party defendant. [**Owen Equipment & Erection Co. v. Kroger,** 437 U.S. 365 (1978)] *Rationale*: If ancillary jurisdiction were permitted in such cases, plaintiffs could circumvent the requirement of complete diversity by suing only diverse potential defendants and waiting for them to implead other nondiverse, potentially responsible, parties.

(b) Contrast—Claim by Third-Party Defendant Against Plaintiff

A number of cases held that there is ancillary jurisdiction over a claim by the third-party defendant against the plaintiff. [*See, e.g.,* **Revere Copper & Brass, Inc. v. Aetna Casualty & Surety Co.,** 426 F.2d 709 (5th Cir. 1970)]

1) Compulsory Counterclaim by Plaintiff

If the third-party defendant filed a claim against the plaintiff, and the plaintiff had a counterclaim arising out of the same events from which the defendant's claim arose, the counterclaim would have been within the court's ancillary jurisdiction because it would be compulsory. (*See supra,* p. 90.) **Caution**: This result may have been changed by the supplemental-jurisdiction statute, discussed *infra,* p. 95.

(3) Crossclaims

Federal Rule 13(g) allows one defendant to assert a crossclaim against another defendant if it arises out of the transaction sued upon by the plaintiff. Because of the relation to the original claim filed by the plaintiff, there was ancillary jurisdiction over the crossclaim. [**LASA per L'Industria v. Alexander,** 414 F.2d 143 (6th Cir. 1969)]

(4) Intervention

Federal Rule 24 allows persons who claim an interest in the litigation to intervene and become either plaintiffs or defendants in the suit. When they could intervene *of right*—because the litigation would inevitably affect their rights or because the present parties would otherwise be subjected to the risk of inconsistent judgments (*see infra,* p. 230 *et seq.*)—it was ordinarily held that *ancillary jurisdiction* covered their participation.

(a) But Note

When intervention was merely *permissive,* an independent jurisdictional basis was required.

(5) Required Parties

Under Federal Rule 19, certain nonparties are considered "required parties" because their rights are implicated in the action or because the present parties run the risk of inconsistent or multiple liabilities if they are not joined. (*See infra,* p. 230 *et seq.*) As to such parties, an *independent basis* for jurisdiction was required. If there was no independent basis for jurisdiction, the court might have had to dismiss the case. [*See* Fed. R. Civ. P. 19(b)—enumerating factors that affect decision whether to dismiss when required party cannot be joined; *see infra,* p. 222]

b. Pendent Jurisdiction

Pendent jurisdiction developed in cases where the plaintiff had both federal and nonfederal claims against a nondiverse defendant arising from the same event. The court was said to have jurisdiction over the state-law claims, which are "appended" to the federal claim. Thus, it referred to the assertion of **nonfederal claims by the plaintiff** that are related to the plaintiff's federal claim.

ANCILLARY JURISDICTION	PENDENT JURISDICTION
A party (usually the defendant) could assert a related claim against **another** defendant, the plaintiff, or a third party, even though the second claim was not itself within the court's jurisdiction.	A plaintiff with a jurisdictionally sufficient claim (usually a federal question) could join a related claim against the **same** defendant, even though the second claim was not itself within the court's subject-matter jurisdiction.

Example: Plaintiff copyrighted a play, revised it, and submitted both versions to Defendant for possible production. After Defendant declined to produce plaintiff's play, but did produce a similar play, Plaintiff sued, claiming that Defendant had stolen parts of both the copyrighted and uncopyrighted versions for use in the play produced by Defendant. Plaintiff asserted a federal copyright claim and two state-law claims of unfair competition, one for use of the copyrighted version and the other for use of the uncopyrighted version. The Supreme Court held that there was pendent jurisdiction over the unfair-competition claim relating to the copyrighted version because it "results from the same acts which constitute the infringement and is inseparable therefrom." But in a narrow ruling, which the Court later rejected as "unnecessarily grudging," it also held that there was no jurisdiction over the unfair-competition claim related to the uncopyrighted version because that claim was "independent of the claim of copyright infringement." [**Hurn v. Oursler,** 289 U.S. 238 (1933)]

Example: Plaintiff claimed that Defendant union violated federal labor laws and committed the state-law tort of interference with contract by pressuring customers of Plaintiff not to employ his services. Both federal and state claims arose from the same series of actions by Defendant's agents. The federal court could grant Plaintiff judgment on the state-law claims even if it decided after trial that Plaintiff had not established a violation of federal law. [**United Mine Workers v. Gibbs,** *supra,* p. 89]

(1) Pendent-Party Jurisdiction

If a plaintiff has a claim within original federal jurisdiction against the first defendant and a claim not within original federal jurisdiction arising out of the same event against the second defendant, the plaintiff might seek to "append" the claim against the second defendant to the claim against the first defendant. Noting that "the addition of a completely new party would run counter to the well-established principle that federal courts, as opposed to state trial courts of general jurisdiction, are courts of limited jurisdiction" [**Aldinger v. Howard,** 427 U.S. 1 (1976)], the Supreme Court took a limited approach to pendent-party jurisdiction.

(a) Diversity Claim

The Supreme Court refused to allow a plaintiff to assert a claim against a nondiverse, third-party defendant because allowing this maneuver would enable plaintiffs to circumvent the complete-diversity requirement. [**Owen Equipment & Erection Co. v. Kroger,** *supra,* p. 90]

(b) Federal Question Claim

Even when there was exclusive federal jurisdiction over a federal claim against one defendant, the Supreme Court held that there could be no jurisdiction over a related, nonfederal claim against a nondiverse party because "a grant of jurisdiction over claims involving particular parties does not itself confer jurisdiction over additional claims by or against different parties." [**Finley v. United States,** 490 U.S. 545 (1989)]

(2) Class Actions

Pendent jurisdiction over class actions was complicated. While the issue of diversity was determined by looking only to the named class representative or representatives (*see supra*, p. 71), the Supreme Court held that when a class action was brought under diversity jurisdiction, *each class member had to have a jurisdictionally sufficient claim* satisfying the amount-in-controversy requirement, unless the claims were legally "joint." [**Zahn v. International Paper Co.,** 414 U.S. 291 (1973)]

(a) Distinguish—Federal-Question Class Action

In a federal-question class action, ordinarily there was no jurisdiction problem since the amount-in-controversy requirement would not apply and each class member would have a claim within the subject-matter jurisdiction of the federal court.

c. Lack of Statutory Basis

In a 1989 decision regarding pendent-party jurisdiction, the Supreme Court stressed that pendent and ancillary jurisdiction appeared to contravene the principle that:

[a]s regards all courts of the United States inferior to this tribunal, two things are necessary to create jurisdiction, whether original or appellate. The Constitution must have given to the court the capacity to take it, and an act of Congress must have supplied it. . . . To the extent that such action is not taken, the power lies dormant.

[**Finley v. United States,** *supra*] Although *Finley* left existing pendent-*claim* precedents undisturbed, it cast doubt on all extensions of ancillary jurisdiction to claims against added *parties* without express congressional authorization.

3. Supplemental-Jurisdiction Statute

In 1990, largely to overcome obstacles to joinder of related matters in the wake of *Finley*, Congress enacted the supplemental-jurisdiction statute. [28 U.S.C. § 1367]

a. Jurisdictional Power to Limit of Constitution

The statute grants federal courts that have original jurisdiction over a claim supplemental jurisdiction over all other claims that form part of the same case or controversy under Article III of the Constitution. [28 U.S.C. § 1367(a)] The focus of the constitutional inquiry is whether the claims sought to be added to those within federal jurisdiction are part of *one constitutional case*. [**United Mine Workers v. Gibbs,** *supra*, p. 91; *and see supra*, p. 89]

(1) Standard for Supplemental Jurisdiction in Federal-Question Cases

In **United Mine Workers v. Gibbs,** *supra*, the Supreme Court articulated the following three-part test to determine whether a federal court has the power to entertain pendent claims:

(a) Substantial Federal Claim

The federal claim must be sufficiently substantial to support federal-question jurisdiction. (*See supra*, p. 88 *et seq.*)

(b) Common Nucleus of Operative Fact

The federal and nonfederal claims must derive from a common nucleus of operative fact.

(c) One Judicial Proceeding

The federal and nonfederal claims must be such that the plaintiff "would ordinarily be expected to try them in one judicial proceeding."

(2) Diversity Cases

The Supreme Court has suggested that the same test may apply to determine the outer constitutional limits of diversity jurisdiction. [**Owen Equipment & Erection Co. v. Kroger,** *supra*, p. 92]

(a) Note

Because only minimal diversity is required by the Constitution (*see supra*, p. 66), as long as one defendant is diverse from one plaintiff, there is no constitutional difficulty with exercise of jurisdiction over the whole case, including nondiverse parties.

(3) Pendent-Party Jurisdiction

Section (a) of the supplemental jurisdiction statute explicitly grants supplemental jurisdiction over "claims that involve the joinder or intervention of additional parties."

(4) Time of Decision

"The question of [constitutional] power will ordinarily be resolved on ***the pleadings***." [**United Mine Workers v. Gibbs,** *supra*]

(5) Contrast to Original-Jurisdiction Statutes

Unlike the statutes granting federal-question and diversity jurisdiction, which have been interpreted not to go to the constitutional limit (*see supra*, pp. 66, 81), subsection (a) of the supplemental-jurisdiction statute ***does go*** to the ***maximum extent*** allowed by the Constitution.

(6) Limited Discretion Not to Exercise

It has been held that federal courts should exercise supplemental jurisdiction granted by 28 U.S.C. section 1367(a) unless a ground for declining jurisdiction exists under 28 U.S.C. section 1367(c) (*see infra*, pp. 96–97). [**Executive Software North America, Inc. v. District Court,** 24 F.3d 1545 (9th Cir. 1994)]

b. Exception for Diversity Cases

When federal subject-matter jurisdiction is founded *solely on diversity of citizenship*, supplemental jurisdiction is limited. [28 U.S.C. § 1367(b)] The legislative history indicates that this limit was included to implement the rationale of *Owen Equipment*, *supra*. This action represents Congress's acceptance of the complete-diversity requirement long ago adopted by the Supreme Court (*see supra*, p. 66).

(1) Claims by Plaintiffs

In diversity-only cases, there is no supplemental jurisdiction over claims by *plaintiffs* against persons made parties under Rule 14 (impleader), Rule 19 (required party joinder), Rule 20 (permissive party joinder), or Rule 24 (intervention).

(2) Claims by Parties Joined as Plaintiffs Under Rule 19 or 24

There is no supplemental jurisdiction over claims by persons *proposed to be joined* pursuant to Rule 19 or 24. *Note*: This limit effects a change. Formerly there was thought to be jurisdiction over claims by plaintiff intervenors of right (*see supra*, p. 91).

(a) Distinguish—Rule 20 Joinder of Plaintiffs

The supplemental-jurisdiction statute has no provision excluding claims by plaintiffs joined permissively pursuant to Rule 20. The Supreme Court has settled that claims by completely diverse plaintiffs in a diversity case when one plaintiff has a claim satisfying the amount requirement, but others with related claims do not, come within supplemental jurisdiction. The Court's opinion, however, indicated that incomplete diversity would still destroy jurisdiction as to all claims. [**Exxon Mobil Corp. v. Allapattah Services, Inc.,** 545 U.S. 546 (2005)—upholding supplemental jurisdiction, in suit by injured child who claimed more than $75,000, over related claims of family members who were diverse from defendant but did not satisfy amount requirement]

(b) Distinguish—Class Actions

The legislative history of the supplemental-jurisdiction statute states that the statute was not intended to affect the requirement in most state-law class actions that each class member had to satisfy the amount-in-controversy requirement. (*See supra*, p. 93.) However, since section 1367(b) does not expressly limit the use of supplemental jurisdiction in diversity class actions, the Supreme Court has held that related claims of class members *may* be appended to the jurisdictionally sufficient claims of plaintiff class representatives, even though the class members' claims could not themselves satisfy the amount-in-controversy requirement. [**Exxon Mobil Corp. v. Allapattah Services, Inc.,** *supra*] Furthermore, under the rule of **Supreme Tribe of Ben Hur v. Cauble,** *supra*, p. 71, which was not affected by section 1367, only named class representatives need be of diverse citizenship from the class's opponents. Thus, supplemental jurisdiction can extend to below-amount claims of diverse and nondiverse unnamed class members alike.

(c) Distinguish—Compulsory Counterclaims by Plaintiffs

Under prior case law (*see supra*, p. 90), there could be ancillary jurisdiction over a compulsory counterclaim by a plaintiff against a nondiverse third-party defendant in a diversity case. [**Evra Corp. v. Swiss Bank Corp.,** 673 F.2d 951

(7th Cir. 1982)] It is **unclear** whether this rule survives the supplemental-jurisdiction statute's prohibition of jurisdiction over "claims by plaintiffs" against such parties. The legislative history's expression of intent to preserve most prior case law, and section 1367(b)'s concluding language making its restrictions applicable only when exercising jurisdiction "would be inconsistent with the jurisdictional requirements of section 1332," suggest that this form of supplemental jurisdiction might survive. [*But see* **Guaranteed Systems, Inc. v. American National Can Co.,** 842 F. Supp. 855 (M.D.N.C. 1994)—although **Owen Equipment & Erection Co. v. Kroger,** *supra*, p. 94, alone would not have forbidden ancillary jurisdiction over diversity plaintiff's compulsory counterclaim against nondiverse third-party defendant, section 1367(b) bars supplemental jurisdiction]

(d) Distinguish—Claims Against Defendants Joined Under Rule 20

Although section 1367(b) does not forbid jurisdiction over claims by plaintiffs joined under Rule 20, as the Supreme Court noted in *Exxon Mobil, supra,* in diversity-only cases section 1367(b) "explicitly excludes supplemental jurisdiction over claims against defendants joined under Rule 20" when, in the words of the statute, "exercising such jurisdiction would be inconsistent with the jurisdictional requirements of section 1332." Thus diversity plaintiffs cannot file incomplete-diversity state-law actions or add a nondiverse defendant on a state-law claim to a diversity action already filed.

c. Discretionary Decline of Jurisdiction

The statute explicitly authorizes district courts to decline jurisdiction in **certain circumstances** that largely implement discretionary factors identified in **United Mine Workers v. Gibbs,** *supra*, pp. 91–93). [28 U.S.C. § 1367(c)]

(1) Grounds to Decline

A federal court may decline to exercise supplemental jurisdiction, but **only** on the basis of one of the following four grounds. [**Executive Software North America, Inc. v. District Court,** *supra*, p. 94]

(a) Novel or Complex Issue of State Law

If the law to be applied to the claim within supplemental jurisdiction is uncertain, the district court may decline to entertain that claim so that the parties can get a "surer-footed reading of applicable law" from a state court. [§ 1367(c)(1); **United Mine Workers v. Gibbs,** *supra*]

(b) Nonfederal Claim Substantially Predominates

The federal court may conclude that the claim within supplemental jurisdiction is the real body of the case. [28 U.S.C. § 1367(c)(2)] The court should not "tolerate a litigant's effort to impose upon it what is in effect only a state law case." [**United Mine Workers v. Gibbs,** *supra*]

(c) All Original Jurisdiction Claims Dismissed

If all claims over which the federal court had original jurisdiction are dismissed, the court may dismiss the supplemental claims. [28 U.S.C. § 1367(c)(3)] In deciding whether to do so, the court should consider the **amount of time invested in the case by the court**.

(d) Extraordinary Circumstances

The federal court may also decline to exercise supplemental jurisdiction in extraordinary circumstances if there are *"other compelling reasons for declining jurisdiction."* [28 U.S.C. § 1367(c)(4)]

1) Complication of Case

In *United Mine Workers*, the Supreme Court said that complication of the case in federal court would justify refusal to entertain the nonfederal claims. It has been held that this ground for declining jurisdiction was limited by the statute to instances in which the district court finds that "exceptional circumstances" exist in the case and that these provide "compelling reasons" for decline of jurisdiction. [**Executive Software North America, Inc. v. District Court**, *supra*]

GILBERT

DISTRICT COURTS MAY DECLINE SUPPLEMENTAL JURISDICTION ON ANY OF THE FOLLOWING GROUNDS:

- ☑ *Novel or complex issues of state law* must be resolved to decide the supplemental claim;

- ☑ *Supplemental* claim *predominates* in the case;

- ☑ *Original jurisdiction* claims have been *dismissed*; or

- ☑ Other *compelling* or *extraordinary* circumstances justify declining supplemental jurisdiction.

NOTE: If one of the above grounds justifies a decline of jurisdiction over the supplemental claim, the court nonetheless must retain jurisdiction over any claim that is within its original jurisdiction. Such a claim is not before the court under supplemental jurisdiction, and it has no discretion under section 1367(c) to decline to a claim over which it has original jurisdiction.

---

(2) Distinguish—State Law Tied to Questions of Federal Policy

When the state-law claim is closely tied to a question of federal policy, this link argues in favor of exercise of supplemental jurisdiction.

e.g. **Example**: When the allowable scope of the state-law claim implicates the federal doctrine of preemption, it is desirable for the federal court to employ supplemental jurisdiction. [**United Mine Workers v. Gibbs**, *supra*]

cf. **Compare—Preemption Defense**: Preemption is usually an affirmative defense and therefore not a ground for exercise of original federal-question jurisdiction under the well-pleaded complaint rule. (*See supra*, p. 86.)

(3) Timing of Decision

The question whether to decline to exercise supplemental jurisdiction remains open throughout the case. However, the longer the court waits, the more effort it puts into the case, and the effort invested by the court may be a reason to retain jurisdiction.

Nevertheless, the court may decide, even after trial, not to entertain nonfederal claims.

d. Tolling of Limitations

The limitations period for any claim asserted under supplemental jurisdiction, or any other claim in the same action voluntarily dismissed at the same time or later, is tolled while the claim is pending in federal court and for 30 days after the federal court dismisses it. [28 U.S.C. § 1367(d)] The rationale for the tolling is that a plaintiff should not be subjected to the risk that her claim will be barred by limitations if the federal court declines to exercise supplemental jurisdiction, or if the plaintiff is mistaken about whether the claim actually falls within supplemental jurisdiction.

(1) Tolling Provision Constitutional

In an action against a county, the tolling provision constitutionally directed that state-law claims could be filed in state court after the limitations period otherwise would have run. The Supreme Court rejected the contention that tolling interfered with the state's sovereign authority to determine the extent to which its political subdivisions are subject to suit, and ruled that section 1367(d) is a legitimate provision in light of Congress's power to establish lower federal courts. [**Jinks v. Richland County,** 538 U.S. 456 (2003)]

(a) Distinguish—Eleventh Amendment Cases

The Eleventh Amendment is an explicit limitation on federal jurisdiction to entertain claims based on state law against states themselves, and Congress did not intend section 1367(d) to apply to dismissals on Eleventh Amendment grounds. [**Raygor v. Regents of the University of Minnesota,** 534 U.S. 533 (2002)]

(b) Voluntary Dismissal of Claim Within Original Jurisdiction

If a claim asserted under supplemental jurisdiction is dismissed, the tolling provision will also apply to any claim that was properly within federal jurisdiction that plaintiff dismisses along with the supplemental claim. *Rationale*: If plaintiff prefers to combine all the claims in state court, limitations should not be an obstacle.

(2) Duration of Tolling

Because § 1367(d) comes into play only when the federal court declines to exercise supplemental jurisdiction, federal courts have not had to determine how long the tolling lasts. State courts have adopted various approaches: (1) the "suspension" approach, under which the remaining time available under the pertinent limitations period when the suit was filed applies, with 30 days added on; (2) the "grace period" approach, allowing 30 days to file in state court without regard to the time remaining under the pertinent limitations period when the suit was filed; or (3) the "substitution" approach, which would require refiling within 30 days no matter how much time remains on the limitations period. [*See* **City of Los Angeles v. County of Kern,** 328 P.3d 56 (Cal. 2014)—adopting "grace period" approach]

E. Removal

1. Introduction

Removal allows a defendant to shift a case from state court to federal court when the plaintiff has chosen to sue in state court. Although there is no mention of removal in the Constitution, some form of removal jurisdiction has existed since the federal-court system was created by the first Congress.

2. Grounds for Removal

In general, if the plaintiff files an action in state court but *could originally have filed in federal court*, the defendant can remove the action to the federal court. [28 U.S.C. § 1441(a)] Note that there are exceptions to this rule (*e.g.*, a defendant who is a citizen of the state in which the federal court is located cannot remove to federal court on grounds of diversity).

a. Federal Question

If the plaintiff's state-court complaint raises a federal question, the defendant may remove.

(1) Federal Defenses Not Considered

The *well-pleaded complaint rule* applies in the removal situation. Thus, that the defendant has raised a federal defense to the plaintiff's state-law claim is not sufficient to support removal. [**Oklahoma Tax Commission v. Graham,** 489 U.S. 838 (1989)]

(2) Federal Counterclaim Not Considered

That the defendant has interposed a counterclaim asserting a federal claim does not provide a basis for removal on federal-question grounds. [**Holmes Group v. Vornado Air Circulation Systems, Inc.,** *supra*, p. 85]

(a) Exception—Counterclaim for Patent or Copyright Infringement

A civil action in which any party asserts a claim, including a counterclaim, for relief under any Act of Congress relating to patents, plant-variety protection, or copyrights may be removed even though a federal statute provides that state courts have no jurisdiction over such claims. [28 U.S.C. §§ 1338(a), 1454]

(3) Plaintiff Omits Federal Claim

If the plaintiff chooses not to assert a possible federal claim, the defendant may not remove the case by citing the unasserted claim.

(a) Amendment to Assert Federal Claim

If after filing in state court, the plaintiff amends the complaint to assert a federal claim, the defendant *can then remove the case*. Note that if the plaintiff does not amend the complaint, the claim-preclusion rule against claim-splitting may bar assertion of the federal claim in a later action.

(b) Exception—Complete Preemption

If federal law completely preempts state law on the matter and converts the plaintiff's claim into one of federal law, that satisfies the well-pleaded complaint requirement and makes the case removable. [**Metropolitan Life Insurance Co. v. Taylor,** *supra*, p. 86]

(4) Effect of Supplemental-Jurisdiction Statute

The Supreme Court has stated that the supplemental-jurisdiction statute [28 U.S.C. § 1367] "applies with equal force to cases removed to federal court as to cases initially filed there." [**City of Chicago v. International College of Surgeons,** *supra*, p. 82] Under the supplemental-jurisdiction statute, any case in which a federal claim is asserted in state court should be removable even though it includes defendants against whom only state-law claims are asserted, as long as the claims against these defendants form part of the same federal constitutional "case."

(5) Effect of Eleventh Amendment Immunity

If a state is a defendant and joins in removing a federal-question case that includes claims barred by the Eleventh Amendment (which limits federal-court jurisdiction over many private claims against state governments—*see* Federal Courts Summary), the federal court may not hear the barred claims, but it still has jurisdiction over the remaining claims against the nonstate parties. [**Wisconsin Department of Corrections v. Schacht,** 524 U.S. 381 (1998)]

b. Diversity of Citizenship

If the plaintiff could have filed the action in federal court using diversity of citizenship jurisdiction, the defendant may remove the case to federal court. Note that the *complete-diversity* requirement applies in this situation.

(1) Local Defendant

However, such removal is not permitted if any defendant is a citizen of the state in which the action is brought. [28 U.S.C. § 1441(b)(2)] *Rationale*: Since diversity jurisdiction is designed to protect against local prejudice, there is no reason to invoke it on behalf of a local party. *Fallacy* in this oft-stated rationale: If local bias is present in state court, it can still have effect in a multi-defendant case by a judge or jury going easy on the in-state defendant and hard on the out-of-stater. *Compare*: A local plaintiff can file an action in federal court invoking diversity jurisdiction.

(a) Exception—Class Action Fairness Act

In class-action claims based on state law that could have been filed originally in federal court pursuant to the Class Action Fairness Act, a defendant who is a citizen of the state in which the action is filed *may remove* to federal court. [28 U.S.C. § 1453(b)]

(2) Fictitious Defendants

If the plaintiff has named fictitious "John Doe" defendants in the complaint, they are disregarded for purposes of determining whether there is complete diversity in cases that are removed from state to federal court. [28 U.S.C. § 1441(b)(1)] Note that the effect of naming a "John Doe" defendant in a case originally filed in federal court is uncertain. (*See supra*, p. 72.)

(3) Fraudulent Joinder

To prevent the defendant from removing the case to federal court, a plaintiff might join a defendant who is a resident of the state the plaintiff lives in or who otherwise would destroy diversity jurisdiction. If the plaintiff joins such a defendant and there really is no basis for the claim against that nondiverse party, the presence of that defendant will not defeat removal.

(4) Jurisdictional Amount

The jurisdictional-amount requirement applies to cases removed on grounds of diversity. (*See supra*, p. 74 *et seq.*) It has been held that the plaintiff can prevent removal by suing in state court for less than the jurisdictional amount, even though the claim could be for a larger sum. [**Vradenburgh v. Wal-Mart Stores, Inc.,** 397 F. Supp. 2d 76 (D. Me. 2005)]

c. Effect of Joinder of Federal-Law and State-Law Claims

State-court rules may allow the joinder of claims arising under federal law with unrelated, nonfederal claims in the same action, even though supplemental jurisdiction would not permit a federal court to entertain the nonfederal claims in the absence of diversity. If the action would be removable had these nonfederal claims not been included, the entire action may be removed, but the court must *sever the unrelated, nonfederal claims* after removal if they are not within the original or supplemental jurisdiction of the federal court, and *remand* those claims to state court. [28 U.S.C. § 1441(c)]

(1) Determining Whether Nonfederal Claims Can Be Retained

The federal court may retain the nonfederal claims only if they fall within the original or supplemental jurisdiction of the federal courts. Under the supplemental-jurisdiction statute, the court must determine whether the nonfederal claims "are so related to the claims [within original jurisdiction] that they form part of the *same case or controversy* under Article III of the United States Constitution." [28 U.S.C. § 1367(a)]

> **cf.** **Compare—Prior Law**: Under the statute before amendment in 2011, an entire action could be removed if it included a *separate and independent claim* arising under federal law. This provision was difficult to apply and raised constitutional concerns about the federal court's authority to entertain the "independent" nonfederal claims between nondiverse parties even though those claims would fall outside Article III's authorization for federal-court jurisdiction. The 2011 amendment was intended to resolve these problems.

(2) Compare—Prior Law

Under the statute before amendment in 2011, an entire action could be removed if it included a *separate and independent claim* arising under federal law. This provision was difficult to apply and raised constitutional concerns about the federal court's authority to entertain the "independent" nonfederal claims between nondiverse parties even though those claims would fall outside Article III's authorization for federal-court jurisdiction. The 2011 amendment was intended to resolve these problems.

d. Special Removal Statutes

In certain cases, special removal statutes apply. For example, when a state-court defendant in a civil or criminal case cannot adequately protect her *federal civil rights regarding racial equality* in state court, she may remove to federal court. [28 U.S.C. § 1443] This provision, however, has been so narrowly interpreted that it is almost never usable. Also, suits against *federal officers* sued for *acts performed under color of office* are removable. [28 U.S.C. § 1442] Additionally, actions that could have been brought in federal court under the ***Multiparty, Multiforum Trial Jurisdiction Act*** (*see supra*, p. 67) may be removed to federal court without regard to whether the defendant is a citizen of the state in which the action is brought, and different timing requirements may apply. [28 U.S.C. §§ 1369, 1441(e)]

(1) Distinguish—All Writs Act

The All Writs Act provides that a federal court may issue any lawful writ necessary in aid of its jurisdiction. [28 U.S.C. § 1651(a)] However, this provision does not give a federal court authority for removal of a state-court action that allegedly frustrates orders the federal court had previously issued. [**Syngenta Crop Protection, Inc. v. Henson,** 537 U.S. 28 (2002)—state-court case instituted in violation of the terms of a settlement in a prior federal-court case could not be removed under All Writs Act]

(2) Criminal Cases

28 U.S.C. section 1441 also provided, until amendment in 2011, for removal of state-court criminal cases. Removal of criminal cases is now covered in a separate statute. [28 U.S.C. § 1455]

e. Removal Forbidden in Employment Injury Cases

Suits brought in state court against a railroad under the ***Federal Employers' Liability Act*** ("FELA") or under state ***workers' compensation laws*** are not removable. [28 U.S.C. § 1445] The rationale for this limitation is to allow injured workers to pick the court in which they wish to have their claims decided.

(1) Distinguish—Fair Labor Standards Act

The Fair Labor Standards Act, which says that an action asserting a violation of its provisions "may be maintained" in *either* a state or federal court, does not guarantee a worker who sues in state court that the suit will remain there. A defendant is denied leave to remove only when a statute "expressly" forbids removal. [**Breuer v. Jim's Concrete of Brevard, Inc.,** 538 U.S. 691 (2003)]

f. Removal Under the Class Action Fairness Act

Class actions making claims based on state law that could have been filed originally in federal court pursuant to the Class Action Fairness Act may be removed to federal court if filed in state court. [28 U.S.C. § 1453]

3. Procedure for Removal

A defendant seeking removal must file a notice setting forth the facts supporting removal in the federal district court and division within which the action is pending. A copy of the notice must be sent to the other parties and to the state court.

a. Only Defendant Can Remove

Only the defendant has the power to seek removal. Even if the defendant asserts a federal claim as a counterclaim, the plaintiff may not remove. [**Shamrock Oil Co. v. Sheets,** 313 U.S. 100 (1941)] Most federal courts also hold that third-party defendants usually may not remove. [*E.g.,* **First National Bank of Pulaski v. Curry,** 301 F.3d 456 (6th Cir. 2002)]

b. All Defendants Must Join

All defendants who have been properly joined and served with process must join in or consent to removal if removal is sought under 28 U.S.C. section 1441(a). [28 U.S.C. § 1446(b)(2)(A)] However, when removal is based on 28 U.S.C. section 1441(c), only the defendants against whom claims based on federal law are asserted need seek the removal.

(1) Exception—Class Action Fairness Act

Class actions governed by the Class Action Fairness Act may be removed by a single defendant *without* the consent of the other defendants. [28 U.S.C. § 1453(b)]

c. Timing

In general, defendants must file a notice of removal within *30 days* after receiving or being served with the initial pleading or summons. [28 U.S.C. § 1446(b)(2)(B)] This time limit is strictly enforced, but subject to certain limitations and exceptions.

(1) Service of Process Required to Trigger Running of Time Limit for Removal

Section 1446(b)(1) says that the time to remove starts when defendant receives a copy of the complaint "through service *or otherwise*." However, the Supreme Court has held that the 30 days do not begin to run until the defendant is *formally* served. [**Murphy Brothers, Inc. v. Michetti Pipe Stringing, Inc.,** 526 U.S. 344 (1999)]

(2) Defendants Served at Different Times

In cases with multiple defendants, it will often happen that service of process occurs at different times for different defendants. Although the requirement that all defendants must join in or consent to a removal notice still applies, if a later-served defendant files a notice of removal within 30 days of being served, any earlier-served defendant may consent to removal even though it did not previously initiate or consent to removal within 30 days of being served. [28 U.S.C. § 1446(b)(2)(C)]

(3) Effect of Later Developments

If the case was *not removable as originally filed*, defendant may remove within 30 days of receiving an amended pleading, motion, or other paper from which it may first be ascertained that the case is or has become removable. [28 U.S.C. § 1446(b)(3)] *Note*: Uncertainty about whether the case was originally removable may sometimes excuse failure to remove immediately.

(4) Uncertainty About Amount in Controversy

Because state-court rules often do not require a plaintiff to state whether the amount sought exceeds the federal amount in controversy, and may sometimes forbid demands for a specific sum, or the complaint may seek nonmonetary relief, defendants may be uncertain whether that requirement of diversity jurisdiction is satisfied.

(a) Sum Demanded in Good Faith

The sum demanded in good faith in the initial pleading in state court should be regarded as the amount in controversy for purposes of removal jurisdiction. But the removal notice may assert the amount in controversy if the state-court pleading seeks nonmonetary relief, or if state practice does not permit a demand for a specific sum, or permits recovery of damages in excess of the amount demanded. [28 U.S.C. § 1446(c)(2)(A)]

(b) Later Developments in State-Court Case

If the sum demanded in the initial pleading in state court does not exceed the federal amount in controversy, information about the amount in controversy in the record or in discovery in the state-court case is treated as an "other paper" triggering a right to remove. [28 U.S.C. § 1446(c)(3)(A)]

(c) Evidence Showing Amount in Controversy Not Required in Removal Notice

The "short and plain statement" required in a notice of removal need not include evidence that the amount-in-controversy requirement is satisfied. [**Dart Cherokee Basin Operating Co. v. Owens,** 135 S. Ct. 547 (2014)]

(d) Compare—Uncertainty About Existence of Diversity

State-court rules may not require that an initial pleading include the information necessary to determine whether complete diversity exists, but there is no comparable statutory removal provision authorizing later removal once that information is obtained. Some courts have, however, treated such discovery as an "other paper" that triggers the right to remove. [*See* **Lovern v. General Motors Corp.,** 121 F.3d 160 (4th Cir. 1997)—citizenship of plaintiff not known until discovery obtained]

(5) General One-Year Time Limit for Diversity Cases

In general, a case may not be removed on grounds of diversity more than one year after commencement of the action in state court. **Exception**: This one-year limitation does not apply, however, when the court finds that "plaintiff has acted in *bad faith* in order to prevent" removal. [28 U.S.C. § 1446(c)(1)] Deliberate *failure to disclose the actual amount in controversy* to prevent removal is bad faith. [28 U.S.C. § 1446(c)(3)(B)]

(6) Exception—Class Action Fairness Act

When removal is permitted under the Class Action Fairness Act, the one-year limitation does not apply. [28 U.S.C. § 1453(b)]

(7) Exception—Multiparty, Multiforum Actions

In multiparty, multiforum actions that could have been brought in federal court under 28 U.S.C. section 1369 (*see supra*), different timing requirements may apply. Notice of removal may be filed within 30 days after a defendant in state court becomes a party to an action in federal court that falls under the statute. However, with leave of the district court, notice of removal may also be filed at a later date. Additionally, the one-year time limit for removal does not apply to these actions. [28 U.S.C. § 1441(e)]

d. Effect of Removal

The case is considered to be removed as soon as the notice of removal is filed and served. After that, the state court may take no further action on the case. The remedy for improper removal is to seek in federal court a *remand* to state court. (*See infra*, pp. 105–106.)

e. State-Court Lack of Subject-Matter Jurisdiction

The federal court has jurisdiction over an otherwise properly removed action even if the state court lacked jurisdiction over the claim. [28 U.S.C. § 1441(f)] Section 1441(f), however, applies only to cases removed "under this section." For cases removed under other provisions, removal jurisdiction is derivative—the federal court lacks jurisdiction if the state court from which the case was removed also lacked jurisdiction. Thus, the rare non-section 1441 removal of an exclusive-federal-jurisdiction case improperly filed in state court is impermissible; the case must, absurdly, be remanded to state court for dismissal and refiling in federal court. [*See, e.g.,* **Barnaby v. Quintos,** 410 F. Supp. 2d 142 (S.D.N.Y. 2005)]

> **e.g.** **Example**: Plaintiff sues Defendant in state court for violation of federal antitrust laws, a claim over which there is exclusive federal jurisdiction. Defendant may remove to federal court under section 1441.

✓ GILBERT

THE KEY REMOVAL ISSUES ARE:

☑ A federal court **must have jurisdiction** over the case; jurisdiction usually need not have been proper in the state court.

☑ Removal is to the federal district court whose **territory encompasses the state court**.

☑ **Only** defendants can remove; **all** defendants must join in the removal

☑ **Notice of removal** must be filed within **30 days** after defendant has been served and receives a copy of the initial complaint, except when another defendant is served later and removes within 30 days, or a subsequent development in the state-court case makes the case removable.

☑ A case may **not be removed on diversity grounds** if any defendant is a citizen of the forum state.

☑ **Notice of removal on diversity grounds** must be filed within **one year** of commencement of the action in state court unless the federal court finds that plaintiff acted in **bad faith** to prevent removal.

☑ If the case contains a **claim arising under federal law** joined with a nonfederal claim, the **entire action** may be removed, but the federal court must **remand** the nonfederal claims unless they are part of the **same case or controversy**.

4. Remand

a. Improper Removal

If the case was improperly removed, the federal court should remand it to state court. [28 U.S.C. § 1447(c)] Remand is required whenever the court determines that removal was improper, unless final judgment has been entered.

(1) Jurisdictional Defect Cured Before Final Judgment Entered

If there was a jurisdictional defect at the time of removal, so that the case should have been remanded but was not, and the defect is cured before final judgment is entered, interests of finality, efficiency, and economy justify *disregarding that defect* on appellate review even if the plaintiff timely moved to remand and the district court erroneously denied that motion. [**Caterpillar, Inc. v. Lewis,** 519 U.S. 61 (1996)—nondiverse defendant dismissed after motion to remand was denied but before trial]

(2) Time Limit for Motion to Remand on Ground Other than Lack of Subject-Matter Jurisdiction

If the ground for the motion to remand is something other than lack of subject-matter jurisdiction (*e.g.,* a defect in removal procedure), the motion must be made *within 30 days* after the notice of removal is filed. [28 U.S.C. § 1447(c)]

b. Supplemental Claims After Dismissal of Federal Claims

When a court would otherwise dismiss the supplemental claims after disposing of the federal claims (*see supra,* p. 96), it may instead remand them to state court. [**Carnegie-Mellon University v. Cohill,** 484 U.S. 343 (1988)]

c. Other Grounds for Remand

The Supreme Court has indicated that remand is *usually not allowed when a case was properly removed.* [**Thermtron Products, Inc. v. Hermansdorfer,** 423 U.S. 336 (1976)—remand improper when based on expectation that there would be greater delay in obtaining a trial date in federal court than in state court]

(1) Distinguish—Addition of Nondiverse Defendants

Under 28 U.S.C. section 1447(e), if the plaintiff seeks to *add additional defendants* whose addition would destroy subject-matter jurisdiction, the court may *permit joinder and remand.* Alternatively, it may *deny joinder and keep the case.*

d. Appellate Review

An order remanding a case to state court *on grounds of lack of subject-matter jurisdiction or a defect in removal procedure* is "not reviewable on appeal or otherwise." [28 U.S.C. § 1447(d)] [**Things Remembered, Inc. v. Petrarca,** 516 U.S. 124 (1996)] However, this prohibition is not as unqualified as it seems. The Supreme Court has upheld *review via mandamus* (a writ procedure seeking an order from a superior court to an inferior court to perform some act) when a district court openly remanded on a ground not authorized by the statute. [**Thermtron Products, Inc. v. Hermansdorfer,** *supra*] In addition, the Supreme Court has upheld review of a remand order based on "abstention" principles under the *collateral-order doctrine.* [**Quackenbush v. Allstate Insurance Co.,** 517 U.S. 706 (1996); *see infra,* pp. 409–433; for a discussion of abstention, *see* Federal Courts Summary]

(1) Distinguish—Discretionary Remand

When, after dismissing the only federal claim in a removed case, the court declines to exercise supplemental jurisdiction and instead remands the state-law claims, that remand is discretionary and not due to lack of subject-matter jurisdiction. The ban on appellate review under 28 U.S.C. section 1447(d) therefore does not apply. [**Carlsbad Technology, Inc. v. HIF Bio, Inc.,** 556 U.S. 635 (2009)]

(2) Distinguish—Remand Motion Erroneously Denied

If a motion to remand is erroneously denied, the plaintiff need not seek interlocutory review to preserve the error for review after final judgment, although denial of the motion to remand will not justify reversal if the jurisdictional defect is cured before entry of final judgment. [**Caterpillar, Inc. v. Lewis,** *supra*, p. 105]

(3) Appellate Review Under Class Action Fairness Act

In class actions making claims based on state law that could have been filed originally in federal court pursuant to the Class Action Fairness Act (*see* discussion of Act, *supra*, p. 71), the court of appeals has ***discretion to accept an appeal*** from an order granting or denying a remand, provided that the application for review is made not more than 10 days after entry of the order. [28 U.S.C. § 1453(c)(1)] The appellate court is directed to complete its review within 60 days, although extensions are allowed under some circumstances. [28 U.S.C. § 1453(c)(2), (3)]

e. Attorney's Fees on Remand

Under 28 U.S.C. section 1447(c), the court has discretion to award attorney's fees to the party seeking remand. [**Martin v. Franklin Capital Corp.,** 546 U.S. 132 (2005)—28 U.S.C. § 1447(c) does not establish a presumption against or in favor of awarding attorney's fees; that decision is left to the discretion of the district court, which should not ordinarily award fees when the removing party had "an objectively reasonable basis for removal"]

5. No "Reverse" Removal

There is presently no method by which a defendant can remove a case originally filed in federal court to state court.

a. Distinguish—Abstention

Federal courts may, however, decline to proceed in certain situations when "abstention" is proper. This situation may be due to the presence of an uncertain issue of state law pertinent to a federal constitutional claim, or to defer to litigation already pending in state court. (For details on abstention, *see* Federal Courts Summary.)

Chapter Three

Relation Between State and Federal Law

CONTENTS

Key Exam Issues

1. *Erie* Doctrine

In many situations and for certain issues, the federal courts must apply state rather than federal law. Determining whether to apply state or federal law is known as an *Erie* problem.

"Erie" problems are a favorite source of examination questions. They usually arise in diversity cases, but can arise in others (*e.g.*, supplemental state claims in federal-question cases are analyzed similarly). In very general terms, in state-law matters in the federal courts, ***state substantive*** and ***federal procedural law*** are followed. However, determining which law to apply is often more complex; the role and definition of the concepts of "substance" and "procedure" vary in different contexts. When either state or federal law might apply, it can help to approach the problem in two stages:

a. ***First, ask whether there is a "true conflict"***—are there both federal and state rules of law that purport to apply and cannot be harmonized? There is no true conflict if a federal rule or practice does not exist and state law is of a substantive nature; or the federal and state rules, while related, do not speak to exactly the same point; or the two rules agree. In such cases, no choice of one or the other is necessary.

b. ***Second, if there is a "true conflict,"*** look to the ***source*** of the potentially applicable ***federal*** rule of law; the test for the federal rule's validity and governing force varies depending on whether it derives from the Constitution, a statute enacted by Congress, a court rule promulgated under the Rules Enabling Act, or purely decisional law (as opposed to interpretation of the Constitution, an Act of Congress, or a Federal Rule).

(1) Is the federal rule of law grounded in the ***Constitution*** itself (*e.g.*, the Seventh Amendment guarantee of jury trial in actions at law in the federal courts)? If so, the ***federal rule governs***, period, without regard to the source, importance, or substantive nature of any contrary state rule.

(2) Is the federal rule of law found in an ***Act of Congress*** (*e.g.*, a federal statute providing for nationwide service of process)? If so, ***it governs*** as long as it is constitutional—*i.e.*, (i) it falls within the broad powers of Congress (which include regulation of procedure and "arguably procedural" matters in the federal courts) and (ii) it does not violate any independent federal constitutional right.

(3) Is the federal rule of law a ***Federal Rule of Civil Procedure*** (or Evidence or Appellate Procedure)? If so, the Rules Enabling Act [28 U.S.C. § 2072] provides the principal test for its validity: It must be "arguably procedural," dealing with practice, procedure, or evidence, ***and*** must not "abridge, enlarge or modify any substantive right." If it passes these tests (and is constitutional, which is practically certain if it satisfies the standards of section 2072), the ***federal rule governs***.

(4) Is the federal rule of law ***judge-made*** (*e.g.*, the equitable doctrine of laches)? If so, it ***should not govern*** in federal court if it fails the "twin-aims" test of *Erie*, as stated in *Hanna v. Plumer. If* the federal courts do ***not*** follow the state rule, will it encourage forum shopping between state and federal courts and produce inequitable administration of the laws by providing different, and possibly outcome-affecting, regimes of applicable law?

Certain "judge-made law" cases involve an "essential characteristic" of the federal-court system, such as relations among the jury, trial judge, and appellate court. In such cases, it might be necessary to balance state interests against those served by a decisional federal rule, or to see whether the state and federal interests both can be accommodated.

2. Federal Common Law

Some civil-procedure courses will also include coverage of "federal common law." Although in *Erie* the Supreme Court stated that "there is no federal *general* common law" (emphasis added), in several areas of special federal authority or interest the federal courts may develop federal common law by borrowing or even preempting state law. You may need to ask whether a case involves: (i) a need to borrow state law (such as a statute of limitations for a federal claim when Congress has enacted none); (ii) an express or implied authorization from Congress for the federal courts to develop federal common law; or (iii) a federal interest significant enough to call for uniform federal decisional law.

A. State Law in the Federal Courts

1. Rules of Decision Act

The starting point for the applicability of state law in the federal courts is the Rules of Decision Act [28 U.S.C. § 1652], originally adopted in 1789. In its present form the Act provides, "The laws of the several states, except where the Constitution or treaties of the United States or Acts of Congress otherwise require or provide, shall be regarded as rules of decision in civil actions in the courts of the United States, in cases where they apply."

2. Former Rule—*Swift v. Tyson*

For almost a century, the prevailing interpretation of the reference to state "laws" in the Rules of Decision Act was that it did not include state common law of a general, as opposed to local, nature. Thus, the federal courts could and did follow their own view of what the "general" common law was or should be. [**Swift v. Tyson**, 41 U.S. (16 Pet.) 1 (1842)] The federal courts' decisions on this "general" common law, however, were not binding precedent on the courts of the states; consequently, different rules of substantive law could apply to the same transaction, depending on whether litigation took place in state or federal court.

a. Note

Even under *Swift*, federal courts **were** bound by applicable state **statutes** (as long as they were constitutional) and **"local" common law** (*e.g.*, state common law regarding rights in real property within the states).

3. Difficulties of *Swift* Regime

The approach taken in *Swift* became vulnerable for several reasons.

a. Changing Attitudes Toward Law

Swift appeared to rest in part on a view that a "true" common law existed and could be "found" by the courts. However, many legal authorities moved away from this view and accepted the idea that each state could have its own internally authoritative common law, and that variations among states on the same point did not mean that some had to be "wrong."

b. Failure to Achieve Uniformity

Swift also became vulnerable because it failed to help develop a uniform common law, due to the disagreement of many state courts with the "general" common law established by the federal courts. Thus, *Swift* came to be seen as allowing the federal courts to add one more regime of common law rather than taking part in the development of one "true" set of common-law doctrines.

c. Practical Difficulties and Unfairness

Swift led to forum shopping. Because the federal courts often applied common-law rules different from the law of the states in which they sat, litigants could manipulate federal jurisdiction to gain favorable substantive law. That is unfair, because parties who are similarly situated except for litigating in different court systems within the same state can be governed by different substantive rules. This disparity undermines the ends of state common-law rules and complicates private planning, because parties cannot be sure what law will govern their affairs.

> **e.g.** **Example—*Black & White Taxicab Co.*:** The height of such manipulation came in **Black & White Taxicab Co. v. Brown & Yellow Taxicab Co.,** 276 U.S. 518 (1928), in which the plaintiff avoided a state common-law anti-monopoly rule by reincorporating in another state and then bringing a diversity action in federal court, which followed a different rule under which the challenged exclusive-dealing agreement was lawful.

d. Doubts About *Swift* Interpretation

Swift also came into doubt because historical research on the adoption of the original Rules of Decision Act questioned whether the drafters had intended to exclude "general" common law from the term "laws of the several states" (*see supra*, p. 111). [Warren, *New Light on the History of the Federal Judiciary Act of 1789*, 37 Harv. L. Rev. 49 (1923)] Later research has raised doubt about whether Professor Warren interpreted the historical materials correctly, but the *Erie* Court relied in part on Warren's view in overruling *Swift*. And the later questioning has not yet played a role in modern *Erie* jurisprudence.

e. Views on the Constitutional Scope of Federal Power

Finally, there seemed to be no constitutional basis for the federal courts' lawmaking authority that existed under *Swift*. The decision appeared to presume a ***general*** law making power in the federal courts of a sort that the Constitution does not grant to Congress, and which Congress had not attempted to confer on the federal courts. (*See infra*, p. 114.)

4. Overruling of *Swift* by *Erie*

The combination of the above problems contributed to the overruling of *Swift* in **Erie Railroad Co. v. Tompkins,** 304 U.S. 64 (1938). *Erie* held that in the absence of an Act of Congress providing governing law, a federal court should follow applicable state common-law principles rather than developing and applying its own "general" common law. At issue was the liability of a railroad for injury to a person who was struck by an object protruding from a passing train. Today the issue of what substantive law governs in cases like *Erie* itself is often simple, but the decision made broad changes whose ramifications are still being worked out in the federal courts today.

a. Reasoning of *Erie*

Erie identified three distinct rationales for the decision.

(1) Statutory Interpretation

The Court accepted the argument that the language of the Rules of Decision Act was not intended to exclude all state "general" common law. (*See supra*, p. 112.) Instead, the term "laws of the several states" includes state common law, general and local, as well as "positive" law like state constitutions, statutes, regulations, and ordinances.

(2) Lack of Uniformity and Resulting Discrimination

The *Erie* majority also noted the persistence of differing views on common-law questions between the state and federal courts, and the possibility that this disparity created for discrimination among litigants depending on the forum in which the case was tried.

(a) Note—"Equal Protection" Red Herring

In this ***nonconstitutional*** portion of its opinion, the Court stated that the *Swift* doctrine had rendered impossible the "equal protection of the law." This misleading phrasing often makes students think that *Erie* rests on the Equal Protection Clause of the Fourteenth Amendment. This conclusion cannot be true because *Swift* was a ***federal***-law ruling; the Equal Protection Clause spoke to the ***states***, and had not yet been held applicable to the federal government at the time *Erie* was decided. Instead, the term "equal protection" here must refer to the serious, but nonconstitutional, problems of nonuniformity in administration of state law and unfairly disparate treatment of litigants depending on whether a case is in state or federal court.

(b) "Discrimination by Noncitizens Against Citizens"

In this second part of the opinion, the *Erie* majority also said that *Swift* had "introduced grave discrimination by noncitizens against citizens," a concept repeated in some later opinions in the *Erie* line of cases. The reference is to the ability that an out-of-state party often has to control the choice of forum—federal or state—in diversity litigation (*e.g.*, an out-of-state plaintiff may decide to sue in the defendant's home-state court, in which case the defendant cannot remove to federal court [28 U.S.C. § 1441(b); *see supra*, p. 100]; an out-of-state defendant often—but not always—can effect removal to federal court if sued in state court; *see supra*, p. 99 *et seq.*). Regardless of who controls the forum choice, discrimination among litigants depending on the forum and what law it may apply remains a concern.

(3) Unconstitutionality of Swift Interpretation

Whatever the persuasiveness of the above two points (erroneous statutory interpretation and resulting discrimination), the Court in *Erie* stated that it would not have been prepared to abandon the long-established *Swift* doctrine were it not convinced of *Swift's* unconstitutionality.

(a) Holding, Not Dictum

Because the Court explicitly said that the constitutional ground was essential to the result in *Erie*, the constitutional portion of the opinion—despite some questioning—qualifies as a ***holding*** rather than dictum.

(b) Basis of Unconstitutionality

The Court did not expressly explain why the *Swift* interpretation of the Rules of Decision Act was unconstitutional. It did not find that *Swift* violated any specific clause, but rather noted the ***absence*** of any clause in the Constitution purporting to confer upon either Congress or the federal courts a general "power to declare substantive rules of common law applicable in a state." The Court explained that the Constitution preserves the autonomy of the states, and supplanting their law with federal law is permissible only pursuant to powers specifically granted to the federal government by the Constitution.

1) Note—Tenth Amendment Alone Not Basis of *Erie*

The Tenth Amendment's reservation of undelegated powers to the states or the people reinforces this argument, but by itself does not establish the unconstitutionality of *Swift*. The *Swift* interpretation probably would be unconstitutional under modern views even if there were no Tenth Amendment, because the interpretation presumes a ***general*** law-making power that has not been granted to the federal government.

2) Commerce Power a Possible Basis?

Because the accident giving rise to the *Erie* litigation involved an interstate railroad, students sometimes wonder whether *Erie* did not overlook a possible basis for federal law in the commerce power. The Constitution does grant Congress pervasive power over interstate commerce. Pursuant to this power, Congress ***could have*** provided for substantive tort law to govern accidents involving interstate commerce or, perhaps, it could have authorized the federal courts to develop applicable common law in the area. However, Congress ***had not done so*** (and still has not). Thus, the Court had to examine whether the federal courts had the power to create a "general" federal common law. It concluded that they did not, leaving state law the only law that could govern in the absence of congressional legislation.

b. *Erie* as Part of a Revolution in Federal-Court Practice

Erie coincided with the adoption of the Federal Rules of Civil Procedure, before which federal courts had largely followed the procedural rules of the courts of the states in which they sat. Thus in the same year, the federal courts moved sharply in opposite directions: (i) under *Erie* toward ***more application of state substantive law*** rather than "general" common law and (ii) under the Federal Rules toward ***uniform federal procedural law*** in place of diverse local practice. (Justice Reed noted in his *Erie* concurrence that "no one doubts federal power over procedure.") The approach to deciding when to apply federal "procedural" law in diversity cases, however, remained problematic for some time.

c. Principal Cases Developing *Erie*

Erie solved many old problems but opened up new ones, especially in cases in which the competing federal and state rules that might apply were in the borderland between substance and procedure. The Supreme Court has repeatedly said that in matters in the federal courts arising under state law, the **general guideline** is that **state substantive law** and **federal procedural law** govern. However, the distinction between substance and procedure is not always clear, unvarying, or mechanical; the role and definition of these concepts vary depending on the context. Major cases in the first decades after *Erie* dealt in differing ways with these problems; two of them—*York* and *Byrd*, *infra*—often receive great emphasis in teaching, but are of limited practical significance today.

(1) *Guaranty Trust Co. v. York*

Guaranty Trust Co. v. York, 326 U.S. 99 (1945), on somewhat complicated facts, presented the question whether a state statute of limitations or the more flexible federal decisional rule of "laches"—which asks whether delay has been excessive and caused the other side prejudice—should determine the timeliness of an equitable state-law claim filed in federal court.

(a) **Specific Holding**

The Court ruled that the New York statute of limitations governed, rather than the federal laches doctrine. This result makes sense because statutes of limitations, although partly reflecting procedural concerns about courts' ability to deal with "stale" claims, also have strong substantive overtones in that they provide for "repose"—when the time to sue has passed, people can stop worrying about being sued, close their books on past transactions, make plans unaffected by the possibility of litigation, and get on with their lives and businesses.

1) **Note**

Regardless of the fluctuations in the *Erie* doctrine since *York*, this holding—treating state statutes of limitations as "substantive" for *Erie* purposes—still stands.

(b) **"Outcome Determination" Test**

In explaining the *York* ruling, the Court articulated what came to be a major test for whether state law should be regarded as substantive for *Erie* purposes: **Will application of federal law** instead of the state law **significantly affect the outcome of the litigation?**

1) **Difficulties of the Test**

It is hard to know where to stop in applying the *York* test. If that test were applied broadly, almost any procedural rule could qualify as substantive because (especially if disobeyed) it could affect the outcome of a case. In fact, some cases applying the test appeared to raise doubts about whether many Federal Rules of Civil Procedure could govern when state law differed, but the Supreme Court has subsequently drawn back from the most far-reaching readings of *York*.

2) **Possible Overreading of Test**

It seems doubtful that the "outcome determination" test should have been read with a vengeance, for it was contrasted with whether a state rule "concerns merely the manner or means" by which a right to recover is enforced (*i.e.*, even under *York*, if a state rule concerned only the manner or means of enforcement, federal law could govern). The opinion also pointed out that the concern was to avoid providing litigants with a second, conflicting body of law. This "dual-regime" concern remains valid and is often a useful tool for discerning whether a serious *Erie* problem exists.

(2) *Byrd* and the "Interest Balancing" Approach

In **Byrd v. Blue Ridge Electric Cooperative, Inc.,** 356 U.S. 525 (1958), the Court appeared to signal another departure by at least demoting the "outcome determination" factor to one among several—to be balanced along with federal and state interests in the rules that could be applied. This view came to be known as an "interest balancing" approach to *Erie* problems.

(a) Specific Holding

Byrd was a federal diversity case. The issue was whether federal or state law should govern the manner of determining an ancillary state-law issue (the status of an outside contractor's employee under a workers'-compensation law). Under state practice, the judge determined status; in federal court, such issues went to the jury. The Court held in favor of the federal rule.

1) Note

A federal court might reach the same result today (if *Byrd* arose as a case of first impression) by application of the Seventh Amendment jury-trial right as it is now interpreted. At the time, though, the Court did not treat the result as required by the Seventh Amendment.

(b) "Balancing" Approach

Byrd discusses three main types of factors that could bear on the choice between the state and federal rules.

1) Relation Between State Rule in Question and Underlying State Right

The Court first asked whether the state practice was "bound up with" the underlying state-law rights and obligations being enforced, and concluded that it was not. The aim of this inquiry seems to have been to determine whether the *state procedural practice was an integral part of the state substantive right*, or if the state system followed it for some *independent reason* that might relate more to state-court internal housekeeping and, therefore, have less call to be followed in federal court.

> **cf.** **Compare—Malpractice Screening Panels**: Several federal courts have followed state-law requirements for screening panels in medical-malpractice suits, on the theory that the procedural mechanism was adopted for purposes related to the legislature's views on the enforcement of the underlying tort claims themselves. [*See, e.g.,* **DiAntonio v. Northampton-Accomack General Hospital,** 628 F.2d 287 (4th Cir. 1980)]

2) Countervailing Interests of the Federal Judicial System

The *Byrd* Court also looked to the strength of the federal policy involved— *i.e.*, the relationship between judge and jury in federal court—and the danger that following the state rule would disrupt that policy. The federal interests relevant to this inquiry fall into a narrow range; they do not pertain to the substance of the law, but rather involve the federal courts' interest in their own smooth functioning and in the uniformity and coherence of the decisional principles they have evolved to govern their procedures.

3) Likelihood of Effect on Outcome

Finally, the Court looked to the *York* "outcome determination" test and decided that following the federal practice would not likely affect the outcome of the suit.

(c) Views on "Balancing" Approach

Byrd drew praise for recognizing the relevance of federal as well as state concerns, for bringing to the surface factors bearing on choices between state and federal law in a complex system, and for reducing the threat that the Federal Rules of Civil Procedure would so often have to yield to state rules as to produce a patchwork and undermine the uniformity sought and achieved by adoption of the Rules. However, *Byrd* suffers from the common difficulties of multifactor balancing approaches: It has the apples-and-oranges problem, for it is hard to find a scale on which to balance state and federal interests of different types, and inconsistency in application can often result.

(d) Status of *Byrd* Test

For many years, starting with *Hanna v. Plumer* (discussed below), the Supreme Court virtually ignored *Byrd* and emphasized other approaches set out in *Hanna* and applied in later cases. However, the Court never disavowed or overruled *Byrd*, thus leaving doubt as to whether that case remained good law in any respect. In 1996, the Court revived *Byrd* to a limited extent, invoking it when the possibly applicable federal rule of law was purely decisional **and** might involve an "essential characteristic" of the federal-court system (*e.g.*, some aspects of the relationship among the jury, trial judge, and appellate court). [**Gasperini v. Center for Humanities, Inc.,** 518 U.S. 415 (1996)] In *Gasperini*, a diversity defendant appealed a jury award, claiming that it was excessive. Had the case been in state court, appellate review would have been de novo and the appellate court would have applied the state standard for excessiveness, which looked to whether the verdict departed materially from what would be reasonable compensation. Federal appellate courts, by contrast, apply the deferential abuse-of-discretion standard when reviewing federal trial courts' rulings on such matters. The Supreme Court held that the state interest in application of its substantive standard, and the federal interest in the relationship between federal trial and appellate courts, could be accommodated by having the federal trial court apply the state's "departs materially" standard, with federal appellate review of the district court's resulting ruling being for abuse of discretion only.

5. Approach Under *Hanna v. Plumer*

Until 1965, the Supreme Court treated many federal- vs. state-law problems as subject to a general *Erie* approach, as developed through *York* and *Byrd*. However, when Federal Rules of Civil Procedure arguably conflicted with the law that would apply in state courts, a parallel but mostly independent line of cases developed. The Court sorted out the different law-choice situations and refined the approaches applicable to each in **Hanna v. Plumer,** 380 U.S. 460 (1965).

a. Specific Holding

In **Hanna,** the Supreme Court held that Federal Rule of Civil Procedure 4(d)(1) [now Rule 4(e)(2)(B)], allowing "substituted" service of process on a defendant's spouse at their home, rather than the personal service required by Massachusetts law, was valid and controlling, even though the "substituted" service would not have sufficed had the same state-law action been brought in Massachusetts state court.

(1) Note

The situation incidentally illustrates the possible overextension of the "outcome determination" test, for if the state rule applied in federal court, the suit would have been dismissed because state requirements had not been met.

b. Two Parts of *Hanna* Opinion

It is perhaps not frequently enough noticed that the majority opinion in *Hanna* has two parts: the first, technically dictum, about the *Erie* rule and the second, being the Court's holding, about the tests for the validity of a rule adopted pursuant to the Rules Enabling Act [28 U.S.C. § 2072].

(1) *Erie* "Dictum" in *Hanna*

The first part of the opinion confirms the scaling back of the *York* "outcome determination" test. It suggests—and later opinions appear to confirm—that while the test survives, it is to be applied in **modified form** in light of "the policies underlying the *Erie* rule." The Court identified these policies as the **"twin aims"** of "discouragement of forum shopping and avoidance of inequitable administration of the laws."

(a) Application

Although the Court decided that *Hanna* was not the type of case to which the modified *York* test applied (*see infra*), the Court implied that if it **did** apply, the Federal Rule would govern because the different rules in federal and state court regarding service of process would neither encourage forum shopping nor cause unfair discrimination among litigants.

(b) Comment on Forum Shopping

Forum shopping is not always an evil; the very existence of diversity jurisdiction, concurrent with state courts' general jurisdiction, reflects an intent to let some litigants choose between forums. By itself, forum shopping seems at most a minor irritant, involving some procedural shuffling. The main difficulty appears to be with what litigants may get when they forum shop—an unfairly different rule of law from what would have governed in state court.

Consequently, although Supreme Court opinions regularly mention the forum-shopping concern, it should not be treated in isolation, but rather should be considered in tandem with the aim of discouraging inequitable administration of the laws.

(2) Holding with Respect to Validity of Federal Rules

In the holding portion of *Hanna*, the Court found that the modified *York* approach (developed in the dictum portion of *Hanna, supra*) applied to the "typical, relatively unguided *Erie* choice," but did not apply here because Congress had provided a different standard in the Rules Enabling Act, under which the Federal Rules are promulgated. That Act gives the Supreme Court the power to adopt Federal Rules regarding practice, procedure, and evidence in the federal courts, as long as the Rules do not "abridge, enlarge or modify any substantive right." Under the Enabling Act, the *Hanna* Court ruled that the Federal Rules are to be applied in federal courts unless they violate the Constitution or the terms of the Enabling Act itself.

(a) Constitutional Restrictions

Recall that the power of the federal courts to create "general" common law was held unconstitutional because it did not rest on a power granted to the federal government by the Constitution. (*See supra*, p. 114.) The power to regulate ***procedure*** in the federal courts, however, has been granted to Congress under the constitutional provision creating lower federal courts [Art. III, § 1], as augmented by the Necessary and Proper Clause [Art. I, § 17] (*see* Constitutional Law Summary), and Congress has delegated part of this power to the Supreme Court through the Rules Enabling Act. The only ***constitutional*** restriction on this power is that the rules be ***"arguably procedural"***: the power to make procedural rules is broad enough to include "matters which, though falling within the uncertain area between substance and procedure, are rationally capable of classification as either." [**Hanna v. Plumer,** *supra*]

(b) Enabling Act Limitations

1) "Practice and Procedure" Requirement

In *Hanna*, the Court reiterated that a rule passes muster under the "practice and procedure" portion of the Enabling Act if it ***"really regulates procedure***—the judicial process for enforcing rights and duties recognized by substantive law and for justly administering remedy and redress for disregard or infraction of them" (emphasis added). It is highly unlikely that any Federal Rule the Court might plausibly promulgate could fail this test.

2) "Substantive Rights" Limitation

The second sentence of the Rules Enabling Act requires that the Rules not "abridge, enlarge or modify any substantive right," and to be valid a rule technically must not transgress this proscription. However, in *Hanna* the Court pointed out that this limitation is not addressed to merely "incidental effects" on the rights of litigants.

(c) Strong Presumption of Validity

The *Hanna* Court made it clear that when there is a conflict between a federal rule adopted under the Rules Enabling Act and state law, there is a very strong presumption in favor of the validity of the Federal Rule. It stated that the Rule is to be applied unless it appears that the Rules Advisory Committee, the Supreme Court, and Congress erred in their initial judgment that the Rule did not transgress the Enabling Act or the Constitution. Indeed, the Supreme Court has never held a Federal Rule invalid on its face or as applied.

	◆GILBERT
YORK OUTCOME DETERMINATION TEST	Will application of federal instead of state law *significantly affect the outcome of litigation*?
BYRD INTEREST BALANCING APPROACH	(1) Is the state practice rule *bound up with the underlying state law rights* being enforced? (2) Would following the state practice rule *interfere with the relationship between the judge and jury* in federal court? (3) Would following federal instead of state practice *affect the outcome of the lawsuit*?
HANNA MODIFICATIONS	Distinguish between situations in which the possibly applicable federal rule has been *promulgated under the Rules Enabling Act* and those in which it is *purely decisional*. If the rule has been promulgated under the Rules Enabling Act (*e.g.*, a Federal Rule of Civil Procedure), it is to be applied in federal court unless it violates the Constitution or the Rules Enabling Act, including its ban on affecting substance (which is *very unlikely*). If the federal rule is purely decisional, in most instances you should analyze the case in light of the twin aims of (i) *discouragement of forum shopping* and (ii) *avoidance of inequitable administration of the laws*.

c. Justice Harlan's Concurrence

Justice Harlan concurred in the *Hanna* judgment, but criticized the majority as going too far in the direction of favoring the Federal Rules. He characterized the Court's approach as: "arguably procedural, ergo constitutional." As to the Federal Rules, this characterization may understate *Hanna's* requirements, at least if the Court were to give some effect to the Enabling Act's substantive-rights limitation. On the other hand, Harlan's characterization seems accurate when Congress itself has enacted legislation regulating procedure in the federal courts (*e.g.*, venue rules, *see supra*, p. 35 *et seq.*). However, such a relaxed standard for validity is not objectionable in the context of a procedural rule for federal courts enacted by Congress. *Rationale*: Congress has broad power over procedure in the federal courts and is not bound by the Enabling Act's restriction against affecting substantive rights.

(1) "Primary Private Activity"

Justice Harlan also argued for an approach to federal vs. state rule choice that would have emphasized state power over "primary private activity" (*i.e.*, state rule would apply if it would affect the primary, out-of-court stages of activity from which a case arises; federal rule would apply if it affected in-court behavior following the "primary" stages). Although thoughtfully advocated, this view has not prevailed; and if turned into a single approach, it would overlook the multiple nature of modern *Erie-Hanna* analyses.

6. Modern Approach Under *Erie* and *Hanna*

The *Hanna* opinion suggests an approach to analysis of many federal-state law-choice issues, amplified in an important article. [Ely, *The Irrepressible Myth of Erie*, 87 Harv. L. Rev. 693 (1974)] First, it is necessary to see whether any choice is needed; there may be no conflict to resolve between federal and state rules. Second, if conflict exists, one should determine the *source* of the arguably applicable federal rule of law—the Constitution; an Act of Congress; a Federal Rule of Civil or Appellate Procedure or Evidence; or a decisional rule developed by the federal courts and not resting on interpretation of one of the foregoing sources. The *source* of the federal rule determines the *test* for its validity and governing force.

a. Conflict-Determination Stage

For several reasons, federal and state rules of law that might apply in a situation may not conflict; *e.g.*, only one system may purport to have an applicable rule at all; or the two rules may address somewhat different, even if closely related, points and may both be applied; or the rules may agree and thus call for the same result, whichever is applied. If so, no *Hanna* analysis is necessary, although in the absence of an applicable Federal Rule of Civil Procedure, the *Erie* concern for inequitable administration of the laws may clinch the case for application of the state rule. [**Walker v. Armco Steel Corp.**, 446 U.S. 740 (1980)]

(1) Illustration—No Federal Rule

After *Erie*, in the absence of action by Congress, there is no federal law that purports to govern in many common tort situations. The only substantive law that can govern is state law.

(2) Illustration—No Direct Conflict

Federal Rule 3, which states that a "civil action is commenced by filing a complaint with the court," need not be read as speaking to when a state statute of limitations is tolled on a state claim. Thus, if state law provides that the statute is not tolled until *process is served*—the service requirement being an integral part of the state limitations statute—the state rule applies in state-law actions in federal court, rendering the *Hanna* analysis inapplicable. [**Walker v. Armco Steel Corp.**, *supra;* **Ragan v. Merchants Transfer & Warehouse Co.**, 337 U.S. 530 (1949)]

(3) Illustration—Parallel Rules or Borrowing

Another reason why no conflict may exist is that many state-court rules closely track the Federal Rules--and some of the Federal Rules were originally modeled on state rules--so that the two provisions may be identical in phrasing or effect. (But state courts are free to interpret state rules that track federal ones differently, so it is important to check not just text but the different systems' treatment even of identically worded rules.) Moreover, Federal Rules, such as Federal Rule 4 on service of process, sometimes borrow certain types of state-law provisions from the state in which the district court sits. Such borrowing precludes the possibility of conflict to the extent that the federal rule is borrowed state law.

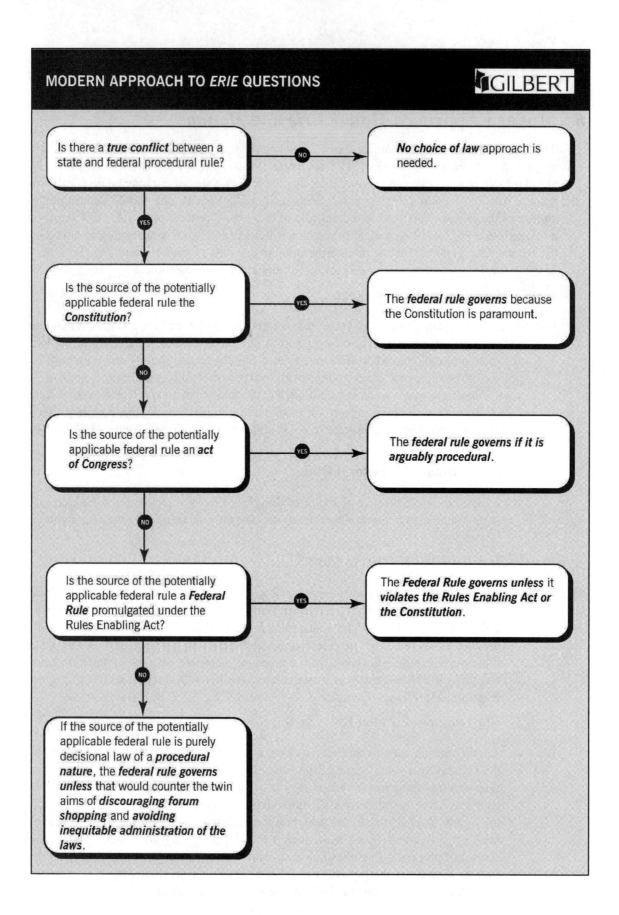

(4) Uncertainty About Construction to Avoid Conflict

The Court has stated that Federal Rules "should be given their plain meaning"; if that reading leads to a direct collision with state law, the *Hanna* analysis applies. [**Walker v. Armco Steel Corp.**, *supra*] This position suggests that a Federal Rule should not be narrowly construed to avoid conflict with state law. However, the Court has indicated that the Federal Rules should be interpreted "with sensitivity to important state interests and regulatory policies" [**Gasperini v. Center for Humanities**, *supra*], which may permit a finding of "no direct conflict" between state and federal laws. The Court has also been willing to adopt limiting constructions of Federal Rules to minimize or avoid problems with the Rules Enabling Act's substantive-rights limitation (*see supra*, p. 119). [**Semtek International Inc. v. Lockheed Martin Corp.**, 531 U.S. 497 (2001); **Ortiz v. Fibreboard Corp.**, 527 U.S. 815 (1999)]

e.g. **Example—*Hanna***: In *Hanna* itself, conflict could have been avoided by reading Federal Rule 4(d)(1) to deal only with service to commence the action and not with tolling the statute of limitations. State law provided for tolling *either* by personal service *or* by filing a notice of claim in probate court; the plaintiff might thus have followed both federal and state law by using substituted service under Rule 4 and tolling the statute by filing a notice of claim. The Court did not take this course, however, saying that the Federal Rule reflected a determination that the notice purposes of state law could be achieved by "less cumbersome" means, and that the Rule implied that in-hand service was not required in federal-court actions.

e.g. **Example—Class Action for Statutory Penalty**: A bare majority of the Supreme Court (with now-retired Justice Stevens providing the fifth vote and the late Justice Scalia writing the majority opinion) found a conflict between Federal Rule 23's authorization for class actions and New York's class-action statute, which generally bars class actions in state court to recover statutory penalties. [**Shady Grove Orthopedic Associates v. Allstate Insurance Co.**, 559 U.S. 393 (2010)] Without a majority opinion, the Court went on to find that Rule 23 governed in a state-law action in federal court, allowing such cases to proceed in class form there even though penalty claims could not be asserted in class form in New York state court (*see infra*, p. 125). Four dissenters would have found no conflict and applied the New York statute to bar such a class action in federal court.

EXAM TIP **GILBERT**

Be alert to ways in which the federal and state rules can be *reconciled or applied in a side-by-side manner* (*e.g.*, no direct conflict, narrow construction to avoid conflict, parallel rules or borrowing). Don't assume that there is always a conflict.

---

b. Conflict-Resolution Stage

If the federal and state rules conflict, it is necessary to proceed to the *Hanna* analysis. In applying that analysis, it is essential first to determine the *source* of the potentially applicable federal rule of law. The answer to that inquiry provides the approach for determining whether the federal rule is valid; if so, under the Supremacy Clause [U.S. Const. art. VI, § 2] it prevails over contrary state law.

(1) Federal Constitution

Some procedural rules that govern in federal court derive from the text and judicial interpretations of the United States Constitution, such as the Seventh Amendment guarantee of the right to trial by jury in suits at common law (which does not apply to state courts). Because the Constitution is our paramount law, if it speaks to a situation before a court, **it governs,** without regard to any contrary state law or practice. This situation provides a possibly oversimplified example of why one should not invariably think in the *Erie* context in terms of "substance" vs. "procedure"; such labels, about either state or federal law, are beside the point if the source of a rule of federal law is the Constitution itself.

(2) Acts of Congress

Because Congress has broad constitutional power over federal courts (*see supra*, p. 119), if Congress passes a statute governing federal-court procedure, that statute is valid and prevails over any contrary state law *if* it is "arguably procedural." Thus, one should look **only** to the "procedural" nature of the **federal** statute in determining whether it is valid and governing; the substantive nature of any contrary state rule would be irrelevant, and there is no place for *Byrd's* balancing of state and federal interests, because Congress has already done the balancing.

> **e.g.** **Example—Federal Transfer-of-Venue Statute**: Although Alabama law that would govern in an action conducted in Alabama state court disfavored contractual forum-selection clauses, 28 U.S.C. section 1404(a) on transfer of venue between federal courts (*see supra*, p. 42 *et seq.*) was sufficiently broad to cover, and governed in a state-law case in Alabama federal court. Thus, the federal court could consider the effect of the parties' forum-selection clause on possible transfer to federal court in New York. [**Stewart Organization v. Ricoh Corp.,** *supra*, p. 47]

(3) Federal Rules

A Federal Rule promulgated pursuant to the Rules Enabling Act is judged by the standards of the Act, as reflected in the holding portion of **Hanna v. Plumer,** *supra*. The Rule (including court interpretations of the Rule) is to be applied instead of contrary state law unless it appears that the relevant Advisory Committee (Advisory Committees on Civil Rules, Appellate Rules, Rules of Evidence, etc., draft proposed rules for the Judicial Conference of the United States, which recommends them for adoption by the Supreme Court), the Supreme Court, and Congress erred in their initial judgment that the Rule did not transgress the Rules Enabling Act or the Constitution. (Congress does not usually vote on proposed Rules, but they must be submitted to Congress at least seven months before they are to take effect. [28 U.S.C. § 2074] If Congress does not act, the rules go into effect.)

> **e.g.** **Example**: Federal Rule of Appellate Procedure 38, which allows *discretionary* penalties for frivolous appeals, prevailed in federal court over an Alabama statute *requiring* penalties for unsuccessful appeals in state court. [**Burlington Northern Railroad v. Woods,** 480 U.S. 1 (1987)]

On your law-school exam, if a question involves a lawsuit in federal court under diversity jurisdiction and there is both a federal law and a state law on a particular issue, be sure to mention the basic rule: Under *Erie*, a federal court sitting in diversity jurisdiction will *apply state substantive law and federal procedural law*. If there is a conflict between the requirements of a Federal Rule of Civil Procedure and a state procedural rule, you should note that, under the modern approach, the federal courts will apply a Federal Rule of Civil Procedure unless the court determines that the rule violates the Rules Enabling Act or the federal Constitution. Think carefully before blazing new trails on this point and arguing that the rule involved is invalid. In most cases, you can probably finish off your answer by stating that it is highly unlikely that the drafters of the rule, the Supreme Court, and Congress erred in their initial judgment that the rule did not violate the Rules Enabling Act and the Constitution.

(a) Rules Enabling Act's "Substantive-Right" Limitation

Whether the Court would ever strike down a Federal Rule for violating the Enabling Act seems to depend primarily on whether it would be willing to give significant independent force to the portion of the Enabling Act that requires that the Rules "not abridge, enlarge or modify any substantive right." Most often, procedural rules will not have anything like the forbidden effect, so the problem will rarely arise.

1) "Incidental" Effects

The Court has disregarded "incidental" effects that leave untouched the content of state substantive law, while providing a somewhat different "manner or means" to enforce it.

e.g. **Example**: The Court has held that any effect on substantive rights resulting from the imposition of Rule 11 sanctions (regarding improper assertion of claims or defenses, *see infra*, p. 169 *et seq.*) is incidental, and that the Rule governs in diversity cases. [**Business Guides, Inc. v. Chromatic Communications Enterprises, Inc.,** 498 U.S. 533 (1991)]

2) Possibility of Conflict with Substantive Right

The Court has not, thus far, entertained the possibility that a generally valid Federal Rule might, in particular contexts, impermissibly conflict with a substantive right. The Court has, however, been willing to adopt limiting constructions of Federal Rules of Civil Procedure to minimize or avoid problems with the Rules Enabling Act's substantive-rights limitation (*see supra*, p. 119). [**Semtek International Inc. v. Lockheed Martin Corp.,** *supra*, p. 121; **Ortiz v. Fibreboard Corp.,** *supra*, p. 121]

3) Fragmented Majority on Possible Conflict with Substantive Right

After holding that Federal Rule 23's authorization for class actions conflicted with New York's general ban on class actions to recover statutory penalties, the five Justices in the majority split without a Court opinion in concluding that the Federal Rule governed. Four Justices agreed, in a plurality opinion by the late Justice Scalia, that if a Federal Rule passes the test of "really regulat[ing] procedure" [quoting **Sibbach v. Wilson & Co.**, 312 U.S. 1 (1941)], "it is authorized by [the Rules Enabling Act] and is valid in all jurisdictions, with respect to all claims, regardless of its incidental effect upon state-created rights." Now-retired Justice Stevens concurred in the result because "the bar for finding an Enabling Act violation is a high one," not cleared in this case. But he agreed with the four dissenters as to the general approach and argued that, in some cases, federal courts must follow state procedural rules "because they function as part of the State's definition of substantive rights and remedies," and a Federal Rule could—if an interpretation avoiding a conflict was not possible—be invalid as applied under the Enabling Act's substantive-rights limitation. [**Shady Grove Orthopedic Associates v. Allstate Insurance Co.**, *supra*, p. 121]

(4) Judge-Made Federal Procedural Rules

If a potentially applicable federal rule is purely *decisional*—i.e., *not* the result of an interpretation of positive law found in the Constitution, an Act of Congress, or a Federal Rule—the "twin-aims" *Erie* test articulated in the dictum portion of the *Hanna* opinion governs: If applying the federal judge-made rule would counter the aims of discouraging forum shopping and avoiding inequitable administration of the laws, the federal court should follow state law.

e.g. **Example**: **Guaranty Trust Co. v. York**, *supra*, p. 115, remains a prime illustration of such a situation, although the Court's analysis when it decided *York* was somewhat different from the modern approach under *Hanna*. Today, federal courts would apply the state rule in a case like *York* because following the federal rule would fail the "twin-aims" test: a party who would be barred by a statute of limitations in state court, but might be able to argue around a more flexible federal judge-made "laches" rule, would be tempted to file in federal court; and entertaining the action in federal court, when it would be barred by limitations in state court, would also deprive the defendant of the benefits of repose meant to be conferred by the state statute.

(a) Note

The "twin-aims" approach might also apply, and cut against the applicability of state law in federal court, if state courts have a rule governing purely internal housekeeping matters—such as judicial attire or length of paper for court filings—and federal courts have nothing that amounts to a rule but do have a practice differing from that followed in state court.

(b) Caution

The Court has also shown a willingness to consider possible outcome variation and forum-choice influence in interpreting a Federal Rule of Civil Procedure, thus possibly making the "twin-aims" approach relevant in at least some cases besides those involving purely decisional federal procedural rules or non-rule practices. [*See* **Semtek International Inc. v. Lockheed Martin Corp.**, *supra*, p. 121—declining to give Rule 41(b)'s provision that most dismissals operate "as an adjudication on the merits" full claim-preclusive effect when the district court dismissed based on the statute of limitations and courts of the state in which the district court sat would not treat such a dismissal as extinguishing the substantive right; the Court noted that otherwise defendants would have an incentive to remove diversity cases to federal court to obtain a broader preclusive effect]

(c) Sufficiency of Evidence

In state-law cases in the federal courts, the lower federal courts are divided on whether to apply state or judge-made federal standards to the issue whether the evidence is sufficient for a case to go to the jury. The trend in the cases, however, appears to be toward the federal standard because the question goes to whether judge or jury should evaluate the sufficiency of the evidence, not to the elements of the claim or the definition of the persuasion burden. [**Mayer v. Gary Partners & Co.,** 29 F.3d 330 (7th Cir. 1994)]

1) But Note—Standard for Reviewing Jury Awards

When a federal trial judge considers a new-trial motion based on alleged excessiveness of a jury's award in a state-law case, state—rather than federal—law supplies the governing standard because it reflects state policy on how much of a check to place on excessive damages. [**Gasperini v. Center for Humanities, Inc.,** *supra*, p. 117]

(d) Relative Infrequency of Problems of This Sort

Because federal statutes and the Federal Rules cover federal procedural issues fairly broadly, and because federal decisional rules often will not conflict with potentially applicable state rules, judge-made federal law infrequently comes into play in state vs. federal law conflicts. Nevertheless, later cases discussing *Hanna* explicitly endorsed the "twin-aims" analysis for this type of situation. [*See, e.g.,* **Stewart Organization v. Ricoh Corp.,** *supra*, p. 124]

1) *NASCO* Case

In 1991, for the first time since before *Hanna*, the Supreme Court faced a case involving what it viewed as a conflict between state law and judge-made federal procedural law. [**Chambers v. NASCO, Inc.,** 501 U.S. 32 (1991)] *NASCO* involved the inherent power of federal courts to impose sanctions for bad-faith conduct in litigation before them, even in state-law cases when the state courts would not have a similar sanctioning power. The majority opinion routinely invoked the "twin-aims" approach, found no forum-shopping incentives or inequity, and upheld the federal rule.

2) Cautionary Note

Because the two prominent intermediate cases of *York* and *Byrd* involved what the Court treated as a conflict between state law and judge-made federal law, students often mistakenly regard them as dominating the field of *Erie* problems. The Court has, however, made it clear that other tests for the validity and governing force of a federal rule apply when the rule is grounded in the Constitution itself, enacted by Congress, or promulgated pursuant to the Enabling Act.

(e) Limited Survival of *Byrd* Approach

The survival of *Byrd's* balancing or accommodation of state and federal interests appears to be limited to a subpart of this category of cases involving judge-made federal procedural law—when an as-of-yet not clearly defined "essential characteristic of the federal court system," likely implicating relations among jury, trial judge, and appellate court, is involved. [*See* **Gasperini v. Center for Humanities, Inc.,** *supra*] Such balancing or accommodation appears uncalled for in cases involving positive federal law, because other authoritative lawmakers—the Constitution drafters, Congress, or the Federal Rules makers—have already done the balancing or accommodating. Even with purely decisional federal rules, the Court's decisions since *Hanna* indicate that the purposive "twin-aims" modified version of the *York* test, rather than *Byrd* interest analysis, is the approach to be followed, unless an "essential characteristic" of the federal-court system is involved.

e.g. **Example—*Hanna*:** In *Hanna* itself, the Court said that the "importance" of a state rule is relevant in the *Erie* context only for purposes of determining whether failing to follow the state rule in federal court would disserve the "twin aims" of discouraging forum shopping and avoiding inequitable administration of the laws.

e.g. **Example—*NASCO*:** In *NASCO* (*supra*), in upholding the federal courts' decisionally established inherent authority to impose sanctions for bad-faith conduct in state-law litigation before them despite contrary state law, the Court relied on *Erie*, *York*, and *Hanna* but ignored *Byrd*.

e.g. **Example—*Gasperini*:** In *Gasperini* (*see supra*, p. 117), the Court relied on *Byrd*, but only concerning the scope of federal appellate review of trial-court denials of motions seeking remittitur, which involves relations among federal juries, trial judges, and appellate courts. In choosing state law over the federal standard for trial judges' review of jury verdicts for excessiveness in state-law cases, however, the Court in *Gasperini* again used the "twin-aims" test and relied on *Erie*, *York*, and *Hanna* while ignoring *Byrd*.

7. Which State's Law Applies?

Because diversity cases—and most of the state-law cases in the federal courts are diversity cases—by definition involve parties from different states, federal courts must often decide *which* state's law is to govern.

a. General Rule

In diversity cases, as to matters for which the federal court is required to follow state law, it will apply the ***law of the state in which it sits***. This law includes the state's choice-of-law rules, *i.e.*, the rules the state courts use to determine what law to apply to cases such as those involving a nonresident party or events that occurred out of state. Thus, if the state's choice-of-law rules require application of another state's law, the federal court is to do the same. [**Klaxon Co. v. Stentor Manufacturing Co.,** 313 U.S. 487 (1941)]

Exam questions involving diversity jurisdiction sometimes are based on a claim involving people or events in several states and include provisions of substantive law from each state. You will have to decide what law the federal district court should apply. Remember to state the basic rule: A federal district court will apply the **law of the state in which it is sitting**, including its conflict-of-laws rules. Thus, if Plaintiff, a resident of State Green, is hit by Defendant, a resident of State Yellow, while driving through State Red, and Plaintiff brings a diversity action against Defendant in State Yellow, the federal district court should apply State Yellow law. However, if the facts tell you that under State Yellow conflict-of-laws rules, a State Yellow court would apply the law of the state where the accident occurred, the federal district court should apply State Red law, because in diversity-jurisdiction cases, the federal court applies the **choice-of-law rules of the state in which it sits**.

b. Questionable Extension of *Klaxon* to Statutory Interpleader

In a companion case decided the same day as *Klaxon* [**Griffin v. McCoach,** 313 U.S. 498 (1941)], the Supreme Court applied the *Klaxon* rule to a case arising within federal statutory-interpleader jurisdiction. (For discussion of interpleader, *see infra*, p. 227 *et seq.*) Although *Griffin* apparently remains the law for federal statutory-interpleader actions, no one has defended its application of the conflicts rules of the state in which the federal court sits, since federal statutory-interpleader jurisdiction was created precisely because it might not be possible to bring scattered claimants before the same state court.

c. Reaffirmance of *Klaxon*

Despite some academic criticism of the *Klaxon* rule, the Supreme Court strongly and summarily reaffirmed it in an extreme case in which the Texas courts would have followed Cambodian law. [**Day & Zimmermann, Inc. v. Challoner,** 423 U.S. 3 (1975)] By contrast, the heavily criticized extension of the *Klaxon* rule to statutory interpleader in *Griffin, supra*, has not been relitigated at the Supreme Court level.

d. Exceptions

In some instances, federal legislation may provide a **federal** choice-of-law rule. [**Richards v. United States,** 369 U.S. 1 (1962)] For example, the Federal Tort Claims Act requires courts to apply the law—including choice-of-law rules—"of the place where the [allegedly tortious] act or omission occurred." [28 U.S.C. § 1346(b)]

8. Determining Applicable State Law

Erie referred to the law of a state as declared by the state's "highest court." Often, of course, because a state statute or supreme-court decision is on point, the state substantive law to be followed by a federal court will be clear. However, in other cases, the state-court system may never have faced a question, or only lower state courts may have ruled, or it may seem likely that the state supreme court would overrule an old precedent if given the opportunity.

a. General Guideline—"Proper Regard" to State-Court Rulings

Although the Supreme Court has not recently spoken directly on how federal courts should approach the problem of determining unclear state law, it has stated that "proper regard" must be given to state-court precedents. In some cases, a **federal court will not be bound** by the ruling of a state intermediate appellate court on a point of state law, and *a fortiori* not by a state trial-court decision. Such courts' opinions are, however, relevant data for ascertaining state law. [**Commissioner v. Estate of Bosch,** 387 U.S. 456 (1967)]

b. **Implementation in Light of *Erie* Aims**

The determination of unclear state law seems best approached with the *Erie* "twin aims" of avoiding forum shopping and inequitable administration of the laws in mind. Adoption of simplistic or rigid tests (*e.g.*, being bound by a recent holding of a state's intermediate appellate court—even if the ruling seems contrary to what the state supreme court would probably do) could encourage forum shopping by making available in the federal system law that would not, ultimately, govern in the state system. Therefore, many lower federal courts look to ***all*** relevant sources, giving due regard to the varying weights of different authorities within the state system, in an attempt to discern how the state supreme court would decide the issue. [*See, e.g.*, **McKenna v. Ortho Pharmaceutical Corp.,** 622 F.2d 567 (3d Cir. 1980)] In any event, a federal court is supposed to ***apply*** state law and ***not*** attempt to change it to what the court thinks might be a better rule.

EXAM TIP   ◼GILBERT

If an exam question involves diversity jurisdiction and you are told that the state supreme court has never ruled on the substantive issue involved or that it has ruled on it but it did so a very long time ago, you should explain that the federal court should give proper regard for state-court rulings. However, "proper regard" does not mean that the court must blindly follow state appellate-court precedent. The court should consider the twin aims of *avoiding forum shopping and inequitable administration of the laws*. It should apply the law it thinks the state supreme court would apply, not the law it thinks is the best rule.

---

c. **No Deference to Local Federal Judges**

The Supreme Court has ruled that federal appellate courts are not to defer to the interpretation of state law by federal trial judges, but must review district courts' state law determinations *de novo*. [**Salve Regina College v. Russell,** 499 U.S. 225(1991)]

d. **State Certification Laws**

Many states authorize their highest courts to answer questions of state law certified by federal courts before which cases are pending. Where this procedure is available, a federal court may seek an authoritative answer to uncertain questions about state law rather than speculating on them. [*See* **Lehman Bros. v. Schein,** 416 U.S. 386 (1974)]

B. Federal Common Law

1. No "Federal General Common Law"

Erie's repudiation of *Swift* (*see supra*, p. 113 *et seq.*) included the flat statement, "[t]here is no federal general common law." However, the very day *Erie* was decided, the Court held that federal common law governed on the specific issue of apportionment of waters in an interstate stream. [**Hinderlider v. La Plata River Co.,** 304 U.S. 92 (1938)] The resolution to this apparent contradiction lies in the fact that the federal courts do have authority to create common law in *particular areas of federal authority or interest,* subject to overruling by Congress.

2. Examples of Federal Common-Law Areas

The range of federal interests and grants of authority that could support federal common law is fairly broad, and the subject receives more extended treatment elsewhere. (*See* Federal Courts Summary.)

a. Borrowed State Law

In some cases, federal statutes may be silent as to particular issues arising under them (*e.g.*, statutes of limitations for older federal claims and definitions of family status for purposes of some federal-law entitlements). In such cases, the federal courts often fill the interstices in federal law by borrowing the law of the relevant state, as long as that law does not undermine the purposes of the underlying federal law.

(1) Illustration—Derivative-Action Demand Requirement

A derivative action is a lawsuit brought by a corporation's shareholder(s) to vindicate corporate rights when the corporation's board of directors has not filed an action. In most states, before filing a derivative action, shareholders must make a demand on the board before they bring the action. However, some states have an exception allowing shareholders to bring an action without making a pre-complaint demand if the demand would be futile (*e.g.*, because the suit would be against members of the board). The federal Investment Company Act allows shareholders to bring certain derivative actions after making demand on the board. The Supreme Court has held that under the Act, the scope of the "futility" exception to the pre-complaint demand requirement should be borrowed from state law. [**Kamen v. Kemper Financial Services, Inc.,** 500 U.S. 90 (1991)]

b. Authorization by Congress

In some areas (*e.g.*, portions of the law of labor relations), the Supreme Court has interpreted congressional legislation as intending that the federal courts develop substantive law to further national uniformity. [*See* **Textile Workers Union v. Lincoln Mills,** 353 U.S. 448 (1957)]

c. Sufficient Federal Interest

The Court sometimes regards the federal government as having a strong enough interest in a transaction that it should be governed by uniform federal common law to further that interest, even in the absence of congressional authorization and despite contrary state law. [*See, e.g.*, **Clearfield Trust Co. v. United States,** 318 U.S. 363 (1943)—federal common law governed on issue of delay in notice of forgery of federal government check] There must, however, be a *significant* federal interest. [*See, e.g.*, **Bank of America v. Parnell,** 352 U.S. 29 (1956)—state law governed in suit between private parties on issue of good faith of holder of previously stolen government bonds; that federal government issued the paper involved in the suit did not by itself suffice to require creating uniform federal common law]

d. Interstate Disputes

In interstate disputes involving governments of, or in, different states (*e.g.*, disputes over interstate pollution), it may be inappropriate for the law of one of the interested states to govern. The federal courts consequently may develop federal common law when no congressional legislation deals with the area. [**Illinois v. City of Milwaukee,** 406 U.S. 91 (1972)]

e. United States Foreign Relations

When questions of American foreign relations are involved, the need for uniform federal common law may be especially clear. [*See, e.g.*, **Banco Nacional de Cuba v. Sabbatino,** 376 U.S. 398 (1964)]

EXAM TIP **GILBERT**

For some reason, almost everyone who has been to law school seems to remember *Erie's* admonition that "there is no federal general common law." This mantra often results in a knee-jerk response whenever students hear the suggestion that a federal court is to apply federal common law. They respond that there is no such thing. This response, of course, is incorrect. Federal common law exists in a significant range of cases, including when Congress has appeared to authorize federal common-law development (*e.g.*, labor relations), when there is a strong federal interest in developing a uniform federal common law (*e.g.*, requirements for notice of forgery on government checks), when interstate disputes are involved (*e.g.*, pollution issues), and when American foreign relations are involved. So don't be fooled on an exam question. Remember, ***federal common law exists in some areas***.

Chapter Four
Pleadings and Motion Practice

CONTENTS	PAGE

Key Exam Issues

The history of pleadings goes back to the common-law "forms of action," which came to require arcane and specific allegations. Reforms sought to get away from these technicalities. First, *code pleading* was introduced in the mid-19th century to require only that a plaintiff set forth the facts underlying the dispute. Many states adopted that form of pleading, and a number still use it. Second, the Federal Rules of Civil Procedure introduced what has been called *notice pleading*, which generally has more relaxed requirements than code pleading. The Supreme Court has tightened those requirements somewhat. Whichever form of pleading applies to an examination question, a range of issues may need to be analyzed:

1. **Sufficiency of the Complaint**

    The defendant may attack the sufficiency of the complaint with a *motion to dismiss for failure to state a claim* in federal court and many state-court systems, or a *demurrer* in a state court using code pleading.

    a. **Elements of the Claim**: The complaint must contain the elements of the claim being asserted (*e.g.*, negligent infliction of injury or breach of contract). The elements of the claim are defined by the *substantive law* that the plaintiff is invoking (*e.g.*, tort or contract law).

    b. **Specificity of Allegations**: In code-pleading jurisdictions, the complaint must include "*facts* constituting the cause of action." In federal court, what is required is "a *short and plain statement* of the claim showing that the pleader is entitled to relief," but this statement generally must include factual matter demonstrating that the plaintiff has alleged the elements of the claim. The *well-pleaded allegations* of the complaint must be accepted as true for purposes of evaluating a challenge to its sufficiency. In code pleading, neither *mere evidence* nor *legal conclusions* are "well-pleaded" and they need not be deemed true for purposes of a challenge to the complaint. Federal courts also may treat conclusory allegations as insufficient to state a claim. Certain types of claims, such as *fraud* claims, usually must be set forth with *more specificity*.

    c. **Materials to Be Considered**: The court is ordinarily restricted to the well-pleaded allegations of the complaint in assessing its adequacy. But it may consider any materials the plaintiff has attached to the complaint as *exhibits*. In addition, if the complaint relies upon documents to support the claim, the court may consider them even though they are not attached to the complaint if there is no dispute about the authenticity of those materials when submitted in connection to a challenge to the sufficiency of the complaint. The court may also consider matters that are the proper subject of *judicial notice* because they are well known and not subject to genuine dispute.

    d. **Alternative of Motion for More Definite Statement or Special Demurrer**: A defendant may also seek clarification of the complaint by making a motion for a more definite statement or filing a special demurrer for uncertainty. Generally, these will be denied unless the defendant shows that the pleading is *too uncertain for the defendant to be expected to frame an answer*. Nonetheless, in some circumstances a defendant may be able to succeed on such a challenge on the ground that the *clarification will show that the claim is subject to dismissal*.

    e. **Alternative of Motion to Strike**: A defendant may also move to *strike extraneous, redundant, or scandalous matter* from a complaint. Such motions are rarely granted. However, if the prayer for relief seeks relief that is unavailable as a *matter of law* (*e.g.*, punitive damages for breach of contract), the defendant may move to strike that portion of the prayer.

2. Adequacy of the Answer

A defendant who does not file a demurrer or motion directed to the complaint must file an answer or risk a default judgment. Issues concerning the answer may arise in a number of ways on an examination:

a. **Default**: Failure to file an answer may result in entry of the defendant's default, foreclosing further defense of the action and entitling the plaintiff to seek a default judgment. At that point, it may be critical to prove that the defendant was *properly served* (*see* Chapter One). In addition, defendants are often able to get their defaults *set aside* by showing that they have a valid defense to the action, some excuse for failure to respond in time, and that the plaintiff has not suffered any prejudice due to their delay.

b. **Admission or Denial of Plaintiff's Allegations**: When the defendant files an answer, any of the plaintiff's allegations that the answer does not deny are *deemed admitted*. The defendant must admit those allegations he cannot deny and may deny on grounds that he lacks sufficient information only if he cannot ascertain the accuracy of the plaintiff's allegations. An improper denial is ineffective and also results in an admission. Denials in an answer in federal court are subject to Rule 11 requirements to have a valid basis after a reasonable investigation (*see* below).

c. **Affirmative Defenses**: The answer may also assert affirmative defenses, which raise legal grounds why the defendant should not be held liable to the plaintiff even if the plaintiff proves the allegations of the complaint. Unless he includes an affirmative defense in the answer, a defendant may not raise that defense at trial, or by pretrial motion, although omitted defenses may be added to the answer by amendment (*see* below).

d. **Waivable and Unwaivable Defenses**: Certain defenses, such as objections to personal jurisdiction or venue (*see* Chapter One), may be waived unless raised at the earliest opportunity, either by pre-answer motion or inclusion in an answer. Other defenses, such as lack of subject-matter jurisdiction (*see* Chapter Two) or failure to join a required party (*see* Chapter Five), may be asserted by motion filed after the answer, even though not included in the answer.

e. **Counterclaims and Crossclaims**: The answer may also raise counterclaims or crossclaims.

   (1) *Counterclaims* are claims by the defendant against the plaintiff. They may be *compulsory* if they arise out of the transaction or occurrence raised in the plaintiff's complaint. Any other counterclaim is *permissive*.

   (2) *Crossclaims* are claims by one defendant against another defendant and are *permissive*.

   (3) *Subject-matter jurisdiction* may be a concern for counterclaims and crossclaims in federal court. (*See* Chapter Two.)

3. May a Party Amend Pleadings?

a. **Amendment as a Matter of Course**: Until a responsive pleading is filed (if one is required), a party usually may amend his pleading *once* as a matter of course.

b. **Amendment by Leave of Court**: Ordinarily, courts will freely allow amendment after the time when it may be made as of course unless there has been *undue delay* or *prejudice to the opposing party*, or the amendment will *delay the trial*.

c. **Effect of Statute of Limitations**: Amendments to assert new claims may be made after the statute of limitations for filing a new suit on the claim has run.

    (1) **As to Original Opposing Party**: If the added claim is asserted against the original opposing party, the amended pleading usually will *relate back* to the date on which the original pleading was filed if the added claim arises out of *the same conduct, transaction, or occurrence* as the one raised in the original pleading. With relation back, the added claim will be treated as though it had been: asserted when the original pleading was filed.

    (2) **As to an Additional or Alternative Party**: Usually, it must be shown that this nonparty *had notice of the action* within (or near) the limitations period.

4. **Has a Party Properly Investigated the Claims or Defenses Asserted in the Pleadings?**

Federal Rule 11 and similar state rules require investigation of claims or defenses before they are asserted in court. In connection with these issues, consider the following:

a. **What Certification Was Made?** The person who signs a pleading (usually an attorney) thereby certifies that she *made a reasonable investigation under the circumstances,* and that:

    (1) The allegations *have evidentiary support* or are likely to have such support after an opportunity for discovery and further investigation;

    (2) The claims, defenses, and other legal contentions are *warranted by existing law or a good faith argument for extending or modifying it*; and

    (3) The claims or defenses are not being presented for an *improper purpose*.

b. **Was the Proper Procedure Used to Challenge the Certification?** Before moving for sanctions, a party claiming that Federal Rule 11 has been violated must serve a sanctions motion and allow the opposing party 21 days to *withdraw the challenged pleading*. The motion may be filed in court only after expiration of the 21 days—this is called *safe-harbor* protection against such sanctions motions.

c. **What Sanctions Should Be Imposed?** If there has been a violation and the proper procedure was used, the imposition of sanctions is *discretionary*, and usually sanctions should be limited to those necessary to *deter repetition* of the offending conduct, rather than being used to punish the wrongdoer or compensate the victim.

A. Introduction

1. In General

The plaintiff begins a civil action by filing in a court of appropriate jurisdiction a *complaint* seeking some sort of judicial relief against specified defendants. The court thereupon issues its process (*e.g.*, summons) directing the named defendants to appear. A defendant "appears" by filing some sort of response (*e.g.*, answer, motion, demurrer), after which other pleadings and motions may be filed until the case is "at issue."

2. Objectives

The basic purpose of pleadings is to give notice of the general character of the controversy between the parties. Under code pleading (*see infra*, p. 137; used in such states as California, Illinois, and New York), the pleadings are also intended to narrow and formulate the issues involved in the case. The pleading process thus helps to determine the scope of the action during discovery and at the trial, and define the scope of any judgment in the action.

3. Background

At common law, the courts relied exclusively on the pleadings to define the issues. The result was that the pleading process was all-important, and pleading rules were extremely technical. Mistakes in the pleading process often proved fatal to the pleader's case, and prevented a hearing on the merits. However, under modern practice, the pleadings are merely one stage of the issue-defining process. Discovery devices and the pretrial conference (*infra*, Chapters Six and Eight) are also available. Consequently, there has been a strong trend toward liberalizing the rules of pleading and streamlining the pleading process.

B. History of Pleading

1. Common-Law Pleadings

The original common-law courts could grant relief only in accordance with certain recognized *forms of action*, each representing a particular theory of substantive law (*e.g.*, trespass, case, trover, assumpsit, etc.), and pleadings had to be drawn in terms of one of these recognized forms. Thus, the plaintiff was forced to fit the out-of-court transaction of which he was complaining into the mold of one of the forms. Amendments to change the form of action were not allowed, so once a plaintiff chose a particular form, he could recover—if at all—only under the substantive theory of law represented by the form; *e.g.*, if the plaintiff chose trespass, but the facts established trover, the plaintiff could not recover.

a. Objective

The basic objective of pleading at common law was to narrow the issues as finely as possible (preferably to a single issue) so that the case could be determined by deciding that issue.

b. Numerous Pleadings

For this purpose, distinct pleadings and counterpleadings were employed; *e.g.*, declaration, answer, replication, rejoinder, surrejoinder, etc. Each party was required to either demur (challenge sufficiency of the pleading responded to; *see infra*, p. 153) or counterplead to each pleading by his adversary. The submission of numerous pleadings was time-consuming, and a defendant could often use the pleading rules for purposes of delay.

c. Distinguish—Equity Pleading

The courts of equity were distinct from common-law courts and were governed by different procedures. Relief was available from the equity courts only when there was no right to recover under any of the forms of action recognized in the law courts (*i.e.*, when the remedy at law was inadequate). Therefore, pleaders in equity had to go outside the forms of action to state their claims; the plaintiff recited *facts* showing that he had a grievance that ought to be remedied. This concept of *fact pleading* was the basis of code pleading (below).

2. Code Pleading

The New York Code of 1848 (known as the Field Code) originated code pleading to relax some of the rigidities of common-law pleading. This code, or adaptations thereof, was subsequently adopted in most states, and is still retained in several today. It incorporates several important departures from common-law pleading rules.

a. Single Form of Action

Unlike the rigid common-law forms, the fundamental requirement of code pleading is that the plaintiff's complaint be in the form of a *statement of facts showing a right to a remedy*. This formulation has been described as abolishing the forms of action and providing for *one form of action*. [Fed. R. Civ. P. 2; Cal. Civ. Proc. Code § 307]

(1) Effect

Under code pleading, the plaintiff no longer has to select and set forth in the pleadings the particular legal theory of his case. He is entitled to recover under *any* legal theory applicable to the *facts* pleaded and proved.

Example: Plaintiff's complaint alleged that Defendant published statements that were injurious to Plaintiff's reputation (that Plaintiff committed a hijacking) and that unnecessarily specified Plaintiff as the person involved. The complaint failed to state a claim for libel because the published statements were admittedly true; but it was held sufficient to state a claim for invasion of privacy. If *any* legal theory will sustain recovery on the facts pleaded, the complaint is sufficient. [**Briscoe v. Reader's Digest,** 4 Cal. 3d 529 (1971)]

Example: A federal statute prohibits states from violating a person's constitutional rights. Plaintiff filed a complaint alleging that the manager of Defendant's store had an arrangement with the local police under which the police would assist the store in refusing service to African Americans at its lunch counter. The complaint was held sufficient to state a claim for violation of Plaintiff's civil rights under federal statutes, since even if the store itself was not governed by the statute, the police were so governed and the complaint alleged concerted action between Defendant (through its manager) and the police. [**Adickes v. S.H. Kress & Co.,** 398 U.S. 144 (1970)]

b. Merger of Law and Equity

Another major aspect of code pleading was the elimination of separate courts of law and equity, and of the separate procedures in each court. This change has persisted under modern practice, in which the same court is vested with jurisdiction to grant both equitable and legal relief. [Fed. R. Civ. P. 1]

(1) Remedies—Distinct

Note that while the distinctions between legal and equitable *procedure* have been abolished, the distinctions between legal and equitable *remedies* remain intact. The nature of the relief available depends upon the circumstances shown (*e.g.*, whether damage has actually resulted).

Example: Equitable relief is generally said to be available only when the legal remedy (damages) is shown to be *inadequate*. This is called the "irreparable injury" rule.

Example: Similarly, various defenses are recognized when an equitable remedy is sought (laches, hardship, unclean hands, etc.), but are not recognized in actions at law.

(a) Jury Trial

Also note that the distinction between legal and equitable remedies is relevant to whether a jury trial is available. While a jury trial is usually available in an action at law, equitable actions are normally tried by the court alone (although the court may impanel a jury for an advisory verdict on disputed questions of fact). (See further discussion *infra*, p. 369 *et seq.*)

c. Limited Number of Pleadings

Far fewer pleadings are allowed under code pleading than in the old common-law system, since there is no objective to reduce the case to a single issue through a pleading "dialogue."

(1) Types of Pleadings

The basic pleadings allowed under existing codes are shown in the chart on the next page. Note that in contrast to the practices in some other code states, California and New York do not permit a reply to matters of affirmative defense in the defendant's answer. Such matter is "deemed controverted" without the necessity of a response by the plaintiff. [Cal. Civ. Proc. Code § 431.20(b)]

d. Fact Pleading

A pleading under the codes must set forth "the facts constituting ***the cause of action*** in ordinary and concise language." [Cal. Civ. Proc. Code § 425.10(a)(1)] This is interpreted as requiring an allegation of the ***"ultimate facts"*** of the cause of action (or defense) involved.

(1) "Ultimate Facts"

Ultimate facts are those facts that describe ***in adequate detail but without legal argument*** the circumstances that the plaintiff believes entitle him to a remedy. If the allegations are too general, they are deemed "conclusions"; and if too much detail is given, it is an impermissible pleading of "evidence."

 Example: Suppose the plaintiff's complaint makes the following allegations in a negligence action:

(i) "Defendant operated her automobile in violation of Vehicle Code section 23101, and injured Plaintiff."

(ii) "Defendant consumed one gallon of wine at the Green Frog Cafe, less than two hours before the accident in which Plaintiff was injured."

(iii) "Defendant drove her car while intoxicated and on the wrong side of the highway, causing it to strike the car in which Plaintiff was riding."

Allegation (i) could be attacked as a conclusion of law. Allegation (ii) might be found to contain only "evidentiary" matter. Allegation (iii) is a sufficient statement of ultimate fact.

PLAINTIFF'S PLEADINGS	DEFENDANT'S PLEADINGS
California Civ. Proc. Code §§ 422.10, 430.30	
Complaint	Demurrer to complaint; Answer
Demurrer to answer	
Demurrer to cross-complaint	Cross-complaint
Answer to cross-complaint	Demurrer to answer to cross-complaint
New York Civ. Prac. Law §§ 3011, 3019, 3211	
Complaint	Motion to dismiss; Answer
Motion to dismiss counterclaim	Counterclaim
Reply to counterclaim	
Illinois Code Civ. Proc. §§ 2–602, 2–608, 2–614, 2–615	
Complaint	Motion to dismiss; Answer
Reply to affirmative matter in answer	
Motion to dismiss counterclaim	Counterclaim
Answer to counterclaim	

(2) Consequences of Improper Pleading of Facts

Failure to allege ultimate facts constituting every essential element of the cause of action (or defense) involved makes the pleading insufficient and subject to a ***general demurrer*** or, under some codes, a motion to dismiss (which is the equivalent of a general demurrer). (*See* discussion, *infra*, p. 153 *et seq.*)

(a) ***If sufficient ultimate facts are alleged***, evidentiary allegations and conclusions of law can be treated as surplusage (but are subject to a motion to strike; *see infra*, p. 156).

(b) ***If the allegations are too vague*** (*i.e.*, mere conclusions), the complaint is also subject to a special demurrer (*see infra*, pp. 155–156).

(3) Criticism

Under the code-pleading system, there is considerable difficulty in determining what constitute the requisite "ultimate facts" (as opposed to "evidentiary matter" or "legal conclusions") in various situations. As a result, pleaders tend to use stereotyped allegations and form complaints that have previously been held sufficient.

3. Pleading Under the Federal Rules

The Federal Rules *further liberalized* pleading standards and have eliminated many of the technical requirements under the Field Code. Today, most states have also adopted rules patterned on the Federal Rules.

a. Pleadings Permitted

The Federal Rules authorize even fewer pleadings than does code pleading (above). The basic pleadings allowed by Federal Rule 7(a) are shown in the chart below.

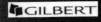

PLAINTIFF'S PLEADINGS	DEFENDANT'S PLEADINGS
Complaint	Answer, which may contain a counterclaim against plaintiff
Answer to counterclaim	

(1) Note

The *demurrer has been eliminated* in federal courts. [See Fed. R. Civ. P. 7(a)] In its place, the *motion to dismiss for failure to state a claim* is used. [Fed. R. Civ. P. 12(b)(6)]

b. Notice Pleading

The Federal Rules eliminate the code requirement of pleading "facts constituting a cause of action." Instead, the Rules simply require a *"short and plain statement of the claim showing that the pleader is entitled to relief."* [Fed. R. Civ. P. 8(a)(2)] This approach has been called "notice pleading."

(1) Rationale

The purpose of pleading under the Federal Rules is to *identify* the transaction out of which the plaintiff's claim arises, so that the defendant has *notice* of the claim. Discovery and other pretrial procedures are relied on for full development of the facts. [**Conley v. Gibson,** 355 U.S. 41 (1957)] Under the Federal Rules, the distinctions among "ultimate facts," "evidentiary facts," and "conclusions of law" (above) are therefore said to be unimportant. Any claim may be stated in general terms, and stylized precision in identifying the cause of action is not required. However, generality can be taken too far. A pleading must "show that the pleader is entitled to relief," and courts may insist that pleadings include sufficient support for the claims included. [**Bell Atlantic Corp. v. Twombly,** 550 U.S. 544 (2007)]

EXAM TIP

If you are asked to write a complaint on your exam under a notice-pleading system, remember that while pleading is generally more relaxed than under a code-pleading system, mere conclusions are not enough. You must set forth *factual assertions* sufficient to support each claim.

C. Complaint

1. In General

In most jurisdictions, a civil action is commenced by the filing of the plaintiff's complaint. [Fed. R. Civ. P. 3; Cal. Civ. Proc. Code § 411.10] (In New York, an action is commenced by service of process; and the complaint can be filed thereafter.)

2. Form

The essential parts of the complaint are: the caption, jurisdictional allegations, body, prayer for relief, and subscription.

a. Caption

The complaint must set forth:

(i)   The *name* of the court;

(ii) The *number assigned* to the action (stamped by the clerk when the action is filed);

(iii) A *designation* of the pleading (*e.g.*, "Complaint for Damages"); and

(iv) The *names* of the parties.

[Fed. R. Civ. P. 10(a); Cal. Civ. Proc. Code §§ 422.30; 422.40]

(1) Note

Suing *"John Doe" defendants* is permitted in some states if the plaintiff does not know the true names of all the defendants. [*See, e.g.*, Cal. Civ. Proc. Code § 474]

(a) Caution—"Doe" Defendants Questionable in Federal Court

Due to subject-matter jurisdiction concerns, use of Doe defendants may not be allowed in cases based on diversity jurisdiction. (*See supra*, p. 72)

(2) Effect of Errors

Under modern rules, pleadings "must be construed so as to do justice." [Fed. R. Civ. P. 8(e)] Accordingly, the courts will disregard errors in the form or caption of the complaint that do not mislead the other party.

(a) Name of Party Wrong or Incomplete

An error or incompleteness in designating a party in the *complaint* is generally harmless error. However, if there is also error in the *summons* and as a result the intended defendant is not adequately warned that he is being sued, the action may be subject to dismissal for insufficient process.

b. Jurisdictional Allegations

In *federal* court, the complaint must contain allegations showing the ground (or grounds) upon which the subject-matter jurisdiction of the federal court is invoked. [Fed. R. Civ. P. 8(a)(1)] Since federal courts are courts of *limited* jurisdiction, a complaint that fails to set forth the jurisdictional grounds must be dismissed unless the ground can be supplied by amendment. (*See infra*, p. 192 *et seq.*)

 Example: If jurisdiction is founded on diversity of citizenship, a sufficient statement might be: "Plaintiff is a citizen of New York and Defendant is a citizen of California. The matter in controversy exceeds, exclusive of interest and costs, the sum of $75,000."

(1) Contrast—State Practice

Jurisdictional allegations generally are **not** required in state-court practice, because state courts usually have general subject-matter jurisdiction.

c. Body

The complaint must also contain a statement of the facts upon which recovery is sought. In code-pleading states, this requires a "statement of the (ultimate) facts constituting the cause of action" (*supra*, p. 139), while under the Federal Rules there must be a "short and plain statement of the claim showing that the pleader is entitled to relief" (*supra*, p. 141).

(1) Separate Claims

Each claim or cause of action should be set forth in a separate group of serially numbered paragraphs; and each paragraph should be limited to a statement of a single set of circumstances. [Fed. R. Civ. P. 10(b)]

(a) **Under code-pleading practice**, this was an essential requirement. A complaint that lumped together several causes of action was subject to demurrer.

(b) **Under modern law**, however, failure to state separate claims separately (*e.g.*, "First Cause of Action," "Second Cause of Action") is merely a formal defect—and is not even a basis of objection in some states (*e.g.*, California).

(c) **Under certain circumstances**, it may be important for the defendant to know exactly the grounds on which the plaintiff is proceeding (*e.g.*, when several different claims have been lumped together and the statute of limitations is different on each claim). In such cases, the defendant's remedy is to file a demurrer for uncertainty under code-pleading practice (*infra*, p. 153) or a motion for more definite statement under federal practice (*infra*, p. 163).

(2) Direct Allegations

The allegations in the complaint should be "simple, concise and direct." [Fed. R. Civ. P. 8(d)(1)]

(a) Recitals

It is improper to allege essential facts only by way of recitals (*e.g.*, an allegation that "Agent, **while acting as Defendant's agent**, executed a contract with Plaintiff"). The proper form is "At all times herein, Agent was the agent of Defendant. On or about _____, Agent made an agreement with Plaintiff."

(b) Exhibits

Essential allegations may appear in an exhibit attached to the complaint if **incorporated by reference** into the complaint. [Fed. R. Civ. P. 10(c)]

> **e.g.** **Example**: When the essential allegation is that P gave D notice to quit the premises by a certain date, P can attach a copy of the written notice as an exhibit to the complaint and incorporate it by reference therein. The date can then be ascertained from the exhibit.

(c) Consequences of Defect

Noncompliance with these rules of form is at most the basis for a *demurrer* or *motion* objecting to the defect. In modern practice, such defects are usually disregarded.

(3) Allegations on "Information and Belief"

Ordinarily, the plaintiff's allegations should be based on personal knowledge. However, if the plaintiff lacks personal knowledge of some element of his claim (*e.g.*, is relying on hearsay or conjecture), in *code-pleading states* the plaintiff may still make the allegation on "information and belief." "Information and belief" may be insufficient under the Federal Rules, however. In federal courts, allegations can be made only after reasonable inquiry and with a belief that the pleading is likely to have evidentiary support. [Fed. R. Civ. P. 11; *see infra*, p. 169 *et seq.*]

(a) Denials

Similarly, in code-pleading states, a defendant may *deny* allegations based on "lack of information and belief." [Cal. Civ. Proc. Code § 431.30] And under the Federal Rules, a statement that the defendant is "without knowledge or information sufficient to form a belief as to the truth of an averment" has the effect of a denial. [Fed. R. Civ. P. 8(b)(5)]

(b) Importance

The use of allegations on information and belief is important when a pleading is to be *verified* by a party (when the pleading party includes an affidavit that the pleading is true to the best of the pleader's knowledge; *see infra*, p. 148*)*, since the plaintiff should not swear that facts are true when she has no personal knowledge thereof.

(c) Limitation

Allegations on information and belief are improper as to matters which the pleader obviously knows or has *reason to know* (*e.g.*, events that she witnessed), or matters as to which she has *constructive knowledge* (*e.g.*, matters of *public record*). In such cases, pleadings on information and belief will be disregarded, leaving the complaint subject to a demurrer or motion to dismiss.

EXAM TIP   GILBERT

Exam questions will sometimes ask you to draft a complaint but tell you that your client has no personal knowledge regarding a necessary allegation. Generally this lack of information should not be a stumbling block. A complaint generally can include allegations based on *"information and belief"* (or in federal court, with a belief that the pleading is likely to have evidentiary support after a reasonable opportunity for further investigation or discovery). Similarly, an allegation can be denied in a code-pleading state based on *"lack of information or belief,"* or under the Federal Rules, on the basis the defendant *"lacks knowledge or information sufficient* to form a belief about the truth of an allegation." *But remember.* If the pleader should have personal knowledge of the matter (*e.g.*, it concerns an event the pleader witnessed), the above allegations may not properly be used.

---

(4) Alternative and Inconsistent Allegations

(a) Inconsistent Legal Theories

A plaintiff *may* properly allege facts based on inconsistent legal theories. Note that Federal Rule 11 may limit this latitude. (*See infra*, p. 169 *et seq.*)

e.g. **Example**: Plaintiff claims damages as the result of surgery performed on him by Dr. Defendant. Plaintiff may plead in one count that the surgery was performed without his informed consent (hence a battery) and alternatively, in a separate count, that the surgery was negligently performed. Plaintiff is entitled to go to trial on *both* theories, so that if the facts do not sustain one theory, they may sustain the other.

e.g. **Example**: Plaintiff claims that Defendant fraudulently induced him to execute a contract. Plaintiff may plead one count for damages based on the fraud and alternatively, in another count, seek rescission of the contract based on the fraud.

1) Limitation—Election of Remedies

However, while a plaintiff may go to trial on both theories and have a verdict on each, he will have to elect one theory *before judgment* because he cannot have two remedies (*e.g.*, duplicate damages) for the same injury. [**Savage v. Van Marie**, 39 Cal. App. 3d 241 (1974)]

a) Time of Election

The plaintiff is not required to make this election until *after* a jury verdict (or fact findings by the court) and before judgment. Otherwise, the plaintiff would have to guess which version of the facts will be sustained and thereby lose the benefit of alternative pleading. [**McCormick v. Kopmann**, 161 N.E.2d 720 (Ill. 1959)]

(b) Inconsistent Facts

A pleader is also permitted to plead inconsistent versions of the facts. [Fed. R. Civ. P. 8(d)(3)] However, some jurisdictions require that the facts alleged indicate some reason why the plaintiff could not know which version was true (*e.g.*, plaintiff was unconscious at the time of the injury, or injury-causing events occurred outside the pleader's observation).

(c) Alternative Defendants

The plaintiff can also plead one version of the facts against one defendant and another version against another defendant. Again, some jurisdictions require a reason why the plaintiff could not know which version is true.

e.g. **Example**: After Plaintiff's husband left a tavern operated by Defendant 2, he was killed in a head-on collision with a truck driven by Defendant 1. In her wrongful-death action, Plaintiff alleged that the accident was caused by the driving of Defendant 1, whom she alleged had crossed the center line. To recover from Defendant 1, Plaintiff had to prove that her husband was free of contributory negligence. But Plaintiff also asserted a claim against Defendant 2, alleging that the accident was caused by her husband's intoxication, which resulted from the drinking her husband did at Defendant 2's tavern. Under this version, Plaintiffs husband would have been guilty of contributory negligence in connection with the crash. [**McCormick v. Kopmann**, *supra*]

 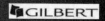
If you are asked to draft a pleading on an exam question, remember that it may include *alternative and inconsistent allegations*. For example, suppose your client in the question tells you facts regarding a contract dispute, and you think the facts support an argument that your client was fraudulently induced into making the contract, and they also support an argument that the other party did not fully perform. The fraud argument essentially seeks to negate the validity of the contract, while the performance argument admits there is a contract, but makes a claim for the other party's failure to perform. Even though these theories are inconsistent, they may be pleaded in the alternative. Similarly, pleadings can make inconsistent factual allegations in different claims if there is some reason why your client might not know which version is true.

---

(5) Defenses Need Not Be Anticipated

Ordinarily, the plaintiff is not required in the complaint to anticipate any defense that the defendant may raise.

(a) Comparison—Well-Pleaded Complaint Rule

The rule regarding anticipating defenses corresponds to the well-pleaded complaint rule for federal-question subject-matter jurisdiction (*supra*, p. 84), which provides that the existence of a federal defense is not considered in deciding whether a plaintiff's claim arises under federal law.

(b) Reply to Affirmative Defense

Although it is not automatically required, a court may order a plaintiff to reply to an answer. [Fed. R. Civ. P. 7(a)(7)] The Supreme Court has observed that requiring a reply may be appropriate in some circumstances [**Crawford-El v. Britton,** 523 U.S. 574 (1998)], and the Fifth Circuit requires trial courts to order that plaintiffs reply to officials' defenses of qualified immunity. [*See* **Reyes v. Sazan,** 168 F.3d 158 (5th Cir. 1999)—district court abused its discretion in failing to require plaintiffs to file reply to defendant's answer containing defense of qualified immunity].

d. Prayer for Relief

A complaint must also contain a prayer for relief, *i.e.*, a statement of the relief sought.

(1) In Default Cases

If the defendant defaults by failing to defend, the relief granted cannot exceed what is prayed for in the complaint or differ from it in kind (*e.g.*, an injunction when the prayer was only for damages). *Rationale*: By failing to appear and contest the action, the defendant has, in effect, acquiesced in the entry of judgment against her; but the judgment entered must conform to the "consent" given. [Fed. R. Civ. P. 54(c); Cal. Civ. Proc. Code § 580; *infra*, p. 201 *et seq.*] Also, when a defendant is considering default, protecting her against liability greater than or different from the relief sought in the complaint gives her an incentive not to contest a case that isn't worth contesting. Otherwise, she might conclude she had to show up not because she had any defenses worth pursuing but just to be sure she wouldn't be ambushed by an award of relief prejudicially differing from that sought in the complaint.

(2) In Contested Cases

In a contested case, the plaintiff is **not** limited to the relief prayed for in the complaint. The court may award **any relief to which a party is entitled** under the pleadings and proof—even if different from or greater than that prayed for in the complaint. [Fed. R. Civ. P. 54(c); Cal. Civ. Proc. Code § 580]

EXAM TIP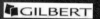

The distinction between damages available in a default case versus a contested case is sometimes tested on law-school exams. Remember that in federal court and in most states in a default case, damages **cannot exceed those asked for in the complaint** because that is what the defendant declined to resist by defaulting. It would be unfair to let a party default when the plaintiff was seeking $1,000 damages and then allow the plaintiff to recover $10,000, for if the defendant knew $10,000 was at stake, she might have defended the action. On the other hand, if the defendant defends and the plaintiff proves damages in excess of those asked for in the complaint, the defendant can't complain, for she had an opportunity to be heard.

(a) Limitation

In a few states, a plaintiff is not permitted to state the amount of his demand in **personal-injury or wrongful-death actions**. [Cal. Civ. Proc. Code § 425.10(b)] *Rationale*: This rule is intended to prevent sensational publicity for large demands. (However, the plaintiff must provide a statement of the damages claimed if the defendant demands one; in any event, such a statement must be made before trial.)

(b) Caution

Some decisions hold that when the complaint alleges **specific amounts** of damages, the allegations may be treated as **binding admissions** with respect to the amount of damage sustained. Hence, it may be error to award a greater sum; and such a judgment may be reduced accordingly. [**Brown v. North Ventura Road Co.,** 216 Cal. App. 2d 227 (1963)]

1) Trial Tactic

When evidence at trial indicates that the verdict may exceed the damages pleaded, the plaintiff should seek leave of court to **amend** the damage allegations and prayer upward. Doing so may prevent the problem noted above. (Note that pleadings may be amended even after trial; *see infra*, p. 200.)

(3) Other Functions of Prayer

The prayer is ordinarily determinative of the **amount in controversy** for purposes of federal subject-matter jurisdiction. (*See supra*, p. 74 *et seq*.) In state courts, it may also determine the nature of the action (legal or equitable) on which the **right to jury trial** depends.

e. Subscription

The complaint must be signed by the attorney (or by the party himself, when he is acting as his own counsel). [Fed. R. Civ. P. 11; Cal. Civ. Proc. Code § 446]

(1) Effect of Signature—Federal Practice

In federal practice, the signature on a pleading by a party or his attorney constitutes a certification by him that to the best of his knowledge, information, and belief, formed after reasonable inquiry, the evidentiary contentions have evidentiary support or are likely to have such support after a reasonable opportunity for further investigation or discovery. The signature also certifies that the claims or defenses are warranted by existing law or a nonfrivolous argument for change in existing law, and that the claim or defense is not being presented for any improper purpose such as harassment, unnecessary delay, or needlessly increasing costs. [Fed. R. Civ. P. 11(b)(1)–(3); *see infra*, p. 169 *et seq.*]

(2) Verification

A verification is an affidavit at the end of a pleading which avers that the pleading is true to the best of affiant's knowledge, information, or belief. The affidavit is made by the party, or by an attorney or other person on her behalf if the pleader cannot do so (*e.g.*, because she is incapacitated), or if another person with better knowledge of the facts is willing to make the verification for the party.

(a) Federal Practice

In view of the importance attached to an attorney's subscription in federal practice (above), verification by a party is the exception rather than the rule in federal courts. Federal Rule 11 expressly provides that pleadings need ***not*** be verified except when specifically required by rule or statute.

 Example: The Federal Rules specifically require verification in shareholders' derivative suits. [Fed. R. Civ. P. 23.1]

(b) State Practice

Some code pleading rules provide that any pleading ***may*** be verified; and verification is frequently required by statute as to certain kinds of proceedings (*e.g.*, quiet-title actions, unlawful-detainer proceedings, divorce suits).

1) Effect of Verification

If a pleading is verified, the responsive pleading must also be verified (*i.e.*, if Plaintiff files a verified complaint, Defendant's answer ***must*** be verified by Defendant). Moreover, a defendant cannot use a mere general denial (*infra*, p. 176) in answering a verified complaint. [Cal. Civ. Proc. Code § 431.30(d)]

2) How to Attack Lack of Verification

If a pleading required to be verified is not verified, the pleading is subject to a ***motion to strike*** (*infra*, p. 156).

A COMPLAINT GENERALLY MUST INCLUDE THE FOLLOWING:
☑ **Caption** (name of court, number assigned to action, designation of pleading, names of parties)
☑ Allegations of **subject-matter jurisdiction** [in federal but usually not state court]
☑ Allegations of **facts upon which recovery is sought**
☑ **Prayer for relief**
☑ **Signature** of attorney or unrepresented party.

f. Form Complaints

In many jurisdictions, form complaints are published for types of complaints that are commonly made.

3. Splitting of Claims

A pleader cannot split a single claim or cause of action into several different parts and file separate suits on each one. If the plaintiff sues on only part of the claim he has against the defendant, he is barred from suing later on the balance. This effect results from the doctrine of **claim preclusion**, *i.e.*, that a judgment on any portion of a single claim merges the claim into the judgment, so that there is nothing left on which to sue (*see* Chapter Eleven). When judgment has not been entered, and two cases are pending, attacks on the pleadings are possible.

a. Obvious Splitting

If the plaintiff is proceeding in two separate actions and the splitting appears **on the face** of either complaint (unlikely), some states permit a special demurrer on the ground that "there is another action pending between the same parties for the same cause." [Cal. Civ. Proc. Code § 430.10(c)]

b. Splitting Not Obvious

More frequently, the splitting will not appear on the face of either complaint, in which case the objection must be raised by the defendant in her answer (again, on the ground that another action is pending between the same parties for the same claim).

4. Joinder of Claims

a. No Compulsory Joinder of Separate Claims

While claim preclusion may prompt the plaintiff to bring suit upon her entire claim or cause of action (above), there is **no** requirement that she join in a single action what are separate and independent claims. Even when the claims are factually related, the plaintiff has the option of instituting a separate suit on each separate claim although, as a practical matter, plaintiffs usually join related claims because of the dangers of **claim preclusion or issue preclusion**. (*See infra*, p. 453 *et seq*.)

b. Permissive Joinder of Claims

(1) Early Common-Law Rules

At common law, the joinder of separate claims was permitted only if all claims were in the same *form of action* and there was *identity* of parties to each claim.

e.g. **Example**: Slander could be joined with nuisance or negligent infliction of bodily injury because both claims had the same form of action (*i.e.*, trespass on the case). Moreover, joinder was permitted regardless of whether there was any factual relationship between these claims.

cf. **Compare**: A claim for slander (trespass on the case) could not be joined with one for assault and battery (trespass)—even when both claims arose out of the same event—because the two claims involved different forms of action.

(2) Equity Rules

In equity suits, it was generally sufficient if the claim arose out of the same transaction or transactions and involved a common question of law or fact—*i.e.*, a requirement of subject-matter relationship.

(3) Code-Pleading Rules

Under the original Field Code, a plaintiff was restricted as to the causes of action that could be joined in a single complaint. All causes joined had to be the *same type* of claim (*e.g.*, all for injury to person, for injury to property, or all contract claims, etc.), or at least arise out of the same transaction; all such causes had to affect all parties to the action; and no cause could require a venue different from the others.

(a) Criticism

These rules frequently prevented a plaintiff from settling all claims against a defendant in a single action, and drastically restricted permissive joinder of parties (because *all* causes joined had to affect *all* parties). In effect, the rules fostered a multiplicity of suits.

(b) Note

To remedy this situation, many code-pleading states have now adopted rules similar to the more liberal Federal Rule on joinder, below. [*See* Cal. Civ. Proc. Code § 427.10]

(4) Federal Rules

The modern viewpoint on joinder of claims is represented by Federal Rule 18(a), which *abolishes all restrictions* on the joinder of claims and provides that a party asserting a claim for relief may join as many claims as she has against an opposing party, regardless of subject matter.

On your exam, remember that a party may assert as many claims as she has against an opposing party, even if the claims are unrelated. This joinder opportunity may be especially important if the plaintiff sues in federal court relying on diversity jurisdiction, for it means that if plaintiff has a $60,000 contract claim against a particular person and a $50,000 tort claim **against the same person** arising from a separate transaction, he can join the actions to meet the jurisdictional amount requirements.

(a) Limitation in Multiparty Cases

While there are no restrictions on the number or nature of claims that may be joined when a *single* plaintiff is suing a *single* defendant, the rules on joinder of parties impose limitations when there are several co-plaintiffs or co-defendants. When there are multiple parties, *at least one* of the claims by or against each party must arise out of "the same transaction, occurrence, or series of transactions and occurrences" *and* must involve a "common question of law or fact" affecting each of the parties joined. [Fed. R. Civ. P. 20(a)]

1) Effect

The party-joinder rules thus limit the joinder of claims in multiparty cases to those among which there is a *subject-matter relationship*.

Example: Plaintiff may sue Defendant 1 and Defendant 2 for personal injuries sustained in a three-car collision, asserting claims against both Defendant 1 and Defendant 2 because the same occurrence is involved. Plaintiff may also join a separate claim she has against Defendant 2 for nonpayment of a promissory note, even though this claim does not affect Defendant 1 in any way, because there are common questions of law affecting Defendant 1 and Defendant 2 in the personal-injury claims.

(b) Separate Trials

In its discretion, the trial court may remedy any possible inconvenience or prejudice caused by the joinder of claims by ordering separate trials. [Fed. R. Civ. R 20(b), 42(b)]

1) Distinguish

If the claims are brought in *separate suits* before the same court, but have related subject matter, the defendant may move to have the trials *consolidated*. [Fed. R. Civ. P. 42(a), *infra*]

(c) Distinguish—Subject-Matter Jurisdiction

In federal court, subject-matter jurisdiction requirements must also be satisfied. For claims that arise out of the same transaction, there would ordinarily be *supplemental jurisdiction* (*see supra*, pp. 93–98) as long as one claim is a federal claim, but otherwise there must be an independent basis for subject-matter jurisdiction (such as diversity of citizenship) with regard to permissively joined claims. That a federal joinder rule says that a claim or party may be joined **does not override** the requirement that federal subject-matter jurisdiction—which may be supplemental in addition to original—must exist.

5. Consolidation of Separate Actions

The trial judge has the power to order separate lawsuits tried together or have them consolidated into a single action if they involve a "common question of law or fact." [Fed. R. Civ. P. 42(a); Cal. Civ. Proc. Code § 1048(a)]

a. Actions Pending in Different Courts

If separate actions involving related facts are pending in different courts, many jurisdictions permit one or more of the actions to be **transferred** so they can be consolidated or joined for trial in the same court. The cases may be transferred in whole or in part.

(1) State Procedure

Transfer in state courts may be ordered when it will promote the just and efficient control of the various cases involved, and may involve transfer of the whole action or only certain issues (*e.g.*, liability). [Cal. Civ. Proc. Code § 404]

(2) Federal Practice

Federal "multidistrict" litigation may be consolidated in one district for all **pretrial** purposes (development of issues, discovery, pretrial conference). [28 U.S.C. § 1407] However, the parties have a right to **trial** in the district where the action was filed unless the action was transferred to another district where it "might have been brought." [28 U.S.C. § 1404(a); *see supra*, p. 42 *et seq.*]

D. Challenges to Complaint

1. In General

Before responding to the factual allegations in the plaintiff's complaint (by admitting or denying them, or setting forth some defense or offset thereto), a defendant may challenge the legal sufficiency of the complaint.

2. Common Law

At common law, defects in the pleadings could be raised by a demurrer. There were two kinds of demurrer:

a. General Demurrer

A general demurrer challenged **the substantive sufficiency** of the cause or causes in the complaint. It did not specifically state the reason for demurring, but asked the court to pause (demur) and look at the complaint to see if it stated a valid case. Otherwise, why prolong the proceeding? This is still the basic idea of a general demurrer.

b. Special Demurrer

This common-law demurrer **specially stated** a matter to be scrutinized in the complaint— *e.g.*, incapacity of plaintiff, allegations that were too vague, etc. Hence, the special demurrer challenged **matters of form**.

3. State Practice

The Field Code, as adopted in states such as California, preserved the demurrer. In other states, such as New York, a motion to dismiss or (when the objection is that the pleading is vague) a motion to make more definite and certain is used instead. (*See infra*, p. 163.) However, the functions of these challenges are similar.

a. Demurrer

A demurrer is a pleading filed by one party for the purpose of challenging the *legal sufficiency* of the other party's pleading.

(1) Pleadings Subject to Demurrer

The most frequent use of the demurrer is to challenge the plaintiff's complaint. However, the plaintiff may demur to an affirmative defense, counterclaim, or cross-complaint filed by the defendant.

(2) Grounds for Demurrer

The grounds for demurrer usually include the following [Cal. Civ. Proc. Code § 430.10]:

(a) *Lack of jurisdiction over the subject* of the action (note that lack of *personal* jurisdiction usually must be challenged by a motion to quash because a demurrer constitutes a "general appearance," which would have the effect of waiving the personal-jurisdiction challenge);

(b) *The plaintiff lacks legal capacity* to sue;

(c) *Another action is pending* between the same parties for the same cause;

(d) *Defect or misjoinder* of parties;

(e) *Failure to state facts sufficient to constitute a cause of action*—the "general demurrer" (below);

(f) *Complaint is uncertain* (ambiguous, unintelligible); *and*

(g) In an action upon a contract, *inability to ascertain whether the contract is oral or written*.

(3) "General" vs. "Special" Demurrer

A demurrer for failure to plead facts sufficient to constitute a cause of action is considered a "general" demurrer. A demurrer on any other ground is a "special" demurrer.

(a) Issue

In ruling on a general demurrer, the court must accept all facts pleaded as though they were true. The issue is whether—assuming that the well-pleaded facts are true—*the facts would entitle the plaintiff to some form of judicial relief*.

(b) Standard

If the complaint alleges facts sufficient to constitute *some* valid cause of action, the general demurrer will be overruled. The test is whether the complaint sets forth *any* good cause of action.

(4) Defect Appearing on Face of Complaint

The demurrer challenges only defects that appear on the face of the pleading or matters of which the court can take *judicial notice* (well-known facts or facts that can readily and reliably be confirmed by resort to, *e.g.*, an almanac; *see* Evidence Summary). A demurrer *cannot* be used to introduce facts to controvert what is alleged in the pleading; *i.e.*, "speaking demurrers" are not allowed.

(a) Note

For this reason, certain grounds of demurrer—*e.g.*, a plaintiff's lack of legal capacity or nonjoinder of parties—are rarely sustained. Such defects rarely appear on the face of the plaintiff's complaint and thus must be raised by motion (*see* below) or by affirmative defense in the answer.

(b) But Note

When the plaintiff's own allegations disclose some *complete defense* (*e.g.*, running of statute of limitations) *on the face of the complaint*, a general demurrer will lie unless the plaintiff has somehow "pleaded around" the defense.

(5) Procedure

A demurrer usually must be filed within the time permitted to answer the complaint. (*See infra*, p. 183.) The defendant may choose to demur and answer at the same time—as when the demurrer goes to only one portion of the complaint.

(a) Demurrer Must Specify Defect

The defendant's demurrer must be in writing and must specify the ground for objection. Unless it does so, it may be disregarded. [Cal. Civ. Proc. Code § 430.60]

> **e.g.** **Example**: "Plaintiff's complaint fails to state a cause of action in that it does not allege what consideration, if any, was given for Defendant's promise" is a sufficient demurrer.

(6) Ruling on Demurrer—Effects

(a) Ruling Limited to Grounds Raised

Usually, the court has no power to raise grounds for demurrer on its own; its ruling must be based on the grounds raised by the demurring party.

1) Exception

However, the court may always raise lack of subject-matter jurisdiction and the question whether the pleading alleges facts sufficient to constitute a cause of action.

(b) When Demurrer Is Overruled

If the demurrer is overruled, the defendant will be ordered to answer the complaint within a period of time designated by the court. The defendant will then have to make a decision either to: (i) file an answer; or (ii) refuse to do so, allow the plaintiff to obtain a *default* judgment, and appeal the default judgment.

1) *If the defendant files an answer*, she *waives* any error in the overruling of a *special* demurrer. However, the defendant retains the right to object that the complaint does not state a cause of action.

2) *If the defendant does not file an answer* and appeals the resulting default judgment, she takes a big risk: An appellate court will not reverse unless the judgment was so plainly erroneous as to constitute an "abuse of discretion." [**Hu v. Fang,** 104 Cal. App. 4th 61 (2002)]

(c) When Demurrer Is Sustained

1) Specify Grounds

In some states, the court must specify the particular ground or grounds upon which the demurrer is sustained. [Cal. Civ. Proc. Code § 472d]

2) Leave to Amend

Having sustained the demurrer, the court normally grants the plaintiff *leave to amend* the complaint.

a) *If the court is convinced that the defect cannot be cured* by amendment (especially when the plaintiff has already tried unsuccessfully to amend), it may sustain the demurrer *without leave to amend*. In that event, a *judgment of dismissal* is entered (from which the plaintiff can appeal).

b) *If the plaintiff is granted leave to amend and amends* the complaint within the time permitted, the defendant again has the choice of answering or demurring to the amended complaint.

c) *If the plaintiff chooses not to amend* (or fails to amend within the time permitted), a judgment of dismissal will be entered. The plaintiff can then obtain appellate review; but the appellate court will affirm the dismissal if:

1/ The complaint was *defective in substance*, even though the trial judge was incorrect as to the ground on which it was defective [*see, e.g.*, **Friendly Village Community Association v. Silva & Hill Construction Co.,** 31 Cal. App. 3d 220 (1973)]; *or*

2/ The complaint was *defective in form and the party failed to use an opportunity* given him in the trial court *to clarify* his pleading [*see, e.g.*, **Cooper v. Leslie Salt Co.,** 70 Cal. 2d 627 (1969)]. *Note*: Appellate courts do sometimes give plaintiffs a second chance to amend in this situation. [*See, e.g.*, **Gillispie v. Goodyear Service Stores,** 128 S.E.2d 762 (N.C. 1963)— remand to allow plaintiff to replead]

(7) Effect of Failure to Raise Ground for Demurrer

Grounds for demurrer are *waived* unless raised in the defendant's *initial pleading*—demurrer *or answer*. (When the defect does not appear on the face of the complaint—*e.g.*, a plaintiff's lack of capacity to sue—it will, of course, have to be raised in the answer.) [Cal. Civ. Proc. Code § 430.80]

(a) Exceptions

Failure to state facts sufficient to constitute a cause of action and the court's *lack of subject-matter jurisdiction* are never waived. These objections can be raised at any time. [Cal. Civ. Proc. Code § 430.80]

(b) Waiver of Objections to Personal Jurisdiction and Process

Since a general demurrer constitutes an appearance in the action, it results in a waiver of objections to *personal* jurisdiction and to sufficiency of process. *Note*: In some code-pleading states, a defendant may be able to preserve objections to personal jurisdiction even though he files a demurrer, by simultaneously filing a motion to quash service of process. [Cal. Civ. Proc. Code § 418.10(e)(1)]

(8) Criticism of Demurrers

Modern writers generally condemn the demurrer as encouraging dilatory tactics by the defendant. Although a general demurrer undoubtedly serves a valuable function in weeding out claims without any legal basis, demurrers that merely attack the form of the complaint can be used for the sole purpose of delay, and thus perpetuate technical objections and technical rules of pleading.

b. Motion to Strike

In code pleading the only other challenge usually permitted against the form or contents of a pleading is a motion to strike, which normally lies to reach defects not subject to demurrer. Filing a motion to strike *extends the time within which to answer* the complaint. This effect enables the defendant to obtain a court order striking improper allegations from the complaint before being obliged to answer them. [Cal. Civ. Proc. Code § 435(c)]

(1) Formal Defects

The usual grounds for a motion to strike are that the pleading attacked contains *irrelevant or redundant matter* (*e.g.*, evidentiary matters or conclusions of law) or has some *defect in form* that is not a ground for demurrer (*e.g.*, lack of verification or subscription, late filing).

(2) Substantive Defects

A motion to strike can also be used to eliminate *part* of a claim that is otherwise valid (*e.g.*, punitive damages sought in a suit for breach of contract). [**Brunius v. Parrish,** 132 Cal. App. 4th 838 (2005)]

4. Federal Practice

The Federal Rules have deemphasized pleadings (*see supra*, p. 141), and accordingly limit the form and manner in which pleadings can be attacked.

a. Motion to Dismiss

Under the Federal Rules, the motion to dismiss is the basic challenge to the legal sufficiency of adversary pleadings. [Fed. R. Civ. P. 12(b)] Making such a motion is *always optional* with the defendant, since he can raise the same objections in his answer (below).

(1) Permissible Grounds

The motion to dismiss can be made *only* on the following grounds (with any other defenses or objections raised in the answer):

(a) *Lack of jurisdiction over the subject matter;*

(b) *Lack of jurisdiction over the person;*

(c) *Improper venue;*

(d) *Insufficiency of process;*

(e) *Insufficiency of service* of process;

(f) *Failure to state a claim* upon which relief can be granted; and

(g) *Failure to join a party whose joinder is required by Rule 19* (necessary or indispensable parties).

GILBERT	
TYPICAL GROUNDS FOR DEMURRER	**GROUNDS TO DISMISS UNDER FEDERAL RULE 12(b)**
Lack of subject-matter jurisdiction	Lack of subject-matter jurisdiction
Plaintiff lacks capacity to sue	Lack of jurisdiction over the person
Another action is pending	Improper venue
Defect or misjoinder of parties	Insufficiency of process
Failure to state sufficient facts	Insufficiency of service
Complaint uncertain	Failure to state a claim upon which relief can be granted
Inability to ascertain whether contract was oral or written	Failure to join a party whose joinder is required

(2) Failure to State a Claim

When the motion is made under Federal Rule 12(b)(6) (failure to state a claim), its function is basically that of a general demurrer (*supra*, p. 153): Assuming the facts pleaded are true, do they constitute a legal claim upon which the plaintiff is entitled to judicial relief?

(a) Test for Sufficiency of Complaint

In testing the sufficiency of the complaint in connection with a Rule 12(b)(6) motion, the following principles are generally applied.

1) "Facts" Not Explicitly Required

The complaint generally need not contain the ultimate facts; Federal Rule 8(a)(2) requires only a "short and plain statement of the claim showing that the pleader is entitled to relief."

2) Liberal Standard for Sufficiency

The Supreme Court stated in 1957 that the complaint should not be dismissed unless the court is certain that the plaintiff can prove no set of facts in support of his claim that would entitle him to relief. [**Conley v. Gibson,** *supra*, p. 141]

e.g. **Example**: A complaint charging "slanderous utterances" by Defendant was held sufficient notwithstanding its failure to state, in so many words, that there had been a ***publication*** of the alleged defamations, because that could fairly be inferred from the allegations made. [**Garcia v. Hilton Hotels,** 97 F. Supp. 5 (D.P.R. 1951)]

a) New Standard—Plausible

However, in 2007 the Court declared that the "no set of facts" directive should be "retired" because a complaint in federal court must show affirmatively that the plaintiff's factual allegations make the plaintiff's entitlement to relief "plausible." [**Bell Atlantic Corp. v. Twombly,** *supra*, p. 141] The requirement of plausibility does not mean that a pleaded claim must meet a standard of probability, but mere conclusory allegations or speculative possibility does not suffice. To show "that the pleader is entitled to relief" as required by Federal Rule 8(a)(2), the claim must include "factual content that allows the court to draw the reasonable inference that the defendant is liable for the misconduct alleged." In making that determination, the court is to disregard "mere conclusory statements": then the court is to apply to the remaining factual allegations the tenet that it is to accept those allegations as true in making the plausibility determination. [**Ashcroft v. Iqbal,** 556 U.S. 662 (2009)]

b) Code-Pleading Standard Compared

Nevertheless, the federal standard is more lenient than the requirements imposed by many state courts under code pleading. For example, former Form 9 of the Federal Rules stated that the following was sufficient to allege negligence: "Defendant negligently drove a motor vehicle against plaintiff." This form relaxed the requirement in some code states that the plaintiff specify the underlying failure of the defendant upon which the claim of negligence was based. The Supreme Court emphasized this form in 2002 in upholding a complaint challenged on a motion to dismiss. [**Swierkiewicz v. Sorema, N.A.,** 534 U.S. 506 (2002)]

3) Continuing Need to Set out Factual Matter

Despite the absence of a specific requirement for allegations of fact in the rules, the plaintiff's complaint must contain factual matter sufficient to show that the plaintiff is entitled to relief against the defendant.

e.g. **Example**: Plaintiffs making an antitrust claim that Defendant providers of local telephone services entered into an agreement to exclude other companies from competition, and also agreed not to compete with each other in providing local telephone services, failed to state a claim for relief. Although Plaintiffs made a conclusory allegation that

Defendants had reached such an agreement, their factual allegations did not make their conclusion of conspiracy plausible. [**Bell Atlantic Corp. v. Twombly**, *supra*, p. 141]

 **Example**: A Pakistani Muslim detained after the September 11 attacks did not state a claim against the Attorney General of the United States and the Director of the FBI for mistreatment while he was in custody. Although plaintiff's claims against prison personnel who allegedly mistreated him appeared sufficient, the factual allegations regarding the Attorney General and FBI Director provided no plausible basis for concluding that these defendants adopted policies for the purpose of discriminating on grounds of religion or national origin. Plaintiff's conclusory allegations of conspiracy did not suffice. [**Ashcroft v. Iqbal**, *supra*]

EXAM TIP  **GILBERT**

It is important to remember the function of a Rule 12(b)(6) motion to dismiss for failure to state a claim. The court will look at the complaint, **assume the facts are true** (provided the complaint sets out sufficient facts to outline the claim), and assess whether, even if all the facts are true, the complaint supports a legal claim that would entitle the plaintiff to relief. If a sufficient claim is not set out, the court is to grant the motion.

---

4) Perfect Statement of Legal Theory Not Required

Although the *factual* allegations must include facts sufficient to show substantive plausibility, a complaint may not be dismissed for imperfect statement of the legal theory supporting the claim asserted. [**Johnson v. City of Shelby**, 135 S. Ct. 346 (2014) (per curiam)—plaintiffs' failure to invoke 42 U.S.C. § 1983 in their complaint did not provide a valid ground for dismissing, given that plaintiffs did adequately provide factual allegations making their claim plausible]

5) Fraud or Mistake

When claims are based on fraud or mistake, the Federal Rules require the plaintiff to plead *"with particularity."* [Fed. R. Civ. P. 9(b)]

a) Claims Affected

This requirement of added specificity applies only when the substantive right to relief depends on proof of fraud or mistake. Examples include common-law fraud, securities fraud, and actions to rescind or modify a contract for mutual mistake. *Rationale*: Courts explain that the added specificity is important to provide added notice and that it protects defendants against unfounded claims that damage their reputations. However, it is difficult to understand why the claims covered give rise to especially troubling problems compared with other claims not covered by the rule.

b) Application

Courts usually look to whether the plaintiff has provided specifics concerning the date and content of representations on which a fraud claim is based. In cases involving multiple defendants, it may be necessary for the plaintiff to specify the involvement of each one that allegedly gives rise to liability, sometimes requiring very great detail. However, some courts say that to satisfy Rule 9(b), the plaintiff need provide only "slightly more" than that which is required by Rule 8(a)(2). [*See*, *e.g.*, **Tomera v. Galt,** 511 F.2d 594 (7th Cir. 1975)]

c) State of Mind

Rule 9(b) also provides that "[m]alice, intent, knowledge, and other condition of mind" can be *averred generally*. This exempts all allegations on these subjects from the particularity requirement of the rule. Nevertheless, some courts apply the particularity requirement to allegations relating to state of mind. [*See*, *e.g.*, **Ross v. A.H. Robins Co.,** 607 F.2d 545 (2d Cir. 1980)—in securities-fraud action, plaintiffs required to plead facts giving rise to a "strong inference" that defendants knew falsity of their statements]

d) Requirements of Private Securities Litigation Reform Act

Under the Private Securities Litigation Reform Act ("PSLRA"), most federal securities-fraud claims must "specify each statement alleged to have been misleading, the reason or reasons why the statement is misleading" and, if the defendant is liable only for acting with a certain state of mind (*e.g.*, knowledge or intent), "state with particularity facts giving rise to a strong inference that the defendant acted with the required state of mind." [15 U.S.C. § 78u–4(b)] Under this standard, plaintiffs must include factual allegations that make the inference of scienter cogent and compelling, and at least as strong as any other inference that could be drawn from the factual allegations. [**Tellabs, Inc. v. Makor Issues & Rights, Ltd.,** 551 U.S. 308 (2007)]

Example: Plaintiffs adequately alleged that defendant pharmaceutical company acted with scienter when it failed to disclose a possible link between its leading cold product and loss of smell, even though they did not allege that defendant knew of a statistically significant number of adverse events involving the product. Although in many instances reasonable investors would not consider adverse-event reports to be material information, this product accounted for approximately 70% of defendant's sales, and the complaint alleged facts that plausibly suggested that reasonable investors would have viewed these reports as material. The complaint included specifics about numerous reports to defendant about loss of smell resulting from use of its product; thereafter defendant nonetheless stated that this product was "poised for growth in the coming cough and cold season," and that the company had "very strong momentum." [**Matrixx Initiatives, Inc. v. Siracusano,** 563 U.S. 27 (2011)]

6) Heightened Specificity for Other Types of Claims

With regard to certain other types of claims, some federal courts have developed pleading requirements that seem to go beyond the liberality of *Conley*.

a) Civil Rights Claims

The most prominent examples are *civil rights claims*. In such claims, courts often insist that plaintiffs allege with specificity the basis for their belief that the defendants acted with forbidden animus. [*See, e.g.,* **Fisher v. Flynn,** 598 F.2d 663 (1st Cir. 1979)—requiring employment discrimination plaintiff to plead basis for believing that firing was in retaliation for her rejection of supervisor's sexual overtures; **Albany Welfare Rights Organization Day Care Center, Inc. v. Schreck,** 463 F.2d 620 (2d Cir. 1972)—plaintiff required to plead basis for believing that defendant officials refused to deal with plaintiff in retaliation for plaintiff's political activities]

b) Other Claims "Analogous" to Fraud

Lower courts have also found that more stringent pleading requirements are appropriate in cases that involve contentions or litigation problems "analogous" to fraud. [*See, e.g.,* **Chiron Corp. v. Abbott Laboratories,** 156 F.R.D. 219 (N.D. Cal. 1994)—particularized pleading required for defense of inequitable conduct by plaintiff in obtaining patent in suit; **Cash Energy, Inc. v. Weiner,** 768 F. Supp. 892 (D. Mass. 1991)—more specific pleading required for claims made personally against corporate officers in environmental-cleanup suit]

c) Qualified Immunity

Another area in which lower courts have required that plaintiffs plead with more specificity are cases in which *government officials* claim qualified immunity against suit. [**Elliott v. Perez,** 751 F.2d 1472 (5th Cir. 1985)—in cases against government officials involving the likely defense of immunity, trial judges must demand that the plaintiff's complaint state with factual detail and particularity the basis for the claim, including why the defendant-official cannot successfully maintain the defense of immunity]

d) Stimulus for Heightened Pleading Requirements

The motivation for this intensification of pleadings scrutiny is *concern about the settlement value of frivolous or groundless claims.* [*See, e.g.,* **Blue Chip Stamps v. Manor Drug Stores,** 421 U.S. 723 (1975)—Court stated that the liberal discovery provisions can give complaints with little chance of success on the merits a disproportionately high settlement value to plaintiff, as long as he can prevent suit from being resolved against him by dismissal]

e) Supreme Court Disapproval of Heightened Specificity Requirements

The Supreme Court has held that in cases not covered by Rule 9(b) the lower courts may *not* impose heightened specificity requirements, but it has also held that giving adequate notice in a complaint can require specifics.

 Example: It was improper to require more specifics from a Hungarian plaintiff who asserted that his French employer engaged in discrimination on grounds of age and national origin, alleging that the employer said he wanted to "energize" the firm and promoted a younger, inexperienced French employee over the plaintiff, who had wide experience in the industry. The lower court had required that the plaintiff plead the facts required to make a prima facie showing of discrimination, but the Supreme Court held that this evidentiary standard did not have to be satisfied at the pleading stage, noting that Rule 9(b) does not apply to employment-discrimination cases. [**Swierkiewicz v. Sorema, N.A.**, 534 U.S. 506 (2002)]

e.g. **Example**: It was improper to require Plaintiffs suing local law enforcement officers to satisfy heightened specificity requirements regarding qualified immunity, because the claims are not governed by Rule 9(b). [**Leatherman v. Tarrant County Narcotics Intelligence & Coordination Unit,** 507 U.S. 163(1993)]

cf. **Compare**: Plaintiffs making an antitrust claim that Defendant providers of local telephone services entered into an agreement to exclude other companies from competition, and also agreed not to compete with each other in providing local telephone services, failed to state a claim for relief. Although Plaintiffs made a conclusory allegation that Defendants had reached such an agreement, their factual allegations did not make their conclusion of illegal conspiracy plausible given the alternative of conscious but nonconspiratorial parallel action, which is not unlawful. [**Bell Atlantic Corp. v. Twombly,** *supra*, p. 141]

cf. **Compare**: In a securities-fraud action, Plaintiffs asserted that the value of the shares they bought was improperly inflated due to Defendants' misrepresentations about the company's financial condition and prospects. Although Plaintiffs alleged that share values had fallen almost 50% after the company announced that its earnings would be disappointing, the Court held that they did not adequately allege "loss causation"—that the decline in the share price was due to the misrepresentations. The Court held that Rule 8(a)(2) required more to give "fair notice of what that plaintiff's claim is and the grounds on which it rests." [**Dura Pharmaceuticals, Inc. v. Broudno,** 544 U.S. 336 (2005)]

f) **Alternative of Requiring Reply or Entertaining Motion for More Definite Statement**

The Supreme Court has stated that in suits involving claims against public officials that require proof of wrongful motive, a district court "must exercise its discretion in a way that protects the substance of the qualified immunity defense . . . so that officials are not subjected to unnecessary and burdensome discovery or trial proceedings." A court has "two primary options" before permitting discovery: (i) "the court may order a reply to the defendant's or a third party's answer under Federal Rule of Civil Procedure 7(a)," or (ii) the court may "grant the defendant's motion for a more definite statement under Rule 12(e)." In this latter connection, "the court may insist that the plaintiff 'put forward *specific, nonconclusory factual allegations*' " that establish the motive causing cognizable injury to survive an early motion for dismissal or summary judgment. [**Crawford-El v. Britton,** *supra*, p. 146]

1/ Reply Required

One lower court has ruled that it is an abuse of discretion for a district court to fail to require a plaintiff to file a reply after the defendants have raised qualified immunity, unless the plaintiff's complaint was pleaded with particularity. [**Reyes v. Sazan,** *supra*, p. 146]

2/ Rule 8(a) Not Applicable to a Reply

The same lower court has concluded that because Rule 8(a) (which requires a "short and plain" statement of the grounds for jurisdiction and of the facts showing a right to relief in a complaint) does not list Rule 7 replies, Rule 8(a)'s "short and plain" standard does not govern Rule 7 replies. [**Schultea v. Wood,** 47 F.3d 1427 (5th Cir. 1995)]

(3) Amendment by Plaintiff If Motion to Dismiss Is Granted

Granting or denying leave to amend rests in the discretion of the court, but leave must be liberally granted. [**Foman v. Davis,** 371 U.S. 178 (1962)]

(a) *If the plaintiff amends*, he waives any error in the ruling on the original complaint, unless he can show that the outcome of the action was prejudiced by the erroneous dismissal of the original complaint.

(b) *If the plaintiff chooses not to amend* (or if leave to amend is denied), the court will enter a judgment of dismissal. The ruling on the motion is not an appealable order, but the judgment can be appealed.

　1) *If the plaintiff appeals and wins*, the complaint is reinstated, and the defendant must answer.

　2) *If the plaintiff loses on appeal* or fails to appeal, any further proceedings in the action are generally barred. However, the appellate court has discretion to remand in order to permit an amended complaint to be filed.

cf. **Compare—Amendment in Response to Motion to Dismiss**: Plaintiff may amend once as a matter of course within 21 days after service of a Rule 12(b)(6) motion to dismiss. [Fed. R. Civ. P. 15(a)(1)(B)]

(4) Answer by Defendant if Motion Is Denied

If the defendant's Rule 12(b) motion is denied, she must answer and proceed with the litigation—*i.e.*, the appellate court will not reexamine the denial of the defendant's motion as such. However, the defendant can raise the same issues on appeal from the final judgment and by subsequent motions (motions for judgment as a matter of law, for directed verdict, for judgment notwithstanding the verdict, etc.), which can also be reviewed on appeal from the final judgment.

b. Motion for More Definite Statement

Rule 12(e) permits a limited attack on the *form* of the pleadings (and to this extent serves somewhat the same function as the special demurrer for uncertainty in code-pleading practice). However, the motion will be granted only when the pleading under attack is *so vague and ambiguous* that it would be *unreasonable* to require the moving party to reply to it. [Fed. R. Civ. P. 12(e)]

(1) When Available

A motion for a more definite statement is appropriate only if the pleading being attacked requires a response. If no response is permitted to the pleading under attack (*e.g.*, a defendant's answer), the motion is *never* proper.

(2) As Predicate for Rule 12(b)(6) Motion

Numerous cases have asserted that the motion for a more definite statement should not be used as a predicate for a Rule 12(b)(6) motion to dismiss for failure to state a claim. [*See, e.g.*, **United States v. Board of Harbor Commissioners,** 73 F.R.D. 460 (D. Del. 1977)] But the Supreme Court has recognized that in some circumstances it is an important way of making plaintiffs "put forward specific, nonconclusory factual allegations." [**Crawford-El v. Britton,** *supra*, p. 162] Thus, although there may be a bias against using a Rule 12(e) motion as a precursor to a Rule 12(b)(6) motion, it appears to be proper to do so if there actually is a substantial threshold question that may be dispositive (*e.g.*, whether the facts are sufficient to overcome official immunity).

(3) Motion Available Even If Complaint States Claim

If a complaint is unduly wordy or otherwise in improper form, a court may require a more definite statement even though the complaint states a claim. Moreover, if the plaintiff fails to comply, the complaint may be dismissed for disobedience of the order even if it is not wholly without merit. [**McHenry v. Renne,** 84 F.3d 1172 (9th Cir. 1996)]

c. Motion to Strike

Either party may move to strike an insufficient defense or any "redundant, immaterial, impertinent or scandalous" matter in the other's pleadings. [Fed. R. Civ. P. 12(f)]

(1) Limited Use

The motion to strike is said to be "disfavored" and generally will be denied unless the allegations attacked have absolutely *no* possible relation to the controversy (*e.g.*, allegations that a tribunal was a "kangaroo court"). [**Skolnick v. Hallett,** 350 F.2d 861 (7th Cir. 1965)] If the alleged matter is merely of doubtful relevance or doubtful legal value, the motion will be denied. *Rationale*: Pleadings are not read to the jury in federal court (except in unusual circumstances when they have special relevance—*e.g.*, when they contain an admission). Consequently, it serves little purpose to strike allegations in the pleadings.

(2) Strike Portions of Complaint

A motion to strike may also be used to attack separate portions of the complaint which are insufficient as a matter of *law*—*e.g.*, when a plaintiff seeks punitive damages in a breach-of-contract action even though, as a matter of law, such damages are not available on such a claim, or when a defendant asserts an affirmative defense that is not applicable to the plaintiff's claim.

d. Procedure on Motions Under Rule 12

A motion under Rule 12 must be *in writing* and must *specify the ground* (or grounds) upon which it is based. [Fed. R. Civ. P. 7(b)(1)]

(1) Facts

If the motion is based on asserted facts, these must be established by accompanying affidavits, declarations, depositions, or other evidence. (The opposing party may, of course, submit controverting evidence.) *Note:* On a Rule 12(b)(6) motion, scrutiny is ordinarily limited to the face of the complaint. (*See infra*, pp. 166–167.)

(2) Time

The motion must be served within the time permitted the defendant to serve the answer (normally 21 days after service of a summons and complaint; *infra*, p. 183). The filing of the motion operates to extend the time within which the answer is due until the court rules on the motion.

e. Effects of Failure to Include Certain Defenses in Motion

The defendant is never compelled to file a motion under Rule 12; but if she does, she must include therein *all defenses and objections that she could then raise by motion*. If she omits an available defense or objection, she may not make a further motion on the omitted ground. [Fed. R. Civ. P. 12(g)] She will, however, be able to raise the ground in her answer, unless it is a ground that is waived by failure to raise in the first responsive pleading or motion.

(1) Waiver

The following defenses are *waived* unless raised by motion or, absent such a motion, in the first responsive pleading [Fed. R. Civ. P. 12(h)(1)]:

Objections to venue, personal jurisdiction, sufficiency of service of process or to *sufficiency of process*.

(a) Rationale

A party who invites the court to pass upon a "threshold" defense should bring forth *all* such defenses, in order to prevent waste of time by piecemeal presentation of defects.

(2) Defenses Not Waived if Omitted from Rule 12(b) Motion or Answer

The following basic defenses may be raised in a Rule 12(b) motion or an answer but are not waived if omitted [Fed. R. Civ. P. 12(h)(2), (3)]:

(a) *Lack of subject-matter jurisdiction*, which may be raised at any time and also requires dismissal on the court's own initiative;

(b) *Failure to join a person required by Rule 19(b);* and

(c) *Failure to state a claim* upon which relief can be granted.

Defenses (b) and (c) may be raised in any pleading allowed or ordered, in a motion for judgment on the pleadings under Rule 12(c), or at trial, as may failure to state a legal defense to a claim.

DEFENSES WAIVED IF NOT RAISED IN RULE 12(b) MOTION OR FIRST RESPONSIVE PLEADING	DEFENSES NOT WAIVED IF NOT RAISED IN RULE 12(b) MOTION OR IN RESPONSIVE PLEADING AND THAT MAY BE RAISED LATER
Objections to *venue*	Objections based on *subject-matter jurisdiction*
Objections to *personal jurisdiction*	Objections based on *failure to join a person required by Rule 19(b)*
Objections to s*ufficiency of service*	Objections claiming *failure to state a claim* upon which relief can be granted
Objections to *sufficiency of process*	

(3) Limitation

Keep in mind that the waiver pertains only to the defenses that *could* be raised by a Rule 12 motion. Thus, there is no waiver of substantive defenses (*e.g.*, release, novation, payment, etc.), which can be raised *only* in the answer. If a defendant fails to raise a given defense in the answer, it is sometimes said that it is "waived," but actually it can later be raised if the defendant obtains leave to amend the answer to add the omitted defense.

(4) Distinguish—Forfeiture of Defense Due to Delay in Asserting

Under some circumstances, even when a defendant complies with Rule 12(h) and includes a preliminary defense in its answer, its failure to assert that defense by motion in a timely fashion may be found to forfeit the defense. [*See, e.g.*, **Hamilton v. Atlas Turner, Inc.,** 197 F.3d 58 (2d Cir. 1999)—defendant's failure to move to dismiss for lack of personal jurisdiction for over four years, while there was substantial pretrial activity in the case, constituted a forfeiture of its objection to personal jurisdiction]

5. Other Procedures

While the demurrer (code-pleading state practice) and Rule 12 motion (federal practice) are the procedures most commonly used to attack the sufficiency of a pleading, other procedures are likewise available—the most important of which is the *motion for judgment on the pleadings* (discussed *infra*, pp. 202–203).

6. Additional Rules of Pleading

In both state and federal practice, the following additional principles apply:

a. Materials Considered

(1) Pleading on Its Face

In general, challenges to the sufficiency of the pleadings are limited to the allegations of the pleadings alone, and consideration of evidentiary materials, no matter how persuasive, is not allowed.

(a) Distinguish—Summary Judgment

Evidentiary materials are the basis for decision on a motion for summary judgment. (*See* Chapter Seven.)

(b) Conversion to Summary Judgment

In federal court, if materials outside the complaint are submitted with a motion to dismiss for failure to state a claim and are not excluded by the court, the motion is to be considered a motion for summary judgment. [*See* Fed. R. Civ. P. 12(d); *and see* **Vesely v. Sager**, 5 Cal. 3d 153 (1971)—motion to strike complaint based on materials outside the complaint treated as motion for summary judgment]

(2) "Speaking" Demurrers

In some code-pleading jurisdictions, there was once a practice of allowing "speaking" demurrers, which went beyond the face of the complaint and called other materials to the attention of the court. This practice has generally been ***disapproved***.

(3) Exhibits

When a document is an exhibit to the complaint, it is "a part of the pleadings for all purposes." [Fed. R. Civ. P. 10(c)] Therefore, it can be considered in connection with a motion to dismiss.

(a) Caution

That the court may consider the exhibit in connection with the motion to dismiss does not mean that all assertions in the exhibit are taken as true for purposes of the motion. For example, in a defamation action based on assertions in a letter, the plaintiff might attach the letter as an exhibit to the complaint without admitting that the assertions in the letter are true.

Example: In a wrongful-death action arising out of the death of an arrestee, plaintiffs attached a transcript of defendants' version of the events as an exhibit to the complaint. But that did not mean they adopted defendants' version, and the exhibit could not be the basis for dismissal in the face of plaintiffs' well-pleaded contrary allegations. But the court did note: "When an exhibit incontrovertibly contradicts the allegations in the complaint, the exhibit ordinarily controls, even when considering a motion to dismiss." [**Jones v. City of Cincinnati**, 521 F.3d 555 (6th Cir. 2008)]

(4) Superseded Pleadings

Reference to earlier pleadings filed by the same party presents several kinds of problems:

(a) Inconsistent Allegations

Because parties may ordinarily make inconsistent allegations within a given pleading (*see supra*, p. 145), that the plaintiff made an inconsistent allegation in a previous complaint does not render the current complaint inadequate.

(b) Omission of Fatal Details

When, however, a party has attempted to "cure" a defect by omitting an allegation, the court may look to the previous complaint to determine the sufficiency of the current complaint. [**Lee v. Hensley**, 103 Cal. App. 2d 697 (1951)—when original complaint showed that claim was barred by limitations, amendment to delete these allegations was ineffective to avoid dismissal]

(5) Matters Judicially Noticed

Finally, a pleading is construed in light of facts that may be *judicially noticed*: historical facts, geography, etc. [Cal. Civ. Proc. Code § 430.30(a); **Greene v. Brown & Williamson Tobacco Corp.,** 72 F. Supp. 2d 882 (W.D. Tenn. 1999)—court takes judicial notice on Rule 12(b)(6) motion that consumers were aware that cigarette smoking posed health risks, rejecting plaintiffs' product-liability claims based on the "consumer expectations" test]

Example: In assessing Plaintiffs' reliance in the complaint on remarks of the CEO of Defendant quoted in an article, the district judge was justified in considering the full contents of the article, and not only the portions quoted selectively by Plaintiffs. [**Bell Atlantic Corp. v. Twombly,** *supra*, p. 141]

(6) Materials Referred to in Complaint but Not Attached

In some instances, the lower courts have considered materials not attached to the complaint in deciding a Rule 12(b)(6) motion (failure to state a claim upon which relief may be granted). In general, the courts explained that these materials were *"central"* to the complaint [**United States v. Ritchie,** 342 F.3d 903, 908 (9th Cir. 2003)—"Even if a document is not attached to a complaint, it may be incorporated by reference into a complaint if the plaintiff refers extensively to the document or the document forms the basis of the plaintiff's claim"; *but see* **Sira v. Morton,** 380 F.3d 57 (2d Cir. 2004)—defendant's submission of hearing transcripts that were neither expressly cited in the complaint, nor integral to the claims asserted, required conversion to summary judgment].

b. Anticipatory Defenses

A complaint need *not* anticipate affirmative defenses that the defendant might raise.

Example: Plaintiff is injured, but executes a release of her claim. Later, Plaintiff sues for her injuries on the premise that the release was given by mistake. Plaintiff should not anticipate the defense of release, but should simply allege her claim for injury, await the defense of release, and then *avoid* it by proof at trial.

Compare: If Plaintiff *does* anticipate a defense in her complaint, the complaint must also plead facts to avoid it. For example, if Plaintiff in the previous example alleges the release, she must also allege facts showing a mistake that would make the release ineffective. [**Powell v. Lampton,** 30 Cal. App. 2d 43 (1938); **Hoshman v. Esso Standard Oil Co.,** 263 F.2d 499 (5th Cir. 1959)]

(1) "Built-In" Defenses

If a defense is "built into" the complaint because the plaintiff's allegations provide support for it, the defendant may *raise the defense on a motion to dismiss for failure to state a claim* even though in general it is an affirmative defense. The common example is the statute of limitations. When the complaint states when the defendant's alleged actions supposedly occurred, the defendant may move to dismiss on statute of limitations grounds. (*See infra*, p. 181.)

(2) Duty to Investigate

Before filing a complaint, the plaintiff's attorney should investigate defenses. (*See* below.)

E. Attorney's Duty to Investigate Claims and Defenses

THE FOLLOWING MATTERS ARE CERTIFIED UNDER RULE 11 BY THE PERSON SIGNING THE PLEADING:

To the best of the signer's knowledge, information, and belief, formed after **an inquiry reasonable under the circumstances**:

☑ The *paper was not filed for an improper purpose*

☑ The position taken in the pleading is **warranted by existing law** or a nonfrivolous argument for a change in existing law or the establishment of new law

☑ The *factual allegations have evidentiary support* or, if specifically so identified, will likely have evidentiary support after the signer has a reasonable opportunity to further investigate and use discovery

1. Introduction

Verification and signature requirements for pleadings have long existed. (*See supra*, p. 148.) Until 1983, the original **Rule 11** of the Federal Rules of Civil Procedure used a **subjective standard** for the obligations of a lawyer signing a pleading. The Rule looked to actual bad faith of the lawyer in signing the pleading. In 1983, the Rule was amended to fortify its requirements and became a major consideration in assessing the obligations of lawyers filing complaints and answers (as well as other papers). In 1993, substantial further revisions were made.

a. Rationale

The rationale for enhanced scrutiny of lawyer behavior was to **promote self-policing by lawyers** and **deter groundless and frivolous claims**.

b. Distinguish—State-Court Provisions

A number of state courts retain **subjective** standards. [*See, e.g.*, Cal. Civ. Proc. Code § 128.5—authorizing sanctions for "bad faith actions or tactics that are frivolous or solely intended to cause unnecessary delay"]

2. Certification Requirement

a. Signature on Paper

Rule 11 focuses on the signature on a paper filed in court, although it may also apply to later oral argument advocating a position in a paper (*see infra*, p. 173).

b. Applicable to All Filings Except Discovery

The rule applies to every filing in court, but may be most important with regard to **complaints** and **answers**.

(1) Discovery

With regard to discovery filings, Federal Rule 26(g) imposes similar certification requirements, and Rule 11 does not apply.

(2) Applicable to Nonattorneys

The rule applies to nonattorneys (*e.g.*, parties appearing pro se and, with regard to certain matters, parties represented by attorneys), as well as to attorneys.

3. Matter Certified by Signature

By signing a paper filed in court, a person certifies the following:

a. Reasonable Inquiry

With regard to the factual and legal grounds for the position taken in the paper, the person signing the paper certifies that she has made an "inquiry reasonable under the circumstances" to support that position.

(1) Attorney Pre-Filing Investigation

Ordinarily, it is expected that a lawyer will investigate factual and legal assertions before making them in a filing. This duty can include factual investigation of allegations and legal research regarding legal assertions.

b. Allegations or Factual Contentions Have Evidentiary Support

Rule 11 provides that signing a paper filed in court certifies that factual assertions "have evidentiary support." [Fed. R. Civ. P. 11(b)(3)]

(1) Option for Party Lacking Evidentiary Support

The rule provides that a party may make allegations without evidentiary support if the allegations *"will likely have evidentiary support after a reasonable opportunity for further investigation or discovery."* This option is available, however, only as to allegations *"specifically so identified."*

(2) Applicable to Denials

These certification requirements apply fully to denials of factual contentions. Denials may, however, be *based on belief or lack of information*, but only *it specifically so identified*. [Fed. R. Civ. P. 11(b)(4)]

(3) Reliance on Client

Reliance on the client for the factual assertions may be dangerous [*see, e.g.,* **Finance Investment Co. v. Geberit AG,** 165 F.3d 526 (7th Cir. 1998)—attorney not justified in accepting client's word that it had a right to pursue the claim asserted; **Southern Leasing Partners, Ltd. v. McMullan,** 801 F.2d 783 (5th Cir. 1986)— "blind reliance on the client is seldom a sufficient inquiry"], although prospective testimony of a client who has personal knowledge of the circumstances may meet the rule's standard.

(a) Possible Shift Under 1993 Amendment

Some courts read the 1993 amendments to Rule 11 as indicating that attorneys need only do "an inquiry reasonable under the circumstances," and that so long as the client provides prospective evidentiary support for allegations, the attorney has acted properly. [**Hadges v. Yonkers Racing Corp.,** 48 F.3d 1320 (2d Cir. 1995)—under the Rule 11 amendments it is clear that an attorney is entitled to rely on the "objectively reasonable representations of the client"]

(b) Distinguish—Sanction on Client When Attorney Reasonably Relies on Client

When the lawyer properly relies on the client, the client can be sanctioned for signing documents filed in court in violation of Rule 11, even if the lawyer committed no violation of the rule. [**Business Guides, Inc. v. Chromatic Communications Enterprises,** 498 U.S. 533 (1991)]

(4) Waivable Affirmative Defense

It is *unclear* whether a lawyer violates the rule by filing a complaint when the investigation shows that there is a valid affirmative defense that could be waived.

(a) Effect on Burden of Pleading

If Rule 11 forbids filing a complaint in such circumstances, it in essence has converted the affirmative defense into a part of the plaintiff's pleading burden, because the plaintiff would not be allowed to proceed despite being able to plead all the affirmative elements of his claim.

c. Supported by Law

The signature also certifies that the claim, defense, or other legal position taken in the paper is "warranted by existing law or by a nonfrivolous argument for extending, modifying, or reversing existing law or for establishing new law." [Fed. R. Civ. P. 11(b)(2)]

(1) Need to Research

The lawyer is expected to do research to determine whether there is a legal basis for claims or defenses that are asserted.

(2) Objective Standard

The rule is intended to create an objective standard. As explained under the 1983 version, it calls for sanctions "where it is patently clear that the claim has absolutely no chance of success under the existing precedents, and where no reasonable argument can be advanced to extend, modify or reverse the law as it stands." [**Eastway Construction Corp. v. City of New York,** 762 F.2d 243 (2d Cir. 1985)]

(a) Conflict Among District Courts

The Supreme Court has held that when there is a conflict on an issue among district courts, it was not frivolous to raise the issue on appeal even if the position was contrary to controlling circuit precedent, when the question had not yet been decided by the Supreme Court. An appeal raising the issue was the only way the party could preserve the issue pending a possible favorable decision by the Supreme Court. [**McKnight v. General Motors Corp.,** 511 U.S. 659 (1994)]

(b) Attorney's Unfamiliarity with Area of Law No Excuse

That the attorney is new to the area of law is no excuse for making a claim or defense that is unwarranted by law. [**Zuk v. Eastern Pennsylvania**

Psychiatric Institute, 103 F.3d 294 (3d Cir. 1996)—although this was attorney's first copyright case, that did not excuse his failure to ascertain that the claim was groundless under copyright law]

(3) Specifying That Existing Law Unfavorable

The courts disagreed under the 1983 version of the rule on whether lawyers were required to state that they were arguing for an extension of existing law. [*Compare* **Golden Eagle Distributing Corp. v. Burroughs Corp.,** 801 F.2d 1531 (9th Cir. 1986)—no need to explain that argument is for an extension of law, *with* **Thornton v. Wahl,** 787 F.2d 1151 (7th Cir. 1986)—failure to clarify that argument was not based on existing law can be sanctioned] The 1993 amendment does not require identification, but the Advisory Committee Notes observe that a contention so identified "should be viewed with greater tolerance under the rule." [146 F.R.D. at 587]

(4) Concern About Chilling Lawyer Creativity

In scrutinizing new arguments, courts are concerned that they might "stifle the enthusiasm or chill the creativity that is the very lifeblood of the law." [**Eastway Construction Corp. v. City of New York,** *supra*]

(5) Monetary Sanction Not Allowed Against Represented Party

A monetary sanction may not be awarded against a represented party for violation of the Rule 11 requirement that claims and defenses be supported by law. [Fed. R. Civ. P. 11(c)(5)(A)]

d. Improper Purpose

The signature also certifies that the paper was not filed "for an improper purpose, such as to harass, cause unnecessary delay, or needlessly increase the cost of litigation."

(1) Collateral Purpose

Some courts have focused on whether a given action seemed to have a collateral purpose (*i.e.*, some objective other than relief in court), finding this to indicate improper purpose. [*See, e.g.*, **Szabo Food Service, Inc. v. Canteen Corp.,** 823 F.2d 1073 (7th Cir. 1987)—objectively reasonable pleading may be sanctioned based on bad intent; **Appeal of Licht & Semonoff,** 796 F.2d 564 (1st Cir. 1986)—litigation used as method for obtaining information to be used in proxy battle between parties; **Whitehead v. Food Max, Inc.,** 332 F.3d 796 (5th Cir. 2003)—flamboyant tactics to enforce judgment designed to embarrass defendant and obtain publicity for plaintiff's counsel could be sanctioned]

(2) Purpose Irrelevant If Complaint Not Frivolous

Other courts have decided that the improper-purpose standard is satisfied as long as the complaint is not frivolous. [*See, e.g.*, **Sussman v. Bank of Israel,** 56 F.3d 450 (2d Cir. 1995)—suit designed to generate adverse publicity about defendant cannot be sanctioned unless frivolous; **National Association of Government Employees, Inc. v. National Federation of Federal Employees,** 844 F.2d 216 (5th Cir. 1988)— "if an initial complaint passes the test of nonfrivolousness, its filing does not constitute harassment for the purposes of Rule 11"]

4. Objective Standard

The Rule 11 standard with regard to the factual and legal basis for the claim is objective, and the actual state of mind of the lawyer is not important. "An empty head but a pure heart is no defense." [**Thornton v. Wahl,** *supra*]

5. Duty to Reevaluate

Although Rule 11 focuses on assertions in written filings with the court, it can be violated by *"later advocating"* a position previously taken in such a paper.

a. Rationale

Oral statements made to the court about matters arising for the first time in court may be made when there is insufficient opportunity to investigate. But litigants' obligations with respect to assertions contained in papers should not be measured solely with regard to what they know at the time they were filed, and later advocacy of those positions should be based on all information reasonably available.

b. No Requirement of Formal Withdrawal

To comply with Rule 11, a party need not formally withdraw an earlier filing; the proscription applies only to later advocacy of the assertion found to be groundless after the paper was filed.

6. Sanctions

a. Discretionary

On finding a violation of the certification requirements, a court *may* impose sanctions. [Fed. R. Civ. P. 11(c)(1)]

(1) Distinguish—Former Law

The 1983 version of Rule 11 provided that a court "shall" impose sanctions for a violation. This term was read to make sanctions *mandatory*, although many courts in practice regarded themselves as having some discretion not only as to the form or amount of sanctions but also whether they should be imposed at all. The 1993 amendment, by using "may," made it explicit that imposing sanctions is discretionary.

b. Nature and Measure of Sanction

The court has substantial latitude in selecting the sanction, which may include measures of a monetary or nonmonetary nature. [Fed. R. Civ. P. 11(c)(4)]

(1) Limited to Deterrence

The sanction is to be "limited *to what suffices to deter repetition of the conduct or comparable conduct by others similarly situated.*"

(2) Ordinarily Paid into Court

If the sanction is to pay money, that money ordinarily is to be paid to the court and not to the opposing party. Thus, Rule 11 sanctions are *not a fee-shifting device* to make the violator pay the victim's attorneys' fees or other legal costs.

(a) Costs of Motion

The court may, however, award the prevailing party the costs incurred in connection with the Rule 11 motion. [Fed. R. Civ. P. 11(c)(2)]

(b) Payment to Movant Warranted for Deterrence

If it is *"warranted for effective deterrence,"* however, the court may direct a payment to the moving party of some or all of its attorneys' fees and other expenses incurred as a direct result of the violation. [Fed. R. Civ. P. 11(c)(4)]

(c) Only Nonmonetary Sanctions Against Represented Party Regarding Legal Basis

Monetary sanctions cannot be imposed on a represented party for violation of the requirement that contentions made be warranted by law. [Fed. R. Civ. P. 11(c)(5)(A)]

(d) Sanctions on Law Firm

Ordinarily, a law firm should be held *jointly responsible* with its partners, associates, or employees for violations of Rule 11. [Fed. R. Civ. P. 11(c)(1)]

7. Procedure

a. Separate Motion

A motion for sanctions must be made "separately from any other motion." Accordingly, parties cannot append a request for sanctions to other papers they file. [Fed. R. Civ. P. 11(c)(2)]

b. Twenty-One Day "Safe Harbor"

The motion is not to be filed with the court until 21 days after it is served on the opposing party, and then only if the challenged paper is not withdrawn or corrected. This requirement provides a safe harbor for parties to reassess their filings without suffering sanctions for realizing that an earlier paper was not supported. [Fed. R. Civ. P. 11(c)(2)] The safe harbor, introduced in 1993, was also intended to reduce heavy "satellite litigation" that had grown up under the 1983 version, which lacked such a provision and had let parties file and serve Rule 11 motions at the same time.

(1) Must Not Be Too Late to Withdraw Challenged Paper

A party may not move for sanctions at a time when it is too late for the opposing party to withdraw the challenged paper. [**Barber v. Miller,** 146 F.3d 707 (9th Cir. 1998)—defendant could not move for Rule 11 sanctions after its motion to dismiss was granted; **Ridder v. City of Springfield,** 109 F.3d 288 (6th Cir. 1997)—defendant could not satisfy safe-harbor requirement by serving motion for sanctions after its summary-judgment motion had been granted]

If an exam question includes facts indicating that a party has violated Rule 11, remember to mention that the court has *discretion* to impose sanctions. The sanction should be limited to what is needed to *deter future similar violations* of the rule, and generally if the sanction is to pay money, the money will be paid to the court. However, if warranted for effective deterrence, the court may order the violator to pay the other party's costs or other expenses related to the violation, including attorneys' fees. Finally, remember that a motion for sanctions must be made separately from other motions, and it must be served upon the party against whom sanctions are sought at least 21 days before filing with the court.

c. Sanctions on Court's Initiative

The court may, on its own initiative, enter an order directing an attorney or party to show that it has not violated Rule 11 (a so-called show-cause order). [Fed. R. Civ. P. 11(c)(3)] But monetary sanctions cannot be imposed under these circumstances unless the court issues the order before voluntary dismissal or settlement of the case. [Fed. R. Civ. P. 11(c)(5)(B)]

d. Sanctions Order

If the court imposes sanctions, it must describe the conduct determined to constitute a violation of the rule and explain the basis for the sanction imposed. [Fed. R. Civ. P. 11(c)(6)]

e. Appellate Review

Rule 11 orders should be reviewed under an *abuse of discretion* standard [**Cooter & Gell v. Hartmarx Corp.,** 496 U.S. 384 (1990)], except when the point at issue is a matter of law such as interpretation of the terms of Rule 11.

8. Sanctions for "Multiplying Proceedings"

A federal statute authorizes courts to impose sanctions on a person who "multiplies the proceedings in any case unreasonably and vexatiously." [28 U.S.C. § 1927] This section looks to *delaying tactics or excessive litigation activity*. Ordinarily such sanctions depend on a finding of *willful bad faith* by the offending person. [**Zuk v. Eastern Pennsylvania Psychiatric Institute,** *supra,* p. 171]

9. Inherent Power to Sanction

Federal courts have inherent power to impose substantial sanctions on a party guilty of bad-faith conduct not involving signing of filings even when Rule 11 does not apply. [**Chambers v. NASCO, Inc.,** 501 U.S. 32 (1991)—repeated acts of deception of court led to imposition of almost $1 million in sanctions] But a monetary sanction under this authority must be limited to the attorney fees or other costs incurred solely because of the misconduct. [**Goodyear Tire & Rubber Co. v. Haeger,** 137 S. Ct. 1178 (2017)]

F. Answer

1. In General

The function of the answer is to put at issue the factual allegations in the complaint. The answer accomplishes this by *denying* the allegations of the claim and/or by setting forth some affirmative defense ("new matter") that *avoids* the effect of the plaintiff's allegations.

2. Denials

To put at issue the allegations of the complaint, the defendant's answer must contain *effective* denials. Allegations not denied are *deemed admitted* (below).

a. Form

(1) General Denials

A single "general" denial will controvert all of the allegations in the complaint (*e.g.*, "Defendant denies each and every allegation in Plaintiff's complaint"). In most jurisdictions, this is no longer good practice.

(a) Federal Pleading

In federal practice, the basic requirement of *good faith* based upon reasonable inquiry in pleading [Fed. R. Civ. P. 11] means that a general denial is rarely proper because there is usually *something* in the plaintiff's complaint (*e.g.*, allegations about the plaintiff's personal identity and jurisdictional allegations) which the defendant in good faith *should* admit. [Fed. R. Civ. P. 8(b)(3)—general denial allowed only if defendant "intends in good faith to deny all the allegations of a pleading—including the jurisdictional grounds"]

(b) State Pleading

In some states a general denial is permitted if the complaint is not verified, but is not allowed in response to a *verified* complaint. In such a case, the answer must also be verified and *specific denials* are required. [Cal. Civ. Proc. Code § 431.30(d); *and see supra*, p. 148]

1) Exception

Verified general denials to a verified complaint may be allowed when the *amount in controversy* is small.

(2) Specific Denials

Anything less than a general denial can be considered a "specific" or "qualified" denial. Several different types of allegations may be used in this regard:

(a) Specific Denial by Parts

The defendant can go through the complaint, paragraph by paragraph or sentence by sentence, admitting or denying each part as appropriate. When only part of a paragraph or allegation therein is true, the defendant should admit that which is true and deny the balance. [Fed. R. Civ. P. 8(b)(4); **Zielinski v. Philadelphia Piers, Inc.,** 139 F. Supp. 408 (E.D. Pa. 1956)]

Example: "Answering paragraph 12 of Plaintiff's complaint, Defendant admits providing medical treatment to Plaintiff on or about May 15, 2016, and, except as expressly so admitted, denies each and every allegation of paragraph 12."

(b) Negativing Plaintiff's Allegations

A denial may be effected merely by repeating the allegation but prefacing it with a word of denial.

1) Caution—Denials in the Conjunctive ("Negative-Pregnant" Rule)

This type of denial, if carelessly employed, may be deemed "pregnant" with an admission of that which the defendant is attempting to deny.

Example: Plaintiff's complaint alleges that Defendant "struck and kicked Plaintiff." Defendant's answer that "Defendant did not strike and kick Plaintiff" is pregnant with an admission that he may have struck *or* kicked Plaintiff.

a) How to Avoid

To avoid the negative pregnant problem, the defendant should make the denial in the *disjunctive*—e.g., "Defendant did not strike or kick Plaintiff."

2) Denials of Times, Dates, or Places

Similarly, if the complaint alleges that an event occurred at a certain time, date, or place *not* material to the statement of the plaintiff's claim, a specific denial thereof may be held pregnant with an admission that the event occurred at some *other* time, date, or place.

Example: Plaintiff's complaint alleges "Plaintiff fully and completely performed the contract *on June 1*." Defendant's answer stating that Defendant "denies that Plaintiff fully and completely performed the contract on June 1" may be held to admit performance on another date.

a) How to Avoid

It is generally a good idea to add "or at any other time," "at any other place," etc., to avoid this negative-pregnant problem.

3) Ease of Avoiding

These problems can be easily avoided by denying ''each and every allegation of the plaintiff'' except as expressly admitted, as indicated on p. 176, *supra*. As a result, the negative-pregnant problem has virtually vanished from the scene under liberalized pleading rules.

(3) Denial on Lack of Information

If the defendant is without sufficient knowledge or information to enable her to form a belief as to the truth of allegations in the complaint, she may so state in her answer. Such a statement has the effect of a denial. [Fed. R. Civ. P. 8(b)(5); Cal. Civ. Proc. Code § 431.30]

(a) Information That Is Peculiarly Within Defendant's Control

If the information of which the defendant claims ignorance is peculiarly within the defendant's control, use of the denial on information and belief may be forbidden.

Example: When Defendant bought out the assets of the company that manufactured a product that injured Plaintiff, information about the extent to which Defendant assumed the tort liabilities of the manufacturer was peculiarly within Defendant's control, and Defendant could not claim to be ignorant of it. [**David v. Crompton & Knowles Corp.,** 58 F.R.D. 444 (E.D. Pa. 1973)]

(b) Public Record

If matters are of public record, the defendant may not deny for lack of information and belief. [**Republic of Cape Verde v. A & A Partners,** 89 F.R.D. 14 (S.D.N.Y. 1980)] *Compare*: In assessing the adequacy of the complaint, the court may refer to matters of which it can take judicial notice. (*See supra*, p. 168 *et seq.*)

b. Effect of Failure to Deny

Failure to make an effective denial of allegations to which a responsive pleading is required constitutes an *admission* of the allegations. [Fed. R. Civ. P. 8(b)(6)]

(1) Exception—Damages

Under federal practice, allegations of *damages* are deemed at issue, even if not effectively denied. [Fed. R. Civ. P. 8(b)(6)] State practice is generally contra—*i.e.*, allegations of damages, like any other material allegation, must be denied.

(2) Material vs. Immaterial Allegations

Note that only *material* allegations are deemed admitted. "Material" allegations are those essential to the claim and which could not be stricken from the pleading without leaving it insufficient. [*See* Cal. Civ. Proc. Code § 431.10(a)]

(a) Distinguish

Failure to deny *immaterial* allegations does *not* constitute an admission thereof, the immaterial allegations being treated merely as "surplusage."

(b) But Note

In practice, few pleaders feel confident enough to decide what is "material" and "immaterial" and hence deny *all* controvertible allegations. Alternatively, the defendant can *move to strike* from the complaint whatever she considers to be "immaterial" allegations before filing her answer (*see supra*, p. 156), so she will not have to admit or deny them.

3. Affirmative Defenses

In addition to or in lieu of a denial, the defendant in her answer must plead any defenses or objections that constitute "new matter" or an affirmative defense. Such matter is *not in issue* (and hence may not be introduced in evidence at trial) *under a simple denial*.

a. Definition

Basically, "new matter" is anything that the defendant must prove in order to *avoid* the plaintiff's claim—*i.e.*, even assuming the plaintiff's allegations were true, an independent reason why the plaintiff cannot recover. The test usually is whether the defendant would bear the *burden of proof* on the issue at trial; if so, it is "new matter."

b. Federal Practice

Although burden of proof is generally deemed to be a "substantive" question for *Erie* purposes (and hence controlled by appropriate state law in connection with a state-law claim), pleading rules are clearly "procedural." Hence, if an affirmative defense falls within Federal Rule 8(c), below, it must *always* be specially pleaded; and this is true whether or not the defendant would have the burden of proof on this issue under state law. [**Palmer v. Hoffman,** 318 U.S. 109 (1943)] Federal Rule 8 does not refer to "new matter," instead requiring that "a party must affirmatively state any avoidance or affirmative defense." [Fed. R. Civ. P. 8(c)(1)]

(1) Rule 8(c)

Federal Rule 8(c) lists various defenses that must be affirmatively alleged, but this list is not all-inclusive. The Rule provides that *"any avoidance or affirmative defense"* must be affirmatively stated.

c. Application

The following are the most common types of "new matter" or affirmative defense in state and federal practice:

(1) Tort Cases

In tort cases:

(a) *Self-defense, consent, justification, or other privilege*, as defenses to intentional torts, are new matter and must be specially pleaded in the answer.

(b) *Contributory negligence and assumption of the risk*, as defenses to negligence, are new matter in most jurisdictions.

(c) *Privilege or license (as a defense to trespass); consent (as a defense to conversion)* are other examples of new matter.

(d) *But lack of causation is not new matter*. Causation is one of the ultimate facts in any tort complaint, and thus *lack* of proximate cause need not be specially pleaded. It is in issue under a general denial of an allegation that the defendant's acts "caused" the plaintiff's injuries.

(2) Contract Cases

In a contract action, new matter that must be specially pleaded (*i.e.*, not in issue under a denial) includes *fraud, mistake, duress, incapacity, release, waiver, and estoppel*.

(a) Illegality

Illegality is of course a "defense" to a contract action, but evidence of the illegality can come in even if not pleaded.

1) Rationale

Public policy to nullify illegal contracts is so strong that it should not require specific pleading. Indeed, the court can raise the issue on its own motion. [**Santoro v. Carbone,** 22 Cal. App. 3d 721 (1972)]

(b) Lack of Consideration

Whenever the plaintiff has alleged consideration, lack of consideration will be in issue under a simple denial. However, consideration need not always be alleged; and when it need not be alleged, lack of consideration is new matter that must be specially pleaded.

(c) Failure of Conditions

1) Condition Subsequent

Occurrence of a condition subsequent that the defendant claims *discharged* his duty to perform is an affirmative defense, and hence must be specially pleaded as new matter. [*In re* **Dibiase,** 270 B.R. 673 (Bankr. W.D. Tex. 2001)]

2) Conditions Precedent or Concurrent

However, because the plaintiff must allege the occurrence or performance of all conditions precedent or concurrent (in order to show that the defendant was under an absolute, unconditional duty to perform), a denial by the defendant sufficiently controverts the plaintiff's allegations concerning such conditions. [*See* Cal. Civ. Proc. Code § 457]

a) But Note

Federal Rule 9(c) requires that the defendant's denial that a condition precedent has occurred or been performed must be made "with particularity"—in effect requiring an affirmative allegation. [**AAR International, Inc. v. Vacances Heliades, S.A.,** 202 F. Supp. 2d 788 (N.D. Ill. 2002)]

(d) Payment

If the plaintiff sues on an obligation for payment of money, she bears the burden of pleading and proving *nonpayment* as part of her case. However, if the defendant intends to rely on payment as a defense in the action, most jurisdictions require that she *affirmatively plead* it in her answer. [Fed. R. Civ. P. 8(c); **Joyner v. Citifinancial Mortgage Co.,** 800 N.E. 2d 979 (Ind. 2003)— "payment is another affirmative defense that must be pled"]

(e) Mitigation of Damages

Although the defendant bears the burden of proof as to mitigation of damages, it does *not* always require special pleading.

e.g. **Example**: Defendant may prove that Plaintiff's damages have been *offset or reduced* by other income (as when a wrongfully discharged employee obtains another job) without special pleading. Such proof goes to the computation of Plaintiff's damages, and is thus in issue under Defendant's denial of the sum demanded. [**Erler v. Five Points Motors,** 249 Cal. App. 2d 560 (1967)]

> **cf.** **Compare**: If Defendant claims that Plaintiff has *failed* to mitigate damages (*e.g.*, failing to seek comparable employment), this contention is treated as new matter in order to alert Plaintiff. [**Erler v. Five Points Motors,** *supra*]

(f) Statute of Frauds

The federal rule (also followed in most states) is that the Statute of Frauds is new matter and must be specially pleaded. [Fed. R. Civ. P. 8(c)]

1) Minority View

Some code-pleading states take the position that the Statute of Frauds is in issue under a simple denial of the contract. This position was originally based on the theory that noncompliance with the Statute of Frauds rendered a contract void, rather than merely voidable; although this theory is no longer recognized (*see* Contracts Summary), the pleading rule has remained. [**Aero Bolt & Screw Co. v. Iaia,** 180 Cal. App. 2d 728 (1960)]

(3) Statute of Limitations

Running of the statute of limitations is new matter and must be specially pleaded.

(a) But Note

If it appears from the dates alleged *on the face of the complaint* that the plaintiff's action is barred, *some* courts allow the defendant to raise this defense (*e.g.*, by a motion to dismiss) even though not pleaded in the answer (*see supra*, p. 168). [**Jones v. Bock,** 549 U.S. 199 (2007)—"If the allegations, for example, show that relief is barred by the applicable statute of limitations, the complaint is subject to dismissal for failure to state a claim."]

(b) Title Obtained by Adverse Possession

If the running of the statute of limitations establishes title in an adverse possessor and the former owner then sues for ejectment, the adverse possessor's title is in issue under a simple denial of the owner's allegations in the ejectment action—since one of the necessary allegations is a claim of title. [**Denham v. Cuddeback,** 311 P.2d 1014 (Or. 1957)]

(4) Pleas in Abatement (Dilatory Pleas)

Pleas in abatement are *not* defenses on the merits, but assert some reason why the present action should be put off or should not be heard. Matters of abatement often appear on the face of the complaint, and when they do, the complaint is subject to demurrer or similar motion. However, when the matter of abatement does not appear on the face of the complaint—which is the usual case—it must be raised in the answer or, in federal practice, by answer or motion; and it must be *specially pleaded* as new matter.

(a) Grounds

The principal pleas in abatement are:

1) *The plaintiff lacks capacity* to sue;

2) *Nonjoinder* of parties;

3) *Another action pending* between the parties on the *same issues*;

4) *An action brought prematurely;* and

5) Lack of *personal jurisdiction* (including improper service of process) and *improper venue*:

    a) *In federal practice*, these issues may be raised by motion or answer, as long as it is in the defendant's first appearance [Fed. R. Civ. P. 12(b)];

    b) *In state practice*, lack of personal service must often be raised by a motion to quash, while improper venue must be raised by motion at or before the time the defendant files a demurrer or answer [Cal. Civ. Proc. Code § 418.10].

GILBERT

TORT	CONTRACT	OTHER
Self-defense	Illegality	Statute of limitations
Consent	Lack of consideration	Pleas in abatement (*e.g.,* plaintiff lacks capacity, nonjoinder of parties, another action on the same issue is pending between the parties, the action is premature, lack of personal jurisdiction, improper venue)
Justification	Failure of conditions	
Privilege	Payment	
Contributory negligence	Statute of Frauds	
	Failure to mitigate damages	

(b) Special Hearing Available

Statutes or rules often require that on motion of either party (or the court itself), matters of abatement be heard first—since they would dispense with the litigation if proved. [*See, e.g.,* Fed. R. Civ. P. 12(i)]

(c) Pleas Disfavored

A plea of abatement is a disfavored defense because it is generally an attempt to "put off" or "hold in abeyance" rather than to defend squarely on the merits. Accordingly, the courts require that such matters be raised *promptly* or the objection will be deemed *waived*. Thus, for example, such defenses generally cannot be raised for the first time in an amended answer. [**Collins v. Rocha,** 7 Cal. 3d 232 (1972)]

d. Effect of Failure to Plead New Matter

If not pleaded in the answer, new matter is not in issue and the *defendant may not offer evidence* of such defenses at the time of trial—unless the plaintiff fails to object to the introduction of such evidence or the court allows leave to *amend* (*see infra*, p. 198). [**Mooney v. City of New York,** 219 F.3d 123 (2d Cir. 2000)]

(1) Personal Jurisdiction, Improper Service, and Improper Venue

In federal practice, objections to personal jurisdiction, venue, or form or manner of service are **permanently waived** unless asserted at the earliest time, so a later motion to amend cannot revive these waived defenses. [Fed. R. Civ. P. 12(h)(1)]

4. Procedure in Answering Complaint

a. Form

The requirements for allegations in a complaint (*supra*, p. 142 *et seq.*) also apply to the allegations of an answer.

b. Signing

In federal practice, the same standards apply to the answer as apply to the complaint. [Fed. R. Civ. P. 11(b)(4); *see supra*, pp. 148, 169 *et seq.*]

(1) Lack of Sufficient Information

Rule 11(b)(4) permits a defendant to deny if the denial is "reasonably based on belief or a lack of information." The Advisory Committee Note accompanying the 1993 amendment explained that a denial would be permissible if "after an appropriate investigation, a party has no information concerning the matter or, indeed, has a reasonable basis for doubting the credibility of the only evidence relevant to the matter. A party should not deny an allegation it knows to be true; but it is not required, simply because it lacks contradictory evidence, to admit an allegation that it believes is not true."

(2) Verification

Under state practice, an answer must be verified if the complaint is verified (otherwise, it may be stricken by the court). [Cal. Civ. Proc. Code § 431.30(d)]

c. Time Limits

Under federal practice, the defendant must file her answer within 21 days after being served with process, except that if she chooses during that time to file a motion under Rule 12(b), her doing so extends the time for filing her answer until 14 days after the Rule 12(b) motion is denied. [Fed. R. Civ. P. 12(a)(1)(A)(i); 12(a)(4)]

(1) Service Waived

If the defendant waives service of process (*supra*, p. 51), the answer is not due until 60 days after the request for waiver was sent, if addressed to a defendant within the United States, or 90 days if the defendant is outside the country. [Fed. R. Civ. P. 12(a)(1)(A)(ii)]

(2) Service on United States

The United States, an agency of the United States, or an officer or employee of the United States sued for actions occurring in connection with the performance of official duties, is allowed *60 days* to file an answer. [Fed. R. Civ. P. 12(a)(2)]

(3) State Practice

State practice is similar. For example, in California, the defendant must answer or demur within 30 days after service of process (although the 30-day period is measured from different dates, depending on whether defendant was served personally, by mail, or by publication). [Cal. Civ. Proc. Code § 412.20(3)]

(4) Effect of Failure to File Timely Answer

See discussion of default procedure *infra*, pp. 201–202.

5. Allegations of Answer Deemed Controverted

Except when the answer contains a counterclaim (*see infra*), no reply to an answer is permitted in federal practice unless the court so directs. [Fed. R. Civ. P. 7(a)] Allegations of new matter in the answer are *"considered denied or avoided"* or *"deemed controverted"*—meaning that the plaintiff has the right, without further pleading, to introduce evidence to defeat or avoid the allegations. [Fed. R. Civ. P. 8(b)(6); *see also* Cal. Civ. Proc. Code § 5431.20(b)]

Example: Plaintiff's complaint charges negligence. Defendant's answer sets up the defense of comparative negligence by Plaintiff. This defense is "deemed controverted," and Plaintiff can introduce evidence to overcome the comparative-negligence defense (*see* Torts Summary) even though he has never formally denied Defendant's allegations of Plaintiff's negligence.

a. Reply Required

The Supreme Court has observed that requiring a reply may be appropriate in some circumstances [**Crawford-El v. Britton,** 523 U.S. 574 (1998)], and the Fifth Circuit requires trial courts to order that plaintiffs reply to officials' defenses of qualified immunity. [*See* **Reyes v. Sazan,** *supra*, p. 163].

6. Challenges to Answer

A plaintiff who desires to challenge the legal sufficiency of an affirmative defense may file a *demurrer* (state practice) or a *motion to strike* "any insufficient defense" under Federal Rule 12(f).

a. And Note

In addition, the plaintiff may employ a motion for judgment on the pleadings or motion for summary judgment to challenge the new matter. (*See infra*, p. 202.)

G. Counterclaims and Crossclaims

1. Federal Practice

a. Counterclaims

As part of her answer, the defendant may set forth by way of counterclaim any claims that she has *against the plaintiff*. Such claims *need not be related* to the claims set forth in the complaint. [Fed. R. Civ. P. 13(b)]

(1) Subject-Matter Jurisdiction

(a) Compulsory Counterclaim

If the counterclaim is compulsory (*i.e.*, based on the same transaction or occurrence as the plaintiff's claim; *see infra*), it is deemed *"ancillary"* to the plaintiff's claim, and therefore within supplemental jurisdiction (*see supra*, p. 93 *et seq.*).

(b) Permissive Counterclaim

However, if the counterclaim is merely permissive (*see infra*), subject-matter jurisdiction requirements must ordinarily be satisfied on some *independent ground* of federal jurisdiction (*e.g.*, if the plaintiff's claim is based on a federal question, the defendant's permissive counterclaim would have to be based on some federal question or on diversity).

It may be, however, that the supplemental jurisdiction statute (*see* Chapter Two) allows assertion of permissive counterclaims that satisfy the "common nucleus of operative fact" standard to be part of the same Article III case as the plaintiff's claim even though not compulsory under Rule 13(a). [**Jones v. Ford Motor Credit Co.**, 358 F.3d 205 (2d Cir. 2004)—in borrowers' suit alleging racial discrimination in violation of the Equal Credit Opportunity Act, defendant's permissive counterclaims for the amounts due on loans satisfied the standard for supplemental jurisdiction]

Criticism: It has been argued that cases such as *Jones, supra*, should be viewed as involving compulsory counterclaims and that supplemental jurisdiction over permissive counterclaims should never be allowed. [McFarland, *Supplemental Jurisdiction over Permissive Counterclaims and Set Offs: A Misconception, 64 Mercer L. Rev. 437 (2013)*]

(2) Venue

Counterclaims have no effect on venue. The venue statutes regulate where the "*action* may be brought"; which refers solely to where the plaintiff files his complaint. By the time the counterclaim is served, the action has already been brought.

(3) Pleading

The sufficiency of a counterclaim is tested by the same rules of pleading applicable to a complaint (*see supra*, p. 156 *et seq.*).

(a) Form

The counterclaim should be set forth as *part of the defendant's answer*, rather than as a separate pleading. [Fed. R. Civ. P. 13(a)]

(b) Caption

A counterclaim should always be labeled as such, since an answer to a counterclaim by the plaintiff is mandatory only if it is so denominated. [Fed. R. Civ. P. 7(a)(3)] However, failure to label a counterclaim as such has no other effect: The court may still treat it as a counterclaim and award whatever relief is appropriate. [Fed. R. Civ. P. 8(c)(2)]

(c) Plaintiff's Answer

A responsive pleading by the plaintiff is required to a counterclaim labeled as such. The answer may contain denials, affirmative defenses, or even a counterclaim to the counterclaim. [**Great Lakes Rubber Corp. v. Herbert Cooper Co.,** 286 F.2d 631 (3d Cir. 1960)]

1) Note

All matters in the answer are deemed "denied or avoided" under Federal Rule 8(b)(6).

2) But Note

The plaintiff can attack the answer by a motion for judgment on the pleadings or a motion to strike under Federal Rule 12.

(4) Joinder of Other Parties to Counterclaim

Although a counterclaim is against the plaintiff, it can be an occasion for the joinder of additional parties.

(a) Permissive Joinder

When making a counterclaim, the defendant may join other persons in accordance with the provisions of Rule 20. [Fed. R. Civ. P. 13(h); *see infra,* pp. 217–220]

1) Caution—Subject-Matter Jurisdiction

Note, however, that when a counterclaim is *permissive*, there must be some independent basis for federal subject-matter jurisdiction (*see supra,* Chapter Two).

(b) Joinder by Order of Court

If the defendant does not join a party that should be joined under Rule 19(a) (*see infra,* pp. 221–222), the court may order that party joined on motion of the plaintiff or, if the party is not joined, proceed to determine whether the case should be dismissed pursuant to Rule 19(b) (*see infra,* p. 222) if it is not possible to join the additional party.

1) Subject-Matter Jurisdiction

If the defendant has asserted a *compulsory counterclaim*, ordinarily supplemental jurisdiction would permit the addition of claims against parties who should be joined under Rule 19(a).

(5) Voluntary Dismissal by Plaintiff

To protect the defendant's right to relief on the counterclaim, Federal Rule 41(a)(2) provides that once a counterclaim is asserted, the *plaintiff cannot dismiss the action without the defendant's consent* (unless the counterclaim can remain pending for independent adjudication; *see infra,* p. 204).

(6) Permissive vs. Compulsory Counterclaims

(a) Permissive Counterclaims

If the defendant's claims against the plaintiff are **unrelated** to the claims set forth in the complaint, it is optional (or permissive) for the defendant to assert them by way of counterclaim; *i.e.*, the defendant may, if she chooses, instead assert the claims in an independent action.

(b) Compulsory Counterclaims

However, if the defendant's claim against the plaintiff arises out of the **same transaction or occurrence** as the claim set forth in the complaint, the counterclaim is **compulsory**—meaning that it must be asserted in the action or it will be barred. (This bar is implicit in Rule 13(a).) *Note*: Courts do not affirmatively require the inclusion of "compulsory" counterclaims. It is up to defendants to plead them, with likely claim-preclusive consequences if they fail to do so and later seek to pursue them separately.

1) When Counterclaim Is "Compulsory"

A counterclaim is compulsory if it:

a) **Arises out of the transaction or occurrence** that is the subject matter of the plaintiff's claim; **and**

b) **Does not require the presence of third parties** over whom the court has no jurisdiction. This provision invokes the requirements of Rule 19 (*see infra*, pp. 221–222).

2) Scope of "Transaction or Occurrence"

In determining whether a counterclaim is compulsory, the phrase "transaction or occurrence" appears to be construed differently, depending on the context:

a) Broad View—Jurisdiction in First Action

When the question is whether the counterclaim is **within a federal court's supplemental jurisdiction**, a **broad** definition of "transaction" is likely to be used—the object being to permit the counterclaim and thereby to avoid multiplicity of suits. [**Albright v. Gates,** 362 F.2d 928 (9th Cir. 1966); *see* 28 U.S.C. $1367(a)]

b) Narrower View: Scope of Preclusion in Later Action

On the other hand, if the question is whether a defendant who **failed** to interpose a counterclaim is barred from later suing on it, a **narrower** definition may be used if it would be inequitable to bar the later suit. [**Bluegrass Hosiery, Inc. v. Speizman Industry, Inc.,** 214 F.3d 770 (6th Cir. 2000)]

(7) Statute of Limitations Problem

An important issue is whether a counterclaim is barred by the statute of limitations if it is filed **after** the statute has run, but the action (*i.e.*, the plaintiff's complaint) was filed before the statute ran. The question is considered "substantive" for *Erie* doctrine purposes, and hence is resolved by appropriate state law. [**Keckley v. Payton,** 157 F. Supp. 820 (N.D. W. Va. 1958)]

(a) Majority View

The general view is that if the counterclaim arises out of the *"same transaction"* as the plaintiff's claim, it will not be barred if the plaintiff's complaint was filed before the running of the statute. *Rationale*: The plaintiff's filing of the complaint places before the court all rights and obligations of the parties to the transaction in question. [**Burger v. Kuimelis,** 325 F. Supp. 2d 1026 (N.D. Cal. 2004)] In addition, in terms of the policies of the statute of limitations, a plaintiff who files suit is on notice of the transaction and has an incentive to preserve evidence about it.

EXAM TIP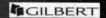

If an exam question sets out grounds for a counterclaim, the statute of limitations for the counterclaim has a shorter limitation period than the plaintiff's claim, and the shorter period has already run, remember to address whether the counterclaim is barred. In most states, the counterclaim will ***not be barred if it arises out of the same transaction or occurrence*** as the plaintiff's claim. For example, if the plaintiff files a malpractice action three years after the defendant provides medical services, the defendant can file a counterclaim that plaintiff never paid for the services, even if the limitations period for such contract claims is two years and has already expired. However, if the counterclaim is unrelated to the plaintiff's claim, it will be barred.

(b) Minority View

A minority view goes further and allows ***any*** counterclaim (same transaction or not) to be used ***defensively***—*i.e.*, as an offset to the plaintiff's claim—even though the statute has run. [**Ruppenthal v. Wyoming,** 849 P.2d 1316 (Wyo. 1993)]

1) "Cross-Demands Deemed Compensated"

Other states reach the same result via statutes that provide that when ***cross-demands for money*** have existed between the parties at any point in time, they are "deemed compensated"—*i.e.*, the plaintiff's claim is ***deemed paid*** to the extent of the defendant's offsetting claim. If the plaintiff later sues the defendant, the defendant can set up her cross-demand to show payment (an affirmative defense), even though an independent action on the defendant's claim would then be barred by the statute of limitations. [Cal. Civ. Proc. Code § 431.70]

2) Limitation

Such statutes apply only if the cross-demands are ***for money***. Thus, if the plaintiff is suing for recovery of property, the statute of limitations will continue to run on any cross-demand which the defendant has against the plaintiff.

b. Crossclaims

In federal court actions, the defendant may set forth in the answer any claims that she has against a *co-defendant* that relate to the *"transaction or occurrence"* or to any property that is the subject of the plaintiff's complaint. Such crossclaims are *never compulsory*, however. [Fed. R. Civ. P. 13(g)]

Example: Plaintiff sues Defendant 1 and Defendant 2, claiming they were jointly negligent in causing his injuries. Either defendant may crossclaim against the other on any claim arising out of the same accident, but is not required to do so. [**Scott v. Fancher,** 369 F.2d 842 (5th Cir. 1966)] Alternatively, either defendant may file a crossclaim *for contribution* against the other, asserting that both are *jointly* liable to the plaintiff and requesting that any judgment be fashioned accordingly. (If one defendant is only secondarily liable, he may crossclaim *for indemnification* against the other who is primarily liable.) [**Lumbermen's Mutual Insurance Co. v. Massachusetts Bonding and Insurance Co.,** 310 F.2d 627 (4th Cir. 1962)]

(1) Jurisdiction

Since the crossclaim must relate to the transaction in the existing action, the better view is that it is within the supplemental jurisdiction of the court, and no independent ground for federal jurisdiction is required. [**LASA per L'Industria del Marmo Societa per Azioni v. Alexander,** 414 F.2d 143 (6th Cir. 1969)]

(2) Pleading

(a) Form

Like a counterclaim, the crossclaim should be set forth as *part of the defendant's answer* rather than as an independent pleading.

(b) Responsive Pleading

The co-defendant against whom the claim is asserted must file an *answer to the crossclaim*. [Fed. R. Civ. P. 7(a)(4)]

(3) Parties

The basic crossclaim must be against a co-defendant. As with counterclaims, however, the crossclaimant may add *new parties* against whom it has claims growing out of the same transaction. [Fed. R. Civ. P. 13(h)]

(a) Note

A crossclaim is also proper when there are several plaintiffs (Plaintiff 1 and Plaintiff 2) and the defendant has counterclaimed against only one of them (P1). In such a case, Plaintiff 1 could crossclaim against his co-party (Plaintiff 2) for contribution or indemnification as to the claim asserted in the defendant's counterclaim.

(4) Other Procedures Compared

(a) Counterclaims and Crossclaims

Counterclaims lie only against the *opposing* party (*e.g.,* the plaintiff), whereas a crossclaim lies against a *co-party* (*e.g.,* Defendant 2).

1) And Note

A counterclaim is sometimes compulsory, whereas a crossclaim is always permissive. [**Priority Records, Inc. v. Bridgeport Music, Inc.,** 907 F. Supp. 725 (S.D.N.Y. 1995)]

(b) Impleaders and Crossclaims

Impleaders are claims against a *third person* who is a stranger to the action, whereas a crossclaim lies against a *co-party* (Defendant 2). Moreover, an impleader claim must be a claim for indemnification or contribution, whereas a crossclaim can be asserted for *any* claim Defendant 1 has against Defendant 2 arising out of the transaction that is the basis for the plaintiff's action.

2. State Practice—Cross-Complaint

Most state rules governing pleading of claims by a defendant against the plaintiff or third parties follow the Federal Rules (above). However, some states (*e.g.,* California) do not recognize the counterclaim or crossclaim, but provide that a defendant's claims against *any* party (plaintiff, co-defendant, or a third person not yet a party to the action) may be asserted in a *cross-complaint*.

a. Form

The cross-complaint is a *separate pleading* (*i.e.,* not a part of the answer). [Cal. Civ. Proc. Code § 428.40]

(1) Procedure

If the cross-complaint is filed *at the same time as the answer*, it may be filed as a matter of right. Otherwise, leave of court must first be obtained for a cross-complaint against current parties to the case. Cross-complaints against new parties can be filed without leave of court until a trial date has been set. [Cal. Civ. Proc. Code § 428.50]

(2) Service

The cross-complaint must be served on *every* party to the action. [Cal. Civ. Proc. Code § 428.60]

b. Joinder of Parties

As noted above, a cross-complaint may be filed against the plaintiff, a co-defendant, *or* a third person not yet a party to the action. In the latter case, a separate summons is issued on the cross-complaint.

(1) Note—Parties Required to Be Joined

The usual rules with respect to Rule 19 parties (*see infra,* p. 221 *et seq.*) apply here as well.

c. Joinder of Claims

(1) Against Plaintiff—Unlimited Scope

The defendant may assert any and all claims she has against the plaintiff. There is *no* requirement of any subject-matter relationship to the plaintiff's complaint. [Cal. Civ. Proc. Code § 428.10(a)]

(a) Compulsory Cross-Complaints

However, if the defendant's cause of action *is* related to the subject of the plaintiff's complaint, failure to assert it constitutes a waiver thereof. [Cal. Civ. Proc. Code § 426.30] Basically, the same rules apply as for federal "compulsory counterclaims." (*See supra*, p. 187.)

(2) Against Other Parties—Subject-Matter Relationship

A defendant can assert a cross-complaint against a co-defendant or third party only if the cause of action sued upon is *related to the plaintiffs complaint*—*i.e.*, arises out of same transaction or series of transactions, or involves the same property or controversy. [Cal. Civ. Proc. Code § 428.10(b)]

(a) Effect

As long as there is *one* such cause of action, the defendant can join with it *any other* causes of action she has against any of the cross-defendants. [Cal. Civ. Proc. Code § 428.30] A defendant may join additional cross-defendants, although they were not formerly parties. [Cal. Civ. Proc. Code § 428.20]

e.g. **Example**: Poppy, while operating a car, collides with Trip, who is operating a car owned by Oliver. Poppy sues Oliver for personal injuries. Oliver may file a cross-complaint against Poppy for the damages to Oliver's car; and against Trip as a third-party defendant, seeking indemnity for any liability that Oliver may be subjected to in favor of Poppy, and also for the damages to Oliver's car.

(b) Note

The California cross-complaint can thus be used to assert the claims asserted under the Federal Rules by compulsory counterclaim (same transaction), permissive counterclaim (different transaction), crossclaim (against co-party), or impleader (bringing stranger in as third-party defendant).

d. Responsive Pleading Required

Each cross-defendant must file an answer (or demurrer) to the cross-complaint. [Cal. Civ. Proc. Code § 432.10] If no such response is filed, a default judgment may be entered on the cross-complaint.

(1) Grounds for Demurrer

The grounds for demurrer to a cross-complaint are the same as for a demurrer to the original complaint.

(2) Additional Cross-Complaints

A cross-defendant, in turn, is permitted to file a cross-complaint against any other party or against any stranger to the action (just as if the cross-complaint filed against him had been the original complaint). [Cal. Civ. Proc. Code § 428.10] *Note*: Consequently, the cross-defendant is subject to the *compulsory* cross-complaint provisions (above).

(3) Note—Indemnification

A special statute in California allows broader defenses when the cross-complaint is for indemnification (*e.g.*, Plaintiff sues Defendant; Defendant cross-complains against Third Party, alleging that Third Party is liable to indemnify Defendant against Plaintiff's claim, so that if Plaintiff wins against Defendant, Third Party is liable to Defendant). In such cases, the cross-defendant (Third Party) is permitted to assert any defenses to the underlying cause of action (Plaintiff vs. Defendant) that could be asserted by the person seeking indemnification from him (Defendant). [Cal. Civ. Proc. Code § 428.70(b)]

(a) Rationale

The purpose of this rule is to protect against collusion on the underlying cause of action (*i.e.*, Defendant admitting or defaulting to Plaintiff's claim, in order to saddle Third Party with the liability).

H. Amended and Supplemental Pleadings

1. In General

Since it is the basic function of pleadings to define the issues in controversy (and thus limit the proof at trial), the rules allowing amendments and supplements to pleadings are of vital importance. The problem is the extent to which a party, by amending or supplementing pleadings, can alter or expand his case from that originally set forth in the complaint or answer. As will be seen, much depends on the *stage of the proceedings* at which an amendment is sought.

2. Amendments Before Trial

a. Amendments as a Matter of Course

Either party in a federal-court action may amend his pleading *once* as a matter of course, either (i) before a responsive pleading (as opposed to a mere motion) is served by the other party or (ii) if the pleading is one to which no responsive pleading is permitted (*e.g.*, the defendant's answer) and the action has not been placed on the trial calendar, at any time within 21 days after the pleading is served. [Fed. R. Civ. P. 15(a)(1)]

(1) Note

Even though there is a right to amend, the alteration must be within the *permissible scope* of amendment (*see infra*, p. 193 *et seq.*) or it is subject to being stricken.

b. Amendment by Permission

In any other situation, a party may amend his pleading *only* with the opposing party's permission or by leave of court; however, such permission is usually *granted liberally* prior to trial.

(1) Rationale

Modern courts stress that the primary function of the pleadings is to give *notice* of the pleader's claim (or defense). As long as the original pleading gave such notice, the claim may be expanded or changed in the course of litigation.

(2) Effect

Leave to amend will usually be granted unless some *actual prejudice* to the other party appears or the *trial schedule* will be disrupted. In the absence of such prejudice or disruption, refusal to permit an amendment may be an *abuse* of the court's discretion. [**Foman v. Davis,** *supra*, p. 163; **Armenta** *ex rel*. **City of Burbank v. Mueller Co.,** 142 Cal. App. 4th 636 (2006)]

e.g. **Example**: When the possibility emerged before trial that Defendant may not have manufactured the water slide on which Plaintiff was injured, the district court did not abuse its discretion in permitting Defendant to amend its answer to change its admission that it had manufactured the water slide to a denial, even though the statute of limitations might prevent Plaintiff from suing another party, should it turn out Defendant had not manufactured the slide. Defendant had reasonably relied on the conclusion of insurance-company representatives that it had manufactured the water slide, and making such a determination was difficult. [**Beeck v. Aquaslide 'N' Dive Corp.,** 562 F.2d 537 (8th Cir. 1977)]

(3) Stipulation

Ordinarily, leave of court is not required when the opposing party stipulates to the amendment.

c. Procedure

(1) Motion for Leave to Amend

Unless the amendment is a matter of course or the parties consent, the party seeking leave to amend must file a formal motion with the court, attaching a copy of the proposed amended pleading, and an appropriate showing (usually by affidavit) of the grounds upon which the amendment is sought.

(2) Service

If leave to amend is granted, the amended pleading must then be filed and served in the same manner as the original pleading.

(3) Response to Amended Pleading

If a response to the original pleading was required (*e.g.*, complaint or counterclaim), then a response to the amended pleading is required as well. The response to the pleading—be it an answer, reply, or motion—must be served within 14 days after service of the amended pleading. [Fed. R. Civ. P. 15(a)]

d. Permissible Scope of Amendment

(1) State Practice

Under the early codes, an amendment would not be permitted if it changed the basic cause of action or defense asserted in the original pleadings. The plaintiff was not allowed to amend his complaint to set up a "wholly new and different cause of action"; neither was the defendant allowed to amend her answer to set up a "wholly new and different" defense.

(a) Modern Rule

Even under code pleading, however, the test now employed is whether the proposed amended pleading is based on the *same general set of facts* as the original pleading. [**Austin v. Massachusetts Bonding Co.,** 56 Cal. 2d 596 (1961)]

(2) Federal Practice

Under the Federal Rules, the basic question is whether (and to what extent) the amendment results in *prejudice* to the opposing party.

(a) Effect

Under federal practice, therefore, it is immaterial that the proposed amendment changes the theory of the case, states a claim arising out of a transaction different from that originally sued on, or causes a change in parties. [**Laber v. Harvey,** 438 F.3d 404 (4th Cir. 2006)]

(b) Amended Answer

The same liberal rules apply to the defendant's answer, *except that* defenses that are waived if not asserted in the defendant's first pleading (answer or motion)—*e.g.*, improper venue, defective service of process—cannot be revived by amendment.

(c) Effect of Trial Date and Rule 16 Limitations on Time to File Motions

Another factor that increasingly bears on whether a party is granted leave to amend is the court's schedule for completion of pretrial activities and trial of the case (*see infra*, p. 347 *et seq*.). If the motion is made after the cutoff for making motions under a Rule 16 scheduling order, or if the scheduled date for trial might be disrupted, the court may deny leave to amend.

e. "Relation-Back Doctrine"—Statute of Limitations Problems

If the plaintiff seeks to amend the complaint after the statute of limitations would otherwise have run on the claim, there is a question whether the amended claim "relates back" to the date of filing of the original complaint.

Example: Plaintiff sues Defendant for breach of contract. Then, after the statute of limitations on an independent fraud action has run, Plaintiff amends his complaint to seek damages for fraud in connection with the same contract. Should the amended claim be deemed filed at the time the original claim was filed?

(1) "Relation Back" Usually Permitted

In most jurisdictions, the amended claim "relates back"—*i.e.*, is deemed filed as of the date of the original complaint—as long as the claim asserted in the amended pleading arose out of the *same conduct, transaction, or occurrence* set forth in the original pleadings. [Fed. R. Civ. P. 15(c)(1)(B); **Branick v. Downey Savings & Loan Association,** 39 Cal. 4th 235 (2006)]

The relation-back doctrine often arises in law-school exam questions. Be sure to mention the basic rule: A plaintiff usually can amend her complaint after the statute of limitations period otherwise would have run on the claim as long as the claim asserted in the amended pleading arose out of the **same conduct, transaction, or occurrence** set forth in the original pleadings.

(a) Effect

As long as the same basic transaction is involved, the plaintiff may therefore amend his complaint to establish new theories of recovery, or even to show new facts entitling him to recover, after the statute of limitations would otherwise have run.

(b) Rationale

The defendant is not prejudiced because she had notice, within the limitations period, that the plaintiff was asserting *some* claim against her on the basis of the transaction involved. Consequently, a change in the nature or theory of the plaintiff's claim does not prejudice the defendant. [**Tiller v. Atlantic Coast Line,** 323 U.S. 574 (1945)]

(c) Rule Regarding New Parties

An amendment of the complaint cannot avoid the statute of limitations with respect to a totally new party (as plaintiff or defendant). *Rationale*: That the plaintiff has filed an action against one defendant does not toll the statute of limitations on such claims as he may have against other defendants. [**Anderson v. Papillion,** 445 F.2d 841 (5th Cir. 1971)]

(d) Federal Rule for Relation Back

In federal court, relation back is permitted if an amendment "changes the party or the naming of the party against whom a claim is asserted." [Fed. R. Civ. P. 15(c)(1)(C)] This relation back is permitted only when the new claim arises from the *same transaction* as that asserted in the original complaint [Fed. R. Civ. P. 15(c)(1)(B); *see supra*, p. 194], and the new party had *notice of the suit*.

1) Liberal vs. Strict Interpretation

Some lower-court cases took a restrictive attitude toward relation back, but the Supreme Court adopted a more liberal attitude in **Krupski v. Costa Crociere S.P.A.,** 560 U.S. 538 (2010), where it held that relation back was required despite the district judge's finding that plaintiff should have realized that she had sued the wrong defendant.

2) Misnamed Defendant

The relation-back provision undisputedly applies when the plaintiff uses the wrong name for the defendant plaintiff wants to sue, providing that the party to be named received notice of the suit within the time for serving the summons and complaint. [Fed. R. Civ. P. 15(c)(1)(C)]

3) Additional Defendant; "Changing" Party Against Whom Claim Is Asserted

Some cases have stressed the rule's statement that the amendment "changes the party or the naming of the party against whom a claim is asserted" and have refused relation back as to an *added* defendant. [**Worthington v. Wilson,** 8 F.3d 1253 (7th Cir. 1993)—"a new defendant cannot normally be substituted or added by amendment after the statute of limitations has run"] Other cases permit addition of defendants and not merely substitution for the original defendant. [**Goodman v. Praxair, Inc.,** 494 F.3d 458 (4th Cir. 2007) (en banc)—rule includes changes in the composition of the parties collectively, and is not limited to situations involving substitution for the original defendant] Courts that had adopted the restrictive view have recognized that the Supreme Court's decision in **Krupski v. Costa Crociere S.P.A.,** *supra*, p. 195, "has cut the ground out from under" the restrictive view. [**Joseph v. Elan Motorsports Technologies Racing Corp.,** 638 F.3d 555, 559–60 (7th Cir. 2011)]

4) Nature of "Mistake"

Although some lower-court cases had held that a "mistake" eligible for relation back did not occur when plaintiff was aware of the "new" defendant at the time the earlier pleading was filed, the Supreme Court has held that the "mistake" provision applies *only to what the defendant should appreciate*, not whether plaintiff should have understood this defendant's involvement earlier. [**Krupski v. Costa Crociere S.p.A.,** *supra*, p. 195.

e.g. **Example:** Plaintiff was entitled to relation back after mistakenly naming defendant's agent as the original defendant, and then amending the complaint to name defendant only after the limitations period had expired. Defendant had been on notice of plaintiff's claim since before suit was filed, and was aware that plaintiff wanted compensation from it. That plaintiff could have identified the correct defendant earlier, or may have delayed in seeking to amend, did not bear on whether defendant should have realized that plaintiff had made a "mistake" about whom to sue. [**Krupski v. Costa Crociere S.p.A.,** *supra*]

5) Time and Nature of Notice

For relation back to apply with regard to a claim against a defendant different from the one originally sued, that defendant must have been on notice *within the time allowed by Rule 4(m)* for service of the complaint— 90 days after the filing of the complaint. The notice need not be by service of the complaint, but may come from any source. However, the notice must alert the new defendant that, but for a mistake concerning the identity of the proper party, the plaintiff would have brought the action against this defendant. This notice may sometimes be found lacking if the theory of the claim against the new defendant is different from that against the original defendant. [**Lundy v. Adamar of New Jersey, Inc.,** 34 F.3d 1173 (3d Cir. 1994)—suit against casino for premises liability in connection with care provided by nurse did not notify doctor who employed nurse, because he had no reason to know he was not sued due to a mistake concerning identity]

6) Relation Back Not Discretionary

Under Rule 15(c), relation back is **mandatory** when the requirements of the rule are satisfied. Unlike Rule 15(a), which gives the district court discretion whether to allow an amendment, the relation-back rule is mandatory. [**Krupski v. Costa Crociere S.p.A.,** *supra*]

7) Added Plaintiffs

Rule 15(c)(1)(C) speaks only of adding defendants, not plaintiffs, so ordinarily relation back is not allowed for claims of new plaintiffs. However, relation back has been allowed when the new plaintiff is the real party in interest [**Tidewater Marine Towing, Inc. v. Dow Chemical Co.,** 689 F.2d 1251 (5th Cir. 1982)], or to permit the original plaintiff to assert a claim in another capacity [**Williams v. United States,** 405 F.2d 234 (5th Cir. 1968)—mother who sued as next friend of her minor son permitted to add claims asserted in her own right for loss of her son's services after limitations period expired].

a) Distinguish—Class Actions

The filing of the class action tolls the running of the statute of limitations for all members of the class. Class members may therefore be included in the suit after a class is certified, or benefit from this tolling of the limitations period if a class is not certified, or if they opt out of a class that is certified. (*See infra*, pp. 256–257.)

(e) Distinguish—"Jane Doe" Defendants Named (State Practice)

Some states permit the filing of a complaint against fictitious defendants ("Jane Does") when the true name of the defendant is not known when the action is filed. In such states, the complaint can be amended to name the defendant when her identity is discovered—even if the new defendant had no prior notice of the action and the statute of limitations has then run! [Cal. Civ. Proc. Code § 474; **Fuller v. Tucker,** 84 Cal. App. 4th 1163 (2000)]

(2) Amendments in Federal Diversity Cases

The Federal Rule permitting "relation back" [Fed. R. Civ. P. 15(c), *supra*] is applied by federal courts in diversity cases even if there is no similar local rule. Thus, a plaintiff may be able to assert a claim in an amended pleading that would be barred by the state court under the same circumstances. [**Heiser v. Association of Apartment Owners of Polo Beach,** 848 F. Supp. 1482 (D. Haw. 1993)]

(a) State Rule May Be More Liberal

When the state rule regarding relation back is more liberal (*e.g.*, by dispensing with the requirement of notice to the new defendant within the limitations period), the state rule should be applied if state law provides the applicable statute of limitations. [Fed. R. Civ. P. 15(a)(1)(A)]

f. Amendment Supersedes Original Pleading

An amended pleading **supersedes** the original, and the original has no further effect as a pleading. The pleader cannot "resurrect" the original pleading by attempting to dismiss or strike the amended pleading; but she can seek leave to re-amend if she wants to return to the claim originally pleaded.

(1) Note

Although superseded as a pleading, the original pleading can still be used *in evidence* against the pleader where appropriate—*e.g.*, as an admission or prior inconsistent statement. (*See* Evidence Summary.)

(2) And Note

In many code-pleading states, if the amended pleading contains *contradictory allegations on material matters without explaining the inconsistency* from the original pleading, the adverse party may move to strike the amended pleading as a sham. This approach applies to both verified and unverified pleadings. [**Oakland Raiders v. National Football League,** 131 Cal. App. 4th 621 (2005)]

3. Amendments at Trial

Because a basic purpose of pleading is to define the scope of the issues at trial, problems arise when a party seeks to amend the pleadings—and thus change the triable issues—during the course of the trial.

a. Common-Law Background—Doctrine of "Variance"

At common law, a party could prevail (if at all) only on the claim stated in the pleadings. Issues outside the pleadings could not be tried; and any "variance" between the facts pleaded and those proved was often fatal to recovery. It made no difference that the other side failed to object or even *consented* to the variance.

b. Modern Code Practice

The common-law rules have been relaxed in most code-pleading states today. When the evidence offered at trial is only a *partial* variance from the pleadings, the court may grant leave to amend the pleadings at trial to conform to the proof. If the variance is prejudicial, however, no such amendment can be permitted.

(1) Nonprejudicial Variance

A nonprejudicial variance exists when the evidence at trial differs from the pleadings but concerns the *same transaction* as that originally alleged *and* the difference was *not prejudicial* to the opposing party (*i.e.*, did not mislead her in preparing her defense). [**County Sanitation District No. 2 v. County of Kern,** 127 Cal. App. 4th 1544 (2005)]

(2) Prejudicial Variance

A prejudicial variance exists when the facts proved at trial show an entirely "new and different" cause of action or theory of recovery, or otherwise differ so materially from the pleadings as to be prejudicial.

> **e.g.** **Example**: Plaintiff's complaint for malpractice alleged liability of Defendant hospital by reason of the negligence of doctors who performed an operation. At trial, Plaintiff sought to prove negligence on the part of members of the hospital's own staff. This was held to be a prejudicial variance, and amendment of the pleadings to assert the new theory was not permitted. [**Rainer v. Community Memorial Hospital,** 18 Cal. App. 3d 240 (1971)]

(3) Determinative Factors

Whether a variance will be deemed prejudicial depends on several factors:

(a) *Surprise* to the opponent—*i.e.*, whether the opponent was put on notice of the new claim or defense, through discovery or pretrial disclosures;

(b) *Whether a continuance* would enable the opponent to meet the new evidence;

(c) *Any elements of inconvenience or unfairness* in granting a continuance (prejudice from delay, extra expense in trial, etc.); and

(d) *Policy favoring amendment*—to obtain complete and final disposition on the merits.

c. Federal Practice

The pleadings are considerably less important in federal than in code-pleading practice, and amendments are therefore allowed more liberally—even during trial. The doctrine of variance is effectively *abolished* in federal practice.

(1) Evidence Received Without Objection

First, any variance between the pleadings and the proof at trial is *waived* unless a specific, timely, and proper objection to the evidence is made when offered. [Fed. R. Civ. P. 15(b)(2)—"When an issue not raised by the pleadings is tried by the parties' express or implied consent, it must be treated in all respects as if raised in the pleadings."]

(a) Aider by Verdict

Rule 15(b)(2) embodies the doctrine of "aider by verdict"; *i.e.*, that evidence received at trial without objection by the adverse party supplies the missing allegations in the pleadings, so that the defective pleadings are "aided" by the verdict.

(b) Tactic—Amend to Conform to Proof

It is still sound practice to seek leave to amend to conform to proof (which can be granted even after trial and judgment)—so there will be a correlation between the judgment and pleadings. However, failure to amend to conform to proof does *not* affect the result of the trial or the validity of the judgment as entered. [Fed. R. Civ. P. 15(b)(2)]

(c) Problem of Relevance

The usual objection that could be made would be relevance—that the proffered evidence is not relevant to the issues made out in the pleading. In many instances, however, irrelevance may not be clear, and one can argue that evidence was relevant even without an amendment. If that is true, failure to object would not necessarily be a waiver of objections to an amendment.

(2) Amendments over Objection

If evidence *is* objected to on the ground that it is outside the issues framed by the pleadings, the proponent of the evidence must seek leave to amend his pleadings. Federal Rule 15(b)(1) provides that the court may allow the pleadings to be amended (during trial) and *should do so freely* if it appears that the amendment will aid in the presentation of the case and will not prejudice the objecting party in the presentation of her action or defense.

(a) Effect

It is up to the objecting party to show *prejudice* on the merits, or the requested amendment must be granted. Refusing leave to amend without such a showing constitutes an abuse of judicial discretion and will be reversed on appeal. [**Laber v. Harvey,** 438 F.3d 404 (4th Cir. 2006)]

(b) Tactic—Continuance

The proper remedy for surprise resulting from a change of theory at trial is a continuance. And in granting a continuance, the court can assess costs against the party at fault. [**Vigilant Insurance Co. v. EEMAX, Inc.,** 362 F. Supp. 2d 225 (D.D.C. 2005)]

(3) Distinguish—Modification of Final Pretrial Order

Due to managerial judging, it often happens that the pleadings are superseded by a final pretrial order that specifies the claims and defenses to be tried. (*See infra*, p. 352.) If so, the final pretrial order is to be modified only *"to prevent manifest injustice."* [Fed. R. Civ. P. 16(e)]

4. Amendments After Trial

In federal practice, the pleadings can be amended to conform to proof at any time, even after trial and entry of judgment (*see* above). [Fed. R. Civ. P. 15(b)] Such a motion for amendment can be made for the first time *on appeal*. However, this possibility is subject to the general rule of appellate practice that a reviewing court will not consider grounds for appeal (other than jurisdictional) that were not reasonably raised in the trial court. (*See infra*, p. 437.)

EXAM TIP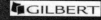

Remember that while the federal rules allow a party to amend a pleading only once *as a matter of course*, in federal courts, pleadings may be amended *by leave of court*, and such leave is liberally granted. Indeed, a party may be given leave to amend even after trial.

---

5. Supplemental Pleadings

The function of supplemental pleadings is to call the court's attention to material facts that have occurred *after* the filing of the original complaint.

Example: In an action for personal injuries, a supplemental pleading might allege aggravation of injuries or increments of damage sustained after filing of the original complaint

a. Discretion of Court

There is *no right* to file a supplemental pleading. The filing of such pleadings is permissive, within the sound discretion of the court. [Fed. R. Civ. P. 15(d)]

(1) But Note

The same policy factors favoring liberality in amendment of pleadings (*supra*) likewise support supplemental pleadings. Indeed, there is even less chance of prejudice to the other party in this situation, since the supplemental pleading does not alter the claim or defense originally asserted.

b. Procedure

The party seeking leave to supplement a pleading must file a ***written motion*** with a copy of the proposed supplemental pleading attached.

(1) Response

Whether a response to a supplemental pleading may be filed is also discretionary with the court. If the court orders a response, it will likewise set the time within which such a response must be served and filed. [Fed. R. Civ. P. 15(d)]

c. Effect on Original Pleading

The function of a supplemental pleading is merely to ***add to***, not modify, the original pleadings. If permitted, it does not replace the original pleading (as would an amended pleading), but it is a supplement to the original.

(1) ***Under state practice***, a supplemental complaint is not permitted to change the basic nature of the case by alleging what amounts to a totally different cause of action. [**Lincoln Property Co., N.C. v. Travelers Indemnity Co.,** 137 Cal. App. 4th 905 (2006)]

(2) ***Federal practice*** is more liberal. Federal Rule 15(d) gives the court discretion to allow supplemental pleadings even though the original pleading is defective, or the supplement would change the nature of the relief sought.

I. Default Procedure

1. In General

As discussed (*supra*, p. 183), if a defendant fails to answer or otherwise plead within the time permitted, the clerk of the court is required to enter a default. [Fed. R. Civ. P. 55(a)]

2. Effect of Default Entry

The defendant's failure to plead is regarded as an ***admission*** of the claim against her. So long as the default stands, any attempt by the defendant to "answer" or file any other pleading in the case will be disregarded.

3. Obtaining Judgment

After entry of default, the plaintiff can proceed to obtain a default judgment. If he is suing on a promissory note or other sum certain, the judgment may be entered directly by the clerk of the court. In all other cases, the plaintiff must present his evidence to the court in order to obtain judgment. [Fed. R. Civ. P. 55(b)(1)]

a. Relief Limited to Prayer

In default cases, the judgment cannot exceed the ***amount or type of relief requested in the prayer of the complaint***. (*See supra*, p. 146.)

b. Defendant Not Entitled to Notice

Unless she made an earlier appearance in the action, the defendant is *not* entitled to any notice of the plaintiff's application for default judgment; nor is she entitled to appear or submit evidence in opposition.

4. Setting Aside Default

If the defendant's default has been entered, her remedy is to move the court to set aside the default (and any judgment entered pursuant thereto).

a. Time Limits

In federal practice, a motion to set aside the default can be made at any time until judgment is entered. [Fed. R. Civ. P. 55(c)] Thereafter, a motion to set aside the judgment can be made at any time within *one year* after the judgment or order is entered. [Fed. R. Civ. P. 60(c)(1)]

b. Grounds

Ordinarily, the defendant must show:

(1) *That she has a valid excuse* for her default (*e.g.*, excusable neglect, fraud, inadvertence);

(2) *That she has a meritorious defense* to the action; *and*

(3) *That the plaintiff will not be prejudiced*.

c. Appellate Review

Review of a trial court's decision on a motion to set aside default is limited. Appellate courts will not overturn the trial-court decision unless both of the above factors (time limit and grounds) are so clearly satisfied or not satisfied that the trial court ruling was an *abuse of discretion*.

J. Judgment on the Pleadings

1. Purpose

A motion for judgment on the pleadings is closely analogous to a demurrer or motion to dismiss under Federal Rule 12(b)(6), and was used at common law for the same purpose—*i.e.*, to challenge the adversary's pleadings on the ground that they are *insufficient to establish any valid claim or defense*.

2. Making of Motion

A motion for judgment on the pleadings may be made *by either party at any time* after the pleadings have closed, but within such time as will not delay the trial. [Fed. R. Civ. P. 12(c)]

3. Issues Raised

a. Legal Sufficiency of Pleading

A motion for judgment on the pleadings challenges only the sufficiency of the adversary's pleading in posing a legally meritorious contention.

b. Matters Beyond the Pleading

Under common-law and code practice, a motion for judgment on the pleadings could not raise defects that did not appear on the face of the pleadings. However, modern practice permits the moving party to present matters beyond the pleadings; and when this is done, the motion is treated as a motion for summary judgment. [Fed. R. Civ. P. 12(d)]

4. Hearing on Motion

As with other pretrial matters, a motion for judgment on the pleadings is generally heard before commencement of the trial (although the court may order the motion deferred until the time of trial). [Fed. R. Civ. P. 12(i)]

5. Adversary's Right to Amend Pleadings

Once a responsive pleading has been filed, a pleader no longer has an absolute right to amend the pleading; any amendment must be by leave of court or by written consent of the adverse party. [Fed. R. Civ. P. 15(a)] For this purpose, a motion for judgment on the pleadings is *not* a "responsive pleading" and hence does not cut off an adversary's right to amend without leave of court if no answer has been filed. [**Harlee v. Hagen,** 538 F. Supp. 389 (E.D.N.Y. 1982); *and see* **Cargo Partner AG v. Albatrans, Inc.,** 207 F. Supp. 2d 86 (S.D.N.Y. 2002)—Rule 12(b)(6) motion, which is not a responsive pleading, does not preclude amendment as a matter of course]

K. Voluntary Dismissal by Plaintiff

1. Common Law

At common law, a plaintiff had the right to dismiss his own action at any time before verdict. While a dismissal ordinarily would result in an award of costs against the plaintiff, the dismissal was without prejudice to a later suit on the same claim.

2. Code Practice

The common-law procedure was subject to some abuse by plaintiffs taking dismissals to prevent decisions on the merits favoring their adversaries. As a result, code-pleading states limited the right of plaintiffs to dismiss their actions without prejudice: Such a dismissal had to occur *before* the commencement of trial; otherwise it was deemed to be with prejudice (*i.e.,* a bar to relitigation). This is still the rule in some states. [*See, e.g.,* Cal. Civ. Proc. Code § 581(b)(1)]

a. Note

The filing of a counterclaim or cross-demand for affirmative relief may also prevent a voluntary dismissal without prejudice. [Cal. Civ. Proc. Code § 581(i)]

3. Federal Practice—Notice of Dismissal (Voluntary)

a. Filing of Notice

Under federal practice, a plaintiff retains the right to dismiss his own action by filing a notice of dismissal. [Fed. R. Civ. P. 41(a)(1)(A)(i)] But the right to do so is even more narrowly limited than in code-pleading states.

b. Time for Filing

An effective notice of dismissal must be filed before the filing of the adversary's *answer or motion for summary judgment*. Thereafter, the plaintiff cannot dismiss without the defendant's consent or court order. [Fed. R. Civ. P. 41(a)(i)(A); 41(a)(2)]

cf. **Compare**: It has been held that a *motion to dismiss for failure to state a claim* is not tantamount to a motion for summary judgment, and does not terminate the plaintiff's right to file a voluntary dismissal. [**Woody v. City of Duluth,** 176 F.R.D. 310 (D. Minn. 1997); **Marques v. Federal Reserve Bank of Chicago,** 286 F.3d 1014 (7th Cir. 2002)—Rule 41(a)(1) motion filed on same day as Rule 12(b)(6) motion attaching extraneous matter was timely because court had not yet considered extraneous materials and the motion could not have been converted into a summary-judgment motion at the time the voluntary dismissal was filed]

c. Number of Dismissals

The plaintiff is limited to one (voluntary) dismissal by notice. Thereafter, any dismissal operates as a dismissal *with prejudice*. [Fed. R. Civ. P. 41(a)(1)(B)]

d. Trial Court Cannot Set Aside Proper Dismissal

An order striking a timely notice of dismissal is reversible error, and any judgment subsequently entered against the plaintiff will be reversed on appeal after trial. [*In re* **Bath and Kitchen Fixtures Antitrust Litigation,** 535 F.3d 161 (3d Cir. 2008)]

e. Effect on Power to Sanction

Unless the court has already issued an order to show cause why sanctions should not be imposed at the time of the voluntary dismissal or settlement, it may not impose monetary sanctions on its own initiative. [Fed. R. Civ. P. 11(c)(5)(B)]

4. Federal Practice—Dismissal by Leave of Court

a. Time for Motion

The court may grant the plaintiff's motion for leave to dismiss without prejudice at any time *before judgment—i.e.,* even after the trial has commenced.

b. Discretion to Refuse Limited

The discretion of the court to refuse a dismissal without prejudice is limited.

e.g. **Example**: "We will affirm dismissals with prejudice . . . only when (1) there is a clear record of delay or contumacious conduct by the plaintiff, and (2) the district court has expressly determined that lesser sanctions would not prompt diligent prosecution." [**Berry v. CIGNA/RSI-CIGNA,** 975 F.2d 1188 (5th Cir. 1992)]

cf. **Compare**: The court would not grant dismissal without prejudice even though the plaintiff claimed that it was his attorney's fault that no action had been taken in the case, and urged that the harsh penalty of dismissal with prejudice should not be used. [**Seabrook v. City of New York,** 236 F.R.D. 123 (E.D.N.Y. 2006)]

(1) Counterclaims Preserved

The court may not dismiss over the objection of a defendant who has filed a counterclaim unless the counterclaim can remain pending for independent adjudication. [Fed. R. Civ. P. 41(a)(2); *see* Chapter Two regarding subject-matter jurisdiction]

c. Number of Dismissals

The court is not limited as to the number of times it may grant motions to dismiss the same action without prejudice—provided, of course, that there is a legitimate reason for the repeated requests. [**American Cyanimid Co. v. McGhee,** 317 F.2d 295 (5th Cir. 1963)]

d. Conditions of Dismissal

A plaintiff seeking dismissal *without* prejudice may be required to bear the full cost of the litigation to date, including the adversary's attorneys' fees. [Fed. R. Civ. P. 41(a)(2)] But such conditions may not be imposed on a plaintiff seeking to dismiss his claim *with* prejudice. [**Aero Tech, Inc. v. Estes,** 110 F.3d 1523 (10th Cir. 1997)] *Note*: Under Rule 11, sanctions may not be imposed on a plaintiff who voluntarily dismisses a groundless suit in response to service of a motion for sanctions. (*See supra*, p. 169 *et seq.*)

e. Continuing Jurisdiction—Stipulated Dismissal

When dismissal by stipulation pursuant to Rule 41(a)(1)(A)(ii) provides that the court shall retain jurisdiction to enforce a settlement agreement, the court has continuing jurisdiction, but otherwise dismissal terminates the court's jurisdiction. [**Kokkonen v. Guardian Life Insurance Co.,** 511 U.S. 375 (1994)—court lacked jurisdiction to enforce provision of parties' settlement agreement after dismissal pursuant to that agreement because the parties' obligation to comply was not made part of the order of dismissal]

Chapter Five
Parties

Chapter Five

Key Exam Issues

Modern procedural rules make available several devices for joinder of parties beyond the "single plaintiff vs. single defendant" paradigm of a lawsuit. The standards for joinder vary with the functions served by the various procedural devices. When you face a problem involving more than just one plaintiff vs. one defendant, consider the following:

1. Before you even get to joinder issues, you may need to think about the requirements of *real party in interest and capacity to sue or be sued*:

   a. Is the action brought in the name of the *real party in interest, i.e.*, the party who has the right to enforce the claim under governing substantive law?

   b. Do the parties have legal competence to be parties to a lawsuit; do they have *capacity to sue or be sued?* Partnerships (as opposed to partners) and infants and incompetent persons, for example, may lack legal capacity.

2. If the situation in your question calls for joinder of someone not a party to the suit, is joinder *required*?

   a. Would failure to join the absentee prevent the granting of *complete relief,* or *prejudice* his or the present parties' interests? If so, the absentee should be joined if joinder is feasible. If it is not feasible (as when joinder would destroy complete diversity in a diversity case in federal court), the court must decide whether it can proceed with only the present parties before it.

      (1) If the court can proceed, the absentee is characterized as merely a *"required"* party, and the action can proceed in his absence.

      (2) If the court cannot proceed, the absentee is regarded as an *"indispensable"* party, and the action must be dismissed.

3. To determine whether *permissive* joinder is appropriate, consider:

   a. Is the relief sought jointly, severally, or in the alternative;

   b. Does the claim arise out of the same transaction, occurrence or series of transactions or occurrences; and

   c. Is there a common question of law or fact?

4. Sometimes someone not already a party to the suit seeks to *intervene*. In that case consider:

   a. Is the case one for *intervention of right,* in which disposition in his absence could impair or impede his ability to protect an interest he claims in the property or transaction sued on, and the existing parties do not adequately represent his interest; or

   b. Is the case one in which the court may allow *permissive intervention,* with the prospective intervenor's claim or defense having a question of law or fact in common with the main action?

5. When you see facts that have two (or more) persons asserting a claim to money or property in the hands of a third party (the "stakeholder"), think of *interpleader*. The stakeholder may deposit the property with the court and seek a ruling as to which of the adverse claimants is entitled to the property.

6. A defendant in your question may seek *impleader* of a third-party defendant. If so, is the third party (*e.g.*, an insurer) one who is or may be liable to the defendant for all or part of the plaintiff's claim against the defendant?

7. In federal court when an effort is made at adding a party, if there is no independent basis of federal jurisdiction, think about whether there is **supplemental jurisdiction** over the added claim or for a claim against the additional party.

8. If the situation seems to call for a **class action**:

   a. Ask:

      (1) Are the class members so **numerous** that joinder of all is impracticable;

      (2) Are there **common questions** of law or fact;

      (3) Are the representative's **claims or defenses typical** of those of the class; and

      (4) Will the representative **adequately represent** the interests of the class?

   b. And in addition, ask:

      (1) Might there be prejudice from separate actions;

      (2) Has the class's opponent acted or refused to act on grounds generally applicable to the class, making classwide injunctive or declaratory relief appropriate; or

      (3) Do common questions predominate over individual ones, and is a class action superior to other methods?

   c. If you find that the case may be conducted as a class action, has **required notice** been given?

   d. If a proposed **settlement** has been reached in a case filed as a class action and it seeks to resolve class claims or defenses, ask:

      (1) Has appropriate **notice** of the proposed settlement been given to members of the class;

      (2) Have any **objections** to the proposed settlement been submitted by members of the class; and

      (3) Have the proponents of the proposed settlement demonstrated that it is **fair, reasonable, and adequate?**

A. Real Party in Interest Rule

1. Background

At common law, only the legal "owner" of a right could bring an action for infringement of that right. Since the common law did not recognize equitable interests (*e.g.*, rights of subrogees, beneficiaries of various kinds of trusts, etc.), the holder of such an interest could not sue at law for its enforcement, but instead had to rely on the legal owner to bring suit. This burdensome practice has been abolished, and today, suit can be brought **only** in the name of the real party in interest. [Fed. R. Civ. P. 17]

2. Definition

The real party in interest rule has two parts; the person who is suing must: (i) use her **own name** as plaintiff, **and** (ii) have a **legal right** to enforce the claim in question under the applicable substantive law.

a. Exception—Permission to Sue Using Fictitious Name

In limited circumstances, a court may permit a plaintiff to proceed under a fictitious name, such as Jane Doe, to protect against serious harm that would result from revealing the party's name. However, this is allowed only if the plaintiff shows a compelling need to proceed anonymously. [*See, e.g.,* **Southern Methodist University Association of Women Law Students v. Wynne & Jaffe,** 599 F.2d 707 (5th Cir. 1979)—female lawyers asserting that law firm discriminated against women could not proceed anonymously]

b. Burden of Proof

The plaintiff has the burden of proving that she is a real party in interest; *i.e.,* that she should be allowed to sue to protect the interest involved.

c. Under Federal Rules and State Rules

The following parties have a right to sue as representative parties even though they may have no beneficial interest in the claims at issue [Fed. R. Civ. P. 17(a)]:

(1) The executor, administrator, guardian, or trustee of an estate;

(2) A party to a contract made for the benefit of another party (e.g., an agent contracting on behalf of the principal or the promisee of a third-party beneficiary contract); and

(3) A private claimant suing in the name of the United States Government, if such a claim is expressly authorized by statute.

d. In All Other Cases

In all other cases, a determination of the real party in interest is made according to applicable substantive law. In a federal diversity action, applicable state law governs.

3. Determination of Real Party in Interest

The following situations illustrate the types of problems encountered in determining the real party in interest.

a. Assignments

Whether an assignee is the real party in interest depends primarily on the nature of the assignment.

(1) Complete Assignment

If the assignor's ***entire interest*** has been transferred to the assignee, the assignee has become the real party in interest. The assignee may then prosecute any action to enforce the assigned right in her own name without joining the assignor.

(a) Gratuitous Assignment

In state and federal practice, the assignee can sue even if she paid nothing for the claim and is merely an ***assignee for collection***. However, in federal court, the citizenship of the ***assignor*** determines whether diversity exists. (*See supra,* p. 73.)

(b) Assignment After Commencement of Suit

If the assignment takes place after suit has been filed, the assignee may either continue the action in the name of the assignor *or* be substituted as the plaintiff. [*See* Fed. R. Civ. P. 25(c)]

(c) Effect of Judgment

A judgment in the assignee's action will *bar any subsequent suit* on the same claim by the assignor, because of the *privity* between the assignee and assignor. [**Nemeth v. Hair,** 146 Cal. App. 2d 405 (1956); *and see* discussion on claim preclusion, *infra*, p. 446 *et seq.*]

(2) Partial Assignments

At common law, the assignee of part of a claim could not enforce the claim at all. However, partial assignees could enforce their claims in *equity* if the assignor and all other partial assignees joined as parties in the same suit.

(a) Modern Rule

Today, the assignor and all partial assignees are considered *"required parties"* in any suit to enforce the claim, and on appropriate motion, the court will order their joinder. [**United States v. Aetna Casualty & Surety Co.,** 338 U.S. 366 (1949)]

(3) Assignment May Create Diversity

When an assignee seeks to base federal-court subject-matter jurisdiction on diversity of citizenship, and there was no diversity between the assignor and the defendant, jurisdiction exists only if substantial consideration was given for the assignment. (*See supra*, p. 73.)

b. Subrogation

Subrogation is an equitable principle through which an assignment occurs by operation of law. Under the doctrine of subrogation, the person who *pays* another for a loss or injury caused by the act of some third person is entitled to enforce whatever claim the injured person had against the third person. Most jurisdictions allow the person who paid (subrogee) to sue in his own name without joining the injured party (subrogor). [**United States v. Aetna Casualty & Surety Co.,** *supra*]

e.g. **Example**: Insurance Co. insures Plaintiff's house and pays Plaintiff for damages to the house caused in a fire. Insurance Co. becomes subrogated to Plaintiff's claims for fire damage to the house and is entitled to sue Plaintiff's neighbors on the theory that they were responsible for the fire damage to Plaintiffs house, [**State Farm General Insurance Co. v. Wells Fargo Bank, N.A.,** 143 Cal. App. 4th 1098 (2006)]

(1) Tactical Problem

An insurance company will usually prefer to sue in the name of its *insured,* rather than in its own name, to avoid any jury prejudice against insurers. Consequently, most insurance settlements contain provisions expressly authorizing the insurer to sue the wrongdoer "in the name of the insured."

(a) Note

The traditional view did not permit such suits because the insured, having been fully paid and having assigned the claim to the company, had no further interest in the matter. [*See* **Sosnow v. Storatti Corp.,** 295 N.Y. 675 (1946)] However, most states now permit suits in the name of the insured. [*See* **Bakowski v. Mountain States Steel, Inc.,** 52 P.3d 1179 (Utah 2002)]

(b) And Note

Even states that do not permit suit in the name of the insured may recognize the "loan receipt" device. Here, the insurer—instead of paying off the insured—makes him a "loan" repayable only out of proceeds from the insured's recovery against the third person. The insured gets his money but still "owns" the claim. The insurance company then brings suit in the name of the insured, and the insurer keeps the proceeds if it wins.

c. Trusts

(1) Trustee

The trustee of a trust holds legal title to the trust estate and is therefore *the real party in interest* for redress of *any wrong to the trust estate*. [Fed. R. Civ. P. 17] Suit is maintained in the trustee's name as trustee (*e.g.*, "John Smith, as trustee of the Mary Doe Trust"). [**Moeller v. Superior Court,** 16 Cal. 4th 1124 (1997)]

(2) Beneficiary

The beneficiary of a trust may *sue the trustee* to protect her rights as beneficiary—*e.g.*, for an accounting, for distributions of assets, etc. [**Harnedy v. Whitty,** 110 Cal. App. 4th 1333 (2003)]

(a) But Note

A beneficiary cannot sue third persons for wrongs to the trust estate unless the trustee refuses to bring suit for such injuries. In the latter situation, the beneficiary can sue the third party by joining the trustee and alleging his failure to act. [**Saks v. Damon Raike & Co.,** 7 Cal. App. 4th 419 (1992)]

d. Executors and Administrators

Executors and administrators are the proper parties to sue on behalf of decedents' estates at law or in equity.

(1) State of Appointment

Problems do arise about the capacity of a representative appointed in one state to sue in another, but such problems do not result from the real party in interest provision. They concern primarily the policy of the forum state of protecting local creditors. This situation has led to the general rule that *an executor or administrator has capacity to sue only in the state of her appointment,* unless she obtains ancillary appointment in another state.

(2) Beneficiary of an Estate Pursuing Claims

Ordinarily, the legatee or distributee of an estate may *not* bring suit to pursue claims of the estate, although exceptions have been recognized in situations parallel to the exceptions for beneficiaries of a trust.

(3) Survival Statutes and Wrongful-Death Acts

Claims under survival statutes are generally part of the decedent's estate and are to be pursued by his executor or administrator just as any other asset of the estate would be. Wrongful-death acts generally specify the proper party to an action under them. Some of them name one or more of the beneficiaries, and in such a case, the party named is, of course, the real party in interest. Many of them require suit to be brought by the personal representative of the deceased—*i.e.*, the executor or administrator. However, when suing under such a statute, the executor or administrator is not acting as a representative of the estate, but rather as a person designated by statute. Consequently, the judgment or recovery under the statute will not be an asset of the estate at all, but instead will belong to the statutory beneficiaries, who may or may not be the same persons who would take as legatees or distributees of the estate.

GILBERT

PARTY	EXAMPLE
ASSIGNEE	Becomes the real party in interest if assignor assigns entire interest; if less than entire interest is assigned, assignor and assignee both are "required parties" and on appropriate motion court will order that both be joined.
SUBROGEE	Most jurisdictions allow a subrogee (i.e., a person who has paid another's obligation to a third party—the subrogor) to sue in his own name without joining the subrogor.
TRUSTEE	The trustee is the real party in interest for redress of any wrong to the trust estate.
BENEFICIARY OF A TRUST	The beneficiary of a trust may sue the trustee to protect her rights as a beneficiary, but may not bring suit against another on behalf of the trust.
EXECUTORS AND ADMINSTRATORS	Executors and administrators are the real parties in interest to sue on behalf of decedents' estates.
PRINCIPAL	If an obligation on a contract made by an agent on behalf of a principal is owed to the principal alone, the principal is the only real party in interest.
AGENT	If an agent enters into a contract on behalf of a principal and the obligation is owed to both the principal and the agent, the agent is a real party in interest in addition to the principal.
THIRD-PARTY BENEFICIARY	If a third-party beneficiary has enforceable rights under a contract, she is a real party in interest and may sue in her own name.

e. **Principal and Agent**

If a contract has been executed by an agent acting for a principal, the following rules apply:

(1) *If the obligation is owed to the principal alone*, the principal is the only proper plaintiff.

(2) **If the obligation is owed to both the agent and the principal**, either party may sue (*e.g.*, if there was a promise to both the agent and the principal). [**Warren Insurance Agency v. Surpur Timber Co.,** 250 Cal. App. 2d 99 (1967)—suit by agent; **Ford v. Williams,** 62 U.S. 287 (1858)—suit by undisclosed principal]

f. Third-Party Beneficiary

If a third-party beneficiary has enforceable rights under a contract, he is the real party in interest and is entitled to sue in his own name to enforce his rights. [**Orcutt v. Ferranini,** 237 Cal. App. 2d 216 (1965)]

(1) Rights of Promisee

The promisee under a contract may also be entitled to sue to enforce the promise given for the benefit of a third party. In such case, **both** the promisee and the third-party beneficiary would have enforceable rights and would be deemed real parties in interest.

4. Attacking Violation of Real Party in Interest Rule

a. If Defect Apparent

(1) Federal Practice

If a violation of the real party in interest rule is apparent on the face of a complaint in federal court, the defendant should make a **motion to dismiss** for failure to state a claim upon which relief may be granted (since the plaintiff has no right to recovery). [Fed. R. Civ. P. 12(b)(6)]

(2) Code Practice (Some States)

Under code-pleading practice, a **general demurrer** is appropriate to attack defects on the face of the complaint. (*See supra*, p. 153.)

b. When Defect Not Apparent

If the defect is not apparent on the face of the complaint, the defendant may move for summary judgment (supported by appropriate affidavits to establish the defect) or may raise the matter as an affirmative defense in her answer.

5. Nonjoinder of Required Party

If the named plaintiff has some kind of interest in the claim (assignor or assignee, principal or agent, trustee or beneficiary), and the objection is that someone else should *also* be the named plaintiff (another partial assignee, principal, etc.), this is an objection to nonjoinder of a *required party*.

a. When Objection Can Be Raised

The objection as to the named plaintiff can be raised by motion before trial or at the trial itself [Fed. R. Civ. P. 12(h)(2)], but delay may result in estoppel against raising it. If the objection is first made on appeal, it is too late unless serious injustice would inevitably result from the nonjoinder. [**Provident Bank & Trust Co. v. Patterson,** 390 U.S. 102 (1968)]

b. No Cause of Action

If the named plaintiff has *no* substantive interest in the claim being enforced, he has no cause of action. This objection is therefore proper at any time before judgment. Note, however, that under the usual rules governing appeal, a claim that the plaintiff has no cause of action cannot be raised on appeal for the first time, and the objection *cannot* be made in collateral attack on the judgment.

B. Capacity of Party to Sue or Be Sued

1. Definition

"Capacity" refers to *legal competence to be a party* to a lawsuit. The plaintiff must have the capacity to sue, and the defendant must have the capacity to be sued.

2. Individuals

The capacity of an individual to sue or be sued is determined by the law of her domicile. [Fed. R. Civ. P. 17(b)(1)] If the plaintiff lacks capacity (as in the case of a minor or an incompetent), suit must be maintained by a duly authorized or appointed guardian. If there is none, the court must appoint one for the particular action (a *"guardian ad litem"*). [Fed. R. Civ. P. 17(c)(2)]

a. Pleadings by Guardian

If a guardian or conservator appears in the action, the pleadings are usually drawn in the name of the guardian "for and on behalf of" the incompetent or minor. [Fed. R. Civ. P. 17(c)(1)] Note that state practice on such pleadings varies. For example, in California, the pleadings are drawn in the name of the minor or incompetent "by a guardian or conservator. . . ." [Cal. Civ. Proc. Code § 372]

b. Incompetent's Right to Disaffirm Judgment

If a minor (or incompetent) is a party to the action but is not represented by a guardian, any judgment rendered is *voidable by him* within a reasonable time after attaining majority (or being restored to competency) *if* it appears that his legal interests were inadequately protected in the action. [**Withers v. Tucker,** 145 N.W.2d 665 (Wis. 1966)—minor represented by attorney]

3. Corporations

The capacity of a corporation to sue or be sued is determined by the law of the state in which it was organized.

Example: Statutes in some states provide for suspension of powers of a corporation that is delinquent in paying its state taxes. [*See, e.g.*, Cal. Rev. & Tax Code § 23301] In such a case, the corporation would have no power to sue, defend itself, or appeal from a judgment as long as it is under the suspension. [**Mather Construction Co. v. United States,** 475 F.2d 1152 (Ct. Cl. 1973)]

a. Limitation

A state cannot impose a disability on a corporation if doing so would violate *federal law*.

e.g. **Example**: An attempt to deny an out-of-state corporation the right to sue in local courts to enforce a contract made in interstate commerce would violate federal law. [**Allenberg Cotton Co. v. Pittman,** 419 U.S. 20 (1974)]

4. Partnerships

Two issues arise with respect to the capacity of partnerships: (i) whether the partnership can (or must) sue as an entity, distinct from its members; and (ii) if the suit is by one or more of the members of the partnership, whether they should be named individually or should sue in the name of the partnership.

a. Federal Practice—Entity vs. Aggregate

In federal courts, a partnership can always *sue or be sued as an entity if the litigation involves a federal question*. However, in other cases—including a diversity action—the partnership's capacity to sue or be sued is determined by the law of the state in which the federal court is located. [Fed. R. Civ. P. 17(b)(3)]

b. State Law Varies

About half the states permit a partnership to be sued, but not to sue, as an entity (in its common name). In those states, actions on a partnership claim must be brought in the names of the individual partners (*e.g.*, "Alistair, Bert, and Chip, as co-partners doing business as Acme Partnership"). Other states allow the partnership to both sue and be sued as an entity. [*See* Cal. Civ. Proc. Code § 369.5(a)]

5. Unincorporated Associations

At common law, unincorporated associations lacked capacity to sue or be sued as entities. [**Ostrom v. Greene,** 161 N.Y. 353 (1900)]

a. State Practice

Many states now treat unincorporated associations like corporations. [*See* Cal. Civ. Proc. Code § 369.5(a); **Wright v. Arkansas Activities Association,** 501 F.2d 25 (8th Cir. 1974)]

b. Federal Practice

In federal courts, an association has capacity to sue or be sued when a *federal right* is being enforced by or against the association. But when a *state*-law right is being enforced, as in a *diversity* action, the capacity of an unincorporated association is determined by the law of the state in which the federal action is brought. [Fed. R. Civ. P. 17(b)(3)]

(1) Existence of Diversity

For purposes of determining the existence of diversity of citizenship, the association is considered a citizen of *each state* of which any one of its members is a citizen. (*See supra*, p. 69.)

cf. **Compare—Residence for Venue**: An entity with the capacity to sue and be sued in its common name under applicable law is deemed to reside, if a defendant, in any judicial district in which it is subject to the court's personal jurisdiction and, if a plaintiff, only in the judicial district in which it maintains its principal place of business. [28 U.S.C. § 1391(c)(2)]

c. Real Party in Interest Rule

Even when an unincorporated association has the capacity to sue, it must assert a claim that belongs to it rather than to its members individually.

> **Example**: An unincorporated association of businesses has standing to seek an injunction against conduct constituting unfair competition to its members, but not to seek damages for past injury to the members, as such rights do not belong to the association. [**Travel Agents Malpractice Action Corps v. Regal Cultural Society,** 287 A.2d 4 (N.J. 1972)]

6. Attacking Lack of Capacity

a. Lack of Capacity on Face of Complaint

If lack of capacity appears on the face of the complaint, the complaint is subject to a *motion to dismiss* (or demurrer, in some states). Usually, however, it does not appear on the face and must be raised by motion for summary judgment or in the *answer*.

b. Lack of Capacity Not Raised by Time of Answer

If lack of capacity is not raised by the time of the answer, the defect is *waived*. The judgment entered will determine the rights of the party despite lack of capacity, unless the party can show that she was inadequately represented (*see supra*, p. 215).

C. Joinder of Parties

1. In General

Determining which parties are to be joined as plaintiffs or defendants requires consideration of the rules of required and permissive joinder. Compulsory-joinder rules cover parties who *must* be joined ("indispensable parties") and those who *should* be joined if possible ("conditionally required parties"). The rules of permissive joinder apply to parties who *may* be joined ("proper parties").

2. Permissive Joinder

At common law and under the early codes, a plaintiff's joinder options were limited. Under the Federal Rules and modern codes, however, a plaintiff may join anyone involved in the *transaction* that is the subject matter of the suit.

a. Early Approach

Under the original codes, parties could be joined only if they each had "an interest" in both the subject of the action and the relief sought. The rules governing joinder of causes of action required that causes joined "affect" *all* parties joined. These rules often prevented joinder even when the need was obvious.

> **Example**: Wife, injured by Defendant's negligence, sues for her injuries. Husband attempts to join his claim for loss of her services. Joinder was not proper under the early approach because Husband had no "interest" in the relief sought by Wife, and vice versa. [**Ryder v. Jefferson Hotel Co.,** 113 S.E. 474 (S.C. 1922)]

b.   Modern Approach

Today, parties may join or be joined in one action if:

(i)   A right to relief is asserted by (or against) them *jointly, severally, or in the alternative*;

(ii) The right to relief *arises out of the same transaction or occurrence or series of transactions or occurrences*; and

(iii) There is *at least one question of law or fact common to all parties* sought to be joined.

[Fed. R. Civ. P. 20(a)]

(1)   Relief Sought

(a)   Separate or Joint

Each plaintiff is not required to have an interest in every claim or in all the relief prayed for. If there are several plaintiffs, they have the option to seek separate relief or joint relief. Likewise, if several defendants are joined, relief may be sought against each separately or against them jointly.

(b)   "In the Alternative"—Plaintiff "In Doubt"

Sometimes, a plaintiff may be in doubt as to which of several defendants is liable for his injuries (*e.g.*, Plaintiff is injured by a bullet fired by either Defendant 1 or Defendant 2). In such a case, it is proper for the plaintiff to set forth a claim against each defendant in the alternative, so that their respective liabilities can be determined.

(2)   "Same Transaction" Requirement

The requirement that the right to relief arise from the "same transaction or occurrence or series of transactions or occurrences" is construed very broadly. *Some causal relationship or interrelation* among the defendants' conduct, or in the interest being asserted by multiple plaintiffs, is sufficient. This requirement tends to merge with the "common question" requirement, below.

e.g. **Example**: Plaintiff was permitted to join a claim against an insurance company for inducing Plaintiff to refrain from suing within the statute of limitations period with a claim against his former attorney for negligently failing to file the suit on time. [**Rekeweg v. Federal Mutual Insurance Co.,** 27 F.R.D. 431 (N.D. Ind. 1961)]

(a)   Note

When defendants are joined *in the alternative* because the plaintiff is in doubt about which one caused his injuries, the injury issue supplies the requisite relationship between the claims joined, even when the conduct of the two defendants is otherwise factually *unrelated*.

e.g. **Example**: When Plaintiff claims permanent back injuries after involvement in two unrelated traffic accidents, alleging doubt as to whether his back injury was caused by accident 1 or accident 2, joinder of both drivers as defendants is proper. [**Landau v. Salam,** 4 Cal. 3d 901 (1971)]

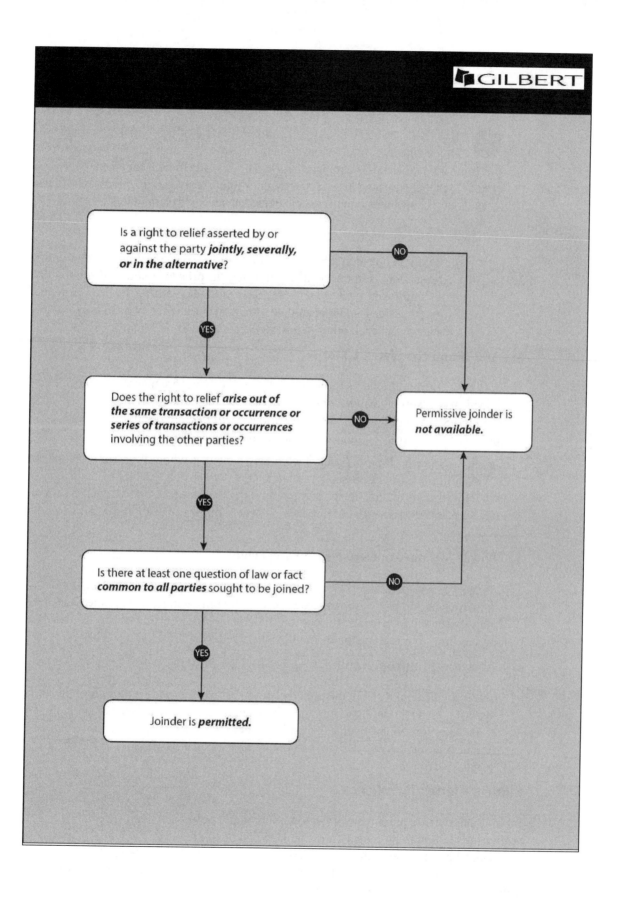

(3) "Common Question" Requirement

It is sufficient if there is a *single* question of law or fact common to all parties joined. However, it is *not* necessary that the "common question" be in dispute.

e.g. **Example**: Plaintiff 1, a driver, and Plaintiff 2, a passenger in the car, sue Defendant for injuries sustained in an auto accident. The "common question" is whether Defendant was negligent. This is sufficient for joinder purposes even though there are also many separate questions involved (*e.g.*, injuries sustained by each, any contributory negligence barring Plaintiff 1's claim, etc.).

(a) Caution

If the common question is relatively unimportant, the court may tend to define the "transaction" somewhat more narrowly to prevent joinder of claims that have no significant *evidentiary relationship* to each other. Hence, a *practical test* for permissive joinder is applied: Are the issues in the two claims *factually intertwined* with each other in any significant way?

(4) Additional Unrelated Claims

As long as the requirements for joinder of parties (above) are met, each of the parties joined may assert as many *claims* as she has against any opposing party. [Fed. R. Civ. P. 18] The policy of the law is to allow *unlimited* joinder of claims as long as there is a transactional connection among all of the parties.

e.g. **Example**: Plaintiff joins Defendant 1 against whom he asserts claims for injuries while a passenger in Defendant 2's vehicle, and Defendant 2 against whom he asserts claims for the same injuries in the accident, and also for failure to pay a promissory note that Defendant 2 executed in favor of Plaintiff. This joinder is proper.

(5) Power of Court to Order Separate Trials

To curb expense or delay, or to avoid prejudice that might result from the joinder of numerous parties asserting numerous separate claims against one another, the court may order separate trials for various claims joined, or otherwise regulate the proceedings to minimize the difficulties involved. [Fed. R. Civ. P. 20(b)]

(6) Attacking Improper Joinder

Under the Federal Rules, a misjoined claim may be *dismissed on motion* of the party against whom it is asserted; and the whole action may be dismissed as to that party if no claim for relief remains against him. [Fed. R. Civ. P. 21] Under code-pleading practice, a *demurrer* will lie for misjoinder of claims. [Cal. Civ. Proc. Code § 430.10(d)]

c. Subject-Matter Jurisdiction

In addition to the requirements of personal jurisdiction over defendants, federal subject-matter jurisdiction requirements must be satisfied as to all parties (whether plaintiffs or defendants) permissively joined. Supplemental jurisdiction does not extend to permissive joinder when the permissively joined matter is not part of the same case or controversy with the claim over which the federal court has original jurisdiction, or in diversity cases when banned by 28 U.S.C. § 1367(b). (*See supra*, pp. 93–96.)

Be sure to remember subject-matter jurisdiction limitations when you encounter an exam question involving permissive joinder in federal courts. *Federal subject-matter jurisdiction requirements* must be met *for all parties*, and supplemental jurisdiction will not help when joinder is of a matter that is not part of the same case or controversy as the claim over which the federal court has original jurisdiction. For example, suppose Plaintiff has a state-law claim against Defendant 1, who is diverse, for breach of Plaintiff's lease of an apartment from Defendant 1. Although Plaintiff may also have a claim against Defendant 2, the leasing agent, that arises from the same transaction, there would not be supplemental jurisdiction to add Defendant 2 if she were not diverse. On the other hand, if there were also a claim of violation of federal anti-discrimination statutes against Defendant 2, the state-law breach-of-lease claim could be in federal court as supplemental to the federal claim. Even then, however, Plaintiff's claim that Defendant 2 also failed to deliver a $300 table to Plaintiff in breach of a contract unrelated to the lease could not be asserted in federal court, because that claim would not be within supplemental jurisdiction, although allowed by claim-joinder rules.

3. Required Joinder

Joinder is required for *any person who has a material interest in the case and whose absence would result in substantial prejudice* to the absentee or to other parties before the court. [Fed. R. Civ. P. 19]

a. Traditional Approach—"Necessary" vs. "Indispensable" Parties

Historically, the statutes and cases drew a distinction between "necessary" and "indispensable" parties.

(1) "Necessary Parties"

Necessary parties were those who *ought* to be joined *if possible*. However, if their interests were *"severable"* and if one or more were not joined (*e.g.*, could not be located), the court could still determine the rights and liabilities of the parties before the court.

(2) "Indispensable Parties"

Indispensable parties, on the other hand, were those whose interests were so unavoidably involved (*i.e.*, nonseverable) that the court could not proceed without them. Failure to join such parties meant that the action had to be dismissed. [**Shields v. Barrow**, 58 U.S. 130 (1855)]

(3) Criticism

A party's interest could always be "severed" somehow, simply by leaving his interests out of the judgment and allowing them to be adjudicated later. Hence, the issue in distinguishing necessary and indispensable parties was not whether the absentee's interests were in fact severable (they always were), but whether they should be adjudicated along with those already present in the action.

b. Modern Approach—Practical Considerations

Modern rules recognize that the labels "necessary" and "indispensable" reflected conclusions arrived at for other reasons. Hence, these rules focus on the *practical consequences* if a party with an interest in the action is not before the court. [**Provident Bank & Trust Co. v. Patterson,** *supra,* p. 214]

(1) Persons to Be Joined if Feasible

Federal Rule 19(a) provides that any person who is subject to service of process and whose joinder will not deprive the court of subject-matter jurisdiction is a "***required party***" (formerly called "necessary party") who must be joined as a party if:

(i) In his absence, ***complete relief*** cannot be accorded those already parties [Fed. R. Civ. P. 19(a)(1)(A)]; ***or***

(ii) He claims an interest relating to the subject of the action and is so situated that disposing of the action in his absence may:

    i. As a practical matter ***impair or impede*** his ability to protect his interest [Fed. R. Civ. P. 19(a)(1)(B)(i)]; or

    ii. Leave an ***existing party*** subject to a substantial risk of incurring double, multiple, or otherwise inconsistent obligations because of the interest. [Fed. R. Civ. P. 19(a)(1)(B)(ii)]

(For examples, *see infra*, pp. 223–225.)

(a) Caveat

Although the modern pragmatic approach has been adopted in the federal courts and in many states, some decisions still assert that ***certain types of parties*** (*e.g.,* partial assignees, *infra*, p. 224) always must be joined—*i.e.,* that these parties are "indispensable." A review of the case law, therefore, reveals two conflicting rules: (i) that required joinder is a pragmatic problem, and (ii) that it is "jurisdictional" in that an action cannot proceed without an "indispensable" party.

(2) Effect of Nonjoinder—Possible Dismissal

If a person to be joined under Rule 19(a) cannot be made a party (*e.g.,* because he is not subject to the court's jurisdiction), the court must determine whether "***in equity and in good conscience***" the action can proceed without him or whether the action should be dismissed. The court's determination is based on the following practical considerations [Fed. R. Civ. P. 19(b)]:

(a) The extent to which any judgment rendered in the action would be ***prejudicial*** to the interest of the absent party, or the interests of those already before the court;

(b) The extent to which such prejudice could be ***lessened or avoided*** by appropriate court action;

(c) Whether relief rendered without the absent party would be ***adequate;*** and

(d) Whether the plaintiff has any ***other adequate remedy*** if the action is dismissed for nonjoinder of the absent party.

e.g. **Example**: An interpleader action was brought to determine whether plaintiffs injured by human-rights violations during the regime of deposed President Ferdinand Marcos of the Philippines could enforce a judgment against Marcos by seizing a New York stock-brokerage account that Marcos had opened. The Republic of the Philippines also asserted a nonfrivolous claim of ownership to that account as looted assets of the nation. The Court held that the action should have been dismissed. The Republic was immune to suit in the United States as a foreign sovereign. Proceeding with the case could nullify the Republic's interest in the account. "Dismissal under Rule 19(b) will mean, in some instances, that plaintiffs will be left without a forum for definitive resolution of their claims. But that result is contemplated under the doctrine of foreign sovereign immunity." [**Republic of Philippines v. Pimentel,** 553 U.S. 851 (2008)]

(3) Application

Situations in which required-joinder issues commonly arise involve:

(a) Joint Obligors

1) Parties to Contract

Joint promisors under a ***contract*** (and other joint debtors) should be joined as defendants whenever feasible. However, if one cannot be joined, the court can still proceed against those before the court. [**Janney Montgomery Scott, Inc. v. Shepard Niles, Inc.,** 11 F.3d 399 (3d Cir. 1993)]

a) Rationale

There is no "substantial prejudice" to the parties before the court that would justify dismissal, since an obligor held responsible on the joint debt has a ***right of contribution*** against the other joint obligors.

2) Tortfeasors

Although the plaintiff may join in one action all defendants potentially liable to her as a result of a given transaction or occurrence (*see supra*, p. 218), ordinarily she is not required to do so, and a joint tortfeasor is ***not considered a required party***. [**Temple v. Synthes Corp.,** 498 U.S. 5 (1990)—"It has long been the rule that it is not necessary for all joint tortfeasors to be named as defendants in a single lawsuit"]

a) Rationale

The plaintiff is the "master of her lawsuit" and can choose to sue as many or as few potential defendants as she desires.

b) Distinguish—Impleader

Often there is a right of contribution among joint tortfeasors. When this is so, those defendants who are sued can file third-party complaints or cross-complaints (depending on the jurisdiction) against the other tortfeasors for ***indemnity*** (*see infra*, p. 226). [**American Motorcycle Association v. Superior Court,** 20 Cal. 3d 578 (1978)] *Note:* This maneuver does not make the new party a defendant on the plaintiff's complaint unless the plaintiff amends to assert a claim against the new defendant, which may be beyond a federal court's subject-matter jurisdiction. *See infra*, p. 228. The only claim asserted against the new defendant is to indemnify the original defendant.

(b) Joint Obligees

Where persons are jointly owed a duty under a contract, the courts have usually held that they are not only required, but also *"indispensable"* parties, and have dismissed for nonjoinder. [**Jenkins v. Reneau,** 697 F.2d 160 (6th Cir. 1983)]

1) Rationale

A promise made to the obligees jointly should be enforced jointly since otherwise there is a risk that the right of the absent obligee to enforce the promise may be prejudiced, that the defendant might be subjected to inconsistent obligations in an action brought by the absent obligee, and that the court would be unable to afford complete relief because it could not provide in its decree for the defendant's obligations to the nonparty while enforcing the same promise for the plaintiff.

(c) Partial Assignees or Subrogees

In an action by a partial assignee or subrogee to enforce its share of a debt, all other partial owners are required parties who must be joined if feasible. [**On-Line Technologies v. Perkin Elmer Corp.,** 141 F. Supp. 2d 246 (D. Conn. 2001); **Peerless Insurance Co. v. Superior Court,** 6 Cal. App. 3d 358 (1970)—insured with claims over policy limit was necessary but not indispensable party in suit by insurer-subrogee who had paid up to policy limit]

(d) Co-Owners of Property

Co-owners of property are required parties when the interests of all should be decided on a consistent basis (*e.g.,* rescission granted to one should be granted to all). [**Feinberg v. Feinberg,** 924 S.W.2d 328 (Mo. 1996)]

1) Conflicting Claims

If the action seeks to determine conflicting claims between persons claiming co-ownership of property, *all co-owners* are required parties (*e.g.,* action for partition by one of several tenants in common, suit to fix shares of beneficiaries in a trust, suit by one of several partners to dissolve the partnership).

2) Suits to Establish Adverse Interest

Similarly, in suits by a *third person* to establish or enforce an interest in the property, all co-owners must be joined if possible (*e.g.,* suits to foreclose a mortgage, remove an easement, and the like).

(e) Third-Party Beneficiary Suits

1) Original Parties to Contract Need Not Be Joined

If a third-party beneficiary sues on a contract, the federal courts have uniformly rejected the argument that the original parties to the contract must be joined. [**Schulman v. J.P. Morgan Investment Management, Inc.,** 35 F.3d 799 (3d Cir. 1994)]

2) Third-Party Beneficiary Need Not Be Joined

If an original party to a contract sues, a third-party beneficiary is not an "indispensable" party. [**Fifth Third Bank of Western Ohio v. United States,** 55 Fed. Cl. 372 (2003)]

(f) Shareholder's Derivative Suit

In a derivative suit by a shareholder (*i.e.*, suing on a cause of action belonging to the corporation because the corporation refuses to sue), the *corporation* is an *"indispensable"* party. Its rights are so inextricably involved that no complete judgment can be rendered unless it is subject to the court's jurisdiction.

	⁍GILBERT
REQUIRED PARTIES	**NONNECESSARY PARTIES**
• Joint obligors	• Joint tortfeasors
• Joint obligees	• Original parties to a contract when third-party beneficiary sues
• Partial assignees and subrogees	• Third-party beneficiary when original party to a contract sues
• Co-owners of property (if case involves interest of all)	
• Corporation in a shareholder's derivative action	

c. Procedure for Compelling Joinder

(1) Must Name All Required Parties

In the complaint, the plaintiff should set forth the names of all required persons who have not been joined, and the reasons for their nonjoinder. [Fed. R. Civ. P. 19(c)] However, this provision is not effective because plaintiffs rarely concede that nonparties are required parties.

(2) Failure to Name All Required Parties

If the plaintiff fails to allege the existence of such parties, the defendant can raise the matter in a motion to dismiss under Federal Rule 12 or in the answer. Failure to object may constitute *waiver*. (*See infra*, p. 226.)

(3) Joinder of Required Parties Ordered If Feasible

If the plaintiff has failed to join required parties, the court will order that they be joined unless it is impossible to do so (*i.e.*, because their joinder would destroy subject-matter jurisdiction or because the court lacks personal jurisdiction over them).

(a) Involuntary Plaintiff

If the absentee should be aligned as a plaintiff, he may be joined as an involuntary plaintiff. [Fed. R. Civ. P. 19(a)(2)]

(b) Required Parties Too Numerous

If the required parties are too numerous to be joined, it is possible that the case might be handled as a *class action*. (*See infra*, p. 239 *et seq.*)

(c) Venue

If addition of the required party would make venue improper, the added party must be dismissed if she objects to venue. Then the court must decide whether to dismiss.

(4) Dismissal if Joinder Not Feasible

If the court cannot order the required parties joined because of lack of personal jurisdiction or because their presence would destroy diversity of citizenship, it must decide whether to dismiss the action. (*See supra*, p. 222 for criteria used to decide whether to dismiss.)

d. Waiver of Right to Compel Joinder

Nonjoinder of an absentee should be raised at the earliest possible opportunity by the parties to the action; otherwise, delay may constitute waiver of the right to compel joinder.

(1) If Absentee Is "Indispensable"

If the absentee is determined to be "indispensable," his nonjoinder can be raised at any time by pleading or motion, even at the trial of the action. [Fed. R. Civ. P. 12(h)(2)] However, delay in raising the objection is one of the factors the court will consider in exercising its *discretion* as to whether to dismiss the action (*i.e.*, in deciding whether the absentee *is* "indispensable"). [**Provident Bank & Trust Co. v. Patterson,** *supra*, p. 221]

(2) No Waiver by Absentee

The failure of the parties to raise the defect of nonjoinder in no way constitutes a "waiver" by the absentee. Since she is not a party to the action, the judgment is not legally binding on her. [**Martin v. Wilks,** 490 U.S. 755 (1989)]

4. Impleader

Impleader is a procedure that permits the defendant to bring into the lawsuit a third person who is or may be *liable for all or part of the plaintiff's claim* against the defendant. [Fed. R. Civ. P. 14] In some states, the same remedy may be secured by a cross-complaint bringing in the third person. Two features of impleader guard against prejudice to the third party: (i) the third party *may plead any defenses* that the defendant might have against the plaintiff's claim and may participate fully in defending against the claim; and (ii) the court may grant a *separate trial on any separate issues* of the third-party claim if needed to prevent undue confusion or prejudice.

a. Limited to Claims for Indemnification

Impleader under the Federal Rules is confined to those situations in which the defending party has a *right to indemnity*, in whole or in part, against the impleaded third party— *i.e.*, when the defendant asserts that if he is held liable to the plaintiff, he would be entitled to collect all or some part of the judgment from the third party. This liability includes a claim to contribution in states where a defendant is allowed to claim contribution from a person that the plaintiff did not originally join as a defendant.

(1) How Right Is Determined

Whether the defendant has any such right to indemnification, etc., is a question of *substantive law*, and under the *Erie* doctrine, the federal court must therefore refer to the appropriate state statutes and case law.

(a) No Right to Indemnification Under State Law

If the appropriate state law does not recognize such a right, the fact that the impleader procedure is available in federal court does not create one for the defendant.

(b) Liability Under State Law May Be "Accelerated"

However, federal impleader may "accelerate" liability created by state law. For example, if, under state law, the defendant can seek indemnity from a third person only after paying a judgment to the plaintiff, the defendant in federal court may implead the third person and *assert his claim conditionally*. If the plaintiff recovers, the defendant should get judgment—thereby closing the time gap between liability to the plaintiff and receipt of an indemnity judgment against the third party. [**Ohio Savings Bank v. Manhattan Mortgage Co.,** 455 F. Supp. 2d 247 (S.D.N.Y. 2006)]

(c) Contribution Among Tortfeasors

Most states allow contribution among tortfeasors only when *judgment* is rendered against *all* of them. For federal impleader purposes, this rule means that the defendant in a personal-injury action *cannot* implead other tortfeasors to seek contribution, because their liability arises only after the plaintiff obtains judgment against all of them. [**Connors v. Suburban Propane Co.,** 916 F. Supp. 73 (D.N.H. 1996)]

1) But Note

If state law allows contribution when judgment is obtained against only one tortfeasor, the situation is essentially one of partial indemnity, and the tortfeasor who is sued can implead the other to recover it. [*See* **American Motorcycle Association v. Superior Court,** *supra*, p. 223]

(2) Potential Liability Sufficient

Rule 14 authorizes impleader of any person who is or *may be* liable for any part of the plaintiff's claim. Thus, impleader is proper before any loss actually has been paid by the defendant.

(a) No Direct Action by Plaintiff Against Defendant's Liability Insurer

In a liability suit, a plaintiff usually would be delighted to join the defendant's insurance carrier as a co-defendant—to let the jury know that the defendant is insured. However, most states do *not* permit this, on the ground that the plaintiff has no right to relief against the defendant's insurance carrier until she has first obtained a judgment against the defendant (after which the plaintiff would have an enforceable claim as third-party beneficiary of the insurance company's promise to indemnify the defendant).

1) Minority Rule Contra

A few states are contra, with "direct-action statutes" that permit joinder of the defendant's insurance carrier in the original action. [*See* **Watson v. Employers Liability Assurance Corp.**, 348 U.S. 66 (1954)—direct-action statute may constitutionally apply despite provision in insurance contract conditioning duty to indemnify on entry of judgment against insured]

EXAM TIP   **GILBERT**

Insurance companies are sometimes lurking in the background of civil-procedure questions. Remember that while Rule 14 authorizes impleader of any person who may be liable for any part of a plaintiff's claim, most courts do *not allow* a plaintiff to implead a defendant's insurance company until after the plaintiff has obtained a judgment against the defendant.

(b) Defendant's Right to Implead Insurer

It may be that the defendant himself will seek to bring his liability insurer into the action—*e.g.*, when the insurer has failed or refused to defend the action. When this is the case, impleader may be permitted to obtain a prompt determination of the defendant's insurance coverage and avoid a multiplicity of suits. [**Government Employees Insurance Co. v. United States**, 400 F.2d 172 (10th Cir. 1968)]

(3) Distinguish—Alternative Liability to Plaintiff

It is not sufficient for impleader that the third-party defendant may be liable to *the plaintiff* for the plaintiff's injuries; only when the law gives the present *defendant a right to relief in the form of indemnity from the third-party defendant* is impleader permitted.

> **e.g.** **Example**: Plaintiff contracted trichinosis and sued Defendant 1, which manufactured a cooker Plaintiff claimed had failed properly to cook pork she ate on July 9. Defendant 1 sought to implead the college that Plaintiff attended, claiming that her trichinosis had actually resulted from eating pork in the college cafeteria on July 8. The court dismissed the third-party complaint because "[c]ontribution will not arise from distinct causes of action, regardless of how similar the events may have been or how close in time they may have occurred." [**Klotz v. Superior Electric Products Corp.**, 498 F. Supp. 1099 (E.D. Pa. 1980)]

(4) Supplemental Jurisdiction over Related Claims

In federal-court litigation, the court has supplemental jurisdiction to adjudicate a claim by the original defendant (third-party defendant in the impleader) for his *own* injuries when joined with a claim for indemnity.

(a) But Note

At least in diversity actions, there is *no* supplemental jurisdiction over a claim by the original plaintiff against the third-party defendant even if it arises out of the transaction originally sued on.

Example: Plaintiff sues Defendant, who impleads Third Party, a citizen of the same state as Plaintiff. Plaintiff may not assert a separate claim against Third Party, because there is no diversity between them and ancillary (now supplemental) jurisdiction will not be permitted. [**Owen Equipment & Erection Co. v. Kroger,** 437 U.S. 365 (1978); 28 U.S.C. § 1367(b)]

b. Pleadings and Procedure

Leave of court is not required for impleader if the defendant (third-party plaintiff) files a third-party complaint of impleader within 14 days after he serves his original answer. Thereafter, leave of court is required, and grant of the motion is at the *discretion* of the court. [Fed. R. Civ. P. 14(a)(1)]

(1) Answer

The impleaded party must file an answer to the third-party complaint, and the answer may raise whatever defenses could be asserted to the *original* cause of action (plaintiff vs. defendant). *Rationale:* The purpose is to prevent collusion between the original parties—the defendant admitting or defaulting to the plaintiff's claim, in order to affix liability on the impleaded party.

(2) Counterclaim or Crossclaim

The impleaded party may also file a *counterclaim or crossclaim* against existing parties, or may implead any person who may be liable to him, subject to the jurisdictional limits noted below. [Fed. R. Civ. P. 14(a)(2)]

c. Possibility of Separate Trials

The trial court has discretion to order a separate trial of the impleaded claim to avoid undue trial confusion or prejudice. [Fed. R. Civ. P. 42(b)]

d. Effect on Jurisdiction and Venue

An impleader claim is usually deemed ancillary to the main claim and has *no* effect on jurisdictional and venue requirements. Thus, an independent ground of federal jurisdiction need not be established, and the impleaded defendant cannot object to venue. [**Grundle Lining Construction Corp. v. Adams County Asphalt, Inc.,** 85 F.3d 201 (5th Cir. 1996); 28 U.S.C. § 1367]

e. Distinguish—Crossclaim

Impleader is somewhat similar to the crossclaim procedure discussed *supra*, p. 189 *et seq.* However, there are significant differences:

(1) *Rule 14 impleader can be asserted only against a person not yet a party*, whereas a crossclaim is filed by one party against another party to the action. However, a crossclaim against a co-party may include a claim that the co-party is or may be liable to indemnify the crossclaimant for all or part of a claim against the crossclaimant. [Fed. R. Civ. P. 13(g)]

(2) *Impleader must be based on a claim for indemnification* or contribution, while there is no such limitation on crossclaims.

5. Intervention

Intervention is a procedure whereby a *nonparty*, upon timely application, may become a party in a lawsuit in order to protect her interests in that action. Whether intervention is allowed depends on a balancing of two conflicting policies: (i) that the plaintiff should be allowed to be "master of his action," in the sense of joining such parties with or against him as he wishes; and (ii) that other interested parties and the court have an interest in avoiding multiplicity of litigation or inconsistency of result, which may require overriding the plaintiff's choice of parties.

a. Types of Intervention in Federal Cases

There are several types of intervention under Federal Rule 24:

(1) Intervention of Right—Federal Statute

Intervention is granted as a matter of right when a federal statute confers an unconditional right to intervene (*e.g.*, 28 U.S.C. § 2403—intervention by United States is a matter of right in any suit in which the constitutionality of an Act of Congress is in question). [Fed. R. Civ. P. 24(a)(1)]

(2) Intervention of Right—To Protect Intervenor's Interest

Intervention of right is also granted when the applicant claims an interest relating to the property or transaction that is the subject of the action, and is so situated that disposing of the action may, as a practical matter, impair or impede the applicant's ability to protect that interest, unless existing parties adequately represent that interest. [Fed. R. Civ. P. 24(a)(2)]

(a) Nature of Interest

The Supreme Court has stated that only a *"significantly protectable interest"* suffices to support intervention of right. [**Donaldson v. United States,** 400 U.S. 517 (1971)] Some lower courts emphasize a direct, substantial, and legally protectable interest to satisfy this standard, while others take a more relaxed attitude.

e.g. **Example**: Opponents of abortion could intervene in an action challenging a city's moratorium on abortion clinics in an area on the ground that they owned houses in the area and were defending their property values, but not on the ground that they were opposed to abortion. "Interests in property are the most elementary type of right that Rule 24(a) is designed to protect." [**Planned Parenthood v. Citizens for Community Action,** 558 F.2d 861 (8th Cir. 1977)]

e.g. **Example**: Rate-payers of a utility could not intervene in a contract action between the utility and a supplier concerning the amounts the utility would have to pay for boiler fuel. Although the outcome of the litigation could affect the rates intervenors would have to pay, they had no legally protectable interest in the contract dispute. [**New Orleans Public Service, Inc. v. United Gas Pipe Line Co.,** 732 F.2d 452 (5th Cir. 1984)]

1) Standing

The Supreme Court has held that an intervening plaintiff must demonstrate standing if it seeks relief not requested by the original plaintiff. [**Town of Chester v. Laroe Estates, Inc.,** 137 S. Ct. 810 (2017)] But the Court has not decided whether an intervenor on the defense side must independently satisfy Article III justiciability requirements to intervene [*see, e.g.,* **Hollingsworth v. Perry,** 133 S. Ct. 2652 (2013); **Diamond v. Charles,** 476 U.S. 54 (1986)], and the lower courts are divided on whether standing is required [*compare* **Ruiz v. Estelle,** 161 F.3d 814 (5th Cir. 1998)—intervenors need not satisfy standing requirements, *with* **Mova Pharmaceutical Corp. v. Shalala,** 140 F.3d 1060 (D.C. Cir. 1998)—party that seeks to intervene as of right must satisfy standing requirements].

(b) Outcome of Litigation May Impair Intervenor's Interests

The intervenor must also show that the resolution of the litigation may as a practical matter impair or impede her ability to protect that interest. This concern is not limited to legally binding effects, such as claim preclusion, but looks to the practical impact of resolution of the litigation on the intervenor's interest.

e.g. **Example**: Plaintiff brought suit against a federal agency, claiming that the agency was improperly allowing the state to issue licenses to run uranium mills without first requiring preparation of environmental impact statements. Companies with license applications pending were allowed to intervene. *Rationale*: As a practical matter, such applicants would be affected by the outcome of the litigation if it caused the state agency to alter its mode of operation and require more of applicants for licenses. [**Natural Resources Defense Council v. United States Nuclear Regulatory Commission,** 578 F.2d 1341 (10th Cir. 1978)]

cf. **Compare**: When a commercial tenant of a shopping center sought to enjoin a lease to another prospective commercial tenant on the ground that the plaintiff's lease limited the number of jewelry stores in the shopping center, interests of the prospective tenant might be affected if it could not compel performance of defendant's commitment to lease space to it, but the court nevertheless held that the prospective tenant was not an "indispensable" party, in part because any threat of inconsistent judgments arose from the defendant's inconsistent lease agreements and not potential court action. [**Helzberg's Diamond Shops, Inc. v. Valley West Des Moines Shopping Center, Inc.,** 564 F.2d 816 (8th Cir. 1977)]

1) Stare Decisis Effect

It is sometimes argued that the stare decisis effect alone is sufficient to justify intervention of right. When a unique issue of law is involved, and there is little likelihood that it will be reconsidered after it is decided in the current litigation, that may be sufficient. [*See* **Atlantis Development Corp. v. United States,** 379 F.2d 818 (5th Cir. 1967)—issue of application of the Outer Continental Shelf Lands Act to specific islands that intervenor sought to develop] More generally, however, that resolution of a question of law might affect cases to which the intervenor is, or may in the future be, a party would more properly be considered a ground for amicus curiae (briefs from "friends of the court") than for intervenor status.

(c) Intervenor Not Adequately Represented by Present Parties

If the intervenor claims the right kind of interest and shows a threat of practical impairment, intervention could be denied on the ground that the intervenor's interest is adequately represented by the present parties.

1) "Minimal" Burden

The Supreme Court has said that the burden of demonstrating inadequacy of representation is "minimal." [**Trbovich v. United Mine Workers,** 404 U.S. 518 (1972)]

2) Factors

A variety of factors can be considered in evaluating the adequacy of representation, including the amount at stake for the intervenor and the present parties, the ability and resources of the present parties to litigate effectively, and the existence of any conflicts of interest between the present party and the intervenors.

3) Concern with Complication of Action

Although it is said that the burden of showing inadequacy is minimal, in order to avoid complication of the action due to the addition of too many new parties, courts will resist multiple intervention applications by parties in similar situations.

(d) Distinguish—Required Joinder

The grounds for intervention of right are analogous to the grounds for finding nonparties to be required parties under Rule 19(a)(1)(B). (*See supra*, p. 222.) As a result, if there is a question on an examination raising issues under one of these rules, the effect of the other should be considered:

1) Intervention More Flexible

Even though the language of the rules for intervention and required parties is similar, courts seem more willing to find a nonparty's interests are of the protected type and are threatened, and therefore protected, when intervention is sought. This is because the nonparty intervenor has indicated a desire to participate in the litigation and the conclusion that intervention of right is proper does not mean that the litigation should not proceed unless all similarly situated nonparties are joined. Under Rule 19, the finding that a person with a certain interest must be joined if feasible means that all others with that interest should also be joined.

2) Adequate-Representation Requirement

This difference in treatment is confirmed by the adequate-representation requirement for intervention. Under Rule 19, the adequacy of the present parties to protect the interests of the nonparty ordinarily does not relieve the court of the duty to add the necessary party. When Rule 19 is invoked but representation seems adequate, treatment as a class action may be in order. (*See infra*, p. 239 *et seq.*)

(e) Conditions on Intervention

Although this form of intervention is designated "of right," the court may nevertheless impose conditions, such as limiting the intervenor to claims already raised by other parties, or requiring that the intervenor obtain permission from one of the original parties to make motions and take discovery. This authority derives from the court's general power to control the litigation before it. [**Stringfellow v. Concerned Neighbors in Action,** 480 U.S. 370 (1987)]

(3) Permissive Intervention

The court has discretion to permit a nonparty to intervene if:

(i)   *A federal statute* confers a conditional right to intervene; *or*

(ii)   *A question of law or fact in common* with the main action is part of the applicant's claim or defense. [Fed. R. Civ. P. 24(b)(1)]

(a) "Common Question"

e.g. **Example**: In a suit to set aside a zoning ordinance, adjoining property owners may intervene if their claims present common questions of law or fact. [**Wolpe v. Poretsky,** 144 F.2d 505 (D.C. Cir. 1944)]

1) Distinguish—Permissive-Joinder Rules

Permissive intervention is the counterpart of permissive joinder under Federal Rule 20(a). The standard for permissive intervention corresponds to that for permissive joinder—*i.e.,* a common question, interpreted as claims arising from the same or a related transaction.

(b) Broad Discretion of Court

The trial court has very broad discretion under Federal Rule 24(b) in granting or denying permissive joinder; and a reversal on appeal is almost impossible to obtain.

(c) Conditions Imposed by Court

The court will often condition intervention in a lawsuit by *limiting* the intervenor's claims to those directly involved in the pending action.

GILBERT

INTERVENTION OF RIGHT	PERMISSIVE INTERVENTION
Federal statute grants a right to intervene	Federal statute grants a *conditional* right to intervene
or	*or*
Intervenor claims an interest in the litigation that may be impaired by the litigation and is not adequately represented by the present parties	A question of law or fact in common with the main action is part of the applicant's claim or defense

(4) Timeliness of Intervention

Whether the intervention sought is of right or permissive, the motion for leave to intervene must be made in a timely fashion. However, since a potential intervenor of right may be seriously harmed if excluded from the action, intervention motions rarely should be denied as being untimely.

b. Effect of Intervention in Federal Cases

(1) Subject-Matter Jurisdiction

If the action is in federal court solely on grounds of diversity, there is no supplemental jurisdiction over claims by intervenors or claims by the plaintiff against persons who intervene. [28 U.S.C. § 1367(b); *see supra*, pp. 93–96] In those circumstances there must be an independent basis for federal-court jurisdiction to permit assertion of the claim. If federal jurisdiction does not depend solely on diversity of citizenship, there would usually be supplemental jurisdiction over claims by or against intervenors of right. [28 U.S.C. § 1367(a)]

(2) Venue

The intervenor cannot question the propriety of venue in the original action, since her act of intervening is a submission to the court in question. [**Pharmaceutical Research & Manufacturers of America v. Thompson**, 259 F. Supp. 2d 39 (D.D.C. 2003)] Venue objections, however, may be raised by someone who is already a party to the action.

(3) Judgment

Any judgment rendered after intervention is binding on the intervening party as if she had originally been a party, and she has a similar right of appeal if injured by the judgment. [**Association of Banks in Insurance, Inc. v. Duryee**, 270 F.3d 397 (6th Cir. 2001)]

But note: Unless the intervenor can demonstrate Article III standing, it can appeal only if a party with standing also appeals. [**Hollingsworth v. Perry**, *supra*— proponents of state initiative to ban same-sex marriage who were allowed to intervene to defend the constitutionality of the provision in the district court when state officials would not defend it could not appeal because they lacked standing]

c. State Practice

Most states have intervention provisions patterned on the Federal Rules. In other states, statutes on intervention provide that a person having an "interest in the matter in litigation *may* intervene" in an action between other parties. [*See* Cal. Civ. Proc. Code § 387(a)]

(1) Broad Discretion of Court

The term "interest" in such statutes is very vague, but usually has been limited to a "legal" interest. The term "may" indicates that intervention is *never of right*. Thus, intervention in state-court actions largely depends on the discretion of the trial court. Often, permission is denied on the ground that the plaintiff has the right to choose the parties to his action.

(2) Modern Trend to Permit Intervention

However, under the influence of federal intervention rules (*supra*), state courts are becoming more liberal in permitting intervention.

6. Consolidation of Separate Actions

Even when joinder rules do not permit the addition of new parties to an action, almost the same result can be achieved by consolidating separate suits pending in the same court. The court has broad discretion, on its own motion or on the motion of a party, to consolidate actions involving **common issues** (*e.g.*, liability of common carrier in mass-accident litigation). Consolidation can be complete so that the separate suits effectively become one, although they are technically not merged; or it may be partial—*e.g.*, consolidation for purposes of determining liability, with separate trials on the issue of damages. [*See* Fed. R. Civ. P. 42]

7. Interpleader

Interpleader is a device that enables a party against whom conflicting claims with respect to the same debt or property are asserted (the "stakeholder") to join all the adverse claimants in the same action and require them to litigate among themselves to determine which, if any, has a valid claim to the debt or property involved. Once the stakeholder's right to interplead is established and he has deposited the funds or property in court, he can be released or "discharged" from the litigation; it is up to the adverse claimants to litigate their claims to the property. (If the stakeholder denies any liability at all, or if he has a claim to the fund, he remains a party.)

e.g. **Example**: An escrow holder may interplead adverse claimants to funds deposited with him. Or a life-insurance company, upon the death of the insured, may, if the policy proceeds are claimed by both the named beneficiary and some third person, interplead the various claimants.

a. Background

Interpleader originated in the equity courts as a way to protect a stakeholder from possible legally inconsistent liability, and to avoid multiplicity of actions and the risk of inconsistent results. Historically, the plaintiff had to admit liability on the obligation in question, and the conflicting claims had to be mutually exclusive, but these limitations are not recognized under modern law. [*See* 28 U.S.C. § 1335; Fed. R. Civ. P. 22]

b. Procedure

The party against whom claims are being made may institute the interpleader action himself (naming all claimants as defendants). If sued by one claimant, or fewer than all claimants, the stakeholder may invoke interpleader by filing a **counterclaim** (*see infra*, p. 237) naming all claimants as counterclaim defendants.

(1) Deposit "Stake" with Court

To invoke federal **statutory** interpleader (*see infra*, p. 236), the plaintiff must deposit (or give security for) the entire amount in his possession that is claimed by the claimants, and may not hold back amounts that he claims. [**Hartford Life Insurance Co. v. Einhorn *ex rel*. Estate of Mehring,** 452 F. Supp. 2d 126 (E.D.N.Y. 2006)]

(a) No Deposit Required for Rule Interpleader

When Rule 22 interpleader is properly invoked (*see infra*, p. 236 *et seq.*), there is no requirement that the stake be deposited in court.

(2) Plaintiff May Claim Interest

As indicated above, interpleader is permitted even if the plaintiff denies **any** liability or claims some offset or defense. Such cases are often referred to as **"actions in the nature of interpleader,"** following old English practice. The difference is that classic interpleader involves a "disinterested" stakeholder, making no claim to the property, while an "action in the nature of interpleader" is brought by an "interested" stakeholder, such as an insurance company denying liability. [*See, e.g.*, **State Farm Fire & Casualty Co. v. Tashire,** 386 U.S. 523 (1967)]

(3) Defendants May File Crossclaims

When the stakeholder initiates interpleader, the adverse claimants can—and usually do—file crossclaims (*see infra*, p. 237) against each other to obtain a judicial determination of their respective rights in the fund or property interpleaded.

c. Types of Federal Interpleader Actions

In federal practice, there are two distinct interpleader remedies:

(1) Statutory Interpleader

Interpleader is permitted by 28 U.S.C. section 1335, which contains special provisions as to jurisdiction, venue, and service of process, if:

(a) *Two or more claimants of diverse citizenship* are making adverse claims to the same debt, instrument, or property owed or held by the plaintiff; *and*

(b) *The debt, instrument, or property has a value of at least $500.*

(2) Rule 22 Interpleader

Federal Rule 22 permits interpleader in any action that meets the normal jurisdictional requirements in federal court—*i.e.*, a sufficient amount in controversy (if applicable) and proper diversity or federal question.

d. Differences Between Statutory and Rule 22 Interpleader

The existence of two forms of federal interpleader can be confusing. Rule 22 interpleader is needed for cases that do not meet the specialized requirements of statutory interpleader. Statutory interpleader is framed to focus on situations involving scattered claimants (below). The basic differences between interpleader under section 1335 and under Rule 22 are as follows:

(1) Requirements for Diversity Jurisdiction

Depending on the type of federal interpleader action, either minimal or complete diversity is required.

(a) Statutory Interpleader

In statutory interpleader, it is sufficient that diversity of citizenship exists between *any two adverse claimants,* but at least two claimants must be diverse. As long as such *minimal diversity* exists, the citizenship of the plaintiff-stakeholder and any other claimants is immaterial. [**State Farm Fire & Casualty Co. v. Tashire,** *supra*]

e.g. **Example**: Insurco, an Illinois insurance company, is confronted by claims to insurance proceeds by Alpha, a citizen of Illinois, Bravo, another citizen of Illinois, and Charlie, a citizen of Wisconsin. There is sufficient diversity for statutory interpleader even though Insurco (as the plaintiff in the action) and Alpha and Bravo (as defendants) are co-citizens, and Alpha and Bravo (as competing claimants) are co-citizens; the required minimal diversity is present because one of the claimants, Charlie, is not a co-citizen of the other claimants.

(b) Rule 22 Interpleader

In an interpleader action under Rule 22, there must be *complete* diversity between the plaintiff-stakeholder and *all* of the adverse claimants, or a federal question must be involved.

(c) Distinguish—All Claimants Citizens of One State

When all the claimants are citizens of one state and the stakeholder is a citizen of another, the suit can be brought *only* under Rule 22, since statutory interpleader requires some diversity among the *claimants* (*see supra*).

(2) Jurisdictional Amount

Statutory interpleader requires only that the debt or property involved be valued at $500 or more. Under Rule 22, if the case relies on diversity jurisdiction, the jurisdictional amount is the same as in any other civil action (more than $75,000).

(3) Limits of Process

In *statutory* interpleader, the reach of process is nationwide. [28 U.S.C. § 2361] Under *Rule 22*, service of process is the same as in any other civil action—*i.e.*, within the territorial limits of the state in which the district court is located, except as extended by any applicable long-arm statute.

(4) Crossclaims and Counterclaims

The interpleaded claimants may (and usually do) crossclaim against each other, counterclaim against the plaintiff, and implead third parties, unless jurisdictional problems prevent their doing so.

(a) Subject-Matter Jurisdiction

Any additional claims that relate to the original interpleaded claim should fall within the supplemental jurisdiction of the court. Any other additional claims may be asserted only if there is an independent basis for subject-matter jurisdiction.

(b) Service of Process

When a defendant is before the court only because of nationwide process under *statutory* interpleader, he is subject to additional claims through crossclaim, etc., only if they are part of "cleaning up" the original interpleader claim.

Example: Annie, a driver insured by Insurco for $20,000, injures Brian and Carrie, each of whom claims more than $20,000 in damages. Insurco interpleads Annie, Brian, and Carrie, contending that there is no liability on Annie's part, but that if there is, the claims of Brian and Carrie to the insurance coverage should be interpleaded. Annie seeks to crossclaim against Carrie for Annie's own injuries. This claim would be disallowed if Carrie was before the court only through nationwide process, because it does not relate to Insurco's interpleader claim. [*See* **Allstate Insurance Co. v. McNeill,** 382 F.2d 84 (4th Cir. 1967)]

	RULE INTERPLEADER (in diversity action)	STATUTORY INTERPLEADER
DIVERSITY REQUIREMENTS	Complete diversity between plaintiff stakeholder and all adverse plaintiffs	Only two claimants need be of diverse citizenship
JURISDICTIONAL AMOUNT	More than $75,000	At least $500
PROCESS	Process is limited to the territorial boundaries of the state in which the district court sits	Process is nationwide
VENUE	In the district where a defendant resides, if all reside in the same state, or where a substantial part of the acts or omissions underlying the claim occurred or in which a substantial part of the property involved is located	Where any claimant resides

(5) Venue

In *statutory* interpleader, venue is proper in the district in which *any* claimant resides. [28 U.S.C. § 1397] With interpleader under *Rule 22*, venue is the same as in any other civil action—*i.e.*, in the district in which a defendant resides, if all reside in the same state, or a district in which a substantial part of the events or omissions giving rise to the claim occurred. [28 U.S.C. § 1391(a)(1)–(2); *see supra*, pp. 36–38] Alternatively, venue is proper in a district "in which a substantial part of the property that is the subject of the action is located." [28 U.S.C. § 1391 (a)(2)] The location of the property may be a convenient venue in many interpleader cases.

EXAM TIP

If an exam question raises the possibility of interpleader, it is, of course, important to keep the two types of interpleader straight. The following mnemonic device may be helpful: *R*ule 22 interpleader must follow the *R*egular *R*ules; *S*tatutory interpleader has *S*pecial, *S*impler *S*tandards.

---

e. *Erie* Doctrine

Whether the interpleader remedy is available is a procedural matter and is decided pursuant to federal interpleader standards. To determine the law to be applied to the merits of the case, the federal court will look to appropriate state law.

D. Class Actions

1. In General

One or more members of a class of persons similarly situated may *sue or be sued* on behalf of all members of that class. Such lawsuits are permitted when considerations of *necessity or convenience* justify an action on behalf of the group rather than multiple actions by (or against) the class members individually.

2. Background

a. Original Development in Equity

Class actions originally were permitted only in equity, and then only if it was shown (i) that joinder of all parties having similar interests was **impractical** because the parties were too numerous, were presently unascertainable, or were not yet in being (*e.g.*, unborn heirs); and (ii) a few members could fairly represent all in the litigation. In such cases, the chancellors in equity permitted suit to be maintained by or against representatives of the class and, in some instances, held that the decree rendered in such an action was binding on **all** members of the class.

(1) Comment

Unless the joinder of all necessary parties was not practical (usually because they were too numerous), the class-action device was not needed, since adequate relief could be obtained in an ordinary action.

b. Class Actions Under Code Pleading

The grounds for maintenance of class suits in equity were carried over in the Field Code, which authorized such suits whenever there were "questions of common or general interest of many persons," or when the parties were "numerous" and it would be "impracticable" to bring them all before the court. [*See* Cal. Civ. Proc. Code § 382]

(1) But Note

The courts usually limited class actions to those asserting what formerly had been equitable (as distinct from common-law) claims—*e.g.*, stockholder derivative suits, creditors' bills to reach the assets of debtors, and injunction suits.

(2) And Note

The decisions were split as to whether the judgment in a class suit was binding on the absent members of the class.

c. Class Actions Under the Federal Rules

(1) Former Federal Rule 23

As originally adopted in 1938, Federal Rule 23 provided for three different kinds of class actions.

(a) "True" Class Action

A "true" class action was one in which the rights of all members of the class were "joint" or "common." A judgment rendered in such an action bound **all** members of the class, including absentees. For example, stockholders' suits and suits by or against the members of labor unions or other unincorporated associations were "true" class actions.

(b) "Hybrid" Class Action

A "hybrid" class action was one in which the subject of the action was a specific fund or property, and the members of the class had "separate" rights therein (*e.g.*, suit on behalf of numerous co-owners of an oil well against a drilling company to enforce a royalty contract). A judgment in such an action was conclusive upon the rights of all members in the specific fund or property involved, but did not otherwise affect or bind class members not before the court. [**Dickinson v. Burnham,** 197 F.2d 973 (2d Cir. 1952)]

(c) "Spurious" Class Action

A "spurious" class action was one in which there was simply a "common question of law or fact" affecting all members of the class, and the claims of each member were separate. A judgment in such an action bound *only* those members of the class actually before the court. Accordingly, this was not really a class action, but rather a permissive-joinder device.

(2) Present Federal Rule 23

In 1966, Rule 23 was completely revised, eliminating the distinctions above and providing that members of a class can sue or be sued *with binding effect on the class as a whole*.

(3) State Courts

Most states have adopted rules based on the 1966 version of Federal Rule 23, sometimes with modifications. In California, the federal approach has been effectively adopted by judicial decisions. [**Vasquez v. Superior Court,** 4 Cal. 3d 800 (1971)]

(4) Class Action Fairness Act

The Class Action Fairness Act expanded federal-court subject-matter jurisdiction to include certain class actions that present claims based on state law (*see supra*, p. 60 *et seq.*). In addition, the Act provides additional protections and limitations regarding the settlement of class actions that are applicable to all class actions in federal court. (*See infra*, p. 263.)

(5) Application of Rule 23 to Cases Based on State Law

The Supreme Court has held that, on the facts before it, Rule 23 would authorize a class action for claims created by state law even though the state's law forbade class action treatment of such claims and the Rules Enabling Act forbids rules from abridging, enlarging, or modifying substantive rights. Four Justices agreed that Rule 23 satisfies the Rules Enabling Act because it "really regulates procedure." Justice Stevens concurred in the result because "the bar for finding an Enabling Act violation is a high one," which was not cleared in that case. But he agreed with four dissenters that in some cases the federal courts would have to follow state procedural rules "because they function as a part of the State's definition of substantive rights and remedies." [**Shady Grove Orthopedic Associates v. Allstate Insurance Co.,** *supra*, p. 121]

3. Prerequisites to Class Action

Under Federal Rule 23(a), ***all four*** of the following conditions must be established in any type of class suit. All class actions must also fit into one of the categories of Rule 23(b) (*infra*, pp. 247–252).

(i) ***Numerous parties***—the class must be so numerous that joinder of all members individually is impractical [Rule 23(a)(1)];

(ii) ***Common question***—the action must involve questions of law or fact common to the class [Rule 23(a)(2)];

(iii) ***Representative's claims typical***—the claims (or defenses) of the persons maintaining the action on behalf of the class must be typical of those of the class generally [Rule 23(a)(3)]; ***and***

(iv) ***Adequate representation***—the persons representing the class must be able fairly and adequately to protect the interests of all members of the class. [Rule 23(a)(4)]

a. Numerous-Parties Requirement

As indicated by the treatment of the real party in interest problem (*see supra*, pp. 209–215), ordinarily litigation is to be conducted by the persons whose rights are involved as named parties. Only when they are too numerous to be joined is class treatment considered justifiable.

(1) No Fixed Minimum

There is no fixed minimum number required to make a class "too numerous" for joinder of all members individually. Some cases have held 25 enough, while others have held that 39 is not enough. If the number is *50 or fewer*, whether a class will be permitted usually turns on the following factors, and note that the trial court has considerable discretion in this matter [**De Marco v. Edens,** 390 F.2d 836 (2d Cir. 1968)]:

(i) The ***size of each member's claim*** (the smaller the claim, the more likely a class suit will be allowed);

(ii) The ***practical likelihood that individual suits will be brought*** (the lower the likelihood, the more likely a class suit will be allowed);

(iii) The ***public importance of the right*** being enforced (the greater the public importance, the more likely a class action will be permitted); and

(iv) The ***geographic location of class members*** (the more difficult the geographic location makes it for class members to intervene, the more likely a class suit will be allowed).

e.g. **Example**: In a case involving a price-fixing conspiracy, the district court found a proposed class of 350 members not numerous enough to justify a class action. The claims involved were large and, based on the district judge's prior experience with decision of such claims, he found that the claims could best be handled by intervention and individual participation. [**American Pipe & Construction Co. v. Utah,** 414 U.S. 538 (1974)]

FIRST DETERMINE WHETHER ALL FOUR CONDITIONS ARE PRESENT:

- ☑ Class members are so *numerous* that joinder of all is impracticable.
- ☑ There are *questions of law or fact common to the class.*
- ☑ The *representative's claims or defenses are typical* of those in the class.
- ☑ The *representative will fairly and adequately protect* the interests of the class.

IF ALL FOUR CONDITIONS ARE PRESENT, A CLASS ACTION MAY BE BASED ON ANY ONE OF THE FOLLOWING GROUNDS:

- ☑ Prosecution of separate actions would create a significant risk of (i) requiring *inconsistent conduct* by the party opposing the class or (ii) *substantially impairing the ability of other members of the class to protect their interests.*
- ☑ *Declaratory or injunctive relief* would be appropriate for the class as a whole.
- ☑ *Questions of law or fact common to the class predominate* over questions affecting only individual members and a class action is *superior.*

If an exam question involves a relatively small number of plaintiffs (*e.g.*, 35) and you must determine whether the court would likely allow a class action, a good ***rule of thumb*** is that the less likely it is that individuals would bring their own suits or intervene (*e.g.*, because damages are small or the individuals are spread out geographically), the more likely the court will allow a class action.

(2) No Fixed Maximum

Similarly, there is no fixed maximum size for a class action. In **Eisen v. Carlisle & Jacquelin,** *supra*, p. 48, for example, the Court dealt with a class of six million members, and while it put severe limitations on the class action, discussed below, it did not disqualify it as a class action because of its size. More recently, a lower court described a class action against tobacco companies on behalf of all "nicotine-dependent" smokers as "the largest class action ever attempted in federal court." [**Castano v. American Tobacco Co.,** 84 F.3d 734 (5th Cir. 1996)]

(a) Limitation—Class Must Be Manageable

In actions brought under Rule 23(b)(3) (*i.e.*, when questions of law or fact common to the class predominate; *see infra*, pp. 249–250), "the likely difficulties in managing a class action" is among the factors that the court must consider in deciding whether to permit the case to proceed as a class action: The larger the class, the greater the problems of manageability are likely to be.

(b) Limitation—Notice Requirements

In some class suits, all identifiable members of the class must be given ***individual notice*** of the action, and the larger the class, the more cumbersome and expensive this requirement becomes.

(3) Need for Class Definition

The class must be defined in an ***objective way*** that will enable the court and the parties to determine who is within it, including the number of class members. [Fed. R. Civ. P. 23(c)(1)(B)] In class actions for injunctive relief only, the problem of ***ascertainability*** has not posed an obstacle to class certification. But in Rule 23(b)(3) actions for monetary relief, particularly on behalf of a class of consumers of low-value retail items, it has prompted divergent judicial requirements. [*Compare* **Carrera v. Bayer Corp.,** 727 F.300 (3d Cir. 2013)—adopting what has been called a "heightened" ascertainability requirement—*with* **Mullins v. Direct Digital, LLC,** 795 F.3d 654 (7th Cir. 2015)—rejecting "heightened" requirement]

(4) Minimum Number of Class Members for Class Action Fairness Act Jurisdiction

Under the Class Action Fairness Act, special jurisdictional provisions apply to certain state law class actions, permitting them to be filed in federal court (*see supra*, pp. 78–80) Under the Act, these jurisdictional provisions are available only if the class has more than *100 members*. [28 U.S.C. § 1332(d)(5)(B)]

b. Common-Question Requirement

There must be "questions of law or fact common to the class." [Fed. R. Civ. P. 23(a)(2)] *Rationale*: Unless there is some common question, there would be no efficiencies to be achieved by adjudicating the rights of the class members in a single proceeding.

Example: In a securities-fraud class action, plaintiff alleged that defendant corporation made misrepresentations and misleading statements regarding two of its flagship drugs, thereby inflating the price of its stock. Common issues included the questions whether defendant made a material misrepresentation or omission with scienter. These common issues sufficed to support class certification, and it was not necessary for plaintiffs also to demonstrate materiality to obtain certification. That individual damages of class members would differ did not defeat class certification. [**Amgen, Inc. v. Connecticut Retirement Plans and Trust Funds**, 133 S. Ct. 1184 (2013)]

Compare: There was no common question applicable to claims on behalf of proposed class of approximately 1.5 million female present or former employees of Wal-Mart Stores, Inc., complaining of gender discrimination in hiring and promotion. Hiring and promotion decisions were made by managers in many different divisions of the company who had discretion in making these decisions. Allowing discretionary decisions by different managers means that proof one manager makes biased decisions does not demonstrate that another manager does. Because allowing discretion is the opposite of a uniform employment practice, there was no common question. [**Wal-Mart Stores, Inc. v. Dukes**, 564 U.S. 338 (2011)]

(1) Predominance of Common Questions

In actions brought under Rule 23(b)(3) (*i.e.*, when questions of law or fact common to the class predominate; *see infra*, pp. 249–250), there must not only be a common question, but also common questions must predominate. Under Rule 23(a)(2), on the other hand, predominance is not required.

(2) Fact Question Needed

As a practical matter, it is usually essential that the common question have factual content that would make common litigation desirable.

(3) Distinguish—Permissive Joinder

Ordinarily, a *closer factual connection* is required to satisfy the class action common question requirement than the common question requirement for permissive joinder. (*See supra*, p. 220.)

(4) Problem of Individual Damages

If class members have suffered individual damages, that presents individual (as opposed to class) questions. However, the need to assess individual damages will not always prevent a class action because there may also be common questions regarding liability.

But see: In some circumstances it may be necessary for plaintiffs to identify a classwide method of determining damages. [**Comcast Corp. v. Behrend**, 133 S. Ct. 1426 (2013)—plaintiffs conceded that they needed to demonstrate a classwide basis for determining damages, but their expert proof provided that with regard to only one of four grounds for recovery]

(5) Problem of Variation in State Law

If the claims asserted in a class action are based on state law, and class members live in a number of states with varying laws, common questions might not be present because the factual questions to be resolved turn on different legal principles. [*See* **Castano v. American Tobacco Co.,** *supra*] The court may not "homogenize" the law of various states to overcome this problem. [*In re* **Rhone-Poulenc Rorer, Inc.,** 51 F.3d 1293 (7th Cir. 1995)] In some cases, however, the laws of the various states will fit into a few patterns so that recurrent common questions are presented. [*In re* **School Asbestos Litigation,** 789 F.2d 996 (3d Cir. 1986)—state laws fit into four basic categories, and the jury could return verdicts based on the four legal standards]

c. Typicality Requirement

The claims or defenses of the representative must be typical of the claim or defenses of the class generally. *Rationale*: Because the class representative acts on behalf of others, the court wishes to be assured that she will have the same objectives as the class members and sufficient motivation to protect their interests. This assurance should flow from the fact that her claim or defense makes her typical of the class members. [*See* **Gonzales v. Cassidy,** 474 F.2d 67 (5th Cir. 1973)] *Note*: Not all state class-action rules include this typicality requirement. It often blends with the common-question and adequate-representation prerequisites and, when included, rarely defeats class certification by itself.

e.g. **Example**: A Mexican-American employee who challenged the denial of a promotion was not typical of a class of Mexican-American job applicants who had not been hired, even though he alleged that the job applicants had, like him, been discriminated against on grounds of national origin. His claim of denial of a promotion in a specific instance was not typical of the claims of job applicants who were not hired. [**General Telephone Co. of the Southwest v. Falcon,** 457 U.S. 147 (1982)]

(1) Size of Claim Relevant

The size of the representative plaintiff's personal claim is relevant to the issue of whether she is properly motivated to protect the interests of the class generally. [**Jenkins v. General Motors Corp.,** 354 F. Supp. 1040 (D. Del. 1973)]

(2) Distinguish—Common-Question Requirement

The Supreme Court has observed that "[t]he commonality and typicality requirements of Rule 23(a) tend to merge. Both serve as guideposts for determining whether under the particular circumstances maintenance of a class action is economical and whether the named plaintiff's claim and the class claims are so interrelated that the interests of the class members will be fairly and adequately protected in their absence." [**General Telephone Co. of the Southwest v. Falcon,** *supra*]

(3) Effect of Mootness of Representative's Claim

When the class representative's claim becomes moot, it may or may not be necessary to locate a new class representative who has a live claim. [*See* **United States Parole Commission v. Geraghty,** 445 U.S. 388 (1980)—named plaintiff whose claim expires before certification may be unable to continue as class representative; **Sosna v. Iowa,** 419 U.S. 393 (1975)—class representative whose claim expired allowed to continue representing class]

d. Adequate-Representation Requirement

This requirement is similar to that of typicality, but also focuses on whether there is any *actual or potential conflict of interest* between the representative and the class she seeks to represent and whether the representative can prosecute or defend the suit with adequate vigor and resources.

(1) Constitutional Requirement

Due process requires that the class representative not have interests adverse to members of the class.

Example: Whites seeking to enforce a racially restrictive covenant forbidding sale of houses in area to blacks could not represent black who desired to buy a house in area. [**Hansberry v. Lee,** 311 U.S. 32 (1940)]

(2) "Future" vs. Present Personal-Injury Tort Claimants

At least in the personal-injury tort claimants context, the Supreme Court has implied that those who presently have claims for current injuries are not adequate representatives of those who may in the future fall ill, because those with current claims would want to maximize payouts presently, while those who may fall ill in the future would want to preserve resources for later compensation. [**Amchem Products, Inc. v. Windsor,** 521 U.S. 591 (1997)]

(3) Present vs. Past Employees

A union representing airline flight attendants in challenging the airlines' policy of discharging pregnant stewardesses could not "adequately represent" former stewardesses who had been discharged on this ground and were seeking reinstatement because their reinstatement might harm those currently employed, thus creating a potential conflict of interest. [**Air Line Stewards Association v. American Air Lines,** 490 F.2d 636 (7th Cir. 1973)]

(4) Failure to Object Does Not Bar Later Objection

If the representative does not meet the adequate-representation requirement but no one objects and the action proceeds to judgment, the traditional rule has been that the judgment can be attacked by an absent member of the class on the ground that his interests were not adequately represented. [**Hansberry v. Lee,** *supra*; *but see* p. 246, *infra*]

(5) Time When Adequate Representation Measured

The adequacy of representation can be measured at two different times:

(i) Before certifying the action as a class action, the judge must believe that the named plaintiff will furnish an adequate representation of the class members.

(ii) After a class action ends, if an unnamed class member sues the party that was the defendant in the class action and the defendant argues that the plaintiff should be bound by the result of the class action, the traditional practice has been that the court will evaluate whether the representation in the class action was in fact adequate. If not, the unnamed plaintiff will not be bound. [**Gonzalez v. Cassidy,** *supra*, p. 245]

Caution: A major split has developed in the lower federal courts over whether there can be such a "collateral attack" in a later, separate proceeding once a class-action judgment in which the court had found representation to be adequate (as it must) has become final. *Compare* **Stephenson v. Dow Chemical Co.,** 273 F.3d 249 (2d Cir. 2001) (collateral attack allowed), *aff'd in part by an equally divided Court and vacated in part,* 539 U.S. 111 (2003), *with* **Epstein v. MCA, Inc.,** 179 F.3d 641 (9th Cir. 1999) (collateral attack not allowed). The Supreme Court has not settled the question; the lower-court cases have been trending strongly toward not allowing collateral attack.

(6) Decertification

Another possibility is that the court will determine, after deciding that the case is a proper class action, that the class representative is not adequate. In that situation, the court can "decertify" the class and change the case back into an individual action.

(7) Subclasses

If an action is otherwise properly brought as a class action, but there is a significant divergence of interest among segments of the overall class, the court may divide the class into *subclasses,* appoint a representative for each subclass, and allow the suit to proceed in that manner. [**Amchem Products, Inc. v. Windsor,** *supra*]

(8) Implicit Requirement That Representative Be Member of Class

Although it is not stated in the text of the adequacy requirement or elsewhere in the class-action rule, it is usually required that a class representative be a member of the class. [*E.g.,* **East Texas Motor Freight System v. Rodriguez,** 431 U.S. 395 (1977)]

4. Three Grounds for Class Actions

If the foregoing conditions are all present, the class action may be based on *any one* of the following grounds. [Fed. R. Civ. P. 23(b)]

EXAM TIP

Be sure to remember that while *all four Rule 23(a) conditions* (numerosity, commonality, typicality, and adequacy) must be satisfied, *only one of the three Rule 23(b) grounds* (prejudice, declaratory or injunctive relief sought, or questions of law or fact common to the class predominate) need be shown.

---

a. Prejudice from Separate Actions

Under Federal Rule 23(b)(1), a class action is permitted if the prosecution of separate actions would create either of the following risks:

(1) Establishing Incompatible Standards of Conduct for Defendant Through Inconsistent Adjudications

To justify a class action on this ground, the court must find that a number of individual actions are otherwise likely to be filed, and that the *conduct* required of the defendant under various judgments might be inconsistent. [Fed. R. Civ. P. 23(b)(1)(A); **Larionoff v. United States,** 533 F.2d 1167 (D.C. Cir. 1976)]

e.g. **Example:** Paradigm examples of proper actions under this part of the rule are actions by taxpayers to invalidate municipal action or by stockholders to compel the declaration of a dividend. In such situations, there is a risk that other similarly situated plaintiffs might sue to compel defendants to take a different course of action (*e.g.*, to proceed with the intended municipal action or to withhold a dividend).

(a) Note

There is no such risk of inconsistency when injured parties are seeking *damages* for separate tort claims arising out of a single occurrence. That the defendant might be held liable in one case and not liable in another is not enough to justify a class action on this basis. [**McDonnell Douglas Corp. v. District Court,** 523 F.2d 1083 (9th Cir. 1975)]

(2) Substantially Impairing the Interests of Other Members of the Class

To permit a class action under this subsection, the court must find that separate actions would interfere with the interests of other absent persons having similar claims. [Fed. R. Civ. P. 23(b)(1)(B)]

e.g. **Example**: (i) One of several beneficiaries of a trust sues the trustee for an accounting and distribution that would affect the interests of all the beneficiaries. [**Redmond v. Commerce Trust Co.,** 144 F.2d 140 (8th Cir. 1944)] (ii) One of numerous claimants to a fund that is not sufficient to pay all claims seeks recovery (since satisfaction of any single claim in full would impair others). [**Bradford Trust Co. v. Wright,** 70 F.R.D. 323 (E.D.N.Y. 1976)]

(a) "Limited Fund" Mass-Tort Situation

An increasingly important, but not sole, occasion for invoking this part of the rule is the situation in which it is claimed that a large number of tort plaintiffs have claims exceeding the assets and insurance of the manufacturer of goods or services that injured them. In this situation, the concern is that if the first successful plaintiffs recover full damages, sufficient assets will not be left to pay compensation to later plaintiffs. The courts have resisted allowing class actions in this situation. [*See, e.g.,* **In re Northern District of California "Dalkon Shield" IUD Products Liability Litigation,** 693 F.2d 847 (9th Cir. 1982)] The Supreme Court has held that a "limited-fund" class action is not permitted when the limitation on the fund is the result of the parties' settlement agreement, as opposed to being limited by law or by the funds actually available, but it has not ruled definitively on whether other limited-fund class actions might be allowed. [**Ortiz v. Fibreboard Corp.,** 527 U.S. 815 (1999)— "fund" created by settlement among plaintiff class, counsel, defendant, and its insurers not acceptable even though agreement provides that claims must be asserted against this fund]

b. Equitable or Declaratory Relief Sought as to Rights Held in Common

Under Federal Rule 23(b)(2), a class action is also warranted if the basis on which the opposing party has acted is generally applicable to the class and *declaratory or injunctive relief would* benefit the class as a whole.

e.g. **Example**: Plaintiff sues on equal-protection grounds to invalidate a statutory provision that divorce actions can be maintained only by persons who have resided in the state for at least a year. The effects on particular members of the class in question (persons who have resided in the state less than a year) may vary; but a class action is proper because the determination will benefit the class as a whole. [**Sosna v. Iowa,** *supra,* p. 245]

(1) Problem of Monetary Relief

The Supreme Court has ruled that Title VII backpay awards may not be certified under Rule 23(b)(2) when they are not incidental to proposed injunctive or declaratory relief. Claims for individualized relief do not fit within (b)(2); individualized monetary claims should be handled under Rule 23(b)(3) instead. This result follows even if one could say that, in some sense, the injunctive or declaratory claims "predominate" over the monetary claims. [**Wal-Mart Stores, Inc. v. Dukes,** *supra*] The Court recognized, however, that (b)(2) certification may be proper for monetary relief that is "incidental to requested injunctive or declaratory relief" in that it will "flow directly from liability to the class *as a whole* on the claims forming the basis for injunctive or declaratory relief." [**Wal-Mart Stores, Inc. v. Dukes,** *supra—quoting* **Allison v. Citgo Petroleum Corp.,** 151 F.3d 402 (5th Cir. 1998)]

c. Predominant Common Questions

The third—and most common—basis for a class suit is under Federal Rule 23(b)(3)—the situation in which questions of law or fact common to the class *predominate* over questions affecting only individual members, *and, on balance, a class action is superior to other available methods* for adjudicating the controversy. The Supreme Court has called this provision "the most adventuresome" innovation in the 1966 amendments to Rule 23. [**Amchem Products, Inc. v. Windsor,** *supra*, p. 246]

(1) Relevant Factors

In deciding whether common issues "predominate" and whether a class action is "superior" to individual litigation, the court will consider:

(i) *The interest of individual members* in personally controlling their cases;

(ii) *The nature and extent of any litigation* in progress involving the same controversy;

(iii) *The desirability or undesirability of consolidating* all claims in the particular forum; and

(iv) *Any likely difficulties* in *managing* a class action.

[Fed. R. Civ. P. 23(b)(3)]

(2) Predominance of Common Questions

To find that common questions predominate, the court must *compare the relative importance* of the common questions and the individual questions presented by the case. It cannot merely compare the number of common and individual questions. Damages, for example, may present individual questions as to each class member, but may not defeat a finding that common questions predominate. Instead, the court is to determine whether the common questions are so important to the resolution of the lawsuit, and whether they will occupy sufficient time and effort in the resolution of the case, that it may fairly be said that they predominate over individual questions.

(a) Existence of Common Issue

It is important to focus carefully on whether there really is a common factual issue. For example, in many products-liability cases, it may be that the common issue regarding liability can be stated only in the most general terms, because so much depends on the individual circumstances of each plaintiff. In such cases, one may conclude that there really is no common factual issue. [*See, e.g.,*

Mertens v. Abbott Laboratories, 99 F.R.D. 38 (D.N.H. 1983)—in action against manufacturer of DES drug, allegedly common issue of defendant's knowledge of risks of DES not important, since "there is nothing to show that knowledge at a given point in time essentially settles anything with respect to liability to a particular claimant"]

(b) Single-Issue Certification

The existence of numerous and important individual issues can be partly solved by certifying the class action as to certain issues only. [Fed. R. Civ. P. 23(c)(4)] However, this device may be in tension with the requirement of predominance of common questions, and in most instances the court should hesitate to sidestep the problem of predominance by limiting the class action aspects to common issues.

EXAM TIP

On exam questions involving class actions, pay particular attention to the *nature of the damages* sought. If individual amounts of damages will have to be proved, that might undercut class certification under Rule 23(b)(3) (for cases in which common questions predominate). But, of course, class certification might still be proper under Rule 23(b)(3) *if other common questions* predominate (*e.g.,* as to liability).

(c) "Maturity" Factor in Tort Class Actions

In mass-tort class actions, courts have resisted finding that there is a predominant common issue when the claim is of a new and untested sort. [**Castano v. The American Tobacco Co.,** *supra,* p. 243—claim that tobacco companies were liable for addicting smokers new and untested; *In re* **Rhone-Poulenc Rorer, Inc.,** *supra,* p. 245—claims by HIV-positive hemophiliacs against producers of blood solids on theory that heat treatment of blood solids designed to remove risk of hepatitis would also eliminate HIV risk] However, when the court is well familiar with the claims, this problem is not present. [**Jenkins v. Raymark Industry, Inc.,** 782 F.2d 316 (5th Cir. 1986)—"state of the art" issue in asbestos litigation very familiar to court due to number of trials that had already addressed it]

(d) Variation in State Law

In Rule 23(b)(3) class actions, the problems of variation in applicable state laws (*see supra,* p. 249) are compounded because the common questions must predominate.

(3) Manageability and Superiority

Assuming that common issues predominate, the court must also ask whether a class action would be manageable, and whether it would be superior to other methods of adjudicating the case.

(a) Comparative Analysis

It is important to understand that manageability is *only one factor in evaluating superiority*. Accordingly, that the case will be difficult to manage as a class action does not necessarily preclude a finding that handling the case as a class action is superior to other methods of adjudicating the dispute. Only in the most extreme instances would problems of manageability alone be decisive in evaluating superiority.

Example—Class Action Superior: In litigation brought on behalf of thousands of military personnel exposed to the defoliant Agent Orange in Southeast Asia, the court recognized that it confronted massive problems of manageability. Nevertheless, it compared the difficulties presented by handling the case as a class action with the enormous problems of handling the litigation as individual cases, and concluded that class-action treatment had advantages over the other methods. [*In re* **Agent Orange Product Liability Litigation,** 506 F. Supp. 762 (E.D.N.Y. 1980)]

Example—Class Action Not Manageable: A suit on behalf of all residents of Los Angeles County (over seven million persons) to enjoin 293 large industrial companies from further pollution of the atmosphere was dismissed as unmanageable because of the number of parties, the diversity of their interests, and the multiplicity of issues involved. [**Diamond v. General Motors Corp.,** 20 Cal. App. 3d 374 (1971)]

(b) Effect of Settlement

A settlement that makes a trial unnecessary may remove manageability obstacles that were present when the case was proceeding as a litigation class action. [**Amchem Products, Inc. v. Windsor,** *supra,* p. 247; *and see* below]

(4) Mass-Tort Class Actions Under Rule 23(b)(3)

In 1966, the Advisory Committee included a note cautioning against use of class actions in mass-accident cases on the ground that individual issues would likely predominate, and the cases would "degenerate in practice into multiple lawsuits separately tried." [Fed. R. Civ. P. Adv. Comm. Note] Nevertheless, since the 1970s, some courts have certified such cases despite the note, and the Supreme Court has recognized this trend with seeming acceptance. [**Amchem Products, Inc. v. Windsor,** *supra*—"The text of the Rule does not categorically exclude mass tort cases from class certification, and district courts, since the late 1970s, have been certifying such cases in increasing number"]

d. Certification for Settlement Only

A court need not conclude that it would certify a class for all purposes, including full trial, in order to approve class certification for the purpose of effectuating a proposed class settlement. The prospect of settlement has on occasion prompted courts to certify cases for settlement discussions only.

(1) Criticism

A lawyer representing a class only with regard to a possible settlement is without significant leverage because she is unable to threaten to proceed to full litigation if settlement demands are not met. Moreover, the defendant may be tempted to "shop" among prospective class counsel to locate one willing to accept a settlement along the lines defendant wants to embody in a court decree. This risk is sometimes described as a *reverse auction*. Rule 23 empowers the court to appoint *interim counsel* in part as a method for dealing with this risk, and also directs class counsel to act in the best interests of the class. [Fed. R. Civ. P. 23(g)(3)–(4)]

(a) But Note

The Supreme Court has recognized that settlement classes are sometimes permissible. [*See* **Amchem Products, Inc. v. Windsor,** *supra*] *Rationale*: The court has at least some role in selecting counsel who will negotiate on behalf of the class if it certifies for purposes of settlement only, even if the case cannot proceed to trial.

(2) Requirements for Certification for Settlement

When certifying a class for settlement only, the court may overlook the likely difficulties of managing a trial. But the judge must still find that all of the Rule 23(a) prerequisites (*see supra*, pp. 241–247) have been satisfied, and that the case falls within one of the Rule 23(b) categories. Subclassing may be necessary to assure adequate representation under Rule 23(a)(4) in the case of a large and disparate class, and in classes certified under Rule 23(b)(3), the fact of settlement does not supersede the rule's requirement that common issues predominate. [*See* **Ortiz v. Fibreboard Corp.,** *supra*, p. 248; **Amchem Products, Inc. v. Windsor,** *supra*]

e. Application of Different Grounds to Same Case

In a given case, the plaintiff may try to satisfy different parts of Rule 23(b) in the alternative, and the case may be certified as to certain matters on one ground while certification is denied as to other parts.

e.g. **Example**: Plaintiffs charged that the Philadelphia police illegally detained persons accused of crimes for as long as 20 hours without food or medical care, and sought declaratory, injunctive, and compensatory relief on behalf of a class. The court certified a class with respect to declaratory and injunctive relief under Rule 23(b)(2), but held that the action could not be certified under Rule 23(b)(3) with respect to damages. [**Rice v. City of Philadelphia,** 66 F.R.D. 17 (E.D. Pa. 1974]

5. "Rigorous" Application of Class-Certification Requirements

The Supreme Court has emphasized that district courts must engage in a "rigorous" analysis of class-certification requirements before certifying a class. [**Wal-Mart Stores, Inc. v. Dukes,** *supra*; **Amgen, Inc. v. Connecticut Retirement Plans and Trust Funds,** *supra*] This scrutiny may include evaluation of aspects of the merits, but only to the extent necessary to apply the certification criteria spelled out in Rule 23, such as commonality.

6. Jurisdictional Requirements in Class Suits

a. Subject-Matter Jurisdiction

In class actions in federal court not involving federal claims, subject-matter jurisdiction issues may arise.

(1) Diversity of Citizenship

For purposes of federal diversity jurisdiction, only the citizenship of the *representative* is considered. This rule facilitates maintenance of a class suit in federal court. Note also that the named representatives must also meet the requirements of venue. [**Supreme Tribe of Ben-Hur v. Cauble,** *supra*, p. 71]

(2) Jurisdictional Amount

Until adoption of the supplemental jurisdiction statute, the rule had been that in any class action in which the individual class members would be entitled to *separate recoveries* (rather than a recovery in common), when the amount in controversy requirement applied, *each member* of the class had to have a claim for *more than $75,000*. [**Zahn v. International Paper Co.,** *supra*, p. 93—refusal to allow ancillary jurisdiction when class representatives' claims satisfied jurisdictional amount requirement, but the claims of unnamed members of the class did not] The effect of the *Zahn* requirement had been to *exclude* from federal court most *diversity* class actions, such as consumer class actions based on state law, because the claims of each member in such cases usually do not exceed $75,000.

(a) Impact of Supplemental-Jurisdiction Statute

The Supreme Court has held that the supplemental-jurisdiction statute [28 U.S.C. § 1367] overrules *Zahn*, allowing *supplemental* jurisdiction over claims of unnamed members of a plaintiff class in a diversity class action even when those claims do not exceed $75,000, provided that there is at least one class member (usually a class representative) whose claim does exceed $75,000. [**Exxon Mobil Corp. v. Allapattah Services, Inc.,** *supra*, p. 95] However, this holding has *no effect* on the rule that the separate claims of individual class members *cannot be aggregated* to satisfy the $75,000 amount-in-controversy requirement for *original* jurisdiction. [**Snyder v. Harris,** 394 U.S. 332 (1969)—no "aggregation" of legally separate claims to satisfy jurisdictional amount requirement] Note, however, that the Class Action Fairness Act (*see* below) allows plaintiffs to aggregate their claims under certain circumstances.

(b) Class Action Fairness Act

The Class Action Fairness Act provides for federal-court jurisdiction for class actions that are based on state law if the *aggregate claims* asserted on behalf of the class *exceed $5 million*, so long as the class has more than 100 members and there is minimal diversity. [28 U.S.C. § 1332(d)(6)]

EXAM TIP

For your exam, remember that after *Exxon Mobil* and the Class Action Fairness Act, federal diversity jurisdiction over class actions based on state law is *quite broad* and allows both *original filing in* and *removal to* federal court of many such suits. As long as the class representatives are completely diverse from all defendants and have claims that satisfy the over-$75,000 jurisdictional-amount requirement, *supplemental jurisdiction can extend to jurisdictionally insufficient, but related, claims of diverse and nondiverse unnamed class members alike*. Furthermore, under the Class Action Fairness Act, class actions with at least 100 class members and minimal diversity of citizenship can be filed in or removed to federal court as long as the aggregate recovery sought on behalf of the class exceeds $5 million. Also, don't forget that federal courts are required or permitted to decline to exercise jurisdiction in some class actions governed by the Class Action Fairness Act, but a court that has jurisdiction without resort to the Class Action Fairness Act may not decline to proceed on the grounds specified in that Act.

---

b. Personal Jurisdiction

It has been held that in an action involving a nationwide class, a state court could assert personal jurisdiction over absent members of the plaintiff class if they were afforded an opportunity to *opt out* and chose not to do so. [**Phillips Petroleum Co. v. Shutts,** 472 U.S. 797 (1985)]

(1) Requirement of Right to Opt Out

It is *unclear* whether the right to opt out is required to justify personal jurisdiction in all cases, such as actions brought under Rule 23(b)(1) or 23(b)(2). The Supreme Court reserved ruling on this point in *Shutts, supra*, and has since declined to decide whether a right to opt out is required. [*See* **Adams v. Robertson,** 520 U.S. 83 (1997)—certiorari dismissed in case raising issue]

(2) Defendant Classes

It is also *unclear* whether the same analysis would apply to a defendant class when the right to opt out was afforded the unnamed members of the class. However, the question may not arise; defendant class actions, while permitted, are not common.

7. Procedure in Conducting Class Suits

a. Certification Decision

At "an early practicable time" after the filing of an alleged class suit, the court must determine whether to certify the action as a class action. [Fed. R. Civ. P. 23(c)(1)(A)] This determination is commonly called "class certification." If the court concludes that class certification is not proper, the suit may be continued as an individual action.

(1) Based on Evidence

In determining whether the suit can proceed as a class action, the court can take evidence on *any* of the issues raised (*i.e.*, it is *not* restricted to the pleadings).

(a) Discovery on Class Certification

Because the class-certification decision is to be based on evidentiary materials, it is said to be necessary to allow precertification discovery relevant to whether the case should be certified as a class action. [**Stewart v. Winter,** 669 F.2d 328 (5th Cir. 1982)] Some courts try to limit such discovery to "class-action" issues, as distinguished from "merits" issues (going to the merits of the case), but so confining the inquiry may prove difficult since commonality and typicality are class-certification issues that depend in large measure on merits information.

(2) Consideration of Merits for Class Certification

The Supreme Court has stated that the "rigorous analysis" it requires for class-certification decisions may overlap with the merits of the plaintiff's underlying claim. In an employment-discrimination case, the question whether a common question was presented overlapped with plaintiffs' underlying claim that defendant employer engaged in a pattern or practice of discrimination against women in hiring and promotion. [**Wal-Mart Stores, Inc. v. Dukes,** *supra*]

e.g. **Example**: The court may determine whether the claim is of a type that would satisfy Rule 23, and to do so it must examine the grounds for the action to identify common issues and decide whether the plaintiff has a typical claim. One court said that the court should look "between the pleading and the fruits of discovery. . . . [E]nough must be laid bare to let the judge survey the factual scene on a kind of sketchy relief map, leaving for later view the myriad of details that cover the terrain." [**Sirota v. Solitron Devices, Inc.**, 673 F.2d 566 (2d Cir. 1982)]

(3) Precertification Decision of Merits

The premise of the 1966 amendments to Rule 23 was that the class action would be binding on all class members, whether or not it was successful. Otherwise, class members could benefit from ***"one-way intervention,"*** finding out how the merits were decided before they elected to remain in the action or to opt out. As a result, it was widely assumed that the court could not decide the merits until it ruled on the certification issue, but the courts have modified this view (see below). However, when the certification process was likely to be protracted and expensive, it might give a plaintiff who added class-action allegations to his groundless complaint undue settlement leverage to prevent defendants from attacking the merits of the case until certification was decided.

(a) Motions to Dismiss

To counteract the risk that plaintiffs will add class-action allegations to groundless complaints, courts generally will entertain motions to dismiss under Rule 12(b)(6) (*see supra*, p. 157) before certification is decided.

(b) Summary-Judgment Motions

Many courts will also allow defendants to move for summary judgment. The theory to support this practice is that defendants can waive the rule's protection against one-way intervention by filing motions for summary judgment if they choose to. [**Cowen v. Bank United of Texas**, 70 F.3d 937 (7th Cir. 1995)]

(4) Certification Order May Be Modified

At any time before trial, the court may revise class certification if it decides changes are necessary, by decertifying or altering the class configuration. Indeed, it may expand class size even after judgment if doing so would not unfairly subject the defendant to liability. [**Payne v. Travenol Laboratories, Inc.**, 673 F.2d 798 (5th Cir. 1982)]

(5) Immediate Appellate Review of Certification Decisions

Rule 23 provides for interlocutory appellate review of orders granting or denying class status. [Fed. R. Civ. P. 23(f)] The court of appeals has discretion to entertain such an immediate appeal if a party applies for review within 14 days after entry of the order.

b. Appointment of Class Counsel

If the court certifies a class, it must also appoint class counsel at the time of certification. [Fed. R. Civ. P. 23(c)(1)(B); 23(g)]

(1) Criteria for Appointment

The court must consider the work counsel has done investigating possible claims in the action, counsel's experience with complex litigation and the type of claim asserted, counsel's knowledge of the applicable law, and the resources counsel will commit to representing the class. The court may also consider any other pertinent matter. [Fed. R. Civ. P. 23(g)(1)]

(a) Multiple Applicants

When multiple applicants seek to be class counsel, the court should select the one best able to represent the class. If there is only one applicant, the court may appoint that applicant only if adequate. [Fed. R. Civ. P. 23(g)(2)]

(2) Terms for Possible Attorney's Fee Award

The court may direct applicants for class counsel to propose terms for an attorney's fee award and may include provisions about a possible fee award in the order of appointment. [Fed. R. Civ. P. 23(g)(1)(D)]

(3) Duty of Class Counsel

Class counsel must *fairly and adequately* represent the interests of the class. [Fed. R. Civ. P. 23(g)(4)]

(4) Interim Class Counsel

The court may designate interim class counsel to act on behalf of the putative class during the period before class certification. [Fed. R. Civ. P. 23(g)(3)]

c. Statute of Limitations

The *filing* of a suit as a class action *suspends the running of the statute of limitations* for all putative members of the class until class certification is decided. [**American Pipe & Construction Co. v. Utah,** *supra,* p. 241] *Rationale*: Unless they could rely on the pendency of the class action to protect their rights, unnamed members of the class would have to file their own suits to guard against the running of the limitations period. Their doing so would defeat the purpose of Rule 23 to achieve the efficient combined resolution of cases suitable for class-action treatment.

(1) Effect

From the date the class action is filed until class certification is decided, the running of limitations is suspended. If class certification is denied, the limitations period begins to run again, and class members have the remainder of the period to file their own actions or intervene. [**Nelson v. County of Allegheny,** 60 F.3d 1010 (3d Cir. 1995)—tolling ceased when district court denied class certification] If class certification is granted, class members who remain in the class action are protected against a limitations defense, provided the class action was filed in time.

(2) Opt-Outs

If class certification is granted and some class members opt out, the limitations period begins to run again and they must file individual actions to protect themselves against the running of limitations.

(3) Tolling Not Dependent on Grounds for Denial of Certification

The suspension of the running of the limitations period applies even if the class-certification motion is denied for lack of commonality or typicality. [**Crown, Cork & Seal Co. v. Parker,** 462 U.S. 345 (1983)] *Criticism*: This rule means that the defendant is really not on notice of the claims that are protected from the running of limitations by the filing of the defective class action.

(4) Defendant Class Actions

The suspension of limitations has been held to apply to a defendant class action in which the unnamed member of the defendant class did not even have notice of the filing of the suit within the limitations period. [**Appleton Electric Co. v. Graves Truck Line, Inc.,** 635 F.2d 603 (7th Cir. 1980)]

(5) Successive Class Actions

The suspension of limitations has been held not to be available in a second class action that is timely only because a deficient class action earlier suspended the running of limitations. [**Basch v. Ground Round, Inc.,** 139 F.3d 6 (1st Cir. 1998)]

d. Notice Requirements

(1) When Notice to Individual Class Members Is Discretionary

If the basis for a class action is to avoid the risk of inconsistent adjudications [Fed. R. Civ. P. 23(b)(1)(A), *supra*, p. 247], or because of possible impairment of interests of nonparties [Fed. R. Civ. P. 23(b)(1)(B)], or the claim is for injunctive or declaratory relief for the class as a whole [Fed. R. Civ. P. 23(b)(2)], the appropriate form of notice to class members is left to the discretion of the court. [Fed. R. Civ. P. 23(c)(2)(A); 23(d)(1)(B)] Individual notice to class members is not required by due process if the class representation is adequate. [**Wetzel v. Liberty Mutual Insurance Co.,** 508 F.2d 239 (3d Cir. 1975)]

(2) When Individual Notice Is Mandatory

(a) Damages Class Action—Individual Notice of Certification Required

In a damages class action based on a predominant question common to the class [Fed. R. Civ. P. 23(b)(3), *supra*, p. 249], when the court certifies the class members of the class must be given "the best notice that is practicable under the circumstances, *including individual notice to all members who can be identified through reasonable effort.*" [**Eisen v. Carlisle & Jacquelin,** *supra*, p. 243—requiring individual notice to 2,250,000 class members; Fed. R. Civ. P. 23(c)(2)(B)]

(b) Compare—Individual Notice Not Required Regarding Proposed Settlement or Dismissal

Once a suit has been certified as a class suit, some type of notice to the class is required before *any* type of class action may be settled or dismissed. [Fed. R. Civ. P. 23(e)(1)]

(c) State Rules May Be More Flexible

State courts usually require individual notice only when members of the class have *"substantial" claims*, because in such cases it is essential for them to decide whether to remain in (and be bound by claim preclusion) or opt out and pursue their independent remedies. When the membership of the class is large and damages to each member small, individual notice might not be required and notice by publication may be sufficient. [**Cooper v. American Savings & Loan Association,** 55 Cal. App. 3d 274 (1976)]

(3) Form and Content of Notice

Federal Rule 23 does not establish any specific form or manner of giving notice.

(a) Form

The notice itself need ***not*** be in the form of a complaint or summons. Letters, bulletins, or circulars mailed to members of the class are commonly used. However, when notice to each member is mandatory, it has been held that notice must be given at least the formality of mail. [**Eisen v. Carlisle & Jacquelin,** *supra*] In other instances, the court has discretion as to form. [**Greenfield v. Villager Industries, Inc.,** 483 F.2d 824 (3d Cir. 1973)]

Note: As means of communication have changed, courts have increasingly considered digital means of giving notice, particularly of proposed class-action settlements.

(b) Contents

The notice must use "***plain, easily understood language***" to advise the class members of the existence of the suit, the nature of the claim and relief requested, provisions for costs of maintaining the suit, and the identity of the person or persons suing on behalf of the class. When based on Rule 23(b)(3)—the predominant-common-question ground—it must also advise each member that he will be bound by the judgment unless he opts out. [Fed. R. Civ. P. 23(c)(2)(B)(vii)]

(c) Effect of Notice

In the ordinary civil action, notice has the effect of making the notified person a ***party*** to the action who will be bound by any judgment in the action (including a default judgment if he does not appear). In a class suit, however, the notified person is already provisionally bound through representation by the class representative. Hence, notice has the following effects:

1) ***If accompanied by an "opt-out" directive*** in a Rule 23(b)(3) suit, the notice allows the notified person to terminate his involvement in the action (*see infra*, p. 259.)

2) ***In other types of class suits***, the notice:

   a) Gives absent members of the class the opportunity to intervene and protect themselves; ***and***

   b) Gives the opposing party more assurance that the eventual judgment cannot subsequently be attacked by an absentee claiming that the representation was inadequate (*see supra*, p. 246).

(4) Plaintiff Must Pay Costs of Notice

Under Rule 23(c), the plaintiff initially must pay the costs of notifying all members of the class. [**Eisen v. Carlisle & Jacquelin,** *supra*] If the plaintiff ***wins*** the action, she can ultimately recover such expenses from the defendant as necessary court costs.

(a) Cost of Identifying Class Members

The plaintiff must also pay the costs of identifying class members. [**Oppenheimer Fund, Inc. v. Sanders,** 437 U.S. 340 (1978)—$16,000 in computer costs to identify certain class members properly charged to plaintiff]

(b) Effect

The cost of notice has inhibited large class actions in federal court, because the larger the class, the less likely it is that any single plaintiff can afford to bear the costs of notice (and thus "fairly and adequately" represent the class).

EXAM TIP

Notice issues may be important in an exam question involving a class action. Recall that if the class is certified under Rule 23(b)(3) (*i.e.*, common questions predominate), class members must be given "the best notice practicable under the circumstances," which includes *individual notice to class members who can be readily identified*. If the class is large, notice may stifle the suit because the plaintiff must bear the costs of notice (although such costs are ultimately recoverable if the plaintiff wins). Also remember: The form of the notice must usually be approved by the court; it should advise class members of the existence and nature of the suit and relief sought, the provisions for costs, and the identity of the class representative. Finally, in common-question class actions, the notice must indicate that members may opt out of the class action.

---

e. Opting Out by Class Members

In class actions under Rule 23(b)(3), unnamed members of the class may opt out, thereby excluding themselves from the binding effects of the class action.

(1) Timing

Usually the decision to opt out must be made *before* the court decides the merits, to avoid the risk of one-way intervention. (*See supra*, p. 255.)

(2) Effect on Statute of Limitations

Once a class member opts out, she loses the class action's effect of suspending the limitations period and must file her own suit within the remainder of the limitations period to protect her rights. (*See supra*, p. 256.)

(3) Rule 23(b)(1) and 23(b)(2) Class Actions

There is no mandatory opt-out right in the rule for actions under Rule 23(b)(1) or 23(b)(2). In some cases, the court may, in its discretion, permit opting out, but that could undermine the purpose of certifying a case of this type in the first place. When class members have monetary claims, however, it may be an abuse of discretion to deny the right to opt out. [**Holmes v. Continental Can Co.,** 706 F.2d 1144 (11th Cir. 1983)]

(4) Constitutional-Right Argument

It may be argued that the Supreme Court's decision that the right to opt out permits exercise of personal jurisdiction over the claims of unnamed class members (*see supra*, p. 254) means that there must always be a right to opt out when unnamed class members are *not subject to the personal jurisdiction* of the court.

(5) Right to Claim Issue Preclusion

It has been held that when class members opt out and the class action is successful, the *opt-outs may not claim issue preclusion* (*i.e.*, claim that the issues decided against the defendant in the class action control here as well). That would be tantamount to one-way intervention. [**Becherer v. Merrill Lynch, Pierce, Fenner & Smith, Inc.**, 193 F.3d 415 (6th Cir. 1999); **Amati v. City of Woodstock**, 176 F.3d 952 (7th Cir. 1998)]

f. Intervention by Class Members

Intervention by class members in the class action is allowed on the same terms that govern intervention otherwise. (*See supra*, pp. 229–234.)

(1) Adequacy of Representation

A problem arises from the inadequate-representation requirement for intervention of right because intervention is not allowed when the intervenor is adequately represented by the present litigant (*see supra*, p. 231), and the court must find the class representative (*i.e.*, the present litigant) adequate to certify the class (*see supra*, p. 246). Some courts solve the problem by saying that the finding of adequacy under Rule 23(a) for class certification does not require a finding of adequacy under Rule 24(a) (dealing with intervention). [**Woolen v. Surtran Taxicabs, Inc.**, 684 F.2d 324 (5th Cir. 1982)]

(2) Role of Intervenor

Rule 23 makes no provision for participation by a class member who is not the class representative. Some courts suggest that when intervention is proper, the certification decision should be reconsidered or the intervenor should be designated a new class representative. [**Lelsz v. Kavanagh,** 710 F.2d 1040 (5th Cir. 1983)]

(3) Entering an Appearance

In Rule 23(b)(3) actions, a class member may "enter an appearance through an attorney." [Fed. R. Civ. P. 23(c)(2)(B)(iv)] This provision does not entitle the class member to take an active role in the litigation, but rather entitles the class member only to receive copies of pleadings and other filings. It is, thus, a way to monitor the progress of the case.

g. Discovery

Class members are treated as "quasi-parties" for discovery purposes. The opposing party is not given the full rights (*e.g.*, to depose each class member) that he ordinarily has against opposing litigants. However, he can obtain fair discovery of the "typicality" of claims, the factual basis for determining inclusion in the class, individual damages, and the like. Interrogatories for these purposes are proper, as are depositions when necessary. [**Brennan v. Midwestern United Life Insurance Co.**, 450 F.2d 999 (7th Cir. 1971)]

h. Communications with Class Members

Courts are concerned about the risk that unnamed members of the class may be victimized by misleading or overreaching on the part of the litigants or their lawyers, and may therefore sometimes limit contacts with class members.

(1) Showing of Need

The Supreme Court has held that limitations on communications with class members by class counsel may be imposed only when there is some showing of need. [**Gulf Oil Corp. v. Bernard,** 452 U.S. 89 (1981)] The showing should indicate a *likelihood of misleading or overreaching class members.*

(2) Effect of Certification

After the class is certified, class counsel is for some purposes the attorney for the class members, and the court's power to interfere with her communications is limited.

(3) Communications by Class Opponent

After the class is certified, the court has broader authority to regulate communications by the class opponent, particularly when there is a risk that the class opponent will try to subvert the class action by pressuring class members to opt out.

e.g. **Example**: In a class action against a bank alleging that it defrauded its borrowers by inflating the prime rate it charged them, the court properly punished the bank for embarking on a campaign to have loan officers call class members and pressure them to opt out of the action. [**Kleiner v. First National Bank of Atlanta,** 751 F.2d 1193 (11th Cir. 1985)]

(a) Attorney Contacts

After certification, class members should be considered "represented by counsel," and the attorney for the class opponent is therefore forbidden by ethical rules to communicate with the class members. [**Resnick v. American Dental Association,** 95 F.R.D. 372 (N.D. Ill. 1982)]

(4) Remedies for Violations

When a valid rule against communication with class members is violated, the court may hold the person who violated the rule in *contempt*. In addition, when the communication resulted in opt-outs, the court can *invalidate the opt-outs* tainted by the communication.

i. Dismissal and Compromise

(1) Court Approval Required

Because of the fiduciary nature of a class action, a proposed class action may not be dismissed or settled by the class representative without court approval. [Fed. R. Civ. P. 23(e)]

(a) Fairness Inquiry Does Not Substitute for Satisfaction of Rule 23(a) Requirements

In a class action that is settled, the Rule 23(a) prerequisites to a class action apply even if the court finds that the proposed settlement is fair and adequate. [**Amchem Products, Inc. v. Windsor,** *supra*, p. 246] Indeed, that class counsel and defendants have reached a settlement without formal certification of a litigation class action may mean that the court should be more exacting with regard to questions of adequacy of representation and typicality.

(2) Notice Required

The court must direct notice in a reasonable manner to all class members who would be bound by the proposed settlement, but individual notice is not required. [Fed. R. Civ. P. 23(e)(1)]

(3) Settlement Before Certification

If a class action is settled before certification, the notice and hearing requirements depend on the nature of the settlement.

(a) Settlement of Class Claims

If the settlement purports to resolve class claims, the settlement-approval *requirements of Rule 23* apply. The settlement may propose that a class be certified, but the court must scrutinize class certification under Rules 23(a) and 23(b) and may not accept it just because it is proposed by the parties. [**Amchem Products, Inc. v. Windsor,** *supra*] Besides evaluating class certification, the court must, when class claims are to be settled, perform a full examination of the fairness of the proposed settlement. [Fed. R. Civ. P. 23(e)]

(b) Settlement of Individual Claims

If the settlement purports to settle only the individual claims of the proposed class representatives, the court need not perform any fairness review. [*Cf.* Fed. R. Civ. P. 23(e)—requiring court approval only for settlement of action involving certified class] Under prior law, most courts held that they should examine the individual settlement to determine whether there was an indication of abuse of the class-action device or prejudice to absent class members. This review is no longer authorized.

(4) Objections by Class Members

Any class member may object that the settlement is not adequate, but an objection may be withdrawn only with court approval. [Fed. R. Civ. P. 23(c)(5)]

(a) Appeal by Objector

If the district court approves the proposed settlement despite objections, an objector may appeal the approval of the settlement without intervening in the case. [**Devlin v. Scardelletti,** 536 U.S. 1 (2002)]

(b) Problem of "Bad Faith" Objector

Concerns have been raised about "bad faith" objectors who threaten to delay consummation of the settlement unless they (or their lawyers) are given substantial consideration for dropping an objection or appeal from approval of a proposed settlement.

(5) Possible Second Opt-Out

The court may refuse to approve a settlement if the time for opting out has expired, unless class members are afforded a new opportunity to opt out. [Fed. R. Civ. P. 23(e)(4)] For example, in Texas state courts, such a second opt-out is mandatory in Rule 23(b)(3) common-question class actions. [Tex. R. Civ. P. 42(e)(3)]

(6) Protections Under the Class Action Fairness Act

The Class Action Fairness Act adds a number of protections that apply to settlements in **all** class actions in federal court.

(a) Coupon Settlements

Sometimes, class-action settlements provide for class members to receive coupons good for purchase of further goods or services from the defendant. The court may approve such a settlement only after **holding a hearing** and **making a finding that the settlement is fair**, and it may also require that **unclaimed coupons be distributed to charitable organizations**. If attorney's fees in such cases are to be based on the value of the settlement to the class, they must be limited to the value of the coupons **actually redeemed** by class members, rather than the total amount available to class members. Alternatively, attorneys' fees can be based on the amount of time class counsel reasonably expended on the action. [28 U.S.C. § 1712]

(b) Protection Against Loss by Class Members

In some consumer class actions, some class members have actually lost money, because attorney's-fee awards required them to pay the lawyers more than they received from the settlement. A court may approve a settlement that would have that effect only if it makes a written finding that nonmonetary benefits to the class member **substantially outweigh** the monetary loss. [28 U.S.C. § 1713]

(c) Protection Against Discrimination Based on Geographic Location

Under CAFA, the court may not approve a settlement that provides larger payouts for some class members than others solely because the benefitted class members are located closer to the court. [28 U.S.C. § 1714]

(d) Notification of Federal and State Officials

Settling defendants are required to give notice of proposed settlements to identified federal and state officials. Final approval of the proposed settlement may not be issued until at least 90 days after the notice is served. A class member who demonstrates that the required notice was not provided may choose not to be bound by the settlement. [28 U.S.C. § 1715]

j. Distribution of Proceeds of Action

(1) Class Members File Individual Claims

Usually, a judgment settlement fund is created, with class members being notified to file individual claims to establish their shares.

(2) Rebate Approach

However, when the class is numerous and the claims are small, this approach may be impractical. In this situation, some courts have adopted what amounts to a rebate approach: When the identity of the class members at the time of the wrong cannot be determined or the amounts of their respective claims are very small, the recovery will be distributed to those persons who are *now* members of the class.

Example: Taxi-fare overcharges to former customers may be refunded by reducing fares to *future customers*. [*See* **Daar v. Yellow Cab Co.,** 67 Cal. 2d 695 (1967)]

(a) Criticism

This approach may distort market structure, resulting in temporary underpricing, overuse, and competitive advantage for the wrongdoer.

k. Award of Attorney's Fees

The court may award attorney's fees as authorized by law or by the parties' agreement. [Fed. R. Civ. P. 23(h)] Although Rule 23(h) itself grants the court no authority to award fees to counsel in a successful class action, federal and state courts generally award fees out of the proceeds recovered by the class. This practice is based on the court's inherent equity powers under the "common-fund doctrine"—*i.e.*, the plaintiff who hired the attorney should not be required to pay the entire amount of legal fees incurred in obtaining a "common fund" benefitting all class members. [**Mills v. Electric Auto Lite Co.,** 396 U.S. 375 (1970)] In many instances, statutory fee-shifting provisions also provide a basis for a fee award in class actions as in other suits. However, the amount of the attorney's-fee award must be carefully examined by the court to protect the interests of the class.

(1) Made on Motion

A claim for an award of attorney's fees must be made by motion, and notice of the motion must be directed to class members in a reasonable manner. [Fed. R. Civ. P. 23(h)(1)]

(2) Objections to Motion

Any class member, or a party from whom payment is sought, may object to the motion. [Fed. R. Civ. P. 23(h)(2)]

(3) Coupon Settlements

The court may grant an attorney's fee award based on the value of coupons in a settlement of a class action only to the extent that the coupons are *redeemed* by class members (*see supra*). [28 U.S.C. § 1712]

(4) Protection Against Loss by Class Members

A court may approve a class-action settlement that would require some class members to pay more in attorney's fees than the benefits that they receive under the settlement only if it makes a written finding that the nonmonetary benefits to the class members substantially outweigh the monetary loss (*see supra*). [28 U.S.C. § 1713]

8. Effect of Judgment in Class Action

A central issue in class actions is whether the judgment binds members of the class who were not actually before the court.

a. State Rules

Some states retain the distinctions between true, hybrid, and spurious class actions (the former Federal Rule), under which the "nature" of the action determines whether the judgment is binding on absentees. (*See supra*, pp. 239–240.)

b. Federal Rule

Under Federal Rule 23, however, these distinctions are eliminated. A valid judgment in any class action (whether or not favorable to the class) *binds all members of the class who do not affirmatively request exclusion (opt out)*. A person who excludes herself from the action will not be bound by an adverse judgment. Conversely, however, she may be unable to assert issue preclusion in her own action if the judgment turns out to be favorable to the class. (*See supra*, p. 260.)

9. Defendant Class Actions

Rule 23 states that suits may be brought against a defendant class. For such actions, the Rule does not provide any procedures different from those for actions on behalf of a plaintiff class. Nevertheless, the *courts tend to approach defendant class actions differently* in ways that should be noted.

a. Adequacy of Representation

There is a risk that a plaintiff will select a weak representative for a defendant class. Adequacy of representation may therefore be *examined more closely*.

(1) Incentive Problem

The defendant class representative may have less incentive to litigate vigorously, and the lawyer for the class lacks the entrepreneurial incentive of a plaintiff's class lawyer, who looks forward to a large fee award if the case is successful.

(2) Courts' Attitude

Despite these problems, many courts realize that defendants will try to escape service as class representative. The courts resist such efforts: "[C]ourts must not readily accede to the wishes of named defendants in this area, for to permit them to abdicate so easily would utterly vitiate the effectiveness of the defendant class action." [**Marcera v. Chinlund,** 595 F.2d 1231 (2d Cir.), *vacated on other grounds*, 442 U.S. 915 (1979)] Hence, when the representatives will adequately protect the class by protecting their own interests, courts will find them adequate.

b. Qualitative Differences Between Plaintiff and Defendant Postures

Many courts view defendants' stakes as qualitatively different. The distinction is that the unnamed plaintiff stands to gain while the unnamed defendant stands to lose. [**Thillens, Inc. v. Community Currency Exchange Association,** 97 F.R.D. 668 (N.D. Ill. 1983)]

(1) Criticism

This leaning represents a skewed view of litigation, because both defendants and plaintiffs stand to lose and gain. The absent plaintiff class member who has a valid claim stands to lose if the class action is decided adversely, and the absent defendant class member stands to gain claim-preclusion protection against future suits if the defendant class is successful.

c. Rule 23(b)(2) Class Actions

Rule 23(b)(2) authorizes actions for injunctive or declaratory relief against "the party opposing the class," seemingly precluding a defendant class action. Nevertheless, there is a division in the courts on whether it is permissible to have a class action seeking an injunction against a defendant class. [*See* **Marcera v. Chinlund,** *supra*—defendant class allowed; **Henson v. East Lincoln Township,** 814 F.2d 410 (7th Cir. 1987)—defendant class not allowed]

d. Personal Jurisdiction

In upholding the authority of a state court to exercise personal jurisdiction over absent plaintiff class members (*see supra,* p. 254), the Supreme Court distinguished the situation of defendants, for "an out-of-state defendant summoned by a plaintiff is faced with the full powers of the forum state *against* it." [**Phillips Petroleum Co. v. Shutts,** *supra,* p. 254] It is uncertain whether this position mandates granting unnamed defendant class members more than the right to opt out to overcome their personal-jurisdiction objections.

e. Bilateral Class Action

Some of the most troubling class-action problems involve "bilateral" class actions, *i.e.,* involving a plaintiff class suing a defendant class. One reaction of courts has been to hold that *each plaintiff class member must have a claim against each defendant class member* in such actions. [**La Mar v. H & B Novelty & Loan Co.,** 489 F.2d 461 (9th Cir. 1973)] There are two principal ways to satisfy this requirement.

(1) Conspiracy

When it is alleged that the defendant class members conspired with each other, that provides a basis for holding each conspirator liable to each plaintiff and solves the problem.

(2) Juridical Link

The courts have also allowed bilateral class actions when there is a "juridical link" among the defendants. Usually this term means that defendants are officers of the same governmental unit, such as the state. [*See, e.g.,* **Marcera v. Chinlund,** *supra*—action against sheriffs of state for denying contact visits to pretrial detainees]

Chapter Six
Discovery

CONTENTS	PAGE

Key Exam Issues

Broad discovery is a 20th-century addition to American litigation. The justification for allowing broad discovery is to afford parties an opportunity to obtain full information to support their own cases and information about what evidence other parties will use to support their cases. Balanced against the interest in fostering a candid exchange of information is the risk of serious costs, due to either invasion of privacy or other confidentiality issues or the sheer expense of responding to discovery requests.

When presented with an examination question involving discovery issues, the following approach should be useful:

1. **What Exactly Is Sought in the Discovery Request?**

   Discovery requests must specify what is sought, and the party seeking discovery must use a mode of discovery suited to obtaining the desired information. On an exam, seemingly innocuous discovery requests may turn out to be overbroad or to seek information not available using the discovery method employed. It is important at the outset to appreciate the breadth of the discovery demand and to focus on the specific operation of the various discovery devices.

   a. **Initial Disclosure**: In federal court and in some states, the parties must exchange certain basic information before formal discovery begins. This exchange, following a discovery conference between the parties, should include the *identities of likely witnesses* the disclosing party will use; *identification of documents* the disclosing party will use; *details about damage claims* made by the disclosing party; and *information about insurance* that may cover the disclosing party's liability in the litigation.

   b. **Document Production**: Discovery often begins with document production to obtain materials that may be used later to question witnesses. These requests can include *electronically stored information* and often are objected to as unduly *burdensome.* A document request (unlike an interrogatory) cannot generally require a party to create responsive materials. But document requests can be very useful—documents don't forget. And recall that with a subpoena, a party can obtain document production by a nonparty.

   c. **Interrogatories**: Interrogatories are written questions that must be answered in writing by a party under oath, and a *reasonable investigation* is required to obtain the requested information. If the answers are from the responding party's records, and the effort involved in obtaining the information is roughly equal for the requesting and responding party, the responding party may make the records available for review by the party seeking discovery. Interrogatories cannot be sent to nonparties.

   d. **Depositions**: Depositions involve live questioning under oath by the lawyer who requested the deposition. Unlike with interrogatories, the lawyer can follow up responses to obtain more information. The witness is usually represented by a lawyer who can object to questions. The testimony is recorded and may in some circumstances be used as evidence at trial. During the deposition, a lawyer may show documents to the witness and ask questions about them. Using a subpoena, a party may compel a nonparty to submit to a deposition.

   e. **Physical or Mental Examinations**: By court order, a party may have another party examined by a suitably credentialed expert if the physical or mental condition of the person is in issue. There is no procedure for obtaining such an examination of a nonparty.

f. **Requests for Admissions**: These devices resemble pleadings in that they are not to discover new information but to establish facts. Unless the recipient party denies the requests, they are *deemed admitted* for purposes of this litigation, although under some circumstances a party who has made an admission will be permitted to withdraw it with an adequate explanation.

g. **Supplementation**: With most disclosure and discovery, there is a duty to supplement after the initial discovery responses are provided if those responses were incomplete or inaccurate.

2. Is the Information Sought Relevant?

The basic standard for discovery is whether the information sought is relevant. This standard calls for consideration of the issues raised by the pleadings; any information that might reasonably prove or disprove those issues is relevant. The scope of relevance is very broad, including information that bears on the credibility of probable witnesses or on the extent of injuries for which compensation is sought. In this common-sense determination, creativity in developing grounds for relevance is often rewarded.

3. Would the Discovery Involve Undue Burden or Expense?

In federal court, discovery must be "proportional to the needs of the case," and the judge is to limit discovery that imposes costs on the responding party that are disproportionate to the importance of obtaining the information for use in the case. The starting assumption is that the responding party must shoulder the expense of responding, but if he can show that the information sought is of marginal relevance to the case, or that he has already produced sufficient information on the issue, he may be able to persuade the judge that further discovery is not warranted due to the expense involved. The requesting party ordinarily must explain the relevance of the information sought, but the objecting party ordinarily must establish the burden that compliance would impose on it, and the court may enter a protective order if so persuaded.

4. Is the Information Sought Protected by a Privilege?

Even though otherwise relevant, information that is protected by a privilege is not discoverable. The most common privilege objection is based on the *attorney-client* privilege, which depends on whether the information is about a *communication between a client and an attorney* relating to *legal advice* that was made *in confidence*. If others have become aware of the communication, there may be a ground for arguing that the privilege protection has been *waived*.

5. Is the Information Protected as Work Product?

Information developed in anticipation of litigation is conditionally protected against discovery. In order to discover such information, a party must demonstrate that it has a *substantial need* for the information and that it is unable to obtain the *substantial equivalent*. Even if it orders production, the court should protect against revelation of *"opinion" work product*.

6. Does the Discovery Seek Information Developed by Experts?

When information is developed for use in litigation by experts retained by the parties, special discovery provisions apply.

a. **Testifying Expert Witnesses**: If the expert will be testifying at trial, the retaining party must provide disclosure identifying the expert before trial, and the expert usually must supply a detailed report concerning the testimony, including all data or information she considered in relation to the opinion. If the testifying expert was not "retained or specially employed to provide expert testimony," only a brief disclosure is necessary. The other side may then take the deposition of the expert witness.

b. **Nontestifying Expert Consultant**: When a party retains an expert to assist in the preparation of the case but not to testify, discovery about the information developed by the expert is allowed only in exceptional circumstances, such as when the expert is the only one to have observed certain events, or when there are no more experts available.

7. **Can a Party Obtain an Order Compelling Discovery or Imposing Sanctions?**

A party that believes another party has not properly responded to its discovery request may move for an order compelling discovery. If the court orders the discovery but the other party does not obey the order, it is possible to obtain sanctions, including dismissal or default, for that disobedience. The party seeking an order must show that the discovery response was inadequate and, to obtain sanctions, that the court's order was disobeyed.

8. **May Discovery Material Be Used at Trial?**

In general, material obtained through discovery may be used at trial.

a. **Depositions**: Ordinarily a deposition may be used at trial in lieu of live witness testimony only if the witness is an opposing party or has been shown to be unavailable.

b. **Undisclosed Information**: When a party tries to use information it should have included in automatic disclosure or in response to discovery, the court on objection should exclude the information unless the failure to disclose it was harmless or was substantially justified. Exclusion should occur on pretrial motions as well as at trial.

c. **Governed by the Rules of Evidence**: In general, the admissibility of discovery information at trial depends on the applicable Rules of Evidence. (See Evidence Summary.)

A. Introduction

1. History of Discovery

a. Common Law

Under common-law procedure, the pleadings were to disclose detailed factual contentions and information to the adversary parties. (*See supra*, Chapter Four.) But neither party could compel the other to disclose additional information that might support his case, even such crucial information as the identity of an eyewitness. A party was not compelled to reveal in advance the evidence he would present at trial; neither were third parties required to make disclosures except pursuant to a subpoena requiring their attendance at trial.

b. Equity

In early equity practice, a bill in equity could be used to compel the adversary to disclose information, and such bills frequently were accompanied by interrogatories which the defendant was required to answer under oath. In addition, parties or witnesses could be required to appear for depositions when interrogation through written questions could be conducted. Since answers to interrogatories and depositions were a part of the record on which the decision was made, they were really part of the trial and not merely preparatory discovery. Live testimony was usually not allowed at the hearing, so cases were decided on the basis of the material developed through discovery.

c. Equity in Aid of Law

A litigant in a law court could sometimes take advantage of the equitable procedures by bringing a bill in equity to compel discovery of information needed to present a claim or defense at law. Such a bill could issue if the evidence sought would be admissible in the specific legal proceeding (*i.e.*, if the moving party was not embarked on a "fishing expedition") and would be helpful to the moving party in meeting a burden of proof imposed on him.

d. Code Procedure

Nineteenth-century reforms merged the bill of discovery into legal proceedings, but did not significantly enlarge its availability. Thus, heavy reliance on the pleadings continued.

e. Federal Rules

Ultimately, the Federal Rules (implemented in 1938) made pretrial discovery an integral part of the process of defining the issues for trial. Similar discovery procedures have now been adopted in almost every state. However, increasing concern about excessive discovery has led to repeated revision of discovery rules.

2. Purpose and Effect of Discovery Procedures

a. Obtaining Factual Information

A party who has made effective use of discovery can go to trial with the best evidence available to prove his contentions and with a good knowledge of the presentation that his adversary will make. Surprise and delay are thus largely avoided, and the chance that the judgment will rest on accurate findings of fact is enhanced.

b. Narrowing the Issues

Discovery can help to eliminate fictitious issues, claims, or defenses by revealing overwhelming evidence on one side, thereby paving the way for stipulations, settlements, and summary disposition. **Caution**: Many lawyers say that broad discovery has not in fact narrowed cases, although it may have facilitated summary judgment (*see infra*, p. 330 *et seq.*).

c. Promoting Settlements

It was hoped that discovery would facilitate more and earlier settlements by providing each side fuller knowledge of the strengths and weaknesses of its case.

d. Simplification of Pleading

The availability of discovery makes it unnecessary to rely heavily upon the pleadings for exchanging information, narrowing issues, or disposing of untenable claims or defenses. Accordingly, where discovery is available, pleading is simplified and technical challenges to pleadings are disfavored.

e. Costs to Litigants

To the extent that discovery produces settlements and stipulations, it can substantially cut down costs to one or both parties. At the same time, the discovery process itself can be very costly in terms of time spent by lawyers, parties, witnesses, and court reporters.

f. Substantive Consequences

The foregoing effects of discovery can have substantive implications as well. Claims and defenses otherwise difficult to establish may be made effective by the availability of discovery. Antitrust claims, for example, are often proved with evidence discovered in the possession of the defense. And the availability of discovery may enable a tenacious and resourceful litigant to wear down one who is weaker or less energetic.

3. Problems in Discovery

a. Collateral Purpose Problem

An ongoing concern with discovery is the risk that litigants may seek to obtain discovery for some purpose other than preparation for trial.

(1) Harassment

Because of its cost, discovery can be used to harass an opponent or club an opponent into settlement. Discovery is limited to material "proportional to the needs of the case." [Fed. R. Civ. P. 26(b)(1)] The court has power to limit discovery having these tendencies [Fed. R. Civ. P. 26(b)(2)] and to sanction the person who misuses it. [Fed. R. Civ. P. 26(g)]

(2) Nonlitigation Use of Information

Alternatively, a litigant may seek information that is pertinent to the litigation to use it for some nonlitigation purpose.

e.g. **Example**: In litigation between business competitors, one litigant may seek to force its opponent to reveal information that can be used to obtain competitive advantages in the marketplace.

e.g. **Example**: In an action between Jacqueline Kennedy Onassis and a professional photographer who specialized in unauthorized candid photos of the Kennedy family, there was concern that the photographer would use Ms. Onassis's deposition as an occasion for photographing her. (**Galella v. Onassis,** 487 F.2d 986 (2d Cir. 1974)—upholding protective order excluding plaintiff from defendant's deposition]

b. "Stonewalling" and Failure to Respond Properly

Another prominent discovery concern is that some litigants do not comply with their obligations to respond to discovery in a timely or thorough manner. Some reportedly withhold materials that should be turned over, while others may use "dump truck" tactics—turning over vast amounts of irrelevant material that the opponent must sift through rather than only the items requested.

B. Basic Discovery Devices

1. Prediscovery Disclosure

Federal Rule 26(a)(1) provides for disclosure of certain information before commencement of formal discovery. *Rationale*: Formal discovery is too time-consuming and expensive as to certain core information that will undoubtedly be revealed during the formal discovery process.

Request for discovery must be **specific** and mode must be **suited to obtaining desired information.** Consider the devices:
- Document inspection
- Interrogatories
- Depositions
- Physical or mental exam
- Request for admission

Scope of discovery is broad but information sought **must be relevant**

Request must be **proportional**, and can be objected to as involving **undue burden or expense**

Privileged information is not discoverable. Consider:
- Attorney-client privilege
- Work product

Discovery of information developed by an **expert** depends on whether expert will testify at trial

Discovery requests may be enforced by an **order compelling discovery.** Failure to obey such an order may result in **sanctions**

Admissibility of discovered material at trial is governed by the **rules of evidence**

a. Early Conference of Counsel

To accomplish the objectives of the disclosure provisions, counsel are to meet and confer "as soon as practicable" after the suit is filed. The purpose of this conference is to allow the parties to "discuss the nature and basis of their claims and defenses," to "discuss any issues about preserving discoverable information," and to "develop a proposed discovery plan," as well as to specify the materials that should be included in the prediscovery disclosures. [Fed. R. Civ. P. 26(f)(2)]

(1) Presented to Court

The discovery plan is to be presented to the court in writing within 14 days, or orally at the court's scheduling conference pursuant to Rule 16 (*see infra*, p. 348).

b. No Formal Discovery Until Meeting of Counsel

Formal discovery may not be undertaken, except on stipulation or court order, until the Rule 26(f) conference has been completed. [Fed. R. Civ. P. 26(d)(1)]

(1) Exception for Witnesses Leaving Country

A party may take a deposition earlier if the witness is expected to leave the country and be unavailable for deposition in this country unless examined before the meeting of counsel. [Fed. R. Civ. P. 30(a)(2)(A)]

(2) Early Rule 34 Requests

Early Rule 34 requests for production and inspection may be served on a party 21 days after the summons and complaint are served on that party. For purposes of the time to respond to the request, it will be considered served at the parties' first Rule 26(f) conference. [Fed. R. Civ. P. 26(d)(2); 34(b)(2)(A)] The objective of this early service is to enable concrete discussion of the demands of Rule 34 discovery during the Rule 26(f) conference.

c. Disclosure of Materials Disclosing Party May Use

Prediscovery disclosure is required regarding witnesses and documents that the disclosing party "may use to support its claims or defenses."

(1) Impeachment Materials Excluded

Materials that a party would use solely for impeachment are not subject to the disclosure requirement. **Caution**: Very few materials fall within this category; if they are relevant for some purpose other than impeachment, a court may hold this exemption inapplicable.

(2) Categories of Cases Exempted

A limited number of categories of cases in which substantial discovery is unlikely are exempted from the disclosure requirement and the accompanying attorney conference and discovery moratorium provisions. [Fed. R. Civ. P. 26(a)(1)(B)] Examples include habeas corpus petitions, actions to enforce an administrative subpoena, and actions on guaranteed student loans.

(3) Objection Suspends Duty to Disclose

If a party objects during the Rule 26(f) attorney conference that disclosure is "not appropriate in this action" and states that objection in the Rule 26(f) report to the court (*see supra*, p. 274), the obligation to disclose is suspended until the court rules on the objection. [Fed. R. Civ. P. 26(a)(1)(D)]

(4) Disclosure by Later-Added Parties

A party first served or otherwise joined after the Rule 26(f) conference must make its disclosures within 30 days. [Fed. R. Civ. P. 26(a)(1)(D)]

d. Material to Be Disclosed

(1) Identity of Witnesses

Each party is to disclose the name and, if known, the address and telephone number of each person whom it may use to support its claims or defenses. [Fed. R. Civ. P. 26(a)(1)(A)(i)]

(2) Documents That May Be Used

Each party is to disclose a copy or description by category of all documents in its possession, custody, or control that it may use to support its claims or defenses. [Fed. R. Civ. P. 26(a)(1)(A)(ii)]

(a) Broad Concept of "Use"

The expected use of a document or witness that mandates disclosure is not limited to use at trial. The expectation that a document or witness will be used in connection with any motion or a pretrial conference is sufficient. Sufficient use even includes certain discovery events, such as questioning a witness by using a document. However, the concept of use here does not extend to the mere use of a document or witness's name to respond to another party's discovery inquiry.

EXAM TIP   **GILBERT**

Whenever a party attempts to make any use of a document or witness (whether at a hearing or through an affidavit) that has not been previously disclosed, consider whether the party may have failed to satisfy its initial disclosure obligations. As noted *infra* (p. 276), failure to do so may result in an "automatic" refusal by the court to permit the use of the material. Keep in mind that the rule calls for disclosure as long as the party "may" use the document; its use need not be certain.

---

(3) Damages Computation

Each party claiming damages should disclose a computation of those damages and produce the documents on which the computation is based. [Fed. R. Civ. P. 26(a)(1)(A)(iii)]

(4) Insurance Agreements

Each party against whom a claim has been asserted should produce for inspection and copying each insurance agreement that might cover the claim. [Fed. R. Civ. P. 26(a)(1)(A)(iv)]

☑ ***Name and (if known) address and phone number*** of any person the disclosing party may use to support its case.

☑ ***Copies or description of all documents*** in the party's possession that it may use to support its position in the case.

☑ ***Computation of damages*** and documents on which computation is based.

☑ ***Insurance agreements*** that might cover the claim.

e. Timing of Disclosures

These disclosures should be made at, or within 14 days after, the meeting of counsel pursuant to Rule 26(f) (*supra*, p. 274) unless otherwise agreed by the parties or ordered by the court. [Fed. R. Civ. P. 26(a)(1)(C)] *Note*: A different period applies to later-added parties. (*See supra*, p. 275.)

f. Form of Disclosures

Every disclosure is to be signed by at least one attorney of record for the disclosing party. The signature represents that to the best of the lawyer's knowledge, formed after a reasonable inquiry, the disclosure is complete and correct as of the time it is made. [Fed. R. Civ. P. 26(g)(1)(A)]

g. Duty to Supplement

If a party learns that its disclosures were incorrect, or if additional or corrective information comes to its attention, the party is to supplement the disclosure with the added information. [Fed. R. Civ. P. 26(e)(1)(A)]

h. Sanctions for Failure to Disclose

A party failing to disclose as required by Rule 26(a)(1) or to supplement as required by Rule 26(e)(1) is subject to sanctions. [Fed. R. Civ. P. 37(c)(1)]

(1) Exclusion of Evidence

Unless the failure to disclose was harmless, the party will not be permitted to use the material in evidence. This sanction is said to be automatic, and it applies not only at trial but also at motion hearings, as on a motion for summary judgment.

(2) Additional Sanctions

In addition, the court may impose the sanctions authorized by Rule 37(b), which usually require an order compelling discovery as a prerequisite (*see infra*, p. 320), and can inform the jury of the failure to make disclosure.

i. Stipulation to Limit Disclosure Obligation

The parties may stipulate to limit or alter the initial-disclosure obligation.

If an exam question focuses on discovery, you will likely need to know not only what constitutes a violation of the rules of discovery, but also what sanctions can be imposed and under what conditions. The sanctions and their prerequisites vary from one discovery device to the next, but it is important to remember that if a party fails to make or supplement a prediscovery disclosure as required by Rule 26 and the failure was harmful, the party who failed to disclose will be prohibited from using the undisclosed evidence. Other sanctions may also be imposed (*e.g.*, contempt) if the court first orders disclosure and the party still does not disclose.

2. Depositions

A deposition is an examination of a witness under oath in the presence of a court reporter, who records the questions and the answers. All parties have a right to be represented by counsel at a deposition; and counsel may examine and cross-examine the witness. The examination may be held in the presence of a judge if the witness is recalcitrant.

a. When Timely

(1) Before Suit Filed

A deposition may be taken before an action is filed, but only by leave of court granted for the purpose of perpetuating testimony based on a showing that the party seeking to perpetuate testimony is unable to cause the action to be brought. [Fed. R. Civ. P. 27(a)]

(2) Moratorium After Commencement of Suit

Federal Rule 26(d)(1) provides that formal discovery (except depositions of witnesses about to leave the country; *see supra*, p. 1350, and early Rule 34 requests for documents, *see supra*, p. 274) must be deferred until after the parties meet and confer on a discovery plan pursuant to Rule 26(f).

(a) Defendant's Head Start

When the moratorium does not apply, as in state court, defendants usually are protected against initiation of formal discovery by the plaintiff until a certain time after service of the complaint [*e.g.*, Cal. Code Civ. Proc. § 2025.210(b)— 20-day period for noticing depositions]

(3) Simultaneous Proceedings

All parties may take depositions simultaneously unless the court otherwise directs. [Fed. R. Civ. P. 26(d)(2)] Hence, neither side is entitled to discovery "priority" before the other side can commence discovery.

b. Optional to Parties

Depositions are optional. Each party has the right to take the deposition of any witness— without a showing of good cause—but is not required to do so. A party is also entitled to interview any willing nonparty witness without court supervision. [**Corley v. Rosewood Care Center, Inc.,** 142 F.3d 1041 (7th Cir. 1998)]

c. Numerical Cap on Depositions

To curb abuse, Rule 30 imposes a 10-deposition limit. [Fed. R. Civ. P. 30(a)(2)(A)(i)]

(1) Limit per "Side"

The 10-deposition limit is not per party, but rather is calculated cumulatively for plaintiffs, defendants, and third-party defendants.

(2) One Deposition per Witness

In addition, the rules provide that a given witness's deposition may be taken only once. [Fed. R. Civ. P. 30(a)(2)(A)(ii)]

(3) Change by Stipulation or Order

The parties may stipulate in writing to vary the deposition limit, and the court may so order.

d. Durational Limit on Depositions

Due to concerns that some depositions may be too long, depositions in federal court are limited to one seven-hour day. [Fed. R. Civ. P. 30(d)(1)] Some states have tighter time limits.

e. Compulsory Appearance of Witness

(1) Issuance of Subpoena

At the request of a party, the court clerk will issue a subpoena commanding the named witness to appear and give testimony at the designated time and place. An attorney admitted to practice before the court may also issue a subpoena. [Fed. R. Civ. P. 45(a)(3)]

(2) Service of Subpoena

A subpoena is served on the witness personally and must be accompanied by a tender of the fee for one day's attendance, plus reimbursement for mileage. [Fed. R. Civ. P. 45(b)(1)]

(3) Place of Deposition

A witness may be required to appear at a deposition at any place within 100 miles of the place where he resides, is employed, or transacts business or, as to a party-witness, within the state where the witness resides, is employed, or regularly transacts business in person. [Fed. R. Civ. P. 45(c); compare Cal. Civ. Proc. Code § 2025.250(a)—75 miles]

(4) Subpoena Not Necessary for Party-Witness

It is not necessary to serve a subpoena on an adverse party, or an officer or managing agent of a party, in order to compel attendance. [Fed. R. Civ. P. 37(d)(1)(A)(i); Cal. Civ. Proc. Code § 2025.280(a)] A deposition of a party-witness may be scheduled at any reasonable place.

(5) Deposition of Corporation or Organization

When a corporation (or an association or governmental body) is to be deposed, the party taking the deposition need not identify the individual who is compelled to give the deposition. She need only state "with reasonable particularity" the matters on which she proposes to examine the organization, and the organization must then designate the appropriate witness. [Fed. R. Civ. P. 30(b)(6)] The adversary need not guess which employee is in possession of the required information; and the organization itself is bound by its deponent's answers.

(a) Scope of Inquiry

Problems can arise when the party taking discovery inquires into matters relevant to the suit but beyond the expertise of the witness or beyond the matters specified in the notice. If the witness has some knowledge of the matters, she may have to answer even though the organization may not be bound by her testimony.

e.g. **Example**: When a defendant manufacturer designated a doctor as its witness in a products-liability action, the doctor could be required to answer questions about company policy as well as technical matters on which he had expertise. [**Lapenna v. Upjohn Co.,** 110 F.R.D. 15 (E.D. Pa. 1986)]

f. Notice to Parties

(1) Form of Notice

A party wishing to depose a witness must give written notice to every other party, identifying the deponent and the time and place of the deposition. [Fed. R. Civ. P. 30(b)(1); Cal. Civ. Proc. Code § 2025.220]

EXAM TIP **GILBERT**

Remember that the effect of notice to a party is different from notice to a nonparty. To compel a party's attendance at the deposition, it is sufficient to give written notice to the parties that a deposition is to be taken. However, a nonparty witness must be commanded to attend by means of a subpoena (*see supra*, p. 278).

---

(2) Time for Notice

In federal proceedings, notice must be given a "reasonable" length of time before the scheduled date for the deposition. [Fed. R. Civ. P. 30(b)(1)] Some state codes are more explicit in regard to the time period. [*See, e.g.,* Cal. Civ. Proc. Code § 2025.270(a)—10 days]

g. Production of Documents

The subpoena (when necessary) or the notice may direct the witness to bring along and produce at the deposition any documents that could properly be sought by a request for production of documents (*see infra*, pp. 288–292). [Fed. R. Civ. P. 30(b)(2); Cal. Civ. Proc. Code § 2025.220(a)(4)]

(1) Effect on Timing

When the witness is to produce documents at the deposition, more notice is required. [Fed. R. Civ. P. 30(b)(2)—time required for Rule 34 document production: 30 days; Cal. Civ. Proc. Code § 2025.270(a): 20 days]

h. Questioning of Deponent

(1) Oral

Ordinarily, the examination of deponents is conducted orally, with the examining party questioning first, and the others in turn.

(a) Examination by Witness's Attorney

Usually the attorney for the witness will not question the witness except to clear up important matters left uncertain by other interrogation. *Rationale*: The witness's lawyer does not wish to assist the other parties by making the content of the witness's testimony at trial more evident to them than their own questions have made it.

(2) Depositions in Writing

The examining party may choose to conduct the examination by means of questions in writing. If so, the questions are submitted in writing; the adversary may review the questions in advance and submit cross-questions to be answered at the same time; and the cross-questions may be followed by re-direct and re-cross-questions. Even though the questions are written, the answers of the deponent are given orally. [Fed. R. Civ. P. 31; Cal. Civ. Proc. Code § 2028.010]

(a) Practicality

This form of deposition may be more economical because it does not require the attendance of lawyers at the place of the deposition. On the other hand, it does not give the examiner an opportunity to follow up answers effectively, and hence is not used when the witness may be evasive or when the subject under examination is complex.

(3) Depositions by Remote Means

In federal practice, depositions may be taken by telephone or other remote means upon leave of court or if both parties so stipulate in writing. [Fed. R. Civ. P. 30(b)(4)]

(4) Objections to Questions

The lawyer for the witness may object to a question, and sometimes may instruct the witness not to answer.

(a) Limitation on Instructions Not to Answer

In federal court, a witness may be instructed not to answer a question only to preserve a privilege (*see infra*, pp. 300–305), to enforce a limitation on evidence imposed by the court in the case, or to present a motion for a protective order. [Fed. R. Civ. P. 30(c)(2)] Furthermore, some federal courts have imposed stricter restraints on the behavior of the lawyer for the witness. [*See, e.g.*, **Hall v. Clifton Precision,** 150 F.R.D. 525 (E.D. Pa. 1993)—deponent's attorney forbidden to talk to deponent between commencement and completion of deposition, except to decide whether to assert a privilege]

(b) Motion to Compel

When a witness is instructed not to answer, the examining party may move for an order of the court compelling an answer. [Fed. R. Civ. P. 37(a)(3)(B)(i); Cal. Civ. Proc. Code § 2025.480(a)]

(c) Failure to Obey Order

If the witness disobeys an order to answer, the witness may be held in contempt; and a party-witness may be subject to other sanctions as well. [Fed. R. Civ. P. 37(b); Cal. Civ. Proc. Code § 2025.480(g)]

(d) Protective Order for Witness

On the other hand, if questioning is conducted in an unreasonably oppressive manner, the witness may move for a protective order limiting or terminating the examination. [Fed. R. Civ. P. 30(d)(3)]

(e) No Waiver

Failure of the witness to object to a question at a deposition does not constitute a waiver of her right to object to the same question or answer at trial. [Fed. R. Civ. P. 32(a)(1)(B); 32(b)]

1) Exception—Matters of Form

Errors in the taking of a deposition that might be cured if promptly presented, but which were not, may not be raised as grounds for exclusion of the deposition evidence at trial. This ban includes objections to the form of questions or answers or in the manner of taking of the deposition. [Fed. R. Civ. P. 32(d)(3)(B)]

GILBERT

A SUMMARY UNDER THE FEDERAL RULES	
WHO	A party may depose *any witness* once, but each side is *limited to* 10 depositions; parties must attend on reasonable notice while nonparties must be subpoenaed to compel their attendance.
WHAT	Usually a deposition involves *oral* questioning of the witness, but an oral deposition may be taken by *written questions* or, upon the parties' stipulation or leave of court, *by phone*. The notice or subpoena may also direct the witness to *produce documents*.
WHERE	The deposition must be taken *within 100 miles* of where the witness resides, is employed, or transacts business.
ENFORCEMENT	If a party refuses to answer, the examining party may *move to compel*. Further refusal can result in *contempt* or other sanctions.

i. Transcript of Deposition

(1) Review of Transcript

If requested before completion of the deposition, a deponent is entitled to review the transcript of her testimony and make corrections in it, subject to the right of the examining party to comment on the changes if the deposition is used at trial. [Fed. R. Civ. P. 30(e)(1)]

(2) Videotape

In federal practice, a deposition may be recorded by audio, audiovisual, or stenographic means if the party noticing the deposition so chooses. [Fed. R. Civ. P. 30(b)(3)] Some states also permit a videotape deposition. [Cal. Civ. Proc. Code § 2025.510(f)]

j. Use of Deposition Testimony at Trial

(1) Generally Inadmissible

Statements in depositions are hearsay and thus are generally inadmissible at trial to prove the truth of matters asserted by deponents.

(2) Exceptions

In the following circumstances, however, statements made in depositions may be admissible:

(a) Party Admissions

Deposition statements by party-witnesses are admissible against those parties. [Fed. R. Civ. P. 32(a)(3); Cal. Civ. Proc. Code § 2025.620(b)]

(b) Impeachment

A deposition by a nonparty witness that contradicts testimony given at trial by that witness may be admitted for the purpose of impeaching the witness who has changed her story. [Fed. R. Civ. P. 32(a)(2); Cal. Civ. Proc. Code § 2025.620(a)]

(c) Unavailability of Deponent

If the deponent is dead, infirm, imprisoned, or beyond the reach of subpoena process at the time of trial, the deposition may be used in lieu of her live testimony. [Fed. R. Civ. P. 32(a)(4); Cal. Civ. Proc. Code § 2025.620(c)(2)]

1) Note

This rule also applies to the deposition of a party seeking to use his own deposition instead of testifying at trial, unless that party is responsible for his own absence. [**Richmond v. Brooks,** 227 F.2d 490 (2d Cir. 1955)]

(3) Objectionable Evidence in Deposition

A party may object to the admission of deposition testimony on any ground that would be available if the witness were testifying in person, except objections to the form of the deposition questions. (*See supra*, p. 281.) This possibility exists even if the objection was not raised when the deposition was taken, except as to matters of form. [Fed. R. Civ. P. 32(b), –(d)(3)]

3. Interrogatories

Interrogatories are written questions from one party to another party requiring written responses. [Fed. R. Civ. P. 33(a); Cal. Civ. Proc. Code § 2030.010]

a. Distinguish—Depositions

Be sure to distinguish interrogatories from depositions:

(1) Depositions can be taken of a party or nonparty witness, while interrogatories may be addressed only to a party to the action.

(2) Deposition questions may be oral or written, but the answers are always given orally before a court reporter or similar official who transcribes what is said, or videotaped or audiotaped. In contrast, answers to written interrogatories are prepared in writing, usually by counsel for the answering party.

(3) A deponent may limit her answers to matters of which she has personal knowledge. Interrogatories require the party to answer not only of her own knowledge, but also on the basis of information to which she has reasonable access.

b. Who Must Answer

(1) Any Other Party

A nonparty witness is not subject to interrogatories.

(2) Co-Parties

Co-parties generally are obliged to respond to interrogatories (although a few states adhere to an older rule that interrogatories may be served only upon an "adverse" party).

(3) Corporate Parties

Interrogatories served on a corporation may be answered by any officer or agent designated by the corporation. [Fed. R. Civ. P. 33(b)(1)(B)]

c. When Served

(1) Federal Practice

In federal practice, interrogatories, like other formal discovery, may be served only after the Rule 26(f) conference on a discovery plan. [Fed. R. Civ. P. 26(d)(1)]

(2) State Practice

Some state rules require the plaintiff to delay service of interrogatories for a fixed period following service of the complaint. [*See, e.g.,* Cal. Civ. Proc. Code § 2030.020(b)—10 days]

d. Numerical Limit

In federal practice parties are limited to 25 interrogatories, including subparts. [Fed. R. Civ. P. 33(a)(1)] This limitation applies to each party, so that co-parties (such as co-plaintiffs) may each use 25 interrogatories even though represented by the same lawyer. The limit may be varied by stipulation or court order. Some states have similar numerical limitations. [*See, e.g.,* Cal. Civ. Proc. Code § 2030.030(a)(1)—35 interrogatories]

e. Duty to Respond

(1) Time for Response

A party must answer or object to interrogatories within 30 days after their date of service. [Fed. R. Civ. P. 33(b)(2); Cal. Civ. Proc. Code § 2030.260(a)]

(2) Duty to Investigate

A party to whom interrogatories are propounded must give all information responsive to the questions that is under her control. This requirement generally includes all information that might be discovered in her own files or by further questioning of her agents or employees.

(3) Option When Extensive Search Required

If an answer can be supplied only by extensive search of the responding party's records and the burden of ascertaining the information is substantially the same for the inquiring and responding parties, the responding party may specify the pertinent records and allow the inquiring party to examine and copy them. [Fed. R. Civ. P. 33(d); and see Cal. Civ. Proc. Code § 2030.230]

f. Failure to Make Adequate Response to Interrogatories

(1) Motion to Compel Response

If an answer to interrogatories is incomplete or evasive, on motion the court will order the responding party to answer fully. [Fed. R. Civ. P. 37(a); Cal. Civ. Proc. Code § 2030.300(a)(1)] If the responding party does not obey the order, she is subject to sanctions. [Fed. R. Civ. P. 37(b)(2)]

(2) Time for Motion

In federal proceedings, a motion to compel an answer may be made at any time. Under state rules, the motion may have to be made promptly after receipt of the unsatisfactory answer or the matter will be deemed waived. [*See*, *e.g.*, Cal. Civ. Proc. Code § 2030.300(c)—45 days after response served]

(3) Objections to Interrogatories

A motion to compel an answer to an interrogatory will be denied if the question propounded is subject to a valid and timely objection.

(4) Costs of Proceedings

A party moving to compel an answer without substantial justification therefor, or a party making an objection that lacks substantiality, is subject to an award to the adversary of costs, including attorneys' fees, incurred in the discovery dispute. [Fed. R. Civ. P. 37(a)(5)(A)]

A SUMMARY UNDER THE FEDERAL RULES	
WHO	Interrogatories may be served only on other parties; each party may be served with up to 25 interrogatories from each other party.
WHAT	Interrogatories are written questions from one party to another requiring written responses.
WHEN	Interrogatories may be served only after the Rule 26(f) meeting of counsel; responses are due within 30 days after the interrogatories are served.
ENFORCEMENT	If a party refuses to answer an interrogatory or gives an incomplete or evasive answer, on motion the court may order the party to respond; further refusal can result in contempt or other sanctions.

4. Requests for Admission

a. Device to Eliminate Issues

A request for an admission imposes a duty on the party served to acknowledge the existence of facts that are not in doubt and that should not be necessary to prove at trial. [Fed. R. Civ. P. 36(a); Cal. Civ. Proc. Code § 2033.010]

b. On Whom Served

A request for admission may be served by any party on any other party, whether or not adverse. [Fed. R. Civ. P. 36(a)(1)]

c. Subject of Request

(1) Facts or Application of Law to Fact

A request may ask the party served to admit the genuineness of a document, the truth of factual allegations, or the applicability of legal concepts to specified facts in issue.

(2) Conclusions of Law

A party may request another party to make an admission about the circumstances underlying the case that includes a legal conclusion, *e.g.*, that a person was acting as an agent, or that the speed limit at a point of impact was 50 miles per hour.

(a) But Note

It is not proper to request an admission to an abstract statement of law (*e.g.*, that speeding constitutes negligence). [Fed. R. Civ. P. 36(a)(1)]

(3) Ultimate Issues

Under the Federal Rules, a party may be requested to admit an ultimate fact—*i.e.*, one that controls the outcome of the controversy (such as causation). [Fed. R. Civ. P. 36(a)(1)(A)] Not all states adhere to this rule, however.

(4) Opinions

A party may also request another party to make an admission regarding a matter of opinion (such as the value of property or the extent of damages). A request is not improper merely because the matter to be admitted is in controversy or in doubt.

(5) Matters Unknown to Responding Party

A party may also be requested to admit a fact that is outside his knowledge.

d. Time Limits

(1) For Serving Requests

Under the Federal Rules, a request to admit may be served at any time after the Rule 26(f) conference. [Fed. R. Civ. P. 26(d)(1)] In some states, leave of court is required if the plaintiff wishes to serve requests within 10 days after service of process. [Cal. Civ. Proc. Code § 2033.020(b)]

(2) For Responses

The party upon whom a request is served must file a response within 30 days. [Fed. R. Civ. P. 36(a)(3); Cal. Civ. Proc. Code § 2033.250]

e. Appropriate Responses

(1) Admit

The responding party may choose to make the requested admission; and if he does so, he will not be permitted to controvert the admission at trial. But the admission is binding only in the present action; it may not be used against the party in any other proceeding. [Fed. R. Civ. P. 36(b)] *Rationale*: If a party's admission could bind it in other proceedings, it might contest a point not worth fighting in the present litigation for fear of the admission's possible consequences in other litigation.

(2) Deny

If the responding party chooses to deny the matter that he is asked to admit, and the matter is subsequently proved, the party may be liable for the full costs of proving that matter, unless the court finds that there were "good reasons" for the denial or that the admissions sought were of "no substantial importance." [Fed. R. Civ. P. 37(c)(2); Cal. Civ. Proc. Code § 2033.420]

(a) Impact

The matter of an award of costs is generally within the court's discretion. The court's power to impose sanctions is not affected by which party ultimately wins the lawsuit. Even the winner may end up having to pay sanctions to the loser if the winner was guilty of a "bad faith" refusal to admit (necessitating extra expenses of proof by the loser). [**Smith v. Circle P Ranch Co.,** 87 Cal. App. 3d 267 (1978)]

(b) Equivocal Denial

An equivocal denial (*e.g.,* "Defendant is not presently certain . . ." or "Plaintiff reserves the right to contest this assertion") may be treated as an admission or, on motion, the court may order a proper response. Alternatively, the court might treat an equivocal denial as a "false denial" and award the full costs of proof to the requesting party.

(3) Reasons for Not Admitting or Denying

If the responding party has good reasons for objecting to the request, she may decline to admit or deny, and instead must state her refusal and the grounds therefor. However, there are few valid objections to be made.

(a) Nature of Matter Sought to Be Admitted

That the matter is one of opinion, or an ultimate issue, or a conclusion of law is not an adequate reason for refusing to admit or deny.

(b) Ignorance of Matter Sought to Be Admitted

However, it is sufficient for a refusal to admit that the responding party is ignorant of the matter in question, provided she has made reasonable inquiry and still found the information unavailable.

EXAM TIP

A few quirks to requests for admissions could be tested on an exam. Be sure to remember that an admission establishes the fact only for the current litigation; it cannot be used in other proceedings. Also remember that a party can be assessed costs if the other party proves the denied matter, even if the proving party loses the case. Finally, remember that for good cause (*e.g.*, ignorance of the matter, to protect the right against self-incrimination, etc.) a party can decline to admit or deny.

(c) Self-Incrimination

A party can refuse to answer on the ground that her response may tend to incriminate herself.

(d) Consequences of Giving Insufficient Reasons

The party seeking the admission may move to determine the sufficiency of any objections to his request. If the reasons are insufficient, the court may order a proper response and may impose other sanctions on the party making the inadequate response. Even if no such motion is made, the party making the request may prove the matter, in which event the court can order the objecting party to pay the full costs of proof.

(4) Failure to Respond

If there is no timely response to a request, the matter is deemed admitted. [Fed. R. Civ. P. 36(a)(3); Cal. Civ. Proc. Code § 2033.280(b)]

f. Withdrawal of Admissions

If presentation of the merits will be served, the court may allow a party to amend or withdraw an admission previously made. [Fed. R. Civ. P. 36(b); Cal. Civ. Proc. Code § 2033.300]

A SUMMARY UNDER THE FEDERAL RULES	
WHO	A request for admission may be served by a party on *any other party.*
WHAT	A request for admission asks the party to *acknowledge the existence of facts* that are not in dispute; the request may even go to an "ultimate fact" (*i.e.,* a fact controlling the outcome of the litigation) or a party's opinion about the application of law to fact.
WHEN	A request for admission may be served *any time after the Rule 26(f) meeting* of counsel; responses must be made within 30 days.
ENFORCEMENT	If a party fails to respond to a request for admission, the matter will be *deemed admitted.* If the party denies the matter and the matter is subsequently proved, the court may order the denying party to pay the proving party's costs unless there was good reason for the denial or the admissions were of no substantial importance.

5. Requests for Inspection of Documents and Other Things

a. Materials Discoverable

A party is entitled to obtain production of a variety of items in the possession or control of another party [Fed. R. Civ. P. 34(a)]:

(1) Documents

A request for production may seek writings, drawings, graphs, charts, or any other documentary information.

(2) Electronically Stored Information

Electronically stored information—including data or data compilations, images, or recordings—may be obtained by request.

(3) Tangible Things

Tangible things, such as an automobile, are also subject to discovery under Rule 34.

EXAM TIP ![GILBERT]

Discovery of e-mail and other computerized information has assumed great importance in litigation and might show up on exam questions. Searching for all e-mail messages or other digital information (*e.g.*, texts or social-media posts) on a given subject can impose an immense burden and also raise confidentiality concerns about the expectations of privacy that attend the use of digital media. Requests for discovery of all interim drafts of documents created on word-processing systems can also raise burden and confidentiality issues. Thus, if you encounter a question seeking discovery of electronically stored information, be prepared to look for facts relating to those issues.

---

b. Scope of Examination

Examination may include testing and sampling of materials, and may involve an entry onto the property of a party. With electronically stored information, this scope may sometimes involve access to an opposing party's electronic information system.

c. Making Request for Inspection

(1) No Court Action Required

The party seeking discovery may serve a request for inspection without prior court order or a showing of good cause.

(a) Inspection of Premises

When inspection of premises is sought, a general showing of "relevance" may not be enough. Since entry upon one's premises may entail greater burdens and risks than mere production of documents or other physical evidence, some degree of necessity is generally required for such inspection. [**Belcher v. Bassett Furniture,** 588 F.2d 904 (4th Cir. 1978)]

(2) Timing

Under the Federal Rules, a request for inspection may be served at any time after the Rule 26(f) conference. [Fed. R. Civ. P. 26(d)(1), 34] Some state rules require leave of court if the request is served concurrently with the initial pleadings. [*See, e.g.,* Cal. Civ. Proc. Code § 2031.020(c)—leave of court required if request served by plaintiff within 10 days after service of summons]

(a) Early Rule 34 Requests

Early Rule 34 requests may be served on or by a party 21 days after the summons and complaint are served on that party. That party may also serve such requests on the plaintiff or any other served party at that time. For purposes of the time to respond to the request, it will be considered served at the parties' first Rule 26(f) conference. [Fed. R. Civ. P. 26(b)(2), 34(b)(2)(A)] The objective of this early service is to enable concrete discussion of the demands of Rule 34 discovery during the Rule 26(f) conference.

d. Designation of Items

The moving party must describe the items to be produced with sufficient certainty to enable a person of ordinary intelligence to know which items are sought. [Fed. R. Civ. P. 34(b)(1)] Other forms of discovery are sometimes needed to identify the real evidence to be inspected.

(1) Designation by Category

Often a party will request all materials that fall within a category (*e.g.,* "all documents that relate or refer to the meeting on January 1, 2017") rather than specifying individual items. Parties do so because the party requesting production cannot know for certain what materials the responding party possesses, and wishes to avoid omitting valuable information.

(2) Relation to Initial Disclosures

The initial disclosures pursuant to Rule 26(a)(1)(A) (*see supra,* p. 275) may enable the requesting party to be more specific in the document request.

e. Timing of Inspection

The request for inspection must specify the proposed time, place, and manner of making the inspection. [Fed. R. Civ. P. 34(b)(2)(A); Cal. Civ. Proc. Code § 2031.030(c)]

The response may state another reasonable time for production, but the production must be completed no later than the time specified in the request or the time specified in the response. [Fed. R. Civ. P. 34(b)(2)(B)]

f. Form for Producing Electronically Stored Information

The request may specify the form or forms in which the party wishes electronically stored information to be produced. [Fed. R. Civ. P. 34(b)(1)(C)]

(1) When Request Does Not Designate Form

If the request does not designate the form for producing electronically stored information, the responding party may choose between a form in which he maintains the information and a form that is reasonably usable to the party seeking production. [Fed. R. Civ. P. 34(b)(2)(E)]

(2) Objecting to Designated Form

When the request designates a form for producing electronically stored information, the responding party may object to using the designated form. [Fed. R. Civ. P. 34(b)(2)(D)]

(3) Stating Form Producing Party Will Use

Whether or not the request specifies a form for production of electronically stored information, the responding party must specify in his response to the request the form he intends to use for production. [Fed. R. Civ. P. 34(b)(2)(D)]

g. Objection to Requests

(1) Timing

In federal actions, the party receiving a request for inspection may file written objections within 30 days following service of the request. [Fed. R. Civ. P. 34(b)(2)(A); *compare* Cal. Civ. Proc. Code § 2031.260—20 days]

(2) Specific Objections

The grounds for objections must be stated with specificity, including the reasons. [Fed. R. Civ. P. 34(b)(2)(B)]

(3) Stating Whether Responsive Materials Withheld on Grounds of Objections

A responding party that makes an objection must also state whether any responsive materials are being withheld on the basis of that objection. [Fed. R. Civ. P. 34(b)(2)(C)]

(4) Motion with Respect to Objections

If objections are made, the requesting party may move for an order compelling the requested inspection; and the merits of the objections will then be determined by the court.

h. Items in Responding Party's Control

The responding party is to produce all requested items (unless objections are interposed) that are within its possession, custody, or control. Some courts hold that the "control" idea requires the responding party to make efforts to obtain documents from others if it has "influence" over the possessor. [*See, e.g.,* **Cooper Industries, Inc. v. British Aerospace, Inc.,** 102 F.R.D. 918 (S.D.N.Y. 1984)]

i. "Inaccessible" Electronically Stored Information

Electronically stored information need not be produced if the responding party identifies it as from a source that is not reasonably accessible because of undue burden or cost. On motion to compel discovery or for a protective order, that party must show to the court's satisfaction that the information from this source is not reasonably accessible. Even then, the court may order the information produced for good cause, but it may also impose conditions such as cost-shifting or cost-sharing. [Fed. R. Civ. P. 26(b)(2)(B)]

j. Organization of Produced Materials

In federal court and in some state courts, the responding party is required to produce the requested materials either as they are kept in the ordinary course of business or organized and labeled to correspond to the requests. [Fed. R. Civ. P. 34(b)(2)(E); Cal. Civ. Proc. Code § 2031.280(a)]

(1) Stimulus for Requirement

This requirement was included to prevent responding parties from "hiding" embarrassing materials among mounds of uninteresting materials (*e.g.,* placing an inculpatory memorandum among thousands of invoices instead of leaving it in the memorandum file where it is normally kept).

(a) Ethical Requirements

"Hiding" relevant material as described above is probably a violation of a lawyer's ethical responsibilities, even if it were permitted by the discovery rules. (*See* Legal Ethics Summary.)

(2) Course-of-Business Format Usually Employed for Documents

Most responding parties will produce records in the way they are kept in the normal course of business. They do so because it is usually difficult to determine exactly which request is the pertinent one for given materials, and several requests may apply to a given item. Therefore, not only would reorganizing the files be a great deal of difficult work, it would often assist the opposing party.

(3) Electronically Stored Information

With electronically stored information, an analogous issue arises regarding the form in which it is produced. The requesting party is initially permitted to specify the form or forms he desires, subject to objection by the responding party. In the event of a dispute, the court is likely to focus on whether a proposed form for production is "reasonably usable." [Fed. R. Civ. P. 34(b)(2)(E)]

k. Failure to Respond

Failure to respond to a request for inspection is a ground for a motion to compel discovery. Failure to comply with an order compelling discovery exposes the nonresponding party to sanctions, including the striking of portions of pleadings and a determination of facts on the assumption that inspection would have provided the requesting party with persuasive evidence.

l. Materials in Possession of Nonparties

(1) Subpoena for Inspection

Under federal practice, a subpoena can order a nonparty to permit inspection and copying of documents in its control, or to permit inspection of premises. [Fed. R. Civ. P. 45(a)(1)(C)] Some states have similar provisions. [*See, e.g.,* N.Y. Civ. Prac. Law § 3120(1)(i)]

(a) But Note

Other states require a showing of good cause in an affidavit (usually a showing of relevance to the claims or defenses raised in the action) as a condition to issuance of a subpoena. [Cal. Civ. Proc. Code § 1985(b)]

(2) Independent Action

Alternatively, evidence not otherwise discoverable may be examined through a suit in equity for discovery in aid of the original action.

GILBERT

A SUMMARY UNDER THE FEDERAL RULES

WHO	A party may request that another party allow him to inspect documents and other things in the control of the other party. The request may designate the material sought by category rather than by individual item. Similar inspection may be sought from nonparties through subpoena.
WHAT	Inspection can be of documents, photographs, maps, records, correspondence, or electronically stored information of any sort. A party may also seek inspection of another party's, or (with subpoena) a nonparty's, premises.
WHEN	A request for inspection can be made any time after the Rule 26(f) conference of counsel.
HOW	The responding party is required to produce the requested materials: (i) as they are kept in the ordinary course of business, or (ii) organized and labeled to correspond to the requests. For electronically stored information, the request may specify a form for production, and disputes about form may focus on what is reasonably usable.
ENFORCEMENT	If a party fails to allow inspection, he is subject to a motion to compel, and if he disobeys an order compelling discovery, to sanctions, including striking portions of his pleadings relating to the items for which inspection was prohibited.

6. Physical and Mental Examinations

a. Court Action Required

If the physical or mental condition of a party is in issue, in federal court a motion is necessary to require a party to submit to examination by experts in the service of other parties.

(1) Distinguish—State Practice

In some states, prior court action is not required for the defendant to obtain a physical examination of the plaintiff in a personal-injury suit. [Cal. Civ. Proc. Code § 2032.220(b)]

b. Condition Must Be in Issue

The condition that is the subject of the examination must be raised directly by the pleadings or by the factual contentions of the parties through discovery; and the court-ordered examination must be limited to such conditions. [**Schlagenhauf v. Holder,** 379 U.S. 104 (1964)]

c. Good Cause

If court action is required, an examination will not be ordered except upon a showing of good cause. [Fed. R. Civ. P. 35(a)(2); Cal. Civ. Proc. § 2032.320(a)] In this context, "good cause" means that the examination sought must be shown to be reasonably likely to produce information about the condition in issue.

d. Only Parties Subject to Examination

Court rules generally provide for the examination only of parties or persons in the custody or control of parties. [Fed. R. Civ. P. 35(a)(1)] Some states also provide for the examination of agents of parties. [*See, e.g.,* Cal. Civ. Proc. Code § 2032.020(a)]

e. Qualifications of Examiner

Historically, court-ordered examinations were done only by medical doctors. In federal court, however, examinations may be ordered by any "suitably licensed or certified examiner." [Fed. R. Civ. P. 35(a)(1); and see Cal. Civ. Proc. Code § 2032.020(b)—"licensed physician or other appropriate licensed health care practitioner"]

(1) Selected by Party

Ordinarily the courts will order examination by the examiner selected by the party wanting the examination, but if reasonable objection is made to the moving party's selection, the court has the power to appoint an "impartial examiner" of its own choosing.

f. Place of Examination

The examination ordinarily will be ordered at the place selected by the examining party; but the court can have the examination conducted elsewhere to diminish the burden on the examinee.

g. Types of Procedure

If the information sought to be obtained is important, the court may permit an examination procedure that is novel or even uncomfortable, as long as it is reasonably safe.

h. Presence of Counsel or Other Observer

Federal and state courts follow widely different approaches when it comes to allowing the presence of counsel or an observer at a physical or mental examination. A majority of federal courts do not permit the presence of the examinee's counsel, a third party, or an unattended videotape machine at a physical or mental examination, absent some compelling circumstance. [*See, e.g.,* **Holland v. United States,** 182 F.R.D. 493 (D.S.C. 1998)] Other courts, however, have found a right to the presence of an observer, and still others decide on a case-by-case basis. [*See* **Galieti v. State Farm Mutual Automobile Insurance Co.,** 154 F.R.D. 262 (D. Colo. 1994)]

i. Copies of Reports

(1) Examinee's Right to Receive Copy

Upon request, the examinee has the right to receive a copy of the examiner's report. [Fed. R. Civ. P. 35(b)(1); Cal. Civ. Proc. Code § 2032.610]

(2) Waiver of Privilege

However, an examinee who requests a copy of the report waives the doctor-patient privilege with respect to any previous examinations of the same condition by his own physician [Fed. R. Civ. P. 35(b)(4); Cal. Civ. Proc. Code § 2032.630]; any reports of such other examinations must be provided on request to the examining party. Note that even absent such a request, a plaintiff in a personal-injury case waives the privilege in regard to medical examinations of the injury for which recovery is sought.

GILBERT

A SUMMARY UNDER THE FEDERAL RULES	
WHO	A party may seek a medical examination only of another party and only if: (i) the condition that is the subject of the examination is in issue, and (ii) the court determines that there is good cause for the exam.
WHAT	The examination can be of physical or mental condition, and can be done by any suitably licensed or certified examiner selected by the party requesting the exam and approved by the court.
WHERE	The examination is usually held at the place selected by the examining party.
HOW	The court may authorize an examination that is novel or even uncomfortable as long as it is reasonably safe.
ENFORCEMENT	A party who refuses an examination may not be held in contempt, but facts that could be proved by the examination can be deemed established by the refusal.

7. Duty to Supplement Responses

a. Federal Practice—Broad Duty to Supplement

Rule 26(e) requires supplementation of prior responses if in some material respect Rule 26(a) disclosures or discovery responses are incomplete or incorrect or if there is additional or corrective information that has been acquired since the response was made.

(1) Inapplicable if Information Otherwise Made Known

The obligation to supplement is satisfied if the additional or corrective information has otherwise been made known during the discovery process or if it is supplied in writing.

EXAM TIP

Don't forget the duty to supplement. Under federal practice rules, if a prior response to a discovery request is incomplete or incorrect, the party who responded has a duty to supplement the response unless the additional or corrective information has otherwise been revealed in the discovery process.

---

(2) Application to Deposition Testimony

The supplementation requirement ordinarily does not apply to deposition answers, but it is applicable to testimony of an expert witness.

b. State Practice Compared

Some states have supplementation requirements similar to those in the Federal Rules, but many do not; in such states, cautious practitioners must attempt to obtain the same information by sending out supplemental interrogatories before the trial. Still other states use different procedures for the same purpose.

(1) Pretrial Conference Orders

If a pretrial conference is held, the court (on a showing of good cause) may require either side to update its responses to earlier interrogatories, particularly in connection with disclosing expert witnesses who will be called to testify at trial. A party failing to disclose an expert at this point may be barred from using that person as a witness at trial, except on such terms as the court finds appropriate. [**Sanders v. Superior Court,** 34 Cal. App. 3d 270 (1973); **Crumpton v. Dickstein,** 82 Cal. App. 3d 166 (1978)]

(2) Demand to Exchange Lists of Expert Witnesses

California has a separate procedure whereby, at the time a case is set for trial, either side may serve the other with a demand to exchange information on the identity, qualifications, and expected testimony of expert witnesses. Failure to disclose the information demanded bars the use of such experts at trial, except for purposes of impeachment or on terms as the court may order. [Cal. Civ. Proc. Code § 2034.210]

DEVICE	PARTY	NONPARTY
DEPOSITION	Yes	Yes, but only by subpoena
DOCUMENT INSPECTION	Yes	Yes, but only by subpoena
INTERROGATORIES	Yes	No
REQUEST FOR ADMISSION	Yes	No
MEDICAL EXAMINATION	Yes	No

C. Scope of Discovery

1. Relation of Discovery to Proof

Generally, discovery may inquire into all information not otherwise privileged that is relevant to the claim or defense of a party and proportional to the needs of the case, whether or not the material would be admissible as proof. The material itself need not be admissible in evidence. [Fed. R. Civ. P. 26(b)(1); Cal. Civ. Proc. Code § 2017.010] However, a few jurisdictions retain the old equity practice, under which discovery is limited to admissible evidence needed by the discovering party to bear his burden of proof.

a. Scope of Discovery in Federal Court

Rule 26(b)(1) defines the scope of discovery as matter "relevant to any party's claim or defense."

(1) Uncertain Dividing Line

Before it was amended in 2000, Rule 26(b)(1) allowed discovery of material relevant to the "subject matter" of the litigation. The Committee Note accompanying the 2000 amendment recognizes that the dividing line between material relevant to the subject matter of the litigation and that relevant to the claims or defenses "cannot be defined with precision." But the Note explains that the change is intended to signify to parties that they are not entitled to use discovery to "develop new claims or defenses that are not already identified in the pleadings." [Fed. R. Civ. P. 26(b)(1) 2000 Committee Note]

(2) Case-by-Case Determination

Determining whether information is "relevant to the claim or defense of any party," depends on the facts of each case, and types of information that are not directly pertinent to the incident in suit could be relevant to the claims or defenses.

e.g. **Example**: Other incidents of the same type, or involving the same product, could be properly discoverable under the revised standard. [Fed. R. Civ. P. 26(b)(1) Committee Note]

e.g. **Example**: Information about organizational arrangements or filing systems of a party could be discoverable if likely to yield or lead to the discovery of admissible information. [Fed. R. Civ. P. 26(b)(1) Committee Note]

Example: Information that could be used to impeach a likely witness, although not otherwise relevant to the claims or defenses, might be properly discoverable. [Fed. R. Civ. P. 26(b)(1) Committee Note]

Keep in mind that the standard for discovery changed again in 2015, so older cases in your casebook might not use the current standard. Before 2000, material was discoverable if it was relevant to the subject matter of the action. The new standard is subtly narrower: To be discoverable, the matter must be relevant to a claim or defense and must be "proportional" (see below).

b. Proportionality—Judicial Limitation of Disproportionate Discovery

In federal court, Rule 26(b)(1) also provides that discovery must be "proportional to the needs of the case," and the court must limit discovery if it finds one of the following circumstances to exist [Fed. R. Civ. P. 26(b)(2)(C)]:

(1) Discovery Unreasonably Cumulative

If the discovery is unreasonably cumulative or duplicative, or if it is obtainable from some other source that is more convenient, less burdensome, or less expensive, the court may limit or forbid the discovery.

(2) Party Has Already Had Opportunity for Discovery

If the party seeking discovery has already had ample opportunity in the action to obtain discovery of the information sought, the court may limit or forbid the discovery.

(3) Discovery Unduly Burdensome

A party may object to the burden of proposed discovery, and the court must then determine whether that burden is warranted by the needs of the case. This issue may be particularly important regarding Rule 34 requests for production, particularly for electronic information. Neither party has the burden to provide all information the court may need to evaluate the proportionality of proposed discovery. The requesting party is likely to be best positioned to explain the importance of the discovery to development of the case, and the responding party is likely best positioned to explain the burdens of complying. The rule provides that the court should consider several criteria in making its decision on the appropriate scope of discovery for the case:

    (a) **Importance of the Issues at Stake in the Action**: As recognized in the pertinent Committee Note, "the significance of the issues, in philosophical, social, or institutional terms" may be considered. "Thus the rule recognizes that many cases in public policy spheres, such as employment practices, free speech, and other matters, may have importance far beyond the monetary amount involved."

    (b) **The Amount in Controversy**: Determining the amount in controversy may be important to deciding whether a federal court has diversity jurisdiction. (*See* Chapter Two) A similar evaluation of the stakes involved in the litigation is pertinent to proportionality of discovery.

(c) **The Parties' Relative Access to Relevant Information**: The pertinent Committee Note explains: "Some cases involve what often is called 'information asymmetry.' One party—often an individual plaintiff—may have very little discoverable information. The other party may have vast amounts of information, including information that can be readily retrieved and information that is more difficult to retrieve. In practice these circumstances often mean that the burden of responding to discovery lies heavier on the party who has more information, and properly so."

(d) **The Parties' Resources**: A general appreciation of the parties' resources is pertinent to proportionality. This factor does not mean that impecunious parties are immune to discovery, or that wealthy parties are subject to unlimited discovery. The Committee Note observes that the court must "prevent use of discovery to wage a war of attrition or as a device to coerce a party, whether financially weak or affluent."

(e) **The Importance of the Discovery in Resolving the Issues**: This factor focuses on the importance of the information sought to the court's resolution of the issues presented in the action. If the information appears cumulative, for example, it may be insignificant even though the issues are of high importance.

2. Scope of Relevant Material

a. Meaning of Relevance

Information will be deemed relevant (and therefore may be discoverable) if the information tends to prove or disprove a given proposition. In federal court, "relevant evidence means evidence having any tendency to make the existence of any fact that is of consequence to the determination of the action more probable or less probable than it would be without the evidence." [Fed. R. Evid. 401; for more detail, see Evidence Summary]

(1) Fact of Consequence

The concept of a "fact of consequence" includes all matters that are pertinent to the decision of the case. This concept would include all issues raised by the pleadings.

(2) Low Threshold for Relevance

The federal standard creates a very low threshold for relevance.

(3) Common-Sense Determination

The determination whether evidence is relevant depends on a common-sense examination of the probative impact of the information in question on the issue it is said to bear upon.

(4) Distinguish—Substantial Evidence

A party with the burden of proof on an issue has the obligation on that issue to produce substantial evidence to justify submitting the issue to the trier of fact. (*See infra*, p. 383, regarding burden to produce evidence.) That such a party has some relevant evidence on the issue does not mean that she has satisfied the burden of production. Put differently, evidence may be relevant, but by itself insufficient to support a jury verdict on a given issue.

b. Relation to Claims and Defenses

Although the scope of federal discovery has narrowed somewhat, discovery may relate to the claims or defenses of either party and is not limited to information that the discovering party needs to satisfy his own burden of proof.

(1) Comment

This scope enables each party to evaluate his adversary's case as well as his own. This consequence in turn may lead to earlier and more realistic settlement efforts—which is one of the main purposes of discovery.

c. Matters Not in Dispute

Information may be subject to discovery even though it bears on issues that are not in dispute. Again, the test is relevance to the claims and defenses rather than admissibility at trial. [Fed. R. Civ. P. 26(b)(1)]

d. Information About Witnesses

The identity and location of witnesses are discoverable facts. Likewise, information bearing on the credibility of witnesses (*e.g.*, possible grounds for impeachment) may be discovered.

e. Insurance Coverage

Although not admissible as evidence, the existence and scope of insurance coverage is discoverable in most jurisdictions. [Fed. R. Civ. P. 26(a)(1)(A)(iv); **Laddon v. Superior Court,** 167 Cal. App. 2d 391 (1959)] *Rationale:* Settlement negotiations are an essential part of the action, and insurance coverage is relevant at least to this aspect of the claims.

f. Financial Status

Financial condition generally is not relevant even though the information might affect settlement negotiations.

(1) Defendant's Financial Status

A general inquiry into the financial ability of the defendant to satisfy a judgment usually is not permitted. However, the defendant's financial condition may be pertinent in some cases, as when punitive damages are sought. In such cases, the defendant may be required to disclose her financial condition. *Rationale:* If the purpose of a damage remedy is punishment rather than compensation, it may take more to make a wealthy defendant feel the sting of punishment than if the defendant has modest means.

(2) Plaintiff's Financial Status

If the plaintiff's loss of earnings is in question, he may be compelled to produce copies of his financial records, including federal income-tax returns.

(3) Bank Records

If pertinent, bank records may be subject to subpoena, although the bank may be under a duty to notify its customer before complying, in order to give the customer an opportunity to resist disclosure. [**Valley Bank v. Superior Court,** 15 Cal. 3d 652 (1975)]

g. Contentions

A party may be asked to particularize his contentions as to the facts (or the application of law to facts) for the purpose of narrowing the issues at trial. However, answers to such questions may be delayed by court order until pretrial, when the party can be expected to know with some precision what his contentions are.

3. Privilege

Privileged material is universally excluded from obligatory disclosure through discovery. Most civil-procedure courses do not examine any privilege in detail, except the attorney-client privilege, which will be the main focus here. It is the oldest and most frequently invoked privilege.

a. Reasons for the Privilege

The traditional rationale for the attorney-client privilege has been labeled the "utilitarian rationale." It justifies the privilege on the ground that it is necessary to promote full and frank disclosure to the lawyer by the client. Unfortunately, there is little evidence that the existence of the privilege is necessary, or perhaps even important, to achieve that objective. Accordingly, some authorities have argued that the privilege is necessary to protect the personal autonomy of persons faced with legal proceedings, because it ensures that there is at least one knowledgeable person from whom they can seek help with the assurance that this person will not become a witness for the other side. (*See* Evidence Summary.)

b. Requirements

(1) Legal Advice Sought

The privilege applies only to communications in which legal advice is sought. Thus, when the client is seeking business advice, no protection exists.

(2) From Lawyer

The privilege applies only to communications seeking legal advice from a professional legal adviser acting in that capacity. In most jurisdictions, it applies whenever the client reasonably believes that the person from whom he seeks advice is a lawyer, even if the belief turns out to be wrong.

(3) Communications Relating to Legal Advice

The privilege applies only to communications relating to obtaining legal advice; communications on entirely different subjects are not protected.

(4) Made in Confidence

The privilege applies only to communications made in confidence. In general, this requirement means that the parties must behave as though they intend the communication to be confidential.

(a) Presence of Other People

The presence of other people during the communication may indicate that the communication is not confidential, unless the presence of these people is necessary to the communication. Thus, the lawyer's secretary or a paralegal might be present to assist the lawyer. Similarly, a friend or close relative might properly be present if the client is unusually young or old or otherwise in need of moral support or guidance.

(b) Eavesdroppers

If the communication is overheard by an eavesdropper, the privilege usually is held not to preclude testimony by that eavesdropper, even if reasonable precautions were taken to protect confidentiality. However, if electronic surveillance was used by the eavesdropper, most courts will forbid use of the fruits of the eavesdropping.

(5) By Client

The traditional formulation of the privilege was that the privilege protected only information communicated to the lawyer by the client. There was no need to protect the information communicated to the client by the lawyer, it was thought, except to the extent that it revealed the content of communications to the lawyer by the client. However, it was often difficult to distinguish communications by the lawyer that revealed client communications from others, and this limitation threatened to intrude into the relationship between the lawyer and the client.

(a) Modern View

The modern view is increasingly that communications by the lawyer to the client are protected also. [*See, e.g.*, **Upjohn Co. v. United States,** 449 U.S. 383 (1981)—privilege exists to protect "the giving of professional advice"]

(b) Distinguish—Communication by Lawyer with Others

When the lawyer communicates with persons other than the client, such as witnesses, the privilege does not apply. [**Hickman v. Taylor,** 329 U.S. 495 (1947)—interviews with witnesses (but other limits on discovery, such as that concerning lawyer work product, may apply)]

GILBERT

THE ATTORNEY-CLIENT PRIVILEGE WILL APPLY ONLY IF THE FOLLOWING CONDITIONS ARE MET

☑ The client must be *seeking legal advice.*

☑ The advice must be sought *from one whom the claimant reasonably believes is an attorney.*

☑ The communication for which privilege is being asserted must *relate to the legal advice sought.*

☑ The communication must have been *made in confidence.*

c. Permanently Protected at Client's Request

(1) Need to Invoke

The privilege is not self-executing and applies only when invoked. Usually, however, the lawyer is under a duty to invoke the privilege on behalf of the client.

In federal court, the claim regarding documents must be made on a privilege log. [Fed. R. Civ. P. 26(b)(5)(A)]

(2) Absolute Protection

The protection is absolute, in the sense that it cannot be outweighed by other considerations, such as the social interest in full disclosure of relevant evidence in the case.

(3) Applies to Disclosure by Client or Lawyer

Once invoked, the privilege precludes disclosure by the lawyer and the client (including employees of the client covered by the privilege; *see infra*, p. 303, regarding corporate clients). Thus the privilege can preclude disclosure by a person who is willing to reveal privileged information.

Caution: Lawyer-client privilege shields only lawyer-client communications, not underlying information

The privilege means that lawyers and clients cannot be required to divulge what they said to each other when the privilege applies. But a client in litigation who has information within the scope of discovery can be required to provide that information, without reference to whether the client and lawyer had communications about it.

(4) Request for Return of Allegedly Privileged Information

When information subject to a claim of privilege or work-product protection is produced in federal-court discovery, the holder of the privilege may notify any party that received the information of the claim of privilege. No other party may use the information unless the court rules that the privilege claim was unjustified or that the privilege was waived. [Fed. R. Civ. P. 26(b)(5)(B)]. If the production was "inadvertent," privilege protection is not waived, as long as reasonable steps were taken to prevent and promptly rectify the disclosure. [Fed R. Evid. 502(b)]

d. Waiver

Just as the client must invoke the privilege, so can the client waive it.

(1) Breadth of Waiver

In general, waiver of the privilege applies to all communications with counsel on the subject matter regarding which the waiver has occurred. *Rationale*: If the waiver did not apply to all related communications, the client could "pick and choose" the favorable pieces of information for revelation while keeping secret unfavorable pieces of information that are necessary to make the picture whole.

(2) No Need for Intentional Waiver

The act that constitutes a waiver need not be intentional, and in litigation unintentional disclosure of privileged material often works a waiver of the privilege.

(3) Application in Other Litigation

Once the privilege is waived, it cannot be revived for other litigation.

e. Federal vs. State Law

(1) Federal Claim or Defense

In federal court the privileges available are to be determined by "principles of common law as they may be interpreted by the courts of the United States." [Fed. R. Evid. 501] Thus, the federal courts may alter the rules governing federal privilege law.

(2) State-Law Claim or Defense

In federal court, when state law supplies the rule of decision with respect to an element of a claim or defense, however, privilege issues are to be determined in accordance with state law. [Fed. R. Evid. 501]

f. Corporate Clients

(1) Privilege Applicable

The Supreme Court early held that the attorney-client privilege applied to corporate clients. This ruling did not answer the question, however, of who was the client.

(2) Control-Group Test

Many courts limited the privilege to communications between the lawyer and those persons who could be considered the "control group" of the corporation, *i.e.*, the persons who controlled the corporation and who could act on the lawyer's advice. But this test was imperfect because often the members of the control group did not have the information the lawyer needed to evaluate the corporation's legal problems, and the lawyer would then be subjected to a "Hobson's choice" about whether to inquire of other employees of the corporation.

(3) *Upjohn* Test

In **Upjohn Co. v. United States** (*supra*, p. 301), the Supreme Court rejected the control-group test as a matter of federal common law of evidence. (*See supra*, p. 303.) Instead, the Court adopted a test that can extend the privilege to any employee. Although the contours of the test are unclear, it turns basically on the following factors:

(a) Matters Within Scope of Employment

The protection extends only to communication about matters within the scope of the employee's job with the corporation.

(b) Information Not Available from Higher Management

The protection is justified for "non-control group" employees when higher management cannot itself supply the information.

(c) Other Requirements Satisfied

In the course of its opinion, the Court emphasized the importance of other requirements of the privilege. Thus, the employee must know that the communication is designed to obtain legal advice for the corporation and that it is to be held in confidence.

(d) Criticism

This new formulation appears to overextend the privilege in that it provides no safeguards for the employee who makes full disclosure to the corporation's lawyer. The corporation can waive the privilege and disclose the employee's confidences without the permission of the employee.

(4) State Law

At least some states have refused to follow the Supreme Court's expansion of privilege protection for corporate clients. Illinois, for example, has continued to adhere to the control-group test. [*See* **Consolidation Coal Co. v. Bucyrus-Erie Co.,** 432 N.E.2d 250 (Ill. 1982)]

g. Other Communicational Privileges

Other privileges protect other communications from disclosure. For more information on these, see the Evidence Summary.

(1) Spousal Communications

Confidential communications between husband and wife during the marriage are privileged at the request of either spouse. [Cal. Evid. Code § 980]

(a) Distinguish—Testimony Against Spouse

A husband or wife also has the privilege not to testify against the other spouse on any subject. [Cal. Evid. Code §§ 970–972; **Trammel v. United States,** 445 U.S. 40 (1980)] Note that no similar privilege is extended to other relatives, such as parents and children of a litigant.

(2) Doctor-Patient

A patient usually has a limited right to prevent disclosure of information she disclosed to her doctor in connection with medical treatment. [Cal. Evid. Code §§ 990–1007]

(a) Easily Waived

This privilege is easily waived, and is usually held waived by a plaintiff who sues for personal injuries and thereby puts her medical condition "in issue." [Cal. Evid. Code § 996]

(3) Psychotherapist-Patient

The Supreme Court has held that there is a psychotherapist/patient privilege for confidential communications even if the psychotherapist is not a doctor. [**Jaffee v. Redmond,** 518 U.S. 1 (1996)—psychotherapy sessions by licensed social worker privileged]

(4) Priest-Penitent

A priest is privileged to refuse to disclose information revealed by a penitent. [Cal. Evid. Code §§ 1030–1034]

(5) Distinguish—Tenure-Review Materials

The Supreme Court has held that universities have no privilege against disclosure of confidential tenure-review materials. [**University of Pennsylvania v. EEOC**, 493 U.S. 182 (1990)]

h. Specificity of Privilege Claim

If a party withholds information—particularly documents—from discovery on grounds of privilege, it should describe the materials withheld with sufficient specificity to enable other parties to assess the applicability of the privilege. [Fed. R. Civ. P. 26(b)(5)(A)]

4. Trial-Preparation Materials

a. "Work Product"—*Hickman v. Taylor* Rule

(1) Qualified Privilege

Materials prepared and information developed by or under the direction of a party or her attorney in anticipation of litigation are subject to discovery only if the discovering party can show a substantial need and an inability to obtain equivalent material by other means. [**Hickman v. Taylor**, *supra*, p. 301; Fed. R. Civ. P. 26(b)(3)(A); Cal. Civ. Proc. Code § 2018.030]

(2) Purpose

This qualified privilege is designed to maintain the adversary process by enabling each party to prepare her own case, with free rein to develop her own theory of the case and her own trial strategy; but this purpose must be reconciled with the overriding need to require full disclosure of the facts.

(3) Matters Protected

The focus of this protection is on the process of preparing for litigation. Thus, it is very broad; the Federal Rule [Fed. R. Civ. P. 26(b)(3)(A)] covers any materials prepared "in anticipation of litigation or for trial."

(a) Possibility of Litigation Foreseen

If there is absolutely no foreseeable possibility of litigation at the time the materials are prepared, then the protection cannot apply.

(b) Regular Reports

When a party makes regular reports of incidents that often lead to litigation (*e.g.*, accidents), it may be held that such reports are not prepared in anticipation of litigation, since they can be used for other purposes and are prepared in situations in which litigation is not foreseen. [*See, e.g.,* **Rakus v. Erie-Lackawanna Railroad**, 76 F.R.D. 145 (W.D.N.Y. 1977)—employees' accident reports to claims department are discoverable]

(4) Showing to Justify Disclosure

To obtain production of material that is protected as work product, a party must make a showing of substantial need and undue hardship.

(a) Substantial Need

The party must show that the material sought is of substantial importance to its case; courts usually do not treat minimal relevance as sufficient.

(b) Inability to Obtain Substantial Equivalent

The party must also show that it is unable to obtain the substantial equivalent without undue hardship.

(5) Special Protection for Mental Impressions of Attorney

If a showing has been made to justify disclosure, materials containing the mental impressions of an attorney are given special protection.

e.g. **Example:** A memorandum prepared by an attorney may include her observations at the scene of the accident, which would be ordinary work product. The memo could also include the attorney's theories about possible grounds of liability and promising avenues of investigation, as well as her assessments of the persuasiveness of various possible witnesses. All this material, except her observations at the scene, would be considered opinion work product and would receive special protection.

(a) Protection Under Federal Rules

Federal Rule 26(b)(3)(B) states that in ordering discovery of work product, the court "must" protect against disclosure of the mental impressions and legal theories of an attorney. This rule has been held to provide absolute protection to such items. [**Duplan Corp. v. Moulinage et Retorderie de Chavanoz**, 509 F.2d 730 (4th Cir. 1974)] The Supreme Court, however, has declined to take this step: "we are not prepared at this juncture to say that such material is always protected by the work-product rule." [**Upjohn Co. v. United States**, *supra*, p. 301] And several lower courts have denied absolute protection. [*See, e.g.,* **Holmgren v. State Farm Mutual Automobile Insurance Co.,** 976 F.2d 573 (9th Cir. 1992)—lawyer's mental impressions a pivotal issue and need for their disclosure compelling]

(b) State Law

Under the law of some states, protection for such materials is absolute. [*See, e.g.,* Cal. Civ. Proc. Code § 2018.030(a)—"A writing that reflects an attorney's impressions, conclusions, opinions, or legal research or theories is not discoverable under any circumstances"]

(c) Method—Redaction

If materials containing opinion work product are ordered produced, the portions containing such material may be "redacted" by covering them over in the copying process so they cannot be read.

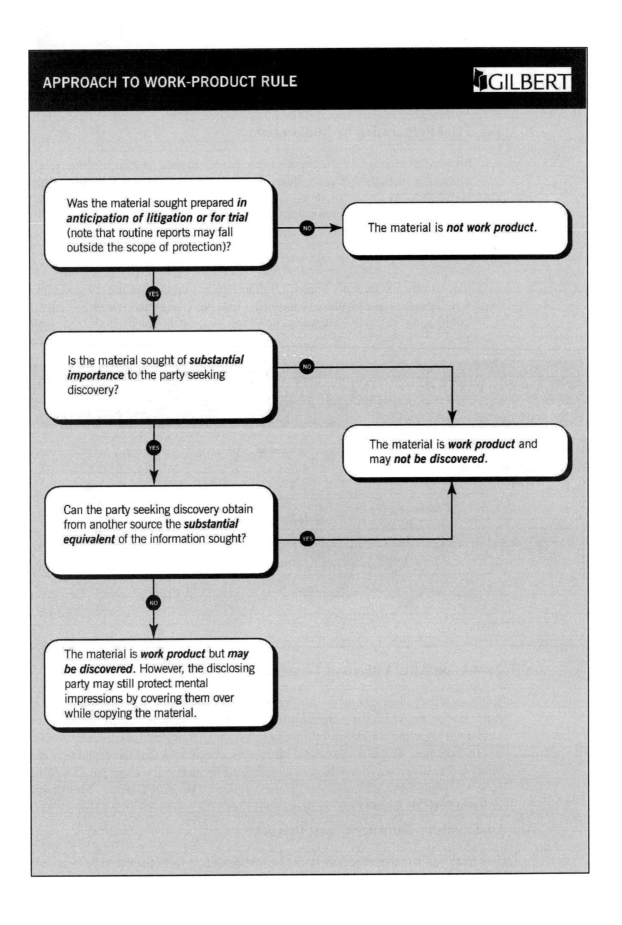

Was the material sought prepared *in anticipation of litigation or for trial* (note that routine reports may fall outside the scope of protection)?

NO → The material is *not work product*.

YES

Is the material sought of *substantial importance* to the party seeking discovery?

NO →

The material is *work product* and may *not be discovered*.

YES

Can the party seeking discovery obtain from another source the *substantial equivalent* of the information sought?

YES →

NO

The material is *work product* but *may be discovered*. However, the disclosing party may still protect mental impressions by covering them over while copying the material.

(6) Rule 26(b)(3) and *Hickman* Contrasted

In federal court, the protections of Rule 26(b)(3) and *Hickman* both continue to apply, although usually they overlap. There are significant differences, however:

(a) Trial Preparation by Nonlawyers

Hickman protects only the work of lawyers. It applies to their assistants, and perhaps to experts hired by them or others acting at their direction. Rule 26(b)(3)(A) is broader; it also includes trial preparation by the party's "consultant, surety, indemnitor, insurer, or agent."

(b) Tangible Materials

Rule 26(b)(3)(A) is more limited than *Hickman*, however, in protecting only "documents and tangible things." It therefore has no application, for example, to a deposition of the attorney inquiring into her trial strategies, etc. *Hickman* would apply in such a situation, however, since it is not limited to tangible items.

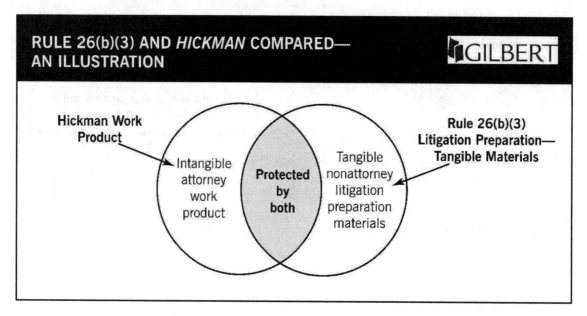

RULE 26(b)(3) AND *HICKMAN* COMPARED— AN ILLUSTRATION

GILBERT

Hickman Work Product → Intangible attorney work product | Protected by both | Tangible nonattorney litigation preparation materials ← Rule 26(b)(3) Litigation Preparation— Tangible Materials

(7) Protection After Litigation Terminated

It is not entirely clear whether work-product protection endures after termination of the litigation for which the material was prepared. The Supreme Court has held in a case involving the Freedom of Information Act that the protection continues. [**FTC v. Grolier, Inc.,** 462 U.S. 19 (1983)] It has also been held that the protection can apply in a case that was not anticipated at the time the material was prepared, as long as it was prepared in anticipation of some litigation. [**Duplan Corp. v. Moulinage et Retorderie de Chavanoz,** *supra*, p. 306]

(8) Distinguish—Attorney-Client Privilege

The qualified work-product rule must be distinguished from the absolute privilege afforded confidential communications from client to counsel.

(9) Witness Statements

Because witness statements illustrate the application of work product and the attorney-client privilege, it is worthwhile to examine them in detail. Some statements of witnesses to lawyers may be subject to the attorney-client privilege, while other communications made to lawyers or investigators may be treated as work product and thus be subject to disclosure only on a showing of substantial need and inability to obtain the substantial equivalent by other means.

(a) Statements Made by Party to Own Attorney

If the statements were made in confidence regarding past events, the communications are privileged under the attorney-client privilege.

1) Attorney's Employees

The privilege may also apply to statements made to an investigator employed by the party's counsel. [**Brakhage v. Graff,** 206 N.W.2d 45 (Neb. 1973)]

2) Caveat

Note, however, that a party cannot put documents beyond the reach of discovery by turning them over to counsel. Nor can a party relieve himself of the obligation to disclose by making disclosure to his own lawyer. All that is protected is the fact of communication from client to lawyer.

(b) Statements by Employees of Corporation

The attorney-client privilege applies to communications made in confidence by employees of a corporation, including nonsupervisory employees in many jurisdictions. (*See supra*, p. 303.)

1) Confidential Reports

The attorney-client privilege may also apply to routine reports that are intended to be confidential records of the corporation, prepared for the corporation's attorney; *e.g.*, accident reports prepared by a truck driver according to company policy that such reports be submitted immediately following any accident for confidential use of the corporation's lawyers. [**D.I. Chadbourne, Inc. v. Superior Court,** 60 Cal. 2d 723 (1964)]

2) Other Reports

Other reports of employees to corporate counsel are not covered by the attorney-client privilege, but may be subject to the qualified work-product privilege if they were made or prepared in anticipation of litigation. [**Xerox Corp. v. IBM Corp.,** 64 F.R.D. 367 (S.D.N.Y. 1974)] However, remember that regular reports may be found not to meet the "in anticipation" requirement. (*See supra*, p. 305.)

(c) Statements of Nonparty Witnesses

Statements obtained from nonparty witnesses are usually held to be work product of the attorney, so they are not subject to discovery by an adversary unless he is not reasonably able to obtain a similar statement from the witness by his own effort and has substantial need for the materials to prepare his case.

1) Note

In federal practice, the witness himself is entitled to a copy of his statement as a matter of right. [Fed. R. Civ. P. 26(b)(3)(C)]

2) Not Covered by Attorney-Client Privilege

Witness interviews are not covered by the attorney-client privilege. [**Hickman v. Taylor**, *supra*, p. 301]

(d) Statements Made by Party to Adverse Counsel

Usually, no privilege (absolute or qualified) protects statements of a party made to adverse counsel. Such statements are subject to discovery without a showing of need—*i.e.*, a party-witness is entitled to a copy of statements given to adverse counsel as a matter of right. [Fed. R. Civ. P. 26(b)(3)(C)]

b. Expert Reports

Lawyers are increasingly dependent on retained experts to help the lawyer prepare for trial and to serve as witnesses who testify at trial. Often the subject matter of a litigation is unfamiliar to the lawyer, and the lawyer therefore needs the assistance of a person schooled in the field to prepare adequately for trial. At trial, the technical subject matter of the litigation may make it essential that an expert testify to support the party's case. (For more detail on the rules governing the presentation of expert testimony at trial, see the Evidence Summary.)

(1) Nontestifying Experts

(a) Role

When the lawyer needs the help of an expert to prepare for trial, she will often retain one to advise her on trial strategy and help develop legal and factual theories for the case. The expert can also help the lawyer prepare to cross-examine the opponent's expert.

(b) Discoverability of Facts Known and Opinions Held

Under Federal Rule 26(b)(4)(D), facts known to and opinions held by nontestifying experts are discoverable only in exceptional circumstances, *e.g.*, when one party has monopolized the qualified experts. *Rationale*: Allowing discovery would give the party seeking it a free ride when it could hire its own expert.

1) Reimbursement for Fees

When discovery is ordered, the court is to require the discovering party to reimburse the party who retained the nontestifying expert for a fair portion of the fees and expenses paid for the facts and opinions developed by the expert. [Fed. R. Civ. P. 26(b)(4)(E)(ii)]

(c) Nontestifying Expert as Witness for Opponent

Experts can differ in their opinions, and when a lawyer hires an expert she will not always know the expert's opinion of her client's case. What happens if the expert develops an opinion unfavorable to the client? The opposing side will likely want to hire the expert because the circumstances tend to make her opinion very believable. One court has held that the opposing party may not do so in the absence of extraordinary circumstances; *i.e.*, Rule 26(b)(4)(D) (*supra*, p. 310) must be satisfied [**Durflinger v. Artiles,** 727 F.2d 888 (10th Cir. 1984)], but other courts might not adopt this rule. The rationale is that if such use of the nontestifying expert's opinions were allowed, lawyers might be deterred from consulting experts whose opinions are unknown.

EXAM TIP   **GILBERT**

An important guiding principle of litigation is that an attorney should never call a witness unless she already knows how the witness will testify. But how will the attorney know? In the case of expert witnesses, she will ask the expert before trial. What happens if, in an exam question, an attorney does this, the expert's opinion is unfavorable, and the attorney's opponent has found out about the expert and can't wait to make the expert his own witness at trial? One court has prohibited such unsporting conduct, holding that the opponent cannot call the expert absent extraordinary need. Your answer should note this view, but should also note the fact that this issue is unresolved.

(d) Discovery of Identity of Nontestifying Expert

The courts are split on whether the identity of the nontestifying expert can be discovered. [*Compare* **Ager v. Jane C. Stormont Hospital,** 622 F.2d 496 (10th Cir. 1980)—discovery not permitted because it subverts protective purposes of the rule—*with* **Baki v. B.F. Diamond Construction Co.,** 71 F.R.D. 179 (D. Md. 1976)—discovery allowed because it does not involve disclosure of facts known or opinions held by expert]

(e) Informally Consulted Experts

The protections of Rule 26(b)(4)(B) apply only to experts who are "retained or specially employed" by a party. The courts have held that discovery regarding experts who were only informally consulted is not available. [**Procter & Gamble Co. v. Haugen,** 184 F.R.D. 410 (D. Utah 1999)]

(2) Testifying Experts

The Federal Rules allow broad discovery regarding testifying experts and impose a requirement to provide a written report that applies to most such experts.

(a) Required Disclosure

Without a formal discovery request, each party must identify each person that party will call to offer expert testimony at trial. [Fed. R. Civ. P. 26(a)(2)(A)] This requirement applies whether or not the expert was "specially retained" by the lawyer.

(b) Timing of Disclosure

In the absence of other direction from the court, this disclosure must be made at least 90 days before trial. [Fed. R. Civ. P. 26(a)(2)(C)] However, courts may stagger the disclosures and the party with the burden of proof may be required to disclose first.

1) Rebuttal

Within 30 days after the disclosure by an opposing party, a party may add another expert intended to offer testimony solely to rebut or contradict expert evidence identified by the opposing party.

(c) Required Report by Specially Retained Expert Witness

In addition to identifying its expert witnesses, a party must ordinarily provide a detailed report from the expert. [Fed. R. Civ. P. 26(a)(2)(B)]

1) Experts Covered

A report must be prepared for any specially retained expert and for any employee of a party whose duties regularly include giving expert testimony. This requirement ordinarily does not include a party's treating doctor if the doctor will offer opinions only on the basis of observations during treatment. [**Riddick v. Washington Hospital Center**, 183 F.R.D. 327 (D.D.C. 1998)]

2) Signed by Expert

The report is to be signed by the witness, although it is contemplated that counsel may assist in drafting the report.

3) Statement of Expert's Opinions

The report is to include a complete statement of all opinions the expert will express in testimony, along with the basis therefor and the facts or data on which they are based. This requirement makes all materials provided to the expert, including privileged materials, subject to mandatory disclosure.

4) Exhibits

Disclosure should also include all exhibits that will be used in connection with the testimony.

5) Expert's Qualifications

The report must include the witness's qualifications, including all publications during the preceding 10 years and a list of all cases in which the expert testified during the preceding four years.

6) Expert's Compensation

The report should include the compensation the expert will be paid.

7) Supplementation

The report should be supplemented with new information that is developed after it is submitted. [Fed. R. Civ. P. 26(e)(2)]

8) Required Disclosure Regarding Expert Not "Specially Retained"

Some expert witnesses have not been "specially retained" to testify. A prominent example is the treating physician of an injured plaintiff. There is no requirement that these witnesses provide detailed reports like those required of specially retained expert witnesses. Instead, the attorney for the party calling the expert witness must disclose the subject matter on which the witness is expected to present evidence and a summary of the facts or opinions the witness is expected to offer.

Note: It is possible that some of the testimony of such a witness may be subject to the more extensive report requirement for a "specially retained" witness. For example, if a treating doctor does additional analysis not involved in treatment of the patient at the request of the patient's lawyer, that additional testimony may be regarded as a matter on which the doctor was "specially retained," and the extensive report requirement would apply.

▟ GILBERT

AT LEAST 90 DAYS BEFORE TRIAL A PARTY ORDINARILY IS REQUIRED TO DISCLOSE:

- ☑ The identity of all experts expected to be called at trial.

- ☑ A statement of all opinions the specially retained expert will express in testimony, along with the basis for the opinions.

- ☑ All exhibits that will be used in connection with the expert's testimony.

- ☑ The expert's qualifications, including a list of anything the expert has published in the last 10 years and cases in which the expert has testified in the last four years.

- ☑ The expert's compensation.

(d) Deposition of Right

Any party has a right to take the deposition of a testifying expert. [Fed. R. Civ. P. 26(b)(4)(A)] When a report is required, however, this deposition may not take place until after the report is provided.

1) Supplementation of Expert's Testimony

Although supplementation is not required with other deposition testimony, a party has a duty to supplement the deposition testimony of its expert witness. [Fed. R. Civ. P. 26(e)(2)]

2) Compensation of Expert for Responding to Discovery

The party taking the deposition must compensate the expert for the time spent on the deposition. *Compare*: There is no requirement to compensate the expert for the time spent on the report.

(e) Work-Product Protection for Attorney-Expert Communications and Draft Reports

Drafts of a retained expert's report are protected as work product, as are communications between an attorney and a retained expert, except to the extent those communications relate to the expert's compensation, facts or data the attorney provided that the expert considered regarding the expert's opinion, or assumptions the attorney provided that the expert relied upon. [Fed. R. Civ. P. 26(b)(4)(B), –(C)]

(f) State Practice Compared

States often have similar statutory procedures for pretrial identification of expert witnesses, including provisions for pretrial depositions. [*See, e.g.,* Cal. Civ. Proc. Code § 2034.260]

(3) Unaffiliated Experts

Rule 26(b)(4) makes no provision for a person who has expertise that may be pertinent to a lawsuit, but who has not consented to assist any party in connection with the case. On occasion, litigants subpoena such persons to compel them to testify. It has been held that they may sometimes be compelled to give such testimony, albeit perhaps only on being paid a fee for it. [*See, e.g.,* **Wright v. Jeep Corp.,** 547 F. Supp. 871 (E.D. Mich. 1982)—professor who prepared report on Jeep rollover problems compelled to testify]

(a) Rationale

Experts should be treated like other witnesses who have information that is pertinent to the resolution of a lawsuit.

(b) Criticism

Society pays a price if such experts are required to spend substantial time attending depositions or trials, and they may not be adequately compensated for being required to reveal their expertise.

(c) Protection Against Subpoenas

Rule 45 provides that if a subpoena requires "disclosing an unretained expert's opinion or information that does not describe specific occurrences in dispute and results from the expert's study that were not requested by a party," the court may quash or modify the subpoena. Alternatively, if the party in whose behalf the subpoena is issued shows a substantial need for the testimony or material that cannot be otherwise met without undue hardship and assures that the person to whom the subpoena is addressed will be reasonably compensated, the court may order appearance or production only upon specified conditions. [Fed. R. Civ. P. 45(c)(3)(C)]

(d) Distinguish—Expert as Fact Witness

Whether or not experts should be protected against being compelled to testify regarding matters within their expertise, they are not immune to the civic duty to testify regarding the facts of the case. Thus, if a Nobel Prize winner witnesses an accident, she must testify about what she saw just like any other witness.

D. Protective Orders

1. Introduction

Protective orders are designed to prevent undue burdens that might otherwise be imposed by discovery. The availability of protective orders recognizes both that discovery can be extremely intrusive and that parties may seek to abuse it. Both concerns can be ameliorated through protective provisions.

2. Requirement of Good Cause

A protective order should be granted only on a showing of good cause by the party seeking protection. [Fed. R. Civ. P. 26(c)(1)] Appropriate grounds include the following.

a. Confidential Information

A protective order may be entered to protect "trade secret or other confidential research, development, or commercial information." [Fed. R. Civ. P. 26(c)(1)(G)]

(1) Showing Required

(a) Confidentiality

Such protection is available only for information that is in fact confidential. To justify an order, the party seeking the order must show that the information has been held in confidence.

(b) Specific Harm from Disclosure

There must also be a showing that a specific harm is likely to flow from disclosure of the information.

(c) Not Limited to Technical Information

The protection is not limited to technical trade-secret information, but rather may extend to wide varieties of commercial data whose disclosure could give commercial advantage to competitors. It has therefore been applied to customer lists [**Chesa International, Ltd. v. Fashion Associates, Inc.,** 425 F. Supp. 234 (S.D.N.Y. 1977)], profit and gross income data [**Corbett v. Free Press Association,** 50 F.R.D. 179 (D. Vt. 1970)], and terms of a contract. [**Essex Wire Corp. v. Eastern Electric Sales Co.,** 48 F.R.D. 308 (E.D. Pa. 1969)]

EXAM TIP

It is not uncommon in real life for a person to seek discovery of information for improper purposes, and this danger could be reflected in an exam question. For example, the Coca-Cola Company might file an unfair-competition action against the bottlers of Dr. Pepper just so it can force the bottlers to disclose Dr. Pepper's secret flavor ingredient during litigation (some say it's cherry; others say it's prune—the debate continues). If such a question appears on your exam, remember that the court can grant a protective order limiting the disclosure and use of the information if the information is confidential and disclosure will likely cause a specific harm.

(d) Privacy Interests

Related arguments can be made to justify the protection of privacy interests of litigants because Rule 26(c)(1) allows protection against annoyance or embarrassment. [*See, e.g.,* **Galella v. Onassis,** *supra,* p. 272—Jacqueline Onassis protected against being photographed by plaintiff during her deposition]

(2) Stipulated Orders

Despite the showing requirement, confidentiality orders are often entered into on stipulation. In such situations, there are no findings regarding either confidentiality or the risk of harm to any person. **Caution**: Some courts question the propriety of such orders.

(3) Format—"Umbrella" Orders

Protective orders to protect confidentiality can take a number of forms. One would be to forbid discovery altogether. More often, however, the information is validly sought for trial preparation and the court places limitations on use and dissemination of the confidential information. Because these orders often are self-executing and apply throughout the discovery process, they are referred to as "umbrella" orders. Such orders often facilitate the discovery process by giving parties and lawyers confidence that what they divulge is unlikely to be publicized.

(a) Designation of Confidential Information

Usually, any person producing information is allowed to designate it as confidential and, therefore, subject to the protection of the order. Often this is done by stamping documents "Confidential."

1) No Judicial Scrutiny

Note that there is no judicial involvement in the designation process, which is left entirely to the parties.

(b) Effect of Designation

Usually, all designated documents are to be held in confidence by the other parties, used only for trial preparation, and disclosed only to specified persons, usually including the client and witnesses.

(c) Challenges to Designation

Any party may move the court to set aside a confidentiality designation on the ground that the material is not in fact confidential.

1) Burden on Producing Party

At this point, the burden is on the producing party to establish that the material is indeed entitled to protection under Rule 26(c).

2) Exception—Blanket Challenges

In some cases when large volumes of material have been designated confidential, however, the court may impose on the challenging party the duty to specify which confidentiality designations are challenged and why. [*See, e.g.*, **Zenith Radio Corp. v. Matsushita Electric Industrial Co.,** 529 F. Supp. 866 (E.D. Pa. 1981)—after summary judgment was entered in favor of defendants, plaintiff sought to unseal hundreds of thousands of documents that had been designated confidential under a stipulated protective order]

(4) Public Access

The public may have an interest in materials covered by confidentiality orders. Were the material to be offered in evidence at trial, there would be a constitutional and common-law right of public access to court trial that would enable the public to have access to the information. Before trial, there are two possible arguments:

(a) Discovery Presumptively Public

Some courts say that discovery is presumptively public unless closed, and that orders limiting access to the public need special justification. This argument appears not to apply to material covered by proper protective orders, and the Supreme Court has stated that there is no tradition of public access to discovery. [**Seattle Times Co. v. Rhinehart,** 467 U.S. 20 (1984)]

1) Filing of Discovery Discontinued

Formerly, discovery materials were automatically filed with the court. However, filing is no longer automatic, and discovery should be filed in court only if it is "used in the proceedings." [Fed. R. Civ. P. 5(d)(1)] This change may further weaken arguments that there should be some presumptive public access to discovery materials because there is no reason to expect them to be in a public file.

(b) Material Involved in Pretrial Rulings

When materials covered by a confidentiality order are involved in pretrial rulings by the court, the public-access argument is stronger because the constitutional and common-law rights are designed to allow the public meaningful access to observe judicial decisionmaking. The application of this concept is not always easy:

1) Access Allowed—Decision on Merits of Case

If pretrial rulings resolve the merits, access to discovery materials relied on should be granted. [*See, e.g.*, **Cianci v. New Times Publishing Co.,** 88 F.R.D. 562 (S.D.N.Y. 1980)—summary judgment granted]

2) Access Denied—Decision That Privileged Materials Should Not Be Produced

If a discovery motion presents the question whether materials sought are privileged, and, based on an in-camera review of the materials, the court decides that they should not be produced, public access should not be allowed because it would undermine the privilege.

3) Intermediate Situations

A problem arises in cases: (i) not involving resolution of the merits, or (ii) involving non-merits decisions that would be undermined by disclosure. Courts tend to deem all materials considered in connection with a motion to be subject to presumptive public access. [*See, e.g.*, **Zenith Radio Corp. v. Matsushita Electric Industrial Co.,** *supra*—public right of access to all materials offered in good faith in connection with summary-judgment motion]

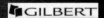

If an exam question involves materials covered by a confidentiality order and a member of the press or public seeks access to the material during discovery, you must assess the procedural context. Generally, the press and public have no right to access material that was disclosed to a party during discovery and is subject to a confidentiality order. However, the United States Constitution provides for open trials, so if a pretrial ruling is based on confidential discovery material, the courts will generally:

- Allow public access if the pretrial rulings resolve the merits of the case;

- Prohibit public access if access would undermine the court's ruling, such as a ruling that the materials are privileged; and

- Refuse public access to unfiled discovery information.

(5) Sharing with Other Litigants

An important issue is the possibility that materials covered by a confidentiality order could be shared with other litigants in similar cases. This sharing would tend to reduce discovery expense for other litigants, which would be a legitimate objective. [**United States v. Hooker Chemical Co.,** 90 F.R.D. 421 (W.D.N.Y. 1981)] Courts often allow such sharing.

(6) First Amendment Limitations on Protective Orders

Protective orders can limit expression by forbidding litigants to disclose information gained through discovery.

(a) Prior-Restraint Analysis

Some courts held that such orders could be justified under the First Amendment only when a prior restraint would be warranted, a very demanding standard. [*See, e.g.,* **In re Halkin,** 598 F.2d 176 (D.C. Cir. 1979)] (For more on the prior restraint doctrine, see Constitutional Law Summary.)

(b) Supreme Court Ruling

The Supreme Court rejected the prior restraint analysis and held that a protective order supported by good cause is valid under the First Amendment. [**Seattle Times Co. v. Rhinehart,** *supra,* p. 317]

(c) Continuing Concern About First Amendment

There is disagreement in the lower courts about whether courts should continue to consider First Amendment values in deciding whether to issue or modify protective orders. [*Compare* **Cipollone v. Liggett Group, Inc.,** 785 F.2d 1108 (3d Cir. 1986)—First Amendment irrelevant—*with* **Anderson v. Cryovac, Inc.,** 805 F.2d 1 (1st Cir. 1986)—First Amendment still a "presence" in protective-order decisions]

b. Inconvenient Place of Examination

If a deposition has been scheduled at a place that is unnecessarily inconvenient for the deponent or adversary, a protective order may issue.

(1) Federal Practice

Under the Federal Rules, protective orders are the only method available for controlling the place at which the deposition of a party can be scheduled, since the adverse party can notice the deposition to be taken anywhere. (*Compare*: A nonparty witness cannot be required to appear except by subpoena, and the range of a subpoena is limited; *see supra*, p. 278.)

(a) Nonresident Defendants

On applications for protective orders as to the place of deposition, courts are inclined to hold that a nonresident defendant should be deposed at his residence rather than at the place where the suit is pending.

1) But Note

A contrary result may be reached if the plaintiff is willing to pay the defendant's expenses to travel to the forum, or if it is shown that the defendant will be in the forum anyway.

(b) Nonresident Plaintiff

The courts appear more inclined to require a nonresident plaintiff to appear locally for his deposition, since he chose to file his action in the local forum.

(2) State Practice Compared

Instead of requiring a nonresident deponent to obtain a protective order, state rules frequently put the burden on the party seeking the deposition to obtain a prior court order if he wishes to compel the other party to give her deposition beyond the range of a subpoena. [Cal. Civ. Proc. Code § 2025.260(a)]

c. Unreasonable Conduct of Deposition

If a deposition is conducted in a manner that is unduly annoying, embarrassing, or oppressive to a witness or party, a protective order may issue. When the court terminates a deposition for this reason, it may not be resumed or rescheduled except by court order. [Fed. R. Civ. P. 30(d)(3)(B); Cal. Civ. Proc. Code § 2025.420(b)(16)]

d. Unduly Burdensome Discovery

When discovery is unduly expensive, unnecessarily burdensome, or otherwise clearly excessive in relation to the importance of the case, a protective order may be sought to limit discovery. (*See supra*, p. 297, regarding judicial limitation of discovery.)

e. Allocation of Expenses

The court has explicit authority to enter a protective order specifying the allocation of expenses resulting from discovery. [Fed. R. Civ. P. 26(c)(1)(B)] This rule provision is not intended to make cost-shifting routine.

3. Relation Between Protective Orders and Other Discovery Orders

a. Effect of Prior Orders

Protective orders are rarely appropriate in regard to discovery conducted pursuant to a prior court order. The circumstances and limitations to be imposed on a medical examination, for example, are generally determined at the time the examination is ordered. Consequently, absent some new information or a change of circumstances, there is no occasion to reconsider the initial order.

b. No Waiver

A party or witness who does not seek a protective order in advance of a deposition, or before the response date for interrogatories, does not thereby waive her right to make objections. She remains free to object to questioning at deposition and she may refuse answers to interrogatories, thereby forcing the discovering party to invoke the power of the court to compel answers to those questions which the court deems proper. [Fed. R. Civ. P. 37(a)]

E. Failure to Disclose or to Comply with Discovery

1. Order Compelling Response—Necessary Prerequisite

Before discovery sanctions can be imposed, a party seeking discovery must usually obtain an order compelling discovery. [Fed. R. Civ. P. 37(a)(1)]

a. Evasive or Incomplete Answer

If a motion to compel discovery is made, an evasive or incomplete answer is treated as a failure to answer [Fed. R. Civ. P. 37(a)(4)], and the responding party can be ordered to provide a proper answer.

b. Exception—Complete Failure to Respond

If a party completely fails to file a response to a discovery request or to attend his properly noticed deposition, discovery sanctions can be sought immediately, without the need for a prior order compelling discovery. [Fed. R. Civ. P. 37(d)]

c. Exception—Failure to Make Required Disclosures or Supplementation

If a party fails to make disclosures required by Rule 26(a), or to supplement disclosures and discovery responses as required by Rule 26(e)(1), the court should usually exclude undisclosed materials from evidence, and it may also impose Rule 37(b) sanctions, which are usually reserved for failures to comply with discovery orders.

(1) Grounds for Declining to Sanction Nondisclosure

The court should not impose sanctions on a party who has substantial justification for its failure to disclose, or when the failure to disclose was harmless.

d. Need to Meet and Confer Before Motion

Before filing a motion to compel discovery, a party must attempt to meet and confer with the opposing party in an effort to secure compliance without court action. [Fed. R. Civ. P. 37(a)(1), (d)]

2. Sanctions for Failure to Comply with Order

If sanctions are authorized because of disobedience of an order compelling discovery, the court has a variety of options available. [Fed. R. Civ. P. 37(b)(2)(A)] Many of them affect the merits of the case and may therefore be called merits sanctions.

a. Order Establishing Facts

The court may order that matters pertinent to the discovery be taken as established in the favor of the party seeking discovery. [Fed. R. Civ. P. 37(b)(2)(A)(i)]

b. Order Disallowing Claims or Defenses

The court may deny the offending party the right to present claims or defenses raised by the pleadings, or exclude certain matters from evidence. [Fed. R. Civ. P. 37(b)(2)(A)(ii)]

Example: When Plaintiff failed to provide adequate answers to interrogatories regarding damages, the court precluded Plaintiff from introducing evidence of damages, leaving it with only a claim for injunctive relief. [**Cine Forty-Second Street Theatre Corp. v. Allied Artists,** 602 F.2d 1062 (2d Cir. 1979)]

c. Dismissal or Default

The court can use the "litigation death penalty" and dismiss or default the offending party, rendering judgment in favor of the party seeking discovery. [Fed. R. Civ. P. 37(b)(2)(A)(v), –(vi)]

d. Contempt

The court may also impose contempt sanctions on the offending party, except for failing to obey an order to submit to a physical or mental examination. [Fed. R. Civ. P. 37(b)(2)(A)(vii)] (*See infra*, p. 324, regarding contempt.)

IF A PARTY DISOBEYS A COURT'S DISCOVERY ORDER OR IF SANCTIONS ARE OTHERWISE APPROPRIATE, THE COURT MAY:

- ☑ Order that *facts pertinent to the undisclosed material be established* in favor of the party seeking discovery.
- ☑ *Deny* the nondisclosing party the *right to present claims or defenses* related to the material sought.
- ☑ *Dismiss or default* the nondisclosing party.
- ☑ Hold the nondisclosing party *in contempt.*

e. Discretion to Select Proper Sanction

The trial court has substantial discretion to select the proper sanction. However, there are some guidelines in the area:

(1) Least Severe Sanction

Some courts of appeals direct district judges to use the least severe sanction, but others do not. [*Compare* **Gonzalez v. Trinity Marine Group, Inc.,** 117 F.3d 894 (5th Cir. 1997)—district court abused its discretion by dismissing because that was not the least onerous sanction that would redress plaintiff's conduct, *with* **Angulo-Alvarez v. Aponte de la Torre,** 170 F.3d 246 (1st Cir. 1999)—district court did not abuse its discretion by dismissing without first considering less severe sanctions] In any case, the district court has discretion to use less severe sanctions if it concludes that would serve the interests of justice.

(2) General Deterrence

The Supreme Court, however, has stated that general deterrence can justify sanctions more severe than would be necessary to deter the offending party from future discovery misconduct (*i.e.*, the courts can impose a harsh sanction against this recalcitrant litigant in order to deter future litigants from similar misconduct). [**National Hockey League v. Metropolitan Hockey Club, Inc.,** 427 U.S. 639 (1976); and *see* **Brockton Savings Bank v. Peat, Marwick, Mitchell & Co.,** 771 F.2d 5 (1st Cir. 1985)—no requirement that lesser sanction first be considered]

3. Culpability Necessary for Sanctions

a. Due Process Requirements

There are due process limits on the power of a court to impose sanctions that affect the merits.

(1) No Merits Sanctions for Misconduct Unrelated to Merits

A party has a constitutional right to have her case decided on the merits, whether or not she obeys every directive of the court. Hence, it is a violation of due process for the court to enter judgment against a party merely for disobeying an order. [**Hovey v. Elliott,** 167 U.S. 409 (1897)] However, if a party's misconduct taints the merits, that is sufficient to justify a sanction order that redresses the effects of the misconduct. Thus, the failure to comply with discovery usually will support an inference that the violator's case lacks merit and justify a merits sanction. [**Hammond Packing Co. v. Arkansas,** 212 U.S. 322 (1909)]

(2) Ability to Comply

Even if the failure to comply relates to the merits of the case, it would violate due process to enter judgment against a party for failing to do something that he was unable to do. [**Societe Internationale v. Rogers,** 357 U.S. 197 (1958)]

b. Willfulness, Bad Faith, or Other Fault

The ordinary formulation looks to whether the party to be sanctioned was guilty of willfulness, bad faith, or other fault in connection with the failure to comply with the court's order. The broadest ground is "other fault," and it is unclear whether, when the most severe sanctions (dismissal or default) are involved, that ground would extend to simple negligence. [*See* **Cine Forty-Second Street Theatre Corp. v. Allied Artists**, *supra*, p. 321—gross negligence sanctionable]

c. Punishing Client for Lawyer's Misconduct

Often it will not be clear that the client (who is directly affected by merits sanctions) was responsible for misconduct by the lawyer.

(1) Lawyer as Agent of Client

The Supreme Court has said that the lawyer is the agent of the client, and that the client is therefore responsible for the conduct of the lawyer. [**Link v. Wabash Railroad,** 370 U.S. 626 (1962)]

(2) Need to Show Client Involvement

Most lower courts, however, insist on some showing of client involvement before imposing harsh sanctions on the client. [*See, e.g.,* **Cine Forty-Second Street Theatre Corp. v. Allied Artists**, *supra*—plaintiff's principal officer "intimately involved" in litigation; **Shea v. Donohoe Construction Co.**, 529 F.2d 1071 (3d Cir. 1986)—trial court to provide direct warning about risk of dismissal to parties before imposing ultimate sanction]

d. Loss of Electronically Stored Information

(1) Information That Should Have Been Preserved Lost

Under rules developed by courts, there is an obligation to preserve material that may be evidence when litigation is reasonably foreseeable. Often this obligation calls for use of a *litigation hold*. If electronically stored information that should have been preserved is lost because a party failed to take reasonable steps to preserve the information, the court may enter an order adverse to the party. [Fed. R. Civ. P. 37(e)]

(2) Curing Prejudice

On finding prejudice to a party resulting from the loss of information, the court may "order measures no greater than necessary to cure the prejudice." But such measures could be significant, such as prohibiting a party from using certain evidence. [Fed. R. Civ. P. 37(e)(1)]

(3) Sanctions for Intent to Deprive Another Party of the Use of Evidence

If the court finds that the party lost the potential evidence "with the intent to deprive another party of the information's use in the litigation," it may presume that the lost information was unfavorable to that party or instruct the jury to do so, or dismiss the action or enter a default judgment as a sanction. [Fed. R. Civ. P. 37(e)(2)]

4. Imposition of Costs of Discovery Proceedings

a. Motion to Compel Discovery

Unless the court finds that the losing party on a discovery motion was substantially justified in taking the position it did, or other circumstances make an award of expenses unjust, the court is to require the losing party to pay the other side the cost of making or defending against the motion to compel. [Fed. R. Civ. P. 37(a)(5)]

b. Failure to Obey Order Compelling Discovery

The party who fails to comply with a discovery order may, in addition to other sanctions, be required to pay the moving party the cost of seeking sanctions. [Fed. R. Civ. P. 37(b)(2)(C)]

c. For Failure to Attend Deposition

Federal Rule 30(g)(1) authorizes the imposition of costs for a party's failure to attend a deposition that he scheduled.

Compare—Protective Order Regarding Allocation of Costs: Effective Dec. 1, 2015, Federal Rule 26(c)(1)(B) authorizes a protective order specifying the allocation of costs of discovery. But such an order may issue only on a showing of sufficient oppression or undue burden to justify the granting of a protective order. This rule is not intended to authorize routine cost-shifting orders.

5. Contempt Power

a. Defiance of Prior Court Order

Failure to comply with a party-initiated discovery notice (*e.g.*, failure to answer an interrogatory to a party) is not in itself a basis for contempt. Contempt is an appropriate sanction only if the party or witness refuses to make disclosure in defiance of a prior court order.

e.g. **Example**: A deponent who fails to submit to a deposition after having been ordered to do so, or who does not comply with a subpoena, may be held in contempt of court. [Fed. R. Civ. P. 37(b)(1), 45(g)]

b. Civil Contempt

The contempt sanction may be civil, and thus coercive in effect (*i.e.*, the witness may "purge" himself of the contempt at any time by providing the information sought). [**International Business Machines Corp. v. United States,** 493 F.2d 112 (2d Cir. 1975)]

c. Criminal Contempt

In a flagrant case, it may also be proper to impose punishment on a contumacious witness, even if he is now willing to submit. [*See* **Gompers v. Bucks Stove & Range Co.,** 221 U.S. 418 (1911)]

d. Limitation—No Contempt to Compel Physical or Mental Examination

In deference to the personal rights of parties, the contempt power may not be used to compel physical or mental examination. [Fed. R. Civ. P. 37(b)(2)(A)(vii)]

6. Distinguish—Sanctions for Improper Certification

Federal Rule 26(g) makes the signature of an attorney on a discovery paper a certificate with respect to the following matters, and directs that if a paper is signed in violation of this requirement, the court shall impose a sanction on the person signing the paper and/or the party on whose behalf it was submitted.

a. Supported by Law

The signature certifies that the request or response is consistent with the Federal Rules and warranted by existing law or a good faith argument for the extension, modification, or reversal of existing law.

b. Proper Purpose

The signature also certifies that the request or response was not interposed for any improper purpose, such as to harass or to cause unnecessary delay or needless increase in the cost of litigation.

c. Reasonable

Finally, the signature certifies that the request or response is not unreasonable or unduly burdensome or expensive, given the needs of the case, the discovery already had in the case, the amount in controversy, and the importance of the issues at stake in the litigation.

 Compare—Rull 11: Rule 26(g) provides guidance for discovery that is analogous to Rule 11 for pleadings. (*See* Chapter Four)

F. Appellate Review of Discovery Orders

1. Orders Usually Not Appealable

a. Discovery Orders Not Final

To further the interest of judicial economy, generally only final orders are appealable. Orders concerning discovery are not final judgments, and hence are not appealable in most jurisdictions.

(1) Not Collateral

Despite the prohibition against appealing non-final orders, many jurisdictions allow immediate appeal of orders that are "collateral" (*i.e.*, not directly in issue) to the main case. Discovery orders are not regarded as "collateral" to the main action and so are not immediately appealable under this principle. (*See infra*, pp. 429–433). [**Cunningham v. Hamilton County**, 527 U.S. 198 (1999)—Rule 37 sanctions orders are not collateral to the merits]

(2) Order Compelling Production of Privileged Material

The Supreme Court has held that an allegedly erroneous order compelling production of privileged material is not immediately appealable as a "collateral order." It concluded that allowing such appeals would apply to all orders involving material claimed to be privileged, that the risk of error in such orders was very small, that such errors could be corrected after final judgment, and that sufficient alternative methods of preserving privilege exist even without a right to an immediate appeal. [**Mohawk Industries, Inc. v. Carpenter**, 558 U.S. 100 (2009)]

b. Not Injunctions

Likewise, discovery orders are not injunctions within the meaning of statutes authorizing immediate appeals from orders granting or denying injunctions. [28 U.S.C. § 1292(a); **International Products Corp. v. Koons**, 325 F.2d 403 (2d Cir. 1963)]

c. Appealable in Some States

In some states, discovery orders are appealable orders—*i.e.*, in those states, no "final decision" requirement is imposed as a condition of appellate jurisdiction. [*See* **Boser v. Uniroyal, Inc.**, 39 App. Div. 2d 632 (N.Y. 1972)]

2. Modes of Review

a. Certified Appeal (Federal Practice)

If the discovery order raises an important question about the controlling discovery rule, the trial court may certify the question to the appellate court if the order involves a controlling question of law as to which there is substantial ground for difference of opinion and an immediate appeal may materially advance the termination of the litigation. [28 U.S.C. § 1292(b); *see*, *e.g.*, **American Express Warehousing Ltd. v. TransAmerica Insurance Co.,** 380 F.2d 277 (2d Cir. 1967)]

b. Mandamus or Prohibition (State and Federal Practice)

An extraordinary writ such as a writ of mandamus (which orders a court to perform an act) may be issued by an appellate court to correct or prevent an abuse of discretion by the trial judge in exercising power over the discovery process. [28 U.S.C. § 1651; **Schlagenhauf v. Holder**, *supra*, p. 293; **Greyhound Corp. v. Superior Court,** 56 Cal. 2d 355 (1961)] Such writs usually are issued only in extraordinary situations.

c. Review After Judgment

If the trial court fails to compel effective disclosure, the appellate court may reverse the judgment on this basis. However, the discovery ruling must be shown to have been "prejudicial" (*i.e.*, likely to have affected the outcome of the case), or there is little likelihood of reversal. [*See* **Burns v. Thiokol Chemical Corp.,** 483 F.2d 300 (5th Cir. 1973)]

d. Sanction as Final

If the discovery sanction takes the form of a final disposition, such as a judgment of dismissal or any entry of judgment by default, that judgment is final and appealable. [**Brennan v. Engineered Products, Inc.,** 506 F.2d 299 (8th Cir. 1974)]

e. Review of Contempt Order

An order of civil contempt is not final and hence is not generally appealable until final judgment is entered. [**International Business Machines Corp. v. United States**, *supra*, p. 324] However, a conviction of criminal contempt is final and appealable. [**Union Tool Co. v. Wilson,** 259 U.S. 107 (1922)] **Caution**: Sometimes the distinction between civil and criminal contempt is difficult to discern. [*See* **United Mine Workers v. Bagwell,** 512 U.S. 821 (1994)—for purposes of right to jury trial, contempt order was criminal, although court announced penalty for violation in advance]

G. Use of Discovery at Trial

1. Statements of Adversary

a. Admissions

A party's admissions (*i.e.*, statements detrimental to his case) in a deposition or in response to an interrogatory are admissible just like any other admission. However, such admissions are not conclusive, as they may be shown to have been inadvertent. [Fed. R. Civ. P. 32(a)(1); Cal. Civ. Proc. Code § 2025.620]

(1) But Note

An admission in a response to a request for admission under Federal Rule 36 is conclusive proof of the facts admitted. [Fed. R. Civ. P. 36(b); *see supra*, pp. 285–287]

b. Right to Object

The party whose statement is being used may object at trial on the basis of its irrelevance or impropriety and is not barred by her failure to interpose objections at the time of discovery. [Fed. R. Civ. P. 32(b), (d)]

2. Statements of Other Witnesses

a. Prior Inconsistent Statement

Depositions may be admitted at trial for impeachment—*i.e.*, to prove a prior inconsistent statement of a witness who testifies at trial. [Fed. R. Civ. P. 32(a)(2); Cal. Civ. Proc. Code § 2025.620(a)]

b. Unavailability

In addition, depositions may be admitted to prove the facts testified to at the deposition if the deponent is "unavailable" at trial (*e.g.*, witness out of state, too ill to testify, deceased, etc.). [Fed. R. Civ. P. 32(a)(4); Cal. Civ. Proc. Code § 2025.620(c)(2)]

c. Party's Own Deposition

A party may use her own deposition in lieu of personal testimony if she is "unavailable" for trial (see above), provided that she has not procured her own absence (*i.e.*, leaving the jurisdiction to avoid being called as a witness by the adversary). [Fed. R. Civ. P. 32(a)(4); *see supra*, p. 282]

H. Private Investigation

1. Formal Discovery Not Obligatory

Civil litigants are entitled to conduct their own private investigation of the facts and are not obliged to use the discovery process to secure information. [**Corley v. Rosewood Cure Center, Inc.,** 142 F.3d 1041 (7th Cir. 1998)]

a. Exception—Contact with Opposing Party

However, ethical rules forbid a lawyer from contacting an opposing party known to be represented by counsel without the permission of that party's attorney.

2. Admissibility of Proof Privately Obtained

Under the Fourth Amendment, the government may not use evidence in criminal trials that was obtained through improper means. Private parties, however, are not subject to the Fourth Amendment limitations on searches or exclusionary rules intended to enforce such constitutional restraints. Thus, at least in the absence of egregious wrongdoing, civil litigants may use material as proof even if it was obtained by tortious means. [**Sackler v. Sackler,** 15 N.Y.2d 40 (1964)]

Chapter Seven

Summary Judgment

CONTENTS	PAGE

Key Exam Issues

Summary judgment is a pretrial device that permits the court to look outside the pleadings to determine whether there is an issue of fact to be tried. In law-school examinations, summary-judgment issues are sometimes raised in connection with disputes about discovery that may bear on the issues raised by the summary-judgment motion. When presented with a motion for summary judgment, ask yourself the following questions:

1. **Has the Moving Party Made a Sufficient Initial Showing?**

    If the moving party would have the burden of proof on the issue at trial, he must initially produce enough evidence for the judge to find that no reasonable jury could find for his opponent. If the moving party would not have the burden of proof, he still must make an initial showing of his opponent's lack of proof. If the initial showing is insufficient, the opposing party need not submit any opposing proof, and the motion should be denied.

2. **Was the Opposing Party Given Notice and an Opportunity to Respond?**

    If the initial showing was sufficient, summary judgment would still be improper unless the opposing party was given notice of the motion and an *opportunity to respond*. Note that the circumstances sometimes justify delay in the decision to give the opposing party an opportunity to gather evidence, especially if the motion is made early in the case or before there has been substantial discovery.

3. **Is There a Triable Issue?**

    Assuming that the moving party's initial burden was met and the nonmoving party was given an opportunity to respond, the court must look at the evidence *in the light most favorable to the nonmoving party* to determine whether there is a *genuine dispute of material fact* to be tried. If the moving party would have the burden of proof at trial, the motion should be granted only if the evidence is so strong that a reasonable jury could find only for the moving party. If the moving party would not have the burden of proof at trial, the court should grant the motion only if the opposing party fails to come forward with sufficient evidence for a reasonable jury to return a verdict in his favor.

Also note that summary judgment may be partial (*i.e.*, only as to some issues or some parties). **Denial** of summary judgment is not immediately appealable. **Grant** of summary judgment, however, may be immediately appealable if it results in a final judgment. Appellate review is de novo; the appellate court does not give deference to the trial judge's decision.

A. Introduction

1. Purpose

Summary judgment is a method for getting beyond the allegations of the pleadings and examining evidentiary material without holding a full-dress trial. If the evidentiary material shows that there is actually no genuine controversy that requires a trial, summary judgment can avoid unnecessary delay and expense in deciding the case.

> **Example**: In the complaint, Plaintiff alleges that Defendant made defamatory statements about him to two people. Defendant moves for summary judgment with affidavits from both people saying that Defendant never made such statements to them, and his own affidavit denying that he ever made such a statement to either. If not somehow countered, this evidentiary material shows that there is no factual dispute warranting a trial

because there was never a "publication," a required element of defamation. [**Dyer v. MacDougall,** 201 F.2d 265 (2d Cir. 1952)]

2. Pleadings Motions Compared

Summary judgment differs from pleadings motions attacking the legal sufficiency of a claim or defense in that *summary judgment allows the court to look at evidentiary material*. Recall that pleadings motions look only at the face of the pleading and test only its legal sufficiency. (*See supra*, pp. 154, 166.) Usually, it is said that consideration of any material beyond the face of the complaint is forbidden on a pleadings motion, or such consideration may convert the motion into a motion for summary judgment. [*See, e.g.,* Fed. R. Civ. P. 12(d)—on motion to dismiss for failure to state a claim, if materials outside pleadings are presented and not excluded by court, motion is to be treated as one for summary judgment]

a. Relevance of Pleadings to Summary Judgment

The pleadings delineate what is in controversy in the case. Thus, if certain allegations have been admitted, those admissions may form part of the basis for summary judgment.

b. Reliance on Pleadings in Response to Summary-Judgment Motion

An opposing party may not rely on the allegations in her pleadings to defeat a summary-judgment motion.

3. Judgment as a Matter of Law Compared

Judgment as a matter of law (*infra*, pp. 383–386) is similar to summary judgment in that it uses essentially the same standard to determine whether there is a triable issue. However, there are some important differences.

a. Timing

The summary-judgment motion can be, and usually is, decided *before trial*. A party may move for summary judgment at any time until 30 days after the close of all discovery unless a different time is set by local rule or court order. [Fed. R. Civ. P. 56(b)] A motion for judgment as a matter of law ordinarily is made *at the close of evidence at trial*, and it may be renewed after a verdict is returned (*see infra*, pp. 400–401).

b. Nature of Material Considered

The summary-judgment motion is based essentially on *pretrial written submissions*, whereas a motion for judgment as a matter of law is based on live testimony and other evidence presented during the trial. However, note that summary judgment may be based on live testimony from depositions, which is usually recorded in a deposition transcript or by videotape.

c. Burden of Proof—Initial-Showing Requirement

Summary judgment also differs from judgment as a matter of law in that on summary judgment the moving party must make an initial showing to justify scrutiny of the evidence, which is not required for the motions at or after trial if the moving party does not have the burden of proof.

(1) Opposing Party with Burden

If the moving party would not have the burden of proof at trial, to obtain judgment as a matter of law he could allow the opposing party to put on her case and then point out the insufficiencies of that case. To obtain summary judgment, such a moving party would have to make an ***initial showing*** of the insufficiency of the evidence of his opponent's case. (*See infra*, pp. 336–339, for discussion of the initial burden.) Only if such an initial showing is made does the opponent then have the burden of bringing forth sufficient evidence to show that there is a genuine dispute for trial.

(2) Distinguish—Moving Party with Burden

If the moving party has the burden of proof on the issue raised at the summary-judgment stage, making that showing before trial does not represent an additional burden on the party because the party would have to put on such evidence at trial to justify judgment as a matter of law. However, such a party must make a compelling case for entry of summary judgment, because a trial should be held if a reasonable jury could disbelieve the moving party's proof.

d. Summary Judgment May Be More Difficult to Obtain

In many courts, it is said that summary judgment is more difficult to obtain than judgment as a matter of law—*i.e.*, it must be clearer to the court that the case can reasonably be decided only one way. However, it appears that courts are gradually becoming more accepting of summary judgment. (*See infra*, p. 333.) Attitudes toward summary judgment in some state-court systems probably remain less favorable than those in the federal system, which can influence some plaintiffs' forum choices toward state court and lead defendants anticipating that they may make summary-judgment motions to seek removal to federal court.

GILBERT

	PLEADINGS MOTIONS	SUMMARY-JUDGMENT MOTION	MOTION FOR JUDGMENT AS A MATTER OF LAW
CAN COURT LOOK TO EVIDENTIARY MATERIAL?	No	Yes	Yes
WHEN MADE?	Before trial; often before answer	Before trial	When opposing party has been fully heard on issues raised by motion
BASIS FOR DECISION	The pleadings	Pretrial written submissions including affidavits, documents, and testimony from depositions	Live testimony and other evidence presented during trial

4. Impact on Right to Trial

The traditional reluctance to grant summary judgment resulted in part from the belief that a litigant has a right to have her claims tested at trial. Nevertheless, there is no right to a trial when there is no genuine dispute about material facts, and the Supreme Court early upheld the validity of summary judgment against arguments that it violated the right to jury trial. [**Fidelity & Deposit Co. v. United States,** 187 U.S. 135 (1902)]

5. Trend Favoring Use of Summary Judgment

Since the mid-1980s, it has seemed that the federal courts have become more receptive to deciding cases on summary judgment. The Supreme Court has observed that "[s]ummary judgment is properly regarded not as a disfavored procedural shortcut, but rather as an integral part of the Federal Rules as a whole" and noted that it has an important role: "with the advent of 'notice pleading,' the motion to dismiss seldom fulfills this function [isolating factually insufficient claims or defenses] anymore, and its place must be taken by the motion for summary judgment." [**Celotex Corp. v. Catrett,** 477 U.S. 317(1986)]

B. Standard for Grant of Summary Judgment

1. Basic Standard

The court is to grant summary judgment when it determines that *"there is no genuine dispute as to any material fact"* [Fed. R. Civ. P. 56(a)], or that there is *"no triable issue as to any material fact."* [Cal. Civ. Proc. Code § 437c(c)]

2. Relation to Standard for Judgment as a Matter of Law

The United States Supreme Court has stated that in federal court the standard for entry of judgment is the same at the summary-judgment stage as at the judgment as a matter of law stage. [**Anderson v. Liberty Lobby, Inc.,** 477 U.S. 242 (1986)] This parallel makes it appropriate to focus on whether the moving party has the burden of proof on the issue raised by the summary-judgment motion.

EXAM TIP   **GILBERT**

Recall that the burden of pleading various issues depends on whether they are considered *elements of the claim* or *affirmative defenses*. (*See supra*, pp. 178–179.) Usually, the party who must raise an issue in the pleadings must also prove it. Accordingly, you should be alert to the question of who has the burden of proof on the specific issue raised by the summary-judgment motion.

---

a. Moving Party with Burden of Proof

If the party moving for summary judgment has the burden of proof on the issue raised by the motion, summary judgment should be granted only if the evidence, including that favoring the moving party and anything submitted by the opposing party, is such that the jury could not reasonably find for the opposing party.

b. Opposing Party with Burden

If the party moving for summary judgment does *not* have the burden of proof on the issue raised by the motion, summary judgment should be granted only if the opposing party fails to present sufficient evidence to permit a jury reasonably to find for him. Put differently, unless the opposing party comes forward with sufficient evidence to support a verdict in her favor, summary judgment should be entered in favor of the moving party.

3. Case-by-Case Determination

The court's evaluation process must be made on a case-by-case basis. As with judgment as a matter of law, therefore, it is difficult to generalize "rules" for making summary-judgment decisions, but there are some general principles that are helpful in approaching problems.

a. All Reasonable Inferences Indulged in Favor of Opposing Party

The court is to make all reasonable inferences in favor of the opposing party, and to view the evidence in the light most favorable to that party.

b. Court May Not "Weigh" Evidence

The court is to determine whether there is a genuine dispute; if there is, it may not choose between two versions of events and grant summary judgment to the party whose version seems more persuasive.

c. Role of Higher Burden of Proof

The Supreme Court has held that when a party will bear a heightened burden of proof at trial, the court should use that higher standard in scrutinizing the evidence at the summary-judgment stage. [**Anderson v. Liberty Lobby, Inc.,** *supra*, p. 333—"clear and convincing" evidence required] *Criticism*: It is difficult to know how the court is to give effect to the higher standard of proof without "weighing" the evidence.

d. Witness Credibility

Ordinarily, the credibility of witnesses cannot be assessed on summary judgment because that assessment is left to the jury at trial.

(1) Uncontradicted Interested Witness

The testimony of an uncontradicted interested witness is usually said not to be sufficient to support summary judgment in favor of a party with the burden of proof. *Rationale*: Even an uncontradicted witness might be disbelieved if he has an interest in the litigation.

(2) Disinterested Witness

In some cases, courts suggest that an uncontradicted affidavit of a disinterested witness is sufficient to support summary judgment for a party with the burden of proof. [*See, e.g.*, **Lundeen v. Cordner,** 354 F.2d 401 (8th Cir. 1966)—affidavit of disinterested witness accepted in absence of a "positive showing that this witness's testimony could be impeached"]

(3) Sham-Affidavit Doctrine

If the deposition of a party or an interested witness is used as the basis for a summary-judgment motion by the other side, and that witness submits an affidavit in opposition to summary judgment repudiating the deposition testimony, the court may *disregard* the affidavit. [**Perma Research & Development Co. v. Singer Co.,** 410 F.2d 572 (2d Cir. 1968)—"If a party who has been examined at length on deposition could raise an issue of fact simply by submitting an affidavit contradicting his own prior testimony, this would greatly diminish the utility of summary judgment as a procedure for screening out sham issues of fact"]

e. "Disbelief" Evidence

Although the jury may ordinarily disbelieve even an uncontradicted witness (*see supra*, p. 334), the logical possibility that this disbelief would persuade the jury that the truth is actually the opposite of what the witness claims is ***irrelevant*** on a motion for summary judgment or a motion for judgment as a matter of law. [*See* **Dyer v. MacDougall,** *supra*, p. 330] *Rationale:* Allowing such credibility determinations to satisfy the burden of proof at trial would immunize the trial court's ruling on judgment as a matter of law from appellate review since demeanor of witnesses is usually not preserved in the record on appeal. In addition, it would mean that summary judgment could never be granted against a party with the burden of proof—even though that party could point to no supporting evidence—when the moving party relied on a witness.

(1) Party's Story Blatantly Contradicted by Record

When the version of the facts offered by one party witness is contradicted by others and also contradicted by unimpeachable evidence in the record, the court may grant summary judgment because no jury could reasonably accept the contradicted story at trial. [**Scott v. Harris,** 550 U.S. 372 (2007)—plaintiff's version of incident in which defendant officer rammed plaintiff's car to end a high-speed chase was "blatantly contradicted" by a videotape of the chase that no party suggested had been doctored or altered. As a result, plaintiff's version of the events was "utterly discredited" and no reasonable jury could have believed him]

Example: In another police-pursuit case, the Supreme Court affirmed summary judgment for defendant police officers. This time the officers shot the suspect to death after the car chase. The car chase had involved speeds over 100 miles an hour. Several other vehicles had to alter course to avoid collisions. Even after he was forced to stop after colliding with a police car, decedent continued trying to escape, including putting the car into reverse. [**Plumhoff v. Rickard,** 134 S. Ct. 2012 (2014)]

Compare: In another police-shooting case, the Supreme Court reversed summary judgment for the defendant officers. After the officers mistakenly identified a car as stolen and had the driver on the ground, an officer forced the driver's mother against the garage door, causing the driver to rise toward his feet shouting that the officer should unhand his mother. The officer then shot the driver. Though the officers claimed that the shooting was justified by what the driver did, there was evidence that the mother was slammed against the garage door and that the son rose only to his knees and was pleading for his mother. [**Tolan v. Cotton,** 134 S. Ct. 1861 (2014)]

f. Motive, Intent, and State of Mind

If issues of motive, intent, or state of mind are presented, it is said that summary judgment is peculiarly ***inappropriate***. [**Cross v. United States,** 336 F.2d 431 (2d Cir. 1964)] *Rationale:* Assessments of a person's motive, etc., are best made on the basis of observing her demeanor while testifying, and the pertinent facts are peculiarly within her knowledge.

g. Cross-Motions for Summary Judgment

If both the plaintiff and the defendant move for summary judgment, it might seem that the court should grant the motion of one or the other, but that is not so. Instead, ***the showing made by each party must be evaluated independently***. It would be entirely consistent to deny both motions if neither party made a sufficient showing; that would only mean that a dispute as to material fact remains and a trial is necessary to decide the case.

h. Complex Cases

For a time, some cases suggested that in complex cases (particularly antitrust cases) summary judgment was to be avoided. [*See, e.g.*, **Poller v. Columbia Broadcasting System, Inc.**, 368 U.S. 464 (1962)] Federal courts have since evinced more willingness to entertain summary judgment in such cases. [*See, e.g.*, **Matsushita Electric Industrial Co. v. Zenith Radio Corp.**, 475 U.S. 574 (1986)]

i. "Slightest Doubt" Standard Contrasted

Under a line of Second Circuit cases, summary judgment was said to be inappropriate whenever there was the "slightest doubt" about the outcome at trial. [*See, e.g.*, **Arnstein v. Porter**, 154 F.2d 464 (2d Cir. 1946)] However, this approach has been repudiated. [*See, e.g.*, **Beal v. Lindsay**, 468 F.2d 287 (2d Cir. 1972)]

C. Procedure

1. Initial Showing

Analytically, the court should not reach the question whether there is a genuine dispute until it has evaluated the moving party's showing to determine whether it suffices to justify pretrial scrutiny of the evidence.

a. Moving Party's Burden

The moving party must demonstrate "that there is no genuine dispute as to any material fact and the movant is entitled to judgment as a matter of law." [Fed. R. Civ. P. 56(a)]

(1) Moving Party with Burden of Proof

If the moving party has the burden of proof, he must produce evidence of such strength that *no reasonable jury could find for the opposing party*.

(2) Moving Party Without Burden of Proof

If the moving party does not have the burden of proof, the matter is more complicated.

(a) Early View

Relying on a decision of the Supreme Court [**Adickes v. S.H. Kress & Co.,** *supra*, p. 138], some lower courts took the position that a moving party without the burden of proof had to make as strong a showing as one with the burden of proof *(supra)* to invoke summary judgment.

(b) Current View

Celotex Corp. (*supra*, p. 333), rejected the early view. However, the exact requirements in this circumstance are unclear, owing to disagreement within the Court on the proper formulation.

1) Mere Conclusory Assertion

It appears that a bald assertion that the opposing party lacks sufficient evidence to support his case is not sufficient. [*See* **Celotex Corp. v. Catrett,** *supra*, p. 333 (White, J., concurring)—"It is not enough to move for summary judgment . . . with the conclusory assertion that the plaintiff has no evidence to prove his case"] *Rationale*: "Such a 'burden' of production is no burden at all and would permit summary judgment procedure to be converted into a tool for harassment." [**Celotex Corp. v. Catrett,** *supra*—Brennan, J., dissenting]

2) Initial Responsibility of Informing Court of Basis for Motion

The majority in *Celotex* stated that the moving party has the initial responsibility of informing the court of the basis for its motion; the party must identify those portions of the record which it believes demonstrate the absence of a genuine issue of material fact. However, it is unclear how much more than a conclusory assertion this is designed to require.

3) Moving Party Need Not Produce Affirmative Supporting Evidence

What *is* clear from *Celotex* is that a moving party without the burden need not (although it may) produce evidence affirmatively supporting a finding in its favor. To provide the required initial showing, it may point, with such specificity as may be possible, to the *absence* from the record of any evidence that would support a finding for the party with the burden.

e.g. **Example**: Celotex may point to the absence of any evidence in the record that the asbestos causing the alleged injury was *its own* product as opposed to that of any other asbestos producer, and its doing so provides the required initial showing. It need not (although it may) produce any evidence that the asbestos came from another producer.

(c) Method of Making Showing

1) Affirmative Evidence

The moving party can offer affirmative evidence that negates an essential element of the opposing party's case.

2) Preview of Opposing Party's Case

If the thrust of the motion is that the opposing party has no evidence, however, the showing should reliably indicate that. Thus, the moving party should be able to point to discovery calculated to elicit from the opposing party any evidence he had to support his case and then demonstrate that this evidence is inadequate. Such a showing invites the argument that the opposing party needs more time to gather facts. (*See infra*, p. 342.)

3) Possible Role for Initial Disclosure

Federal Rule 26(a)(1) requires each party to disclose witnesses and documents that it "may use to support" its claims or defenses. (*See supra*, p. 274.) In some cases, the content (or absence) of such disclosures may be used to satisfy the initial-showing requirement by providing a preview of the opposing party's case.

(d) Support for Showing

A party asserting that a fact cannot be disputed must support the assertion by citing materials in the record or additional materials submitted with the motion, or showing that the materials cited do not establish a genuine dispute, or that no admissible evidence can be offered to support a fact. [Fed. R. Civ. P. 56(c)(1), –(2)]

b. Opposing Party's Burden

(1) Initial Showing Not Made

If the moving party has not made the required initial showing, there technically is *no burden* on the opposing party to make any showing in response to the motion, which should be denied.

(a) No Advance Determination of Sufficiency of Initial Showing

However, the opposing party is not entitled to advance notice of the court's attitude toward the sufficiency of the moving party's showing. Thus, to be prudent, the opposing party should submit opposing evidence unless he is absolutely sure of the insufficiency.

(b) Attacking Showing

The opposing party can call the court's attention to other material in the record that demonstrates the existence of a genuine issue. [Fed. R. Civ. P. 56(c)(1)]

e.g. **Example**: In *Celotex*, plaintiff claimed that her husband died due to exposure to asbestos that defendant manufactured. Defendant moved for summary judgment on the ground that there was no evidence in the record linking its products to plaintiff's husband's death. On remand, the court held that summary judgment should not be granted because plaintiff was able to point to material in the record suggesting that at trial she would have a witness to support her claim—a letter from an official of a former employer of plaintiff's husband indicating that company records showed that plaintiff's husband had been exposed to defendant's products. [**Catrett v. Celotex Corp.,** 826 F.2d 23 (D.C. Cir. 1987)]

(2) Initial Showing Made

If the moving party has made the initial showing, the burden is on the opposing party to *come forward with evidentiary material* that establishes the existence of a triable issue, *i.e.*, *sufficient evidence to support a jury verdict in his favor*.

2. Notice

The opposing party is entitled to *notice* of the motion for summary judgment and an *opportunity to submit opposing materials*. Federal Rule 56 does not include any minimum notice duration, but the Committee Note to the 2010 amendment says that "[a]lthough the rule allows a motion for summary judgment to be filed at the commencement of an action, in many cases the motion will be premature until the nonmovant has had time to file a responsive pleading or other pretrial proceedings have been had. Scheduling orders or other pretrial orders can regulate timing to fit the needs of the case." In addition, local rules usually prescribe a minimum notice period (such as 28 or 35 days) for all motions. In California, the notice period is 75 days, which was designed to ensure that the opposing party has sufficient time to respond. [Cal. Civ. Proc. Code § 437a(c)]

a. Summary Judgment Independent of Motion

A federal court may enter summary judgment for a nonmovant, or grant it *on grounds not raised by a party*, or consider summary judgment *on its own*, provided that it gives *notice* to the parties of its intent to take one of these actions and *affords a reasonable time for the parties to respond*. If the court is considering summary judgment on its own, the notice to the parties must identify the material facts that may not be genuinely in dispute. [Fed. R. Civ. P. 56(f)]

(1) Distinguish—Cross-Motions for Summary Judgment

This situation is different from a case in which there are cross-motions for summary judgment. (*See supra*, p. 335.) In that situation, each side is on notice that the other side is seeking summary judgment.

b. Contrast—Notice of Need to Submit Opposing Material

The opposing party generally is *not* entitled to notice of the need to submit opposing material to avoid summary judgment, even if there is a question about the sufficiency of the moving party's initial showing. However, some courts require that pro se litigants be advised, either by the court or by the moving party, about the general requirements of Rule 56 regarding the submission of materials to support their claims in response to summary-judgment motions. [*See* **Vital v. Interfaith Medical Center,** 168 F.3d 615 (2d Cir. 1999)—pro se plaintiff must be given such notice; **Rand v. Rowland,** 154 F.3d 952 (9th Cir. 1998)—pro se prisoner litigants must be given notice] The Committee Note to the 2010 amendments to Rule 56(e) observes that "[m]any courts take extra care with pro se litigants, advising them of the need to respond and the risk of losing by summary judgment if an adequate response is not filed."

3. Time for Motion

The earliest moment for filing motions for summary judgment varies by jurisdiction, and efforts have sometimes been made to protect defendants against having to respond to such motions before they have a reasonable time to obtain representation and investigate the case. In federal court, however, any party may move for summary judgment at any time until 30 days after the close of all discovery. [Fed. R. Civ. P. 56(b)] The assumption is that the court can, by order, protect against premature motions and ensure that the responding party has time to prepare to meet the motion. In California, by way of contrast, the motion is not allowed until 60 days after the general appearance in the action of each party against whom it is directed. [Cal. Civ. Pro. Code § 437c(a)(2)]

4. Materials Considered on Motion

a. Pleadings

Admissions contained in the pleadings may be used to decide summary-judgment motions, but otherwise the pleadings do not bear on the summary-judgment decision except to identify the issues in contention in the lawsuit.

b. Affidavits

Affidavits made on *personal knowledge* of facts, showing that the affiant would be competent to testify to these facts in court, may form the basis of a ruling on a motion for summary judgment. [Fed. R. Civ. P. 56(c)(4)] Affidavits are probably the *most common* materials submitted in support of (or opposition to) motions for summary judgment. However, *the moving party is not required to submit affidavits*. [Celotex Corp. v. Catrett, *supra*, p. 337]

c. Discovery Materials

Material developed through discovery, whether by interrogatory, document request, deposition, or request for admission, may be used in connection with a summary-judgment motion. [Fed. R. Civ. P. 56(c)(1)(A)] Often, affidavits of attorneys are used as vehicles to bring such materials to the attention of the court by "authenticating" true copies of the discovery materials.

(1) Distinguish—Materials Improperly Withheld from Discovery or Disclosure

Materials that should have been disclosed or turned over through discovery, or to supplement prior disclosures or discovery responses, may *not* be used as evidence on a motion for summary judgment. [Fed. R. Civ. P. 37(c)(1); *see supra*, p. 276] Thus, if either party submits such material, the opposing party may argue that the material should be disregarded in ruling on summary judgment for this reason.

d. Oral Testimony

Oral testimony may be heard on a motion for summary judgment, but this is done very rarely, since the objective is to decide the case without holding a trial, and hearing oral testimony might defeat that purpose. Moreover, the need to present matters orally may suggest that a credibility determination is necessary.

EXAM TIP　　　　　　　　　　　　　　　　　　　　　　**GILBERT**

Summary judgment issues often appear in law-school exams. Be sure that your answer notes the basics. A court will grant summary judgment only if there is *no genuine dispute as to any material fact*. In determining whether there is such an issue, the court should consider any admissions that were made; affidavits based on personal knowledge of relevant facts; and relevant material obtained through discovery (*e.g.*, copies of relevant documents, such as the contract in a contract case). Generally, oral testimony is not taken.

---

e. Admissibility

Materials considered in connection with a motion for summary judgment must generally be capable of admission into evidence. [Fed. R. Civ. P. 56(c)(4); Cal. Civ. Proc. Code § 437c(d)]

(1) Possible Relaxation for Opposing Party

Although the moving party must present material that would be admissible, it may be that the opposing party is not held to such requirements, as long as he can show that he will have admissible evidence at trial. For example, after remand in **Celotex Corp. v. Catrett,** *supra*, a dissenting judge argued that the court denied summary judgment in part based on a letter from an official, even though there was no showing that this official had personal knowledge on the subject or that there was admissible evidence to support the assertions in the letter. Critics argue, however, that relaxing the requirement that the opposing party present admissible evidence may erode the value of summary judgment in weeding out groundless claims and defenses.

(a) Material Need Not Be in Admissible Form

Affidavits are usually not admissible at trial because they are hearsay, but they suffice to oppose a motion for summary judgment when they indicate that the affiant would be able to testify at trial to the facts recited. Thus, the nonmoving party need not produce evidence in a form that would be admissible at trial in order to avoid summary judgment.

(2) Determination of Admissibility

Before evaluating the evidentiary materials to determine whether summary judgment should be granted, the court can entertain objections to the admissibility of some of the materials and exclude them from consideration if they are not admissible. [*See, e.g.,* **In re Japanese Electronic Products Antitrust Litigation,** 723 F.2d 238 (3d Cir. 1983), *rev'd on other grounds sub nom.* **Matsushita Electric Industrial Co. v. Zenith Radio Corp.,** *supra*, p. 336—Court commended district court's hearing on evidentiary objections because it would afford fuller consideration of them than would be possible at trial]

(3) Waiver of Evidentiary Objections

Evidentiary objections not made in connection with summary-judgment proceedings may be waived, at least as to those proceedings. [Cal. Civ. Proc. Code § 437c(b)]

f. Judge May, but Need Not, Consider Materials in Record That Were Not Properly Cited by Parties

If the parties do not properly cite materials in the record, the court may—but need not—consider other materials in ruling on the motion. [Fed. R. Civ. P. 56(c)(3)]

5. Partial Summary Judgment

A party may move for summary judgment with regard to a part of a claim or defense. [Fed. R. Civ. P. 56(a)]

On your exam, it is important to remember that summary judgment can be directed to *individual claims*, even if it is not appropriate for the *entire case*. Thus, if a plaintiff's complaint alleges three claims (*e.g.*, unfair competition, trademark infringement, and breach of contract), the defendant may move for summary judgment on any one or more of the claims. If the defendant moves for summary judgment on all claims, the court may grant the motion as to all claims or fewer than all.

6. Order Establishing Material Facts

If the summary-judgment motion cannot be entirely granted, the court may enter an order determining that certain facts are established, and this order will govern the further course of the action. [Fed. R. Civ. P. 56(g); Cal. Civ. Proc. Code § 427c(g)]

a. Statement of Undisputed Facts

In some jurisdictions, the court requires that each party to a summary-judgment motion list all facts it claims are undisputed. [*See, e.g.*, Cal. Civ. Proc. Code § 437c(b)]

7. Inability to Provide Responsive Materials

When the opposing party cannot provide opposing materials, *the court may continue the hearing* to allow materials to be obtained. [Fed. R. Civ. P. 56(d); Cal. Civ. Proc. Code § 437c(h)] *Rationale*: The Supreme Court identified the concerns behind this option in *Celotex* (*supra*, p. 340): "no serious claim can be made that respondent was in any sense 'railroaded' by a premature motion for summary judgment. Any potential problem with such premature motions can be adequately dealt with under Rule 56(f)" [redesignated 56(d) by amendment]. Rule 56(d) states that the court may defer ruling on a summary-judgment motion when the opposing party "shows by affidavit or declaration that for specified reasons, it cannot present facts essential to justify its opposition." Courts usually apply this provision under the following criteria:

a. Showing Required

The opposing party is said to be required to make a showing that continuance is appropriate. *Note*: In practice, courts may be liberal in treating contentions about the need for more discovery as sufficient to justify continuances.

b. Facts Material and Important

A continuance is appropriate only if the additional facts appear important to the disposition of the summary-judgment motion.

e.g. **Example**: In an action for damages for personal injuries, defendant's need to do more discovery on the issue of damages would not be a reason for deferring ruling on plaintiff's motion for partial summary judgment on the question of liability.

c. Facts Can Be Obtained

A continuance is appropriate only if there is some reasonable possibility that the additional facts the opposing party wishes to present can be obtained.

e.g. **Example**: In an action growing out of an accident in which the issue is whether the light was red for defendant and the only two witnesses known to the parties both have testified that the light was green for defendant, plaintiff's hope that another witness will be discovered may be insufficient to justify delaying a ruling on summary judgment. [*See* **Dyer v. MacDougall**, *supra*, p. 335—all alleged witnesses to slander assert that defendant never made statement]

d. Prior Opportunity

If the opposing party has had a reasonable opportunity to obtain the facts but has not done so, that may cause the court to refuse the continuance.

e.g. **Example**: When Intervenor moved for summary judgment on the basis of affidavits by a disinterested witness, the court noted that Plaintiff had not taken the opportunity to take the deposition of this witness. [**Lundeen v. Cordner**, *supra*, p. 334]

e. Relevance of Amount of Advance Notice

The opposing party's claim that he was unable to produce affidavits or other materials in time for the hearing on the summary-judgment motion may be evaluated with skepticism if it had notice of the motion well in advance. In California, for example, notice must be given *75 days* before the hearing, with the expectation that this amount of lead time would permit the opposing party to obtain needed information to respond. [Cal. Civ. Proc. Code § 437c(a)]

8. Effect of Summary-Judgment Decision

If the motion is granted as to the entire case, judgment is entered for the prevailing party. If the motion is denied or granted only in part, the litigation continues.

9. Statement of Reasons for Granting or Denying Motion

The court should state on the record its reasons for granting or denying the motion. [Fed. R. Civ. P. 56(a)] The 2010 Committee Note explains that this provision "can facilitate an appeal or subsequent trial-court proceedings," but added that "[t]he form and detail of the statement of reasons are left to the court's discretion."

10. Appellate Review

a. Standard

The appellate court uses a de novo standard of review, and gives no deference to the trial court's decision, because summary-judgment rulings turn on whether the movant is entitled to judgment as a matter *of law*.

b. Timing

Unless summary judgment is entered as to the entire case, appellate review of the summary-judgment decision may be delayed until the final decision of the case. (*See infra*, pp. 425–433, for discussion of the final-judgment rule.)

c. Order Denying Motion

If summary judgment is denied, no judgment results, so the order is not reviewable until after the trial. By that time, a mistaken denial of summary judgment may be treated as *harmless error* if the trial was properly conducted and the judgment after the trial is supported by the evidence at trial.

CIRCUMSTANCES	No genuine dispute as to any material fact and movant is entitled to judgment as a matter of law.
SUPPORT FOR MOTION	Pleadings, affidavits, discovery materials, oral testimony (rare).
TIMING	In federal court, at any time until 30 days after the close of all discovery. State practices vary.

Chapter Eight

Managerial Judging, Settlement Promotion, and Arbitration

CONTENTS	PAGE

Key Exam Issues

1. Until recently, pretrial conference and settlement promotion were considered beyond the scope of a first-year course, and they still are more likely to be given intense attention in an advanced course on complex litigation. Nevertheless, they have increasingly been covered in the basic first-year civil procedure course. Moreover, they may play an increasing role in examinations involving challenges to actions by judges that fall outside the traditional realm of judicial activity. In connection with such examination questions, there are two basic questions to be asked:

   a. **Did the Court Have Authority to Take the Action It Took?**

      Except for "inherent authority," a slippery idea, courts must usually ground their right to take nontraditional actions in some statute or court rule. Many jurisdictions allow or require scheduling conferences and orders to set time limits for joining parties, amending pleadings, limiting discovery, etc. Status conferences and final pretrial conferences are allowed to discuss issue simplification and promote settlement. Courts have also been given some power to use mandatory nonbinding arbitration and summary jury trials to promote settlement without trial.

   b. **Did the Court Abuse Its Discretion?**

      Assuming that there was authority, an appellate court could still reverse on the ground that under the circumstances this authority was abused. The main point to remember is that the court cannot club a party into submission.

   In addition, examination questions may ask for evaluation of the *policy questions* that surround the innovations that are discussed in this chapter. Indeed, an examination question may ask the student to evaluate a proposed new program of expediting litigation by comparing it to current practices and considering the arguments for and against adopting the new regime. The main arguments for most procedures are that they streamline cases by simplifying issues and make trial results less uncertain and therefore promote early settlement. The main disadvantages are that the procedures: (i) take some control away from the parties over their own cases; (ii) may force important decisions early, before the parties have had a chance to fully investigate issues; and (iii) often force judges to "prejudge" a case or issue, before all the facts are in.

2. Formal Offers of Judgment -- Is there a rule or statute applicable to authorize such a formal offer with potentially adverse consequences? [*E.g.,* Fed. R. Civ. P. 68] If so,

   a. Did the offer made conform to the rule or statute?

   b. Did the opposing party accept the offer? If so, judgment is entered in accordance with the offer.

   c. If the opposing party did not accept the offer, does that failure to accept result in adverse consequences?

      (i) Was the eventual outcome of the case not more favorable to the offeree than the offer? This determination may be difficult in cases involving nonmonetary relief.

      (ii) Did the offeree prevail in court? The Supreme Court has held that Federal Rule 68 has no application to cases in which the defendant prevails.

      (iii) What is the adverse consequence of not accepting a formal offer and failing to do better in the eventual outcome? In federal court, it is generally limited to the offeree having to pay the offeror's post-offer "costs." But when a pertinent statute makes attorney's fees awardable "as part of costs," the non-accepting offeree loses its entitlement to its post-offer attorney's fees. Under the law of some states *(e.g.,* California) other consequences may follow, such as liability for the offeror's expert-witness expenses.

3. Application of the Federal Arbitration Act (FAA) – The FAA makes written arbitration provisions in contracts involving commerce "valid, irrevocable, and enforceable, save upon such grounds as exist at law or in equity for the revocation of any contact." Such arbitration agreements usually require that a dispute be resolved in private arbitration and that it not be taken to court.

   a. Does a provision affecting arbitration apply to contract validity generally, or does it single out arbitration for special treatment or disfavor? If the latter, the provision is invalid under the FAA.

   b. Can an arbitration proceed on a class basis? Class arbitration can and does occur, but the Supreme Court has held that application of state unconscionability law to hold a waiver of class arbitration invalid impermissibly treats the arbitration agreement's specification for individual arbitration with disfavor. The Court has also held that a class-arbitration waiver in a credit-card contract did not impermissibly limit plaintiffs' ability to pursue federal antitrust claims.

   c. Can state unconscionability law apply to invalidate aspects of arbitration provisions other than class-arbitration waivers? Relying on the Supreme Court's statement that the FAA permits invalidation by "generally applicable contract defenses, such as fraud, duress, or unconscionability," a leading lower-court decision has held invalid a one-sided cost- and fee-shifting provision in an arbitration agreement.

A. Pretrial Conferences and Managerial Judging

1. Historical Background

a. Federal Rule 16

The original Federal Rule 16 authorized a pretrial conference to be held shortly before trial to organize the trial. However, concern arose that the relaxed pleading requirements and broadened discovery of the Federal Rules (and the state systems that emulated the Federal Rules) had led to amorphous lawsuits involving excessive discovery expense because they were not focused. In response, and due to rising caseload pressures, federal judges in metropolitan districts began, during the 1970s, to experiment with more active pretrial control of litigation. Sometimes this control was handled on a judge-by-judge basis, and sometimes it was implemented by district-wide local rules. This expanded judicial role in the pretrial process was explicitly built into the Federal Rules, which provide for mandatory conferences among the parties [Fed. R. Civ. P. 26(f)], numerous pretrial conferences [Fed. R. Civ. P. 16(a)–(c)], and a final pretrial conference. [Fed. R. Civ. P. 16(e)]

b. State-Court Practices

In state courts, such pretrial control was less prominent, in part because in many states, cases were not assigned to a single judge for all purposes. Nevertheless, some added emphasis on pretrial supervision has emerged. [*See, e.g.,* Cal. Civ. Proc. Code §§ 575–

76—regarding pretrial conferences for judicial management] Moreover, more and more state courts employ a single-assignment procedure.

2. Scheduling

Under Rule 16, federal district-court judges have an expanded pretrial role in the control and development of civil cases.

a. Mandatory Scheduling Order

Except in categories of cases exempted by local rule, federal district courts are *required* to enter a *"scheduling order"* within 60 days after a defendant's appearance and within 90 days after service of the complaint. This order is to set time limits for joining parties, amending pleadings, completing discovery, and filing motions. [Fed. R. Civ. P. 16(b)(2)]

b. Conference

The scheduling order is to be entered after the parties have provided their discovery plan under Rule 26(f) or the court has consulted with the parties at a scheduling conference. [Fed. R. Civ. P. 16(b)(1)]

c. Other Scheduling Limitations

Beyond the mandatory scheduling limitations, the court may impose much more specific scheduling requirements regarding a variety of matters as part of its pretrial management of a case. These orders can come at periodic pretrial or status conferences.

d. Significance

Limitations on timing of discovery and other matters can be extremely significant to the parties, because they can no longer exercise unilateral control over the sequence and timing of pretrial litigation activities. In particular, this control may be especially significant when the parties wish to defer formal litigation activities for some reason (*e.g.*, to discuss settlement), but the court's schedule requires the case to proceed expeditiously.

e. Exempted Categories of Cases

A district court may, by local rule, exempt categories of cases from the scheduling-order requirements on the ground that those requirements would be inappropriate in such cases. [Fed. R. Civ. P. 16(b)(1)]

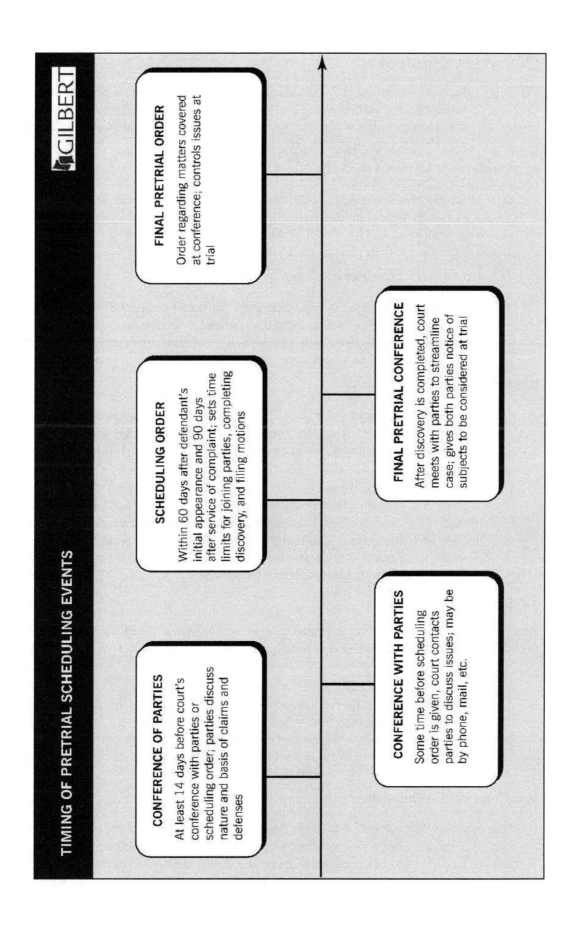

TIMING OF PRETRIAL SCHEDULING EVENTS

CONFERENCE OF PARTIES

At least 14 days before court's conference with parties or scheduling order; parties discuss nature and basis of claims and defenses

SCHEDULING ORDER

Within 60 days after defendant's initial appearance and 90 days after service of complaint; sets time limits for joining parties, completing discovery, and filing motions

FINAL PRETRIAL ORDER

Order regarding matters covered at conference; controls issues at trial

CONFERENCE WITH PARTIES

Some time before scheduling order is given, court contacts parties to discuss issues; may be by phone, mail, etc.

FINAL PRETRIAL CONFERENCE

After discovery is completed, court meets with parties to streamline case; gives both parties notice of subjects to be considered at trial

GILBERT

3. Discovery Control

The Federal Rules now limit the scope of discovery to material "proportional to the needs of the case," considering such factors as the importance of the issues, the amount at stake, the parties' access to relevant information, the parties' resources, and the relation of burden and expense to likely benefit. [Fed. R. Civ. P. 26(b)(1)]

a. Conference by Parties

At least 21 days before the Rule 16(b) scheduling conference or order, the parties are to confer regarding "the nature and basis of their claims and defenses" and to develop a discovery plan. [Fed. R. Civ. P. 26(f)] After this meeting, they are to submit a written report to the court of their plan within 14 days.

(1) Exempted Categories of Cases

Cases falling in categories exempted from the initial-disclosure requirements by Rule 26(a)(1) are also exempt from the conference requirement. [Fed. R. Civ. P. 26(a)(1)(B); 26(f) *see supra*, p. 274] Courts may not exempt categories of cases from the initial-disclosure requirements by local rule.

b. Court's Pretrial Order

Based on the parties' report under Rule 26(f), the court is to enter an order that should limit the time to complete discovery [Fed. R. Civ. P. 16(b)(3)(A)] and may include provisions "controlling and scheduling discovery." [Fed. R. Civ. P. 16(c)(2)(F)]

(1) Criticism

Such precise discovery limitations impinge on the parties' freedom to control the lawsuit. Moreover, the task of designing such limitations requires the judge to develop a much greater familiarity with the action than would otherwise be necessary, and raises the risk that the judge may misapprehend what is important (and therefore worthy of pursuit through discovery).

4. Issue Simplification

At a pretrial or status conference, the court can discuss *simplification of the issues* and seek to obtain *stipulations and admissions of fact* to simplify the case. [Fed. R. Civ. P. 16(c)(2)(A)]

a. Rationale

By the time the matters are raised in the pretrial conference, it is said that the parties know more about their case and that, therefore, it is fair to pressure them to commit to binding positions for purpose of the litigation. However, there is concern that early pressure toward issue simplification may undermine the supposed benefits of relaxed pleading and unduly constrict cases before the facts are out.

b. Compelled Admissions

The court may not compel admissions from an unwilling party, but the court does have the right to pressure parties to abandon positions that seem unsupported. *Criticism*: Again, the judge may not adequately appreciate the circumstances of the case based on the explanation given at the pretrial conference and may unjustifiably curtail legitimate litigation opportunities.

5. Settlement Promotion

It has long been recognized that more active judicial involvement in pretrial activities could affect settlement of cases, but for some time many judges were reluctant to become overtly involved in settlement discussions, because that might seem to erode their impartiality. This reluctance has waned, and Rule 16(c)(2)(I) now explicitly authorizes discussion of the possibility of settlement.

a. Tactics

Judges use a variety of tactics to foster settlement, including meeting separately with each side (with the permission of both sides), requiring attendance of clients at settlement conferences, and meeting with clients outside the presence of their lawyers.

b. Mandatory Attendance

Rule 16(c)(1) authorizes the court to require that a party or its representative be present or reasonably available by telephone to consider settlement.

c. No Power to Dictate Terms of Settlement

The court is not authorized to dictate the terms of the settlement. [**Kothe v. Smith,** 771 F.2d 667 (2d Cir. 1985)—Rule 16 "was not designed as a means for clubbing the parties—or one of them—into an involuntary compromise"] Nevertheless, the court may suggest terms for a settlement that the parties may follow.

d. Ambiguity of Judicial Role

The judge's role in settlement is hard to square with the traditional notion that the judge decides disputed matters according to standards set out by the law.

(1) Evaluating Terms of Settlement

It is unclear whether the judge should promote *any* agreement that seems likely to obtain the consent of the parties, or insist that the agreement correspond, somehow, to the strengths and weaknesses of the merits of the parties' positions.

(2) Absence of Trial

The judge would usually reach conclusions about the strengths and weaknesses of the parties' positions on the merits only after a trial. To the extent that the judge is to rely on her opinion about the strength of the case in suggesting proper terms for settlement, involvement in settlement seems to circumvent the normal decisionmaking process.

Example—the Weak Case for Plaintiff: If the case for the plaintiff appears weak, the judge's role becomes difficult to comprehend in traditional terms of decisions according to the law. For example, if the plaintiff has a strong case on liability, but little in the way of provable damages, the judge may be able to suggest a reasonable compromise based on the rules governing damages and her experience with awards in similar cases. However, when the plaintiff's case is weak on liability, it is hard to identify any benchmarks. There is no legal standard or reference point in decided cases for determining the "right" settlement amount when the plaintiff has a small chance of success on liability, but large provable damages, since the result at trial would essentially be all or nothing for the plaintiff.

e. Promotion of Alternative Dispute Resolution

The judge may also explore the "use of special procedures [*e.g.*, mini-trials, summary jury trials, mediation, etc.] to assist in resolving the dispute" during pretrial conferences when authorized by local rule or by statute. [Fed. R. Civ. P. 16(c)(2)(I)] The Alternate Dispute Resolution Act of 1998 (*infra*, p. 354 *et seq*.) directs district courts to adopt some of the same procedures.

6. Final Pretrial Conference

a. Purpose

The final pretrial conference is intended to *simplify* and *streamline* the trial and resolve as much as possible before trial. In addition, it serves to give both sides advance notice of the subjects to be covered at trial, so that they can be prepared.

b. Required Pretrial Disclosures

The final pretrial conference will ordinarily follow the pretrial disclosures. At least 30 days before trial, each party is to make further disclosures regarding *evidence the party may present at trial*. [Fed. R. Civ. P. 26(a)(3)]

(1) Matters to Be Disclosed

The following types of evidence should be disclosed, *except for evidence used solely to impeach witness testimony*:

(a) The *names of the witnesses* the party "expects to present" and those it "may call if the need arises" [Fed. R. Civ. P. 26(a)(3)(A)(i)];

(b) The *witnesses whose testimony will be presented by deposition* [Fed. R. Civ. P. 26(a)(3)(A)(ii)]; and

(c) The *documents or other exhibits* the party expects to offer or which it may offer if the need arises. [Fed. R. Civ. P. 26(a)(3)(A)(iii)]

(2) Waiver of Objections

As to the indicated exhibits, the other parties must object *within 14 days* or waive most objections to the admissibility of the exhibits or to the presentation of a witness by deposition in lieu of live testimony. [Fed. R. Civ. P. 26(a)(3)(B)]

(3) Additional Local Requirements

A number of courts, as a matter of local rule, require more detailed pretrial submissions.

c. Topics Covered

Local requirements vary, but courts may require delineation of a variety of matters, including the following.

(1) Undisputed Facts

The parties may be required to list all undisputed facts relevant to the case in pretrial filings.

(2) Disputed Facts

Similarly, the parties may have to list all factual issues that need to be resolved at the trial.

(3) Witness Lists

The parties are usually required to identify all witnesses they will call during their direct cases. (*See supra*, p. 352.) In some instances, they are required also to provide a summary of the substance of the testimony that each witness will give.

(a) Direct Testimony in Writing—Court Trials

Some courts require that in cases to be tried to the court, the entire direct testimony of witnesses be submitted in writing before trial.

(4) Legal Issues

The parties are often required to identify and brief all legal issues that are likely to arise in the case.

d. Final Pretrial Order

Following the final pretrial conference, the court will usually enter a final pretrial order with regard to the matters covered at the conference. This order is to control the trial, and can be *modified only "to prevent manifest injustice."* [Fed. R. Civ. P. 16(e)]

(1) Exclusion of Evidence and Witnesses

The consequence of failure to list a witness or piece of evidence in the pre-trial order can be that the evidence will not be allowed in at the trial.

(2) Distinguish—Amending Pleadings

Ordinarily, the courts take a liberal attitude toward amendment of the pleadings, and it is uncertain how much more restrictive Rule 16 is than Rule 15 (dealing with pleading amendments). [*See* **Wallin v. Fuller,** 476 F.2d 1204 (5th Cir. 1973)—"It is unlikely that the pretrial order under Rule 16 was intended to make the pleadings, and therefore Rule 15, obsolete"; *compare* **United States v. First National Bank of Circle,** 652 F.2d 882 (9th Cir. 1981)—"Unless pretrial orders are honored and enforced, the objectives of the pretrial conference . . . will be jeopardized if not entirely nullified"]

7. Sanctions

The federal courts have *explicit authority* to use sanctions to enforce their authority with regard to pretrial supervision of cases. [Fed. R. Civ. P. 16(f)]

a. Failure to Appear

If a party fails to appear through counsel at a pretrial conference, sanctions may be imposed. In some instances, the court may be able to require that the party appear personally. (*See supra*, p. 351.)

b. Appearing Substantially Unprepared

If a party or lawyer appears, but is not prepared to participate meaningfully in the conference, sanctions are appropriate.

c. Failure to Participate in Good Faith

A party can also be sanctioned for failure to participate in good faith. It is unclear whether the determination of good faith can be based on the court's disagreement with the party's views about proposed settlement terms or stipulations. (*See supra*, p. 351, regarding absence of judicial power to require stipulations or impose terms of settlement.)

d. Sanctions Available

The court can impose the sanctions available for violation of discovery orders [Fed. R. Civ. P. 37(b)(2); *see supra*, pp. 320–324] and also impose expenses, including attorneys' fees, resulting from the failure to comply with responsibilities.

8. Effect on Work-Product Protection

Information such as the identity of witnesses and the subject matter of their testimony would ordinarily be protected work product, yet courts routinely require revelation of this material as part of the final pretrial process. It has been held that work-product protection does not limit the power of the court to require revelation of pertinent information in pretrial preparation under Rule 16. [*In re* **San Juan Dupont Plaza Hotel Fire Litigation,** 859 F.2d 1007 (1st Cir. 1988)]

B. Court-Annexed Settlement Devices

1. Introduction

Because informal settlement promotion seemed not to exhaust the potential for judicial promotion of settlement, judges began to experiment with other ways of facilitating settlement. Such efforts usually involved some simulation of a trial as a method of predicting the outcome of trial.

a. Rationale

A primary rationale for this form of judicial activity is that uncertainty about the outcome of a trial is a major impediment to settlement. Simulated substitutes, therefore, could erase much doubt and give the parties a more reliable basis for negotiations. In addition, there are reports that such proceedings enhance litigant satisfaction and permit prompt resolution of cases.

b. Initial Development at Local Level

In the federal-court system, court-annexed programs initially developed at the local level as various districts experimented with different methods. The eventual federal statute (*see* below) built on and validated these methods.

2. Mandated Alternative Dispute Resolution in Federal Court

Under the Alternative Dispute Resolution ("ADR") Act of 1998, district courts are directed to mandate in their local rules that, subject to certain exceptions, litigants in *all civil cases* **"consider the use of an alternative dispute resolution process at an appropriate stage in the litigation."** [28 U.S.C. § 652(a)] The Act further directs that each district devise and implement its own ADR program, and that it *"encourage and promote the use of alternative dispute resolution in its district"* [28 U.S.C. § 651(b)] Because these activities occur in connection with cases proceeding in court, and under the auspices of the court, they are often referred to as *court-annexed ADR*.

a. ADR Methods

The Act authorizes use of *mediation, early neutral evaluation, summary jury trial, and, subject to certain limitations, arbitration*. All these devices will be discussed in detail below.

b. Exempted Categories of Cases

Each district court may exempt categories of cases from the ADR requirements. [28 U.S.C. § 652(b)]

c. Panel of Neutrals

Each district is to maintain, and arrange for the training and evaluation of, a panel of neutrals to serve in ADR proceedings in the district. [28 U.S.C. § 653] A neutral is usually a lawyer experienced in the legal field giving rise to the case.

d. Confidentiality

Each district must, by local rule, provide for confidentiality in ADR proceedings conducted pursuant to the Act. [28 U.S.C. § 652]

3. Mediation

Mediation involves a neutral third party who attempts to find common ground on which the parties can reach an agreement and resolve their dispute. This role is very different from that of a judge or other person who "decides" a dispute.

a. Formal Legal Rules Not Binding

Because the goal is to reach an agreement, the legal rules that might apply in court are not binding in mediation. They may, however, cast a "shadow" over the mediation and influence the result.

b. Creativity in Devising Solutions

Because formal legal rules limiting court awards do not apply in mediation, the mediator can attempt to devise a solution that would not be available in an action litigated to judgment.

c. Goal Is Agreement of the Parties

If the mediator is successful, the parties will reach an agreement that should be *embodied in a contract between them*. These agreements are usually legally binding in accordance with principles of contract law.

d. Separate Meetings with Parties

Mediators may often find it helpful to meet separately with the contending parties to try to develop solutions that warrant discussion. Separate meetings are permitted.

e. Mediation in State Courts

Mediation occurs in connection with state-court actions as well as in federal-court cases. In some states, statutory provisions authorize court-annexed mediation. [*See* Cal. Civ. Proc. Code §§ 1775–1775.15]

4. Early Neutral Evaluation

Early neutral evaluation originated in the United States District Court for the Northern District of California, and it relies on an experienced neutral lawyer (the neutral) to advise the parties on their prospects in the case after both sides have presented their positions. The parties get the advantage of an early, frank, and thoughtful assessment of their positions.

a. Experienced Lawyer

The neutral should be a lawyer with substantial experience in the field of law that gave rise to the suit.

b. Evaluative Orientation

The neutral is to bring a critical eye to the positions of the parties and offer them her assessment of the likely success of those positions. The goal is that this third-party assessment will ***encourage the parties to be realistic about their chances of success***. This effort may include an indication by the neutral of her expectation of an award in the case.

c. Occurs Early in Case

As suggested by the title of this ADR device, early neutral evaluation should occur early in the case, and before the parties have expended substantial resources on litigation.

d. Suggestions for Future Conduct of Case

Beyond assessing the likely outcome of the case, the neutral may offer the parties suggestions about the future conduct of the case to prepare it for trial should it not settle. These suggestions are conveyed only to the parties and are ***not conveyed to the court***.

5. Summary Jury Trial

The summary jury trial ("SJT") was invented in 1980 by a federal district judge in Cleveland.

a. Timing

The SJT is usually deferred until all normal pretrial activities have been completed. All motions in limine (*i.e.*, limits on evidence to be presented at trial) and other similar pretrial matters should be disposed of and a final pretrial order entered.

b. Nature of Hearing

The specifics on summary jury trials may vary from place to place, but generally they have similar procedures:

(1) In Courthouse

The proceedings occur in the courthouse, in a regular courtroom, with a judge (or magistrate judge) presiding.

(2) Before Jury

The case is presented to a jury summoned to appear in the normal manner for juries.

(3) Lawyer Presentations

The bulk of the case is based on summaries by the lawyers of the evidence developed in the pretrial phase.

(a) Limitations on Content

Some guidelines will apply to limit the content of the summaries. The presentations may have to be based on material developed during discovery, or upon the attorney's representation that she has talked to the witness and that the witness would testify as described.

(b) Live Testimony

In some courts, limited live testimony may be allowed.

(4) Instructions by Court

After the lawyers have completed their summaries, the court gives the jury abbreviated instructions on the law applicable to the case.

(5) Verdict

The jury is to render a consensus verdict, if possible, and if not, to report on reactions to the case on a juror-by-juror basis.

(6) Effort to Settle

With the added information provided by the jury verdict, the parties try to settle the case.

c. Secrecy

Generally, the SJT is held in secret, and the public is not allowed to attend.

Example: In a suit claiming that builders of a nuclear power plant were liable for poor design because the facility leaked radioactive steam, a newspaper was denied access to the SJT on the ground that it was merely a settlement procedure. [**Cincinnati Gas & Electric Co. v. General Electric Co.,** 854 F.2d 900 (6th Cir. 1988)]

d. Binding Effect

In some instances, the parties can *stipulate* that the summary jury trial will be binding.

e. Compulsory Participation

There has been a split among the courts on whether an unwilling party can be compelled to participate in an SJT before being afforded an opportunity to have a regular trial in court. [*Compare* **Strandell v. Jackson County,** 838 F.2d 884 (7th Cir. 1987)—no power to compel, *with* **In re Atlantic Pipe Corp.,** 304 F.3d 135 (1st Cir. 2002)—court has inherent power to order mediation but must set limits on duration and cost]

6. Court-Annexed Arbitration

In the late 1970s, federal courts in some districts began experimenting with *mandatory nonbinding arbitration* in some cases. In 1988, Congress expressly sanctioned these experiments in 10 districts where such experiments had begun and authorized further experiments in 10 other districts. [28 U.S.C. §§ 651 *et seq.*] This authorization was further extended until Congress included arbitration in the 1998 Act, subject to certain limitations. Some states have authorized similar procedures in their courts. [*See, e.g.,* Cal. Civ. Proc. Code §§ 1141.10 *et seq.*]

a. Cases Affected

(1) Federal Court

With the consent of the parties, a federal court may allow the referral for nonbinding arbitration of *any civil action* before it *except* cases involving *civil rights claims*, alleged *violations of constitutional rights*, or *damages* relief sought in an amount *exceeding $150,000*. [28 U.S.C. § 654(a)]

(a) Safeguards on Giving of Consent

District courts that authorize arbitration as an ADR device are required to adopt safeguards (*e.g.*, that no party or attorney be prejudiced for refusing to participate) to ensure that parties who are asked to consent do so freely and knowingly. [28 U.S.C. § 654(b)]

(b) Presumption Regarding Damages Sought

Unless counsel certifies that more than $150,000 is involved, the court may presume that damages do not exceed that amount. [28 U.S.C. § 654(c)]

(2) State Courts

In state courts where arbitration is authorized, eligibility may turn on the amount claimed, as in federal courts. In California superior courts, for example, all civil actions in which the amount in controversy, in the opinion of the court, will not exceed $50,000 are subject to arbitration. [Cal. Civ. Proc. Code § 1141.11(a)]

(a) Dispute About Amount Claimed

Under the California approach, there can be disputes about whether over $50,000 is really in controversy. [*See* Cal. Civ. Proc. Code § 1141.16(a)— conference to be held to determine whether over $50,000 is actually in controversy]

(b) Equitable Relief

In California, arbitration may not be compelled if equitable relief is sought, unless the prayer for equitable relief is frivolous. [Cal. Civ. Proc. Code § 1141.13]

b. Timing

Arbitration generally occurs early in the litigation process.

c. Hearing

The arbitration decision is based on a hearing, which resembles a trial, but may be more relaxed. The rules of evidence might not be applied with full force, and relaxed rules about the form of presentation of evidence (*e.g.*, narrative answers) may be allowed.

(1) Subpoena for Witnesses

Subpoenas under Federal Rule 45 are available to compel attendance of witnesses and production of documentary evidence for arbitration hearings. [28 U.S.C. § 656]

(2) Oaths of Witnesses

Arbitrators may administer oaths and affirmations. [28 U.S.C. § 655(a)(2)]

d. Award

After the hearing, the arbitrator is to enter an award, which briefly identifies the prevailing party and (if necessary) the amount of damages. This award is filed in court and *becomes the judgment* of the court *unless a trial de novo is demanded*. [28 U.S.C. § 657(a); Cal. Civ. Proc. Code § 1141.20]

e. Trial de Novo

On timely demand, any party may insist that the case be restored to the regular trial calendar for trial de novo, which is conducted as a regular trial, unaffected by the arbitration proceedings. [28 U.S.C. § 657(c); Cal. Civ. Proc. Code § 1141.20]

(1) Less Favorable Result

In some jurisdictions, if the party who demands a trial de novo does not obtain a more favorable result in that trial, it can be required to *reimburse the opposing party for certain costs*. [Cal. Civ. Proc. Code § 1141.21]

f. Refusal to Participate

If a party refuses to participate in the arbitration or fails to participate in good faith, the court may have authority to deny a trial de novo. [*Compare* **New England Merchants National Bank v. Hughes,** 556 F. Supp. 712 (E.D. Pa. 1983)—trial de novo denied, *with* **Lyons v. Wickhorst,** 42 Cal. 3d 911 (1986)—no authority to deny trial de novo under California statute]

GILBERT

MEDIATION	EARLY NEUTRAL EVALUATION	SUMMARY JURY TRIAL	NONBINDING ARBITRATION
- Neutral third party helps parties find common ground on which to resolve a dispute - Formal rules of evidence and procedure not binding - Third party may meet with parties together or separately	- Neutral lawyer experienced in the type of case between the parties advises the parties on their chances of success in the case after hearing both sides present their positions	- Trial-like hearing before a jury; public not allowed - Lawyers present evidence to jury in a summary form based on discovery - Parties may try to settle based on information learned from jury verdict, or parties may stipulate that verdict is binding	- Trial-like hearing before an arbitrator - Available in civil actions when damages are less than $150,000, except civil rights or constitutional claims - Rules of evidence and procedure are relaxed - Arbitrator's award will be entered as the court's judgment unless a trial de novo is timely demanded

C. Formal Offer-of-Judgment Rules

1. Federal Rule of Civil Procedure 68

a. Basic Provisions

Federal Rule of Civil Procedure 68(a) provides that a defending party may, "[a]t least 14 days before the date set for trial, . . . serve on an opposing party an offer to allow judgment on specified terms, with the costs then accrued." The opposing party has 14 days from when it is served in which it may serve a written notice of acceptance. If it accepts, either party may file the offer and notice of acceptance, in which case the clerk must enter judgment.

Absent timely acceptance, under Rule 68(b) an offer "is considered withdrawn." Rule 68(d) further provides that if the judgment finally obtained by the offeree is not *more favorable* than an unaccepted offer, "the offeree must pay the costs incurred after the offer was made."

b. Purposes

Federal Rule 68 is regarded as intended to encourage settlements. But it applies only to formal offers served on the claimant, not to settlement offers made in negotiations. The rule also promotes fairness to offerors by awarding them post-offer costs when they are forced to continue litigating after offering all that the offeree turns out to obtain at trial.

c. Incentive Effects

Rule 68 gives claimants an incentive to consider formal offers seriously because of the threat of having to pay post-offer costs even if they win. In American practice a prevailing party in civil litigation is usually entitled to an award of "costs" such as docketing fees, reporters' charges, printing and copying costs, etc., but not including attorneys' fees. If an offeree does not accept a Rule 68 offer, the offeree is entitled to post-offer costs only if it obtains a judgment better than the offer. If it does not, its usual entitlement to such costs is reversed, and an award of post-offer costs to the offeror is mandatory.

d. Applicability

The cost-shifting feature of Rule 68 comes into play only if the offeree wins *some* recovery, but not more than the unaccepted offer. The Supreme Court has settled that Rule 68 does not apply if the offeror wins outright. [**Delta Air Lines v. August,** 450 U.S. 346 (1981)] In that event the offeror will likely receive an award of all its costs under Federal Rule of Civil Procedure 54(d)(1), although the trial judge has some discretion to reduce a costs award or make no award.

e. Effect on Liability for Attorneys' Fees

Absent a statute authorizing an award of attorneys' fees as part of "costs," Rule 68 does not affect the parties' entitlement to a fee award. But many federal statutes, such as one applicable in civil rights cases, do authorize fee awards to a prevailing plaintiff as part of costs. The Supreme Court has decided that an offeree in such a case who wins a judgment not better than an unaccepted offer loses its entitlement to post-offer attorneys' fees.

[**Marek v. Chesny,** 472 U.S. 1 (1983)] Such an offeree remains liable for the offeror's post-offer non-fee costs.

The Supreme Court has not settled whether such an offeree can be liable for the offeror's post-offer attorneys' fees. Most lower federal courts that have faced the question, however, have held that the offeree, having obtained *some* recovery, cannot be liable for the offeror's post-offer fees. [*E.g.*, **Crossman v. Marcoccio,** 806 F.2d 329, 333–34 (1st Cir. 1986)]

f. No Mooting of Offeree's Claim by Non-Acceptance of Full-Satisfaction Rule 68 Offer

A significant issue had been whether an unaccepted Rule 68 offer of all that or more than an offeree could legally gain in a judgment mooted the offeree's claim. Defendants, particularly in putative class actions involving small individual claims, had frequently made full-satisfaction Rule 68 offers to individual plaintiffs, then argued that the individual claims were moot so that the litigation could not proceed. The Supreme Court, relying on principles of contract law and Rule 68(b)'s language that an "unaccepted offer is considered withdrawn," has held that an unaccepted full-satisfaction Rule 68 offer does not moot either individual or putative class claims. [**Campbell-Ewald Co. v. Gomez,** 136 S. Ct. 663 (2016)] The Court left open the possibility that deposit of a full-satisfaction amount in an account payable to the plaintiff might lead to a different result. Lower courts have so far been holding that a plaintiff in that situation must still have a "fair opportunity to move for class certification." [*E.g.*, **Chen v. Allstate Ins. Co.,** 819 F.3d 1136 (9th Cir. 2016]

g. Other Key Features of Federal Rule 68

Four other significant features of Federal Rule 68 are (i) that successive offers are permissible; (ii) that it can apply in cases seeking other forms of relief than money damages; (iii) that it authorizes formal offers of damages after a judgment of liability; and (iv) that it is available only to parties defending against claims, not to claimants.

(1) Successive Offers Permissible

Rule 68(b) offsets its provision that an "unaccepted offer is considered withdrawn" with the specification that "it does not preclude a later offer."

(2) Rule 68 Offers in Cases Seeking Injunctive or Declaratory Relief

Offers under Federal Rule 68 are by far most common in cases seeking money damages. But it is well settled that such offers can be made in cases seeking injunctive or declaratory relief, and in cases seeking a mixture of damages and other forms of relief. Such offers can raise issues of how to compare an unaccepted offer to the relief obtained for purposes of Rule 68(d) cost-shifting when an offeree does not obtain a judgment more favorable than the offer.

(3) Rule 68 Offer of Damages After Judgment of Liability

Rule 68(c) covers situations in which "one party's liability to another has been determined but the extent of liability remains to be determined by further proceedings." Then, "the party held liable may make an offer of judgment" at least 14 days "before the date set for a hearing to determine the extent of liability."

(4) Availability Only to Parties Defending Against Claims

Only parties defending against claims may make offers under Federal Rule 68. That includes plaintiffs defending against counterclaims, parties defending against crossclaims, and parties defending against Rule 14 indemnity claims. But it means that parties in the status of claimants cannot make Rule 68 offers or demands. That apparent one-sidedness sometimes leads to criticism of Rule 68. But what Rule 68 mainly affects is entitlement to post-offer non-fee costs; prevailing claimants are already entitled to such costs under general American costs provisions, and Rule 68 affects only liability for post-offer costs when an offeree does not accept an offer and does not do better in the final judgment.

2. State Offer Rules and Their Applicability to State-Law Claims in Federal Court

Many states have offer statutes or rules that are similar to, or variants on, Federal Rule 68. Some such rules permit demands by plaintiffs with cost or fee consequences when a defendant does not do better in the final judgment than a formal demand by the plaintiff. The dominant trend in the federal cases is that such state rules do not apply on state-law claims in federal court to defending parties' offers, which are covered by Federal Rule 68, but that state rules on claimants' formal demands under state counterparts to the federal offer-of-judgment rule may apply. [*See, e.g.*, Cal. Code Civ. Proc. § 998—either party may make an offer, and failure to accept obligates a plaintiff who fails to obtain a better judgment must pay defendant's post-offer expert-witness costs]

D. The Federal Arbitration Act and Its Impact on Regulation of Arbitration

1. Introduction

In 1925, Congress adopted the Federal Arbitration Act (FAA) to counter what was then judicial hostility to private arbitration agreements. Such agreements took contract disputes away from courts and put them before arbitrators chosen by the parties, usually with little scope for judicial review of the arbitrators' decisions and little if any public openness about these private arbitration proceedings. Parties to such contracts were often seeking benefits such as speed, informality, low cost, and privacy.

2. Applicability of General Contract-Validity Provisions Under FAA

The FAA makes written arbitration provisions in contracts involving commerce "valid, irrevocable, and enforceable, save upon such grounds as exist at law or in equity for the revocation of *any* contract." [9 U.S.C. § 2 (emphasis added)] In other words, generally applicable law regulating contract validity can apply to arbitration provisions in contracts just as it can to other aspects of contracts, but is not to single out arbitration provisions for special treatment or disfavor.

3. Supreme Court Decisions on FAA Applicability

Beginning in the late 1970s, the Supreme Court decided several significant cases about the scope of the FAA and its impact on other state- or federal-law provisions bearing on the enforceability of arbitration agreements. These decisions have been especially significant as they have pertained not just to peer-to-peer situations (two businesses agreeing in advance to arbitrate rather than adjudicate a dispute that might arise from their dealings) but in contracts of adhesion requiring arbitration between the likes of consumers or employees and their service providers or employers.

Example: The FAA extends to most employment contracts. Hence when employers require employees to agree to arbitration provisions in their contracts of employment, the FAA preempts state law restricting such agreements. [**Circuit City Stores v. Adams,** 532 U.S. 105 2001)]

Example: A clause in an arbitration agreement requiring the arbitrator to determine any dispute relating to the enforceability of the agreement is valid, so that the arbitrator rather than a court rules on enforceability. [**Rent-a-Center, West, Inc. v. Jackson,** 561 U.S. 63 (2010)]

4. Decisions Affecting Class Arbitration

A significant recent development has been businesses' including in contracts of adhesion (like those of cable-TV or cell-phone services) of provisions not just requiring arbitration rather than court adjudication but specifying that arbitration cannot take the form of a class proceeding. When valid such provisions mean that the person claiming against the business, often with a small claim, may proceed only in what may be an uneconomical individual arbitration. Starting in 2010 the Supreme Court has decided several key cases concerning such agreements, often by close 5–4 votes with the late Justice Scalia in the majority.

Example: An arbitration panel may not require a party "to submit to class arbitration unless there is a contractual basis for concluding that the party *agreed* to do so." [**Stolt-Nielsen S.A. v. Animal Feeds Int'l Corp.,** 559 U.S. 662 (2010)]

5. *Concepcion* Decision

In its most important class-arbitration decision to date, the Supreme Court ruled that the FAA preempts state law holding waivers of class arbitration to be unconscionable. [**AT&T Mobility LLC v. Concepcion,** 563 U.S. 333 (2011)] Given the specification of individual arbitration in the contract, the majority viewed a change from individual to class arbitration proceedings as involving a departure from the chosen advantages of individual arbitration. The dissent viewed the relevant comparison differently, seeing the state law as impartially disfavoring waivers of class proceedings in both arbitration and court adjudication.

6. Supreme Court Decisions Since *Concepcion*

The Court has unanimously held that an arbitrator did not exceed his power by interpreting an arbitration agreement to allow class arbitration. [**Oxford Health Plans LLC v. Sutter,** 133 S. Ct. 2064 (2013)] But given *Concepcion*, businesses can validly draft arbitration agreements to exclude class arbitration.

After *Concepcion* dealt with state unconscionability law and class-arbitration waivers, a question remained whether some *federal*-law provisions might bar such waivers. The Supreme Court held, 5–3, that an arbitration agreement waiving class-wide arbitration in a credit-card arbitration clause did not impermissibly limit plaintiffs' ability to pursue their possible antitrust claims. [**American Express Co. v. Italian Colors Restaurant,** 133 S. Ct. 2304 (2013)]

The Kentucky courts, in light of state constitutional provisions on access to the courts and the right to a jury trial, required an explicit statement in a power of attorney that the person holding the power had authority to waive those rights of the principal. The Supreme Court held, 7-1, that this "clear-statement" rule disfavored arbitration agreements and was preempted by the FAA. [**Kindred Nursing Centers Limited Partnership v. Clark,** 137 S. Ct. ---- (2017)]

7. Leading Lower-Court Decision on State Unconscionability Law After *Concepcion*

The Supreme Court in *Concepcion* noted that the FAA permits arbitration agreements to be invalidated by "generally applicable contract defenses, such as fraud, duress, or unconscionability." The Eleventh Circuit has held that a state unconscionability provision can invalidate a one-sided cost- and fee-shifting provision in an arbitration agreement. [***In re* Checking Account Overdraft Litigation,** 685 F.3d 1269 (11th Cir. 2012)] But the court found the invalid provision severable so that the rest of the arbitration agreement could still be enforced.

Chapter Nine
Trial

Key Exam Issues

Because a variety of trial-related issues can arise on an exam, it is important to be alert to determine which ones are actually raised. Some that are particularly likely to arise are:

1. **Is There a Right to Jury Trial?**

    For a party to have a right to trial by jury, he must make a ***timely demand for jury trial***. Then the question whether there is a right to have the case submitted to a jury depends largely on the constitutional scope of that right. In federal court, it is important to focus on the following issues:

    a. **Equitable vs. Legal Relief**: In general, there is a right to jury trial when a party seeks "legal" relief—generally money damages—and there is no right to a jury trial when equitable relief is sought. Often, the ***historical test*** is used to determine whether the action should be deemed equitable—*i.e.*, by looking to how such an action would have been classified in England at the time of the adoption of the Seventh Amendment in 1791.

    b. **Statutory Rights to Sue**: When the right being asserted was created by statute, the question is usually whether it corresponds to rights asserted at law in the 18th century. When a new right analogous to a right asserted at law in 1791 is created, there is a right to jury trial if suit is in federal court, but Congress may assign initial adjudication to an administrative agency that does not provide a jury trial.

    c. **Actions Combining Legal and Equitable Claims**: Some suits may include both legal and equitable claims. In those cases, the ***sequence of decisionmaking*** is important—the common issues must be tried first to ensure a right to jury trial of those issues.

    d. **Equitable Proceedings Seeking Legal Relief**: Even if the historical origin of the form of proceeding lies in equity (as with interpleader or shareholder derivative actions), the ***nature of the underlying claim*** determines whether there is a right to jury trial. Juries are rarely used, however, in bankruptcy proceedings, which are historically equitable.

    e. **No Right to Jury Trial of Issues of Law**: Issues of law—such as construction of a patent—are determined by the court.

2. **Jury Selection**

    The method used to select prospective jurors may not systematically exclude people on religious, racial, ethnic, or political grounds. For any given jury, prospective jurors are subject to ***voir dire***, to ***challenges for cause*** when there is ground to suspect that they may not render a fair verdict, and to a limited number of ***peremptory challenges*** that need not be justified by cause.

3. **May a Party Obtain Judgment as a Matter of Law?**

    Formerly called directed verdict, in federal-court judgment as a matter of law permits a party to avoid having an issue or claim submitted to the jury.

    a. **Time for Motion**: In federal court, the motion can be made whenever the opposing party has been ***fully heard on the issue*** raised by the motion.

    b. **Standard for Decision**: Like a motion for summary judgment (*see* Chapter Seven), the question depends in part on which party has the ***burden of proof*** on the issue raised:

        (1) ***If the opposing party has the burden of proof***, the motion should be granted only if the opposing party (*i.e.*, the party who wants the issue submitted to the jury) has not

presented *substantial evidence* that would permit a jury reasonably to accept its position.

(2) *If the moving party has the burden of proof*, she must present such *compelling evidence* that no jury could reasonably fail to find in her favor.

c.   **Reserving Decision**: The judge may reserve decision on the motion until after the jury returns its verdict. Even if the court denies the motion, the moving party may renew the motion after an unfavorable jury verdict.

4.   Post-Verdict Motions

Ordinarily, the verdict winner will not want to make post-verdict motions, but the verdict loser often will. If such motions are on your exam, there are several issues to consider:

a.   **Renewed Motion for Judgment as a Matter of Law**: Providing that the verdict loser made a motion for judgment as a matter of law after the victorious party had been fully heard on the issue raised, it may renew the motion. The issue of the sufficiency of the evidence will usually be the same after the verdict as before it.

b.   **Motion for New Trial**: Either together with or instead of making a post-verdict motion for judgment as a matter of law, the verdict loser may move for a new trial. Several grounds exist for such motions:

(1) **Error in Evidence Rulings**: If the court erroneously admitted or excluded evidence during the trial, that may be a ground for granting a new trial. To preserve that ground, the moving party must have objected to the admitted evidence, or made an "offer of proof" with regard to the excluded evidence, during the trial.

(2) **Error in Instructions**: If the court made an error in instructing the jury, that is a ground for granting a new trial. To preserve that ground, the moving party must have *proposed a correct instruction or objected* to the instruction the court proposed to give.

(3) **Misconduct of Counsel**: If prevailing counsel engaged in serious misconduct during the trial, that misconduct may be a ground for granting a new trial if it appears to have *seriously prejudiced* the jury.

(4) **Error in the Verdict**: If the court has used *special verdicts* or a *general verdict accompanied by written questions*, the jury's responses may have been inconsistent. The court may direct the jury to return to deliberations to cure such an inconsistency if the inconsistency is called to the court's attention before the jury is discharged. Otherwise, the court may grant a new trial, but it will usually search for an interpretation of the verdict that permits entry of judgment.

(5) **Newly Discovered Evidence**: If the verdict loser can show that it now has *critically important* evidence that it *could not have obtained* in time to present at trial, that new evidence may justify granting a new trial. Courts are likely to focus on the importance of the evidence and scrutinize the moving party's justification for failing to obtain it earlier, an inquiry that can raise discovery issues (*see* Chapter Six).

(6) **Verdict Against the Weight of the Evidence**: Even if there was no demonstrable error in the conduct of the trial, the court may grant a new trial if it concludes that the verdict winner's evidence was so weak that entry of judgment based on the verdict would result in a *miscarriage of justice*. This standard is not as demanding as the standard for granting a post-verdict judgment as a matter of law, but is relatively close to that standard.

(7) **Excessive or Insufficient Verdict**: If the amount of damages awarded is either excessive or insufficient, that may be a ground for a new trial. In connection with

such a new trial, consider whether a ***partial new trial*** limited to determination of the damages could fairly be held. In addition, in cases of excessive damages consider whether ***remittitur*** would be appropriate. In some state courts (but not federal court), ***additur*** is permissible when the amount of damages is insufficient.

(8) **Harmfulness of Error**: Often, particularly with erroneous rulings on admission of evidence or objections to opposing counsel's conduct during trial, it may be difficult to demonstrate that harmful error occurred. Trials must be fair, but they need not be perfect; the party seeking a new trial must show that the matter raised on the post-trial motion was actually likely to have ***tainted the result***.

(9) **Conditional Ruling on New Trial if Judgment as a Matter of Law Granted**: In federal courts, when both judgment as a matter of law and new-trial motions are made, the district court is to make a conditional ruling on the new-trial motion even if it grants the motion for judgment as a matter of law (thereby making the new-trial issue moot unless that ruling is reversed on appeal).

A. Right to Trial by Jury

1. Source of Right

a. Federal Courts

(1) Federal Constitution

The Seventh Amendment to the United States Constitution provides: "In suits at common law, where the value in controversy shall exceed twenty dollars, the right of trial by the jury shall be preserved." This requirement applies to diversity cases regardless of whether there would have been a jury trial if the case had been in state court. [**Simler v. Connor,** 372 U.S. 221 (1963)]

(2) Legislation

In matters not covered by this constitutional provision, there may also be a statutory right to trial by jury when Congress has so provided.

b. State Courts

(1) No Federal Constitutional Right

Unlike many other Bill of Rights guarantees, the Seventh Amendment right to trial by jury in civil cases has not been held "incorporated" into the Due Process Clause of the Fourteenth Amendment. Hence, the federal Constitution does not assure such a right in state-court proceedings. [**Walker v. Sauvinet,** 92 U.S. 90 (1875); **Minneapolis & St. Louis Railroad v. Bombolis,** 241 U.S. 211 (1916) The Seventh Amendment remains inapplicable to civil cases in state court, although the Supreme Court has noted that the cases establishing this rule were decided long before the Court adopted its current "selective-incorporation" approach. [**McDonald v. City of Chicago,** 561 U.S. 742, 765 n.12 (2010)]

(2) Federal Legislation

However, there may be a federal right to a jury trial in state-court actions involving matters governed by federal law, when Congress has so provided.

Example: State-court civil action based on claims under Federal Employers Liability Act. [*See* **Dice v. Akron, Canton & Youngstown Railroad,** 342 U.S. 359 (1952)]

(3) State Constitutions

Also, most state constitutions have provisions similar to the Seventh Amendment that apply to civil actions in state courts. [*See, e.g.,* Cal. Const. art. 1, § 16]

2. Cases in Which Right Exists

a. Basic Historical Test

Because the Seventh Amendment and many state constitutional jury guarantees refer to "preserv[ing]" the right to a civil jury trial, a major factor in applying the guarantees is historical inquiry into practice at the time of their adoption. The right to jury trial existed in the English law courts but *not* in chancery, where the system of equity was administered. Accordingly, with a traditional type of claim a federal court will consider whether the claim is *"legal"* or *"equitable"* as such terms were understood in 1791 (the year in which the Seventh Amendment became effective). [**Dimick v. Schiedt,** 293 U.S. 474 (1934)]

(1) Jury Right After "Merger" of Law and Equity

With the abolition of separate law and equity court systems in the federal courts and nearly all states, the availability of a jury can no longer depend on the system in which a case is heard. Generally speaking (although with many qualifications), today if a claim would have gone before the law courts before merger, the constitutional jury right applies; if a claim would have been within equitable jurisdiction, there is no constitutional right to trial by jury.

(2) Criticism—Vague Distinction

The line between "law" and "equity" was somewhat vague and shifting, and depended on the evolution of early English court systems. The main distinction related to the *remedy* sought. *Equity* generally afforded remedies such as *injunctions* that imposed duties directly on the parties, subjecting them to contempt sanctions in the event of disobedience. *Law courts*, on the other hand, usually afforded *monetary damages* and other remedies (*e.g.*, ejectment, replevin) that could be enforced by court officers with or without the cooperation of the parties.

RIGHT EXISTS		NO RIGHT EXISTS
Tort action seeking money damages for personal injury	⟷	Tort action seeking injunction against defendant's misconduct
Contract claim seeking money damages for breach	⟷	Contract claim seeking specific performance
Property action seeking replevin or ejectment	⟷	Property action seeking foreclosure of a mortgage

GILBERT

b. Present Federal Standards for Right to Jury Trial

(1) Counterparts to Actions at Law—Right to Jury

Modern actions that are counterparts to actions at law, such as personal-injury damage claims or claims to recover damages for breach of contract, are triable to a jury.

(2) Counterparts to Suits in Equity—No Right

However, there is no right to a jury in actions that are counterparts to suits in equity—*e.g.*, actions to foreclose mortgages, to enjoin misconduct, or for specific performance of a contract.

(3) Statutory Remedies

With types of claims that existed when a constitutional guarantee was adopted, the historical inquiry is usually easy and determinative. Legislatures, however, regularly redefine common-law rights, replace traditional claims with new forms, and create novel statutory rights. A simple historical test usually cannot resolve the jury-right question in such cases, although historical analogies to traditional claims remain a significant factor.

(a) Statutory Substitutes for Actions at Law

Legislation cannot impair the right to jury trial in federal court when the right and remedy afforded fit the historical pattern of a judicial proceeding at law.

e.g. **Example**: An action to evict a tenant for nonpayment of rent is triable to a jury, even when legislation has substituted a statutory remedy for the old common-law remedy of ejectment. [**Pernell v. Southall Realty,** 416 U.S. 363 (1974)]

e.g. **Example**: Suits by bankruptcy trustees to recover fraudulent conveyances from parties who had not submitted claims against the bankruptcy estate are "quintessentially suits at common law," and Congress could not remove the right to jury trial by assigning jurisdiction over such actions to bankruptcy courts. [**Granfinanciera, S.A. v. Nordberg,** 492 U.S. 33 (1989)]

1) Note

Federal bankruptcy judges (who lack Article III status) may conduct jury trials in proceedings within their authority, but only if they are "specially designated to exercise such jurisdiction by the district court and with the express consent of all the parties." [28 U.S.C. § 157(e)]

2) But Note

Proceedings under the federal Bankruptcy Code are mostly equitable, and a creditor who files a claim against the bankruptcy estate submits to the jurisdiction of the bankruptcy court. Such a creditor cannot insist on a jury trial should the trustee assert a claim to recover a preferential transfer. [**Langenkamp v. Culp,** 498 U.S. 42 (1990)]

(b) When "New Right" Involved

Congress may provide for nonjury trials when the right to be enforced is one *not known* at common law and practical considerations justify withholding the right to a jury in order to assure efficient disposition, especially if initial adjudication and enforcement of the right are assigned to a *federal administrative agency* rather than an Article III court. When an action on a new statutory right that can be initiated in *federal court*, the approach in such cases requires examining "both the nature of the issues involved and the remedy sought." There is to be a comparison of the statutory action to 18th-century, pre-merger English actions, and an examination of whether the remedy sought is legal or equitable in nature. The second *remedial inquiry is more important*. [**Chauffeurs, Teamsters & Helpers Local 391 v. Terry,** 494 U.S. 558 (1990)]

Example: Congress could create new duties of employers regarding employee safety and assign disputes to an administrative agency with which a jury trial would be incompatible. [**Atlas Roofing Co. v. Occupational Safety & Health Review Commission,** 430 U.S. 442 (1977)]

Compare: Proceedings to enforce new statutory rights *in federal court* are triable to a jury when the *remedy* sought is a legal remedy, such as damages (*e.g.*, claims under federal copyright or civil rights statutes). [**City of Monterey v. Del Monte Dunes at Monterey, Ltd.,** 526 U.S. 687 (1999); **Feltner v. Columbia Pictures Television, Inc.,** 523 U.S. 340 (1998); **Curtis v. Loether,** 415 U.S. 189 (1974)] Similarly, an employee who seeks back wages for a union's alleged breach of its duty of fair representation has a Seventh Amendment right to trial by jury in federal court. [**Chauffeurs, Teamsters & Helpers Local 391 v. Terry,** *supra*]

1) Civil Penalty

When a statute provides a civil penalty for violation (*e.g.*, a certain amount per day of violation), that is sufficient to create a right to jury trial in an action for a civil penalty. [**Tull v. United States,** 481 U.S. 412 (1987)—action for civil penalties for violation of Clean Water Act]

2) Distinguish—Amount of Penalty

While holding that there is a right to jury trial *with regard to liability* for a civil penalty, the Supreme Court has held that there is no right to a jury trial on the *amount* of the penalty. [**Tull v. United States,** *supra*]

EXAM TIP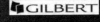

If you see a question on your exam in which Congress creates a new right enforceable in court and provides that a jury trial shall not be available, chances are good that your professor wants you to discuss the Seventh Amendment right to a jury trial. Remember that the right is preserved *only as it existed in the 18th century;* if an 18th century citizen would not have had a right to a jury trial for a similar action, then Congress doesn't have to provide one now. A good rule of thumb to determine whether a right to a jury would have existed in the 18th century is to *look at the remedy sought*. If it is payment of money damages, there probably would have been a right to a jury. If it was an injunction or order for specific performance, there probably would not have been that right.

(4) Actions for Declaratory Relief

Actions for declaratory judgments pose special problems because declaratory relief is a *statutorily created remedy* unknown to early English law or equity and thus neither legal nor equitable in nature. In general, the federal courts look to what the underlying nondeclaratory claim would have been and determine the jury right accordingly. [*See, e.g.,* **Terrell v. DeConna,** 877 F.2d 1267 (5th Cir. 1989)—declaratory judgment plaintiff's insurance coverage claim if brought for nondeclaratory coercive relief would have been equitable garnishment action, so no jury trial right existed]

(a) But Note

Issues in declaratory-judgment actions will often be questions of law for the court rather than of fact for the trier of fact, so no jury right may exist, whether the action would be classified as legal or equitable.

(5) Punitive Damages

A jury's determination of the amount of punitive damages does not involve fact-finding within the Seventh Amendment. Accordingly, appellate review of a district court's determination that a punitive award is consistent with due process would not involve reexamination of a jury finding of fact forbidden by the Seventh Amendment. [**Cooper Industries, Inc. v. Leatherman Tool Group, Inc.,** 532 U.S. 424 (2001)]

3. Proceedings in Which Right to Jury Applies in Part

a. Actions Joining Legal and Equitable Claims

Determining whether the right to trial by jury exists on a *claim* may be only part of the problem, for some cases involve both legal and equitable claims (*e.g.,* a contract action in which a plaintiff seeks damages at law for past breach and an equitable order compelling future specific performance). In general, federal courts are to structure their proceedings to preserve a jury trial on issues common to the legal and equitable aspects of a case. [**Beacon Theatres, Inc. v. Westover,** 359 U.S. 500 (1959)] This is usually true even if the equitable aspects of the case predominate [**Dairy Queen, Inc. v. Wood,** 369 U.S. 469 (1962)], which entirely or virtually eliminates in federal court any modern effect of the old equitable "clean-up" doctrine that allowed nonjury disposition of minor legal matters in a mainly equitable case. However, the clean-up doctrine survives in some states.

EXAM TIP   **GILBERT**

Remember that in federal courts, the right to a jury trial is paramount. Thus, if some issues in a case are jury triable and others are not, a jury trial should be granted *for the jury-triable issues*, even if those issues are minor in comparison to the non-jury-triable issues. This is not true in many states, however, which follow the equitable clean-up doctrine. The doctrine allows an equity court (without a jury) to hear minor jury-triable issues that are tied up with a case that is predominantly equitable.

---

(1) Priority of Issues at Trial

It may make a great deal of difference which issues in a case are tried first, since adjudication of the issues raised by the equitable claim may render meaningless the claim for legal relief, or vice versa. For example, suppose the plaintiff sues for rescission of a contract for fraud, while the defendant countersues for damages for breach of the contract. If the court tries the rescission claim first and holds the contract unenforceable, it thereby disposes of any claim for damages by the defendant.

(a) State Practice

In state courts, the order of trial is usually within the *discretion* of the trial judge, who may order either the equitable or legal aspects tried first.

(b) Federal Practice

In federal courts, however, all issues affecting the claim for legal relief must ... arily be tried *first* to the jury. The possibility of irreparable harm to a party ... delay in granting an injunction can usually be handled by grant of *...locutory injunctive relief* (*i.e.*, a temporary restraining order ("TRO") or ...minary injunction), which requires only provisional findings that will not ... the jury or dispose formally of the legal claims.

> **Example**: The federal court was not to try equitable claims first in an antitrust case involving a complaint for declaratory judgment and ...nction, and a counterclaim and crossclaim for antitrust treble damages, ...n final determination of common issues between the legal and equitable ...ects of the case might prevent the jury trial of the counterclaim and ...ssclaim. [*See* **Beacon Theatres v. Westover,** *supra*]

Erroneous Dismissal of Legal Claims

The Seventh Amendment bars giving preclusive effect to a district court's determinations of issues common to legal and equitable claims when the court resolves the equitable claims first solely because it wrongly dismissed the legal claims. [**Lytle v. Household Manufacturing, Inc.,** 494 U.S. 545 (1990)]

b. Equitable Proceedings Seeking Legal Relief

One historical role of equity was to provide procedural mechanisms for the resolution of complex disputes. Thus interpleader, class actions, and shareholder derivative suits were "inventions" of equity. However, in determining the right to jury trial, federal practice now focuses on the *nature of the underlying claim* rather than the procedural mechanism by which the claim is to be adjudicated.

(1) Shareholder Actions

In a shareholder derivative action in federal court, there is a right to jury trial on all issues that would have been tried by jury if the claim had been brought by the corporation itself. [**Ross v. Bernhard,** 396 U.S. 531 (1970)]

(2) Interpleader

Similarly, an interpleader action would be triable to a jury when the underlying claims against the stakeholder would have been actions at law if brought by the interpleader claimants. [**Hyde Properties, Inc. v. McCoy,** 507 F.2d 301 (6th Cir. 1974)]

c. Issues of Law and Fact Bearing on Same Claim

Even when the right to trial by jury applies, some *issues* in a case may be questions of law for the judge while others are issues of fact for the jury. And if the issue of law is dispositive, the case is not decided by the jury. [**Markman v. Westview Instruments, Inc.,** 517 U.S. 370 (1996)—in a patent-infringement case, construction of the patent is a question of law for the judge and may result in judgment as a matter of law against the patent holder, even though whether infringement occurred would be an issue of fact for the jury]

e.g. **Example**: In a trademark-infringement case, when the applicable legal standard requires a determination of an ordinary consumer's understanding of what the mark conveys, that determination is for the jury. Because the legal test relies on "an ordinary consumer's understanding of the impression that a mark conveys" it falls "within the ken of a jury." [**Hana Financial, Inc. v. Hana Bank,** 135 S. Ct. 907 (2015)]

4. Right to Jury Trial Depends on Timely Demand

Various rules govern how the right to jury trial must be asserted. Failure to comply with these rules operates as a waiver of the constitutional right.

a. State Practice

In state-court proceedings, the right to jury trial usually must be exercised by a demand in writing at the time the case is set for trial. Otherwise, the right is waived.

(1) Note

If cases are set for trial by request of the parties (*e.g.*, in a motion for trial setting), the demand must be made as part of that request. Where cases are set for trial automatically by the court, the parties ordinarily have a limited period of time after receipt of the notice of trial setting within which to file the written demand for jury trial. [Cal. Civ. Proc. Code § 631]

(2) And Note

Frequently, a deposit of jury fees is required at the time of jury-trial demand. Failure to make the deposit likewise waives the right (although the other party may "pick up the tab" to preserve a jury trial).

b. Federal Practice

In federal actions when the right to jury trial applies, a party must demand a jury trial in writing with regard to any issue within 14 days of the service of the last pleading directed to that issue. [Fed. R. Civ. P. 38(b)] Ordinarily, parties include the demand as an addendum to their pleadings: "Plaintiff demands a trial by jury of all issues triable by jury herein."

e.g. **Example**: If Defendant's answer contains a counterclaim denominated as such, Plaintiff must file an answer to the counterclaim. [Fed. R. Civ. P. 7(a)] If the counterclaim and answer deal with issues as to which a jury trial is available, either party has until 14 days following the filing of Plaintiff's answer to demand a jury trial.

(1) Amended or Supplemental Pleadings

The filing of amended or supplemental pleadings does ***not*** revive the right to a jury trial if no demand was made when the original pleadings were filed (unless the amended or supplemental pleadings raise ***new issues*** that are triable to a jury).

(2) Withdrawal of Demand

Once a party has timely and properly demanded a jury, the case is to be tried to a jury unless all parties stipulate to trial to the court. [Fed. R. Civ. P. 39(a)]

5. Jury Trials Discretionary with Court

a. When Jury Previously Waived

The court may order a jury trial on any or all issues in a case in which the right has been waived (*e.g.*, by failure to make timely demand therefor). [Fed. R. Civ. P. 39(b)]

b. By Consent

Even when no right to a jury exists, the court may order a binding jury trial with the consent of both parties. [Fed. R. Civ. P. 39(c)]

c. Advisory Jury

And the judge may order a trial by jury to obtain an "advisory" verdict. [Fed. R. Civ. P. 39(c); *see* **Cutter Labs v. R.W. Ogle & Co.**, 151 Cal. App. 2d 410 (1957)]

B. Selection of the Jury

1. Summons of the Venire

Trial juries are selected from a larger panel of citizens, commonly known as the ***venire***. Prospective jurors are summoned by the court.

a. Historical Background on Selection

In earlier times, the clerk or jury commissioner selected veniremen by personal contact; the officer of the court was charged with identifying citizens of good repute to serve as jurors.

(1) The "Key Man"

Members of the clergy and other professional people known favorably to the clerk or commissioner would frequently be asked to serve as "key men" to identify appropriate prospective jurors.

(2) Talesmen

If the court was short of veniremen, the clerk or commissioner might go into the corridors of the courthouse for willing volunteers, known as "*talesmen*."

b. Constitutional Requirements

(1) Systematic Exclusion Prohibited

The systematic exclusion from jury panels of any religious, racial, ethnic, or political group is an unlawful denial of equal protection of the laws. [**Eubanks v. Louisiana,** 356 U.S. 584 (1957); *and see* Constitutional Law Summary]

(2) Cross Section Not Required

On the other hand, the Constitution does *not* require that juries be strictly representative. Jury service may be confined to persons meeting certain standards of education, intelligence, judgment, and character, as long as the standards are not administered in a discriminatory manner. [**Carter v. Jury Commission of Greene County,** 396 U.S. 320 (1970)]

(3) "Blue Ribbon" Juries

Neither does the Constitution proscribe the use of "blue ribbon" juries selected on the basis of special intelligence or experience to handle complicated cases. [**Fay v. New York,** 332 U.S. 261 (1947)]

c. Contemporary Selection Practice

(1) Federal Courts

(a) Local Plans

Jury-selection methods in federal courts now conform to plans promulgated by local district courts in conformity with national standards. [28 U.S.C. § 1863]

(b) Fair Cross Section Required

The national policy requires that juries be "selected at random from a fair cross section of the community." [28 U.S.C. § 1861]

(c) Use of Voter Registration Lists

Every district uses voter registration lists as the basic source from which potential jurors are summoned. Some districts supplement these lists when necessary to foster the national policy (above). [28 U.S.C. § 1863(b)(2)]

1) When Supplementation Required

The voter registration list *must* be supplemented if it underrepresents any group identified by race, color, religion, sex, national origin, or economic status. [28 U.S.C. §§ 1862, 1863(b)(2)]

(d) Challenge to Array

If the venire has not been selected in strict compliance with statute and the local plan, either party may challenge the array (the whole group of prospective jurors) and require that a new venire be summoned. [28 U.S.C. § 1867(c); *and see* **Thiel v. Southern Pacific Co.,** 328 U.S. 217 (1946)]

1) Single Nonrepresentative Panel

It is not a basis for challenging the array that a single panel or venire is not cross-sectional, as long as the *method* by which the group was selected is random.

2) Nonrepresentative System

However, if it can be shown that the system regularly produces panels or venires that are substantially nonrepresentative in the same way, that is an adequate basis for challenge.

(2) State Courts

Many state courts select juries in a manner similar to the federal system, others retain vestiges of the traditional practice, and some states continue the use of "blue ribbon" jury panels (*supra*).

2. Qualifications of Prospective Jurors

a. Exclusions

Statutes generally provide that certain classes of citizens shall be excluded from juries. Categories typically excluded include minors, felons, aliens, and illiterates. [28 U.S.C. § 1865; Cal. Civ. Proc. Code § 203]

b. Excuses

A prospective juror may be excused for good cause, such as extraordinary financial loss from service.

c. One-Day or One-Trial Service

Some courts are now summoning jurors to attend court for jury selection for only one day or to serve as a juror (if selected) for only one trial. Where this practice is used, exemptions and excuses are likely to be more sparingly recognized.

3. Number of Jurors Required

a. Typical Size of Venire

The venire usually consists of at least two or three times the number of persons who will be selected to serve as jurors.

b. Traditional Jury of Twelve

Common-law juries were composed of 12 members, and for some time it was assumed that this number was required in federal courts by the Seventh Amendment. [**Capital Traction Co. v. Hof,** 174 U.S. 1 (1899)]

c. Twelve Not Required by Sixth Amendment in Criminal Cases

The common-law requirement of 12 jurors has been held not to be required by the Sixth Amendment. [**Williams v. Florida,** 399 U.S. 78 (1970)—criminal case] However, the amendment requires at least six jurors in a criminal case. [**Ballew v. Georgia,** 435 U.S. 223 (1978)] [p. 378]

(1) Civil Cases

The minimum number of jurors required by the Seventh Amendment in federal-court civil cases has not been finally resolved. Local district rules providing for *six-member* juries in civil cases have been upheld—on the rationale that the outcome of the verdict is not likely to be affected substantially by the number of jurors (at least as between 12 and 6). [**Colgrove v. Battin,** 413 U.S. 149 (1973)]

(2) State Practice

Since the United States Constitution does not require states to provide jury trials at all, the number of jurors in state-court civil trials depends entirely on state law. Many states have long used juries with fewer than 12 members in civil cases, particularly when the amount in controversy is small.

d. Jury Size in Federal-Court Civil Cases

Federal Rule 48 provides that the court shall seat a jury of not fewer than 6 nor more than 12 jurors.

e. Appointment of Alternate Jurors

Traditionally, courts appointed alternate jurors in addition to regular jurors to provide for the possibility that a regular juror may be unable to serve for the full term of the trial. Alternates would sit through the trial, but would be excused before jury deliberations started unless needed to take the place of incapacitated or excused jurors. However, the institution of the alternate juror was abolished for federal courts. Instead, under Rule 48 the court may seat from 6 to 12 jurors, and may excuse some for good cause during trial or deliberations, as long as *at least six* remain (unless the parties agree otherwise).

EXAM TIP

If an exam question involves the number of jurors in a federal case, be sure to point out that the Constitution does ***not require a jury of 12***—juries of six have been upheld, and the Federal Rules provide for juries of between 6 and 12. Alternate jurors are no longer appointed; instead the court may excuse some jurors for good cause, as long as at least six remain.

---

4. Voir Dire Examination of Jurors

After the venire has been initially screened by the court to remove persons who should be excluded, exempted, or excused, the prospective jurors are generally subject to further interrogation about their possible biases. This examination is known as ***voir dire***.

a. Challenge for Cause

A party may challenge a prospective juror if it appears that the juror has a financial stake in the case or in similar litigation, if members of the juror's immediate family have such an interest, or if there is other sufficient reason to believe that the juror may be unable to render impartial service. [28 U.S.C. § 1866(c)] There is ***no limit*** to the number of challenges for cause.

b. Peremptory Challenge

Each "side" is also entitled to a limited number of challenges ***without*** a showing of cause—*i.e.*, a peremptory challenge. *Rationale*: The purpose of the peremptory challenge is to give each side the opportunity to act upon intimations of bias that may not be demonstrable or even rationally explainable. In this way, those persons most distrusted by either side are removed from the jury.

(1) Number in Federal Courts

In federal courts, each side is entitled to three peremptory challenges. [28 U.S.C. § 1870]

(2) Number in State Courts

The number of peremptory challenges allowed in state-court proceedings *varies*. In California, six challenges are allowed, with more permitted in multiparty litigation. [Cal. Civ. Proc. Code § 231(c)]

(3) Racial Grounds for Exercise

The equal-protection component of the Fifth Amendment Due Process Clause precludes a private party in federal civil litigation from using peremptory challenges to excuse potential jurors on grounds of their race. [**Edmonson v. Leesville Concrete Co.,** 500 U.S. 614 (1991)] The same rule would apply to state-court actions under the Fourteenth Amendment's Equal Protection Clause.

(4) Gender Grounds for Exercise

The Equal Protection Clause forbids use of peremptory strikes to remove jurors on the basis of their gender. [**J.E.B. v. Alabama ex rel. T.B.,** 511 U.S. 127(1994)]

c. Questioning by Court

In most jurisdictions, the judge may control the voir dire examination by asking all questions of the jurors. [**United States v. Cummings,** 400 F. Supp. 2d 822 (W.D. Pa. 2005)] However, the judge must ask all proper questions submitted by counsel, in order to enable them to make good use of their peremptory challenges. [**Butler v. City of Camden,** 352 F.3d 811 (3d Cir. 2003)]

(1) Limited to Grounds for Challenge for Cause

In most jurisdictions, the inquiry on voir dire examination of jurors is limited to grounds that might provide a basis for excusing jurors for cause. (*See supra*, p. 378.) In some jurisdictions, however, in criminal cases counsel may inquire into any matter that may bear on their exercise of peremptory challenges.

d. Questioning by Counsel

Some courts permit counsel to ask questions directly, and in some states (*e.g.*, Texas), counsel have a right to do so. In other states (*e.g.*, New York), the examination may be conducted by counsel outside the courtroom, with the judge called in only to rule on objections.

(1) Improper Questioning

It is not proper to use the voir dire examination to put before jurors comments or hypothetical evidence that would not be admissible at trial. If such questioning has been allowed, a new trial should be ordered.

e.g. **Example**: When Plaintiff is not allowed to offer proof of Defendant's insurance at trial, Plaintiff's counsel should not be allowed to interrogate prospective jurors about the subject of insurance.

(2) Tactic

Counsel may use the voir dire examination as an occasion to preview the case by asking prospective jurors whether they "could believe" proof of the sort described, or "could in good conscience award" damages of the amount or type being sought.

C. Disqualification of Judge

1. Grounds for Disqualification

The judge assigned to a trial proceeding may be disqualified if her impartiality might reasonably be questioned. Bases for disqualification would therefore include the following. [*See generally* 28 U.S.C. § 455; Cal. Civ. Proc. Code § 170.1]

a. Personal Bias

If the judge has a personal bias or personal prejudice concerning a party, she may be disqualified.

b. Personal Knowledge of the Facts

If the judge has personal knowledge of disputed evidentiary facts, she may be disqualified.

c. Previous Involvement as Lawyer

If the judge served as counsel in connection with the controversy, or a lawyer with whom she practiced so served during the period of their association, she may be disqualified.

d. Financial Interest

A judge may be disqualified if she knows that she, her spouse, or her minor child has a financial stake in the controversy or an interest that could be substantially affected by the outcome. In federal court, corporate parties must file a disclosure statement identifying any related corporations to assist in revealing such an interest. [Fed. R. Civ. P. 7.1]

e. Family Relationship

If the judge's spouse (or a relative of the judge or the judge's spouse) is a party, an officer of a party, or a lawyer for a party or is known to have a financial interest, or is likely to be a material witness, she may be disqualified.

f. Disqualification Must Be Based on Extrajudicial Matters

The judge's adverse reaction or hostility to the parties or the evidence generally as a result of presiding over the case is *not* a basis for disqualification. [**Liteky v. United States,** 510 U.S. 540 (1994)]

2. Duty of Judge

The judge has a duty to be informed about possible bases for disqualification and to disqualify herself on her own motion if adequate grounds for disqualification exist.

3. Procedure for Disqualification

a. Federal Practice

In federal court, a party seeking to disqualify a judge must do so by filing an affidavit of bias—*i.e.*, a sworn statement setting forth the facts that are the basis for disqualification. [28 U.S.C. § 144] Factual averments in such an affidavit are *not* open to challenge (except in a criminal proceeding to punish the affiant for perjury). If the facts set forth are legally sufficient to disqualify the judge, she ***must*** excuse herself and assign the case to another judge.

b. State Practice

State procedures vary greatly.

(1) Traditional Rule

Most states require an actual showing by affidavit of grounds for disqualification, as in federal practice.

(2) Peremptory Challenge

In some states, each party has an absolute right to disqualify ***one*** judge by filing, in a timely fashion, an affidavit that he believes he cannot obtain a fair trial before that judge. As to any subsequent judge, a party may make a motion to disqualify and is entitled to a hearing on the facts in front of still another judge, who must determine whether the second should be disqualified. [*See, e.g.*, Cal. Civ. Proc. Code § 170.6] However, this system has been criticized as permitting too free an attack on judges and as a source of delay.

EXAM TIP

It is important to remember that not only can a litigant seek to have jurors disqualified for bias or prejudice, a litigant can also seek to have a ***judge*** disqualified for these reasons as well. Some states give litigants an absolute right to disqualify one judge. Additionally, the judge should disqualify herself if she knows a reason why she should be disqualified. The federal courts require the party seeking disqualification to file an affidavit alleging bias, and the judge cannot challenge the accuracy (as opposed to the sufficiency) of the affidavit; she must excuse herself. The only protection against lying In such an affidavit is the threat of a perjury charge.

D. Order of Trial

1. Right to Speak First and Last

a. General Rule

Ordinarily, the party opening and closing each phase of a trial is the party who has the ***burden of proof*** with respect to the principal issues. This party usually will be the plaintiff—but it may be the defendant if the plaintiff's prima facie case has been established by the pleadings and pretrial order.

b. Discretion of Court

The decision to accord the right to speak first and last is ultimately one for the discretion of the trial judge. [Cal. Civ. Proc. Code § 607—court may order different order of presentation for "special reasons"]

2. Stages of Jury Trial

The usual sequence of a civil jury trial is as follows:

a. Opening statement of the plaintiff;

b. Opening statement of the defendant;

c. Presentation of direct evidence by the plaintiff, with cross-examination of each witness by the defendant, followed by redirect and recross examination (*the plaintiff rests*);

d. Presentation of direct evidence by the defendant, with cross-examination, redirect, and recross examination (*the defendant rests*);

e. Presentation of rebuttal evidence by the plaintiff;

f. Presentation of rebuttal evidence by the defendant;

g. Argument of the plaintiff to the jury;

h. Argument of the defendant to jury;

i. Final closing argument of the plaintiff to the jury;

j. Instructions to the jury by the judge;

k. Verdict of the jury.

3. Nonjury Trial

The order of a nonjury trial is essentially the same up to the point at which all evidence has been presented. Before the presentation of argument, or during argument, the parties may propose specific findings of fact and conclusions of law to the court. After the close of arguments, the judge will render the decision, which will take the form of specific findings of fact and conclusions of law. [Fed. R. Civ. P. 52(a)(1)]

E. Presentation of Evidence

1. Control over Presentation

Ordinarily, presentation of the evidence at trial is the responsibility of the parties and their counsel, subject to control by the court. [Fed. R. Evid. 611(a)] Even so, most jurisdictions acknowledge the discretionary power of the trial judge to call witnesses on his own motion. [*In re* **Eric A.**, 73 Cal. App. 4th 1390 (1999)]

2. Rules of Evidence

Proceedings in federal court are governed by the Federal Rules of Evidence. In some respects, these rules incorporate provisions of state law (*e.g.*, what privileges are recognized). Many states have adopted evidence rules that follow the Federal Rules. Some states, like California, have evidence codes, while others rely in varying degrees on common-law rules. (*See* detailed discussion in Evidence Summary.)

3. Objections and Exceptions

a. Failure to Object

Failure to object to the admission of an item of evidence generally waives the ground for objection.

b. Amendment by Proof

If no objection is made to evidence that goes beyond the pleadings or the pretrial order to raise new issues, the pleadings or the order will be treated as if they had been amended to allege the facts proved by the evidence admitted. [Fed. R. Civ. P. 15(b), 16; *and see supra*, pp. 198–200]

c. Exceptions Unnecessary

In modern practice, it is sufficient to state an objection to the admission of evidence and the basis for the objection. It is not necessary, in order to preserve the issue for appeal, to take exception to rulings on such objections. [Fed. R. Civ. P. 46]

4. Burden of Producing Evidence

The plaintiff must produce sufficient evidence tending to prove each element of the *prima facie* case. If the plaintiff fails to do so, the defendant is entitled to a dismissal or a judgment as a matter of law at the close of the plaintiff's evidence. Similarly, if a defense is to be considered by the trier of fact, the defendant must produce sufficient evidence tending to prove each element of the defense. *Note*: A party may be relieved of this burden by the adversary's admissions in pleadings, discovery proceedings, or at pretrial. (*See* Evidence Summary.)

5. Judicial Notice

It is unnecessary to plead or prove facts that are not subject to reasonable dispute; the court must take judicial notice of such facts. (*See* Evidence Summary.)

F. Pre-Verdict Motions

1. In General

At the close of proof, motions may be used to determine whether a party has carried the burden of producing evidence, *e.g.*, motion for judgment as a matter of law, for nonsuit, or for involuntary dismissal.

2. Jury Trial—Motion for Judgment as a Matter of Law (Directed Verdict)

In a jury trial, either party may move for judgment as a matter of law when the adversary has been fully heard with respect to the issue in question. [Fed. R. Civ. P. 50(a)] Some courts have developed acronyms for this motion. [*See, e.g.*, **Weese v. Schukman,** 98 F.3d 542 (10th Cir. 1996)—JML; **McKeel v. City of Pine Bluff,** 73 F.3d 207 (8th Cir. 1996)—JAML]

a. Terminology

Before Federal Rule 50(a) was amended in 1991, what is now called a "motion for judgment as a matter of law" was called a "motion for a directed verdict." *State courts* usually still refer to such a motion as a *"motion for directed verdict."*

b. Standard for Grant

The general standard for whether to grant a motion for judgment as a matter of law looks to whether there is a *legally sufficient evidentiary basis* on which the jury could find for the nonmoving party. The application of this standard depends on whether the moving party has the burden of proof on the issue raised.

(1) Moving Party with Burden of Proof

If the moving party has the burden of proof, judgment as a matter of law is appropriate only if the evidence favoring the moving party is of such *compelling strength* that the jury could not reasonably find for the opposing party. Accordingly, to defeat the motion it is sufficient that the jury could reasonably disbelieve the witnesses upon whom the moving party relies.

(a) State-Court View

In some states, a directed verdict cannot be entered if the movant has the burden of proof unless the facts are totally uncontroverted or the parties agree to them. [**Allstate Insurance Co. v. Miller,** 553 A.2d 1268 (Md. 1989)]

(2) Opposing Party with Burden

If the party moving for judgment as a matter of law does not have the burden of proof, the motion should be granted only if the opposing party has *no substantial evidence* to permit a jury reasonably to find in its favor.

(a) Scintilla Rule Contrasted

In some jurisdictions the "scintilla rule" still is invoked. Under this rule, a party with a scintilla of evidence would be allowed to have her case presented to the jury. The federal courts have rejected the scintilla rule. [**Galloway v. United States,** 319 U.S. 372 (1943)]

c. Case-by-Case Determination

The court's evaluation process must be made on a case-by-case basis, and discussion of given cases should involve careful examination of the facts presented and inferences from them. Consequently, it is difficult to present "rules" governing judgment as a matter of law. There are, however, several governing principles that are helpful in analysis, and these are discussed below.

(1) All Reasonable Inferences Indulged in Favor of Opposing Party

The court is to make all reasonable inferences in favor of the opposing party, and to view the evidence *in the light most favorable to that party*.

(2) Court May Not "Weigh" Evidence

The court is to determine whether there is a genuine issue to present to the jury; it may not choose between two versions of events and grant judgment as a matter of law to the party whose version seems more persuasive.

(a) Role of Speculation

Within limits, that the jury's decision will involve some speculation is not a ground for taking the case from the jury. If facts are in dispute or reasonable people may draw different inferences from the evidence, the jury may use speculation and conjecture to settle the dispute by choosing what seems to be the most reasonable inference. [**Lavender v. Kurn,** 327 U.S. 645 (1946)]

(b) "Equal Possibilities" Analysis

It is sometimes said that the case should be taken from the jury when the evidence presented on any essential fact by the party with the burden of proof shows only an equal possibility of the existence of that fact. [*See, e.g.,* **Pennsylvania Railroad v. Chamberlain,** 288 U.S. 333 (1933)] This analysis has been *rejected* in most jurisdictions, as long as there is some basis on which the jury could choose between conflicting versions of events.

(3) Evidence to Be Considered

(a) Only Opposing Party's Evidence

Some courts limit their examination to the evidence offered by the opposing party, at least when the opposing party has the burden of proof, and the courts may say that the moving party's evidence is irrelevant. [**Lavender v. Kurn,** *supra*—defendant's evidence was "irrelevant upon appeal, there being a reasonable basis in the record" to support the jury's verdict for plaintiff]

(b) All Evidence Presented in Light Most Favorable to Opposing Party

The *federal rule* is that the court should "review the record as a whole," but "it must disregard all evidence favorable to the moving party that the jury is not required to believe." [**Reeves v. Sanderson Plumbing Products, Inc.,** 530 U.S. 133 (2000)]

(4) Demeanor Evidence

The jury has observed the witnesses while testifying, and may draw conclusions about their truthfulness from their demeanor.

(a) Moving Party with Burden of Proof

If the moving party has the burden of proof and relies on witnesses whom the jury could disbelieve, it is not entitled to a judgment as a matter of law, even if there is no conflicting evidence offered. (*See supra*, p. 384.)

1) Possible Exception—Disinterested, Unimpeached Witness

The above rule may not apply if the witness relied upon is disinterested and has not been impeached. Under these circumstances, there may be no reasonable basis for disbelieving the witness. [*See* **Lundeen v. Cordner,** *supra*, p. 343]

e.g. **Example**: Plaintiff, the executor of Decedent's estate, sues Defendant, the executor of Driver's estate, to recover for Decedent's injuries in the head-on automobile collision in which both were killed. The physical evidence at the scene of the accident does not show who drove over the center line and caused the accident, but Plaintiff charges that Driver drove over the line and must prove this fact to collect. Plaintiff relies on the testimony of a highway patrol officer that she was driving behind Driver's car and observed Driver drive across the center line and collide with the car driven by Decedent. There are no other witnesses and no other evidence, and the officer is not impeached in any way. Plaintiff should be granted a judgment as a matter of law.

2) Opposing Party with Burden of Proof

Demeanor evidence, sometimes called *disbelief evidence*, is not sufficient to satisfy the opposing party's burden of producing evidence. [**Dyer v. MacDougall,** *supra*, p. 335]

(5) Distinguish—Renewed Motion for Judgment as a Matter of Law (Judgment N.O.V.)

If a motion for judgment as a matter of law is made before a verdict is rendered but is denied and the verdict goes against the moving party, the party may make a "renewed motion for judgment as a matter of law" (formerly called a judgment n.o.v.). (*See infra*, pp. 400–401.) Whether resolved before or after the verdict, the motion uses the *same standard* and thus asks the same question at different times— whether the case should be (or should have been) submitted to the jury.

(a) Pre-Verdict Motion as Predicate for Renewed Motion

In federal court, a party may not make a renewed motion unless she moved for a judgment as a matter of law after the opposing party was *fully heard on an issue* and before submission of the case to the jury. [Fed. R. Civ. P. 50(b)]

1) Constitutional Justification

This requirement of a pre-verdict motion is a result of the Supreme Court's early decision that judgment n.o.v. violated the right to jury trial [**Slocum v. New York Life Insurance Co.,** 228 U.S. 364 (1913)], which the Court modified to permit a renewed motion if there was first a directed-verdict motion on which the judge "reserved" ruling. [**Baltimore & Carolina Line v. Redman,** 295 U.S. 654 (1935)] Thus, Rule 50(b) states that whenever there is a motion for judgment as a matter of law, to satisfy *Redman* the judge will be deemed to have reserved later ruling on it.

2) Opportunity to Cure Deficiencies in Proof

Some argue that the requirement of a predicate motion for judgment as a matter of law permits parties to cure omissions from their proof before the case is submitted to the jury, and that there is good reason to give parties an incentive to call such problems to the attention of the other side.

3) Timing of Motion

Until it was amended in 2006, Rule 50(b) permitted a post-verdict motion for judgment as a matter of law only if the moving party made such a motion before the verdict "at the close of all the evidence." The rule now requires only that the pre-verdict motion be made after the opposing party has been *fully heard on the issue* raised by the motion, which may be much earlier in the trial, perhaps even before the opposing party has completed offering all its proof in the case.

(b) Deferring Decision Until After Verdict

Judges presented with motions for judgment as a matter of law may consider a variety of factors, including the following, in deciding whether to defer decision when they find the motions persuasive.

1) Jury Will Agree

If the judge feels that one side's case is so weak that judgment as a matter of law is proper, it is likely that the jury will also feel that way, and a jury verdict to that effect will be *harder to overturn on appeal*.

2) Judge May Be Wrong

If the judge grants judgment as a matter of law before jury verdict and is reversed on appeal, it will be necessary to hold a *second trial*, whereas the appellate court may be able to reinstate the jury verdict if it reverses a post-verdict decision to grant judgment as a matter of law, and avoid thereby the need for a retrial.

3) Time Savings

By granting a pre-verdict motion for judgment as a matter of law, the judge saves the time that would be needed for the rest of the trial. At a minimum, granting the motion can save the time required for closing arguments to the jury, the judge's instructions to the jury, and jury deliberations. But there may be even greater time savings, depending on when the motion is made. In federal court, the motion can be made when the opposing party has completed its proof on a given issue. For a motion by the defendant, this could be before the plaintiff has even finished its case in chief; granting the motion in such a case would avoid the time needed for the remainder of the plaintiff's case in chief, for the defendant's case in chief, and for all rebuttal evidence.

3. Jury Trial—Motion for Nonsuit

In some states, the defendant may move for a nonsuit at the close of the plaintiff's opening statement (or at the close of plaintiff's proof).

a. Test Applied

Such a motion should be granted if the opening statement or proof reveals the plaintiff's case to be *legally insufficient*. For example, the plaintiff's failure to produce any credible evidence of damages might justify a nonsuit in a negligence case. [**Seivell v. Mines,** 116 A. 919 (Pa. 1922)]

b. Judgment on Merits

Historically, a judgment of nonsuit was not a judgment on the merits, and thus did not bar a new action on the same cause. [**Oscanyon v. Arms Co.,** 103 U.S. 261 (1880)] However, this rule has been changed in most states by legislation or court rule. [Cal. Civ. Proc. Code § 581c(c)]

4. Nonjury Trial—Motion for Judgment as a Matter of Law

In a nonjury trial, after any party has been fully heard with respect to an issue, the court may enter judgment as a matter of law against that party on that issue. [Fed. R. Civ. P. 52(c)]

a. Early Common-Law Treatment

The historical analogue to this motion was a ***demurrer to the evidence***, which required the trial judge to accept all of the plaintiff's evidence as true for the purpose of ruling on the demurrer.

b. State Practice

Nomenclature for this motion varies among the states. In some, it is referred to as a ***motion to dismiss;*** while in others it is a ***motion for judgment***. [Cal. Civ. Proc. Code § 631.8—motion for judgment]

c. Test Applied

In modern practice, the court may grant the motion if it finds that the plaintiff's proof is ***unpersuasive*** on issues as to which plaintiff had the burden of persuasion. [**Huber v. American President Lines,** 240 F.2d 778 (2d Cir. 1957)] The rationale is that, in a nonjury trial, the judge is the ultimate trier of fact; and if she is already convinced, there is no reason to require further proof by the defendant.

MOTION	GROUNDS	TIMING
MOTION FOR JUDGMENT AS A MATTER OF LAW	Evidence viewed in light most favorable to motion's opponent leads reasonable person to conclusion in favor of moving party	After opponent has presented case but before submission of case to jury
MOTION FOR NONSUIT	Opening statement or proof reveals plaintiff's case to be legally insufficient	At close of plaintiff's opening statement or proof

GILBERT

G. Argument to Jury

1. Time for Argument

In federal court and most state courts, counsel's argument to the jury takes place at the close of the evidence and *before* the judge instructs the jury (so that the last words the jurors hear are those of the judge, rather than the impassioned pleas of counsel). [Fed. R. Civ. P. 51]

2. Right to Argue

Counsel have an absolute right to argument in a jury trial. [**Nishihama v. City and County of San Francisco,** 93 Cal. App. 4th 298 (2001)]

3. Control of Argument by Court

However, the trial judge in his discretion may control the duration and manner of argument.

4. Limitations on Argument

In arguing to the jury, counsel is subject to the following constraints:

a. ***Comment must be based on the evidence***, and counsel may not distort the facts or assume facts not in evidence.

b. ***Argument must be within the limits of the substantive law*** governing the action. Thus, for example, counsel may not argue for the use of an improper method of calculating damages (*e.g.*, to "punish" a defendant in an ordinary negligence case).

c. ***Counsel may not appeal to the passions or prejudices of the jurors***. [**Pingatore v. Montgomery Ward & Co.**, 419 F.2d 1138 (6th Cir. 1969)] However, less restraint is imposed on counsel when the dispute is one fraught with emotion (such as a defamation trial). [**Curtis Publishing Co. v. Butts**, 351 F.2d 702 (5th Cir. 1965)]

5. Effect of Improper Argument

Not every improper argument requires a reversal of the judgment obtained and a new trial. A new trial is in order only if the argument is not adequately corrected by the judge, so that an incorrect verdict is likely to have resulted.

H. Instructions to Jury

1. In General

Before a case is submitted to the jury for a verdict, the trial judge instructs the jury on certain relevant matters.

2. Issues of Fact

The jury's role is to decide ***issues of fact*** identified by the judge in the instructions, whereas the judge must decide questions of law (such as the meaning of statutes and documents).

a. "Law" vs. "Fact"

Issues of law can be said to be general and to pertain to interpretation of the controlling law, while issues of fact are specific and pertain to past events. However, the boundary between the two may be unclear at times—in which case the matter must be resolved by reference to historic policy regarding the role of the jury.

e.g. **Example**: The law of negligence is usually expressed in general terms (*e.g.*, "a failure to exercise reasonable care") that minimize the role of the judge in defining the issues and maximize the role of the jury in deciding cases.

cf. **Compare**: If a decision necessarily requires that some additional meaning be attributed to the legal standard by the jury applying it, a law issue is inevitably intertwined with the fact issue, and such matters are sometimes said to present a ***mixed issue*** of law and fact. [*See* Wiener, *The Civil Jury Trial and the Law-Fact Distinction*, 54 Cal. L. Rev. 1867 (1966)]

b. Jury Decides *Disputed* Facts Only

There is an issue of fact for the jury only if there is a genuine dispute about past events or the interpretation of those events.

(1) Facts Not in Dispute

If only one reasonable inference can be drawn with respect to a matter, the judge should give instructions that *assume* the necessarily inferred fact. Thus, in a contract dispute in which a written contract is proved and the evidence presented by the defense bears only on the amount of damages, the court should not ask the jury to decide whether there was mutual assent.

(2) Disputed Facts

The judge may *not* give an instruction that assumes a fact in *dispute*. Each party is entitled to have the jury instructed to consider her version of matters that have been disputed. For example, if the defendant in a contract dispute offers proof tending to show that the defendant did not sign the written contract presented by the plaintiff, the court must put the issue of mutual assent to the jury, however much the judge may doubt the denial.

3. Burden of Persuasion

a. Assigning the Burden

The judge must explain to the jury which party has the burden of persuasion on each issue of fact that the jury must decide. The burden of persuasion will generally be assigned to the party having the burden of producing the evidence on that issue; but this may not be the case if there is an applicable legal *presumption*. (*See* Evidence Summary.)

b. Degree of Persuasion

(1) Preponderance of the Evidence

In a *civil* case, the trier of fact usually must be persuaded that a fact is more probable than not in order to resolve an issue in favor of the party bearing the burden of persuasion. [**Sullivan v. Nesbit,** 117 A. 502 (Conn. 1922)]

(2) Clear and Convincing Proof

In regard to issues of *fraud, duress, or undue influence*, however, the trier of fact generally is instructed to find for the party having the burden of persuasion only if the evidence is "clear and convincing." This rule evolved in equity, which was said to *presume* honesty and fair dealing, thus requiring a greater amount of evidence to overcome the presumption.

(a) Note—Rejected by Some Modern Courts

Some modern courts have rejected this principle, holding that a mere preponderance is sufficient with respect to *any* issue in a civil case. [**Weiner v. Fleishman,** 54 Cal. 3d 476 (1991)]

Students who have watched much television are probably very familiar with the standard of proof required in criminal cases—proof beyond a reasonable doubt. But TV shows usually give short shrift to the standard of proof *in civil cases*. If this issue comes up in an exam question, remember the general rule: The party with the burden of persuasion generally need only convince the trier of fact that his version of the facts is *more probable than not* (*i.e.*, just slightly more likely than any other version of the facts). For certain issues (*e.g.*, fraud, duress, or undue influence) some courts require a higher standard—*clear and convincing proof*—but even this higher civil standard is much lower than that standard required in criminal cases.

4. Comment on the Evidence

a. Majority Rule

In most courts, the judge may comment on the quality of proof bearing on issues that the jury must decide, provided she informs the jury that it is the final decisionmaker. [**Acevedo-Garcia v. Monroig,** 351 F.3d 547 (1st Cir. 2003); Cal. Const. art. VI, § 10]

b. Minority Rule

Some states do not permit *any* comment on the evidence, on the ground that a judge's comments are too likely to prejudice the jury.

5. Instructions Requested by Counsel

a. Responsibility for Preparation

While the ultimate responsibility for instructions rests with the judge, counsel has the duty of proposing instructions that present her theory of the case. [Fed. R. Civ. P. 51(a); **Willden v. Washington National Insurance Co.,** 18 Cal. 3d 631 (1976)]

b. Form of Requests

Proposed instructions must be *in writing* and must be *served* on opposing counsel.

c. Time for Filing

The Federal Rules provide that requests for instructions must be filed at the close of the evidence or at such earlier time as the court reasonably requires. [Fed. R. Civ. P. 51(a)] In a complex case, the judge often orders such proposals to be filed before trial (at the time of pretrial conference).

(1) State Practice May Vary

In California, for example, requests for instructions covering the legal issues raised by the pleadings must be filed before the first witness is sworn. [Cal. Civ. Proc. Code § 607a]

d. Objections

Each party must be given the opportunity to object to instructions proposed by his adversary. Failure to make objection before the jury retires is generally a waiver of any error not pointed out to the judge. [Fed. R. Civ. P. 51(c)(2)]

e. Notice to Counsel of Court's Action on Requests

Before counsel make their arguments to the jury, they are entitled to be informed of the judge's rulings on their requests for instructions. [Fed. R. Civ. P. 51(b)(1)] *Rationale*: Counsel need to know what the judge will say during instructions so that they can structure their closing arguments accordingly.

6. Appellate Review of Jury Instructions

a. Plain Error

Ordinarily, any error in the jury instructions is waived unless a timely objection was made in the trial court (*see* above). A federal trial or appellate court may, however, "consider a plain error in the instructions" that has not been preserved as required, if the error affects substantial rights. [Fed. R. Civ. P. 51(d)(2)]

b. Harmless Error

On the other hand, if it appears unlikely that the jury was misled by a minor error in instructions, the error may be deemed harmless. [Fed. R. Civ. P. 61; Cal. Civ. Proc. Code § 475] In applying this rule, the appellate court will consider the impact of the instructions as a whole. [**Marshall v. Ford Motor Co.,** 446 F.2d 712 (10th Cir. 1971)]

(1) Note

When alternative theories are advanced, the instructions given are correct as to one theory but incorrect as to the other, and the jury returns a *general verdict* (with no indication as to which theory was accepted), reversal is generally required, because there is no certainty that the error was harmless. [**Pacific Greyhound Lines v. Zane,** 160 F.2d 731 (9th Cir. 1947)]

(2) But Note

A minority of courts adheres to the principle that a jury should be presumed to have based its verdict on the correct portion of the instruction. [**State v. Hills,** 113 N.E. 1045 (Ohio 1916)]

I. Jury Deliberation and Verdict

1. Types of Verdicts

Verdicts may take several forms, depending on the form of jury instructions.

a. General Verdict

The traditional and still most common form of verdict is the general verdict, in which the jury makes a decision in favor of one party or the other, with amount of damages if claimant prevails. Such a verdict *implies* a finding in favor of the prevailing party *on every material issue of fact* submitted to the jury. [Cal. Civ. Proc. Code § 624]

> **e.g.** **Example**: In the typical negligence case, a general verdict for the plaintiff traditionally was thought to rest on findings that the defendant was negligent, that the negligence proximately caused harm to the plaintiff, and that the plaintiff was free of contributory negligence. [**Sassano v. Roullard,** 27 Cal. App. 2d 372 (1938)]

(1) Criticism

At the same time, a general verdict may conceal a misunderstanding of the instructions or even a disregard of them. It has been called "the great procedural opiate" because it "draws the curtain upon human errors and soothes us with the assurance we have attained the unattainable." [Sunderland, *Verdicts, General and Special*, 29 Yale L.J. 253 (1920)]

b. Special Verdict

A special verdict consists of the jury's **answers to specific factual questions** that it is instructed to decide. In this situation, the jury does not decide directly which party should prevail on the law. Instead, the special verdicts should resolve all the material issues so the court can enter judgment. [Fed. R. Civ. P. 49(a)(1); Cal. Civ. Proc. Code § 624]

(1) Verdicts Required on All Disputed Issues

To serve their purpose, special verdicts should usually be fashioned to cover **all disputed issues**, so that the judge can determine the proper judgment from them.

(2) Advantages

A special verdict reduces the burden on the judge of instructing the jury on the law and reduces the jury's need to understand the law.

(3) Disadvantages

If a special verdict is used, the jury may find it harder to reach a unanimous verdict. Moreover, **inconsistent** findings on crucial issues may necessitate a new trial. However, the court has the power to interpret the jury's findings in order to "mold" them to a judgment. [**Gallick v. Baltimore & Ohio Railroad,** 372 U.S. 108 (1963)]

(4) Disclosure to Counsel

Some courts hold that counsel should be given access to the special verdicts and an opportunity to comment on them. [**Sakamoto v. N.A.B. Trucking Co.,** 717 F.2d 1000 (6th Cir. 1983); **Clegg v. Hardware Mutual Casualty Co.,** 264 F.2d 152 (5th Cir. 1959)]

(5) Advising Jury of Legal Consequences of Answers

Since the judge is to draw the legal conclusions from the special verdicts, it is not required that the jury be instructed on them. However, the district court may decide to inform the jury. [**Beul v. ASSE International, Inc.,** 233 F.3d 441 (7th Cir. 2000)—it "would be difficult to conceive" that a judge's decision to provide a jury with legal information could constitute reversible error] *Rationale*: The jury is likely to deduce from the lawyers' arguments which party will be benefitted from a particular resolution of an issue, and so the judge should have the right to make it clear to the jury.

c. General Verdict with Written Questions

The trial judge may combine the two foregoing forms of verdict by instructing the jury to return a general decision as to which party should prevail, and simultaneously to answer specific questions of fact posed by the evidence. [Fed. R. Civ. P. 49(b)(1); Cal. Civ. Proc. Code § 625]

(1) Purpose

The idea of this combined form of verdict is to permit the jury to decide the whole case, while obtaining a "cross-check" that the jury understood and adhered to the instructions on the law.

(2) Disadvantage

Like special verdicts, the general verdict with written questions carries the risk of inconsistency necessitating a new trial.

(a) Inconsistency Between Finding and Verdict

If there is an inconsistency between the special findings and the general verdict, the judge in her discretion may disregard the general verdict and enter judgment according to the special findings. [Fed. R. Civ. P. 49(b)(3)(A); Cal. Civ. Proc. Code § 625]

(b) Inconsistency Among Findings

However, if there are inconsistencies among *several* of the special findings, the judge must order a new trial unless she can reconcile the inconsistencies. In doing so, there is a presumption in favor of the general verdict; and special findings should be reconciled so as to support the general verdict, if possible. [**Law v. Northern Assurance Co.,** 165 Cal. 394 (1913)]

(3) Failure to Respond

A jury's failure to respond to a written question is not necessarily fatal to the verdict. The court in its discretion may assume that the missing answer would be consistent with the general verdict. [**Gulf Refining Co. v. Fetschan,** 130 F.2d 129 (6th Cir. 1942)]

(4) Inability to Agree on an Issue

And even when the jurors announce their inability to agree on a particular issue, the verdict may be sustained if there is agreement on an alternative finding sufficient to support the general verdict (*e.g.,* jurors could not agree on which among several negligent acts by defendant caused plaintiff's injury, but agreed that one of those acts was responsible). [*But see* **Jazzabi v. Allstate Insurance Co.,** 278 F.3d 979 (9th Cir. 2002)—to hold defendant liable, jury must unanimously reject affirmative defense]

GENERAL	Jury simply makes a *decision in favor of one party*; judge must instruct jury on how to apply law to facts; no guarantee that jury acted properly when reaching its decision.
SPECIAL	Jury is to resolve *all disputed fact issues* so court may apply law to facts; can eliminate need for jury to understand law, but can also lead to inconsistent fact findings.
GENERAL VERDICT WITH WRITTEN QUESTIONS	Combination of the two above, with jury giving general verdict *and* answering specific fact questions so judge can cross-check that jury understood and adhered to the instructions and the law, although inconsistencies are still possible.

2. Requirement of Unanimity

a. General Rule

In federal and most state courts, the jury must render a unanimous decision, unless the parties otherwise agree. [Fed. R. Civ. P. 48]

(1) Purpose

This requirement forces the jurors to deliberate in any case in which one of the group has serious doubt about the outcome.

(2) "Dynamite Charge"

If the jurors, after deliberating, announce that they are unable to reach a verdict, it is not improper for the court to emphasize to the jury the expense of a new trial and the unlikelihood that another jury would reach a better verdict, and to ask each juror to make a renewed effort to reach unanimity. [**Allen v. United States,** 164 U.S. 492 (1896)] Such a charge is sometimes referred to as a "dynamite charge."

b. Minority Rule

Some states permit nonunanimous verdicts. In California, for example, only three-fourths of the jury in civil cases must concur. [Cal. Civ. Proc. Code § 618]

c. Tactic

The unanimity requirement generally favors the defense, at least insofar as the plaintiff has the burden of persuasion on the disputed issues. Thus, if nonunanimous verdicts are allowed in state court, the plaintiff may prefer to litigate there, whereas the defense may seek to remove to a federal court.

3. Jury Deliberation and Impeachment of Verdict

a. Standards of Jury Conduct

(1) Materials Taken into Jury Room

During its deliberations, a jury normally has access to exhibits or other papers received in evidence. [Cal. Civ. Proc. Code § 612] The judge may allow jurors to take notes during the trial, and such notes may also be used during deliberations.

(2) Consideration of Matters Outside the Record

The jury is not permitted to receive any information that was not presented at trial and made a part of the record.

(a) *Any communication from the judge* must be received in court in the *presence of counsel*. [Cal. Civ. Proc. Code § 614] For example, it is error for the judge to provide the jury with a dictionary in counsel's absence, when it appears that jurors may use the dictionary definition of important terms in arriving at their verdict. [**Palestroni v. Jacobs,** 77 A.2d 183 (N.J. 1950)]

(b) *It is improper for jurors to fraternize with counsel* during the trial or during deliberation.

(c) *And it is likewise improper for the jury to conduct its own investigation* of the facts by calling experts in the absence of counsel, conducting experiments with the exhibits, or independently taking a view of the premises of an accident. [**Sopp v. Smith,** 59 Cal. 2d 12 (1963)]

(3) Each Juror Shares in Decision

Consistent with the requirement of unanimity, each juror must make up her own mind on the verdict.

(a) Chance Verdicts

Accordingly, the jury may not decide by lot or other method of chance. [Cal. Civ. Proc. Code § 657(2)]

(b) Quotient Verdicts

Nor may the jury reach a decision by taking an average of several awards of the jurors. Such an average *may* be computed as a means of assisting each juror to appraise the appropriate award; but the jurors may not bind themselves in advance to the result of the computation. [*See* **McDonald v. Pless,** 238 U.S. 264 (1915)]

(c) Coercion by Judge

The judge may not coerce the jury to agree. In this regard, it may be reversible error, at least in a criminal case, to *repeat* a "dynamite charge" (*see supra*, p. 384) urging unanimity. [**United States v. Nickell,** 883 F.2d 824 (9th Cir. 1989)]

EXAM TIP   **GILBERT**

On your exam, don't snap at bait. The facts of a question might tell you that the jurors were deadlocked in a case. They all agreed on the defendant's liability, but each wanted to award the plaintiff a different amount. Eventually, the jury foreperson wrote down the 12 amounts, added them up, and divided the total by 12. She then asked the jurors if they all agreed to the quotient amount. They all agreed. An improper quotient verdict? *No!* That was a perfectly legitimate way for the jury to arrive at a damages figure. The verdict would have been an improper quotient verdict *if the jurors agreed beforehand* that they would add up the various amounts, divide by 12, and use the quotient as a verdict.

---

b. Impeachment of Verdict for Misconduct

(1) Common Law-Rule

The traditional common-law rule was that a juror could not impeach his own verdict. Thus, any misconduct in the deliberation had to be established by the testimony of someone *other than* the jurors, such as a bailiff or court attendant.

(a) Rationale

This rule safeguarded the secrecy of jury deliberations and protected jurors from harassment by counsel urging repudiation of verdicts. [*See* **McDonald v. Pless,** *supra*]

(b) Criticism

At the same time, the rule made enforcement of the standards of conduct described above very difficult.

(2) Federal Rule

The Federal Rules of Evidence now permit a juror to testify to any *"extraneous prejudicial information"* or *"outside influence"* that may have altered the verdict. [Fed. R. Evid. 606(b)]

(a) Scope

This rule does *not* authorize the use of juror testimony to attack the deliberative process (matters occurring *inside* the jury room), as by showing a quotient verdict. [*See* **Scogin v. Century Fitness, Inc.,** 780 F.2d 1316 (8th Cir. 1985)] It is possible, however, to use juror testimony to show gross misconduct, such as taking of a bribe or fraternizing with a party. [*See, e.g.,* **Jorgensen v. York Ice Machinery Corp.,** 160 F.2d 432 (2d Cir. 1947)]

Example—Use of Intoxicants: When jurors drank heavily during lunch, some smoked marijuana or took cocaine during the trial, and jurors generally approached their task as "one big party," juror affidavit was inadmissible to impeach the verdict on these grounds, because they were "internal" to the verdict. [**Tanner v. United States,** 483 U.S. 107 (1987)]

Example—Evidence of Juror Statements During Deliberations to Prove False Answer by Juror During Voir Dire: A juror affidavit asserting that, during deliberations in a case growing out of an auto accident, another juror made statements suggesting that she did not answer questions honestly during voir dire *could not be considered*. The challenge to the verdict on the ground that the juror answered falsely during voir dire involved an "inquiry into the validity of the verdict" within the exclusionary rule. The statements allegedly made—about an experience her daughter had after an auto accident—was not "extraneous" information but information of the sort jurors are expected to bring to the jury room. [**Warger v. Shauers,** 135 S. Ct. 521 (2014)]

But see: The Supreme Court has held that in a criminal case, the Sixth Amendment requires that impeachment be allowed for alleged juror reliance on expressed racial stereotypes or animus in deliberations to convict a defendant. [**Pena-Rodriguez v. Colorado,** 137 S. Ct. 855 (2017)]

(b) Distinguish—Determining What Was Decided for Issue-Preclusion Purposes

The rule of exclusion applies to challenges to the validity of a verdict, but does not forbid use of juror affidavits to determine what was actually decided in order to give proper issue-preclusion effect to the verdict. (For discussion of issue preclusion, see *infra*, p. 453 *et seq.*)

(3) State Rules

Some states are much more permissive than the federal courts with respect to use of juror testimony to attack verdicts. In California, for example, *any improper influence*—inside or outside the jury room—may be shown. [**People v. Hutchinson,** 71 Cal. 2d 342 (1969)]

e.g. **Example**: Juror testimony may be used to show that jurors were coerced to change their views or that improper consideration was given to the fact of insurance.

(a) Rationale

Assuring the "purity" of a verdict is more important than protecting its stability.

(b) Limitation

However, affidavits may not be used merely to show that a juror's reasoning or mental process was faulty.

EXAM TIP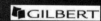

If an exam question poses the possibility of challenging a verdict for juror misconduct, remember that while some states are receptive to such challenges, other states and the federal courts will usually allow a juror to testify *only to extraneous* prejudicial information (*e.g.*, some jurors made a visit to the accident site and told the others about it). The juror may not testify to matters occurring inside the jury room. Thus, for example, even if jurors improperly entered a quotient verdict (*see supra*, p. 396), it could be difficult to have the verdict overturned on this ground because the jurors usually cannot testify to what went on in the jury room.

---

c. Impeachment of Verdict for Inaccurate Response on Voir Dire

A juror's failure to respond correctly to voir dire may be a ground for impeaching the verdict.

(1) Showing Required

The party challenging the verdict must show that the juror *refused to answer honestly* a material question and that a correct response would have *provided a valid basis for challenge* for cause. [**McDonough Power Equipment, Inc. v. Greenwood,** 464 U.S. 548 (1984)]

e.g. **Example**: A juror in a personal-injury case was asked whether any member of his family had suffered "injuries . . . that resulted in any disability or prolonged pain or suffering." He failed to reveal that his son had once been injured when a truck tire exploded, but because the juror honestly did not understand that describing this event was called for by the question, his failure to answer did not provide a ground to set aside the verdict. [**McDonough Power Equipment, Inc. v. Greenwood,** *supra*]

(2) Contempt

When a juror intentionally withholds disqualifying information, he may be held in contempt for doing so. [**Clark v. United States,** 289 U.S. 1 (1932)]

d. Announcement of Verdict

To help ensure that deliberations were proper, the jury verdict must be announced in open court.

(1) Polling the Jury

At the request of either party, the jury may be "polled"—*i.e.*, each juror may be asked if he concurred in the verdict. If a juror fails to concur, the jury must resume its deliberations or a new trial must be ordered. [**Fox v. United States,** 417 F.2d 84 (5th Cir. 1969)]

(2) Correction of Verdict

Likewise, if the verdict returned is insufficient or incomplete, the court may direct the jury to continue and complete its deliberations. [Cal. Civ. Proc. Code § 619]

(3) Effect of Discharge of Jury

Ordinarily, once the jury is discharged, it cannot be reassembled to cure a defect in the verdict. [**Mendoza v. Club Car, Inc.,** 81 Cal. App. 4th 287 (2000)] But federal judges have limited "inherent authority" in civil cases to recall a discharged jury to deliberate further. This power must be exercised "with restraint," taking into account the length of delay, whether jurors had spoken to anyone about the case, whether jurors witnessed emotional reactions to the verdict, and whether they had accessed their smartphones or the Internet. [**Dietz v. Bouldin,** 136 S. Ct. 1885 (2016)—jury recalled only a "few minutes" after discharge, when all jurors but one were still in the courthouse, the one juror had left only to retrieve a hotel receipt, and no juror had discussed the case with any nonjuror]

e. Investigation of Jury Misconduct

Counsel may sometimes question jurors after they have given their verdict to ascertain any possible bases for impeachment.

(1) Limitation

However, hostile interrogation of jurors may be enjoined [**Rakes v. United States,** 169 F.2d 739 (4th Cir. 1948)], and some courts routinely limit post-trial interrogation of jurors.

(2) And Note

Jurors cannot be subpoenaed unless there is some reason to expect that their testimony may reveal a ground for impeachment. The rationale is that jurors should not routinely be subject to being "placed on trial by defeated litigants." [**Linhart v. Nelson,** 18 Cal. 3d 641 (1976)]

J. Motions After Verdict or Judgment

1. Renewed Motion for Judgment as a Matter of Law (Judgment Notwithstanding the Verdict)

Judgment *non obstante veredicto* ("n.o.v." or "notwithstanding the verdict") is a traditional device for nullifying a jury verdict that is not supported by the evidence. In 1991, the name was changed in federal court to renewed motion for judgment as a matter of law. [Fed. R. Civ. P. 50(b)]

a. Test Applied

The standard applied for a renewed motion is the same as for such a motion at the close of all the evidence; *i.e.*, the motion should be granted only if there is *no substantial evidence to support the decision* of the jury. [**Montgomery Ward & Co. v. Duncan,** 311 U.S. 243 (1940)] (*See supra*, pp. 382–386, regarding standard on motion before the verdict.)

b. Procedural Requirements

(1) Motion

In federal court, a renewed motion for judgment as a matter of law may *not* be entered by the court on its own motion. If no motion is made, not even an appellate court has power to enter judgment for the losing party. [**Cone v. West Virginia Pulp & Paper Co.,** 330 U.S. 212 (1946)]

e.g. **Example**: When defendants moved unsuccessfully for summary judgment on qualified-immunity grounds but did not file a Rule 50(b) motion after losing at trial, the appellate court was powerless to review the sufficiency of the evidence on appeal. Defendants' argument that the immunity issues were "purely legal" did not change the result because the dispute was about the sufficiency of the evidence, not the substance or clarity of preexisting legal rights, which are often important to decisions on qualified immunity. [**Ortiz v. Jordan,** 562 U.S. 180 (2011)]

(a) Some States Contra

In at least some states, judgment n.o.v. *can* be entered *sua sponte*. [Cal. Civ. Proc. Code § 629]

(2) Timeliness of Motion

(a) Federal Rule

In federal court, a renewed motion for judgment as a matter of law must be made within 28 days after the entry of judgment on the verdict. [Fed. R. Civ. P. 50(b)]

(b) State Practice

Time limits in state practice may vary. [Cal. Civ. Proc. Code § 629—15 days following notice of entry of judgment]

(3) Prior Motion for Judgment as a Matter of Law

In federal court, a motion for renewed motion for judgment as a matter of law cannot be considered unless the moving party made a motion for judgment as a matter of law after the opposing party had been fully heard on the issue raised by the motion. [Fed. R. Civ. P. 50(b)]

(a) Rationale

Judgment n.o.v. was not known at common law, and hence presumably was forbidden by the Seventh Amendment. But a directed verdict *was* permitted at common law; and since the judge can reserve his ruling on that motion, a motion for judgment n.o.v. can be viewed as a renewal of the motion for a directed verdict. [**Baltimore & Carolina Line v. Redman,** *supra*, p. 386]

(b) Practice in Some States Contra

Some states do not require a prior motion for directed verdict in order to move for judgment n.o.v. [Cal. Civ. Proc. Code § 629]

(4) Joined with Motion for New Trial

A post-verdict motion for judgment as a matter of law may be joined with a motion for new trial.

(a) If Judgment Granted

If judgment as a matter of law is granted, the trial court should nevertheless rule in the alternative on the motion for new trial. In that way, if there is an appeal, the appellate court will have full knowledge of the trial judge's decision. [Fed. R. Civ. P. 50(c)(1)]

(b) If Judgment Denied

1) Appeal

The party whose motion is denied may appeal from the judgment as entered (but not from denial of the motion itself, which is a non-appealable order; *see infra*, p. 425 *et seq.*).

2) Responding Party's Ground for New Trial

If the moving party does appeal, the party seeking to preserve the verdict should assert in the alternative any grounds he may have for a new trial (*i.e.*, why the appellate court should stop short of ordering entry of judgment contrary to the verdict and order a new trial instead). Otherwise, the issues may not be preserved for consideration by the appellate court, which might reverse and order entry of judgment contrary to the verdict. [Fed. R. Civ. P. 50(e); *and see* **Neely v. Martin K. Eby Construction Co.,** 386 U.S. 317 (1967)]

3) Appellate Court May Enter Judgment for Verdict Loser

If a federal appellate court determines that some trial evidence was erroneously admitted and that the remaining evidence did not suffice to put the case before the jury, it may direct entry of judgment as a matter of law for the verdict loser. [**Weisgram v. Marley Co.,** 528 U.S. 440 (2000)]

2. Motion for New Trial

The trial judge has the power to order a new trial on all or part of the factual issues in dispute. [Fed. R. Civ. P. 59(a)(1); Cal. Civ. Proc. Code § 657]

a. Grounds for Motion—Jury Trial

A federal court may order a new trial in a jury case "for any reason for which a new trial has heretofore been granted in an action at law in federal court." [Fed. R. Civ. P. 59(a)(1)(A)] Some state statutes are more explicit in enumerating grounds. [Cal. Civ. Proc. Code § 657] In any case, appropriate grounds would include the following:

(1) Prejudicial Misconduct

A new trial may be granted if the court, the jury, or the adversary engaged in misconduct that prevented a fair trial.

Example: *Counsel's improper jury argument* was a basis for granting a new trial. [**Minneapolis, St. Paul & Sault Ste. Marie Railway v. Moquin,** 283 U.S. 520 (1931)]

Example: *A false answer by juror on voir dire examination* allowed for a new trial. [**Estate of Mesner,** 77 Cal. App. 2d 667 (1947)]

Example: *An improper delay* or continuance for personal convenience of the trial judge was also a basis for a new trial. [**Citron v. Aro Corp.,** 377 F.2d 750 (3d Cir. 1967)]

(a) No New Trial for Harmless Error

A new trial should not be ordered for misconduct that was not prejudicial or was adequately corrected by appropriate instructions from the judge. [Fed. R. Civ. P. 61]

(b) Waiver of Prejudicial Error

And a party moving for a new trial may not rely on misconduct known to him *before* the verdict, but which he did not point out to the court. *Rationale:* Allowing the party to gamble on the outcome of the verdict would impose an unfair risk on the adversary, who would face the alternative of an adverse verdict or a new trial. [**DeCato v. Goughnour,** 73 N.E.2d 1042 (Ohio 2000)]

(2) Accident or Surprise

A new trial may be granted when a party is unfairly surprised by the evidence presented at trial.

(a) Prejudicial Effect

The surprise must have had a *material* effect on the outcome of the trial. [**Dostal v. Curran,** 679 N.W.2d 192 (Minn. 2004)]

(b) Diligence

The party also must have been *diligent* in guarding against the surprise.

Example: A party who relies on a witness's promise to appear voluntarily and who fails to subpoena the witness is *not* entitled to a new trial when the witness fails to appear. [**Rudin v. Luman,** 53 Cal. App. 212 (1921)]

1) Incompetent Counsel

A party is charged with the mistake of his counsel, so that a new trial generally will *not* be granted on the ground that counsel was negligent or incompetent. [**Calarosa v. Stowell,** 32 S.W.3d 138 (Mo. Ct. App. 2000)]

(c) Timely Application

When surprise occurs, counsel must move for a mistrial or continuance at the earliest opportunity. [**Mitchell v. Mt. Hood Meadows,** 99 P.3d 748 (Or. 2004)]

(3) Newly Discovered Evidence

A new trial also may be granted to consider evidence discovered after the trial.

(a) Requirements

1) *The new proof must pertain to facts in existence at the time of trial*, not facts occurring later. [**Rivera Pomales v. Bridgestone Firestone, Inc.,** 224 F.R.D. 52 (D.P.R. 2004)]

2) *The new proof must be highly significant*, not merely cumulative. [**Willard v. Fairfield Southern Co.,** 472 F.3d 817 (11th Cir. 2006)]

3) *And the moving party must show* that the evidence *could not have been obtained by due diligence before trial.* [**Toledo Scale Co. v. Computering Scale Co.,** 261 U.S. 399 (1923)]

(b) But Note

A new trial should *not* be ordered when the "discovery" results from the failure of counsel earlier to appreciate the significance of available proof. [**Slemons v. Paterson,** 14 Cal. 2d 612 (1939)]

(c) And Note

Generally, "newly discovered evidence" is a *disfavored* ground for new trial; and parties should not withhold or fail to develop proof in hopes of getting a second chance at a favorable verdict. [**Estate of Emerson,** 170 Cal. 81 (1915)]

(4) Improper Evidence

A new trial may be granted to correct an erroneous ruling on the admissibility of evidence, provided the error was prejudicial and was the subject of timely objection.

(5) Verdict Contrary to Law

A new trial likewise may be granted if the evidence is *not legally sufficient* to support the verdict. An order granting a judgment n.o.v. may also be appropriate if the procedural requirements for such a motion were met. (*See supra*, p. 401.)

(6) Weight of the Evidence

Finally, a new trial may be ordered if the judge finds the verdict to be contrary to the manifest weight of the evidence. [**Aetna Casualty & Surety Co. v. Yeatts,** 122 F.2d 350 (4th Cir. 1941)]

(a) Standard for Decision

The standard for decision has been expressed in different ways. An underlying policy concern is that motions for new trials on this ground not undermine the right to jury trial; if the judge can invalidate a jury decision on the ground that she does not like it, the right to jury trial becomes insignificant.

1) Directed-Verdict Standard

Some courts phrase the standard in terms of whether there was substantial evidence to support the verdict—the directed-verdict standard. *Criticism*: This view seems overly narrow because the motion for new trial on this ground is intended as an additional safety valve in the jury system.

2) Thirteenth-Juror Standard

At the opposite extreme is the thirteenth-juror standard: The judge may grant a new trial whenever she disagrees with the jury. *Criticism*: This standard seems too easy to satisfy. It would constrict the right to jury trial because a litigant must persuade the judge, as well as the jury, in order to prevail.

3) Majority Rule—Miscarriage of Justice

Between the thirteenth-juror and directed-verdict standards is the standard applied by most courts—the miscarriage-of-justice standard. Under this standard, the judge is to ask whether the jury has reached a seriously erroneous result. In answering this question, she may weigh the evidence, assess the credibility of witnesses, and draw inferences from the evidence.

a) Possible Exception

It has been held that as to nontechnical matters, the court should not grant a new trial on the basis of *credibility determinations* because those are peculiarly within the province of the jury. [**Lind v. Schenley Industries, Inc.**, 278 F.2d 79 (3d Cir. 1960) (en banc)]

(b) Constitutionality

Because the motion for a new trial on this ground existed at common law, there has been no serious challenge to its constitutionality, even though it may seem to erode the value of the right to jury trial. [*See* **Galloway v. United States**, 319 U.S. 372 (1943)—discussing existence of motion for new trial at common law]

EXAM TIP

If the jury in an exam question reaches a result that seems to be at odds with the facts, be sure to consider discussing the possibility of moving for a new trial on the ground that the verdict was against the manifest weight of the evidence. Explain that such a motion should *not be granted lightly* because courts want to protect the jury-trial right. Nevertheless, if after assessing the credibility of witnesses and weighing the evidence, the judge believes the jury has reached a *seriously erroneous result* so that there has been a miscarriage of justice, a new trial may be ordered.

(c) Appellate Review

1) Traditional Rule

The traditional rule was that the weight of the evidence was to be assessed only by the trial judge—*i.e.*, whether he granted or denied a new trial on this ground, his decision ordinarily was not reversible. The trial judge's ruling would be reversed only if a new trial was denied and there was *no* substantial evidence to support the verdict—*i.e.*, if there should have been a directed verdict. [*See* **Portman v. American Home Products Corp.,** 201 F.2d 847 (2d Cir. 1953)]

2) Modern Rule

Today, appellate courts may reverse the grant of a motion for new trial if it is determined that granting the motion was an *"abuse of discretion."* This means that if the evidence was seriously arguable, the trial judge should not substitute his view of the evidence for that of the jury. [**Lind v. Schenley Industries, Inc.,** *supra*]

3) Review of Grant of New Trial

An order granting a new trial is *not immediately appealable* because it is not a final judgment. On appeal from the final judgment following the second trial, however, the appellant may claim error in the grant of the new trial. If the appellate court agrees, it can *reinstate the verdict* from the first trial, although this rarely happens.

4) Excessive or Inadequate Damages

The trial judge may find that the jury's award of damages is against the weight of the evidence. In such cases, a partial or conditional new trial may be ordered. (*See* discussion of remittitur and additur, *infra*, pp. 408–410.) Such rulings are generally reviewable only for abuse of discretion. State law on the standard for review of excessiveness or inadequacy of damage awards by the trial court, however, may supplant federal decisional law on that issue in state-law cases in federal court. [**Gasperini v. Center for Humanities, Inc.,** *supra*, p. 127]

GILBERT

A NEW TRIAL MAY BE GRANTED AFTER A JURY VERDICT ON THE FOLLOWING GROUNDS

☑ *Prejudicial misconduct* by the court, jury, or adversary, such as: *improper attorney argument to jury; false answer by juror* on voir dire; or *improper delay* or continuance for personal convenience of judge.

☑ *Incorrect rulings* during the trial *on admission or exclusion* of evidence.

☑ A party was *unfairly surprised* by evidence presented at trial that affected the outcome in a material way, despite the party's diligence in guarding against the surprise.

☑ *New evidence* is discovered that is highly significant, pertains to facts that existed at the time of trial, and could not have been obtained by due diligence before trial.

☑ Verdict was *contrary to law or weight of evidence*.

b. Grounds for Motion—Nonjury Trial

If the trial was conducted without a jury, a motion for new trial is essentially a motion for rehearing. Such a motion may be granted on the following grounds:

(1) *Newly discovered evidence;*

(2) *Erroneous findings of fact;* and/or

(3) *Error in the conduct of the trial* (*e.g.,* erroneous rulings on admissibility of evidence).

c. Procedural Requirements for New-Trial Motion

(1) Necessity for Motion

(a) Federal Rule

A federal court may grant a new trial on its own motion. [Fed. R. Civ. P. 59(d)] However, if the losing party does not make a post-verdict motion, and the district court does not grant a new trial on its own motion, the appellate court may not grant a new trial even though the losing party made a pre-verdict Rule 50(a) motion for judgment as a matter of law. [**Unitherm Food Systems, Inc. v. Swift-Eckrich, Inc.,** 546 U.S. 394 (2006)]

(b) State Courts

In some states, the court may order a new trial only on motion by a party. [Cal. Civ. Proc. Code § 659]

(2) Timeliness of Motion

(a) Federal Rule

In federal courts, a motion for new trial must be served within 28 days after entry of the judgment. [Fed. R. Civ. P. 59(b)]

(b) State Courts

State court time limits vary. In California, for example, the motion must be made within 15 days after notice of entry of the judgment. [Cal. Civ. Proc. Code § 659]

(3) Affidavits

A motion for new trial may be accompanied by affidavits if proof is necessary to establish the grounds.

(a) Time for Filing

In federal court, the movant's affidavits must be filed at the time of filing the motion. [Fed. R. Civ. P. 59(c)] State rules may allow later filing. [Cal. Civ. Proc. Code § 659a]

(b) No Oral Testimony

Most courts refuse to accept oral testimony in support of a motion for new trial. [**Linhart v. Nelson,** 18 Cal. 3d 641 (1976)]

(4) Hearings

A motion for new trial must be heard by the judge who conducted the trial, unless she is disabled.

(5) Time for Decision

There is no time limit for the judge's ruling on a motion for new trial, at least in federal practice.

(a) State Laws

Some state statutes impose a limit. [Cal. Civ. Proc. Code § 660—failure to grant motion within 60 days after filing operates as a denial]

d. Order

(1) In Nonjury Cases

In ruling on a motion for new trial in a nonjury case, the court may order a full retrial or only a *partial* new trial (*i.e.*, it may order the reopening of the judgment for the taking of additional proof, after which it may amend its findings of fact and conclusions of law or make new findings and conclusions and direct the entry of a new judgment). [Fed. R. Civ. P. 59(a)(2)]

(2) In Jury Cases

In a jury case, the court must grant or deny the motion, but it may do so in parts or on conditions (*e.g.*, new trial on damages only).

(a) Specification of Grounds

1) Federal Practice

A federal court need not specify the grounds on which new trial is granted.

2) State Practice

State rules on specifications of grounds vary. In California, if the ground is *insufficiency of the proof*, the judge must specify the respect in which the proof is deficient (and this specification is reviewable on appeal). [Cal. Civ. Proc. Code § 657]

(b) Excessive or Inadequate Damages

If the judge finds that the jury's damage award is inappropriate, there are several alternatives:

1) Full New Trial

The judge may order a full new trial. This would be the only appropriate order if the award is so excessive that the judge concludes that the verdict is the result of passion. [**New York Central Railroad v. Johnson,** 279 U.S. 310 (1929)]

2) Partial New Trial

As a *time-saving move*, the court may order that the new trial be limited to certain issues. However, such a limited new trial may be used only when "it clearly appears that the issue to be retried is so distinct and separable from the others that a trial of it alone may be had without injustice." [**Gasoline Products Co. v. Champlin Refining Co.,** 283 U.S. 494 (1931)]

e.g. **Example**: When the low verdict for Plaintiff indicates that it was a compromise verdict in which jurors who favored exonerating Defendant altogether went along with a low award to Plaintiff, a new trial limited to the issue of damages would be unfair to Defendant.

3) Conditional New Trial

a) Remittitur

A remittitur is an order for a new trial, not to be held if the plaintiff consents to *reduction* of the damage award. If the plaintiff so consents, a new trial is denied.

1/ Constitutional

Remittitur was recognized at common law and has been held consistent with the Seventh Amendment. [**Northern Pacific Railroad v. Herbert,** 116 U.S. 642 (1886)]

2/ Proper Sum

Courts vary in their approach to what is the proper sum for a remittitur.

a/ Fair Amount

Many courts hold that the verdict should be reduced to whatever amount the trial judge determines to be fair and reasonable (*i.e.*, her estimate of what a properly functioning jury would have found)—on the theory that this gives the plaintiff adequate incentive to avoid the costs and risks of a retrial. [**Powers v. Allstate Insurance Co.,** 102 N.W.2d 393 (Wis. 1960); Cal. Civ. Proc. Code § 662.5(b)]

b/ Lowest Amount

However, a few courts have reduced the verdict to the lowest amount that an impartial jury reasonably could have awarded—on the theory that this best protects the defendant from an improper award and that plaintiff can always protect himself by accepting a new trial. [**Meissner v. Papas,** 35 F. Supp. 676 (E.D. Wis. 1940)]

c/ Highest Amount

Still other courts reduce the verdict to the *highest* amount deemed not excessive—on the theory that the jury's verdict should be upheld insofar as possible. [**Gorsalitz v. Olin Mathieson Chemical Corp.,** 429 F.2d 1033 (5th Cir. 1970)]

d/ Note—Effect on Plaintiff's Election

Note that remittitur gives the plaintiff the choice whether to proceed to a new trial or accept a reduced award. Using the lowest-possible-award standard (p. 408, *supra*) signals to the plaintiff that this amount is the worst he can do at the second trial if he prevails on liability. Using the highest-possible-award standard (p. 408, *supra*) signals to the plaintiff that he cannot expect to do better at the new trial and keep that result. Thus, adoption of the highest-possible-award standard will be more likely to induce plaintiffs to accept remittitur than the lowest-possible-award standard.

3/ Waiver

If the plaintiff agrees to a remittitur, most courts hold that he waives the right to appeal the propriety of the remittitur (except that if the defendant thereafter appeals, the plaintiff may cross-appeal from the reduction of damages ordered by the trial judge). [**Donovan v. Penn Shipping Co.,** 429 U.S. 648 (1977)] *Exception*: It has been held that a plaintiff did not waive the right to appeal when a court reduced a punitive-damage award pursuant to a constitutionally mandated reduction in such damages, and the plaintiff did not have a choice between consenting to the reduction or going to a new trial. [**Johansen v. Combustion Engineering, Inc.,** 170 F.3d 1320 (11th Cir. 1999)]

4/ Appellate Court

A federal appellate court may review a district judge's denial of a motion seeking remittitur, but only for trial-court abuse of discretion in applying the governing standard. [**Gasperini v. Center for Humanities, Inc.,** *supra*, p. 405] State practice varies. For example, California Rule of Court 8.264(d) expressly recognizes remittitur and additur by appellate courts of the state.

a/ Constitutional Right to Retrial

In federal court, if the appellate court directs recalculation of damages due to excessiveness, the plaintiff has a right under the Seventh Amendment to reject the recalculated figures as too low and insist on a new trial. [**Hetzel v. Prince William County,** 523 U.S. 208 (1998)]

b) Additur

An additur is an order granting a new trial unless the defendant consents to an *increase* in the amount of the verdict.

1/ Federal Practice

Additur was not known at common law and has therefore been held forbidden in federal courts by the Seventh Amendment (*i.e.,* as violating the plaintiff's right to jury trial on the issue of damages.) [**Dimick v. Schiedt,** *supra*, p. 369] The modern Court has hinted, however, that it might be willing to rethink sympathetically the constitutionality of additur. [**Gasperini v. Center for Humanities, Inc.,** *supra*]

2/ State Practice

Many state statutes and constitutions allow additur as well as remittitur. [*See, e.g.,* Cal. Civ. Proc. Code § 662.5]

4) Entry of Reduced Judgment

Some jurisdictions limit the amount of punitive damages available in tort cases and give courts power to reduce excessive awards. In the special and limited circumstance of a constitutionally mandated reduction of excessive punitive damages, one circuit takes the view that a trial court may bypass the usual remittitur procedure of granting a conditional new trial if the plaintiff accepts a reduction in the damage award. Instead, the court may enter judgment for the amount of punitive damages it finds to be constitutionally permitted. [**Johansen v. Combustion Engineering, Inc.,** *supra*]

3. Motion to Alter or Amend Judgment

A motion to alter or amend judgment may be used to reopen judgments in both jury and nonjury cases. [Fed. R. Civ. P. 59(e); Cal. Civ. Proc. Code § 663]

a. Errors of Law Only

The purpose of the motion is to correct errors of law, and it cannot be used to secure a retrial on the facts.

Example: Vacating a judgment would be proper: when the judgment rests on *erroneous conclusions of law;* when *necessary conclusions of law were omitted;* or when the court *erroneously asserted jurisdiction.*

b. Time Limitations

A motion to alter or amend judgment is subject to the same time limits as a motion for new trial. [Fed. R. Civ. P. 59(e); Cal. Civ. Proc. Code § 663a; *see supra*, p. 406]

4. Motion for Relief from Judgment

a. For Clerical Mistakes

If the judgment as entered by the clerk differs from that ordered by the court, the mistake can be corrected. [Fed. R. Civ. P. 60(a); Cal. Civ. Proc. Code § 473(d)]

(1) Procedure

Corrections can be made on motion or *sua sponte.*

(2) Timing

There is no time limit on the power to correct.

(3) "Clerical" Mistake

Clerical mistakes subject to correction by this motion may be those of either clerk or counsel who drafted the order or judgment, but *not* those of the judge. Judicial errors should be attacked by a motion to alter or amend (above).

b. Other Grounds

The court likewise may relieve a party from judgment on the following grounds:

(1) Mistake, Inadvertence, or Surprise

A judgment may be reopened for these reasons, but the circumstances must be *extraordinary*. The standard of care to which the moving party is held is much higher than would be applied in a motion for new trial. [Fed. R. Civ. P. 60(b)(1); **Bershad v. McDonough,** 469 F.2d 1333 (7th Cir. 1972); Cal. Civ. Proc. Code § 473(b); **Martin v. Taylor,** 267 Cal. App. 2d 112 (1968)]

(2) Excusable Neglect

The court may reopen a default judgment for excusable neglect. However, gross negligence of counsel is *not* a sufficient ground for relief. [**Universal Film Exchanges, Inc. v. Lust,** 479 F.2d 573 (4th Cir. 1973)]

(3) Newly Discovered Evidence

The court may reopen a judgment to receive additional proof, but it must be shown that the moving party, by reasonable diligence, could not have discovered the new evidence in time to move for a new trial under Federal Rule 59. And the proof must be more than cumulative; *i.e.*, it is not enough that the moving party has now devised a new factual theory to explain the proof. [*See* **Stilwell v. Travelers Insurance Co.,** 327 F.2d 931 (5th Cir. 1964)] The standard is essentially the same as that used on a motion for a new trial on this ground. (*See supra*, p. 403.)

(4) Fraud or Misconduct

A judgment may be reopened for fraud or other misconduct (*e.g.*, a judgment obtained by the use of perjured testimony). [Fed. R. Civ. P. 60(b)(3); **Peacock Records, Inc. v. Checker Records, Inc.,** 365 F.2d 145 (7th Cir. 1966)]

(a) Burden on Party Guilty of Fraud

The responding party then has the burden of showing that the fraud did not affect the outcome. [**Hazel Atlas Glass Co. v. Hartford Empire Co.,** 322 U.S. 238 (1944)]

e.g. **Example**: When Defendant in a products-liability action failed to produce a document called for by an order compelling production of documents, its failure to do so constituted misconduct. Since production of the document might materially have affected Plaintiff's presentation of the case, judgment for Defendant was vacated. [**Rozier v. Ford Motor Co.,** 573 F.2d 1332 (5th Cir. 1978)]

(5) Void Judgment

A judgment may be reopened if it is void (as when no notice was given before the entry of a default). [**Bass v. Hoagland,** 172 F.2d 205 (5th Cir. 1949)]

However, a judgment can be set aside as void only in the rare instance when it is premised on jurisdictional error or a violation of due process that deprives a party of notice or the opportunity to be heard. [Fed. R. Civ. P. 60(b)(4); **United Student Aid Funds, Inc. v. Espinosa,** 559 U.S. 160 (2010)—bankruptcy court's discharge of student-loan debt could not be set aside as void on motion of creditor that was given prejudgment notice of possible loss of its rights and an opportunity to object, even though a statute required that such a debt be discharged by an adversary proceeding and there was no such proceeding; the bankruptcy court's lack of statutory authority to discharge in the absence of an adversary proceeding was not of the "jurisdictional" type that made its judgment void]

(6) Change of Circumstances (Equitable Relief)

When the judgment provides for continuing equitable relief, as when an injunction is granted, the court may reopen the proceedings to consider whether supervening events make the old decree inequitable. [Fed. R. Civ. P. 60(b)(5); **De Filippis v. United States,** 567 F.2d 341 (7th Cir. 1977)]

(a) Note

This ground is generally not applicable in the case of money judgments. [**Ryan v. United States Lines,** 303 F.2d 430 (2d Cir. 1962)]

(b) And Note

The parties may not contract to bar the court from considering the continuing equity of a decree; it is an abuse of discretion to refuse to modify a decree that no longer fairly serves its original purpose. [**System Federation No. 91, Railway Employees Department v. Wright,** 364 U.S. 642 (1961)]

(7) Relief Otherwise Justified

Under the Federal Rules, the court may also reopen a judgment for "any other reason that justifies relief." [Fed. R. Civ. P. 60(b)(6)] However, this rule has been *sparingly* applied, and the courts have frequently emphasized that it is *not* an alternative to appeal. [**Ackermann v. United States,** 340 U.S. 193 (1950)]

e.g. **Example**: Subsequent state-court interpretation of state law different from a federal court's interpretation of the same state law in a federal case that has become final is *not* by itself an extraordinary circumstance justifying relief under Federal Rule 60(b). [*See, e.g.,* **Kansas Public Employees Retirement System v. Reimer & Koger Associates,** 194 F.3d 922 (8th Cir. 1999)

(a) Exception

A federal court interpreted a state law differently from the way the state supreme court subsequently interpreted the same state law in a case involving another claimant injured in the *same accident* as the plaintiff in the federal case. The need to correct the federal court's erroneous interpretation of the state law in this exceptional circumstance was held sufficient to justify overriding the usual rule that mere error does not warrant disturbing a final judgment. [**Pierce v. Cook & Co.,** 518 F.2d 720 (10th Cir. 1975)]

c. Time Limits

(1) Federal Practice

A motion for relief from judgment must be made within a "reasonable" time. This cannot be more than one year from the entry of judgment if the ground asserted is mistake, inadvertence, surprise, excusable neglect, newly discovered evidence, or fraud. [Fed. R. Civ. P. 60(c)(1)]

(a) But Note

There is no fixed time limit when the ground is that the judgment is void or satisfied, or that there are "other reasons justifying relief" (*see* above).

(2) State Practice

Time limits in state courts vary. In California, the period is six months from the entry of judgment. [Cal. Civ. Proc. Code § 473(b)]

d. Distinguish: Independent Suit to Set Aside Judgment

A motion for relief from a judgment must be distinguished from an independent suit in equity based on similar grounds. The motion is addressed to the court that entered the judgment, whereas the independent suit may be filed in a different court. In addition, the grounds for an independent suit in equity tend to be narrower and more strictly scrutinized than those for a motion for relief from judgment. [**Lapin v. Shulton, Inc.,** 333 F.2d 169 (9th Cir. 1964)]

(1) Grounds for Independent Action

The two basic grounds for an independent equity suit for relief from judgment are:

(i) Jurisdictional defects; and

(ii) Fraud—as when a plaintiff was induced not to appear or contest the case by a false promise of settlement. [See **United States v. Throckmorton,** 98 U.S. 61 (1878); **Kulchar v. Kulchar,** 1 Cal. 3d 467 (1969)]

(a) Former Limitation

At one time, relief through an independent suit could be obtained only if the fraud was *extrinsic*, as distinguished from fraud such as perjury. However, this distinction has now been repudiated by most courts. [**Publicker v. Shallcross,** 106 F.2d 949 (3d Cir. 1939)]

(b) Modern Limitation

Relief from a federal-court judgment by an independent action is authorized only *"to prevent a grave miscarriage of justice."* [**United States v. Beggerly,** 524 U.S. 38 (1998)—alleged failure of adversary to search its records thoroughly and to make a full disclosure did not provide sufficient basis for vacating the judgment]

(2) State-Federal Relations

A federal court may refuse to entertain an independent action in equity to set aside a state-court judgment. [**Maicobo Investment Corp. v. von der Heide,** 243 F. Supp. 885 (D. Md. 1965)]

(3) Relation to Motion for Relief

Seeking relief by motion in the main action is ***not*** a prerequisite to the independent action. However, if such relief is still available in the main action, the equity court may choose not to act because there is an adequate direct remedy.

(a) Note

If the ground for relief asserted in the equity suit was previously presented to the court that entered judgment and was held insufficient to reopen the judgment, that decision has ***preclusive*** effect.

(4) Jurisdictional Basis

A federal court has subject-matter jurisdiction to entertain an independent action to set aside a federal-court judgment ***ancillary*** to its jurisdiction over the original action (*see supra*, pp. 90–91). [**United States v. Beggerly,** *supra*]

GILBERT

MOTION	CIRCUMSTANCES	TIMING
RENEWED MOTION FOR JUDGMENT AS A MATTER OF LAW	The verdict returned could not have been reached by reasonable jurors. Moving party must have previously sought judgment as a matter of law after verdict-winner fully heard on issue.	Within 28 days after entry of judgment.
MOTION FOR NEW TRIAL	Prejudicial misconduct, accident, surprise, newly discovered evidence, improper evidence, verdict contrary to law, verdict contrary to weight of the evidence.	**Federal**: No later than 28 days after entry of judgment. **State**: Timing varies among state courts.
MOTION TO ALTER OR AMEND JUDGMENT	Corrects errors of law.	**Federal**: No later than 28 days after entry of judgment. **State**: Timing varies among state courts.
MOTION FOR RELIEF FROM JUDGMENT	Clerical mistakes, mistake, inadvertence, surprise, excusable neglect, newly discovered evidence, fraud, misconduct, void judgment, change of circumstances, other reason justifying relief.	**Federal**: Within a reasonable time, but no more than one year from entry of judgment if the ground asserted is mistake, inadvertence, surprise, excusable neglect, newly discovered evidence, or fraud. **State**: Timing varies among state courts.

5. Coram Nobis

a. State Practice

In some states, the common-law writ of coram nobis is still available. The purpose of the writ is "to declare as false a fact previously determined to be true . . ."—as when a witness recants perjury, or evidence previously concealed by a party comes to light.

(1) Cautiously Applied

Writs of coram nobis are granted only if no other remedy is available and it is absolutely clear that the evidence involved was crucial to the outcome of the case. [**Rollins v. City and County of San Francisco,** 37 Cal. App. 3d 145 (1974)]

b. Federal Practice

In federal practice, the writ of coram nobis has been ***abolished***.

Chapter Ten
Appeal

CONTENTS	PAGE

Chapter Ten

Key Exam Issues

Procedural issues in connection with appeal mostly fall under one of two headings: appealability and reviewability. *Appealability* concerns whether the action of the lower court is one that permits the case to be taken to a court of appeals *at that point.* *Reviewability* deals with *what issues*, once a case is before an appellate court, the court may consider, and what *standard of review* (de novo or deferential) governs the appellate court's consideration of the trial court's rulings.

1. **Appealability**

   In most court systems, the main question is whether the lower court has entered a *final judgment*. If not, a decision is usually not appealable at that time.

   a. There are *exceptions* to the final-judgment rule permitting *interlocutory review*:

      (1) Has the lower court granted or denied a *preliminary injunction?*

      (2) Has the lower court *certified* a ruling for discretionary interlocutory review?

      (3) Has the lower court made a ruling that qualifies as a *collateral order?*

      (4) Is the order being appealed a grant or denial of a *class certification?*

      (5) Is there a basis for review by *extraordinary writ*, such as mandamus or prohibition (ordinarily for serious abuse of discretion by the trial court)?

2. **Reviewability**

   What may be considered by the appellate court depends on the issue involved:

   a. Was the objection *properly preserved* or was it *waived*, as by failure of counsel to make timely objection? If proper objection was not made, is there nonetheless *plain error?*

   b. Is the challenge to a ruling on a *question of law?* If so, review is *de novo*.

   c. Is the challenge to a *finding of fact?* If so, the appellate court will generally accord a degree of deference to the trier of fact.

   d. Is the action one committed to the *discretion of the trial judge?* If so, the trial court can usually be reversed *only* for abuse of discretion or failure to apply the correct legal standards.

   e. Was the alleged error one with *prejudicial effect*, or was it *harmless error?*

A. Right to Appeal

1. Appeal Reviews Lower-Court Rulings

An appeal is the usual procedure for obtaining review by a higher court. The function of the appeal is to assure that the litigation has been conducted in a proper manner and that judgment conforms to the law. An appeal ordinarily does not involve a retrial of the case in the higher court (except in some systems that allow for "appeal" of inferior-court decisions by providing trial de novo in a trial court of general jurisdiction), but rather is limited to a consideration of the rulings by the lower court in light of the record on which those rulings were made.

2. Status as Right

The right to appeal in civil matters is a creature of statute.

a. Common Law

There was no right to an appeal at common law. A *writ of error* could issue from a higher court, but was discretionary with that court.

b. Constitution

Similarly, the Due Process Clause does not guarantee a right of appeal—at least in civil cases. [**National Union of Marine Cooks v. Arnold,** 348 U.S. 37 (1954); **Cobbledick v. United States,** 309 U.S. 323 (1940)—"the right to a judgment from more than one court is a matter of grace and not a necessary ingredient of justice"]

c. Statutory Foundation of Right

(1) State Law

Legislation in every state creates a civil appellate jurisdiction in some court of the state.

(2) Federal Law

There is, likewise, a statutory right of appeal in civil proceedings in federal district court. [28 U.S.C. §§ 1291 *et seq.*]

3. Waiver of Right

The statutory right of appeal may be lost through any of the following:

a. *Express waiver*,

b. *Untimely assertion*;

c. *Voluntary compliance with judgment* (*e.g.*, a party who pays the amount of a judgment or performs the act ordered by a decree may be held to have waived the right to appeal). However, performance must be voluntary. When a judgment is executed by officers of the court and thereby satisfied, the judgment debtor's right of appeal survives [**Reitano v. Yankwich,** 38 Cal. 2d 1 (1951)]; and

d. *Acceptance of benefits*—when the plaintiff recovers a judgment and voluntarily accepts payment of the amount recovered, he may not thereafter appeal (*e.g.*, on the ground that the award was inadequate). [**Schubert v. Reich,** 36 Cal. 2d 298 (1950)]

B. Courts of Review

1. The Federal System

a. United States Courts of Appeals

There are 13 United States Courts of Appeals. Twelve have a territorial jurisdiction; in addition, the Federal Circuit, seated in Washington, D.C., has subject-matter appellate jurisdiction in patent cases and tort and contract claims against the United States. Appeals to the courts of appeals come from:

(1) District Courts

Most appeals from district-court decisions are taken to the courts of appeals.

(2) Administrative Agencies

Proceedings to review decisions by many federal administrative agencies must be taken to the courts of appeals. Some go to district courts.

b. Supreme Court of the United States

The Supreme Court has a limited original jurisdiction, as authorized by Article III of the Constitution. However, the Court performs primarily an appellate function, as follows:

(1) Direct Review of District Courts

There is a statutory right of appeal from a district-court decision *directly* to the Supreme Court when an act of Congress requires the case to be heard and determined by a *three-judge district court* (a rare thing) and the court *granted or denied injunctive relief*. [28 U.S.C. § 1253]

(2) Review of Courts of Appeals

Decisions of the United States Courts of Appeals may be reviewed by the Supreme Court as follows:

(a) By Certiorari

The Supreme Court may grant a writ of certiorari before or after judgment is entered (although review before final judgment is extremely rare). [28 U.S.C. § 1254(1)] The Court has *complete discretion* to deny review without explanation, and the denial has no precedent effect—it just means that the decision below stands.

(b) By Certification

A court of appeals may certify a question of law to the Supreme Court. [28 U.S.C. § 1254(2)] This route is used very rarely, the courts of appeals generally taking the view that they have the responsibility to decide issues of federal law themselves, without seeking the Supreme Court's assistance.

(3) Review of Decisions of State Courts

The Supreme Court may also review decisions of state courts by certiorari. [28 U.S.C. § 1257]

(a) Highest Possible State Court

The Supreme Court will not review a state-court decision while further review is still possible in the state-court system. Thus, the litigant seeking Supreme Court review must first exhaust state-court appeal procedures.

(b) Involving Federal Law

The Supreme Court can review a state-court decision only to the extent that it involves issues of federal law.

UNITED STATES SUPREME COURT—APPELLATE JURISDICTION

UNITED STATES SUPREME COURT
(also has limited original jurisdiction)

DIRECT REVIEW OF DISTRICT COURTS:

- When required by Congress to be heard by three-judge district court; and

- Lower court granted or denied injunctive relief.

REVIEW OF COURTS OF APPEALS:

- By certiorari, at the Court's discretion; or

- By certification from a court of appeals.

REVIEW OF STATE-COURT DECISIONS:

- State-court appeals must be exhausted; and

- Only issues of federal law.

GILBERT

(c) Distinguish—State-Law Issues

The Supreme Court has *no authority* to review state-court decisions on issues of state law. The state courts are the highest authorities on the meaning of state law, as long as state law does not infringe on matters protected by federal law.

EXAM TIP   **GILBERT**

Remember that while the Supreme Court can hear appeals from a state's highest court, it may take the appeal only to adjudicate *federal law*. Thus, if an exam question involves a state-law claim decided by the state's supreme court, your answer should not suggest that the decision can be appealed to the United States Supreme Court unless there is an argument that *federal law*, such as the Constitution, forbids the state court's reading of state law.

---

2. State Appellate Systems

There are substantial differences in the organization of court systems among the various states, and no particular structure can be regarded as typical.

a. New York

In New York, the principal *trial* court of general jurisdiction is called the Supreme Court.

(1) Appeals

There is an Appellate Division of the Supreme Court, which hears appeals of right from proceedings and orders of the trial courts. The Appellate Division is divided into four departments, each serving a different area of the state.

(2) Highest Court

The highest court is the Court of Appeals of New York. Appeals of right to this court may be taken in constitutional matters and pursuant to various statutes. In addition, the Court of Appeals has the power of discretionary review over many types of lower-court decisions.

b. California

In California, the trial court of general jurisdiction is the superior court, which also exercises appellate jurisdiction with regard to "limited civil cases," suits formerly heard by the municipal courts. [Cal. Code Civ. Proc. §§ 904.1, 904.2]

(1) Appeals

The courts of appeal, which are six in number, each serve a separate area of the state called a district. Three of the six are further divided into divisions. The courts of appeal hear all appeals of right from superior-court judgments, except that death-penalty cases go directly to the state supreme court.

(2) Highest Court

The Supreme Court of California exercises discretionary jurisdiction over proceedings in civil cases in the courts of appeal. Review in the supreme court may be granted on petition for review by a party or by the court on its own initiative.

(a) ***If a case is heard in the Supreme Court***, the decision of the court of appeal is vacated.

(b) ***The purpose of Supreme-Court review*** is to secure uniformity of decision among the courts of appeal or to settle important questions of law. [Cal. Rules of Court 8.500(b)]

c. Texas

The Texas courts of general civil jurisdiction are district courts.

(1) Appeals

Appeals from district courts in civil cases are taken to the courts of appeal, which are 14 in number, each serving a different area of the state and reviewing particular district courts, except that two courts of appeal review decisions from Houston district courts.

(2) Highest Court

Review of civil decisions of the courts of appeals is by the Supreme Court of Texas, which exercises civil jurisdiction only. (Criminal appeals go to the Court of Criminal Appeals, a court of last resort, directly from trial courts in capital cases and from the courts of appeals in other cases.)

d. Michigan

Michigan is typical of several states that have a unified intermediate court, the Court of Appeals, which is subject to review in the Supreme Court of Michigan.

e. South Dakota

South Dakota is typical of some less populous states that have only one appellate court, the supreme court, to which all appeals are taken.

C. Appellate Procedure

1. Filing of Appeal

An appeal is commenced by filing a ***notice of appeal***. The notice is filed in the appellate court or trial court, depending on the specific court rules. The notice of appeal is a ***written statement*** that the appellant invokes the jurisdiction of the appellate court to review a specified judgment from the court below. Formality in the notice is not essential; and the instrument will be ***liberally construed*** to prevent waiver. Indeed, under Federal Rule of Appellate Procedure 3(c)(4), which provides that an appeal "must not be dismissed for informality of form or title of the notice of appeal," a document meant as an appellate brief can qualify as the notice of appeal if it is filed within the time for filing notice and if it contains the information required in a notice of appeal. [**Smith v. Barry**, 502 U.S. 244 (1992)]

a. But Note—Need to Name All Appellants

However, if there are multiple appellants, each one must be named in the notice of appeal. An attorney representing multiple appellants may satisfy this requirement by using such terms as "all plaintiffs" or "the plaintiffs Alpha, Bravo, *et al.*," but it must be clear which parties intended to appeal. [Fed. R. App. P. 3(c)(1)(A)] Mere use of "Alpha *et al.*" will not suffice, and the lower court's judgment will be final as to the unspecified parties even if it is reversed as to those specified with adequate clarity. [*See* **Torres v. Oakland**

Scavenger Co., 487 U.S. 312 (1988)—when some of the 16 plaintiffs whose suit was dismissed for failure to state a claim were not named in the notice of appeal, they were bound by the dismissal even though the court of appeals reversed]

2. Time Limits

a. Federal Courts

In federal court, a notice of appeal in a civil case must be filed within 30 days after entry of judgment (or within 60 days, if the United States is a party). The trial judge may extend this period for not more than 30 days, upon a showing of excusable neglect. [Fed. R. App. P. 4]

(1) Premature Notice of Appeal

Under Federal Rule of Appellate Procedure 4(a)(2), a notice of appeal filed between announcement and entry of a judgment or order is treated as filed immediately after its entry. Under this rule, a premature notice of appeal ripens and becomes effective after eventual entry of judgment even if the notice is filed with respect to a ruling that is not appealable if the decision would have been appealable if followed immediately by entry of judgment, because the party filing the notice reasonably (though mistakenly) could have believed the decision to be final. [**FirsTier Mortgage Co. v. Investors Mortgage Insurance Co.,** 498 U.S. 269 (1990)]

b. State Practice

State time limits for noticing an appeal vary. In California, the notice must be filed within 60 days after notice of entry of judgment or 180 days after actual entry, whichever is later. The court has *no* power to extend the time. [Cal. Rules of Court 8.104(a)]

c. Limits Affect Jurisdiction

The time limits for an appeal are often jurisdictional and ordinarily cannot be waived.

e.g. **Example**: When the district court granted Petitioner's motion to extend the time to appeal denial of his habeas corpus petition, the judge mistakenly said in the order that Petitioner had two more days to file his appeal than he actually did. Petitioner filed his notice of appeal the day before the date specified by the judge, but that was one day after the actual due date; the appeal was dismissed because the time limit was jurisdictional. Even the judge's mistake could not excuse Petitioner's late filing. [**Bowles v. Russell,** 551 U.S. 205 (2007)]

3. Appeal Bonds

a. Costs

To perfect an appeal, the appellant generally must post a *bond* to secure the payment of his adversary's costs on appeal in case the judgment is affirmed. [Fed. R. App. P. 7]

(1) Possible Constitutional Limitation

In limited circumstances, due process and equal protection may forbid conditioning the right to appeal upon payment of charges such as record-preparation fees. [**M.L.B. v. S.L.J.,** 519 U.S. 102 (1996)—state that allows appeal from decision terminating parental rights may not deny right of appeal because of appellant's inability to pay a $2,300 record-preparation fee]

b. Supersedeas

If the appellant wishes to stay execution of the judgment pending appeal, he must usually assure that the judgment will be satisfied if it is ultimately affirmed. This assurance may be given in the form of a *supersedeas* bond, which is generally executed by a surety company. [Fed. R. App. P. 8]

(1) Possible Constitutional Limitations

There may be a constitutional requirement that it be possible to obtain a supersedeas bond. In **Pennzoil Co. v. Texaco, Inc.,** 481 U.S. 1 (1987), Texaco argued that the Texas requirement that it post such a bond to avoid execution of a judgment for more than $10 billion violated its due-process rights, because such a bond could not then be obtained. The Supreme Court held that the federal courts should not intervene in this matter, which should have been handled in the state courts.

4. Record on Appeal

Review on appeal is limited to proceedings in the trial court.

a. Clerk's Record

It is the duty of the clerk of the trial court to assemble and transmit the record on appeal, which will include the pleadings, motions, orders, verdict, and judgment in the case. [Fed. R. App. P. 11]

b. Reporter's Transcript

At the request of a party, the record may also include a transcription of the testimony at trial or such portions of the testimony that the party seeks to place before the appellate court. [Fed. R. App. P. 10]

5. Stay of Proceedings Below

The taking of an appeal ousts the trial court of jurisdiction. While the appeal is pending, the trial court generally has *no power* to alter or vacate its judgment and limited power to make any other order or decree affecting rights of the parties with respect to the case on appeal. [Cal. Civ. Pro. Code § 916(a)]

D. Rulings Subject to Appeal

1. Final-Decision Requirement

Generally speaking, only a final decision may be appealed.

a. General Rule

(1) At Common Law

At common law, a writ of error could be taken only from a "final" judgment—*i.e.,* a written order of the trial court, which stated the outcome of its proceedings and manifested that those proceedings were complete.

(a) Rationale

The purposes of the rule were:

1) To avoid the cost and delay of multiple appeals in the same action;

2) To avoid needless effort by appellate courts in considering issues that may be rendered moot by subsequent proceedings in the trial court; and

3) To avoid the demeaning effect on the status of the trial judge that results from excessive review of her decisions.

(2) Modern Practice

Today, the final-decision rule is the basic rule, but it is subject to exceptions.

(a) Federal Courts

Appeals to the United States Courts of Appeals may generally be taken only from final decisions of the district courts. [28 U.S.C. § 1291]

(b) State Courts

Similarly, all but a few states adhere to the final-decision requirement. The notable exception is New York, which includes trial-court actions "involv[ing] some part of the merits," or "affect[ing] a substantial right," among appealable orders. [N.Y. Civ. Prac. Law & Rules § 5701(a)(iv), –(v)]

(c) Separate-Instrument Rule

The final decision must also be embodied in a separate instrument that unequivocally manifests that the trial-court proceeding is complete and that a disposition has been made. [Fed. R. Civ. P. 58(a)]

(3) Unappealable Orders

As a result of the final-decision requirement, no immediate appeal may be taken from most orders of trial courts—including such important rulings as discovery orders, pretrial orders, orders denying summary judgment, and the like.

Example—Bankruptcy Court's Refusal to Confirm Plan Proposed by Debtor: A bankruptcy court's refusal to confirm a plan proposed by a debtor in a Chapter 13 proceeding was not an appealable order. Under the Bankruptcy Act, the debtor was free to propose a different plan. True, he could obtain review of the rejection of the first proposed plan by permitting dismissal of the bankruptcy proceeding. But allowing appeal without dismissal would mean that the automatic stay in bankruptcy would remain in effect, providing an incentive for taking appeals despite a low likelihood of success on appeal. Ordinarily trial courts rule correctly, and the cost of choosing between submitting a new plan and permitting dismissal would have to be borne by the debtor. [**Bullard v. Blue Hills Bank,** 135 S. Ct. 1686 (2015)]

(a) Orders After Judgment

1) Orders Granting New Trial

a) Federal Practice

An order granting a new trial is *not* appealable in the federal courts—the case must proceed to retrial and a new judgment before an appeal is allowed.

b) State Practice

In some states, an order granting a new trial *is* an appealable order. [Cal. Civ. Proc. Code § 904.1(a)(4)]

c) Review After Second Trial

In those jurisdictions when an order granting a new trial is not immediately appealable, the issue may be raised on appeal after final judgment in the second trial. If the appellate court finds that the grant of new trial was improper, it can order that the first judgment be reinstated.

2) Orders Denying New Trial

An order denying a new trial is not itself a final appealable order, but it leaves intact the final judgment from which an appeal can be taken.

3) Appealable Orders

An appeal may be taken from other orders made after judgment that have the effect of *vacating* the judgment or *staying* its execution.

(b) Extraordinary Review

In exceptional circumstances, unappealable orders may be reviewed by means of *extraordinary writs* (*see infra*, p. 439).

(c) Orders Not Immune from Review

That an order is not immediately appealable does not mean that it is immune from review. If a judgment adverse to the party aggrieved is later entered, an appeal from the judgment can contest the correctness of the previous unappealable order. As to some orders, such as discovery orders, it is unusual for an appellate court to find that they were sufficiently prejudicial to warrant reversal.

EXAM TIP  **GILBERT**

Remember that the basic rule in most jurisdictions is that appeals may be taken only from *final decisions*. Thus, most trial-court orders regarding pretrial matters, discovery, denial of summary judgment, etc., are not immediately appealable. This rule does not mean that the orders can never be reviewed; it means only that review must wait until the entire case can be reviewed.

---

b. "Jurisdictional" Character of Rule

The final-decision requirement is jurisdictional in the sense that it cannot be waived by the appellee. Thus, an appeal taken from an unappealable order will be dismissed by the appellate court *sua sponte*. [*In re* **Grand Jury Subpoenas Duces Tecum,** 85 F.3d 372 (8th Cir. 1996)]

2. Exceptions to Final-Decision Requirement

a. Partial Final Decisions

If multiple claims or parties are involved in the action, an order disposing of fewer than all of the claims ordinarily is not a final judgment and, hence, is not appealable until the remainder of the claims are disposed of. [Fed. R. Civ. P. 54(b)]

(1) Appeal at Discretion of Trial Court

However, if the trial judge finds that there is no just reason for delay, she may enter a partial final judgment, which is then appealable. [Fed. R. Civ. P. 54(b)] Generally, this power is exercised only when hardship would result if the appeal from the partial disposition were delayed. [**Cullen v. Margiotta,** 618 F.2d 226 (2d Cir. 1980)]

(2) State Practice

State rules often permit an appeal when the claims of a single party are severed and determined apart from the others. [Cal. Civ. Proc. Code § 579]

> **cf.** **Compare—Final Decision in One of a Group of Consolidated Cases**: A final judgment of dismissal in one of number of cases consolidated for combined pretrial management by the Judicial Panel on Multidistrict Litigation is immediately appealable although other consolidated cases remain pending before the district court. [**Gelboim v. Bank of America Corp.,** 135 S. Ct. 897 (2015)]

b. Review of Equitable Remedies

(1) In Chancery

The final-decision rule was not applied in early equity practice. One reason was that equity often issued personal orders to the parties which, if erroneous, might result in consequences that could not be corrected later by review. Therefore, immediate appellate review was permitted even as to "interlocutory" orders.

(2) Modern Statutory Exception

Modern practice generally preserves the right to interlocutory review of equitable remedies that are not final orders but that might result in irreparable consequences. Thus, 28 U.S.C. section 1292(a) provides the following *exceptions* to the final-decision requirement:

(a) Interlocutory orders *granting, modifying, refusing, etc., injunctions*;

(b) Orders *appointing receivers;*

(c) Decisions in *patent-infringement actions* that are final except for an *accounting;* and

(d) Certain orders in *admiralty proceedings.*

c. Ruling on Remand of Case Under Class Action Fairness Act

When a case is removed from state court to federal court under the Class Action Fairness Act (*see supra*, p. 67), an order granting or denying a motion to remand to state court may be reviewed if application for review is made to the court of appeals "not more than 10 days" after entry of the order. [28 U.S.C. § 1453(c)(1)]

d. Liability Determination in Removed Multiparty, Multiforum Cases

In cases removed from state court under the Multiparty, Multiforum Trial Jurisdiction Act (*see supra*, p. 67), if the district court issues an order determining liability and certifies its intention to remand to state court, an appeal may be taken within 60 days after that order is entered. [28 U.S.C. § 1441(e)(3)]

e. Discretionary Review

Interlocutory appeals may also be permitted by leave of court. Thus, 28 U.S.C. section 1292(b) permits an appeal if:

(i) *The trial court certifies* that a determination by the appellate court of a *controlling question of law* as to which there is *substantial ground for difference of opinion* would speed the ultimate resolution of the case; *and*

(ii) *The court of appeals grants leave to appeal.*

(1) Entirely Discretionary

The court of appeals may decline leave to appeal for *any* reason, including calendar congestion.

(2) Reexamination of Propriety of Certification by District Court

Some courts of appeals also feel bound to reexamine the determination of the district court that an immediate appeal is warranted under the statute. [*See, e.g.,* **Garner v. Wolfinbarger,** 433 F.2d 117 (5th Cir. 1970)]

(3) Rationale for Review

When the district court is genuinely uncertain about the correct interpretation of the law, and it would materially advance the conclusion of the litigation to have this uncertainty cleared up, deferring appellate review would not be desirable.

(4) Scope of Appellate Jurisdiction

Appellate jurisdiction extends to any question included within the order certified for review, and is not limited to the particular question formulated by the district judge. [**Yamaha Motor Corp. v. Calhoun,** 516 U.S. 199 (1996)]

f. Orders Regarding Class Certification

Interlocutory orders granting or denying class certification may be reviewed immediately if application for review is made within 14 days. [Fed. R. Civ. P. 23(f)] Although this provision resembles the discretionary review available under 28 U.S.C. section 1292(b) (*see supra*, p. 429), it differs in that *district-court certification is not required*. The appellate court has complete discretion to determine whether to accept the application for immediate review. [*See* **Blair v. Equifax Check Services, Inc.,** 181 F.3d 832 (7th Cir. 1999)—immediate appeal usually warranted only in cases in which (i) denial of class status is "death knell" of suit because the individual plaintiff's claim is very small, (ii) grant of class status raises the stakes so much that the defendant will feel pressure to settle, or (iii) an immediate appeal will clarify a fundamental issue of law; *and see* **Waste Management Holdings, Inc. v. Mowbray,** 208 F.3d 288 (1st Cir. 2000)—restricting third category to cases in which an immediate appeal will resolve an unsettled legal issue important to other cases and likely to escape appellate review if deferred until final judgment]

g. Collateral Orders

A qualification established by case law in the federal courts allows an immediate appeal from orders that are final with respect to certain "collateral" matters. [**Cohen v. Beneficial Industrial Loan Corp.,** 337 U.S. 541 (1949)] For a collateral matter to be reviewed, the following requirements must be met:

(1) Important Issue Completely Separate from the Merits

The issue resolved by the court's order must be an important one that is completely separate from the merits of the underlying case. *Rationale*: The proper time to review all decisions related to the merits is after final decision of the case, and unimportant matters do not justify circumvention of the finality requirement.

e.g. **Example—Requiring Derivative-Suit Plaintiff to Post Security for Expenses**: In a derivative action, the district court decided that federal rather than state law should apply to determine whether Plaintiff had to post a bond to secure Defendant's costs of litigation. This decision was appealable because it raised issues of choice between state and federal law, which were completely separate from the merits of Plaintiff's claims of misconduct by corporate officers. [**Cohen v. Beneficial Industrial Loan Corp.,** *supra*]

e.g. **Example—Involuntary Medication of Criminal Defendant to Render Him Competent to Stand Trial**: An order that Defendant, who was charged with fraud and attempted murder, be given anti-psychotic medication involuntarily could be appealed immediately. The issue raised—whether Defendant had a right to refuse medication—was important and completely separate from his guilt of the crimes charged, and the harm Defendant sought to avoid could not be undone by acquittal. [**Sell v. United States,** 539 U.S. 166 (2003)]

cf. **Compare—Order Refusing to Certify Class**: The decision whether to certify a class is closely tied up with the merits of the case, in the sense that the court must decide whether there are common questions of law and fact and whether the common questions predominate (in a Rule 23(b)(3) class action). Thus, the decision was not immediately appealable as a collateral order. [**Coopers & Lybrand v. Livesay,** 437 U.S. 463 (1978)] However, the subsequent adoption of Rule 23(f), permitting immediate review of class-certification orders in the discretion of the court of appeals (*see supra*, p. 429) provides a new avenue for review of such orders.

(2) Order Effectively Unreviewable on Appeal from Final Judgment

Early review should be allowed only if deferring review until entry of final judgment would effectively destroy the appellant's claimed rights.

(a) Illustration—Denial of Official Immunity

An order rejecting a government official's claim of immunity from suit could not be reviewed effectively on appeal from a final judgment because the immunity is designed to protect the defendant from having to stand trial. [**Osborne v. Haley,** 549 U.S. 225 (2007)—immunity is "a measure designed to immunize covered federal employees not just from liability, but from suit"; **Mitchell v. Forsyth,** 472 U.S. 511 (1985)]

1) But Note—Inapplicable to Denial Based on Finding of Sufficient Evidence

When a defendant seeks summary judgment based on a *fact-related* official-immunity defense asserting that the record shows insufficient evidence of a genuine issue for trial, as opposed to a *legal* basis, such as that given facts show no violation of clearly established law, denial of the motion is not appealable. [**Johnson v. Jones,** 515 U.S. 304 (1995)]

cf. **Compare**: When defendants move for summary judgment on qualified-immunity grounds and there is no significant dispute about the evidence, the motion presents a question of law and denial of the motion is immediately appealable. [**Plumhoff v. Rickard,** 134 S. Ct. 2012 (2014)—the record conclusively disproved plaintiffs' claim that a high-speed car chase was over before officers fired their weapons, so their use of deadly force was not unconstitutional]

2) Multiple Appeals Allowed

If a defendant's Rule 12 motion to dismiss based on official immunity is denied, he may appeal that ruling and then appeal a second time if the district court later denies a Rule 56 motion for summary judgment on immunity grounds. [**Behrens v. Pelletier,** 516 U.S. 299 (1996)]

3) Not Required in State Court

State courts need not follow the rule of **Mitchell v. Forsyth,** *supra*, and thus may decline to allow interlocutory review of denials of qualified immunity. [**Johnson v. Fankell,** 520 U.S. 911 (1997)—state provisions regarding appellate review did not confer right to immediate review of denial of official immunity]

4) Inapplicable to Judgment Bar in Tort-Claims Actions

The "judgment bar" that forbids suits against government agents after judgment is entered in the government's favor in an action under the Federal Tort Claims Act is not analogous to official immunity, and denial of such a defense does not qualify for immediate appellate review. [**Will v. Hallock,** 546 U.S. 345 (2006)]

(b) Illustration—Eleventh-Amendment Objection

An order rejecting a claim of immunity from suit under the Eleventh Amendment could not be effectively reviewed after final judgment because the value of the protection afforded by that amendment against suit in federal court would be lost if the litigation proceeded past the motion stage. [**Puerto Rico Aqueduct & Sewer Authority v. Metcalf & Eddy,** 506 U.S. 139 (1993)]

(c) Distinguish—Order Refusing to Disqualify Counsel

An order refusing to disqualify counsel for an alleged conflict of interest can be reviewed after trial is completed, at which time the actual course of events will permit a better judgment of whether there was a conflict. [**Firestone Tire & Rubber Co. v. Risjord,** 449 U.S. 368 (1981)—whether counsel sacrificed interests of his client to earn business from defendant's insurer]

(d) Distinguish—Refusal to Enforce Forum-Selection Clause

An order refusing to dismiss on the ground of a contractual forum-selection clause could be reviewed effectively after final judgment, because defendant objected only to defending in a particular place and not to having to defend at all. [**Lauro Lines, Inc. v. Chasser,** 490 U.S. 495 (1989)]

(e) Distinguish—Discovery Sanction Against Counsel

A Rule 37 discovery sanction against counsel will often be inextricably intertwined with the merits of the action because review would require assessment of the completeness of the discovery responses in question. Thus, such an order can be reviewed after final judgment. [**Cunningham v. Hamilton County,** 527 U.S. 198 (1999)]

(3) Conclusively Determines Disputed Issue

The collateral-order doctrine requires that the trial court have made its final decision on the issue challenged on the appeal. *Rationale*: If the trial court has not had its final say, the appellate court should not interfere.

e.g. **Example—Order Imposing Notice Costs on Defendant**: In a class action, an order imposing on defendant 90% of the cost of notifying class members of their right to opt out was held to be the trial court's final determination of this issue. [**Eisen v. Carlisle & Jacquelin,** *supra*, p. 233]

EXAM TIP ▐**GILBERT**

Remember that while orders as to collateral matters may be appealable before the whole case is resolved, such orders still ***must be final*** with respect to the issue involved. If they do not appear to be the court's final word on the issue, they are not appealable even though they involve a matter collateral to the main issue.

---

(4) Exception Narrowly Limited

The Supreme Court has repeatedly emphasized that the collateral-order exception applies to a *"small class" of cases* [**Cohen v. Beneficial Industrial Loan Corp.,** *supra*, p. 430], and it has been used in a restrictive manner.

e.g. **Example—Discovery Orders Involving Privileged Material**: Discovery orders compelling disclosure of allegedly privileged material seem to satisfy the requirements of the rule, because they conclusively determine claims of privilege, which are separate from the merits, and which cannot effectively be reviewed after the materials are turned over to the opposition. Nevertheless, the Court has adamantly refused to entertain appeals from such orders, noting that the party resisting discovery could refuse to comply, be held in criminal contempt, and appeal immediately from the judgment of criminal contempt. (*See supra*, §§ 1667–1675 for discussion of appealability of discovery rulings.)

In 2010, the Supreme Court held that an order that concededly privileged material (as to which privilege may have been waived) be turned over through discovery was not appealable as a collateral order. It reasoned that the question whether review should be allowed must be made in reference to all orders involving allegedly privileged material, and most such rulings involve routine application of settled legal principles that are unlikely to be reversed on appeal. It added that alternative protections for the party resisting production exist, including reversal of a judgment based on erroneously admitted privileged materials, mandamus relief from the appellate courts, and review from a contempt citation if the party refuses to comply with the court's order that the material be produced. [**Mohawk Industries, Inc. v. Carpenter,** *supra*, p. 325]

(5) No "Pendent-Party" Appellate Jurisdiction

An appellate court that has appellate jurisdiction over a collateral order against one party ordinarily may not exercise "pendent appellate jurisdiction" over otherwise unappealable interlocutory orders against other parties in the case, even though doing so might result in judicial efficiency. [**Swint v. Chambers County Commission,** 514 U.S. 35 (1995)]

h. Practical Construction of "Finality"

The Supreme Court has stated that it will accord a "practical rather than a technical construction" to the finality requirement. [**Gillespie v. United States Steel,** 379 U.S. 148 (1964)] However, this view does not cause a significant expansion of appealability.

e.g. Example—**"Death Knell" Doctrine**: The Supreme Court rejected a plaintiff's argument that refusal to certify a case as a class action is final (the "death knell") when the named plaintiff cannot afford to maintain the action alone. [**Coopers & Lybrand v. Livesay,** *supra*, p. 430]

E. Scope of Appellate Review

1. In General

Appellate review must be sufficiently broad to assure that the trial court properly applied the controlling substantive law and that the procedure conformed to the applicable standards. However, appellate review does not extend to retrying the facts or supplanting the trial judge's decision in matters committed to her discretion.

2. Findings of Fact Subject to Limited Review

It is not the function of an appellate court to make factual determinations; yet the appellate court must examine factual determinations to assure that the trial court has not rested its decision on unsupportable factual assumptions.

a. Jury Verdicts

When the findings below are embodied in a jury verdict, the role of the appellate court is essentially the same as that of the trial judge—*i.e.*, to oversee the jury's adherence to the law.

(1) Substantial-Evidence Test

The accepted test is that a jury verdict must be upheld if supported by substantial evidence, so that reasonable jurors could have found as they did—even if the reviewing judges think they would have found differently as triers of fact.

(2) Cases Taken from Jury

When the trial judge has taken the fact-finding function away from the jury—*e.g.*, by granting a motion for judgment as a matter of law—the appellate court must examine the record to determine whether there is any substantial evidence to support a finding contrary to that of the trial judge. If it finds such evidence, the judgment will be reversed. The appellate court gives no deference to the trial court's decision.

b. Judicial Findings in Nonjury Trials

(1) Explicit Findings Required

When a case is tried without a jury, the trial judge usually is required to make explicit findings of fact to facilitate review of her decision by the appellate court. [Fed. R. Civ. P. 52(a)(1)]

(2) Clear-Error Test

A judge's finding of fact may not be set aside unless the appellate court finds that it is "clearly erroneous." To find clear error, it is not enough that the appellate court is convinced that it would have decided the case differently. [**Anderson v. City of Bessemer City,** 470 U.S. 564 (1985)] Rather, the reviewing court must be left "on the entire evidence . . . with the definite and firm conviction that a mistake has been committed." [**United States v. United States Gypsum,** 333 U.S. 364 (1948)] Due regard must be given to the opportunity of the trial court to appraise the credibility of the witnesses [Fed. R. Civ. P. 52(a)(6)], although the requirement of deference is not limited to findings that rest on credibility determinations. [**Anderson v. City of Bessemer City,** *supra*]

(a) Distinguish—Substantial-Evidence Test

The clear-error test does not constrict appellate review as much as the substantial-evidence test, since a finding may be clearly erroneous even though there is substantial evidence to support it.

1) Rationale

A jury verdict is the product of a deliberative process and reflects democratic political values that assign special worth to the participation of lay decisionmakers. On the other hand, the findings of a trial judge are the product of a single mind, which may be more vulnerable to bias or idiosyncrasy. Still, considerable deference to trial judges' fact findings is due because of the judges' expertise in fact determinations and the costs of extensive review to the parties and to the system. [**Anderson v. City of Bessemer City,** *supra*]

c. "Fact" and "Law" Distinguished

It is only findings of fact, as opposed to matters of law, that are entitled to deference.

(1) Errors of Law (Jury Trial)

If the jury was erroneously instructed on the *law* on a point significant to the its decision, the verdict cannot stand, even if there is substantial evidence to support findings that could have been made pursuant to correct instructions.

(2) Erroneous Conclusions (Nonjury Trial)

(a) Explicit Conclusions Required

In a nonjury trial, the judge must state conclusions of law, either in a recorded oral statement or in writing, in order to facilitate appellate review. [Fed. R. Civ. P. 52(a)(1)]

(b) Effect of Erroneous Conclusions

If the conclusions are erroneous, so that the judge's findings rest on a false legal premise, the judgment cannot stand (even if the findings themselves are not clearly erroneous).

(3) Mixed Issues of Law and Fact

The distinction between a finding of fact and a conclusion of law is not always clear. Sophisticated observers have long noted a circularity in making this distinction for purposes of appellate review; *i.e.*, matters may tend to be treated as issues of fact if the appellate court feels less competent to resolve them and as issues of law if the court feels competent to resolve them without help from the lower court.

(a) Interpretation of Legal Documents

The interpretation of a contract, deed, will, or other legal document is generally regarded as a question of law if the trial court interpreted the document without judging the credibility of extrinsic evidence. But if the trial court did so, the appellate court may disregard any conclusions reached by the trial judge as to the meaning or effect of the document and substitute its own interpretation. [**Cordi-Allen v. Halloran,** 470 F.3d 25 (1st Cir. 2006)]

1) Distinguish—Findings Based on Documentary Evidence

Note the difference between review of legal documents (*e.g.*, contracts, wills) and review of documentary evidence (*e.g.*, receipts, letters). Findings of fact based on documentary evidence (or on oral evidence) are reviewed under the clearly-erroneous standard. [Fed. R. Civ. P. 52(a); **Anderson v. City of Bessemer City,** *supra*, p. 434—disapproving the much-cited contrary case of **Orvis v. Higgins,** 180 F.2d 537 (2d Cir. 1950)]

2) Distinguish—Interpretation of Term Used in Patent

Although the interpretation of a patent is a question of law for the judge and therefore reviewable de novo, the district court's factual findings about the meaning of the terms used in the patent are reviewed only for clear error. [**Teva Pharmaceuticals USA v. Sandoz, Inc.,** 135 S. Ct. 831 (2015)—appellate review of district court's interpretation of term "molecular weight," based on expert evidence, is governed by the clearly-erroneous standard in Fed. R. Civ. P. 52(a)(6)]

(b) Negligence

It is arguable whether a finding of negligence represents a legal or factual conclusion. In either event, appellate courts generally defer to a jury determination on negligence—even when there is no dispute as to the basic events.

1) But Note

In a nonjury trial, the judge's findings with respect to "negligence" are subject to the clear-error standard of review (*supra*).

(c) Other Issues—Suggested Approach

In other areas, a question usually will be treated as one of fact if it:

(i) *Pertains to the occurrence or nonoccurrence of a past event*,

(ii) *Is of specific interest* to the parties to the dispute and has no bearing on the rights or liabilities of others;

(iii) *Is determined on the basis of the testimony of witnesses;*

(iv) *Is not appropriately determined by reference to general policy;*

(v) *Is determined on the basis of intuitive instinct* about the application of some general morality to a specific event.

e.g. **Example**: One business person transfers a new automobile to another. Whether the transfer results in taxable income to the recipient, or instead is a "gift," is an issue of fact. [**Commissioner of Internal Revenue v. Duberstein,** 363 U.S. 278 (1960)]

1) Criticism

Reliance on the "intuition" of the trier of fact in such matters is the result of judicial unwillingness or inability to formulate explicit rules of decision to govern future like cases.

3. Review of Discretionary Rulings

Especially with regard to procedural matters, many decisions by trial judges are entrusted by law to their discretion. In such cases, an appellate court will not substitute its discretion for that of the trial judge in the absence of clear abuse.

e.g. **Example**: Whether to *delay or continue a trial* on account of the unavailability of a witness is a matter for the discretion of the trial judge. [**Napolitano v. Compania Sud Americana de Vapores,** 421 F.2d 382 (2d Cir. 1970)] Likewise, *setting the amount of a security bond* to be required of a party seeking a preliminary injunction is a matter of discretion. [Fed. R. Civ. P. 65(c)] And whether to grant a new trial on the ground that the verdict is *contrary to the weight of the evidence* is within the sound discretion of the trial judge, although the modern trend is away from earlier rulings that the trial judge's discretion was virtually unlimited. [**Coffran v. Hitchcock Clinic, Inc.,** 683 F.2d 5 (1st Cir. 1982)]

a. Limitation

The appellate court may properly review a discretionary ruling by a trial judge to determine whether she has *abused* her power. [**Allis-Chalmers Corp. v. Philadelphia Electric Co.,** 521 F.2d 360 (3d Cir. 1975)]

4. "Harmless-Error" Standard

a. General Rule

The appellate court may not reverse a lower-court judgment unless the trial court committed an error that was **prejudicial**—*i.e.*, one that affected the substantial rights of the parties. [Fed. R. Civ. P. 61; 28 U.S.C. § 2111] State law is similar. For example, the

California Constitution provides that: "No judgment shall be set aside ... for any error as to any matter of pleading or procedure, unless after an examination of the entire cause, including the evidence, the appellate court shall be of the opinion that the error ... resulted in a *miscarriage of justice*." [Cal. Const. Art. VI, § 13]

Example—Harmless: Erroneous rulings on the *pleadings or on matters of discovery* will rarely be sufficiently prejudicial in their effect on the trial that a reversal would be warranted.

Example—Harmless: The admission of *improper evidence* in a *nonjury* trial is generally regarded as harmless, since it is assumed that a professional trial judge will discount the improper evidence and not permit it to influence his findings of fact. [**First American State Bank v. Continental Insurance Co.,** 897 F.2d 319 (8th Cir. 1990)]

b. Burden

The burden of showing prejudice is usually on the party claiming it. There is no presumption of an impairment of substantial rights merely from the fact that error occurred.

c. Distinguish—Jury Verdict

The rule is to the contrary in *jury* trials: It is assumed that jurors *will* be influenced by improper evidence, at least if they are not cautioned by the trial judge to disregard it.

d. Limitation

The harmless-error rule will not prevent reversal when the *error is "egregious."* In such cases, the appellate court may reverse as a means of disciplining the trial judge, even though her error would not likely have had an adverse effect on the rights of the appellant. [**Thiel v. Southern Pacific Co.,** 328 U.S. 217 (1946)—discrimination in selection of jury panel]

e. Legal Theory Sustaining Judgment

An appellate court may review a legal theory *not previously presented* to the trial court if considered for the purpose of sustaining the decision below. Thus, if the findings of fact below clearly support application of the correct legal principle to reach the result achieved below, the judgment will be affirmed even if the correct legal theory was never presented to the trial court. Any error in articulation of legal theory was *harmless*. [**Xiloj-Itzep v. City of Agoura Hills,** 24 Cal. App. 4th 620 (1994)] Put differently, the trial court's decision must be affirmed even if its reason was wrong, as long as the outcome it reached was correct under applicable legal principles.

5. Waiver of Objections in Lower Court

a. General Rule

An appellate court may not reverse a judgment to correct an error that might have been avoided or corrected had the appellant made timely objection in the trial court. [**Security Pacific National Bank v. Geernaert,** 199 Cal. App. 3d 1425 (1988)] *Rationale:* The appellant should not be permitted to withhold objection and await the outcome of further proceedings before deciding whether to take advantage of a mistake by the court.

b. Specific Applications

(1) Jury Instruction

An error in instructing the jury usually will not be the basis for reversal unless the appellant made a timely objection to the charge and proposed a correct instruction. [Fed. R. Civ. P. 51(d)(1)]

(2) Admission of Evidence

Similarly, an error in admitting evidence generally will not be grounds for reversal unless the appellant made a timely and specific objection to the admission.

(3) Invited Error

If the aggrieved party *induced* the error of the trial court (*e.g.*, by proposing incorrect jury instructions or by offering inadmissible evidence), the case for waiver is strongest. [**Horsemen's Benevolent Association v. Valley Racing Association,** 4 Cal. App. 4th 1538 (1992)]

(4) New Matter

Newly discovered evidence, evidence of jury misconduct, or other matters coming to light *after trial* may not be presented directly to an appellate court. Such matters must be presented to the trial court by motion for a new trial or for relief from judgment. [*See* Fed. R. Civ. P. 60(b)(2)]

c. Exceptions

An appellate court may review notwithstanding the failure of an appellant to make timely objection in the following situations:

(1) Subject-Matter Jurisdiction

When the court below lacked subject-matter jurisdiction, no objection is necessary, since the jurisdictional issue can be raised belatedly or even *sua sponte*. [Fed. R. Civ. P. 12(h)(3)]

(2) Clear and Fundamental Error

No objection is necessary when the error is so clear and fundamental that the trial court should have avoided it, even without timely objection, and it would be *unjust* to permit the judgment to stand.

> **e.g.** **Example**: In the course of a long trial, the judge took a long recess for his own vacation, causing a serious hiatus in the presentation of the case to the jury. When the judge declared that under no circumstances would he consider a change in his plans, no objection was necessary to preserve the issue on appeal. [**Citron v. Aro Corp.,** 377 F.2d 750 (3d Cir.1967)]

6. Trial de Novo

Legislation may sometimes authorize a trial *de novo*, which is in effect a new trial in a higher court. This form of review is generally limited to review of trial courts that exercise minor jurisdiction (*e.g.*, small-claims courts) and that make no records of their proceedings.

STANDARD	USED TO REVIEW	TEST
SUBSTANTIAL-EVIDENCE TEST	Jury verdict	Verdict must be supported by substantial evidence, so that reasonable jurors could have found as the jury did
ABUSE-OF-DISCRETION STANDARD	Case-management decisions and some other rulings such as those on preliminary injunctions	Deference to trial court ruling unless action was outside range of judgment committed to discretion of trial judge
CLEAR-ERROR STANDARD	Judicial findings of fact in nonjury trials	On reviewing all the evidence, the appellate court is left with the definite and firm conviction that a mistake has been committed
HARMLESS-ERROR STANDARD	Lower-court judgment	If the trial court committed an error, its judgment may be reversed only if the error was prejudicial, *i.e.*, affected the substantial rights of the parties
PLENARY REVIEW	Lower-court judgment as to matters of law	Trial-court decision accorded no deference; appellate court decides afresh how case should be resolved

F. Appellate Review by Extraordinary Writ

1. Prerogative Writs

In exceptional cases, review of unappealable orders may be had by means of a prerogative writ issued by the appellate court to direct the conduct of trial judges. The available writs, depending on the court system, are:

a. *Mandamus*—an order directing the judge to perform her legal duty; and

b. *Prohibition*—an order enjoining the judge from conduct that exceeds her lawful authority.

2. Source of Power to Issue Writs

a. State Courts

Writs in state court tend to be based on common-law practice. In some states, statutes or constitutional provisions establish alternatives. In Michigan, for example, the appellate courts have power to issue "writs of superintending control."

b. Federal Courts

The United States Courts of Appeals have power to issue prerogative writs by reason of statute, which authorizes all federal courts to issue writs as necessary "in aid of their respective jurisdictions and agreeable to the usages and principles of law." [28 U.S.C. § 1651(a)]

3. Discretionary Character of Writ

An important distinction between writs and an appeal is that the issuance of a prerogative writ is always discretionary with the appellate courts. The petitioner has *no right* to a hearing. [**Kerr v. United States District Court,** 426 U.S. 394 (1976)]

4. Grounds for Issuance

a. Conduct Exceeding Limits of Power

A prerogative writ may issue to prevent misuse of judicial power, such as:

(1) *An abuse of discretion;*

(2) *An excess of jurisdiction;* or

(3) *A refusal to exercise jurisdiction.*

b. Necessity for Immediate Review

When the petitioner has no right to review by appeal at the present time, and would suffer undue hardship or substantial prejudice if appellate review was delayed until after a final judgment, a writ may properly issue.

(1) But Note

Extraordinary writs will not issue when adequate review by appeal is available to the petitioner. [*In re* **McDonald,** 489 U.S. 180 (1989)]

5. Common Uses of Writ

United States Courts of Appeals use discretionary writs:

a. *To correct the erroneous denial of a right to jury trial* [**Beacon Theatres, Inc. v. Westover,** 359 U.S. 500 (1959)];

b. *To prevent improper delegation of judicial power* with respect to special matters [**LaBuy v. Howes Leather Co.,** 352 U.S. 249 (1957)]; and

c. *To prevent unlawful remand to state court* of actions properly removed to federal court. [**Thermtron Products, Inc. v. Hermansdorfer,** 423 U.S. 336 (1976)]

6. Supervisory Mandamus

In rare circumstances, mandamus may be used to resolve *issues of first impression* that may be important in a significant number of cases. [**Silva v. Superior Court,** 14 Cal. App. 4th 562 (1993)]

e.g. **Example**: When the question of the proper treatment of physical examinations of defendants under Federal Rule 35 was presented, mandamus was available to review an order requiring a defendant to submit to a physical examination, because issue had never been resolved. [**Schlagenhauf v. Holder,** 379 U.S. 104 (1964)]

a. Availability

In a few jurisdictions, such as California, the grounds for issuing prerogative writs have been greatly expanded. In effect, the writ proceeding becomes a device for granting or refusing immediate appellate review of important interlocutory orders. [**Omaha Indemnity Co. v. Superior Court,** 209 Cal. App. 3d 1266 (1989)]

Chapter Eleven

Preclusive Effects of Judgments

CONTENTS   **PAGE**

Key Exam Issues

After a court has entered judgment, related matters may come up in later litigation involving the same or different parties. For several reasons—including economy, prevention of harassment, and avoidance of inconsistent rulings—doctrines of former adjudication sharply limit the extent to which *relitigation* is permitted. When relitigation is not permitted, parties cannot argue in a new proceeding that the prior ruling was erroneous; the point is taken as established in accord with the prior decision.

This field of law has two main components: (i) *claim preclusion* (or, in older terminology still in widespread use, *res judicata* in its narrow sense), which bars reassertion of the same claim; and (ii) *issue preclusion* (in the older terminology, direct or collateral estoppel), which bars relitigation of the same issue, whether it arises in connection with the same claim (*direct estoppel*) or a different claim (*collateral estoppel*).

1. Claim Preclusion

Key questions are:

a. Is the judgment on the *same claim*? Most jurisdictions now define "claim" broadly to prevent the bringing of one aspect of a related matter in one action and another aspect in a second proceeding against the same party (rule against splitting claims).

b. Is the judgment *final*?

c. Is it *valid*—was it rendered by a court of competent jurisdiction, and was constitutionally adequate notice given?

d. Is it *"on the merits"*—did the court rule on the merits of the claim, dismiss with prejudice, or enter a default judgment? **Caution**: "On the merits" is often overread, and many judgments that are not literally "on the merits"—such as final judgments entered as sanctions for discovery abuse—can have claim-preclusive effect. The "on the merits" mantra is common in statements about claim-preclusion requirements, but the widely followed Restatement (Second) of Judgments does not use the term in this connection.

e. Did the plaintiff in the prior action *prevail*? If so, the doctrine of *merger* precludes a second try—the original claim is merged in the judgment.

f. Did the plaintiff *lose* in the first action? If so, the doctrine of *bar* precludes the second suit, with the plaintiff's claim regarded as barred by the defeat.

g. Is the plaintiff guilty of *"claim-splitting,"* which involves suing on a related claim that could have been brought in the prior action but was not?

h. Was the party now asserting a claim a defendant in a prior action in which that claim was an omitted compulsory counterclaim? If so, failure to assert that claim before is likely to preclude its pursuit in the later action.

2. Issue Preclusion

Key questions are:

a. Is the party against whom issue preclusion is sought to be invoked one who was a *party* to the prior litigation or *in "privity"* with such a party?

b. Was the issue *actually litigated and determined*, *identical* to the issue in the present action, and *essential* to the prior judgment?

c. Can *nonmutual estoppel* be applied?

(1) Are the **stakes** so much higher in the present case that it would be unfair to apply estoppel?

(2) Could the party asserting estoppel **easily have joined** in the earlier action?

(3) Are **procedural opportunities** available to the party against whom estoppel is asserted in this action that were not available in the earlier action?

(4) Have there been **inconsistent determinations** of the same issue in other cases?

A. Introduction

1. In General

Preclusion doctrine has two main components: (i) claim preclusion, and (ii) issue preclusion.

2. Claim Preclusion (Also Called Res Judicata)

A final judgment on a claim or cause of action **precludes reassertion of that claim** or **cause of action** in a subsequent suit.

a. Merger

If judgment was for the plaintiff on the claim, there is a **merger** of the claim in the judgment—*i.e.*, the prejudgment claim is transformed into the judgment claim. The claimant cannot sue on the same claim again but can only enforce the judgment, even if it is for less than the claimant had sought.

b. Bar

If judgment was for the defendant, it is a **bar** against the plaintiff's suing again on the claim.

3. Issue Preclusion (Also Called Collateral Estoppel)

Preclusion prevents not only relitigation of a claim, but also, in some circumstances, relitigation of issues of fact resolved in a prior proceeding, even when the later case involves a different claim. A decision on an issue of fact may be binding in subsequent litigation between the same parties or, in some circumstances, between one of the parties and a different adversary.

4. Purposes

The purposes of these doctrines are twofold: (i) to avoid the time and expense of multiple litigation over the same matter; and (ii) to give stability to the results of adjudication—to prevent inconsistent results.

B. Claim Preclusion

1. In General

Before any judgment can have claim-preclusive effect, it is often said that the judgment must be (i) **final**, (ii) **"on the merits,"** and (iii) **valid**. The quotation marks around "on the merits" are deliberate because the term must not be taken too literally, as is explained below (*see infra*, pp. 449–450).

2. Policy Basis

The basis for claim preclusion is that litigants should be compelled to litigate their entire claim on the first occasion they bring it before the courts. This requirement can serve the following policy objectives:

a. Judicial Efficiency

Resolving all claims in a single lawsuit avoids waste of judicial resources on repeated litigation of the same claim. It also gives parties an incentive to present all pertinent evidence and issues in the first case.

b. Avoiding Vexation of Defendants

Allowing plaintiffs to sue defendants repeatedly on the same claim by changing their legal theories would raise the risk of oppression of defendants. Defendants should be assured that they will not be forced to answer a given claim more than once.

c. Consistency

Although it would often be legally consistent for a plaintiff to lose on one theory and then prevail on another with different elements, requiring litigation of all theories for a claim in a single action promotes the reality and public appearance of consistency.

d. Effect—Foreclosing Matters That Were Never Litigated

The net effect of claim preclusion is, therefore, often to foreclose matters that were never litigated because they were never raised in the first litigation.

e.g. **Example**: Plaintiff sues Defendant car salesperson for common-law fraud in connection with Defendant's sale of a used car to Plaintiff. After judgment is entered in this action, Plaintiff files a second suit against Defendant, this time charging violation of the state Automobile Consumer Protection Act in connection with the sale of the same car. Even though the question of violation of the Act has never been litigated, the second suit is precluded by the first.

(1) Distinguish—Issue Preclusion

Estoppel (particularly issue preclusion or collateral estoppel) applies preclusion only to matters that were *actually litigated and determined* in the first lawsuit.

3. Meaning of Claim—Breadth of Preclusion

Determining the scope of the claim in the first lawsuit is often difficult. Unless the claim in the second lawsuit is the "same," claim preclusion does not apply (although issue preclusion may).

a. Traditional Tests

The traditional tests were derived from the code-pleading concept of the cause of action. The idea was that the first litigation was res judicata only as to the same cause of action. The courts developed tests to give effect to this concept:

(1) Same Primary Right and Duty

If the plaintiff asserted a violation of the same basic right in the second case as in the first, preclusion applied. *Criticism*: Distinguishing between differences in the law that mattered (in terms of the elements of the second claim compared to those of the first claim) made it hard to determine if the second suit involved the same "primary right."

(2) Same Evidence

If the second claim turned on essentially the same evidence as the first claim, preclusion was said to apply. *Criticism*: Because there was usually some difference in the evidence that could be presented, this test was also difficult to apply.

(3) Mere Change of Legal Theory

If the second suit merely changed the legal theory upon which the earlier suit relied, preclusion applied. *Criticism*: Although this test accurately portrays one concern of preclusion doctrine, it provides little guidance in determining whether something more than the legal theory has changed.

b. Modern Approach—Transactional Test

The Restatement (Second) of Judgments adopts a transactional approach to the scope of claim preclusion: Claim preclusion applies to "all or any part of the transaction, or series of connected transactions, out of which the action arose." [Restatement (Second) of Judgments § 24(1)] A claimant who omits a transactionally related, available claim from a first suit is guilty of *"claim-splitting"* and may not bring a second action on the omitted claim. Whether claim-splitting is involved is probably the most-litigated type of claim-preclusion issue, since parties tend not to make rank second efforts on what they litigated already.

(1) Flexible Definition

The definition is flexible: "What factual grouping constitutes a 'transaction,' and what groupings constitute a 'series,' are to be determined pragmatically, giving weight to such considerations as whether the facts are related in time, space, origin, or motivation, whether they form a convenient trial unit, and whether their treatment as a unit conforms to the parties' expectations or business understanding or usage." [Restatement (Second) of Judgments § 24(2)] This analysis requires an examination of the facts underlying the claim similar to that called for in assessing permissive joinder of parties under Federal Rule 20. (*See supra*, pp. 217–220.)

e.g. **Example**: After a pre-enforcement challenge to a state abortion restriction, a post-enforcement challenge to the same provision brought by several plaintiffs, including some of the original ones, was not barred by claim preclusion because developments since the first challenge, showing concreteness of harms suffered, made the second challenge a new claim. The second action also included a challenge to another, different provision in the same statute, which was not barred by the claim-preclusion rule against splitting related claims because the challenge to the distinct provision was a distinct claim. [**Whole Woman's Health v. Hellerstedt**, 136 S. Ct. 2292 (2016)]

c. Claims by or Against Different Parties Usually Not Foreclosed

Ordinarily a claim by one plaintiff is considered a different claim for preclusion purposes from that of another plaintiff, and so is a claim against a different defendant. However, these rules may not apply if the parties are in privity (*see infra*, pp. 457–459), but closely similar claims can survive a final adjudication.

e.g. **Example**: In the first suit, Plaintiff sought to recover for his own personal injuries in an auto accident but lost on a finding that Defendant was not negligent. He then brought a second suit as representative for his wife and three minor children to recover for their injuries in the accident. He was allowed to pursue these claims because they were not the same as his personal claim. [**Freeman v. Lester Coggins Trucking, Inc.,** 771 F.2d 860 (5th Cir. 1985)]

(1) Successor in Interest

If the first plaintiff's claim is assigned to the second plaintiff, or passes by action of law, the second plaintiff is precluded. Thus, if before death a victim of an accident sues the other driver and recovers for her injuries, the executor of her estate cannot file a second suit against the other driver to recover wrongful death damages for the estate. (*See infra*, p. 458.)

(2) Liability of One Defendant Depends on Liability of Another

In some situations, one potential defendant may be held to be responsible for the conduct of another (*see infra*, pp. 460–461). In such cases, a judgment exonerating one potential defendant precludes an action on the same claim against the other.

4. "Final"

A ruling at a pretrial hearing or the determination of an issue severed for trial does not decide a claim until judgment is rendered. However, if a claim has been separately determined in the course of an action, it may be treated as the equivalent of a final judgment for preclusion purposes, even if the action is still pending. The question for issue preclusion is whether the "prior adjudication of an issue in another action . . . is determined to be sufficiently firm to be accorded conclusive effect." The finality requirement is interpreted somewhat more strictly for purposes of merger and bar, since the question then is the creation of a new claim based on the judgment (merger) or the extinguishment of the claim (bar). [Restatement (Second) of Judgments § 13, comment g]

a. Effect of Appeal

Whether a judgment on appeal is final for purposes of claim preclusion is determined by the *law of the jurisdiction in which the judgment was rendered*.

(1) Federal Practice

In federal practice, for preclusion purposes once a judgment is entered in the district court it is deemed to be final even though an appeal therefrom is pending. The judgment remains final and valid until reversed or modified by the appellate court. In such jurisdictions, preclusion attaches immediately upon entry of the judgment. [**United States v. Nysco Laboratories, Inc.,** 318 F.2d 817 (2d Cir. 1963)]

(a) Note

As a practical matter, however, any suit to enforce the judgment, or in which the preclusion issue is otherwise involved, is likely to be abated or continued until the pending appeal is determined.

(b) And Note

Even courts that have somewhat expanded the notion of finality for preclusion purposes may look to whether there was an opportunity for appellate review. A partial summary judgment followed by a settlement that prevents appellate review, for example, will ordinarily not be given preclusive effect. [**American Casualty Corp. v. Sentry Federal Savings Bank,** 867 F. Supp. 50 (D. Mass. 1994)]

(2) State Practice

In many states, the taking of an appeal *automatically* postpones finality until the appeal is determined. Until then, no preclusive effect attaches. [**Sosa v. DIRECTV, Inc.,** 437 F.3d 923 (9th Cir. 2006)—applying California law]

b. Modifiable Judgments

Many civil judgments are nonfinal in the sense that they are subject to modification (*e.g.,* alimony awards, child-custody determinations, and some kinds of injunctions). Such judgments do not prevent reconsideration of the relief granted, for example, when conditions have changed. But they are *preclusive until modified.* [Restatement (Second) of judgments § 13, comment *c*]

c. Conflicting Judgments

If two judgments are in conflict, usually the later in time controls. [Restatement (Second) of Judgments § 15]

Example: If a judgment is rendered in action 1, but is not raised or established in action 2 (or the court in the second action holds that the earlier judgment is not entitled to preclusive effect) and both judgments are otherwise final, the second judgment is controlling. Hence, it (rather than the earlier judgment) is entitled to preclusive effect in any third proceeding on the same claim. [**Treinies v. Sunshine Mining Co.,** 308 U.S. 66 (1939)]

5. "On the Merits"

a. General Rule

A judgment is deemed to be "on the merits" if the claim has been tried and determined—*i.e.,* if the court has ruled that the *plaintiff has (or has not) established his claim.* This rule includes a determination by summary judgment, judgment on the pleadings, nonsuit, and directed verdict, as well as a determination after trial and verdict.

(1) Note

Rulings not "on the merits" generally are preclusive only as to issues. If the court dismisses on a ground that *does not* relate to the merits (*e.g.,* for lack of jurisdiction, improper venue, or a dismissal expressly "without prejudice" to a new action), the judgment of dismissal usually does not bar a subsequent action. [Restatement (Second) of Judgments § 20]

(2) But Note

Such a judgment is determinative of *issues decided. Example*: A dismissal for improper venue because the defendant is not a resident of the county where sued is determinative of that *issue* in a subsequent suit (*see infra*, p. 452 *et seq.*). When the second suit is on the *same claim*, this relatively uncommon form of issue preclusion is known as *direct estoppel.*

(3) Caution

While the term "on the merits" is often used in descriptions of the requirements for claim preclusion, the widely followed Restatement (Second) of Judgments does not use it. The phrase can be dangerously misleading, because various types of judgments that do not involve adjudications that truly reach the merits, including defaults, settlements, and disciplinary dispositions such as dismissals for pretrial misconduct, can have claim-preclusive effect. So if you use it, which you need not, do not take it too literally.

b. Meaning of "On the Merits"

If an action is dismissed on a ground closely related to the merits, the following approaches apply:

(1) Dismissals

If dismissal is for failure to state a claim, but it is possible that the complaint could be amended to state a valid claim, or if there was a dismissal for failure to diligently prosecute the action, earlier cases held that the judgment was not on the merits and hence not a bar.

(a) But Note

Today, such a dismissal is *considered a bar*—on the theory that the plaintiff had a *fair opportunity* to get to the merits (by amending his pleading, appealing, etc.). [**Rinehart v. Locke**, 454 F.2d 313 (7th Cir. 1971)]

(2) Default and Consent Judgments

Default and consent judgments terminate the claim and hence *have claim-preclusive* effect (*i.e.*, result in merger or bar of the claim). Note, however, that a default judgment may be less effective in regard to issue preclusion. (*See infra*, p. 454.)

(3) Punitive Dismissals

A punitive dismissal is a dismissal based on a party's refusal to obey trial-court orders—*e.g.*, a dismissal of a plaintiff's action for failure to prosecute diligently, or a default judgment against a defendant for refusal to obey a discovery order. Because such judgments terminate the claim, they have claim-preclusive effect; but they do not involve issue preclusion regarding issues going to the merits.

EXAM TIP

On your exam, be sure to remember the basics of claim preclusion (*i.e.*, res judicata in the narrow sense—the term is also used to refer to the whole preclusion area): Once a *final judgment "on the merits"* has been rendered, the plaintiff is barred from filing a new suit based on any claim against the defendant that arose out of the occurrence upon which the final judgment was entered. Generally, this preclusive effect does not bind third parties, but it may if the third party is in *privity* with the plaintiff in the first action (*e.g.*, an assignee of plaintiff's claim).

---

6. "Valid"

The third requirement for claim preclusion is that the judgment be valid. A judgment is valid *unless*:

(i) The court lacked *subject-matter jurisdiction* of the case (*see supra*, Chapter Two.);

(ii) The notice given to the defendant failed to conform to ***due process requirements***, or substantially departed from the requirements of statute or court rule concerning the ***form of notice*** (*see supra*, p. 48 *et seq.*); ***or***

(iii) The court lacked ***personal jurisdiction*** over the defendant (*see supra*, Chapter One).

a. Determination of Validity

If the question of validity was ***litigated*** in the original action, that determination is itself preclusive. [**Baldwin v. Iowa State Traveling Men's Association,** 283 U.S. 522 (1931)] This is an illustration of direct estoppel (*see supra*, p. 449).

Example: A court exercises jurisdiction in an action concerning land on the basis that the land is within the state, rejecting Defendant's contention that the land is across the state boundary and hence in another state. This determination of jurisdiction is conclusive, and the judgment may not thereafter be attacked as invalid. [**Durfee v. Duke,** 375 U.S. 106 (1963)]

(1) And Note

Preclusion also applies to decisions concerning the court's subject-matter jurisdiction [**Stoll v. Gottlieb,** 305 U.S. 165 (1938)] and the adequacy of notice. [**Gordon v. Gordon,** 227 S.E.2d 53 (Ga. 1976)]

7. Claim Preclusion When Jurisdiction Is in Rem or Quasi in Rem

a. Definition

Jurisdiction ***in rem*** or ***quasi in rem*** is based on the presence of the property about which the lawsuit is concerned (*see supra*, p. 20). For example, a state can exercise jurisdiction to determine rights under a mortgage pertaining to land in that state.

b. Preclusive Effect

If jurisdiction is exercised ***in rem*** or ***quasi in rem***, the rules of claim and issue preclusion apply essentially as they do in ***in personam*** judgments, except that the preclusion is limited to claims in the property.

(1) Claim Preclusion

Suppose Anne brings a suit to foreclose a mortgage on property in State X, serving notice in State X on Beth, the mortgagor. A judgment for or against Anne is preclusive as to her claim to foreclose. However, if no jurisdiction was exercised to determine Beth's in personam indebtedness to Anne, that claim is not determined and still may be sued upon by Anne.

(2) Issue Preclusion

Any issues determined in the in rem proceeding (*e.g.*, the enforceability of the mortgage note) are conclusive in subsequent litigation.

8. Attachment Jurisdiction

Attachment jurisdiction is exercised by seizing local property as a basis for collecting on an obligation allegedly due from its owner, the obligation being unrelated to the property.

a. Preclusive Effect

(1) Claim Preclusion

A judgment based on attachment jurisdiction does *not* extinguish the claim, except to the extent of the property seized.

(2) Issue Preclusion

However, the issues actually litigated are conclusive on the parties if the amount of the property attached was large enough to give them a fair incentive to litigate.

b. Restriction

Attachment jurisdiction has been considerably restricted by **Shaffer v. Heitner**, *supra*, p. 77, but it has not been eliminated.

9. Exceptions to Claim Preclusion

Only under ***extraordinary*** circumstances may a party relitigate a claim that has been reduced to judgment. The losing party would have to establish grounds for setting aside the judgment (*e.g.*, fraud on the court) and that she has a good case on the merits. The policy is ***very strongly against*** relitigation. (*See supra*, pp. 445–446.)

> **Example**: Seven consumers brought actions under the federal antitrust laws charging defendant department stores with conspiring to fix prices of women's clothing. The actions were dismissed on the ground that consumers had no standing to sue for price fixing. Five of the plaintiffs appealed, and the other two filed new actions asserting claims under state antitrust law. The Supreme Court then held that consumers did have standing to sue, and the judgments against the five plaintiffs who appealed were reversed and remanded for further proceedings. In these circumstances, the Ninth Circuit created an exception to claim preclusion so that the other two plaintiffs could proceed with their actions. The Supreme Court reversed, stressing that claim preclusion serves the vital interest "that there be an end to litigation." [**Federated Department Stores, Inc. v. Moitie**, 452 U.S. 394 (1981)]

10. Defenses and Counterclaims

a. Effect of Compulsory-Counterclaim Rules

A compulsory-counterclaim rule or statute requires that the defendant set up any counterclaim she has against the plaintiff arising out of the same transaction as the plaintiff's claim. [Fed. R. Civ. P. 13(a)] If she fails to do so, she is barred from thereafter asserting the counterclaim, either as a defense or as the basis for affirmative relief in an independent action. Hence, the judgment in the former action is preclusive as to claims that were or should have been asserted as compulsory counterclaims in that action. [**Baker v. Gold Seal Liquors, Inc.,** 417 U.S. 467 (1974)]

b. When No Compulsory-Counterclaim Rule Is Involved

If no compulsory-counterclaim rule or statute applies, claim preclusion does not prevent the defendant from asserting the same matter first as a defense to the plaintiff's action, and later in a separate suit as a basis for independent relief against the former plaintiff.

> **Example**: Contractor sues Owner for money due under a construction contract. Owner successfully defends by showing that the work was not properly done, but no counterclaim is asserted. Owner may subsequently file an independent damage action for the improper work (assuming no compulsory-counterclaim statute or rule is in effect).

(1) But Note

Because of issue preclusion (below), the *issues actually litigated* and decided in the first action may not be relitigated.

(2) Exception—Nullifying Initial Judgment

If a former defendant seeks relief in a later suit based on a claim that could have been asserted as a counterclaim, and the relief sought would nullify the judgment entered in the earlier suit, the later action is barred even if there was no applicable compulsory-counterclaim rule in the earlier action. [Restatement (Second) of Judgments § 22(1)(b)]

e.g. **Example**: In the first action, McDonald's sued in a state court without a compulsory-counterclaim rule to terminate its franchise agreement with Plaintiff under a provision forbidding any member of Plaintiff's family to acquire an interest in a competing fast-food business. Plaintiff's son had bought a Burger Chef franchise in a nearby town. After judgment was entered in the first action finding a breach of the franchise agreement and directing sale of the franchise, Plaintiff sued McDonald's, alleging that application of the noncompetition provision of the franchise agreement violated the antitrust laws. The court held the second action foreclosed because "its prosecution would nullify rights established by the prior action." [**Martino v. McDonald's Systems, Inc.**, 598 F.2d 1079 (7th Cir. 1979)]

C. Issue Preclusion

1. Direct Estoppel

Issues actually litigated and determined *between the parties* are binding on them in subsequent actions concerning the *same claim*. *Example*: In a child-support suit in which several modification proceedings have been held, issues actually litigated and determined in an earlier proceeding (*e.g.*, legitimacy of the child) are binding on the parties in subsequent proceedings.

e.g. **Example**: A determination by the Patent and Trademark Office that respondent's proposed trademark was so similar to petitioner's mark that it created a serious risk of consumer confusion was binding in a later litigation in court between the two parties about whether respondent was guilty of infringement. [**B & B Hardware, Inc. v. Hargis Indus., Inc.**, 135 S. Ct. 1293 (2015)]

Note: The Restatement (Second) of Judgments does not use the traditional terms "direct estoppel" and "collateral estoppel." Instead, its section 27 sets out the requirements for issue preclusion—that "an issue of fact or law is actually litigated and determined by a valid and final judgment, and the determination is essential to the judgment"—and bars relitigation of the issue whether a later action is "on the same or a different claim." Thus one may speak of issue preclusion without distinguishing between direct and collateral estoppel, although those traditional terms—especially the latter—are still in wide use.

2. Collateral Estoppel

If the second lawsuit involves a *different* claim (and hence no merger, bar, or direct estoppel), the first judgment may be invoked as to all matters *actually litigated and determined in the first action and essential to the judgment*. [**Cromwell v. County of Sac**, 94 U.S. 351 (1876); Restatement (Second) of Judgments § 27] *Example*: Plaintiff sues Defendant to collect interest that has become due on a promissory note. Defendant defends on the ground that she was induced by fraud to sign the note, and wins. If Plaintiff later sues to collect the principal amount of the note after it matures, the prior determination on the question of fraud is conclusive against him.

a. "Actually Litigated and Determined"

The issue-preclusive effect of a prior judgment applies to issues *actually litigated and determined* in the former action, but not to those that merely *could* have been litigated therein.

e.g. **Example**: Landlord sues and recovers judgment against Tenant for rent owed. Later, Landlord sues again for additional rent owed under the same lease. Tenant now interposes the defense that the lease was invalid at all times. The earlier judgment is *not* preclusive as to this issue, since the only thing litigated in the first action was the rent claim, and the court was not called upon to determine the validity of the lease.

(1) Default Judgments

There is a split of authority on whether a default judgment creates issue preclusion.

(a) Conclusive

Many decisions hold that a default judgment is conclusive as to all issues that were necessarily involved in the former suit, even though the action went by default and there was no actual litigation thereof. [**Norex Petroleum Ltd. v. Access Industries, Inc.,** 416 F.3d 146 (2d Cir. 2005)]

(b) Not Conclusive

However, there is substantial authority contra, including Restatement (Second) of Judgments, holding that "actually litigated and determined" requires evidence presented to, and a decision by, a trier of fact (so that default judgments do not qualify). [Restatement (Second) of Judgments § 27, comment *e*]

1) Rationale

The Restatement's is believed to be the better view, because a person defaulting to a complaint may not have foreseen that the admissions created thereby would return to haunt him in a subsequent, unrelated lawsuit.

(2) Stipulated Judgments

There is likewise a split of authority on whether a stipulated (consent) judgment is issue preclusive.

(a) Comment

Even if an issue conceded through a default or consent judgment is not treated as within the rule of issue preclusion, it may be admissible under the law of evidence as an *admission*. (*See* Evidence Summary.)

(3) Jury vs. Nonjury Trial

The presence or absence of a jury in the first trial is a "neutral" factor—*i.e.*, matters actually litigated in action 1 may be held precluded in action 2, even if there was no right to a jury in the earlier action (*e.g.*, a suit in equity) and the present suit is jury triable (*e.g.*, action for damages). [**Parklane Hosiery Co. v. Shore,** 439 U.S. 322 (1979)]

b. "Essential to the First Judgment"

Issue preclusion applies only to those matters decided in the earlier lawsuit that were *essential to the court's determination*—*i.e.*, essential to the claim (or defense) established by the judgment therein. Other matters involved in the earlier lawsuit, even though "actually litigated and decided," are not binding in a later action. [Restatement (Second) of Judgments § 27]

(e.g.) **Example**: Plaintiff sues Defendant over personal injuries sustained in an auto accident. The court finds that: (i) Plaintiff was contributorily negligent; and (ii) Defendant was also negligent. The finding that Defendant was negligent may not have been "necessary" (it would be immaterial if Plaintiff's claim is barred by his own contributory negligence). Consequently, when Defendant later sues Plaintiff for his injuries in the same accident, the finding in the earlier action that Defendant was negligent is not binding against Defendant.

(1) Test

An issue is "essential" to the court's determination in the former action only if it appears that the judgment could not have been reached without determining the issue. [**Mansoldo v. State,** 898 A.2d 1018 (N.J. (2006)] One federal decision divided over the standard for "essential," with a majority requiring that a finding be "critical and necessary" to the judgment, at least in the context of offensive nonmutual issue preclusion (*see infra*, pp. 461, 462). A partial dissent, claiming support from two other circuits, argued for a slightly lower standard of " 'distinctly put in issue and directly determined' and a material element of" the judgment. [***In re* Microsoft Corp. Antitrust Litigation,** 355 F.3d 322 (4th Cir. 2004)]

(2) Alternative Findings

There is a ***split of authority*** on whether alternative findings at the trial level, either of which would have been sufficient to support the judgment, should have issue-preclusive effect in other proceedings. [*Compare* **Halpern v. Schwartz,** 426 F.2d 102 (2d Cir. 1970), *and* Restatement (Second) of Judgments § 27, comment *i*—no preclusion, with **Jean Alexander Cosmetics, Inc. v. L'Oreal USA, Inc.,** 458 F.3d 244 (3d Cir. 2006)—preclusion allowed]

(e.g.) **Example**: In an action to declare involuntary bankruptcy, Debtor was found to have committed three acts of bankruptcy misconduct, each of which would be sufficient to support the determination that involuntary bankruptcy was proper. In a subsequent action concerning her discharge, estoppel was asserted on the basis of one of the three findings because it involved fraud. The court held that preclusion should not apply because the finding was merely an alternative basis for the decision. [**Halpern v. Schwartz,** *supra*]

(a) Significance of Appeal

Some courts distinguish between cases in which the earlier judgment was appealed and those in which it was not. If no appeal was taken, they will hold that neither finding is preclusive. If an appeal is taken, however, there is preclusion with respect to those issues that the appellate court reaches that support its judgment. [Restatement (Second) of Judgments § 27, comment *o*]

Rationales: Preclusion law should not create an incentive for a party who lost on more than one independent ground—and who might generally think an appeal not worth it—to appeal just to avoid the threat of future issue preclusion. Also, alternative grounds may not all have been as carefully considered as when there was a single finding.

(3) "Ultimate" vs. "Evidentiary" Facts

Some cases have held that the previous determination of an issue is conclusive when the "ultimate" facts in the two actions are the same, but not when the first finding is simply a step (*i.e.*, a "mediate or evidentiary fact") toward the ultimate fact in the second action. [**Evergreens v. Nunan,** 141 F.2d 927 (2d Cir. 1944)]

e.g. **Example**: In a personal-injury action, a finding that Defendant was "negligent" would be an ultimate fact, whereas a specific finding that Defendant had failed to maintain or repair her vehicle in a safe condition might be treated as "evidentiary."

(a) Modern Approach Contrary

This distinction generally is *not* accepted. [*See* **Synanon Church v. United States,** 820 F.2d 421 (D.C. Cir. 1987)—issue preclusion applies to *any* fact determination actually litigated and determined and essential to the judgment, without any distinction between "ultimate" and "mediate" or "evidentiary" facts]

c. "Identical" Issue

The issue decided in the prior adjudication must be identical to the one presented in the instant action. Mere similarity of issues is not enough.

e.g. **Example**: When the first suit involved an alleged breach of contract by defendant, there was no issue preclusion in a second action involving securities-act violations because the issues were different, even though the same conduct by defendant was involved in both actions. [**Watson v. Roberts, Scott & Co.,** 466 F.2d 1348 (9th Cir. 1972)]

e.g. **Example**: In the first action, the court held that a worker could recover for injuries from defendant manufacturer of asbestos. This decision did not provide the basis for issue preclusion against the manufacturer in a later action brought by another worker, because issues raised in the later action were not identical and depended on the actual (and different) circumstances under which the later plaintiff was exposed to asbestos products. [**Hardy v. Johns-Manville Sales Corp.,** 681 F.2d 334 (5th Cir. 1982)]

e.g. **Example**: When a proceeding before the Patent and Trademark Office between the same parties about the same trademarks involved in later litigation had determined that there was an undue risk of consumer confusion due to the similarity of the marks, that issue was the same as the one involved in the litigation. True, the PTO used slightly different factors from the court, but they were both applying the same statutory provision. [**B & B Hardware, Inc. v. Hargis Indus., Inc.,** *supra*]

d. Decision by Administrative Agency

The Supreme Court has held that it will assume that Congress intends that determinations by administrative agencies based on trial-type proceedings should be accorded binding effect in court unless there is an evident reason why Congress did not want certain types of administrative decisions to have such preclusive effect. [**B & B Hardware, Inc. v.**

Hargis Indus., Inc., *supra*—decision by Patent & Trademark Office after "lengthy proceeding" that there was a serious risk of consumer confusion between two trademarks should be given preclusive effect in court in trademark-infringement litigation between the parties to the PTO proceeding]

e. **Exceptions**

Issue preclusion is not as strictly applied as claim preclusion.

(1) ***When the two actions involve the same parties***, under Restatement (Second) of Judgments section 28 the loser may be allowed to relitigate an issue in a subsequent action if, for example:

(a) As a matter of law, ***appellate review*** of the initial action was ***unavailable*** [**Kircher v. Putnam Funds Trust,** 547 U.S. 633 (2006)];

(b) Even if review was available, the ***nature of the proceedings*** in the court handling the first action was ***informal or expedited***, as in a small-claims court;

(c) The ***stakes involved*** in the second suit are much larger, as when the first action was in small-claims court and the second involves a major personal-injury claim;

(d) The ***issue is one of law*** and the claims in the two actions are substantially unrelated [**American Casualty Co. v. Sentry Federal Savings Bank,** 867 F. Supp. 50 (D. Mass. 1994)];

(e) The ***burden of proof is*** materially different or has shifted; or

(f) There is a clear and convincing need for a new determination because, for instance, the party who lost on the issue ***could not have been expected to foresee*** that the issue would arise in a later action.

(2) ***When the second action involves a different party***, all these exceptions apply and, in addition, the loser may relitigate if there are other factors that justify allowing her to do so. (*See infra*, p. 462.)

D. Persons Precluded by Judgments

1. Parties and Privies

Judgments may have a preclusive effect on parties and those in privity with a party.

a. Parties

A party to a judgment is bound by ***claim preclusion*** (so that she cannot relitigate the claim) ***and issue preclusion*** (so that, ordinarily, she cannot relitigate an issue determined in the first action).

b. Privies

A person in "privity" with a party is usually bound to the ***same extent*** as the party. "Privity" is a legal conclusion, indicating that the person in question has a relationship to the party such that he should be bound. Whether "privity" exists depends in part on the type of claims involved. There are two general categories of privity:

(1) Procedural Privity

If the party acted in the first action as the *representative* of the nonparty, the judgment therein binds the nonparty. [Restatement (Second) of Judgments § 41]

e.g. **Examples**: A party appearing as the representative of a class in a class suit [**King v. International Union,** 114 Cal. App. 2d 159 (1952)]; a trustee or guardian representing a beneficiary or ward [**Armstrong v. Armstrong,** 15 Cal. 3d 942 (1976)—parent for child]; *or* a party whose interests are represented by an executor or administrator.

(2) Substantive Privity

Privity may also arise out of *substantive* legal; relationships, with the nonparty bound because of a prior legal relationship to the party. [Restatement (Second) of Judgments § 41] Examples include the following:

(a) Bailment

Either the bailee or the bailor can sue a third party for injury to the bailed chattel; and an action by one precludes an action by the other. [**Anheuser-Busch, Inc. v. Starley,** 28 Cal. 2d 347 (1946)]

(b) Medical Losses of Child or Spouse

In most states, medical expenses (*e.g.*, hospital bills) paid by a parent or spouse can be recovered either by the injured person or by the parent or spouse who paid them. Hence an action by one of those who could recover the expenses precludes an action by any of the others. [Restatement (Second) of Judgments § 48]

(c) Successor in Interest

A successor in interest to property is bound by a judgment regarding that interest to which his predecessor was a party. [**Kartheiser v. Superior Court,** 174 Cal. App. 2d 617 (1959)]

e.g. **Example**: Plaintiff sues Defendant, an adjoining landowner, to determine the boundary between the properties. After judgment, Plaintiff transfers the property to Third Party. Third Party is bound by the prior determination of the boundary.

(d) Beneficiary of Estate

A beneficiary of an estate is bound by an action litigated on behalf of the estate by the trustee. [Restatement (Second) of Judgments § 41(a)]

(e) Public Official Authorized by Law to Act on Person's Behalf

If a public official is authorized by law to act on a person's behalf, the person is bound by the official's litigation on his behalf. [Restatement (Second) of Judgments § 41(d)]

(f) "Virtual" Representation

Several lower courts had held that in some circumstances a nonparty was bound by the outcome of an earlier litigation even though no traditional ground for "privity" applied. The Supreme Court has rejected the "virtual" representation ground for binding nonparties. [**Taylor v. Sturgell,** 553 U.S. 880 (2008)]

e.g. **Example**: It was improper to bind a plaintiff who made a Freedom of Information Act request to the Federal Aviation Administration for documents regarding repairs on an antique aircraft by the result of an earlier litigation that denied a request by another plaintiff for the same documents. Although the later litigant was a "close associate" of the loser in the first case, and had agreed to help him obtain the information, those facts alone would not justify binding the later litigant. Binding effect could occur only if defendants proved that the later litigant was really acting as the agent of the unsuccessful earlier litigant in bringing the second case. [**Taylor v. Sturgell,** *supra*]

(3) Distinguish—Family Relationships

That parties have a legal relationship with each other does not of itself make them "privies." Thus, a husband's lawsuit is not binding on his wife (unless, in a community-property state, the husband represents the community in maintaining the suit); neither does a parent necessarily represent a child. Whether "privity" exists depends on whether there is a *representative* capacity arising out of the relationship.

e.g. **Example**: In a divorce action with Wife, Husband litigated the question whether he had given half ownership of the family farm to his sons. The sons were not bound by the result, even though they testified as witnesses in the divorce action. [**Searle Brothers v. Searle,** 588 P.2d 689 (Utah 1978)]

e.g. **Example**: Parent and Child are both hurt in an automobile accident with Defendant. If Parent sues Defendant for his injuries and loses, that does not bar Child from suing Defendant for Child's injuries.

cf. **Compare**: If Parent sues as Child's *guardian* for Child's injuries, that precludes a suit by Child (because she was represented in the first suit) (*see supra*, p. 458)—although it would not preclude a suit by Parent for *his own* injuries, because that is a different claim (*see supra*, p. 447).

EXAM TIP ◤GILBERT

Issue preclusion (collateral estoppel) is a fairly common exam topic. Remember the basics: If an issue is actually litigated and determined in a proceeding and essential to the judgment, that determination is binding in any subsequent action between the parties, even if the subsequent action is unrelated to the first action. This preclusive effect applies only to issues that were **actually litigated and determined** and only if the issue was **essential to the first judgment**. The preclusive effect extends to persons in privity with the parties. But remember that issue preclusion will not apply if it would be unfair because, for example, the stakes in the first suit were low (*e.g.,* a few hundred dollars) and the stakes in the second suit are much higher.

---

2. Nonparties

a. Nonparty Not Bound

In general, a nonparty is **not bound** by a judgment. Such a person has not had his day in court and, as a matter of **due process,** he cannot be denied a valuable interest (his right of action) without one. [**Parklane Hosiery Co. v. Shore,** *supra*, p. 454] Instances of "privity" (above) are exceptions to the rule, justified on the ground that the nonparty's interests were adequately represented by the party to the first action.

Example—No Binding Effect on Nonparties: White firefighters, who had not been parties to a prior litigation between a city and civil rights claimants that resulted in consent decrees establishing minority hiring and promotion goals, were not precluded from bringing a discrimination suit against the city for promotion decisions it made under the decree. It was immaterial whether the white firefighters could have intervened in the first litigation; the burden of joining additional parties to secure binding effect against them is on those already parties. [**Martin v. Wilks,** *supra*, p. 226]

(1) Federal Statutory Exception

For cases involving federal employment-discrimination claims, Congress, in the Civil Rights Act of 1991, changed the ruling of *Martin*, *supra*, to give binding effect to a litigated or consent judgment or order when the nonparty had adequate notice and opportunity to present objections, or when the nonparty's specific interests had been adequately represented by another. [42 U.S.C. § 2000e–2(n)]

(2) Due Process Limits on Extreme Application of State Preclusion Law

Although states are generally free to decide the content of their own preclusion law, federal due process principles impose some limits on extreme applications to nonparties. [**Postal Telegraph Cable Co. v. City of Newport,** 247 U.S. 464 (1918)] Thus, individual taxpayers who sought to challenge a county occupation tax levied upon them could not be bound by a prior, unsuccessful nonclass action brought by a city against the county challenging the same tax, when the taxpayers received no notice of the first action and the court and parties had done nothing to assure adequate protection of their interests. [**Richards v. Jefferson County,** 517 U.S. 793 (1996); **South Central Bell Telephone Co. v. Alabama,** 526 U.S. 160 (1999) (corporation's challenge to state tax not precluded by other suit involving unrelated taxpayer); *compare* **Hansberry v. Lee,** *supra*, p. 246]

b. Nonparty May Benefit

A nonparty may sometimes **benefit** from the judgment in an action to which he was not a party.

(1) Claim Preclusion

In some situations, two potential defendants will have a relationship such that one is responsible for the conduct of the other. Examples include employer and employee (under the principle of respondeat superior) and insurer and insured (the insurer being liable, up to the policy limits, for acts of the insured). When this relationship of vicarious responsibility exists, a judgment *exonerating either* potential defendant precludes an action on the same claim against the other.

Example: Plaintiff claims injuries as the result of negligence by Employee, who was acting in the course and scope of his employment for Employer. If Plaintiff sues either Employee or Employer alone, a judgment *exonerating* that defendant (on a finding of no negligence by Employee) will preclude a claim against the other, since Employer's liability is derivative in nature. *Note*: This form of preclusion existed even before the widespread (but still not universal) abandonment of the requirement of mutuality of estoppel (*see infra*, p. 461), to prevent anomalies in some indemnity situations such as that above involving Employer's possible respondeat-superior liability. It was then often regarded as a form of claim preclusion. Today, in jurisdictions that have abandoned the mutuality requirement, the same result would likely be reached if Plaintiff sued, say, Employee and lost, then sued Employer, by issue preclusion against Plaintiff on the issue of Employee's negligence.

(a) Not Applicable to Joint or Concurrent Liability

This form of claim preclusion applies **only** in situations of **vicarious responsibility**, and not in cases of joint or concurrent tort liability. Thus, if Plaintiff is injured by the **concurrent negligence** of Driver 1 and Driver 2 (each of whom operates his own car) and Plaintiff sues Driver 1 and loses, that judgment does not bar Plaintiff from suing Driver 2. But if Driver 1 was driving Owner's car, and Plaintiff lost in an action against Driver 1, Plaintiff could not sue Owner based on Driver 1's conduct.

(2) Issue Preclusion

(a) Basic Rule

The majority rule is that a party who litigates an issue against one party **and loses** may not relitigate that issue with another party. This form of preclusion is known as "nonmutual" issue preclusion because a prior nonparty cannot be bound when a prior party in another case against someone else litigates an issue **and wins**. About two-thirds of the states, plus federal courts when federal preclusion law governs, allow nonmutual issue preclusion; the remainder usually do not.

e.g. **Example**: Driver and Passenger are injured when Driver's car is hit by Defendant's car. Driver sues Defendant, contending that Defendant was negligent, and wins. If Passenger then sues Defendant, Defendant is bound by the first action and cannot relitigate whether he was negligent.

1) Rationale

If a party has had a **full and fair opportunity to litigate an issue** in one action, there is no reason to waste the time of the court and other persons in relitigating that issue. [**Blonder-Tongue Laboratories, Inc. v. University of Illinois Foundation,** 402 U.S. 313 (1971); **Bernhard v. Bank of America,** 19 Cal. 2d 807 (1942)] The rule is often referred to as the *"Bernhard"* rule.

(b) Background—Mutuality Rule

Before *Bernhard, supra,* the mutuality rule prevented a nonparty from having the benefit of issue preclusion in his favor. The theory was that an estoppel should apply only if it was mutual—*i.e.,* since the nonparty would not have been bound by the issue had it been decided the other way (because he had not had his day in court), he should not be able to invoke estoppel in his favor based on the earlier judgment. *Bernhard,* which rejected this mutuality rule, is now the majority view. [Restatement (Second) of Judgments § 29]

Clarification: Students sometimes find the old mutuality requirement (still followed in some states) mind-bending. It helps if you realize that you don't have to figure out mutuality in every case. In a jurisdiction requiring mutuality, the effect is a general rule that nonmutual issue preclusion is usually not allowed.

(c) Offensive vs. Defensive Use of Prior Judgment

Some earlier decisions held that nonmutual issue preclusion could be used defensively against a prior plaintiff, but not offensively against a prior defendant (to block defendant's attempt to relitigate issues on which he had lost in the earlier trial). However, the Supreme Court has held that this is *not* a critical distinction. [**Parklane Hosiery Co. v. Shore,** *supra*, p. 459] The Restatement (Second) of Judgments also draws no general distinction between defensive and offensive uses of nonmutual issue preclusion. [Restatement (Second) of Judgments § 29]

Example—Defensive Use: Plaintiff claims to have been injured by the concurrent acts of Defendant 1 and Defendant 2. In an action by Plaintiff against Defendant 1, it is found that Plaintiff suffered no actual injury. If Plaintiff later sues Defendant 2 for the same loss, Defendant 2 can invoke issue preclusion defensively. [**Ponce v. Tractor Supply Co.,** 29 Cal. App. 3d 500 (1972)]

Example—Offensive Use: Passenger 1 and Passenger 2, passengers in a bus, are hurt when the bus collides with a train. Passenger 1 wins in his suit against the railroad. Most decisions would give issue-preclusive effect on common issues in Passenger 2's later suit against the railroad.

Example—Offensive Use: In action 1, the SEC files suit against Corporation for false statements in a proxy solicitation in connection with a proposed merger (*i.e.*, mailings to the shareholders seeking their votes to approve the merger). Judgment is rendered against Corporation. In action 2, shareholders file suit against Corporation seeking damages as a result of their reliance on the same proxy solicitation. The judgment rendered against Corporation in the SEC action may be held to bar Corporation from relitigating the issue whether the solicitation was false and misleading. [*See* **Parklane Hosiery Co. v. Shore,** *supra*]

(d) Limitations

Although nonmutual issue preclusion can be used offensively or defensively, the benefits of such preclusion may be denied under certain circumstances.

1) Issue Would Not Be Conclusive Between Parties

If the issue would not be treated as conclusive between the *parties* to the first action (*see supra*, p. 457), it cannot be conclusive in *favor of a third person* not a party to the first action.

 Example: Plaintiff is slightly injured while a passenger in Driver 1's car when it collides with Driver 2's car. Plaintiff sues Driver 1

for $300 in doctor's bills and wins on a finding that Driver 1 was negligent. Driver 2 then sues Driver 1 for $250,000 in personal injuries. The finding in the first action does not preclude Driver 1 from relitigating the negligence issue because the first case was so small that it would not be treated as conclusive even between Plaintiff and Driver 1 in a second action.

2) Unjust Under Circumstances

In addition, a third person cannot have the benefit of issue preclusion against a party to the first action if it would be unjust in the circumstances. In deciding whether preclusion would be "unjust," the court may consider relevant factors such as the following: [*See* Restatement (Second) of Judgments § 29]

a) Whether the person seeking the benefit of preclusion *could have joined in the prior action*, but decided instead to "sit it out";

b) Whether the prior determination was itself *inconsistent with an earlier determination* of the same issue;

c) Whether the party to be precluded has *procedural opportunities* in the second action (*e.g.*, broader discovery, ability to compel live testimony of important witnesses) that were not available in the earlier action;

d) Whether the prior finding was apparently a *compromise verdict*;

e) Whether the issue is one of law whose *reconsideration should not be foreclosed* [**United States v. Mendoza,** 464 U.S. 154 (1984)— federal government not subject to issue preclusion from prior determination in litigation with different party]; and

f) Whether *other compelling circumstances* justify relitigation.

CLAIM PRECLUSION	ISSUE PRECLUSION
Judgment must have been:	Issue decided in prior action was:
• On the *same claim* (transactionally defined—related claim omitted before is barred by rule against *claim-splitting)*;	• *Actually litigated and determined* by a *valid and final judgment* (with "final" including some sufficiently definite issue rulings even when no final judgment has been entered);
• *Final*;	
• *Valid*;	• *Essential* to the first judgment;
• *On the merits* (remembering that some decisions not literally "on the merits" can have claim-preclusive effect); and	• *Identical* to the issue presented in the instant action; and
Party against whom claim preclusion is sought was a *party* to the prior litigation or *in privity* with such a party.	Party against whom issue preclusion is sought was a *party* to the prior litigation or in *privity* with such a party.

E. Interjurisdictional Preclusive Effects of Judgments

1. Introduction

In the United States, there are 50 state-court systems as well as the federal-court system. Although preclusion issues often arise when the later case is in the same court system as the earlier case, it also happens frequently that the second case is in a different court system. When that occurs, the attitudes toward preclusion of the first court system and the second court system may differ, and a decision will have to be made about which principles to apply.

2. Basic Rule

The basic rule regarding interjurisdictional preclusive effects of judgments is that the *preclusion principles of the court system that rendered the judgment* should be used to determine its preclusive effect.

a. State-Court Judgments Constitutionally Entitled to Effect in Other State Courts

Under the Full Faith and Credit Clause, Article IV, section 1 of the federal Constitution, "Full Faith and Credit shall be given in each State to the . . . judicial Proceedings of every other State."

b. State-Court Judgments Given Effect in Federal and State Court by Statute

The *Full Faith and Credit statute*, 28 U.S.C. section 1738, directs that state-court judgments "shall have *the same full faith and credit* in every court within the United States and its Territories and Possessions *as they have by law or usage in the courts* of such State, Territory or Possession *from which they are taken*." This statute requires federal courts, and courts of other states, to give effect to state-court judgments, and also directs that the preclusion principles of the rendering jurisdiction be applied.

e.g. **Example**: Plaintiffs filed suit in an Illinois state court, alleging a violation of a "common law right of association" resulting from denial of their applications to join a professional group. Their suit was dismissed, and Plaintiffs thereafter sued in federal court asserting that there had been a federal antitrust violation. The state court could not have entertained the federal antitrust claim because it was subject to exclusive federal jurisdiction. The federal district court nevertheless did not consider whether claim preclusion would apply under Illinois preclusion law, and instead dismissed based on general preclusion principles. This action was error because section 1738 requires the federal court to look to state preclusion law. [**Marrese v. American Academy of Orthopaedic Surgeons,** 470 U.S. 373 (1985)]

e.g. **Example**: Even though federal common law of preclusion permitted relitigation if an earlier case ended in default judgment, a California state-court judgment was binding in a subsequent federal bankruptcy-court proceeding because California law treated default judgments as binding. [**Bay Area Factors v. Calvert,** 105 F.3d 315 (9th Cir. 1997)]

(1) Caution

In practice, some state courts seem unaware of the obligation to follow the preclusion law that would govern in the courts of the system that rendered a judgment, and they may apply their own preclusion principles instead. Because preclusion doctrines are often similar in different systems, however, such ignorance of the proper source of applicable preclusion law will usually make no practical difference.

c. Federal-Court Judgment Generally Given Effect According to Federal Principles of Preclusion

Even though there is no explicit constitutional or statutory provision to this effect, it is accepted that federal-court judgments are entitled to preclusive effect, and that this effect is determined according to the *federal common law* of preclusion. [**Stoll v. Gottlieb,** 305 U.S. 165 (1938)—judgment of a federal court in a federal-question case entitled to preclusive effect as determined by federal common law of preclusion]

(1) Diversity Cases

Federal common law governs the preclusive effect of federal courts' judgments in diversity cases; but, because state substantive law is at issue, no uniform federal rule is needed. Hence, absent a federal interest such as enforcement of sanctions for discovery misconduct, the federal common law governing the preclusive effect of a federal court's diversity judgment is the law that would be followed by the courts of the state in which the federal diversity court sat. [**Semtek International Inc. v. Lockheed Martin Corp.,** *supra*, p. 126]

d. Scope of Effect of First Judgment

Although the preclusive effect of a judgment is determined in the first instance by the preclusion law of the court that entered it, that effect cannot exceed the scope of what the judgment could legitimately conclude, *e.g.*, it could not bind persons not parties to the judgment. [**Baker v. General Motors Corp.,** 522 U.S. 222 (1998)—Michigan state-court injunction that prohibited witness from testifying without GM's permission in later cases in which GM was a party did not preclude subpoenaed testimony of that witness in suit against GM by unrelated plaintiff in federal court in another state]

3. Prohibition Against Giving Broader Preclusive Effect than Required

Ensuring that judgments of sister states are given due respect might seem to permit giving them more effect than would the courts of the state where the judgment was rendered. Nonetheless, the Supreme Court has interpreted the Full Faith and Credit Statute to forbid a federal court to give more effect to a state-court judgment than is called for by the preclusion rules of that state. [**Marrese v. American Academy of Orthopaedic Surgeons,** *supra*] The rule is to give no more *and* no less preclusive effect to the judgment than the courts of the forum rendering the judgment would give it.

Examples: A court in a state that allows nonmutual issue preclusion, dealing with a judgment from a court in a state that does not, should not recognize any nonmutual preclusive effect. And a court in a state that does not allow such preclusion, dealing with a judgment from a court in a state that allows it, should follow the first forum's rule and allow nonmutual issue preclusion.

4. Preclusion Regarding Claims Within Exclusive Federal Jurisdiction

A frequent problem arises when a federal suit asserts a claim that could not have been raised in an earlier state-court action because it was subject to exclusive federal jurisdiction, and a party argues that the federal claim is nevertheless precluded by the judgment in the state-court case.

a. Rule of Jurisdictional "Competence" for Claim Preclusion

The law of most states is that *claim preclusion* is not available with respect to a claim over which the court does not have subject-matter jurisdiction. [Restatement (Second) of Judgments § 26(1)(c)] *Rationale*: If the court cannot entertain the claim, it should not be able by its judgment to extinguish the claim.

b. Distinguish—Issue-Preclusive Effects

If the state-court decision of a state-law claim resolves issues that are also presented by a federal claim, those determinations can be given effect in a later federal suit asserting the federal claim even if that claim is within exclusive federal jurisdiction. [**Kremer v. Chemical Construction Corp.**, 456 U.S. 461 (1982)—issue preclusion applicable to Title VII employment-discrimination claim although it was unclear whether there is exclusive federal jurisdiction over such claims; **Becher v. Contoure Laboratories, Inc.**, 279 U.S. 388 (1929)—issue preclusion from state-court suit bars subsequent federal patent suit]

c. Possible Argument for Exception to Full Faith and Credit Statute

If state law indicates that a state-court judgment should be given preclusive effect even with regard to a claim within exclusive federal jurisdiction, there may be a basis for finding an exception to section 1738 if the grounds for prohibiting state courts from adjudicating such claims support finding a *partial repeal* of the statute. But the Supreme Court has said that this is a "relatively stringent standard" for finding such a repeal, depending on an "irreconcilable conflict" between section 1738 and the Congressional grant of exclusive federal jurisdiction. [**Matsushita Electric Industrial Co. v. Epstein**, 516 U.S. 367 (1996)]

Review Questions and Answers

Review Questions

PERSONAL JURISDICTION

1. Plaintiff is a resident of State A. Defendant is a resident of State B. Plaintiff files suit against Defendant in an appropriate State A court, serving Defendant personally while Defendant is in an airplane flying over State A. Defendant has no other contacts with State A. Should the court grant Defendant's motion to dismiss for want of jurisdiction over his person?

2. Plaintiff is a resident of State A. Defendant is a doctor in State B. Plaintiff commenced an action against Defendant in the court of State A, alleging that he had been injured in an auto collision in State A caused by a loss of consciousness in a patient of Defendant, which in turn had resulted from an act of professional malpractice committed in State B. Defendant moved to dismiss the action for want of jurisdiction over his person. Should the motion be granted?

3. Hypochondriac is a resident of State A. Pharmco is a drug manufacturer in State B that sells its products in State A. Hypochondriac commenced an action against Pharmco in the court of State A, alleging injury from a defective drug purchased by Hypochondriac in State A. Pursuant to the law of State A, Hypochondriac served Pharmco by mail at its place of business in State B. Pharmco moved to dismiss the action for want of jurisdiction over its person. Should the motion be granted?

4. Plaintiff is a resident of State A. Defendant is a resident of State B and is not itself subject to service of process in State A. Plaintiff brings an action against Defendant in a court of State A for breach of contract. Process is served in State A on Hand, a resident of State A, who was designated as Defendant's agent for service of process in a contract made between Plaintiff and Defendant. Defendant moves to quash the service of process and to dismiss for want of jurisdiction. Should the motion be granted?

5. Brenda is a resident of State A. Dylan is a resident of State B and is not subject to service of process in State A. Brenda commenced an action against Dylan in a court of State A. After a contested trial, the jury rendered a verdict for Brenda. Dylan then raised want of jurisdiction over his person and moved to dismiss. Should the court grant the motion?

6. Plaintiff is a resident of State A. Defendant is a resident of State B and is not subject to service of process in State A. Plaintiff writes Defendant offering to settle a dispute on very reasonable terms if Defendant will meet Plaintiff in State A to discuss it. Defendant arrives and is met at the appointed place by a process server in an action brought in a court of State A by Plaintiff on the dispute. Defendant moves to quash service of process and to dismiss for want of jurisdiction. Should the court grant the motion?

   _____

7. Martha files a diversity suit against Ben in federal court in New York, claiming damages arising out of an accident which occurred in New Jersey. Martha resides in Connecticut and Ben resides in Pennsylvania, but Martha chose to file in New York because most of the witnesses reside there. Is venue proper in New York?

   _____

8. Can the action in the previous question be transferred to New Jersey? If transferred to New Jersey, can the action be transferred back again to New York for the convenience of the parties and witnesses under 28 U.S.C. section 1404(a) if Ben does not agree to that transfer?

   _____

9. If a transfer for convenience of parties and witnesses was proper, could the transfer be made on the motion of *Plaintiff?*

   _____

10. Plaintiff, a resident of New York, wishes to sue Defendant, a resident of New Jersey, for injuries suffered in an auto accident in Pennsylvania. Would venue be proper for a federal action in New Jersey (which has only one federal district) and some district in Pennsylvania?

    _____

11. Plaintiff Co. is incorporated in Delaware and has its principal place of business there. Its employee is a citizen of Pennsylvania. Plaintiff and Employee wish to join as plaintiffs in a suit against Defendant 1 (a citizen of Florida) and Defendant 2 (a citizen of Georgia) for damage done in a ship collision that occurred in international waters. In what state would venue be proper for an action in federal court?

    _____

12. Plaintiff is a resident of State A and Defendant is a resident of State B. After negotiations that occurred in both State A and State B, Plaintiff and Defendant entered into a contract for Defendant to provide services in State A. The contract provided that any dispute between them under the contract would be resolved by a court in State B. Plaintiff later sued Defendant in federal court in State A, properly invoking diversity jurisdiction. Can Defendant have the action dismissed for lack of personal jurisdiction based on the contract provision calling for disputes to be resolved by a court in State B? Can Defendant have the action transferred based on that contract provision?

    _____

13. Plaintiff is a citizen of State A. Defendant is a citizen of State B. Plaintiff files a diversity suit against Defendant for $150,000 in a federal court located in State A. Copies of the summons and complaint are mailed to Defendant in his home state of B. Has Defendant been effectively served? _____

14. Plaintiff is a resident of State A. Defendant is a resident of State B. Defendant is subject to service of process in State A and has a bank account in that state. Plaintiff files an action against Defendant in a court of State A and serves a writ of garnishment on Defendant's bank, thereafter notifying Defendant of the proceedings. Defendant moves to quash the writ of garnishment and to dismiss for want of jurisdiction. Should the court grant the motion? _____

FEDERAL SUBJECT-MATTER JURISDICTION

15. Plaintiff, a citizen of Texas, files a diversity action in federal court against "XYZ, Inc."

    a. Assume that "XYZ, Inc." is in fact a partnership, having its principal place of business in Oklahoma, and consisting of three partners (X, Y, and Z), one of whom is a citizen of Texas. Does the requisite diversity of citizenship exist? _____

    b. Assume that "XYZ, Inc." is a corporation incorporated in Delaware, having its principal place of business in New York with branch offices nationwide, including one in Texas. Does the requisite diversity of citizenship exist? _____

16. George, a citizen of Virginia, takes a vacation trip to Mexico City, where he negligently injures Vincent. Vincent sues George for $150,000 damages in the federal court in Virginia, claiming diversity jurisdiction. Which, if any, of the following factors would justify the court's dismissing the action for *lack* of diversity? _____

    (A) Vincent is a Mexican national.

    (B) Vincent is a United States citizen living permanently in Mexico City.

    (C) Vincent is a citizen of Virginia, but has been mentally incompetent since birth, and his longtime guardian is a citizen of Maryland.

17. Plaintiff files suit against Defendant in federal court, claiming diversity of citizenship jurisdiction. Which, if any, of the following facts would justify the court's dismissal of the action for *lack* of diversity? _____

    (A) Plaintiff and Defendant were both citizens of State A at the time the claim arose. Plaintiff moved to State B just before filing suit against Defendant, for the apparent purpose of *creating* diversity of citizenship.

(B)   Plaintiff and Defendant were citizens of different states at the time the claim arose. Just before Plaintiff filed his suit, Defendant moved into the state where Plaintiff resided, for the apparent purpose of *preventing* diversity of citizenship.

(C)   Plaintiff and Defendant were citizens of different states at the time the claim arose and at the time the suit was filed. Shortly thereafter, however, Defendant moved into the state where Plaintiff resided.

(D)   Plaintiff and Defendant are citizens of different states at all times. However, neither of them resides in the state in which the federal court is located.

(E)   Plaintiff and Defendant are citizens of different states at all times, but Plaintiff is suing on a claim assigned to him for collection by a citizen of the state in which Defendant resides.

18.   Pam, a citizen of State A, and Jim, a citizen of State X, join in an action against Dwight, a citizen of State B, and Michael, a citizen of State X. Federal jurisdiction is invoked on grounds of diversity of citizenship. Michael moves to dismiss for want of federal jurisdiction. Should the motion be granted?   _____

19.   Plaintiff is a citizen of State A. Defendant is a citizen of State B, but is subject to service of process in State A. Plaintiff brought an action against Defendant in the federal court in State A, alleging diversity of citizenship, and asserting a tort claim for damages in the amount of $65,000. After trial, the jury rendered a verdict for Plaintiff in the amount of $40,000. Defendant then moved to dismiss for want of subject-matter jurisdiction. Should the court grant the motion?   _____

20.   Plaintiff files a diversity suit against Defendant, alleging $125,000 damages for invasion of privacy. The jury subsequently awards Plaintiff only $500 damages. Does the federal court have jurisdiction to enter such a judgment?   _____

21.   Hunter sues Blair in a diversity suit for $60,000 owed on a promissory note and $50,000 in personal injuries. Has the required jurisdictional amount for diversity purposes been met?   _____

22.   Plaintiff sues Defendant 1 and Defendant 2 as co-defendants in a diversity suit. Plaintiff alleges that Defendant 1 owes her $60,000 on one promissory note, that Defendant 2 owes her $50,000 on another promissory note, and that both promissory notes were executed at the same time and as part of the same transaction. Is the jurisdictional-minimum requirement satisfied?   _____

23. Plaintiff 1 and Plaintiff 2 join as plaintiffs to sue Defendant in a diversity suit to recover for an auto accident in which Plaintiff 1 and Plaintiff 2 were both riding in a car hit by a car driven by Defendant. Plaintiff 1 seeks to recover $60,000 and Plaintiff 2 seeks to recover $50,000. Is the jurisdictional minimum requirement satisfied?

_____

24. Same facts as in the previous question, except that Plaintiff 1 makes a claim for $100,000. Assuming complete diversity, is there jurisdiction for Plaintiff 2 to join in the suit with a claim for $50,000?

_____

25. Same facts as in the previous question, except that Plaintiff 2 has the same citizenship as Defendant. Can Plaintiff 2's claim be joined in Plaintiff 1's suit?

_____

26. Plaintiff is a citizen of State A. Defendant is a citizen of State B. Plaintiff brought an action against Defendant in the federal court in State B, praying for a decree of divorce. Defendant moved to dismiss for want of federal jurisdiction. Should the motion be granted?

_____

27. Britney and Kevin, both citizens of State A, were divorced pursuant to an agreement providing for alimony payments by Kevin to Britney in fixed amounts "after taxes." Britney was held liable for federal income taxes on payments received. She now brings an action in federal court to recover on the promise of Kevin to bear the income-tax liability, alleging that it arises under federal law. Kevin moves to dismiss for want of subject-matter jurisdiction. Should the motion be granted?

_____

28. Plaintiff brought an action against Defendant in federal court for defamation, alleging federal jurisdiction based on the federal question presented by Defendant's defense that his speech was constitutionally protected by the First Amendment. Defendant moved to dismiss for want of federal jurisdiction. Should the motion be granted?

_____

29. Plaintiff claims that his business has been damaged by monopolistic practices by Defendant, which allegedly violate **both** the Sherman Act and a state "fair practices" act.

    a. Can Plaintiff file an action asserting both claims in either state or federal court?

_____

    b. If Plaintiff files in federal court, can the federal court grant relief under the state act even if no violation of the Sherman Act is proved?

_____

30. If there are **several** co-defendants in a state-court action, must they **all** join in the notice of removal to the federal court for removal to the federal court to be proper?

_____

31. Smith, a citizen of Nevada, sues Jones, a citizen of California, in a California state court to enforce a promissory note for $100,000. Jones files a counterclaim against Smith for $1 million.

    a. Can Smith remove the action to the federal court in California?

    b. Can Jones remove the action to the federal court in California?

32. Black, a citizen of New Jersey, sues Brown, a citizen of New York, in a state court in New York. The claim is for copyright infringement, which is subject to exclusive federal-court jurisdiction. Can Brown remove the action to the federal court in New York?

33. Plaintiff is a citizen of State A. Defendant is a citizen of State B. Plaintiff files an action against Defendant for violation of the federal civil rights laws in a state court of general jurisdiction in State A. Should the court grant Defendant's motion to dismiss for want of jurisdiction over the subject matter of the claim?

RELATIONSHIP BETWEEN STATE AND FEDERAL LAW

34. On July 14, Parker files an action against Meredith in federal court in State X, properly invoking diversity jurisdiction, to recover for injuries sustained in an automobile accident on the previous July 15. One week after the suit was filed, Meredith was personally served with the summons and complaint. Meredith defends on the ground that the action is barred under the applicable one-year statute of limitations, citing a provision of State X law that the limitations period continues to run until a defendant is personally served. Is Meredith's defense valid?

35. Plaintiff files a diversity action against Defendant in federal court in State X. To prove her right to recover, Plaintiff must rely on certain hearsay evidence that would be inadmissible in state court in State X, but which is admissible under the Federal Rules of Evidence, which provide a number of exceptions to the hearsay rule. Should the evidence be admitted?

36. In Plaintiff's diversity suit against Defendant in federal court in State X, Defendant moves for judgment as a matter of law at the close of all the evidence on the ground that Plaintiff has failed to produce substantial evidence as required by federal precedents interpreting Rule 50(a)(1). Plaintiff responds by invoking the rule of the courts of State X that such a motion should be denied if plaintiff has produced a scintilla of evidence, a lower requirement. Should the court apply the federal requirement?

37. Plaintiff files a diversity suit against Defendant in federal court in State X. Under a 30-year-old decision of the intermediate appellate court of State X, Defendant has an absolute defense to the case, but the more "modern" view is that this defense is no longer valid. Defendant moves to dismiss, citing the state appellate-court decision. Should the court grant the motion? _____

PLEADING

38. Polly files an action in a code-pleading state against Riding Stable to recover for injuries sustained when Polly was thrown from a horse rented from Riding Stable. Polly's complaint is captioned "for breach of contract," and alleges that "Riding Stable allowed Polly to ride an unruly horse without adequate warning." Riding Stable demurs because the complaint nowhere alleges the existence of any contractual relationship. Should the court sustain the demurrer? _____

39. Plaintiff files a complaint against Defendant, a restaurant owner, alleging that he suffered food poisoning as the result of consuming "improperly prepared" food in Defendant's restaurant.

    a. Is this sufficient to state a claim for relief in federal court (apart from jurisdictional allegations)? _____

    b. Is this sufficient to state a claim for relief in a code-pleading state? _____

40. Plaintiff sues Defendant to quiet title to certain real property. Plaintiff alleges "on information and belief" that Defendant has recorded a document that clouds Plaintiff's title. Is such an allegation sufficient to state a claim for relief? _____

41. Plaintiff files a diversity action against Defendant in federal court, claiming $125,000 damages for a battery. In one claim of the complaint, Plaintiff alleges that Defendant himself struck and battered Plaintiff; but in a later claim he alleges that Defendant did not do it personally, but rather paid a third person to batter Plaintiff. Defendant files a motion to dismiss for failure to state a claim. Should the court grant the motion? _____

42. Henry sued Brad seeking to enjoin Brad's operating an amusement park as a nuisance interfering with Henry's enjoyment of his property. Brad filed no answer to Henry's complaint, and his default was entered. At the hearing on entry of judgment, the court found that an injunction would be harsh and unnecessary, and instead awarded Henry $50,000 damages for interference with the use and enjoyment of his property. Can Brad successfully appeal this judgment, having defaulted in the trial court? _____

43. Plaintiff has three separate and distinct claims against Defendant: (i) for nonpayment of a promissory note; (ii) for personal injuries; and (iii) to quiet title to certain property.

a.   Can Plaintiff join all three claims in a single action against Defendant in federal court?   _____

b.   Would the answer be the same if Plaintiff named Defendant's wife as a co-defendant on the promissory-note claim alone?   _____

44.   Spencer files a breach of contract action against Brody. Brody files a general denial and also alleges, "Spencer is a millionaire, and is bringing this suit hoping to force Brody into bankruptcy, so that he can pick up all of Brody's assets for a pittance." Spencer moves to strike this allegation from Brody's answer. Should the court grant the motion?   _____

45.   Plaintiff files a diversity suit in a federal court not having proper venue. Defendant does not file a motion to dismiss, but raises the improper venue in his answer. At the time of trial, he moves to dismiss for improper venue. Is Defendant's motion timely?   _____

46.   Plaintiff files a diversity suit in a federal court not having proper venue. Defendant files a motion to dismiss for failure to state a claim. When this motion is denied, Defendant files an answer in which he raises the venue objection. Plaintiff moves to strike this portion of the answer because the issue was not raised in Defendant's earlier motion to dismiss. Should the court grant the motion?   _____

47.   Plaintiff files a diversity suit in a federal court. Defendant moves to dismiss for improper venue, but his motion is denied. Defendant then files an answer in which he raises the objection that Plaintiff's complaint fails to state a claim upon which relief can be granted. Plaintiff moves to strike this portion of Defendant's answer because the issue was not raised in Defendant's earlier motion to dismiss. Should the court grant this motion?   _____

48.   Plaintiff's complaint in a federal action shows on its face that the action is barred by the statute of limitations, but otherwise sets forth all elements of the claim sued upon. Defendant moves to dismiss for failure to state a claim upon which relief can be granted. Plaintiff counters that the allegations of time were surplusage and asks the court to disregard them in ruling on Defendant's motion. Should the court grant Defendant's motion?   _____

49.   Jacqueline files a verified complaint in a state-court action in a code-pleading state. Lilly's answer (also verified) contains a general denial. Jacqueline moves to strike Lilly's answer on the ground that a general denial to a verified complaint is improper. Should the court sustain the demurrer?   _____

50. Plaintiff sues Defendant for nonpayment of a promissory note. Defendant's answer contains only the following allegation: "Defendant neither admits nor denies Plaintiff's charge, and puts Plaintiff to his proof at trial." Plaintiff moves for a judgment on the pleadings on the ground that Defendant has admitted liability. Should the court grant the motion?

_____

51. Plaintiff files a federal-court action against Defendant for breach of contract, claiming $125,000 damages. Defendant files an answer containing only a general denial. Is Defendant's answer an admission that some other sum is owed Plaintiff?

_____

52. Plaintiff files a defamation action against Defendant. Defendant's answer contains only a general denial. At trial, which, if any, of the following matters may be proved by Defendant?

_____

(A) That Defendant's utterance was true.

(B) That no one in fact heard what Defendant said about Plaintiff.

(C) That Plaintiff and Defendant later entered into a contract settling the matter.

(D) That Plaintiff's reputation was already so bad that no harm was done by the utterance.

53. Plaintiff sues Defendant for personal injuries in a federal action. Defendant's answer contains only a general denial. Later, Defendant seeks leave of court to amend his answer to object to improper venue. Should the court permit such an amendment?

_____

54. In answer to Alton's complaint, seeking to recover for injuries allegedly caused by food improperly prepared by Emeril's restaurant, Emeril alleges: "Whatever food poisoning Alton suffered resulted from his consuming food elsewhere than at Emeril's restaurant." What sort of pleading is now required from Alton in order to preserve the issue (as to where he consumed the food) for trial?

_____

55. Darien files a counterclaim to Porter's complaint in a federal-court action. Which, if any, of the following would be a valid ground for striking Darien's counterclaim if Darien and Porter are of diverse citizenship?

_____

(A) The counterclaim was pleaded as part of Darien's answer rather than as a separate pleading.

(B) Porter's complaint was for copyright infringement, while Darien's counterclaim was for $1 million for personal injury; hence no subject-matter relationship.

(C) Porter's complaint was for $125,000 damages for breach of contract. Darien's counterclaim was for $5,000 for personal injury. Hence, no federal jurisdiction on the counterclaim.

(D)   Several other parties would have to be joined for a complete determination of Darien's counterclaim.

56.   Plaintiff filed a complaint against Defendant on June 1 for back injuries arising out of a highway truck accident. Defendant filed a counterclaim on July 1 for damages to his own truck arising out of the same accident. Plaintiff moves to strike on the ground that the statute of limitations on Defendant's counterclaim ran on June 15. Should the court grant the motion?   _____

57.   Plaintiff has filed a personal-injury action in federal court against Defendant 1 and Defendant 2, claiming they were jointly responsible for causing a traffic accident in which he was injured. On which, if any, of the following grounds would it be proper for Defendant 1 to *crossclaim* against Defendant 2?   _____

(A)   Defendant 1 claims that the accident was entirely the fault of Defendant 2.

(B)   Defendant 1 claims that his car was damaged in the accident, and Defendant 2 was responsible therefor.

(C)   Defendant 1 claims that if Plaintiff recovers a judgment against him, it should be made payable against Defendant 2 jointly.

(D)   Defendant 1 claims that Defendant 2 owes him $15,000 on a promissory note.

58.   Same facts as in the previous question. Suppose Defendant 2 claimed that he lost control of his car due to defective repairs made by Repair Shop. Could Defendant 2 file a crossclaim for indemnification against Repair Shop?   _____

59.   Peggy sues Dalton for personal injuries resulting from Dalton's alleged negligence in causing an auto accident. Shortly before trial, Peggy discovers that Dalton had been driving under the influence of alcohol, and had been performing an errand for XYZ Co. By this time, however, the statute of limitations has run on all claims arising out of the accident.

a.   If Peggy seeks leave to amend her complaint to allege that Dalton was driving while intoxicated so as to entitle Peggy to punitive damages, should the court deny the motion on limitations grounds?   _____

b.   If Peggy seeks leave to amend her complaint to name XYZ Co. as a co-defendant, asserting liability against it on respondeat-superior grounds, should the court deny the motion on limitations grounds?   _____

60. Plaintiff sues Defendant 1 in state court in State X for an auto accident in State X, and Defendant 1 properly removes to federal court on grounds of diversity. Three years later, Plaintiff amends the complaint to add Defendant 2 as a defendant. Defendant 2 had no notice of the suit until it was served with the amended complaint, and it moves to dismiss on the ground the claims against it are barred by the applicable two-year statute of limitations. Under the law of State X, added defendants who are not on notice have no limitations defense if the plaintiff sues some defendant within the limitations period. Should the court grant Defendant 2's motion to dismiss?

    _____

61. Paula files suit against "Alfred A. Albertson," alleging that Albertson negligently operated a model airplane so as to cause it to fly through an open window of Paula's house, striking Paula in the head and causing serious injury.

    a. At trial, the evidence shows that the real name of the person sued as "Alfred A. Albertson" is "Albert T. Albrittson." Paula seeks leave to amend her complaint to conform to proof. Defendant resists on the ground that the statute of limitations has run. Should the court grant the motion?

    _____

    b. The evidence also shows that the model airplane destroyed a valuable vase in Paula's home worth $10,000. Paula seeks leave to amend to conform to proof. Defendant objects. What ruling?

    _____

    c. The evidence also shows that since the time the original complaint was filed, Paula's injuries have worsened, and she is now blind in one eye. Paula seeks leave to plead these additional facts. Defendant objects. Should the motion be granted?

    _____

62. On the date set for trial in a federal diversity suit, Plaintiff discovers that a crucial witness is unwilling to testify. Plaintiff moves for a dismissal of the action, hoping to sue again later. Defendant objects, wanting to obtain a judgment in his favor so as to bar any later suit. Can the court simply refuse to grant a dismissal and force Plaintiff to go to trial?

    _____

PARTIES

63. Which of the following parties would be entitled to sue in his own name on the claim in question without joining any other party as a plaintiff?

    _____

    (A) A collection agency on a debt assigned to it for collection.

    (B) The beneficiary of a trust on a claim against a third person for wrongs to the trust estate.

(C) A third-party beneficiary on a contract made expressly and primarily for his benefit.

(D) The promisee of a contract made expressly and primarily for the benefit of a third person.

(E) The undisclosed principal on a contract entered into on his behalf by an agent.

64. If someone other than the real party in interest files suit, and the defendant fails to raise a timely objection, can the resulting judgment be attacked? _____

65. In a federal action by a partnership asserting a state-law claim, does federal law determine the partnership's capacity to sue as an entity (rather than as an association of individual partners)? _____

66. Samantha, a minor female, wants to play baseball in the Little League system. After being refused, she files suit against Little League for injunctive relief. Little League moves to dismiss, on the ground that Samantha's father is the real party in interest. Should the motion be granted? _____

67. Bruce went into the hospital for surgery. He claims that Surgeon was negligent in performing the operation, causing him damages in the sum of $110,000. He also claims that the hospital was negligent in caring for him after surgery, for which he seeks $50,000 damages.

   a. Can Bruce join both defendants in a single action? _____

   b. Assume that Bruce cannot prove whether his injuries were attributable to improper surgery or to improper care after surgery. Is it permissible for him to join both defendants under such circumstances? _____

68. Plaintiff brought an action against Defendant 1 and Defendant 2 alleging that each had defrauded him in separate securities transactions. Defendant 2 moves to dismiss the action for improper joinder. Should the motion be granted? _____

69. Plaintiff brings an action against Defendant 1 on a promissory note signed by Defendant 1 and Defendant 2. Defendant 1 moves to dismiss the action for failure to join Defendant 2. Should the motion be granted? _____

70. Plaintiff brings an action as a holder in due course against Defendant to collect a portion of Defendant's liability on a note. The remainder of the obligation had been assigned by the payee to Assignee, who has not joined in the action. On motion by Defendant, should Assignee be joined? _____

71. Plaintiff, a citizen of State A, brought a federal diversity action against Defendant, a citizen of State B, to recover for alleged mismanagement of a corporation partially owned by Plaintiff. The corporation is a citizen of State B. Defendant moves to dismiss the action for failure to join the corporation. Should the motion be granted?

      _____

72. Chloe files a diversity suit in federal court against Tod, claiming damages for breach of contract. Tod claims that he was prevented from performing the contract by reason of tortious interference by Martha.

    a.   Can Tod join Martha as a party to the action?

      _____

    b.   Can the federal court retain the case if it appears that Martha is a citizen of the same state as Chloe?

      _____

73. Paul files a diversity suit against Duchess Sandwich Co., alleging that he became violently ill after consuming a sandwich purchased from Duchess which he alleges contained impure ingredients, thereby sustaining damages exceeding $110,000.

    a.   Tom, a co-worker in Paul's office, purchased a similar sandwich from Duchess on the same day as did Paul, and also became violently ill. If Tom moves to intervene in Paul's lawsuit against Duchess, should the court grant the motion?

    b.   XYZ is the company that furnishes Duchess with all of its ingredients, and has contracted to indemnify Duchess for any loss due to impurities in the ingredients furnished. If XYZ moves to intervene in Paul's lawsuit against Duchess, should the court grant the motion?

      _____

74. Don's life was insured for $500,000 by Apex Insurance Co., which has its principal place of business in California. Don is now dead. Apex has received conflicting claims for the insurance benefits from Don's wife, Wilma, a citizen of California, and Don's brother, Bob, a citizen of New York.

    a.   If Apex pays the $500,000 into federal court, can the federal court exercise jurisdiction to determine who is entitled to it?

      _____

    b.   Can the federal court in California exercise jurisdiction even though Bob is not subject to personal service in California?

      _____

75. Andy sues on behalf of himself "and all other students paying nonresident-rate tuition at State University" to enjoin collection of the higher tuition charged nonresidents on equal protection grounds, and seeking an injunction against continued higher tuition charges for nonresidents. Approximately 500 students are affected. May the case proceed as a class action?

      _____

76. Summer, a citizen of California, files suit in federal court against Victor Vacuum Co., incorporated and having its principal place of business in New York. Summer sues "on behalf of herself and all other customers of Victor Vacuum Co." alleging various deceptive advertising and sales practices, causing aggregate losses exceeding $110,000. Which, if any, of the following arguments justify granting Victor's motion to dismiss the action?

   (A) No diversity of citizenship, because some of Victor's customers reside in New York.

   (B) No diversity jurisdiction, because none of the individual claims involved is for more than $75,000 each.

   (C) Improper as class suit because each customer has a separate contract with Victor, hence no common question "predominates."

77. In determining whether an action should proceed as a class action, is it proper for the court to consider the suit's likelihood of success on the merits?

78. Assume that federal class-action status is granted on the ground that there is a "predominant common question."

   a. Is it mandatory that all members of the class who can be identified with reasonable effort be notified, no matter how many of them there are?

   b. Is it mandatory that the plaintiff initially pay the costs of giving such notice?

   c. Will a resulting judgment necessarily bind all members of the class?

79. Lisagh owns a Blizzo Snowmobile. Lisagh sues Blizzo in state court on behalf of herself and all other owners of Blizzo Snowmobiles, alleging that the vehicles have defective parts that make them unsafe to ride in and cause an unusually fast depreciation in value. Blizzo offers Lisagh $15,000 to settle the claim, and to create a fund that will assure that any other owner can recover $100 if a claim is made within one year. Lisagh then consents to entry of judgment in favor of Blizzo. Several months later, another owner, Tom, sues Blizzo for the same kind of damages. Is Tom bound by the judgment in Lisagh's action against Blizzo?

DISCOVERY

80. Must a party to a federal civil action disclose to an adversary, without having received any discovery request, the contents of a document in the party's possession that is harmful to its case?

81. Kiki files an action against XYZ, Inc. in federal court. Kiki wishes to conduct discovery by deposition, but is unsure which of the XYZ employees has the information she seeks, and therefore does not know whose name to put on the notice of deposition. Is it necessary for Kiki to file interrogatories to find out the employee's name before sending out the notice of deposition?

_____

82. Plaintiff sues XYZ, Inc. for personal injuries sustained in a traffic accident with a truck belonging to XYZ and driven by Employee (who is not a party to the action).

   a. Plaintiff took Employee's deposition before trial, with proper notice to XYZ, and obtained some admissions of negligence. Can Plaintiff introduce Employee's deposition as substantive evidence of negligence at the time of trial?

_____

   b. Plaintiff also took the deposition of Mr. X, the president of XYZ, Inc., who admitted that Employee was driving within the course and scope of his employment. Can Plaintiff introduce Mr. X's deposition testimony at trial as substantive evidence of this fact?

_____

83. Which, if any, discovery procedure is available under the Federal Rules to obtain the information indicated in the following cases?

   a. Plaintiff was involved in a traffic accident with Defendant, but is in doubt whether Defendant was at fault. Hence, *before* filing suit, she wants to obtain the testimony of Witness, who has refused to talk to Plaintiff about the matter.

_____

   b. Plaintiff sues Defendant for personal injuries sustained in a traffic accident. Plaintiff claims she was off work for several weeks. Defendant wants to check Plaintiff's time card maintained by Plaintiff's employer, but the employer has refused to provide this information.

_____

   c. An eyewitness to the Plaintiff-Defendant traffic accident claims to have observed the collision from his living-room window. Defendant wants to take photographs from inside the witness's living room to check the credibility of the witness's claimed observations.

_____

   d. The same eyewitness was wearing thick lenses at the time in question. Defendant has reason to doubt whether the witness's vision is sufficient to have seen what he claims to have seen. Therefore, Defendant asks for a court order to have the witness submit to a reasonable eye examination by Defendant's doctor. Should the court grant Defendant's motion?

_____

84. Carol sues Murray to quiet title to certain land. After considerable investigation, Murray's attorney obtains an old deed, which tends to support Carol's claim of title and to undermine Murray's defense. Somehow, Carol finds out about the deed and serves a request to produce on Murray. Which, if any, of the following are valid grounds for objection under the Federal Rules?

   (A) Murray does not have possession of the document.

   (B) The document is privileged as attorney's work product.

   (C) The request is improper because it was served without prior court order or any showing of good cause.

85. In a personal-injury case, Plaintiff is examined by Defendant's doctor. Plaintiff's attorney requests and obtains a copy of the report made by Defendant's doctor. Is Defendant now automatically entitled to copies of all medical reports by Plaintiff's doctors about the same condition?

86. Patron filed action against Restaurant for $75,000, claiming food poisoning from impure food prepared by Restaurant. Patron served on Restaurant the following interrogatories, to which Restaurant objected on the grounds stated. Patron now moves to compel answers. How should the court rule on the motion to compel regarding each of the following interrogatories and objections?

   a. Interrogatory: "Have you obtained statements in writing from other customers in the restaurant concerning the food served on the night in question?" Objection: Such statements are hearsay and inadmissible at trial.

   b. Interrogatory: "Do you claim that Plaintiff's food poisoning resulted from consumption of food elsewhere on the date in question?" Objection: Calls for a conclusion.

   c. Interrogatory: "Has any other customer ever filed a lawsuit against you claiming food poisoning as the result of food you served?" Objection: Irrelevant.

   d. Interrogatory: "In the event Plaintiff recovers a judgment for the full amount of his claim, do you have assets sufficient to pay such a judgment?" Objection: Irrelevant.

   e. Interrogatory: "Has your attorney caused any tests to be performed on the food in question to determine its purity, and if so, what are the results of the tests?" Objection: Calls for nondiscoverable expert opinion.

87. Ian has sued Shep and served and filed a set of interrogatories on Shep and Shep's wife. Which, if any, of the following are valid grounds for objection under the Federal Rules?

(A) The interrogatories were served concurrently with the summons and complaint, and without court order authorizing such service.

(B) Shep's wife is not a party to the action.

(C) This is the third set of interrogatories served on Shep, and many of the questions were answered in earlier interrogatories.

(D) The set of interrogatories includes 40 questions.

88. Puffy sues Ditty in federal court for copyright infringement of Puffy's musical composition. Puffy sends Ditty a request to admit that a designated portion of a song published by Ditty is in fact identical to a designated portion of Puffy's song. Ditty makes no response to this request. Which, if any, of the following statements is true?

(A) Upon motion, the court may adjudge Ditty in contempt and order Ditty's answer stricken.

(B) Ditty's failure to respond constitutes a binding admission that the designated portions are identical.

(C) No admission or denial was required because whether the designated portions are "identical" is the ultimate fact in issue for the trier of fact to determine.

89. Plaintiff brings an action against Defendant for personal injury. Defendant's lawyer goes to Plaintiff's place of employment, without notice to Plaintiff and without permission of the employer, and interrogates Plaintiff's employer and co-workers about the extent of his physical impairment. Which, if any, of the following statements are true?

(A) The employer and co-workers may lawfully refuse to talk to Defendant's lawyer.

(B) On motion, the court will order Defendant to desist from this practice because the proper way to get the information is by deposition.

(C) On motion, the court will exclude any information secured because it was the product of an unlawful trespass.

(D) Plaintiff is at least entitled to a copy of all statements signed by the informants.

SUMMARY JUDGMENT

90. Plaintiff files an action against Defendant for personal injuries arising out of a traffic accident. Defendant files a motion for summary judgment on the ground that he was not negligent. Defendant's motion is supported by affidavits signed by all the other eyewitnesses, and by the police officer who investigated the accident. The only opposing affidavit is that of Plaintiff, who simply controverts everything the eyewitnesses and police officer say. May the court grant Defendant's motion? _____

91. Becky files an action to rescind a deed for fraudulent misstatements made by Robbie. Robbie files a motion for summary judgment supported by his own affidavit to the effect that he believed the statements were true at the time he made them. No opposing affidavit is filed by Becky. Should the court grant Robbie's motion? _____

92. Plaintiff sues Defendant for copyright infringement of his musical composition. Defendant's answer denies Plaintiff's allegations. In deposition testimony, however, Defendant admits that a significant portion of his song is identical to Plaintiff's.

    a. Can the court grant Plaintiff's motion for a summary judgment as to the issue of infringement only? _____

    b. If Defendant files an affidavit denying the similarity, could the court grant Plaintiff's motion based on its own comparison of the songs? _____

MANAGERIAL JUDGING

93. Carter brings an action against Daisy in a federal court.

    a. Thirty days after the complaint was served, the court directed the parties to appear for a pretrial conference at which it would set deadlines for completion of discovery and the filing of all motions. Does the court have authority to require the parties to attend such a conference and to impose such restrictions? _____

    b. At a later pretrial conference, the court determines that there is a possibility of settlement and orders both Carter and Daisy to appear in person for a settlement conference. Are Carter and Daisy required to attend if they are represented by counsel? _____

    c. At the final pretrial conference, the court directs Carter and Daisy to submit their cases to a summary jury trial. Carter objects that such a proceeding would require revelation of trial strategy and that the parties are too far apart in their settlement negotiations to make it worthwhile. Is Carter required to attend and participate in the summary jury trial if the judge insists? _____

d. After the final pretrial conference, the court enters an order listing the issues in the case and witnesses for each party. At trial, Carter calls a witness not listed in the final pretrial order. Daisy objects. Should the court allow Carter's added witness to testify? _____

TRIAL

94. In which, if any, of the following cases is there a right to a jury trial in federal courts? _____

   (A) Audrey sues Cameron for damages for trespass to land.

   (B) Audrey sues Cameron to enjoin future trespasses upon her land.

   (C) Audrey sues Cameron to enjoin future trespasses and for damages for past trespasses.

   (D) Cameron sues Audrey for declaratory relief that his past entries were privileged and not actionable trespasses.

95. Plaintiff files a federal suit to rescind a contract on the basis of fraudulent misrepresentations by Defendant. Defendant counterclaims for damages based on Plaintiff's nonperformance of the same contract. Plaintiff's reply alleges that Defendant's fraud excused his performance under the contract. Defendant demands a jury trial on the counterclaim and moves for an order that the counterclaim be tried first. Should the court grant the motion? _____

96. Plaintiff sues Defendant for medical malpractice in federal court. At the close of Plaintiff's case, Defendant moves for a judgment as a matter of law. The trial judge recognizes that Plaintiff has made out a prima facie case technically, but believes that Plaintiff's witnesses are not worthy of belief and hence that the jurors should not hold Defendant liable. Should the court grant Defendant's motion for a judgment as a matter of law? _____

97. Plaintiff sues Defendant for medical malpractice in federal court. At the close of Plaintiff's case, Defendant's counsel recognizes that Plaintiff's witnesses are not likely to be believed, and she rests her case without presenting evidence. Plaintiff moves for a judgment as a matter of law. Should the court grant the motion? _____

98. The trial of Patient's medical malpractice lawsuit resulted in a verdict for Doctor. Which, if any, of the following would be a valid ground for appeal? _____

   (A) The trial judge on her own motion called a medical witness to testify as to the standard of care in the community, which testimony hurt Patient's case.

(B)   At the close of the trial, the judge told the jury that while they were the triers of fact, she personally did not believe Patient's testimony as to damages.

(C)   In instructing the jury, the judge stated: "In determining whether Doctor is liable, you should use your own common sense, as well as the standard of care in the community." Patient made no objection to this instruction in the trial court.

99.   Paige sues Dennis for personal injuries arising out of an auto accident. Dennis's answer raises several affirmative defenses: contributory negligence; assumption of the risk; and Paige's execution of a release. The case goes to trial and there is evidence to support each of Dennis's defenses. The judge's instructions to the jury are correct, except that he defines contributory negligence in a manner which is overly favorable to Dennis. The jury returns a general verdict for Dennis. Paige appeals on the ground that the contributory-negligence instruction was incorrect, even though the instructions on the other defenses admittedly were correct. Should the appellate court reverse?

_____

100.   A jury returns a general verdict in favor of Plaintiff but also answers written questions which are inconsistent with a verdict for Plaintiff and consistent with a verdict for Defendant. The court thereupon enters judgment in favor of Defendant. Plaintiff appeals. Should the appellate court reverse?

_____

101.   Patient sues Doctor for medical malpractice. The jury returns a verdict for Doctor. Patient files a motion for new trial, claiming jury misconduct. Which of the following evidence is admissible in support of Patient's motion?

_____

(A)   An affidavit by Juror 1 that Juror 2 admitted during the course of deliberations that he was a former patient of Doctor. Juror 2 had denied knowing Doctor during voir dire questioning.

(B)   An affidavit by Juror 3 that Juror 4 had been belligerent throughout the deliberations and had badgered and bullied him into voting for Doctor.

(C)   An affidavit by the bailiff that he overheard the jurors say that in order to reach a unanimous verdict they would all vote for whomever the majority of them wanted.

102.   Patient sued Doctor for medical malpractice in federal court, and the jury returned a unanimous verdict for Patient for $100,000. Doctor moves for a new trial. Which of the following evidence, if any, is sufficient to support the granting of Doctor's motion?

_____

(A)   An affidavit by Doctor's attorney that during the course of the trial, he discovered that several of the jurors had lunched and visited with Patient's wife, although he did not mention it to the court at the time.

(B) An affidavit by Doctor that after the verdict had been returned, he overheard Patient admit that he had been faking his injuries all along.

(C) An affidavit by noted physician, Witness, that he had been prepared to testify as a witness for Doctor, but had been called out of town just before the trial.

103. Plaintiff sued Defendant for medical malpractice in federal court. Although the witnesses for Plaintiff gave testimony that the judge found extremely unlikely, the judge denied Defendant's motion for judgment as a matter of law, and the jury rendered a verdict for Plaintiff. Defendant renews the motion for judgment as a matter of law and moves, in the alternative, for a new trial. What ruling should the court make?

_____

104. The jury returned a $30,000 verdict for Patient in a medical-malpractice case in federal court. This amount was considerably less than the special damages proved by Patient. Patient moved for a new trial on the ground of inadequate damages. Can the court grant the new trial on condition that if Doctor consents to increase the verdict to $85,000, a new trial will be denied?

_____

105. Piper filed a federal suit against Talbot for personal injuries sustained in a traffic accident. Talbot was ill and upset at the time and forgot to turn the pleadings over to his attorney. Piper obtained a default judgment against Talbot for $120,000, but did nothing to enforce the judgment for over a year. It was only when Piper executed on the judgment that Talbot remembered the matter; and he then moved promptly to set aside the judgment on the ground that he had a valid defense to Piper's action, and that he failed to answer only through inadvertence and excusable neglect. Should the trial court grant the motion?

_____

106. Petunia sues Dudley in federal court claiming diversity of citizenship. Dudley lacks the funds to employ an attorney, and files no answer. Petunia obtains a default judgment against Dudley for $125,000. Several years later, Dudley decides he wants to attack the judgment on the ground that he and Petunia were at all times citizens of the same state, and hence the federal court lacked jurisdiction. However, all time limits for appeal or relief in the trial court have now expired. Is there any remedy available to Dudley?

_____

APPEAL

107. If a party inadvertently fails to file a notice of appeal within the required time limit, can he obtain an extension of time to file from the appellate court?

_____

108. Plaintiff obtains a jury verdict for $10,000 in a medical-malpractice case, in which he had proved special damages of over $50,000. If he accepts payment of the $10,000 from Defendant, can he appeal the judgment on ground of inadequacy of damages (giving Defendant credit for the $10,000)? _____

109. Plaintiff sues Defendant for personal injuries. Defendant moves to compel Plaintiff to submit to a physical examination, but the trial court erroneously denies the motion. In view of the importance of the exam, can Defendant immediately appeal the trial court's order? _____

110. After trial to the court, the court made findings of fact and conclusions of law, and entered judgment in favor of Defendant. Plaintiff appeals, arguing that the evidence supported findings favorable to him. Which of the following is the appropriate standard of review? _____

   (A) The appellate court may reverse only if it finds that there is no substantial evidence to support the judgment below.

   (B) The appellate court may reverse if it finds that the findings below were clearly erroneous.

   (C) The appellate court may reverse if it determines that the findings were against the weight of the evidence.

111. Plaintiff sues Defendant for copyright infringement. At the outset of the action, the federal court grants a preliminary injunction against any further publication by Defendant of the material that allegedly infringes Plaintiff's copyright, pending trial of the case. Can Defendant appeal the order granting this injunction? _____

112. Potter sues Draco to quiet title to certain real property. At a trial to the court, Potter introduces both hearsay and nonhearsay evidence to support his claim. Draco objects to the hearsay, but his objection is overruled. The court grants judgment for Potter. Draco appeals on the ground that the judgment rests as much on inadmissible hearsay as it does on nonhearsay. Should the appellate court reverse? _____

PRECLUSIVE EFFECTS OF JUDGMENTS

113. Plaintiff unreasonably delays prosecution of his lawsuit against Defendant, resulting in the court's dismissing his action. If the statute of limitations has not run, can Plaintiff file a new action against Defendant on the same claim and obtain a judgment? _____

114. Alpha sued Bravo for damages for breach of contract and obtained a judgment. Thereafter, Bravo sued Alpha for damages, alleging that Alpha had fraudulently induced him to enter into the contract sued upon in the first case. Alpha moves for summary judgment on ground of claim preclusion. Should the court grant the motion? _____

115. Wife sued Husband for installments due under their divorce property-settlement agreement. Husband defended on the ground that Wife was in breach of the agreement. However, the court granted judgment for Wife. Later, Wife sues Husband for other installments coming due under the agreement. Husband now raises the defense that the agreement was void and illegal because of fraud perpetrated by Wife at the time it was signed. Wife moves to strike Husband's defense, claiming issue preclusion. Should the court grant the motion?

    _____

116. Alpha sued Bravo for $500 damage to his car sustained in a traffic accident. Bravo defended on the ground that he was not negligent and that even if he were, Alpha was contributorily negligent. The jury returned a general verdict for Alpha. Meanwhile, Bravo had filed a $50,000 suit against Alpha in a superior court for personal injuries sustained in the same accident. When the judgment in the Alpha-Bravo action became final, Alpha moved for summary judgment against Bravo's suit on the ground of issue preclusion. Should the court grant the motion?

    _____

117. A bus owned and operated by Buslines, Inc., and driven by Driver was involved in a traffic accident. Several passengers were injured, including Plaintiff and Mr. X.

    a.   Plaintiff sued Driver for negligence, and the jury returned a verdict for Driver. Plaintiff thereupon filed suit against Buslines, alleging that it was vicariously liable for Driver's negligence (respondeat superior) and was also negligent in hiring Driver. Buslines moves for summary judgment against Plaintiff's suit. Should the court grant the motion?

    _____

    b.   Assume that Plaintiff sued Buslines first on the respondeat-superior theory and lost. Plaintiff then files suit against Driver for negligence. Driver claims that Plaintiff is precluded by the first suit. Should the court sustain the defense?

    _____

    c.   Assume that Plaintiff sued Driver and won a judgment. Plaintiff now files suit against Buslines on a respondeat-superior theory and moves for a ruling that Buslines's liability was established by the judgment against Driver. Should the court grant the motion?

    _____

    d.   Assume that Plaintiff sued Buslines on a respondeat-superior theory and won. Now another passenger on the same bus, Mr. X, brings suit against Buslines on the same theory and moves to establish liability on the basis of Plaintiff's judgment against Buslines. Should the court grant Mr. X's motion?

    _____

Answers to Review Questions

1. **PROBABLY NOT**   Tradition holds that personal service within the state is always adequate to sustain personal jurisdiction and the Supreme Court has upheld "transient jurisdiction" over a nonresident temporarily within a state (although there was no majority opinion and some Justices expressed doubt if the presence were not intentional or voluntary). [p. 5]

2. **PROBABLY**   The action of Defendant's patient in driving to State A probably establishes no meaningful contact between Defendant and State A. *See* **World-Wide Volkswagen v. Woodson,** in which plaintiffs drove a car purchased from one defendant in New York to Oklahoma, where they had an accident; the Supreme Court found there was no constitutional basis for jurisdiction in Oklahoma. [p. 11]

3. **NO**   Distribution of the drug in State A establishes a minimum contact between Pharmco and the forum state; and as long as the state has authorized the method of service of process used here through long arm legislation, there is no constitutional objection to the exercise of jurisdiction. [p. 12]

4. **PROBABLY NOT**   An agreement appointing an agent is a valid means of forum selection by contract unless, perhaps, the contract was an overreaching by a powerful party. [p. 26]

5. **NO**   Lack of jurisdiction over the person is a defense which is waived if not raised at the first opportunity. Dylan appeared and defended at trial, and thereby waived the objection. [p. 28]

6. **PROBABLY YES**   If Defendant was induced to enter the state by fraud, which seems to be the case here, the service of process is invalid. [p. 29]

7. **NO**   Ben does not reside there, and it is not where a substantial part of the events or omissions giving rise to the claim occurred. [pp. 36, 37]

8. **YES, NO**   When an action is brought in a federal district court where venue is improper, under 28 U.S.C. section 1406(a), the court may either dismiss it or transfer it to a district where the action could have been brought. [p. 42] Transfers for the convenience of parties and witnesses can be made only to a district in which venue *would be proper originally* (and here, venue was never proper in New York) or to a district to which all parties have consented. [p. 42]

9. **YES**   Unlike motions to transfer for improper venue, motions for convenience transfers can be made by *either* party. [p. 43]

| 10. | **YES** | In diversity suits, venue is proper *either* in the district where any defendant resides, if all defendants reside in the same state, *or* in a district where a substantial part of the acts or omissions giving rise to the claim occurred. [pp. 36, 37] |

| 11. | **PROBABLY NONE** | There is no state in which *all* defendants reside, nor any judicial district in which a substantial part of the acts or omissions giving rise to the claim occurred. There might, however, be venue in a district where either ship involved in the collision has its home port, or perhaps where it is located, or (lacking any other basis for venue) in a district where a defendant was subject to personal jurisdiction when the action was commenced [pp. 36, 37]. Plaintiffs could satisfy venue requirements for separate actions against each defendant in that defendant's home state. |

| 12. | **NO, YES** | The contract provision does not deprive the State A federal court of personal jurisdiction, assuming that Defendant has sufficient contacts due to the negotiations there and the fact that Defendant was to provide services there. Venue would similarly be proper in the place where Defendant was to provide services. The forum-choice clause in the contract does not change that result. But the Supreme Court has ruled that federal courts must transfer to the selected forum in all but the most exceptional cases, and that party interests may not be invoked to resist such transfer. [p. 43] |

| 13. | **POSSIBLY** | Service may be made by any method authorized by state law where the court is located or process is served. In some states, such as California, service by mail on nonresidents is allowed. Moreover, under Federal Rule 4, Plaintiff may request waiver of service by mailing the request and complaint to Defendant, and Defendant has a duty to waive to avoid costs. Thus, under either approach service might be proper or waived (although if Defendant refuses to waive service and state law does not allow service by mail, Plaintiff must serve Defendant in person or by leaving a summons and complaint with a "person of suitable age and discretion" residing at Defendant's home). [pp. 30, 50–52] |

| 14. | **PROBABLY** | Defendant was constitutionally entitled to notice and hearing before the attachment of his property. This rule generally applies even when the attachment is for the purpose of establishing jurisdiction. Once the garnishment is quashed, there is no jurisdictional basis for the proceeding, although the lack of jurisdiction could be cured by service of process. [p. 55] |

| 15.a. | **NO** | Diversity jurisdiction is determined by the citizenship of the *members* of the partnership. Under the complete-diversity rule, all plaintiffs must be diverse from all defendants. [p. 69] |

15 b.	**YES**	A corporation is a citizen of any state where it is incorporated, *and* of the state where it has its principal place of business, but not of every state in which it has an office. [p. 68]
16.	**(B) and (C)**	Diversity can be based on *alienage*—*i.e.*, all citizens of American states on one side and all aliens on the other (A). [p. 65] In (B), a United States citizen living abroad permanently *cannot sue or be sued* on the basis of diversity of citizenship (no United States domicile). [p. 68] On claims belonging to an incompetent person, diversity depends on the state citizenship of the incompetent person. In (C), George would have acquired Virginia citizenship at birth, and due to mental incompetence been unable to change it. [p. 71]
17.	**(B) and (E)**	As long as diversity exists *at the time suit is filed*, the federal court has diversity jurisdiction. Thus, it makes no difference that Plaintiff moved into a state for the purpose of creating or preventing such jurisdiction as long as Plaintiff genuinely changed citizenship (A and B) [p. 72] or that after the suit was filed, diversity terminated (C) [p. 69]. That neither party resides in the state where the court is located (D) may be relevant as to *venue* [pp. 36–37], but has no effect on diversity jurisdiction. [p. 66] When claims are *assigned* for collection (E), the residence of the *assignor* determines diversity. [p. 73]
18.	**PERHAPS**	There is diversity, but it is not complete. The jurisdictional defect might be cured by dismissal of one of the diversity-destroying parties, if he is not required for disposition. But if all are "indispensable," dismissal must result. [p. 74]
19.	**YES**	The jurisdictional amount is lacking, and lack of subject-matter jurisdiction can be raised at any time. [pp. 60, 74]
20.	**YES**	As long as the claim was filed in good faith, jurisdiction is not affected by the fact that the judgment ultimately recovered does not exceed the jurisdictional minimum. (But in such a case the court has discretion to deny costs to the plaintiff.) [p. 75]
21.	**YES**	Unrelated claims by a single plaintiff against a single defendant *can* be aggregated. [p. 76]
22.	**NO**	Claims against several defendants can be aggregated only if it is shown that they are *jointly* liable on each claim. [p. 76]
23.	**NO**	Claims by multiple plaintiffs against a single defendant can be aggregated only when plaintiffs assert a *joint* right to relief. [p. 76]
24.	**YES**	Plaintiff 1 and Plaintiff 2 could join their claims under the permissive joinder provisions of Rule 20(a). Because both claims arise out of the same accident, they would be regarded as part of the same "case or controversy" under the supplemental jurisdiction statute. The court would have

original jurisdiction over Plaintiff 1's claim, which is large enough to satisfy the jurisdictional minimum. Even though this is a diversity suit, there is no limitation on supplemental jurisdiction for claims that do not satisfy the jurisdictional minimum by plaintiffs joined under Rule 20. [p. 77]

25.	**NO**	Although the Supreme Court held that supplemental jurisdiction can be used to add the claim of a plaintiff joined under Rule 20 that does not satisfy the jurisdictional minimum, the Court strongly indicated that there should not be supplemental jurisdiction to add a claim by a nondiverse plaintiff. [p. 95]
26.	**YES**	Although there is diversity of citizenship, under a decisional exception to diversity jurisdiction, the federal courts lack jurisdiction over divorce, alimony, child custody, and probate cases. [p. 77]
27.	**YES**	The involvement of federal law is merely incidental to the claim, which is essentially one of simple contract arising under the common law of the state. [p. 83]
28.	**YES**	To the extent that the federal issue is raised by the complaint, it is not "well pleaded," but anticipates a defense. Only the defense, not the claim, arises under federal law. [p. 84]
29.a.	**NO**	Antitrust claims under the Sherman Act are within the *exclusive* jurisdiction of federal courts. [p. 63]
29.b.	**YES**	Under supplemental jurisdiction. [p. 94]
30.	**YES**	When the right exists, it belongs to all defendants *jointly*, except when one defendant can remove on the ground that it is the subject of a "separate and independent claim" or pursuant to the provisions of the Class Action Fairness Act. [p. 103]
31.a.	**NO**	A plaintiff is *never* entitled to removal. Having filed in the state court, Smith must remain there. [p. 102]
31.b.	**NO**	Removal is not allowed in diversity actions in which any properly joined and served defendant is a citizen of the state in which the action is filed. [p. 100]
32.	**YES**	On removal, the federal court has jurisdiction even if the state court lacked subject-matter jurisdiction; the federal court's jurisdiction is no longer viewed as "derivative." Because removal is based on federal-question jurisdiction, Brown may remove even though he is a citizen of New York. Brown could, however, move to dismiss in state court for lack of subject-matter jurisdiction rather than removing. [p. 105]
33.	**NO**	Unless there is statutory provision for exclusive federal jurisdiction, state courts exercise concurrent jurisdiction over

claims based on federal law and must accept such cases. [p.62–63]

34. **YES** The Supreme Court has held that, although Federal Rule 3 says that an action is commenced by the filing of a complaint, it was not intended to provide thereby for "tolling" of the limitations period in a state-law action. Because the duration of limitations is a matter of state law, the definition of the events that toll it is also governed by state law, which can coexist with Rule 3, because there is no conflict between the rule and the state-law provisions. [p. 121]

35. **YES** There appears to be a clear conflict between the state and federal provisions. The Federal Rules of Evidence were passed by Congress, so they are valid if "arguably procedural." Determinations about the admissibility of hearsay evidence seem to be arguably procedural, so that under *Hanna* the federal rule should be applied. [p. 123] (Note, however, that with regard to issues of privilege, Federal Rule of Evidence 501 directs that state law should be applied in federal court with regard to issues governed by state law.)

36. **YES** Rule 50(a)(1) applies because it is "arguably procedural." Even if the courts' interpretation of that rule is regarded as judge-made, the cases are divided—the majority view favors the federal standard, especially when the question goes to whether judge or jury should evaluate the sufficiency of the evidence, rather than to the elements of the claim or the definition of the persuasion burden. Relations between judge and jury in federal court are an appropriate subject for determination by federal law. [p. 124]

37. **UNCLEAR** The task for the federal court is to determine how the state supreme court would now resolve the issue, not to select the "better" legal rule. But a federal court should not be blind to trends in the law, and if there is reason to believe that the state supreme court would not adhere to the older rule, the federal court should not do so. On the other hand, state appellate decisions are, in general, good indications of the content of state law, and the court should have some reason grounded in more recent, analogous state-court decisions for disregarding the earlier decision squarely on point. [pp. 127–129]. If the state's procedure permits, the federal court could certify the question to the state supreme court.

38. **NO** The court looks to the *facts* alleged, not the caption of the complaint or even the pleader's apparent legal theory. The complaint sufficiently pleads negligence (failure to give warning of known danger), and hence sufficiently states facts supporting a cause of action. [p. 138]

39.a. **PROBABLY** The allegations are sufficient if they give Defendant *notice* of the *general nature* of the claim against him and make a "plausible" claim. These allegations would likely be viewed as a plausible basis for Plaintiff to sue Defendant. After the pleading stage, however, the federal courts would demand sufficient factual matter to satisfy all elements of the claim. A court might grant a motion for a more definite statement, seeking clarification of the allegations. [p. 141]

39.b.	**NO**	The allegations are not of "ultimate facts"—*i.e.*, the word "improperly" does *not* present a legal issue (negligence, warranty, strict liability). [pp. 139–140]
40.	**NO**	Allegations on information or belief are proper only if the pleader lacks personal knowledge. Where, as here, Plaintiff has **constructive knowledge** (*i.e.*, matters of public record), the allegation is insufficient. [p. 144]
41.	**NO**	In federal court, pleaders may state their claims or defenses "regardless of consistency." (*Compare*: The result is contra in many code-pleading states, particularly if the complaint is verified.) Plaintiff might, however, face sanctions under Federal Rule 11 if the factual allegations were made without "evidentiary support." [pp. 137, 145, 148]
42.	**YES**	In a default case, the relief granted cannot exceed or differ in kind from that prayed for in the complaint. [p. 146]
43.a.	**YES**	There is no requirement of subject-matter relationship among the claims joined against a *single* defendant. (State rules not modeled on the Federal Rules are often contra.) [p. 150]
43.b.	**YES**	If there are multiple parties, one claim by or against them must arise out of the same transaction and involve a common question of law or fact. [p. 151]
44.	**PROBABLY**	Some courts deny a motion to strike when *no responsive pleading* is due. But the better view is to strike immaterial allegations to prevent such matters from being read to the jury at trial. [p. 164]
45.	**PROBABLY**	Defendant is never compelled to file a motion to dismiss. Raising the venue objection in his answer sufficiently preserves it. [p. 165]. But assuming Defendant participated in preparation for trial, that activity might be treated as having forfeited the right to dismissal on the eve of trial. [p. 166]
46.	**YES**	When the defendant *does* make a motion to dismiss, his failure to raise certain defenses and objections which he could raise by the motion, including venue, results in waiver of those defenses. [p. 165]
47.	**NO**	Failure to state a claim can be raised at any time until judgment is entered. [p. 165]

48.	**YES**	A court may grant a motion to dismiss premised on a defense that appears on the face of the complaint. [p. 166]
49.	**YES**	The rule in code-pleading states is that the defendant must file *specific* denials to a verified complaint, because there is usually something which ought to be admitted. (*Note*: The federal rule is contra, but a general denial is appropriate in federal court only when even the jurisdictional allegations can be denied in good faith.) [p. 176]
50.	**YES**	A failure to deny constitutes an admission. [p. 178]
51.	**NO**	In *federal* actions, allegations of damages are deemed controverted even if not denied. *Compare*: The rule in *state* courts in code-pleading states is usually contra—*i.e.*, when a sum of money is alleged to be due, it must be *specifically* denied. [p. 178]
52.	**(B) and (D)**	Truth (A) is an affirmative defense and must be specially pleaded as new matter. So must any release or settlement (C). However, proof that no one heard (B) is admissible under the general denial, as it contradicts the element of publication, which is a part of Plaintiff's case. Likewise, evidence as to the extent of damages (D) contradicts Plaintiff's case and is admissible under the general denial. [pp. 178–179]
53.	**NO**	In federal actions, objections to venue are waived if not raised in the initial answer. Subsequent amendments to add such objections are *not* allowed. [pp. 41, 165]
54.	**NONE**	Allegations of Emeril's answers are *deemed controverted*. No responsive pleading by Alton is required to preserve the issues raised thereby. [p. 184]
55.	**ONLY (C)**	(A) is wrong because the counterclaim *should be* a part of Darien's answer. [p. 184] (B) is wrong because no subject-matter relationship is required for assertion of a permissive counterclaim, such as this one, and there is an independent ground for subject-matter jurisdiction. [p. 184] (C) is right because when a counterclaim is only *permissive* (not arising out of same transaction as complaint), there must be an independent ground for federal jurisdiction (here the parties are diverse, but the claim is for only $5,000). [p. 185] (D) is wrong because other parties can be joined when necessary. [p. 186]
56.	**NO**	Plaintiff's filing of a complaint *tolls* the statute of limitations for counterclaims arising out of the same transaction. For limitations purposes, Defendant's counterclaim "relates back" to the time Plaintiff filed his complaint and hence is timely. (A minority view allows *any* counterclaim to be used defensively, even after the statute has run.) [pp. 187–188]

57.	**(B) and (C)**	(A) is wrong because no affirmative relief is sought; Defendant's "claim" is merely a defense. (D) is wrong because there must be a subject-matter relationship to Plaintiff's complaint. (B) and (C) are proper because there is the requisite subject-matter relationship; claims for indemnity or contribution are permissible. [p. 189]
58.	**NO**	Crossclaims lie only against co-defendants. Claims against an outside party must be asserted by *impleader*. (Most courts permit impleader only if indemnification or contribution is sought; under this view, Defendant 2 would be permitted to implead Repair Shop only if there were a claim for indemnification, but might then be permitted also to seek affirmative relief—*i.e.*, to recover for damage to his car.) [p. 226]
59.a.	**NO**	Amendments relating to the same transaction "relate back" for limitations purposes. A change in the nature or theory of the action does not prejudice Dalton. [p. 194]
59.b.	**PROBABLY NOT**	Amendments to bring in *new parties* after the statute of limitations has run are permitted only in limited circumstances. This amendment involves adding a party, not changing a party or the naming of a party against whom a claim is asserted, which is generally allowed. But it is permitted in federal court only when the added party had notice before expiration of limitations. If there is reason to believe XYZ Co. was aware of the suit, that could satisfy the notice requirement. Some states (*e.g.*, California) do not require notice. [pp. 195–197]
60.	**NO**	Federal Rule 15(c)(1)(A) allows relation back when it is permitted by the law providing the applicable statute of limitations. [p. 194]
61.a.	**PROBABLY NOT**	Here, the defendant appears to have had notice of the pendency of the action, and probably knew or should have known of the naming mistake. [p. 195]
61.b.	**DISCRETIONARY**	Even though such an amendment would be freely allowed *before* trial, courts are more reluctant to permit such amendments at the time of trial. In state practice, they may find a "material variance" when the relief sought by the amendment differs significantly. Federal practice is more liberal, putting the burden on the objecting party to show *prejudice* (although a continuance to enable Defendant to prepare would usually remedy such prejudice). [pp. 198–200]
61.c.	**YES**	Paula should be permitted to file a *supplemental complaint* to allege occurrence of developments after the date of her original complaint, when no alteration of the basic claim is involved. [pp. 200–201]

62.	**PROBABLY NOT**	The federal court has *discretion* to refuse; but such a refusal here is likely to be an abuse of discretion, at least if Plaintiff could not have known sooner about the witness's unwillingness. [p. 204]
63.	**ALL EXCEPT (B)**	The person having the *right to sue* (*i.e.*, legal title to the claim) is the "real party in interest," (B) is wrong because usually only the trustee has the right to sue third persons for wrongs to the trust estate. [pp. 209, 212]
64.	**PROBABLY NOT**	Unless serious injustice would result, the defendant may be estopped to raise the issue by direct or collateral attack. [p. 214]
65.	**NO**	In a diversity action, capacity of such a party is determined by the law of the state in which the federal court is located. [p. 216]
66.	**NO**	Samantha *is* the real party in interest. The correct challenge would be that she lacks capacity (as a minor). However, this challenge is *waived* if not timely made. [pp. 209, 215]
67.a.	**YES**	Under modern rules, joinder of claims against multiple parties is proper as long as the claims arise out of the same transaction, occurrence, or series of transactions or occurrences; there is a common question of fact or law; and the defendants may be jointly or severally liable (or liable "in the alternative"). [p. 218–220]
67.b.	**YES**	By alleging the facts showing *why* he is "in doubt," Plaintiff is entitled to join defendants and claims *in the alternative*. [p. 218]
68.	**NO**	Under Rule 21, misjoinder is not a ground for dismissal. But the actions should be severed because there is no connection between the transactions. [pp. 218, 234]
69.	**PROBABLY NOT**	If Defendant 2 can be joined, there may be an argument she should be joined in order to give effective protection to Defendant 1's right to contribution. However, the court can and should proceed to enforce Plaintiff's right if the joinder of Defendant 2 is not feasible or if it would destroy the jurisdiction of the court. If the obstacle to joinder is incomplete diversity, some federal courts might dismiss, leaving Plaintiff to sue both Defendant 1 and Defendant 2 in state court. [pp. 222–223]
70.	**YES**	In federal court, and in most states, partial assignees or subrogees are required but not indispensable parties who should be joined if feasible to prevent a multiplicity of actions or inconsistent results, and the court can compel joinder of Assignee as an involuntary plaintiff. [p. 224]

71.	**YES**	The corporation must be joined as a plaintiff, but its joinder destroys diversity of citizenship, the basis for federal jurisdiction; and the action must therefore be dismissed for want of federal jurisdiction. [pp. 225, 226]
72.a.	**YES**	Tod should file a third-party complaint against Martha, showing why Martha should be held liable on a theory of *indemnification* for whatever liability Tod has to Chloe. [p. 226]
72.b.	**YES**	Because the impleader claim is made by the defendant, supplemental jurisdiction is allowed, and Martha's citizenship has *no* effect on jurisdiction and venue. [p. 229]
73.a.	**PROBABLY NOT**	There is clearly no *right* to intervene. Permissive intervention can be granted when there is a "common question of law or fact," but here, there is only an inference that Tom's illness was caused by the same condition that caused Paul's. [p. 229, 233]
73.b.	**PROBABLY NOT**	In this situation, intervention is unnecessary because a finding that Duchess is liable to Paul for selling a sandwich containing impure ingredients would not be binding on XYZ or affect its ability to defend against Duchess's claim for indemnification in a separate action, if Duchess fails to implead XYZ in the suit brought by Paul. [pp. 229, 231]
74.a.	**YES**	The Federal Interpleader Act permits a stakeholder to deposit a disputed debt with the court if the amount is at least $500 and diversity exists between the adverse *claimants*. [p. 236]
74.b.	**YES**	Nationwide service is authorized in statutory interpleader. [p. 237]
75.	**YES**	A class action is appropriate under Rule 23(b)(2), since the issues and relief are identical for all members of the class. The number of students involved (and possibly the relatively modest amount of their individual claims) also makes a class suit the most practical way of resolving the issue, because nothing would be gained by requiring each member to litigate the same issue separately. [pp. 248–249]
76.	**(B)**	In federal class actions not coming within the Class Action Fairness Act, at least one class member's claim (probably the class representative's) claim must exceed the jurisdictional minimum. (A) is wrong because diversity is determined only from citizenship of the *representative*. (C) is wrong because the common sales practices, if proved, could be the requisite "common question," although that might be more difficult with oral representations. [pp. 244, 252–253]
77.	**NO**	It is reversible error for the court to premise its certification decision on the likelihood of Plaintiffs' success on the merits. [p. 254] But in order to decide whether there are common

questions, the court may have to assess the need for individual proof on the merits.

78.a.	**YES**	*See* Fed. R. Civ. P. 23(c)(2). [p. 257]
78.b.	**YES**	This is the impact of the *Eisen* case. [p. 258]
78.c.	**NO**	Those who opt out are not bound. [p. 256]
79.	**NO**	Because (i) there is no showing that adequate *notice* of the pending settlement was given to the class members, and (ii) the special recovery obtained by Plaintiff indicates that she did *not* adequately represent the interests of other class members. In federal courts, the court would have to decide whether to approve any settlement of class claims. [pp. 261–263]
80.	**NO**	The Rule 26(a)(1) obligation of disclosure applies only to materials the disclosing party "*may use to support its claims or defenses.*" Although that could be true of a document that contained harmful information, it usually would not be, and in any event Rule 26(a)(1) does not require disclosure of the contents of documents; it requires only a listing of them. [pp. 274, 275]
81.	**NO**	In federal practice, Kiki may serve notice on a corporate party stating the *matters* upon which the deposition will be based. It is then up to the corporation to produce employees having knowledge as to such matters. [p. 278]
82.a.	**DEPENDS**	If Employee is *unavailable* to testify, his deposition is admissible; otherwise, it is not. [p. 282]
82.b.	**YES**	The deposition of the adverse party or the officer of an adverse corporate party is admissible as substantive evidence. [p. 282]
83.a.	**NONE**	Depositions to perpetuate testimony are proper before filing suit only when Plaintiff can show that she is *unable* to sue now. Such depositions cannot (in federal practice) be used simply to determine the merits of Plaintiff's claim. Rule 11 does not pose an obstacle to Plaintiff's ability to bring suit now if she can assert that allegations against Defendant are likely to have evidentiary support after an opportunity for investigation or discovery. [p. 277]
83.b.	**SUBPOENA FOR PRODUCTION OR DEPOSITION**	A *nonparty* cannot be required to produce documents by a *request* to produce under Rule 34, but he can be *subpoenaed* under Rule 45 to produce them or to attend a deposition and to bring with him evidence in his control. [p. 292]
83.c.	**SUBPOENA FOR INSPECTION**	A nonparty may be subpoenaed to permit inspection of premises in his control. [p. 292]

83.d.	**NO**	A motion to compel a physical examination applies only to *parties* or someone in a party's custody or control (such as a child when a parent is suing for the child's injuries). [p. 293]
84.	**NONE**	(A) is wrong because a party is deemed in control of that which is in his attorney's possession. [p. 291] (B) is wrong because the work-product privilege does not apply to evidence unearthed by the attorney. [p. 288] (C) is wrong because a request to produce requires neither a court order nor a showing of good cause. [p. 289]
85.	**YES**	By so requesting, the examined party becomes bound to provide copies of his own medical reports on the condition at issue. [p. 294]
86.a.	**MOTION GRANTED**	Discovery is proper even though the information itself is not admissible. So the fact that witness statements are hearsay is no bar to discovery. [p. 296] Note that there might be a valid work-product objection.
86.b.	**MOTION GRANTED**	A party's factual contentions are usually discoverable in order to flush into the open all claims or defenses. [p. 300]
86.c.	**MOTION DENIED**	The test for the outer limits of discovery relevance is whether the information is relevant to the claim or defense of a party. Unless Plaintiff can somehow show that an earlier lawsuit relates to *his* claim of food poisoning, the discovery appears to be improper. [p. 299]
86.d.	**MOTION DENIED**	Even though many courts permit discovery of insurance coverage (and the federal courts require disclosure without a discovery request of insurance agreements), most do *not* permit discovery of a defendant's financial status except in connection with claims for punitive damages. [p. 299]
86.e.	**MOTION DENIED**	The testing would probably be treated as opinions obtained from experts retained to advise counsel. Unless they are going to testify, discovery from such experts may be allowed only in exceptional circumstances. No such circumstances have been stated, although it might be possible to justify discovery if the allegedly tainted food no longer exists, so that Plaintiff cannot test it now. [pp. 310–311]
87.	**ALL EXCEPT (C)**	(A) is right because parties generally may not initiate discovery in federal court without first meeting to discuss, among other matters, a discovery plan. [p. 283] (B) is right; interrogatories can be served only on parties (though these need not be adverse parties). [p. 283] Unless the 25-question limit has been reached, (C) is not a ground for objection, although it may be grounds for a protective order. [p. 303] (D) is right because interrogatories, including discrete subparts, may not exceed 25 in number without leave of court. [p. 283]

88.	**(B)**	(A) is wrong because no such sanction may be imposed when there has been no prior court order to answer. [p. 324] (B) is correct. [p. 287] (C) is wrong because, in federal practice, requests can be directed even as to the ultimate issues in the case. [p. 285]
89.	**ONLY (A)**	A nonparty is not required to answer questions unless subpoenaed. [p. 278] But Defendant has the right to conduct an investigation [p. 327], and the exclusionary rule has no application to this situation [p. 327]. The statements are work product and there is no apparent reason for requiring them to be disclosed. [pp. 305, 309] *Note*: In federal practice, the witnesses themselves have a right to a copy of their own statements. [p. 309]
90.	**NO**	A motion for summary judgment must be **denied** if the essential facts are controverted by a witness competent to testify. If Plaintiff claims to have seen the accident, that should suffice. Credibility cannot be determined at this stage. [p. 334]
91.	**PROBABLY NOT**	Assuming Becky has the burden of proving Robbie's knowing deceit at trial (at least a debatable issue if there is no question that the statements were in fact false), it is likely that the court would find the surrounding circumstances sufficient to support the inference that Robbie knew of their falsity, despite Robbie's protestations of innocence. [p. 334] Nevertheless, Becky cannot rely entirely on the jury's disbelief of Robbie's testimony to satisfy Becky's burden of producing evidence of Robbie's knowledge. [p. 335]
92.a.	**YES**	*Partial* summary judgment can be granted as to certain claims or issues, reserving the balance for trial. [p. 340]
92.b.	**YES**	A summary judgment can be based on any admissible evidence, including comparison of the songs. [pp. 340–341] Moreover, Defendant's affidavit might be rejected as a sham. [p. 334]
93.a.	**YES**	The court not only has the power to set such deadlines, but under Rule 16, it is required to set such deadlines early in the action. [p. 348]
93.b.	**YES**	If the court so orders, under its authority to require that a party or its representative be present or reasonably available by telephone to discuss settlement. [p. 351]
93.c.	**PROBABLY**	Rule 16 authorizes trial judges to use "special procedures to assist in resolving the dispute when authorized by statute or local rule." [p. 357]
93.d.	**PROBABLY NOT**	The final pretrial order should be amended only to avoid "manifest injustice." Unless there is some justification for Carter's failure to list this witness in the final pretrial order, the court would be justified in excluding the witness unless he

is essential to Carter's case. Because the matter is discretionary, however, the court would have the power to allow the witness to testify. [p. 353]

94. **ALL EXCEPT (B)** The right to jury trial extends to all actions "at law." Historically, (A) was "at law," while (B) was in equity. When legal and equitable claims are joined (C), the *federal* rule is that the jury right must be preserved as to the legal claims (damages). There is a jury right in (D) because the court looks to the basic substance of the relief sought—here, to prevent tort liability (damages) for past acts. [pp. 368, 372]

95. **YES** In federal practice, the claim for legal relief (damages) *must* be tried first, to preserve the right of jury trial on the fraud issue free of binding prior adjudication on the equitable claim. [p. 373]

96. **NO** As long as a prima facie case is made out, a motion for judgment as a matter of law *must* be denied. The court may not weigh the testimony in ruling on the motion. [pp. 383–387]

97. **PROBABLY NOT** To prevail on a motion for judgment as a matter of law, the party with the burden of proof must put on such a strong case that the jury could not reasonably disbelieve it. Ordinarily, the jury could disbelieve witnesses on the basis of their demeanor while testifying; given the fact that Defendant's lawyer thinks the witnesses are not likely to be believed, this does not seem to be a case in which the jury would have to believe them. [pp. 384, 385]

98. **NONE** A trial judge may call and interrogate a witness on her own (A). [p. 382] The judge may also comment on the evidence, including the credibility of a witness (B) in *most* states (minority contra). [p. 391] Failure to object to a jury instruction (C) is usually considered a waiver of any objection thereto, unless the error is so fundamental that it deprives a party of a fair trial. The instruction here is somewhat confusing, but does not seem to be fundamental in the foregoing sense. [p. 392]

99. **PROBABLY** Since the jury may have based its verdict solely on the one defense as to which the instructions were incorrect, most courts would reverse. [p. 392]

100. **NO** When inconsistent with the verdict, the jury's answers to written questions may control over their general verdict. [p. 394]

101. **(C) (most courts)** The Supreme Court has ruled that concealed grounds for disqualification (A) may not be proved by juror affidavit regarding statements during deliberations. [p. 398]. Some states (*e.g.*, California) would allow use of the affidavit. Few courts, however, would permit juror affidavits to attack the deliberations themselves (B). [p. 397] On the other hand,

affidavits by outsiders (C) are generally admissible to show improper deliberations, and an agreement to be bound by majority rule when unanimity is required is clearly improper. [pp. 395, 397]

102.	**NONE**	(A) does not establish "juror misconduct" because it was known to Doctor **during** the trial and he chose to do nothing about it (such as a motion for mistrial). [p. 402] (B) might amount to fraud on the court, but usually trial verdicts may not be set aside on the basis of allegedly false testimony. [pp. 402–403] (C) does not establish "accident or surprise" because it fails to show that Doctor had done all he could to procure Witness's attendance—*i.e.*, subpoenaing him. [p. 402]
103.	**NEW TRIAL GRANTED**	Judgment as a matter of law cannot be granted because there is some evidence to support the verdict. [p. 400] But the trial judge may order a new trial if he finds that the verdict is contrary to the weight of the evidence. In making this determination, in contrast to ruling on a motion for judgment as a matter of law, the judge may weigh the evidence. [p. 403]
104.	**NO**	In federal practice the trial court does **not** have the power of "additur." [p. 409]
105.	**NO**	There is a **one-year limitation period** in federal practice for a motion for relief from judgment. [p. 413]
106.	**YES**	Dudley can bring a separate suit in equity to set aside the judgment. [p. 413]
107.	**NO**	Time limits for filing appeals are usually jurisdictional. The Federal Rules permit the *trial* court to extend time for 30 days, but the appellate court cannot do so. [p. 424]
108.	**NO**	Plaintiff's voluntary acceptance of the benefits of a judgment *waives* his right to appeal therefrom. [p. 419]
109.	**NO**	The final-judgment rule bars any appeal of most interlocutory orders, and interlocutory review of discovery orders is especially rare. (However, appellate review by extraordinary writ may be available.) [pp. 425–427]
110.	**(B)**	Clear error is the correct test. [p. 434]
111.	**YES**	Review of preliminary injunctions is one of the generally recognized "exceptions" to the final judgment rule. However, appellate review is generally limited to whether the trial court abused its **discretion** in granting the injunction. [pp. 428, 436]
112.	**PROBABLY NOT**	In **nonjury** cases (quiet title) it is presumed that the trial judge considered only the legally admissible evidence in arriving at his decision. [p. 436]

113.	**NO**	An involuntary dismissal is usually treated as a judgment on the merits, so it bars any later action on the same claim. [p. 450]
114.	**YES**	Bravo's fraud claim would have been a ***compulsory counterclaim*** in most jurisdictions, and since it was not raised in the first suit, it is ***barred***. [p. 452]
115.	**NO**	The first judgment is a bar with respect to the installments then in question. But it is preclusive only as to the issues ***"actually litigated."*** Since the fraud issue was not litigated, it can be raised with respect to the ***later*** installments. [pp. 453–454]
116.	**YES**	The general verdict in the Alpha-Bravo action necessarily found that Bravo was negligent and Alpha was not. The issue-preclusion effect of those findings is fatal to Bravo's claims against Alpha in the second action. [p. 455]
117.a.	**YES**	Buslines's liability, if any, is ***derivative***, *i.e.*, predicated on a showing that Driver was negligent. Plaintiff litigated and lost this issue in the first action and, thus, is barred from relitigating it in the second action. [p. 461]
117.b.	**DEPENDS**	If the sole issue in the first suit was Driver's negligence, the first judgment should preclude Plaintiff. However, if Buslines raised some other defense (*e.g.*, Driver was not acting in course and scope of employment), the result would be contra. [p. 455]
117.c.	**NO**	Buslines should not be bound because it had no opportunity to litigate in the first case. Driver may or may not have defended it properly. [p. 459]
117.d.	**PROBABLY**	Even offensive use of issue preclusion by a stranger to the prior action is usually permissible in most jurisdictions, absent any of several special circumstances (such as much smaller damage exposure in the first action) that might make it unfair to give issue preclusive effect to rulings in the first action. [p. 462] About a third of states have not followed this abandonment of the mutuality requirement.

Exam Questions and Answers

Question I

Mitsui Machinery Co., a Japanese manufacturer, makes high-temperature ovens for heating nonferrous metals. The ovens are shipped from Japan to Mitsui-American Co., a California corporation that is a wholly owned sales subsidiary based in Los Angeles. Mitsui-American sells the ovens to various metals fabricators in the United States, including Pot Line Co., a Delaware corporation whose principal place of business is in Utah. John Worker, a citizen of Utah, is an employee of Equipment Service Co., a Utah corporation that services manufacturing equipment, including the equipment at Pot Line.

A. Worker is injured while engaged in repairing a Mitsui oven at the Pot Line plant. Under Utah law, Worker's only remedy against Equipment Service Co. is under the workers'-compensation law. Under Utah law, it is also arguable that his only remedy against Pot Line is limited to the workers'-compensation law. Apart from any claim that Worker might have against Mitsui and Mitsui-American, what proceedings should he initiate? Explain.

B. Worker wishes to sue on the basis that the oven was defectively designed. Can he join Mitsui Machinery and Mitsui-American, and if so, in what court or courts? Explain.

C. Assume that Worker named Mitsui Machinery and Mitsui-American as defendants in an action in Utah state or federal court, and in connection with that action filed a writ of attachment upon Pot Line, asserting attachment jurisdiction over $35,000 due from Pot Line to Mitsui in payment for the oven.

   1. Assuming that Utah has state rules modeled on the Federal Rules of Civil Procedure in relevant respects, by what procedure may Mitsui Machinery and Mitsui-American challenge the attachment?

   2. Would the challenge be sustained?

D. Assume that the First National Bank of Utah had financed Pot Line's purchase of the oven and, upon learning of the attachment, is concerned that its rights under a chattel mortgage on the oven may be jeopardized by the attachment. What procedures might the bank use to protect its interest?

E. Assume that Worker sued Pot Line for damages on the theory that the oven was defective and that Pot Line impleaded the Mitsui entities ("Mitsui") for indemnity. While discovery was being conducted, Pot Line settled with Worker for $200,000 and Worker's action against Pot Line is dismissed "with prejudice." What effect does that judgment have on Pot Line's claim against Mitsui?

Question II

The Republican Party is an unincorporated association with headquarters in Washington, D.C. Paul Buchan, a member of the Party who lives in Virginia, decides to run as the Reform Party candidate for President. The National Committee of the Republican Party expels Buchan. He brings suit for reinstatement in the United States District Court for the Eastern District of Virginia, alleging that the expulsion violates the First Amendment and also his rights under the common law governing unincorporated associations. He also asks for damages. Analyze whether and on what basis a damages award would be binding against the Republican Party as an organization and against individual members of the Party.

Question III

John Moline is a citizen of Illinois; Harry Duffalo is a citizen of New York. They enter into a joint venture for buying machinery in the United States and selling it in various parts of the world, Moline doing the buying and Duffalo doing the selling. The venture has an office in Chicago, Illinois, at which Moline works regularly and which Duffalo visits from time to time. After the business has been going for a while, Moline becomes suspicious that Duffalo has been cheating him by holding back payments from sales. By September 2016, Moline has collected enough evidence to convince himself of Duffalo's cheating, but on September 15, 2016, he suddenly dies of a heart attack.

On May 1, 2017, Moline's widow, as executor of his estate, commences an action in U.S. district court in Chicago against Duffalo to recover $550,000 of payments allegedly held back. Process is served on Duffalo in New York on May 5, 2017. On May 15, 2007, Duffalo commences an action in New York state court for (i) $100,000 of profits from the joint venture that he alleges are due him but unpaid and (ii) a declaratory judgment that no sums are owing out of the joint-venture accounts except the $100,000 mentioned in his first claim. Duffalo serves process on Mrs. Moline in Illinois and also garnishes Allstate Life Insurance Co., which had issued a life-insurance policy for $250,000 on John Moline's life.

A. Does the Illinois court have jurisdiction of this action filed by Mrs. Moline?

B. Does the New York court have jurisdiction of the action filed by Duffalo?

Question IV

Plaintiff brought an action in a federal district court for (i) specific performance of a contract and incidental damages for defendant's failure to perform on time, or (ii) full damages in case the court refused to order specific performance. Defendant filed an answer denying plaintiff's material allegations and counterclaimed for damages arising out of the same contract dispute.

A. If plaintiff demands a jury trial, what issues, if any, should be tried by a jury?

B. Assume that plaintiff does not demand a jury trial, but defendant does. What issues, if any, should be tried by a jury?

C. Assume that the court strikes defendant's jury demand and sets all the issues of the case for a court trial. Is the order then reviewable? If so, by what means?

Question V

The sole issue being tried by the jury in a condemnation action was the issue of just compensation. After lengthy deliberation, the jurors advised the court that they could not agree on a verdict. The judge then instructed them that each juror should write his or her valuation on a piece of paper, that they should then divide the total by 12, and that should be their verdict. After returning to the jury room, the jury shortly came in with a verdict of $375,000 in favor of the landowner. Was the instruction proper? Assume that neither the United States (the condemnor) nor the defendant landowner had objected to the court's instruction. On appeal by the defendant-landowner from the judgment entered on the verdict, may the appellant raise the giving of the instruction as error?

Question VI

A Santa Fe railroad freight train hit a school bus at a grade crossing in Lumpe, Texas. The crossing had a sign but no light or gate. Two children were killed and three others and the bus driver were injured. The locomotive engineer was killed by flying debris. An action was brought in federal district court against Santa Fe, a Kansas corporation, on behalf of the children who were killed and injured. In discovery, depositions were taken of the bus driver, the fireman on the locomotive, and the brakeman on the train.

The fireman said that the train was going "about normal speed, which at that place on the route would be 60 miles an hour." He said that he was at his regular seat in the front of the locomotive cab, looking ahead, when the bus "came up to the tracks and just kept going." He said there is a speedometer in the control panel at his seat but "can't recall" looking at the speedometer in the interval just before the crash.

The brakeman said the train was going "about usual speed, which is supposed to be 60 miles an hour." He did not see the bus until after the collision.

The bus driver says that he slowed down as he approached the grade crossing, did not see the train, and nearly got across the tracks before the train hit the rear of the bus. He admits he did not stop, as required by state law.

Also through discovery, the railroad was compelled to produce the paper tape from the train's speed recorder, an automatic device that records the speed at which the train is going at each moment of a run. The tape indicates that the train was going 80 miles per hour at the time of the collision.

Plaintiff moves for summary judgment on the issue of liability, requesting that its previous demand for jury trial be applicable only to the issue of damages. In support of the motion, plaintiff appends the depositions and speed tape described above.

The Texas Constitution provides that in actions at common law, "the jury shall be the judge of the facts and the law."

Should summary judgment be granted?

Question VII

The following is a complaint filed in United States District Court for the District of Connecticut:

1. Plaintiff Jane Smith is a citizen of Connecticut. The amount in controversy herein exceeds $75,000, exclusive of interest and costs.

2. Defendant Electronics Institute, Inc. is a Delaware corporation with its principal place of business in New York. It operates an establishment in New Haven, Connecticut.

3. Defendant advertised a course in electronics technology at a tuition of $12,500. The advertisements claimed that "completion of the course could lead to big money in electronics." Plaintiff enrolled in and completed the course and paid $12,500 in tuition therefor.

4. Plaintiff has been unable to find any employment in electronics at a wage exceeding the minimum wage. Plaintiff is informed and believes and therefore alleges that there are no jobs paying more than the minimum wage in the New Haven area for which the training provided by Defendant is necessary and useful.

5. Plaintiff was induced to believe that employment at a high wage would result from taking the course provided by Defendant. As a result of thus being misled by Defendant, Plaintiff suffered embarrassment, humiliation, and loss of self-respect, to her damage of $500,000.

6. The training provided by Defendant was substantially worthless.

Wherefore, Plaintiff prays for restitution in the amount of $12,500; for additional damages in the amount of $500,000; and for interest and costs.

You represent Defendant. Write a memorandum for the file, analyzing motions that you might have good basis for asserting by way of attack on the complaint.

Question VIII

Sierra Club, Inc. is a nonprofit corporation incorporated in California, having its headquarters in San Francisco and an office in Washington, D.C. It has 25,000 members who pay annual dues varying from $25 to $500 and who elect its board of directors. The Club organizes hikes and treks, promotes conservation through public education, and lobbies in Washington and in various state capitals for environmental regulation. In 2016, the Club discovered that persons employed by oil and coal companies were joining in large numbers and suspected an "infiltration" intended to oppose its political activism. In January 2017, Nelson Oil Bunker, a citizen of Texas and a member of the Club and president of Gusher Oil Co., sent a letter to the board demanding that the Club cease lobbying efforts because those efforts could jeopardize the Club's status as a tax-exempt organization under the Internal Revenue Code. In February, the Club board adopted a resolution that no person could become or continue as a member except by subscribing to a "statement of principles" that affirmed the Club's involvement in environmental regulation. Bunker refused to sign the statement and demanded a list of Club members to contest the next election of Club directors. In April 2017, the Club board voted to cancel Bunker's membership. Litigation is imminent.

A. If the Club wishes to bring suit against Bunker individually to determine the validity of the cancellation of his membership, in what court or courts could it effectively do so? Identify the court(s) and the legal basis for it (their) being proper court(s).

B. Assume that on April 15, 2017, the Club brought a class suit in California Superior Court, San Francisco County, against three members, one from Texas, one from Nevada, and one from Oklahoma, named individually and as representatives of a class constituting those members who object to the requirement of signing the "statement of principles." The suit asks for a declaratory judgment that the requirement is valid. State a legal argument for the proposition that a judgment for the Club would be binding on Bunker.

C. Assume that, in the situation described in B, Bunker wished to become an individual party to the action. State the basis or bases upon which he could do so, with a supporting legal argument, if he acted (i) while the action was pending in state court and (ii) after the action was removed to federal court (described in D. below).

D. Assume that the suit mentioned in B was removed to federal court and that the question of giving notice to the members of the class was then presented. Must notice be given to all class members? State reasons. Should Sierra Club be required to pay the cost of giving such notice? State reasons.

Answers to Question I

A. Worker should bring a workers'-compensation proceeding against Equipment Service, a remedy limited in amount but very sure of recovery. Worker should also sue Pot Line on the theory that he is not an employee of Pot Line and, therefore, is not limited to a workers'-compensation remedy against it. If this theory loses, he may seek a workers'-compensation remedy (*see supra*). The tort suit should be in Utah state court, not in federal court, because Pot Line has its principal place of business in Utah and, hence, is a co-citizen of Worker, who is also a Utah citizen. Thus, there is no diversity, so the federal court would lack subject-matter jurisdiction.

B. Multiple tortfeasors may be joined as defendants under Federal Rule 20 and analogous state rules. Presumably, Utah and California have such provisions.

Subject-matter jurisdiction: If the action is to be against Pot Line as well as Mitsui-American and Mitsui Machinery, Worker must proceed in Utah state court because there is no diversity with Pot Line (*see* above), and Pot Line is apparently not amenable to suit in California (there being no apparent contact between Pot Line and California). There is also a question of personal jurisdiction for Worker's claims against the Mitsui companies (*see* below). Diversity exists between Worker and Mitsui-American, because Mitsui-American is a California corporation and its principal place of business is not in Utah. Diversity also exists between Worker and Mitsui Machinery, because it is an alien corporation.

Personal jurisdiction: Personal jurisdiction over Mitsui-American can be established in Utah if Utah has a typical long-arm statute. *International Shoe* contacts of Mitsui-American are plainly sufficient. Hence, Mitsui-American is amenable to suit in Utah state or federal court. Depending on whether Mitsui Machinery exercises a high degree of control over Mitsui-American, the parent may be subject to Utah personal jurisdiction on the theory that contacts of its wholly owned subsidiary should be attributed to it. Ordinarily, though, contacts of parent and subsidiary are considered separately. Federal venue is based on where a substantial part of the events giving rise to the claim occurred, which should be satisfied by the injury in Utah.

If jurisdiction cannot be obtained in Utah, California should be considered. Personal jurisdiction over Mitsui-American can be established in California, where it is incorporated. California personal jurisdiction over Mitsui Machinery is more problematic: Mitsui Machinery's contacts with California are more intense than with Utah, but the tort involved here apparently did not occur in California. However, contacts seem sufficient, as Mitsui Machinery apparently ships all the ovens it exports to the United States to its California distributor. Worker could sue in California state court or in federal court in California.

C. 1. The Mitsui entities should challenge jurisdiction and service with a Rule 12(b) motion on the basis of *Shaffer v. Heitner*, the line of cases culminating in *Connecticut v. Doehr*, and the lack of necessity for using attachment procedures.

2. Generally, under *Shaffer*, attachment jurisdiction can be established only if in personam jurisdiction could be established. (There may be exceptions to this general view if there is a connection between the property and the claim, but that is not true here.) If analysis of personal jurisdiction in part B (*supra*) is correct, the "contacts" requirement is satisfied, at least as to Mitsui-American. Hence, the motion to dismiss should be denied as far as *Shaffer* is concerned. However, that means attachment is not necessary to establish jurisdiction and hence a valid *Fuentes-Doehr* objection may exist: Seizure without notice has occurred without the possible justifying circumstance that it was necessary to establish jurisdiction, which also violates Rule 4(n)(2) on assertion of jurisdiction by seizing assets.

If "contacts" are insufficient for in personam jurisdiction, attachment is permissible only under an exception that the *Shaffer* doctrine would recognize. No such exception appears as to Mitsui-American, which is a United States corporation clearly amenable to suit in California. As to Mitsui Machinery, the possibility that it might not be amenable to suit in California (*see supra*) might justify attachment jurisdiction, to give an American injured party an American forum.

D. *Intervention*: The bank might seek intervention by arguing that its interest in securing Pot Line's indebtedness is jeopardized by the attachment of the debt, because that might give Mitsui-American cause to reclaim the oven. Were that to happen, the bank's security would be impaired, and it is not clear how it could protect this interest absent intervention. On the other hand, it is not clear what role it would play in the suit itself, as it has no interest in the issues being litigated at present, nor is it clear that Pot Line would fail to represent the bank's interest adequately, as it can be expected to contest tort liability to Worker vigorously.

Subject-matter jurisdiction: If the case is in federal court, the bank's participation in the case might raise subject-matter jurisdiction problems, depending on the identities of the other parties and how the bank is aligned as a party. If it is considered adverse to Worker, there is no diversity between them, but there is no bar to supplemental jurisdiction over the state-law claims of a nondiverse intervenor-defendant in a diversity case.

E. The claim was settled without adjudication, so no issues were litigated and hence issue preclusion is inoperative. The judgment extinguishes Worker's claim against Pot Line, but not Pot Line's claim against Mitsui. Hence, there is no claim preclusion either. If Mitsui participated in the settlement or manifested acquiescence in the reasonableness of the amount, it could possibly be estopped from disputing the existence of Pot Line's liability to Worker or the amount of that liability, but that would result from Mitsui's stance in the negotiations and not from the judgment as such.

Answers to Question II

Buchan's first claim is based on federal law. Federal Rule 17 seems to say that an obligation created by federal law against an unincorporated association and members of such an association rests against the association as an entity. If so, and if the entity concept is applied consistently, Buchan's damages claim based on the First Amendment would be binding on the Republican Party as an entity if the expulsion was the act of the organization's management, as it appears to have been. The claim would not be binding on any member of the Party, except for officers or directors who might be found individually to be co-wrongdoers with the entity, in the same way that an officer of a corporation can be held personally liable for a wrong committed in the course of corporate employment.

The binding effect of the state-law claim is determined by applicable state law, which could be Virginia or District of Columbia. If that law treats an unincorporated association as an entity, then the analysis above applies. Whether that law treats an association as an entity may depend on whether the claim is in tort (open-ended damages) or contract (limited damages). If the association is not treated as an entity, the situation is essentially a suit against a large number of joint wrongdoers, some of whom (the officers and board) acted personally and others of whom (the members at large) are chargeable only on principles of vicarious liability. Buchan would have to prove liability on one or the other such bases against individuals to bind them.

Procedurally Buchan should treat the "defendant" both as an entity and as an aggregate of individuals. That is, process under Federal Rule 4 and designation of the defendant under Federal Rule 23.2 should be modeled after both a suit against a corporation and a suit against a class under Federal Rule 23.

Answers to Question III

"Jurisdiction" can mean subject-matter jurisdiction or jurisdiction over the person. Both will be analyzed.

A. As for subject-matter jurisdiction, the federal court in Illinois appears to have such jurisdiction. The amount in controversy exceeds $75,000. There appears to be diversity of citizenship: Duffalo is a citizen of New York and Moline was an Illinois citizen. Note that it is the decedent's citizenship (Mr. Moline's), and not that of his executor (Mrs. Moline), that controls diversity. Whether the federal court in Illinois has personal jurisdiction depends on whether Duffalo has "minimum contacts" with Illinois and whether Illinois has a long-arm statute that reaches him, which it probably does. It appears that Duffalo's contacts with Illinois are sufficient. He had a continuous business relationship based in Illinois, and the lawsuit arises out of that business. It may be assumed that Illinois has a typical long-arm statute. If so, such a statute very likely extends jurisdiction to persons "doing" or "engaging in" business in the state or entering into contracts in the state. Any such provision would be a sufficient statutory basis for asserting personal jurisdiction over this claim arising out of Duffalo's local business.

B. As for subject-matter jurisdiction of the New York state court, there is no diversity requirement. The only possible question with regard to subject-matter jurisdiction is whether the suit is filed in the proper court in New York. Given the size of the claim asserted by Duffalo, that would be the trial court of general jurisdiction. [In New York that happens to be the Supreme Court, but this is a fact that students outside New York would not ordinarily be expected to know.]

The problem of personal jurisdiction in New York is less clear. It may be assumed that New York can extend process to the decedent's representative if and only if it could extend process to the decedent himself, because there is no indication that the executor, as such, had any contacts with New York. Mr. Moline had only very tenuous connections with New York: He was a joint venturer with Duffalo, and Duffalo evidently conducted much of the venture's business from New York. On that basis, it could be said that Moline himself was engaged in business in New York and hence subject to its process. On the other hand, the venture had its headquarters outside New York and Moline himself does not appear to have gone regularly to New York in the course of the business. The question could also be affected by the precise terms of the New York long-arm statute. If it required that the defendant have "done business" in New York, it might be said that Moline did not personally do business in New York and that it would be a bootstrapping maneuver to say that he did business in New York because Duffalo did. On balance, personal jurisdiction probably would not be sustained.

As for the garnishment of Allstate, the problem is similar to, but not identical with, *Rush v. Savchuk*. In that case, the policy sought to be attached was a liability-insurance policy in which the obligation or "debt" came into being only if the merits of the controversy at hand were resolved in favor of the plaintiff. Here the policy is a life-insurance policy and is an existing debt, regardless of the outcome of the Duffalo-Moline litigation. Hence, the insurance proceeds can properly be considered "property" that might be subject to attachment.

However, even so, the attachment is probably insufficient to support jurisdiction in New York. The Allstate Company is subject to process in New York and the "debt follows the debtor," so that the property is "in" New York for purposes of attachment. Nevertheless, simple presence of property is not a sufficient basis for exercise of attachment jurisdiction, at least when the property is not real property. *Shaffer v. Heitner* requires, in general, that the principal defendant (Moline's executor in this case) have "minimum contacts" with the state in which the attachment is made. On the analysis above, such minimum contacts are missing. Other possibly justifying circumstances recognized in *Shaffer* are not present. (For example, there is no indication that Duffalo could not sue in Illinois to enforce his claim, or that the "presence" of the property somehow supports jurisdiction because the property is related to the claim asserted.) Thus, the attachment of the life-insurance policy in New York would not meet the requirement of *Shaffer* and could not provide a basis for jurisdiction in New York.

Answers to Question IV

A.   Under *Beacon Theatres v. Westover* and related cases, for purposes of determining the right to jury trial, a pleading is read with attention to its "legal" claims and with a presumption in favor of jury trial. Viewed in this way, the complaint in this case is an action for damages (the second claim) with an alternative claim for specific performance (the equitable claim). On this analysis, plaintiff has an action for damages, which is therefore triable by jury as to all issues of liability and measures of damages. The only issue triable to the ***court*** would be the propriety of granting specific performance, and the terms upon which it is granted, if liability is found by the jury.

B.   The foregoing applies whether the demand for jury trial is by plaintiff or by defendant. Hence, the issues of liability and damages should be tried by a jury regardless of which party made the demand for jury trial.

C.   If the court rejected the defendant's demand for a jury, the order is reviewable. Most obviously, the order would be reviewable on appeal from a final judgment after the case had been tried to the court. The more important question is whether the order could be subject to appellate review before the case goes to trial. The order is not a final judgment, and hence an appeal would not ordinarily lie from the order. However, the order is one that can be certified for interlocutory appellate review under 28 U.S.C. section 1292(b). To obtain review by this method, the trial judge would have to certify the question as warranting immediate review and the appellate court would have to agree to accept the case on that basis. If the trial judge refuses to certify the order, section 1292(b) review cannot be obtained.

Furthermore, defendant may be able to obtain immediate review of the order by means of extraordinary writ, specifically, mandamus to compel the judge to put the case on the jury trial calendar. Review by extraordinary writ is generally disfavored in the federal courts, although the attitude varies considerably from one circuit to another. Nevertheless, when there is a plain and serious error going to important procedural rights (particularly the right to jury trial), the writ has often been granted. In light of *Beacon Theatres v. Westover* (itself a mandamus proceeding), the error here is serious. Hence, review by extraordinary writ might well be afforded.

Answers to Question V

The instruction was error. The procedure adopted is known as a quotient verdict, *i.e.*, one in which the jury sums up the jurors' individual proposed awards and then divides the total by the number of jurors. It is error for a jury to do this on its own initiative, and error for the court to instruct the jury to follow such a procedure. The vice of the quotient verdict is that the process of jury discussion and mutual consideration of the issue of damages is displaced by the simple averaging of individual views.

So far as raising the objection on appeal is concerned, the general rule is that a party may not complain on appeal of a ruling or action of the trial court unless the party raised timely objection in the trial court. The crucial questions therefore are whether the parties knew of the special instruction by the court and, if so, whether the circumstances were such that they did not have fair opportunity to object. For example, if the instruction was given without advance notice to counsel (required in most courts), then the party is excused from the requirement of timely objection. Similarly, if the judge allowed no time for objection or had notified the parties but had made it clear that he would tolerate no objection, the "timely objection" requirement might be excused. And even if the parties had knowledge of the instruction and opportunity to object, in this exceptional case an appellate court might regard the instruction as "plain error" subject to review despite the parties' failure to object.

Answers to Question VI

The first question is whether federal law or state law should govern the question of granting or denying summary judgment. If state law is applied, it would be arguable that summary judgment should be denied. Summary judgment is proper only when there is no genuine issue of material fact and, as a matter of law, the movant is entitled to judgment. Under Texas law, as stated, it appears that all issues are decided by the jury. Hence, under state law, summary judgment could not be granted on these facts. It thus is necessary to analyze whether this provision of state law is applicable in federal court.

The argument for applying state law is as follows: This is a diversity case, governed by state law in its substantive aspects. *Erie*, as construed in such cases as *Guaranty Trust v. York*, requires that a federal court, when not applying governing federal law, apply not only state "substantive" law, but also "outcome-determinative" state law. Since the Texas rule on scope of jury authority could have an "outcome determinative" effect in this case, it could be argued that the state rule should be applied in determining whether there is an issue for trial.

Although this argument has support in some of the cases, the Supreme Court in *Hanna v. Plumer* and other decisions has established approaches that make it likely federal law should govern. If the source of the potentially applicable federal rule of law is regarded as being the "no genuine dispute as to any material fact" language of Federal Rule 56 itself, then the test for the validity and governing force of the federal standard is provided by the Rules Enabling Act [28 U.S.C. § 2072]. The federal rule qualifies as procedural within the terms of the Act, especially given the Supreme Court's broad definition of federal-court rulemaking authority as including even "arguably procedural" rules in the border area between substance and procedure. And the Court's tolerance for "incidental" substantive impacts of Federal Rules makes it highly probable that the Court would not regard the summary-judgment rule here as impermissibly abridging, enlarging, or modifying any substantive right.

Perhaps one could argue that the federal standard for sufficiency of the evidence to go to the jury should be regarded as purely decisional, and thus subject to the "twin aims" approach articulated in *Hanna* for the "relatively unguided *Erie* choice" between a federal decisional rule affecting federal court procedure and a conflicting state rule. But because Rule 56 states its own standard, that argument seems weak.

Applying the federal standard, a "genuine dispute as to material fact" exists if, given the material presented in the summary-judgment motion, it can be reasonably foreseen that a sufficient evidentiary basis will exist at trial for the case to go to the jury. Here the case looks very strong against the railroad, but there remains a "genuine dispute." First, it has not been established in the affidavits that the speed recorder was operating properly. If it was not working properly, the indicated speed of 80 miles per hour may not have been the actual speed. Second, even if the train had been going 80, it is a question for the jury whether that speed was excessive under the circumstances. Third, even if the train was going at an excessive speed, that would not have been the proximate cause of the accident if the bus driver's conduct is regarded as a supervening cause. Although the bus driver's testimony in deposition is not contradicted, he is so situated that his testimony is self-serving. The jurors therefore could disbelieve the testimony. If they did, they could find the railroad was not responsible for the collision.

Answers to Question VII

Since the action is in federal court, the Federal Rules of Civil Procedure apply. There is no demurrer under the Federal Rules, so the question becomes what kind of motion should be prepared.

Possibly, a motion for more definite statement would be effective, but such motions are disfavored and rarely granted under the "notice pleading" approach of the Federal Rules. The complaint is very vague as to the details of the alleged advertisement. The gist of the claim seems to be fraud, which must be alleged with particularity under Rule 9. The pleading does not meet this standard.

Furthermore, the allegations as to the availability of jobs in the field of electronics are also very vague. Even if a motion to make them more definite and certain were to be granted, however, it would provide only a temporary respite, because plaintiff would probably file a more definite pleading. There is little chance the suit would be dismissed on the ground that the complaint is uncertain, for under the Federal Rules an action may be dismissed only when it appears that the claim is not plausible.

A motion to dismiss for failure to state a claim would probably not be effective. While there is grave doubt whether plaintiff states a claim entitling her to $500,000 in damages for emotional distress, the claim for restitution of $12,500 does not seem substantively baseless. Since the plaintiff states a valid claim to this extent, the complaint would not be vulnerable to a motion to dismiss for failure to state a claim. Although the Supreme Court has supported dismissal if the factual allegations fail to make the claim plausible, particularly if a more definite statement elicited more details this claim would likely survive.

The most promising motion would be to dismiss for want of subject-matter jurisdiction. There seems to be no basis at all for an argument on the part of plaintiff that her action is based on federal law. (If there were a valid federal claim, the amount in controversy requirement would not be applicable.) There is no problem with diversity of citizenship, but the amount in controversy in a diversity action in the federal courts must exceed $75,000. To meet the $75,000 amount-in-controversy requirement, the pleader must have a good-faith basis upon which she might conceivably recover a judgment exceeding $75,000, exclusive of interest and costs. Although plaintiff may state a valid claim for restitution of $12,500, the defendant has a strong argument that no basis exists for recovery in excess of that amount. The allegations of fraud, which could lead to punitive damages, are insufficient. In particular, there is no allegation that defendant knew that employment of the type advertised would be virtually impossible to obtain by a graduate of the Institute. If the action is regarded as one for breach of contract, as opposed to fraud, the measure of damages under generally prevailing law does not include "embarrassment, humiliation," etc. The damage recoverable by plaintiff on a contract claim would be limited to the difference between the amount paid and the value of the education actually received. Given these flaws, a motion to strike the references to humiliation in paragraph five and to strike the request for $500,000 in additional damages might be successful. The more telling point is that a damages award could not exceed $12,500, and therefore the amount-in-controversy requirement is not met, and the federal court does not have jurisdiction of the action.

Answers to Question VIII

A.   A suit individually against Bunker would seek to cancel his membership on the ground that he refused to abide by the rules governing membership. This claim is based essentially on the common law of unincorporated associations. A federal question might arise in the case, but it would be a defensive contention by Bunker that the Club rule requiring subscription to the "statement of principles" is a violation of his First Amendment rights. The fact that a federal question may arise defensively does not make the case one that "arises under" federal law. Therefore, the claim in an action by the Club to terminate Bunker's membership would be a state-law claim.

Such a claim could be brought in federal court only if the requirements for diversity jurisdiction could be met, since the federal question basis of jurisdiction does not exist. There is diversity between the Club and Bunker. Bunker is a citizen of Texas, while Sierra Club is a citizen of California, where it is incorporated. (It does not appear that Sierra Club is also a citizen of the District of Columbia, because its principal place of business is in San Francisco.) However, diversity jurisdiction requires that the amount in controversy exceed $75,000. There is nothing to indicate that the value of the membership to Bunker is of that amount, nor that the value to the Sierra Club of excluding Bunker from membership would be in that amount. Possibly, the Club could meet the amount-in-controversy requirement by allegations that

Bunker threatens disruption of the Club and that the disruption would damage it to the extent of more than $75,000. However, on the facts given, there seems no basis for making nonfrivolous allegations to this effect. Accordingly, the action could not be brought in federal district court.

The action could be brought in a state court where personal jurisdiction could be obtained over Bunker. That would include an appropriate state court in Texas, where presumably Bunker is subject to service of process. Possibly the action could also be brought in California on the ground that Bunker is subject to service of process there for any claim concerning his membership in the Club. His joining the Club was a voluntary action and he knew that the Club was headquartered in California. With regard to a claim arising out of the membership activity itself, Bunker's "contact" with California seems sufficient to meet the constitutional standard applied in such cases as *International Shoe* and *Burger King Corp. v. Rudzewicz*. Because California's long-arm statute goes to the limits of due process, service of process on Bunker is authorized by the statute.

There seems to be no basis upon which Bunker could be subject to process in the District of Columbia. There is no indication that he had any contact with the District or that he carried on activities relating to membership there. That the Club has an office in the District is not a sufficient basis for subjecting members of the Club to jurisdiction.

B. The class suit names as defendants individuals who object to the requirement of signing the "statement of principles." Such individuals would adequately represent the class if they can defend the litigation with reasonable competence and diligence. On that assumption, the litigation would probably meet the requirements for a binding class suit: The Sierra Club would have to show that the group of affected individuals is so large that it is impractical to join all those who are similarly situated (which might prove difficult); that the individuals actually named are representative of the class; and that they are typical of class members and appear to be able to defend the litigation on behalf of the class. Under the principles of *Hansberry v. Lee*, they can represent the class as a whole. There does not seem to be a problem under *Phillips Petroleum Co. v. Shutts* with the California state court's exercising jurisdiction over out-of-state defendant class members, because of the members' voluntary contact with California in joining the club. All this being so, the judgment would be binding on all members of the class, including Bunker.

C. If Bunker sought to become a party to the action as an individual, the proper procedure under either federal or state practice is to seek to intervene. If the action was pending in state court, his petition for intervention should state the essentials of intervention. These are that the pending action will or may determine his legal rights; that there is risk that the action will be defended by the class less effectively than Bunker could defend his own interest individually; that his petition is timely and his becoming a party will not unduly delay the progress of the litigation.

If the action were removed to federal court, the procedure would be essentially the same. However, Bunker should frame his petition in the alternative, first as a petition for intervention of right, and second as a petition for permissive intervention. There is no fundamental distinction between the two, except that intervention of right is permitted when the proposed intervenor stands in risk that his rights will be legally or practically affected by the judgment, whereas permissive intervention requires only that the petitioner show that his claim and the claims already pending in the action involve a common question of law and fact, although allowing permissive intervention is a discretionary decision for the trial court. The allegations outlined above establish that the judgment in the pending action may affect Bunker's interest. They also show that his claim involves a common question of law and fact with the claim pending in the existing action. But since the court would need to find that the class representatives adequately represent the class members in order to certify a class, Bunker might have difficulty showing that he would not be adequately represented if denied intervention.

D. When a class action is pending in federal court, the question of notice to the class is determined under the Federal Rules. Under Rule 23, individual notice to each member of the class who can be identified with reasonable effort is required when the class suit is of the (b)(3) or damages type, when each individual member has the right to opt out. However, individual notice may not be required in other types of class suits, including those in which an injunction or declaratory judgment is sought regarding the rights and duties of the class as a whole. The present suit falls into the latter category and, therefore, individual notice is probably not required. It would be within the discretion of the court to require individual notice even in this type of class suit, but to do so might be regarded as an abuse of discretion in this case. The question involved is a legal issue common to all members of the class. Published notice to the class as a whole, plus perhaps individual notice to members known to oppose the "statement of principles," might be sufficient.

With regard to the cost of giving notice, the party opposing the class is not required to pay that cost in a "damages" type of class suit. [*See Eisen v. Carlisle & Jacquelin*] However, this is not a damages class suit so the court has broader discretion in determining whether the party opposing the class should be required to pay the cost of notice. And because this case involves a plaintiff seeking to invoke the class-action procedure to sue a defendant class, it should not be a problem to make the plaintiff at least initially bear the notice costs.

Table of Cases

Table of Citations to the Federal Rules of Civil Procedure

Index

questioning by counsel, 379–380
questioning by court, 379

"KEY MAN," 375
See also Jury

LIMITED APPEARANCE, 28, 35

LONG ARM LEGISLATION, 31–32
See also Personal jurisdiction
Specific acts, 31–32

MANAGERIAL JUDGING
See Pretrial conferences and managerial judging

MANDAMUS, 439–441
See also Appeal

MEDICAL EXAMINATION, 293–294, 324
See also Discovery

MERITS
See Res judicata

MINIMUM CONTACTS, 7–20
See also Personal jurisdiction
And First Amendment, 18
Domicile, 24
In rem jurisdiction, 21
Purposeful availment, 9–16
Reasonableness requirement, 16–18
Transacting business, 31

MODIFIABLE JUDGMENTS, 449
See also Res judicata

MOTIONS
After verdict or judgment, 400–415
For directed verdict, 383–387, 401
For failure to state claim, 157–163
For judgment as a matter of law, 383–388
For judgment n.o.v., 400–401
For judgment on the pleadings, 166, 202–203
For leave to amend pleadings, 193
For more definite statement, 163–164
For new trial, 401, 402–410. *See also* New trial
For nonsuit, 387
For relief from judgment, 410–414
For summary judgment, 336–341
Pre-verdict, 383–388
Renewed, for judgment as a matter of law, 400–401
Rule 12 procedure, 165
To alter or amend judgment, 410
To compel response, 284
To dismiss, 156–163
To strike
    federal, 164–165
    state, 156
Waiver of defenses, 165–166

MULTIPARTY, MULTIFORUM TRIAL JURISDICTION ACT
Appeal, 429
Diversity exception, 67
Removal, 101–102, 104

MULTIPLE DEFENDANTS
Jurisdictional amount, 76
Removal, 40
Venue, 36

MULTIPLE PLAINTIFFS
Jurisdictional amount, 76

MUTUALITY RULE, 461
See also Res judicata

NECESSARY PARTIES, 91, 221
See also Joinder

NEGATIVE PREGNANT RULE, 177
See also Answer

NEW MATTER, FAILURE TO PLEAD
See Answer

NEW TRIAL, MOTION FOR, 401, 402–410
Additur, 409–410
And judgment n.o.v., 401
And renewed motion for judgment as a matter of law, 401
Grounds for, 402–406
Harmless error, 402
Jury trial, 402–405
Nonjury trial, 406
Order, 407–410
Procedure requirement, 406–407
Remittitur, 408–409, 410
Standard for ruling on, 404
Timeliness, 406
Weight of evidence, 403–405

NONSUIT, 387

NOTICE
See also Service of process; Personal jurisdiction
Class actions, 48, 49
Constructive, 50
Contents, 49
Depositions, 279
Due process requirements, 48
Duty to make further efforts, 50
Failure to receive, 50
Identification efforts, 49
In rem cases, 7, 48
Methods of, 48
Notice to prisoner, 48
Prejudgment seizures, 52–56
    common law, 7, 52
    due process requirements, 53–56
        chattels, 53–54
        garnishment, 53, 54
        real property, 55–56
Service of process, 50–52
Service via e-mail, 49

NOTICE OF APPEAL
See Appeal

NUMEROUS PARTIES REQUIREMENT
See Class actions

OBJECTIONS AND EXCEPTIONS, 383

OBJECTIONS TO JURISDICTION, 34–35, 61–62
See also Personal jurisdiction

ON THE MERITS
See Res judicata

PARTIAL FINAL DECISIONS, 428
See also Final decision rule

PARTIES
See Impleader; Interpleader; Intervention; Joinder; Real party in interest rule; Res judicata

6/17/18